# Memory from a Broader Perspective

# Memory from a Broader Perspective

❖

**Alan Searleman**
*St. Lawrence University*

**Douglas Herrmann**
*National Center for Health Statistics*

**McGraw-Hill, Inc.**

New York   St. Louis   San Francisco   Auckland   Bogotá   Caracas
Lisbon   London   Madrid   Mexico City   Milan   Montreal   New Delhi
San Juan   Singapore   Sydney   Tokyo   Toronto

This book is printed on recycled paper containing a minimum of 50% total recycled fiber with 10% postconsumer de-inked fiber.

1 2 3 4 5 6 7 8 9 0   DOH   DOH   9 0 9 8 7 6 5 4 3

ISBN 0-07-028387-7

This book was set in Palatino by Ruttle, Shaw & Wetherill, Inc.
The editors were Jane Vaicunas and Fred H. Burns;
the production supervisor was Paula Keller.
The cover was designed by Joan Greenfield.
The photo editor was Elyse Rieder.
R. R. Donnelley & Sons Company was printer and binder.

**Library of Congress Cataloging-in-Publication Data**

Searleman, Alan.
   Memory from a broader perspective / Alan Searleman, Douglas
Herrmann
      p.    cm.
   Includes bibliographical references and index.
   ISBN 0-07-028387-7 (alk. paper)
   1. Memory.    2. Learning, Psychology of.    I. Herrmann, Douglas J.
II. Title.
BF371.S465       1994
153.1'2—dc20                                                93-21686

# About the Authors

❖

**ALAN SEARLEMAN** is professor and chair of psychology at St. Lawrence University. He received his B.S. in psychology from the University of Massachusetts at Amherst in 1973, where he was elected to Phi Beta Kappa. His Ph.D. in experimental psychology was from the State University of New York at Stony Brook (1978). He has taught courses in memory, statistics, research methods, neuropsychology, learning, sensation and perception, and introductory psychology. Dr. Searleman has published numerous articles and book chapters (particularly in the area of left-handedness and cognitive ability), has served as a National Science Foundation grant reviewer, and has been a consulting editor for the *Journal of Experimental Psychology: Human Perception and Performance*. Recently, he was a coeditor (along with D. Herrmann, H. Weingartner, and C. McEvoy) for a book, *Memory Improvement: Implications for Memory Theory*. He lives in Canton, New York with his wife Janice, a computer scientist, and enjoys reading science fiction, and playing with his children Jason, Adam, and Alana.

**DOUGLAS HERRMANN** is currently a senior research psychologist in the "cognitive methods group" at the National Center for Health Statistics (NCHS) in Hyattsville, Maryland. He was trained as an engineer at the U.S. Naval Academy (1964) and later received both his M.S. (1970) and Ph.D. (1972) in experimental psychology from the University of Delaware. He taught at Hamilton College until 1990 when he joined the federal government. In addition to his work at NCHS, he teaches courses for University College at the University of Maryland. He has taught courses in memory, cognition, psycholinguistics, improving memory and thinking, statistics, and introductory psychology. Dr. Herrmann has published extensively, especially in the areas of memory and the comprehension of semantic relations. He served as the North American editor of the journal *Applied Cognitive Psychology* and on the editorial board of the *Zeitscrift für Psychologie*. He has also written a textbook called *Improving Student Memory*. Dr. Herrmann lives in Gaithersburg, Maryland, with his wife Donna and their 16-year-old daughter Amanda and 6-year-old son Zachary.

v

*For their phenomenal support and love,*
*we dedicate this book to our families.*

*To Janice, Jason, Adam, and Alana*
*&*
*To Donna, Amanda, and Zachary*

# Contents

———— ❖ ————

vii

# Preface

————— ❖ —————

This textbook differs markedly from any previous books written about human memory. The first hint of this comes from the title we have chosen—*Memory from a Broader Perspective*. When experienced teachers of memory courses scan the table of contents of the book, we expect that many will be surprised in a positive way.

Why do we think our memory book is so different from its predecessors? First of all, in keeping with our multimodal approach to memory functioning and performance (e.g., Herrmann & Searleman, 1990, 1992), it is our belief that human memory is affected by a wide range of factors, and that truly to appreciate this multitude of influences our book had to incorporate topics that have never appeared before in a traditional memory textbook (or if they have appeared, were covered only in a cursory fashion). So, for instance, we devote a full chapter to the biological bases of memory, a dynamic area of memory research that is of major theoretical interest and that holds great promise for helping brain-injured people suffering from memory disorders. The chapter describes the effects that various drugs, neurotransmitters, hormones, and stimulants, as well as REM sleep, can have on memory performance and consolidation. Another chapter describes the important effects that arousal, stress, and emotion can have on memory accuracy and performance. Also, a full chapter is allotted to describing the fascinating ways in which various social groups affect memory performance and the social factors that can influence the types of memory tasks people choose to undertake.

In addition to presenting many research findings that clearly demonstrate the multimodal nature of memory, the book contains other topics that have been largely neglected by more traditional memory textbooks. For example, there is considerable coverage of topics such as prospective memory, memory for the timing of events, memory during anesthesia, dissociative disorders of memory, and clinical memory assessment tests. Not only do we believe such topics deserve to be included, but we also have data showing that students find these topics quite captivating (from a group of fifty students at the University of Maryland who read an early version of the book).

In recent years the field of memory has grown tremendously in the types of memory tasks that are given to subjects or memory-impaired patients. For instance, while memory researchers have certainly not abandoned the more traditional laboratory tasks and procedures that measure explicit remembering (e.g., serial learning, cued recall, paired-associate learning), newer memory tasks that tap implicit remembering have vastly proliferated (e.g., priming tasks such as word-stem completions and deciphering word fragments). More so than other books on memory, we repeatedly demonstrate throughout the text the importance of assessing both explicit and implicit memory to get an accurate picture of what a person truly remembers. This is accomplished by acquainting students with a very wide range of memory tasks and techniques in a variety of different contexts.

Perhaps the fastest growing and most influential trend in memory research has been the growth of the *everyday/applied memory movement*. This movement underscores the value of studying memory in naturalistic settings and the investigation of memory tasks that have an applied focus. The present book showcases the strengths inherent in the more traditional basic laboratory approach to memory research, and yet at the same time, tries to convey to students the value of extending laboratory findings to the real world.

The chapters have been ordered in the way in which we are inclined to teach them. We suggest that the first six chapters be assigned in order. For the remainder of the book, since the chapters are each fairly self-contained, the instructor should feel free to vary the order of assigning chapters according to his or her own orientation and preference.

*Alan Searleman*
*Douglas Herrmann*

# To the Student

---------- ❖ ----------

You would be hard pressed to overstate how important your memory is to you. After all, everything you know about *anything* is stored in your memory. And for most people, their memories are among their most cherished possessions.

Our primary intention in writing this book was to provide college students with the latest information and theories concerning how human memory works. We have purposely tried to select topics and provide examples that will show students how memory research applies to their daily lives and can be a fascinating area to study. Although we expect that most of you have already taken other psychology courses, when writing the book we did not assume that you had any specialized knowledge about psychology, and, in particular, the field of memory. To help you learn (and remember!) what you have read, each chapter concludes with a comprehensive summary. We have also included an extensive glossary at the end of the book to help you better understand the myriad terms and theories of modern-day memory research.

# Acknowledgments

◆

We first wish to thank Jim Anker for having faith in us and for convincing us to write a new kind of memory book for McGraw-Hill. After Jim left the company, Chris Rogers became our editor for a time and provided us with needed encouragement and good cheer. During the last year, Jane Vaicunas took over for Chris and has done a wonderful job in skillfully guiding and helping us finish and polish the manuscript. Jane's advice and counsel have been terrific and we want her to know that they are much appreciated. Other McGraw-Hill people, such as Kathy Bendo, Beth Kaufman, Jill Gordon, Yanett Peña, Elyse Rieder, and Nomi Sofer also provided valuable assistance to us. During the last few months before publication, it seems like we were in almost daily contact with Fred Burns, senior editing supervisor, who worked tirelessly in helping to produce the book (and didn't panic like we did when it first appeared that all of the copyedited art work was lost in the mail).

Either directly or indirectly, several people influenced our thinking while the book was being written, and we want to acknowledge their contributions. These people include Miriam Bendikson, Ivan Bendikson, Stephen Ceci, Tom Crook, Tom Cunningham, Ken Deffenbacher, Rick Gardner, Jordan Grafman, Tom Greene, Mike Gruneberg, Paula Lipman, Cathy McEvoy, Dick Neisser, Dana Plude, Mike Pressley, Jonathan Schooler, Jim Wallace, and Herb Weingartner. We also wish to thank several people who reviewed the entire manuscript and provided us with very valuable comments, insights, and suggestions: Deborah Best, Wake Forest University; David Burrows, Skidmore College; James Nairne, Purdue University; David Pillemer, Wellesley College; Janice Searleman, Clarkson University; and Steven Smith, Texas A&M University. Jan Searleman deserves special recognition for reading all three versions of the manuscript and also for providing exceptional sketches for many of the figures that appear in the book. Our thanks to Robin Lock for posing as a mad slasher in Chapter 8; normally he is more likely to be found teaching statistics in the St. Lawrence Math Department. As anyone who has written a book will attest, having excellent secretarial help is a tremendous plus. We were very fortunate and grateful to have the services and experience of Sandi Licht, psychology department secretary at St. Lawrence. And finally, a special debt is owed to our families—they gave us the time, encouragement, and unflagging support we needed (sometimes desperately) to complete this book. We can never fully repay them.

*Alan Searleman*
*Douglas Herrmann*

# PART 1

———— ❖ ————

# Overview

# 1

# *Introduction: History and Themes*

———— ❖ ————

The telephone rings, and upon answering it, you effortlessly recognize the voice of a friend whom you haven't spoken with for some time. How do you do this? Or perhaps at a party one time, much to your embarrassment, you quickly forgot the names of the people with whom you were talking, even though you were introduced only moments before. What caused this case of seemingly instant forgetting? Finally, consider this common experience: an old, familiar song comes on the radio, and suddenly, long-buried memories come unbidden to mind. Why do these memories come streaming back to consciousness, and why is it often next to impossible to stop them?

When situations like those described above occurred, you may have wondered about the mysterious workings of your memory. In addition, haven't you ever thought about *how* or *where* memories are stored in your brain? Wondered what your earliest memory is? Questioned if it is really possible to greatly improve your memory by studying memory-improvement books or tapes, as the advertisements promise? Marveled at your ability to remember trivial facts learned years ago? Been chagrined at your inability to remember a few simple facts on yesterday's exam? Or asked if it is true, as some believe, that we never really forget anything?

Clearly, memory is a fascinating topic to explore, if for no other reason than to simply satisfy one's curiosity. But beyond just satiating a natural inquisitiveness, it is also very important to carefully examine memory processes because of the immense role they play in our lives. For instance, consider how difficult daily life would be if people couldn't recognize the faces of family members, were unable to remember which foods were good to eat and which were not, failed to recall that it is wise to avoid snarling dogs or not to touch

3

hot objects, had no recollection of how to find the way home again, or couldn't learn and retain information necessary to keep a job.

Obviously, there's a close link between the processes of *learning* and *memory*. Learning has been said to involve the acquisition of new skills or information, whereas memory pertains to the retention of what has been learned over time (Squire, 1987). Without a well-functioning memory system, learning is of little importance. All the information you have about everything you know is stored in your memory. One estimate of the vastness of human memory is that by the time an average person dies, the amount of information that he or she will have stored will be approximately 500 times the amount of information contained in the entire *Encyclopaedia Britannica* (Hunt, 1982). Most people take memory for granted; only when it fails us do we pay it proper attention. Without the ability to remember past events and information, life as we know it would be impossible.

When you have finished reading this book, you will be aware of the latest findings and theories about memory. We believe that this book is unique in that it has a much broader scope than any previous memory textbook. You should have a very good sense of where memory is headed in the near future and what memory phenomena deserve the most attention by your generation of psychologists.

## MEMORY THROUGH THE AGES

Hermann Ebbinghaus (1908) once remarked that "psychology has a long past, but only a short history." This has become a famous saying in psychology; however, he could just as easily have substituted the word *memory* for the word *psychology,* and the statement would still be just as accurate. For while it is generally agreed that the scientific study of memory first began in the 1880s with the work of Hermann Ebbinghaus, it is also true that scholarly thought about memory processes dates back thousands of years. One purpose of this chapter is to review some of the major philosophical conjectures and intuitions about memory before the time of Ebbinghaus. Next, we will mention some of the seminal work of Ebbinghaus and try to explain why his research on remembering and forgetting had such a remarkable impact on the nature and scope of future memory research for many decades afterward. Finally, we will briefly summarize the major approaches, theories, and trends of modern-day memory research.

As you will come to understand, the study of memory has been approached in many different ways. At a very general level, these approaches may be classified into the following four categories: (1) the *pragmatic* approach—which seeks ways to improve a person's ability to learn and remember, (2) the *experimental* approach—which documents the existence and nature of memory phenomena with observations that are systematically collected, (3) the *atheoretical* approach—which characterizes memory in an intuitive and informal matter, and (4) the *theoretical* approach—which attempts to explain the mechanisms of memory with either theories, models, or metaphors that capture part of a phenomenon. Many investigators combine these approaches; for instance, modern memory researchers often adopt an experimental/theoretical perspective.

## MEMORY BEFORE EBBINGHAUS

Several histories were written about memory scholarship prior to Ebbinghaus's work (Beare, 1906; Burnham, 1888; Edgell, 1924; Herrmann & Chaffin, 1987, 1988; Marshall & Fryer, 1978; Mitchell, 1911; Murray, 1976; Yates, 1966). What these histories indicate is that surprisingly few scholars studied memory until the Renaissance. Figure 1.1 shows the development of memory scholarship prior to Ebbinghaus [based on a count of the memory scholars cited in Yates's *The Art of Memory* (1966) and Young's *Bibliography of Memory* (1961)].

It certainly appears that even the earliest societies in recorded history placed a high value on memory ability. Indeed, they regarded memory so highly that they created gods or goddesses to handle the memory problems of

FIGURE 1.1

The frequency of memory scholarship in the era before Ebbinghaus.
*Herrmann & Chaffin, 1987. Reprinted by permission of Lawrence Erlbaum Associates, Inc.*

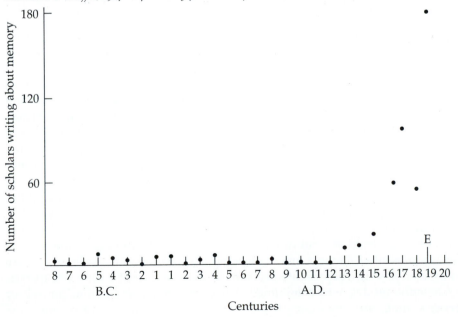

(a)                                    (b)

mere mortals. Figure 1.2 presents images of Thoth, Mnemosyne, and Minerva, the god and goddesses of the ancient Egyptians, Greeks, and Romans, respectively, who were responsible for memory functions.

Some of the earliest written documents were concerned with the practical aspects of how to improve memory performance. For instance, a fragment written in the fifth century B.C., known as *Dialexis,* advised that attentiveness and rehearsal aided learning (Yates, 1966). In the same century, the Greek philosopher Heraclitus made the practical observation that "the eyes are more exact witnesses than the ears." Aristophanes, the Greek dramatist and author of many satirical comedies (ca. 450–385 B.C.), pointed out the importance of motivation to memory when he observed that memory is of two sorts: "If I'm owed anything, I'm mindful, very. But if I owe, (Oh, dear!) forgetful, very."

In the fourth century B.C., the celebrated Greek philosophers Plato and Aristotle formulated several different memory models: the wax tablet model, which represented memory traces as being like impressions made in wax; an aviary model, which represented each memory as a bird of a different species; and a scribe model, which assumed that each person has within himself or herself a miniature scribe (or private secretary) who records our personal ex-

(c)

FIGURE 1.2
(a) Thoth, the god of learning, memory, and wisdom in ancient Egypt (circa 3000–4000 B.C.); (b) Mnemosyne, the goddess of memory in ancient Greece (circa 1000 B.C.); (c) Minerva, the goddess of learning, memory, and wisdom in ancient Rome (circa 1000 B.C.).
*Page 6, right: Painting by Dante Gabriel Rossetti, Delaware Art Museum, Samuel and Mary R. Bancroft Memorial, 1935; left: Douglas Herrmann. Page 7: Bettmann.*

periences. Plato also proposed a process for the retrieval of innate knowledge, while Aristotle advanced basic ''laws'' of associationism. (The laws of associationism describe why certain things tend to be remembered together. Aristotle maintained that the most important principle was the *Law of Contiguity*—two events or experiences occurring closely in time will likely come to be associated with each other. A good example would be the pairing of thunder and lightning during a thunderstorm.) In addition, both of these individuals correctly identified various memory phenomena such as the rapid forgetting of things to which we don't actively attend (Plato) and the decline of memory performance with age (Aristotle).

Interest in the practical aspects of memory grew in the Roman period. Both the eminent statesman and orator Cicero and the anonymous author of *Ad Herennium* championed the use of the first *mnemonic technique* to assist in public speaking. A mnemonic technique is a way of remembering something new by relating it to something you already know (see Chapter 13 for more information on mnemonics). The mnemonic technique suggested was the *method of loci*, which requires a person to mentally place items to be memorized in certain places in an area well known to the person, such as his or her own house. Usually when people do this, they are able to easily recall the items by imagining the well-known places (*loci* means "places" in Latin), mentally "walking" around them and recalling the items to be remembered as they are "seen" there.

In the first century, Quintilian, the renowned rhetorician (a person well versed in the art of using words effectively in speaking and writing), also taught Cicero's methods but with a note of skepticism not held by Cicero. Quintilian feared that the method of loci imposed a "double task" on memory; that is, the person had to remember not only the original items but also the places. In the fifth century, the theologian Augustine suggested metaphorical models of memory that likened remembering to the exploration of caverns. Additionally, Augustine discussed the relationship between memory and emotions, noting that the knowledge of the emotion held during an experience "clung to my memory so that I can call it to mind."

During the dark ages (from approximately the fifth to the twelfth century), work on memory (and all other topics, for that matter) markedly decreased. Substantive writings on memory from the fifth century into the medieval period were very rare (or have since been lost; Yates, 1966). In the thirteenth century, although the Italian theologian Thomas Aquinas brought Aristotle's views on memory into prominence again, theoretical interests were unusual for Aquinas's time.

Very few people could read or write during this time. And even for those privileged few who could, written documents were rare, so many villages depended on traveling entertainers or troubadours for their news. Because the audience typically would hear the stories or news only once, the troubadours had to make sure that their presentations were easily remembered. For this reason, their entire performance was usually in rhyme, which made it easier for both the audience and the performer to remember. In France, regular meetings were held in which these troubadours would exchange stories and demonstrate their memory prowess by engaging in poetry competitions. It was said that well-trained troubadours could memorize several hundred new lines of poetry after hearing them spoken only three times (Burke, 1985). The value placed on rhyming as an aid to memory was so great that until about the fourteenth century, except for legal documents, almost all other material was written in rhyme. For example, French merchants concocted a poem made up of 137 rhyming couplets that contained all the rules necessary to conduct commercial arithmetic (Burke, 1985).

During the Renaissance period, the focus was primarily on the practical use of memory, often involving the use of the visual arts (Yates, 1966). For example, artists of this era often painted the seating inside of a cathedral, numbering the seats in each pew so that a person would have hundreds of loci available with which to work. These artists would also be commissioned to paint elaborate and dramatic scenes on the walls and ceilings of cathedrals, often depicting Bible stories. These magnificent scenes acted as triggers to help people remember important dates, names, and events. By the sixteenth century, however, interest in the *arts of memory* had waned again. In its place there was a new spurt of *theoretical* interest in memory. Scholars such as Francis Bacon, Thomas Brown, John Locke, David Hume, Immanuel Kant, John Stuart Mill, and Thomas Reid proposed that ideas, and memory for them, are made up of smaller ideas that are associated with each other. Subsequently, many people thought that it was associations, rather than visual images, that were of primary importance for understanding memory.

## *H*ERMANN EBBINGHAUS, 1850–1909

In 1885 Ebbinghaus published his now classic monograph *Memory: A Contribution to Experimental Psychology (Über Das Gedächtnis: Untersuchugen zur Experimentellen Psychologie),* which presented the first experimental study of memory. The impact of his monograph on his contemporaries was swift. Now, instead of relying on just natural observation and conjecture, people interested in memory phenomena began to conduct experiments. The influence of Ebbinghaus was so great that soon after the publication of his pioneering monograph, the study of memory using an experimental approach largely replaced the previously fashionable philosophical approach. The philosophical approach to the study of memory survived and continues today to elucidate important properties of memory, but it is true that Ebbinghaus's monograph produced a pronounced shift in memory scholarship toward the experimental method (Klix, 1986; Kuhn, 1962).

To fully understand and appreciate today's scientific approach to memory, it's important to understand how Ebbinghaus so quickly convinced his contemporaries that the scientific approach was so well suited to the study of memory.

FIGURE 1.3
Hermann Ebbinghaus (1850–1909).
*Courtesy National Library of Medicine.*

In the next section, we will look briefly at Ebbinghaus's life and then consider why Ebbinghaus's work became so important so fast. Finally, we will briefly review Ebbinghaus's major empirical findings (see Chapter 5 also), which in many ways are as important today for understanding memory as they were when they were first published over a century ago (Eysenck, 1984; Slamecka, 1985; Wertheimer, 1986).

## Ebbinghaus's Life

Hermann Ebbinghaus was born in 1850 in what was then called Prussia and which now is western Germany. He studied history and philology (historical linguistics) at Bonn and philosophy at Halle and Berlin. In 1873 he finished writing a dissertation on the unconscious and obtained his doctorate at Berlin.

From 1873 to 1878 Ebbinghaus traveled about Europe. One day in 1875, while browsing in an old-book store in Paris, Ebbinghaus came upon a copy of Gustav Fechner's *Elements of Psychophysics,* which had been published several years earlier (1860). Fechner's work demonstrated that it was possible to scientifically study the perception of sensory stimulation. For example, Fechner had shown that the degree of brightness or loudness that a person perceives ($P$) in a light or sound is systematically related to its physical intensity ($I$). He even proposed a quantitative expression for this relationship ($P = K \log I$, which means that perceived intensity equals a constant times the logarithm of the physical intensity of the stimulus). Immediately, Ebbinghaus recognized that Fechner's experimental methods could be applicable to the study of memory.

On returning to Berlin, Ebbinghaus began his now famous investigations into memory. He conducted these investigations on himself in his own home with stimulus materials he devised. Perhaps his most famous creation is what became known as the *nonsense syllable.* Nonsense syllables are three-letter combinations of a consonant, a vowel, and a consonant that were supposedly devoid of meaning (hence the term *nonsense syllable*). *Nuh, veg, kar, zof,* and *tud* would all be examples of the kinds of nonsense syllables that Ebbinghaus used. Ebbinghaus invented nonsense syllables because he wanted to study the unadulterated properties of learning and memory. To him, this meant the study of stimuli that were brand-new (such as nonsense syllables) and that had no inherent meaning that could complicate the interpretation of his results. Contrary to what Ebbinghaus thought at the time, it was later demonstrated that nonsense syllables were not really nonsense after all—they *do* vary in meaningfulness (Glaze, 1928). For instance, the nonsense syllable *veg* could easily bring to mind the word *vegetable,* making it more likely to be remembered.

On a daily basis he would study lists of these nonsense syllables and would then attempt to recall them. His presentation of the nonsense syllables to himself was extremely exacting—each new syllable was presented for study when Ebbinghaus heard the beat of a metronome (a device used to mark time at a steady beat) or when he heard the tick of his watch. He studied the nonsense syllables until he could recall the entire list. Ebbinghaus referred to this procedure as the "method of complete mastery."

To measure how much he could retain, at varying intervals following the initial learning Ebbinghaus tried to recall all the nonsense syllables in correct order. If his recall was not perfect, he would restudy the list until he had mastered it once again. As described in more detail in Chapter 5, Ebbinghaus calculated a *savings score* that was a quantitative measure of the effort "saved" in relearning the list owing to what was retained from the original learning.

In 1880 he became a Dozent (lecturer) at Berlin University. He continued his work on memory and published in 1885 his monograph on memory. This monograph, a small book of a mere 123 pages (in the English translation), turned out to be the means by which Ebbinghaus produced a revolution in the study of memory (Bringmann & Bringmann, 1986; Hoffman, Bringmann, Bamberg, & Klein, 1987). Almost as soon as memory scholars finished reading the monograph, they either wrote about Ebbinghaus's experiments or performed ones to follow up on his work—a tradition of experimentation that has never ceased. Consequently, one historian of psychology has even suggested that "Ebbinghaus's monograph represents perhaps the most brilliant single investigation that has ever been made in experimental psychology" (Flugel, 1933, p. 200).

Ebbinghaus's monograph impressed scholars almost immediately because it contributed to psychology in three major ways. First, it made it clear that memory could be studied experimentally. A researcher could vary certain aspects of a memory task, such as the number of rehearsals given to the study material, and then observe a change in memory performance, such as the number of syllables correctly recalled.

Second, Ebbinghaus's monograph reported some experiments whose findings were new and revealed important properties of memory. These findings are as relevant today as when they were first empirically demonstrated a century ago. For instance, Ebbinghaus established that the ease of learning and the amount to be learned are not related in a simple one-to-one fashion. Instead, difficulty increases *disproportionately* with length. In other words, the number of repetitions needed to learn a list of syllables greatly increases as more syllables are added to the list. He also showed that the amount of subsequent retention depends on the degree of original learning. If he overlearned the material, the savings score would inevitably be much higher than if he had only barely mastered the list of syllables. Furthermore, Ebbinghaus was one of the first to draw attention to the powerful effects of *distribution of practice*. As discussed in Chapter 4, if a person spaces or distributes over time his or her studying, instead of cramming all the studying in at one time, the typical result is greater retention. Ebbinghaus is also credited with carefully measuring the *forgetting curve* for the first time (see Chapter 5). It should be noted that other findings of Ebbinghaus also live on through various lines of research and could, if more space were available here, be described as well.

The third major way in which Ebbinghaus's monograph was important was in its influence in establishing psychology as a bonafide science. Many in the late nineteenth century regarded Fechner's earlier success with psychophysics as having been due to the physical nature of his subject matter: eyes, ears, and skin. These skeptics of the new scientific approach to psychology argued that a rigorous, experimental, quantitative approach to mental phenomena—such as human memory—was not possible in the same way that Fechner had shown was possible for studying the senses. Ebbinghaus showed that the skeptics were wrong by providing undeniable evidence that mental phenomena were amenable to experimentation.

Ebbinghaus continued to be an active scholar after the publication of his monograph. He was promoted at Berlin University to Extraordinary Professor in 1886. In 1890 he and a colleague founded the *Zeitschrift fur Psychologie* (i.e., the *Journal of Psychology*), which became, and continues to be, a major journal in Europe for psychology. Around this time Cornell University attempted to lure him away from Germany to head its psychology laboratories. Ebbinghaus apparently concluded, however, that such a move would create a hardship for his family, and so he remained in Berlin (Bringmann & Bringmann, 1986). In 1894 he moved to the university at Breslau. He continued doing research in psychophysics, memory, and educational psychology until 1909, when he died of pneumonia.

Few would dispute that if it were not for the work of Ebbinghaus on memory over a century ago, scientific psychology would probably not be as well developed as it is today (Klix, 1986; Sprung & Sprung, 1986). In 1985, to commemorate and celebrate the 100th anniversary of the publication of Ebbinghaus's monograph on memory, the publishers of the *Journal of Experimental Psychology* produced a special issue—*Journal of Experimental Psychology: Learning, Memory and Cognition* (vol. 11, no. 3)—in which 13 current memory scholars commented on Ebbinghaus's influence on the scientific study of memory. In addition, three international conferences were held in his honor (in New York, Berlin, and Prague).

# MEMORY AFTER EBBINGHAUS

## Approaches

Since Ebbinghaus, while all the major approaches (i.e., pragmatic, experimental, atheoretical, and theoretical) continue to be used, the experimental approach has been by far the primary way that researchers have attempted to study memory. This approach has developed in several different directions. Some researchers have been *atheoretical* in their work; their concern has been to simply determine the conditions that produce or alter certain memory phenomena. However, most experimentalists since Ebbinghaus have employed an experimental/theoretical approach (i.e., one in which experiments are routinely used to test hypotheses about memory). Some investigators have focused their research and theorizing on *specific* kinds of memory phenomena, such as short-term memory or our ability to recognize familiar objects. In contrast, others have addressed the organization and functioning of memory phenomena in general. For instance, some of these latter researchers have attempted to explain all memory phenomena on the basis of subsystems—similar to the way a tape player involves the operation of components (i.e., tape reader, amplifier, speakers, etc.). Finally, some approaches have more specific concerns about the kinds of methods used in experiments and/or the types of people most deserving of study (studying the progressive memory loss in Alzheimer's sufferers or the development of memory strategies in young children). These trends are very much alive today.

The section below reviews the movements that have evolved since Ebbinghaus. This review will not provide much detail on the experimental or theoretical issues mentioned. The chapters that follow will do that. Instead, an overview of the major themes that have influenced the investigation and interpretation of different issues concerning memory will be presented.

## Atheoretical Work

Ebbinghaus's work is generally regarded as having been atheoretical in nature. The variables he manipulated, such as the number of repetitions or the delay between study and test, were ones that were thought to be related to memory performance. Ebbinghaus certainly understood the general relationship of these variables to performance and thus in some sense could be said to have been theoretically minded. However, Ebbinghaus did not consider the different kinds of outcomes that might have resulted from his experiments and what these outcomes might indicate about the functioning of human memory. Since his research did not attempt to test which hypotheses about memory functioning were supported or not, it has been thought of as being atheoretical.

The reasons that Ebbinghaus took an atheoretical approach are unclear. The most likely reason is that he had the wisdom to recognize that a new science needs to be grounded in reliable observations. Until a critical mass of observations exists, it is often not possible to discriminate one theory from another (Bruce, 1985; Neisser, 1985). Many of the researchers who followed Ebbinghaus in the late nineteenth and early twentieth centuries followed his experimental/atheoretical approach to memory as well. Investigator after investigator sought out the most obvious variables and determined how memory performance depended on these variables.

Several methodological developments occurred at the beginning of the twentieth century. While Ebbinghaus always tested himself for *serial memory* (i.e., for a list of items in the order of presentation), other researchers who followed him tested memory differently. Some of these people examined memory for pairs of items, a procedure called *paired-associate learning* (e.g., Calkins, 1894, 1896; Müller & Pilzecker, 1900); for the free recall of a list of words regardless of order (Kirkpatrick, 1894); and for visual patterns (Wlf, 1922; see Wertheimer, 1986).

Not every researcher immediately following Ebbinghaus had an atheoretical orientation. As the early experimental work progressed, more and more researchers started to put their work into a theoretical context. Let's briefly examine some of this research.

## Durability of Memory

**Sensory memory.** Sir William Hamilton observed in 1859 that he could not recall very much of what he saw when briefly glancing at an array of items. In the 1960s, a methodology was developed to quantify how much information is retained from a single glance and how that information decays in memory (Sperling, 1960). Each sense modality is now thought to have its own sensory memory system.

**Short-term memory.** William James (1890), one of this country's most influential and famous early psychologists, proposed that the momentary memory that serves our conscious activities differs a great deal from the less accessible memory we have for vast amounts of information and events. What is surprising is that interest in the distinction between short-term and long-term memory did not attract intense investigation until the late 1950s. Since then there has been a great deal of research on such phenomena as the decline in accuracy over short time intervals (Brown, 1958; Peterson & Peterson, 1959), the speed of information retrieval from short-term memory (Sternberg, 1966), how information is coded for short-term storage (Conrad, 1963; Shepard & Metzler, 1971; Shulman, 1972), and the form and capacity of short-term memory (Baddeley, 1992; Miller, 1956).

**Long-term memory.** Many scholars and researchers who followed in Ebbinghaus's footsteps were concerned with memories established long ago in a person's life. In the past twenty to thirty years it has become increasingly clear that many factors influence our long-term memory capabilities. In a very influential paper that will be discussed in some detail in Chapter 3, Atkinson and Shiffrin (1968) proposed that memory processes were affected by two major factors. One of these factors depended on the actual biology of the memory system, while the other depended on processes under the person's voluntary control (such as the creation and rehearsal of a rhyme to help remember new information).

Research also began to strongly suggest that the nature of the control that a person exercised in a memory task depended in large measure on what the person knew, or thought he or she knew, about the memory process or the

"*The matters about which I'm being questioned, Your Honor, are all things I should have included in my long-term memory but which I mistakenly inserted in my short-term memory.*"

FIGURE 1.4
Cartoon distinguishing between short- and long-term memory.
*Drawing by Ed Fisher; © 1983 The New Yorker Magazine, Inc.*

sought-after memory (Brown & McNeill, 1966; Flavell, 1977; Hart, 1965). For instance, if a person knew an effective memory strategy for recalling some information (e.g., concentrating on the sound of the first letter) and also knew when to apply it, this knowledge could certainly affect memory performance. Knowledge about the memory process is called *metamemory* ("memory about memory"). Since the recognition of the importance of metamemory, considerable research has shown that this kind of knowledge is essential to the development of effective memory skills (Hertzog, 1992; Pressley & El-Dinary, 1992). This area of research, among others, also demonstrates the increasing attention that investigators have paid to the topic of consciousness and the influence that voluntary processes have on memory performance. In fact, a new journal (*Consciousness and Cognition*) was recently inaugurated to explicitly explore the role that conscious processes play in our thinking and remembering.

In 1932, Bartlett criticized research done with nonsense syllables for not dealing with meaningful memories like those formed in everyday life. Nonetheless, psychologists paid little attention to Bartlett's plea, and memory for one's personal past received very little notice until the 1970s (Tulving, 1972). During the past decade, however, interest in memory for one's past has reawakened, and considerable research has been done on *autobiographical memory* (Conway, 1990; Neisser, 1988; Ross, 1991; Rubin, 1986).

Another kind of long-term memory that psychologists have only recently begun to devote serious attention to is *prospective memory*. This kind of memory is concerned with our ability to remember to carry out future actions (such as remembering to go to the dentist's office next Thursday). Theories have been proposed to account for how we realize our obligations and responsibilities in order to remember to perform them at the right time (Harris, 1984; Meacham, 1988; Winograd, 1988).

## Factors Affecting Remembering

**Interference.** Müller and Pilzecker (1900) were among the first to describe how one memory can interfere with the remembering of another memory. For example, suppose you learn to drive a car in the United States and then you move to England. If you are typical, during your first few outings you will likely experience considerable problems in driving, even (and perhaps especially) if you have had lots of previous driving experience. Why? Because in the United States people are taught to drive a car on the right side of the road, but in England drivers are taught just the opposite. Therefore, there will be interference between your old memories of driving on the right and the new memories you are trying to form (i.e., learning to drive a car on the left side of the road). As you will learn in more depth later, not only can old memories interfere with newer memories (such as in the car example), but the reverse is also true—more recent memories can interfere with the recall of older memories.

**Emotions and motivations.** Sigmund Freud proposed in his book *Psychopathology of Everyday Life* (Freud & Brill, 1916) that many memory errors are produced by unconscious motivations. For instance, according to Freud, extremely unpleasant emotional experiences or events are sometimes banished from conscious awareness by the process known as *repression*. Although Freud's notions were largely ignored by early memory researchers, in recent years they have resurfaced (especially to account for some forms of clinical amnesia; see Chapter 14).

**Acquisition of memory skills.**  As you learned earlier in this chapter, people have long tried to learn techniques to improve their ability to remember things. Ideally, people would be able to learn a small set of memory skills that would work in a variety of different situations. Unfortunately, research has shown rather convincingly that any particular memory skill is usually of limited usefulness (see Chapter 15). In other words, learning a technique to remember your grocery list (such as the *method of loci*) will not likely help you memorize your social security number.

In addition, in contrast to what many people believe, memory is *not* a muscle—exercising it on one type of material will not affect your ability to memorize other types of information. For example, William James and some of his colleagues attempted to improve their ability to memorize poetry and prose by repeated attempts at such memorization. They found no evidence that practice at memorization *per se* had any beneficial effect on memory ability. Other early investigators, such as Thorndike and Woodworth (1901), also explored this issue and came to the same conclusion.

## General Theoretical Perspectives

Besides the investigation of specific memory phenomena, a variety of general theoretical perspectives in the field of memory has also developed. Some of the major perspectives are as follows.

**Biological.**  It has long been held by many researchers that memory is ultimately a biologically based process. As you will learn in Chapter 7, many different types of drugs, hormones, and neurotransmitters, as well as the application of electrical stimulation, can dramatically influence memory performance or alter physiological structures involved in the formation, storage, and retrieval of memories.

**Associationism/connectionism.**  In its simplest form, the associationism/connectionism approach maintains that memory involves making and storing associations, or connections, between items. This approach was already more than 2000 years old by the time of Ebbinghaus's work. By and large, the memory tasks that the early psychologists chose to study focused on simple associations, such as learning a list of words in order or learning to pair two items in memory.

**Information-processing/cognitive.**  Largely because of the influence of the Gestalt psychologists (e.g., Koffka, 1935; Kohler, 1947; Wertheimer, 1912), almost all psychologists came to accept the view that context, organization, and meaning are very important factors for both learning and memory. Inspired by the computer age, the information-processing/cognitive perspective further assumes that our memory for new information is dependent on how this information is processed. It is suggested that the memory system, like many computers, is controlled by a central processor. One of the major jobs of this central processor is to govern the distribution of attention and to aid in the retrieval of stored information (Atkinson & Shiffrin, 1968). The distribution of attention is directed by a previously learned program called a "routine" or "strategy." For example, a strategy for item rehearsal might direct a person to first read the item, then repeat the item to himself or herself, and then finally say the item aloud (Rundus, 1971; Underwood, 1978).

Many researchers became interested not only in the act of processing information but also in the nature of what was being processed (Neisser, 1967, 1976). These theorists were concerned with the kinds of knowledge held in memory and the different ways that knowledge could be processed or represented (Baddeley, 1982; Chase & Ericsson, 1982; Craik & Lockhart, 1972). Most recently, the roles of conscious and unconscious awareness in the retrieval of memories has attracted considerable attention (Graf & Schacter, 1985; Jacoby & Witherspoon, 1982; Tulving & Schacter, 1990).

**Multimodal.**  Because of societal pressures in the last decade or two to aid the field of education, the cognitive difficulties of the elderly, and the problems of the neurologically impaired, many researchers have looked for ways to facilitate learning and memory. As a result, many psychologists have begun to pay attention not only to variables that *directly* affect memory (e.g., the amount of time a person has to study and learn the material) but also to the *indirect* influences on memory performance. These indirect influences include a person's unique perception and interpretation of the world, his or her motivations and social interactions, and various physiological and emotional states (Herrmann & Searleman, 1990; Herrmann, Weingartner, Searleman, & McEvoy, 1992; Poon, 1986).

## Movements

In recent years, the study of memory has seen the growth of various memory trends or movements. These wide-ranging movements involve both psychologists and nonpsychologists who have joined together to address certain issues of common interest or concern. Although the theoretical perspectives of the people in a particular movement may differ considerably, these people choose to work together to help solve problems that otherwise may slow the progress of research. At least three movements in recent years have affected the evolution of memory research.

**The everyday/applied memory movement.**  The everyday/applied memory movement is arguably the most influential movement currently within the field of memory. As the name implies, this movement emphasizes the value of studying memory in naturalistic settings and the investigation of memory tasks that have an applied focus (Baddeley, 1982; Neisser, 1976, 1982). Psychologists interested in memory have been involved in many different types of applied problems, ranging from determining the reliability of eyewitness accounts in legal testimony, to designing memorable telephone numbers and postal codes, to evaluating how well people can recall information in television commercials. The rapid growth of this movement has been encouraged by two international conferences on the practical aspects of memory (Gruneberg, Morris, & Sykes, 1978, 1988) and by the creation of a journal intended as an outlet for ecologically valid memory research (*Human Learning,* broadened and renamed *Applied Cognitive Psychology* in 1987). Recently, there has been considerable debate about how useful it is, or is not, to do memory research in natural settings (e.g., Bahrick, 1991; Banaji & Crowder, 1989; Ceci & Bronfenbrenner, 1991; Gruneberg, Morris, & Sykes, 1991).

**The life-span approach memory movement.** From Chapter 12, you will discover that there is now good evidence that humans have the capacity to learn and remember certain information (such as the sound of their mother's voice) even before they are born! Elementary school teachers, as well as child psychologists, have long been fascinated by the memory abilities and limitations of children. Many researchers now realize the importance of exploring the vast developmental changes in memory capability that occur between infancy and old age. Researchers have begun to develop new techniques to help people suffering from memory difficulties that come naturally with age or with neurological problems that often attend advanced age (Poon, Rubin, & Wilson, 1989; Rybash, Hoyer, & Roodin, 1986).

**The neurological memory movement.** Because of advances in medical science, more people than ever before are being kept alive who have profound memory disorders due to brain injuries. To help these individuals better cope with their memory problems, clinically oriented psychologists have been devising new methods of remediation. These methods are specifically appropriate for those whose memory problems originate from disease, head injury, or environmental factors (Stollery, 1988; Wilson, 1987; Wilson & Moffat, 1984). This movement has grown rapidly in the past few years and is likely to continue to gain momentum.

# *THE FUTURE OF MEMORY RESEARCH*

History reveals that people have been thinking and speculating about how human memory works for thousands of years. The field has become much more diverse in the past two decades in the theoretical issues it chooses to explore and in the methodologies that are used for these investigations.

In our opinion, the current study of human memory is in a volatile phase.

Analysis of the history of memory since Ebbinghaus indicates that more general theories are competing for the title of "the best or most important explanation of memory" than ever before. There are also many more specific theories competing for the title of "most important explanation of —————" (you can fill in the blank with almost any specific memory phenomenon that you want). Research has only recently begun in many emerging areas such as autobiographical memory, prospective memory, and the unconscious awareness of past memories.

It's too early to tell which of today's movements and theories will have the greatest effect in the long run. It is equally uncertain what new movements and theories will arise. Clearly, the field of memory is in a state of flux. Many findings are well established, but their interpretations are not. Thus, researchers are open to new ideas, far more so than a couple of decades ago, and perhaps more than will be so a few decades from now (after the best theories and most persuasive movements have become entrenched). It is for these reasons that we believe that now is an especially exciting time to explore and study memory.

# *S*UMMARY

### I. Memory through the Ages
- Although the scientific study of memory started only about a century ago with the remarkably influential work of Hermann Ebbinghaus, scholarly thought concerning memory processes has occurred for thousands of years.
- Many different ways have been used to study memory, including the *pragmatic*, *experimental*, *atheoretical*, and *theoretical* approaches.

### II. Memory before Ebbinghaus
- Memory ability was highly valued by early societies, as is evidenced by their creation of various gods and goddesses of memory.
- Early thinking about memory involved the pragmatic need to improve memory performance. The Greek philosophers Plato and Aristotle wrote extensively about possible models of memory and memory phenomena.
- Little substantive work on memory appears to have occurred during the dark ages. During the Renaissance, interest in the pragmatic aspects of memory revived, but it then waned during the sixteenth century as interest in the theoretical nature of memory blossomed.

### III. Hermann Ebbinghaus
- The publication of Ebbinghaus's short book on memory in 1885 had a dramatic and almost immediate effect. The experimental approach to memory that he demonstrated was quickly adopted by others as the primary way to study memory phenomena.

- Ebbinghaus's monograph revealed many new properties of memory. Although Ebbinghaus certainly championed the experimental approach to studying memory, his research was also mainly atheoretical. Today, most researchers use an experimental/theoretical approach when exploring memory processes.

## IV. Memory after Ebbinghaus

- A large number of different memory phenomena have been investigated since the time of Ebbinghaus. Many of these concern the *durability of memory, factors that affect remembering,* and the *acquisition of specific memory skills.*

- Several general theoretical perspectives have developed over the years with regard to the study of memory. These include the following approaches: *biological, associationism/connectionism, information-processing/cognitive,* and *multimodal.*

- In recent years, three movements in memory research have been identified. These movements (*everyday/applied, life span,* and *neurological*) will likely play a major role in the future of memory research.

# 2

# *Methodology of Memory Research*

❖

Many memory phenomena that have intrigued people are ones that occur during normal, everyday living. Examples include *memory slips* (when a person accidentally recalls something other than what was intended, such as inadvertently addressing your teacher by her more colorful nickname rather than by her real name); *memory blocks* (when a person tries repeatedly to recall something but is unable to succeed—something that happens all too often for some people when taking exams); *absentmindedness* (when a person intends to do one thing but unintentionally does another—planning to meet a friend for an early breakfast but instead reading the morning paper); and the frustrating *tip-of-the-tongue phenomenon* (when a person fails to recall a word or name, feels confident that he or she knows the correct response, but can't quite recall it at the moment—meeting an acquaintance and not being able to dredge up the person's name during the conversation).

This chapter begins by examining the nature of the memory process and the factors that influence memory performance. Then a number of different types of research techniques that are frequently used to evaluate memory capability are discussed.

## THE MEMORY PROCESS

The way that people behave on a particular memory task is called their *memory performance*. The term *memory performance* can refer to many different things. For instance, at various times, we may be interested in the accuracy of recall, or the speed of recognition, or more subjective aspects of performance such as the degree of effort people judge they have given to a memory task. The memory process is composed of three main phases: *registration* (which involves the transforming of information presented to a person into a form that can be retained), *retention* (which is the storage of information), and *remembering* (which involves the retrieval of information).

Memory for stimuli or events can occur either intentionally or incidentally. For instance, a memory researcher can explicitly direct one group of subjects to learn a list of words for subsequent recall. For a different group of subjects, the researcher might have them perform another kind of task (such as a rhyming task) that includes the same list of words the first group was given. By later testing each group's recall of the items, the experimenter can compare performance between an intentional memory task and an incidental one. When a memory task is *intentional* (i.e., the person is deliberately trying to commit the material to memory), the process of registration is referred to as *explicit encoding*. In contrast, during an *incidental* memory task, when the person is not deliberately trying to learn the material, the registration process is called either *incidental encoding* or, more generally, *incidental learning*. The generic term *encoding* is often used when no distinction is being made between intentional and incidental registration. Generally speaking, explicit encoding results in better memory performance than does incidental learning. This makes sense, since you would expect to have a more detailed memory for things that you consciously intended to remember.

## Explicit Remembering

If the process of remembering involves the *conscious* recollection of previous experiences, it is called *explicit remembering*. Explicit remembering can occur either intentionally or involuntarily. For instance, if you want to, you may be able to intentionally recall the date of your mother's birthday or your social security number. Sometimes, however, a past memory may enter your conscious awareness completely unbidden and spontaneously (such as when you are unable to stop dwelling on a recent argument you had with your best friend). Both cases are considered instances of explicit remembering because conscious recollection is involved.

Explicit remembering is typically assessed by measuring a person's *recognition* or *recall* ability. During recognition a person decides whether or not something has been encountered before. When your parents smiled at you during your high school graduation ceremony, it was because they could recognize your face in the crowd. To do so, they probably scanned the facial characteristics of all the people in the ceremony, and when a match was found with information already stored in their memories about your particular facial features, they "recognized" you. In contrast to what is essentially a matching process during recognition, the process of recall requires a person to generate or retrieve information from memory. As will be described in more detail later in this chapter, this process can be either aided (cued recall) or unaided (free recall) by retrieval cues. Most psychologists think that the process of retrieving information from memory that occurs during recall requires more extensive mental processing than occurs during recognition. This means that with some exceptions (e.g., Watkins & Tulving, 1975), recognition is usually easier than recall and results in better performance.

Everyday life experiences provide good evidence that recognition is generally easier than recall. For instance, many people claim that while they often have trouble remembering names, they never forget a face. This is because a person's face is a great retrieval cue if all you have to do is simply judge whether or not the person is familiar (recognition of the person). Recalling a person's name from memory, however, often requires a better retrieval cue than seeing the person's face. This is particularly true if the person is seen in an unexpected context. The tip-of-the-tongue phenomenon is another good example of how recognition is easier than recall. Even when someone can't recall a particular name or word, he or she can almost always recognize it if the correct response is suggested.

Most students also prefer to take a multiple-choice exam over an essay exam. This is because a multiple-choice exam only requires the ability to recognize the correct answer, whereas an essay exam requires the recall of information. However, as many of us know from personal experience, this doesn't mean that all multiple-choice tests are easy. These tests can be extremely difficult if the alternatives are very similar to the correct answer (this makes it more challenging to recognize the right response). As you will see in Chapter 12, the meager differences in recognition ability between children and adults pale in comparison to the vast differences in recall performance. Again, this supports the notion that in most circumstances recognition is easier than recall.

## Implicit Remembering

The process of remembering, however, does not always involve conscious recollection. For example, suppose that yesterday you saw the funny cartoon on the next page about a frog who, both literally and figuratively, had something on the tip of his tongue. Now today, while working on a term paper for your English literature class, you decide that you need a good synonym for the word *flatterer*. To your surprise, the word *toady*, which you rarely use, comes to mind quickly. This could be an instance of *implicit remembering*. Evidence for implicit remembering occurs whenever a person has no conscious recollection of information or past events but, nevertheless, is affected by such material. This influence is most often reflected in the performance of some task. If you had no conscious awareness of the frog cartoon, but it nevertheless did influence your choice of a synonym, then implicit remembering was operating. The importance of distinguishing between explicit and implicit remembering will be highlighted throughout the book.

FIGURE 2.1
Cartoon about a frog.
*Reprinted by permission: Tribune Media Services*

## The Nature of Independent Variables in Memory Research

A critical goal in memory research is to identify the factors that influence memory performance. These factors are called *independent variables*. Some independent variables have been found that affect almost all memory tasks, and anyone who is truly interested in becoming knowledgeable about memory should become familiar with these independent variables. They can be classified into three groups: *organismic variables, antecedent variables,* and *task variables.* One of the major scientific challenges in current memory research is to determine just how these different types of independent variables combine, and under what circumstances, to affect memory performance. Let's briefly describe these variables (you will see them in operation throughout the book).

*Organismic variables* refer to permanent or relatively permanent characteristics of a person that affect general memory performance. Examples of such personal characteristics include the individual's degree of intelligence, ability to concentrate, normal attention span, and general motivation to do well, as well as whether the person is physically and psychologically healthy or not. *Antecedent variables* are independent variables that have recently altered (usually temporarily) a person's typical organismic level. For instance, antecedent variables that would influence a person's normal ability to concentrate on a memory task include the amount of sleep the person has recently had and whether or not the individual is under the influence of any drugs (like alcohol) or medications (like sleeping pills). Promising to pay a subject 50 cents for every word correctly recalled from a list to be studied would be a powerful antecedent variable to raise most people's typical level of motivation to be alert and attentive to the task.

*Task variables* consist of the particular characteristics that are unique to a given situation. There are four main types of task variables. *Instructional variables* influence how a person performs a memory task by giving explicit or implicit instructions to the subject. For example, on a subsequent surprise memory test, subjects told to form bizarre visual images between words on a list will usually outperform subjects not given such instructions. *Presentational variables* affect memory performance by means of the way stimuli are presented. For instance, varying the amount of time a subject has to study and learn the material to be remembered can markedly determine how much a person will ultimately remember. Another example of a presentational variable is whether the stimuli are presented orally or in written form. *Stimulus variables* refer to the different types of material that a subject might be expected to remember. It is well known that more meaningful or familiar stimuli (such as common English words) are easier to recall than are less meaningful or unfamiliar stimuli (such as groups of unrelated letters).

The fourth type of task variable pertains to the *context* in which a task occurs. The context of a given situation can vary widely and may greatly affect memory performance (Davies & Thomson, 1988). For example, although the context for many memory studies is still the laboratory, other contexts can involve a person's workplace, his or her home, or even where the individual goes for enjoyment (e.g., when you are at the beach and you are selected to purchase ice cream, you may have to remember several different requests simultaneously). It should be noted that not all research laboratories are alike. And even the same laboratory on different days can present subjects with widely varying contextual conditions (e.g., different experimenters involved in the same research projects may test different subjects and may affect subjects differently because of their particular moods, personalities, and gender). Context effects also can be seen when the memory task is embedded within different activities: using the phone, driving a car, keeping track of finances, dieting, and so on. As you will learn later, some memory investigations have even involved the context of a formal Senate hearing (Neisser, 1981)!

# EVALUATING MEMORY PERFORMANCE

## Primary Measures

There are numerous ways to measure what someone can remember about something. All *primary measures* reflect the amount of information held in memory. One typical way to operationalize the term *amount of information* is in terms of accuracy. A person who can answer all the questions on a topic with 100 percent accuracy will generally be thought of as having mastered all the relevant information. Now contrast this performance with that of someone who answers all the questions incorrectly. This unfortunate individual will be considered as knowing absolutely nothing about the topic. Sometimes the degree to which a primary measure adequately reflects what is in memory is open to debate (as when a student complains to a teacher that an exam was unfair in that the questions didn't really allow the student to demonstrate what he or she *really* knew about the material).

Procedures for judging someone's memory may give credit only if every response is produced precisely and in the same order as originally presented. Alternatively, scoring procedures may give credit if memory adequately represents the central ideas (often called the *gist*) of the material originally presented. A complicating factor in scoring for gist is that memory may contain items (known as *intrusion errors*) that were not part of what was originally presented. Items that a person omits are usually judged as simply not in memory (that is the implicit assumption of most teachers when failure to answer a question is scored as a zero). However, there may be reasons to believe that an omission does not in fact always represent ignorance. For example, people may fail to remember something that they truly know because they are too tense and their memory is temporarily blocked. Some students often claim that this happens to them on final exams. In other cases, as will be explored in more detail in Chapter 10, people will sometimes pretend not to remember something because it may be in their best interests in terms of their social interactions with others. (For example, you might tell your mother that you simply forgot to write that thank-you note to your maiden aunt for the birthday present she gave you. In reality, however, you didn't forget at all—you just didn't want to do it, but you cannot openly admit this to your mother without starting a big fight.)

When people do not know the answer, they may decide to guess. Therefore, it is often helpful to estimate the likelihood that the guess might be correct by chance alone. Judging the likelihood of guessing is usually difficult with recall unless you have independent evidence that the person may have known the information (as your teacher may have if he or she remembers that you described the information in class that you failed to later recall on the exam). Similarly, when people know an answer they do not wish to disclose (such as when recalling a sensitive or an embarrassing episode from their past), they may claim ignorance or fake an answer. Judging the likelihood of nondisclosure again requires other data. The likelihood of guessing is much easier to determine with recognition tests. If a question on a recognition test contains three incorrect answers and one correct one, then a guess, on the average, will be correct 25 percent of the time.

## Secondary Measures

Memory performance can also be evaluated by means of *secondary measures*. These measures are concerned with aspects of memory other than the quantity of information correctly retrieved by someone. Instead, these measures involve an assessment of the *quality* of information remembered. One type of secondary measure is the time needed to either recall or recognize an item. It is usually the case that the stronger the memory, the faster is the reaction time (RT) to respond. The RT refers to the time interval between the onset of a stimulus and the beginning of a response to that stimulus that is made as quickly as possible. For example, after learning a list of words, a subject may be presented with the word *helicopter* and be asked to decide as fast as possible if this word appeared on the original list. The person's RT for responding to the word *helicopter* can be determined by having the individual depress a button or key on a computer that is connected to a timer. If a subject is very accurate in his or her responding, then faster RTs typically mean stronger memories. Another kind of secondary measure assesses subjective feelings and attitudes present during learning or retrieval. For instance, subjects may be asked to indicate the degree of confidence they have in their answers.

## Primary-Secondary Relationships

Secondary measures often provide insights into the memory processes that underlie the primary measures. But the relationship between primary and secondary measures is not always straightforward. For example, the speed of a memory response typically increases with a person's familiarity with the material learned. Although fast responses occur when memory is strong, they can also occur when memory is absent and a person just guesses. When people try too hard to answer quickly, they are more likely to make errors (anyone who has had to rush to finish an exam can vouch for this). Thus, in such situations, people sometimes *trade off* accuracy for speed (Murdock, 1982). To the extent that different people feel different degrees of pressure, it becomes very hard to untangle the relationship between speed (a secondary measure) and accuracy (a primary measure).

# TRADITIONAL MEMORY TASKS

In the past, most researchers examined memory performance using only explicit remembering procedures and tasks. People were usually tested in laboratory settings, and the testing was for the conscious recollection of previously presented material. The testing involved some form of recall or recognition of either verbal items (words, numbers, nonsense syllables, sentences, or paragraphs) or geometric shapes, faces, or pictures.

## Varying Independent Variables

For several decades following Ebbinghaus, most psychologists investigated how people performed a few elementary memory tasks. Frequently, these tasks involved learning lists of nonsense syllables or words. In order to ensure that

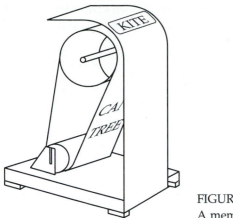

FIGURE 2.2
A memory drum.

the list items were presented in a precise and consistent fashion, devices such as the *memory drum* (shown in Figure 2.2) were invented early in this century. This machine presents materials in front of the subject's eyes for a set amount of time by rotating a drum on which the stimuli to be studied are attached. In the past 20 years, the memory drum has been largely replaced by microcomputers that achieve the same effect.

With a memory drum the experimenter can vary a whole host of different independent variables to examine their effects on memory performance. For instance, the *familiarity* of the words to be remembered can be varied (e.g., the word *green* versus the word *chartreuse*), as well as their *relatedness* to each other (i.e., the words could all be body parts like *arm, leg, foot,* and *nose,* or they could be completely unrelated to each other like the words *door, book, ice,* and *goat*); their *relative frequency of occurrence* in everyday living can be manipulated (e.g., the word *house* is more frequently used than the word *chateau* to refer to a dwelling), or the words chosen can be *concrete* or *abstract* in nature. Words that are classified as concrete denote something that can be perceived by the senses and that a person can easily picture or imagine (words such as *bird, tree,* and *coin*). In contrast, abstract words typically denote ideas or concepts and are not easily imagined or reflected in pictures (words such as *truth, justice,* and *dignity*).

To help researchers classify words appropriately, sources exist that contain hundreds of different words, each rated on various dimensions. For example, Toglia and Battig (1978) had dozens of college students from the University of Colorado rate a total of 2854 words on several different dimensions (such as *concreteness, meaningfulness,* and *familiarity*). Each word was rated on a 7-point scale, with 1 indicating a low rating and 7 a high rating. The typical subject rated 480 words on one dimension only. The results were published in a book that researchers can consult to select words with specific characteristics. For example, by using the book, an investigator could select the following 10 words for a memory experiment, half of which are high in both concreteness and familiarity and half of which are low in concreteness but high in familiarity:

| High concreteness/high familiarity | Low concreteness/high familiarity |
| --- | --- |
| blush | authentic |
| cook | good |
| guest | infinite |
| punch | social |
| temple | wise |

Factors such as concreteness and familiarity are not independent of each other; for example, in general, words that are concrete are also more likely to be frequently seen and familiar to people than is true of abstract words. Therefore, the memory researcher must be careful in the selection of the particular items used so as not to misinterpret the results and claim that one independent variable (such as familiarity) affected performance when in reality it was a different variable (such as concreteness). Memory performance is usually enhanced when the stimuli to be remembered are either familiar, frequent, related to each other, or concrete (and especially if these attributes are combined).

## Evaluating Memory Ability

Several standard methods were developed by early memory researchers to evaluate a person's memory ability. As mentioned before, these methods (which are still in use today) usually involve learning items in a list. For instance, sometimes people are required to recall the items in the exact order in which they were studied. This procedure is called *serial learning*, and every-day examples of serial learning abound. These include tasks such as memorizing poetry, Bible verses, nursery rhymes, and songs, as well as learning the correct order of the days of the week, months of the year, and letters of the alphabet. For decades, the most popular way to measure a person's short-term memory capacity has been to determine the maximum number of items the person can correctly recall in order. This capacity is known as the *memory span*, and it is determined by using a serial learning procedure that is widely used to assess the capability of people with known or suspected memory disorders (see Chapter 14 for an in-depth discussion of memory assessment techniques for clinical populations).

To determine your own memory span for digits, try the following exercise: Using the array of digits below, have a friend (or you can do it yourself) read out loud the first row of digits at the rate of 1 digit per second. Immediately after hearing the last digit in the sequence, try to repeat the digits in correct order. If you can do so, follow the same procedure for each succeeding line. At some point—if you're a typical college student, it will occur for a row with seven or eight digits—you will make a mistake. Your memory span for digits is equal to the highest sequence length that you can repeat back perfectly.

2 8
6 9 1
0 4 7 3
8 7 4 5 4
9 0 2 4 8 1
5 7 4 2 2 9 6
6 4 7 1 9 3 0 4
3 5 6 7 1 8 4 8 5
1 0 2 8 8 3 4 7 2 9
4 7 2 0 8 2 7 4 2 6 4
7 3 1 0 9 3 4 3 5 1 3 8

Sometimes subjects are allowed to recall list items in any order they wish. This is referred to as *free recall learning,* and as you will read in the next chapter, free recall procedures often give rise to what are called *serial-position curves,* in which the items from the beginning and end of the list are best recalled. At other times subjects are given retrieval cues to help them during testing. This is called *cued recall,* and the nature of the cue is a potent independent variable that can vary on a number of dimensions (Watkins & Gardiner, 1982). For instance, to help a person recall the word *red,* the cue could be semantic (*it's a color*); the cue could be graphic (it's spelled like *r _*); or the cue could be phonemic (it rhymes with *bed*). In general, cued recall results in significantly better memory performance than does free recall, and the more cues given the better.

A procedure called *paired-associate learning* is a very common type of cued recall that was extensively used during the 1950s and 1960s. In this procedure, subjects are given a series of pairs of items to remember. The first item of a pair is called the *stimulus* and the second item the *response.* Subjects are expected to learn to associate each stimulus with the appropriate response. After numerous study trials to learn the correct associations, the stimulus items are presented later in a random order, and the subjects are expected to recall the proper response to each stimulus. Memory researchers have varied many characteristics of the item pairs, such as their relatedness, confusability, and concreteness, to investigate the effects on learning and memory.

Table 2.1 presents a typical study list of paired associates and shows what a test trial might look like. The paired-associate paradigm has been used extensively to investigate the acquisition of foreign language vocabulary. For example, one may pair in memory a foreign term with an English word, such as the Latin word *puer* with its English equivalent, *boy.*

Two popular forms of testing recognition (that all students are familiar with) are the *multiple-choice test* and the *true-false test.* A multiple-choice test is also an example of a *forced-choice test.* This is a test in which a set of alternatives is presented and the subject must choose one or more of the items. A true-false

**TABLE 2.1** AN EXAMPLE OF A TYPICAL PAIRED-ASSOCIATE EXPERIMENT

| Study list | Test trial (new order) |
| --- | --- |
| horse—desk | pen—? |
| plant—wrench | water—? |
| stamp—picture | button—? |
| pen—clock | horse—? |
| needle—glass | grass—? |
| puck—cereal | plant—? |
| button—brain | puck—? |
| award—floor | case—? |
| grass—cheese | note—? |
| water—handle | stamp—? |
| case—science | needle—? |
| note—eraser | award—? |

test is sometimes called a *yes-no test* because the subject must respond in a binary fashion to an item or question ("Was the color purple on the list?" or "Is a bird a mammal?").

A common laboratory method that uses a forced-choice or yes-no response for testing recognition is known as the *study-test procedure*. It entails presenting a subject with a series of items, only half of which were presented originally during learning. The subject's task is to classify each item as being either "old" (having been previously presented) or "new" (not having been previously presented). With this procedure there are two ways to get a correct answer. You may score a *hit* by identifying an old item as having been previously presented, or you may score a *correct rejection* by identifying a new item. Similarly, there are two ways to be mistaken. You can overlook an old item and thus score a *miss*, or you can incorrectly classify a new item as being an old one, in which case you are marked with a *false alarm*. A variant of the study-test procedure is sometimes called the *single-item probe technique*, made popular by Sternberg (1966, 1969, 1975). In this procedure the subject is given a short list of items to learn, followed by a single-item probe. The subject's task is to respond "yes" if the probe was on the list and "no" if it wasn't. The response is typically made by pressing a button or key as fast as possible. Since accuracy is usually quite high, the subject's response time (or latency) is usually the critical dependent variable (see Chapter 3 for a more complete discussion).

# NEWER MEMORY TASKS

During the past two decades many memory researchers have concluded that the traditional memory tasks described above, while certainly useful and informative, are not sufficient to fully understand the range and diversity of human memory. One reason for this shift is that it is now recognized that many memory phenomena are very task-specific. In other words, independent variables—such as the effects of rehearsal, drugs, or mood on memory—often differ in important ways across different tasks. Therefore, memory researchers must carefully select the tasks used to study a memory phenomena and compare across tasks the effects of their independent variables.

Since the current prevailing view is that discovering the facets of memory can best be achieved by utilizing a much larger group of tasks, most memory researchers are now much more inclined to use research methods other than just the traditional laboratory ones. These newer methods include, but are certainly not limited to, the following: asking people to keep diaries of their activities and then testing them for selected items, having people fill out questionnaires about their general knowledge of the memory process itself or concerning their own memory problems, examining the effects of priming memory with pictures or words on future performance (see below), having people undergo brain-imaging procedures to examine brain structures that are known to be critical for normal memory functioning, and exploring how people remember to perform future actions.

In addition, psychologists have greatly broadened the types of stimuli that they are interested in investigating. One area that has drawn particular attention, and that is described in detail in Chapter 11, is *autobiographical memory*. Research in this area involves testing a person's knowledge for personal past memories. Examples of this kind of research include testing for the memory of old television show titles (Squire & Cohen, 1982), long-term retention of Spanish learned in school (Bahrick, 1984), famous faces (Albert, Butters, & Levin, 1980), famous voices (Meudell, Northen, Snowden, & Neary, 1980), public events (Brown, Rips, & Shevell, 1985), events that occurred during anesthesia (Bonke, Fitch, & Millar, 1990) or hypnosis (Pettinati, 1988), and recognition of high school classmates decades after graduation. [In case you were wondering, you'll probably recognize a lot of people at your twenty-fifth high school reunion, especially if you look at your yearbook before attending (Bahrick, Bahrick, & Wittlinger, 1975).]

## The Emergence of the Value of Implicit Memory Testing

In addition to the growing realization that many memory phenomena were task-specific and needed to be explored using a wider variety of stimuli and procedures, there was another major reason that researchers decided that it made sense to start using some new types of memory tasks. This change in attitude can largely be attributed to some startling findings concerning the memory capabilities of people suffering from amnesia. To appreciate why this change in direction occurred, let's preview some of the research you will learn more about in Chapters 7 and 14.

Until around 1970, it was believed that people suffering from certain types of amnesia could not learn or remember anything new after the onset of the amnesia. This conclusion, however, was based only on using *explicit* tests of memory—standard tests of recall or recognition. But Warrington and Weiskrantz (1968, 1970), in some pioneering research, showed convincingly that amnesics could learn and remember things *if* their memory was tested in the right way. The right way turned out to be by using *implicit* tests of memory.

In one study, they compared 4 amnesics with 16 control patients matched for age and intelligence (Warrington & Weiskrantz, 1970). All the subjects were presented with word lists to learn. When tested for their recall of the words, or their ability to recognize the words, the amnesics were much inferior to the control patients. This was not surprising. Recall and recognition both require the conscious recollection of information (they are both tasks involving explicit remembering), and it was well known that amnesics had great trouble with such tasks.

But Warrington and Weiskrantz also assessed memory for the words with two nontraditional tasks. One test involved identifying *word fragments* (see Figure 2.3), which were difficult to identify if the words were not previously seen on the word list. The other was a *word-stem completion* task in which the subjects had to complete a word when given the first three letters (e.g., *cha* for *chair*). The sets of three letters came from words on the original study list; without having seen the list, a person would find this task very difficult. These latter two tasks are both examples of implicit tests of memory, and they were presented to the subjects as being word-guessing games. Good performance does not depend on conscious recollection of the previously studied words.

The results astounded many people—the amnesics performed as well as the controls on both implicit memory tests. This means that the memory ability of such patients had been greatly underestimated. Not only were these new findings of major theoretical importance (they were instrumental in establishing the need to assess implicit remembering and the value of such assessment), but they also had considerable implications for helping amnesics in terms of rehabilitation (see Chapter 14). These results have now been replicated many times with similar tasks and types of patients (e.g., Graf & Schacter, 1985; Graf, Squire, & Mandler, 1984; Jacoby & Witherspoon, 1982; Shimamura, 1986; Warrington & Weiskrantz, 1974).

As you might imagine, it didn't take long before the investigation of implicit remembering became a very hot area of memory research (Jacoby, 1988; Jacoby & Kelley, 1987; Lewandowsky, Dunn, & Kirsner, 1989; Richardson-Klavehn & Bjork, 1988; Roediger, 1990; Schacter, 1987; Tulving & Schacter, 1990). Many studies, using a variety of clever tasks, have demonstrated that normal people also show evidence of retention without conscious remembering. And although still somewhat controversial, similar findings have recently revealed that subjects can also learn and remember things without conscious

FIGURE 2.3
An example of a word fragment for the word *RAINBOW*.

awareness even while fully anesthetized (see Chapter 11 for a full account of this fascinating work).

## Comparing Explicit and Implicit Memory Tests

**Priming effects.** The term *priming* is often used to describe the effect that prior learning has on subsequent behavior or performance. In explicit memory tasks a person is consciously aware that priming has occurred. For instance, in a *lexical decision* task a subject has to decide if a string of letters forms a real word. The speed at which this can be done increases if the subject is first presented (in other words, primed) with a letter string that is semantically related to the second letter string (Meyer & Schvaneveldt, 1971, 1976). So if the first letter string is BUTTER, subjects respond faster to the second letter string if it is BREAD than if it is NURSE. In these types of lexical decision tasks the subjects are aware that priming has taken place.

Priming can also occur without conscious awareness. In fact, this is one of the defining characteristics of tasks measuring implicit remembering. The subject performs a task better than if he or she had not previously been exposed to something (such as a list of words or pictures of objects), yet the person has no conscious recollection of the prior experience. Although priming can have similar facilitating effects for both explicit and implicit remembering, there are, as described in the next section, some important differences or dissociations in how certain variables affect explicit and implicit memory tests.

**Dissociations.** Some *dissociations* have been found between explicit and implicit memory tests (Parkin, Reid, & Russo, 1990; Schacter, 1987). A dissociation occurs when a variable can be shown to affect one type of test differently than it affects another. One major dissociation has already been described in terms of a subject variable; amnesics perform very poorly on explicit memory tests but perform as well as normals on tasks tapping implicit remembering. Another dissociation is that while pictures are generally remembered better than words in using explicit measures of memory (Madigan, 1983), words provide better priming than do pictures on word-fragment implicit memory tasks (Weldon & Roediger, 1987).

Currently there's considerable debate over how best to account for dissociations between explicit and implicit tests of memory. Some researchers, particularly those who have worked either with people who have memory disorders or with animals, have proposed that separate neural systems underlie the differences between explicit and implicit remembering (e.g., Cohen & Squire, 1980; Squire, 1987; Tulving & Schacter, 1990; Weiskrantz, 1987, 1989). These people suggest, for example, that the best way to account for the types of memories that are preserved in amnesics is to assume that the neural system for explicit memory processing has been destroyed or damaged but that the neural system for implicit remembering remains intact.

Others have argued that the dissociations can best be explained by the fact that different types of cognitive processing are required to perform most explicit and implicit memory tasks (e.g., Craik, 1983; Graf & Mandler, 1984; Jacoby, 1983, 1988; Moscovitch, 1984; Roediger, 1990; Roediger & Blaxton, 1987). For instance, it has been claimed that explicit memory tests are primarily *conceptually driven* in that people take an active role in processing information by organizing it and elaborating on it. This is also sometimes referred to as *top-down processing* to reflect the fact that prior knowledge and expectations affect our cognitive processing. Implicit tests are more likely to be *data-driven* (involving *bottom-up processing*) and do not involve active manipulation of the information. Instead, what matters most is the perceptual appearance of the information (Jacoby, 1983).

Since there's evidence to support each theoretical approach, it has recently been suggested that both may be right. In other words, there may exist separate memory systems in the brain, and some of these memory systems primarily rely on conceptually-driven processing, while others rely on data-driven processing (Hayman & Tulving, 1989a, 1989b; Schacter, Cooper, & Delaney, 1990; Tulving & Schacter, 1990).

**The future.** It should be noted that instead of using the terms *explicit* and *implicit* memory tests (Graf & Schacter, 1985; Schacter, 1987), some researchers have preferred to use such terms as *direct* and *indirect* memory tasks (Johnson & Hasher, 1987) or *intentional* and *incidental* tests of memory (Jacoby, 1984). But rest assured that in the years to come, regardless of the terms used, memory capability will be assessed when people can, and when they cannot, consciously recollect experiences and events. Only by using both types of procedures will memory researchers be able to fully gauge the richness of human memory performance.

# INTERPRETATION OF MEMORY PHENOMENA

All too rarely does any scientific research area yield completely consistent findings. And some would even lament that the field of memory has suffered more than its fair share of contradictory results! Regardless of whether memory is probed using explicit or implicit procedures, we believe that the best overall approach to discovering valid and reliable facts about memory phenomena involves the critical examination and reexamination of empirical observations and the conclusions about these observations.

An important part of this process of reexamination is the *adversarial* method, in which different investigators take opposite sides regarding the explanations or theories that account for various memory phenomena. This is somewhat analogous to the way a courtroom trial proceeds. As in court, where the prosecutor and defense counsel oppose each other, memory researchers with different perspectives or theoretical backgrounds will advance different explanations for a particular phenomenon. Over time, as in a court of law, the correct explanation of a phenomenon usually emerges by the thorough airing of different points of view backed by all the available evidence that is reliable and valid.

A good scientist prepares to understand the subtleties of the phenomena he or she investigates by careful reading of prior investigations of the phenomena of interest. Not only will this provide you with fresh ideas to test and techniques to employ, but it will also save you from doing research that has already been done. In addition, as will be discussed in Chapters 12 and 13, it is easier to remember new information about a topic when you already know a great deal about it. This is referred to as building a good *knowledge base*.

The French philosopher and mathematician Blaise Pascal (1623–1662) once noted that "chance favors the prepared mind." Discoveries occur *deliberately* after a careful search, but they also occur *serendipitously* when a researcher is looking for something else but is prepared to appreciate the value of the unexpected. An excellent way to become prepared for both the expected and the unexpected is by building your knowledge base by consulting the primary source material (i.e., the firsthand account of the research) for your area of interest.

This primary source material will most often be found in scientific journals and the published proceedings of conferences. Because of the widespread importance of memory research, most journals in psychology have an occasional article concerning some aspect of memory. In addition, many journals either have memory research as a focus or typically contain one or more important articles about memory in each issue. Listed in Table 2.2 are the names of many journals that fall into this latter category. Periodically reading as many of these journals as possible will keep you abreast of the exciting new findings and theories about memory.

# *S*UMMARY

## I. The Memory Process

- The three main phases of the memory process are, in order of occurrence, *registration*, *retention*, and *remembering*.
- It is called *explicit encoding* when people intentionally try to register information. When the process of registering information is unintentional, this is known as *incidental learning*.
- *Explicit remembering* involves the conscious recollection of past events or information and is assessed by tests of recall and recognition. In most everyday situations, recognition is easier than recall.
- *Implicit remembering* occurs when a person who has no conscious recollection of a past event or of some information is nonetheless affected by the material. Typically, this is demonstrated by later performance on some task.

**TABLE 2.2** JOURNALS THAT OFTEN CONTAIN ARTICLES ABOUT MEMORY

*American Journal of Psychology*
*Applied Cognitive Psychology*
*Brain and Cognition*
*British Journal of Psychology*
*Canadian Journal of Psychology*
*Child Development*
*Cognition*
*Cognition and Emotion*
*Cognitive Development*
*Cognitive Psychology*
*Cognitive Rehabilitation*
*Developmental Psychology*
*International Journal of Cognitive Psychology*
*Journal of Experimental Child Psychology*
*Journal of Experimental Psychology: Human Learning, Memory and Cognition*
*Journal of Gerontology: Psychological Sciences*
*Journal of Memory and Language*
*Journal of Personality and Social Psychology*
*Memory*
*Memory and Cognition*
*Neuropsychologia*
*Psychology and Aging*
*Quarterly Journal of Experimental Psychology*
*Review of Educational Research*

- Factors that influence memory performance are called *independent variables*.
- Changing the value of some independent variables has been found to alter memory performance in almost all tasks. These independent variables are categorized as *organismic variables, antecedent variables,* and *task variables*.
- A major goal of current memory research is to discover how these independent variables combine and interact to influence memory performance.

## II. Evaluating Memory Performance
- When a person's memory performance is evaluated, a distinction is often made between *primary* and *secondary* measures.
- A primary measure reflects the amount of information held in memory, while a secondary measure involves an assessment of the quality of recall or recognition. A full appreciation of an individual's memory performance often involves having knowledge from both primary and secondary measures.

## III. Traditional Memory Tasks

- For decades after Ebbinghaus, only a few different stimuli and tasks measuring explicit remembering were used.
- The majority of these memory tasks used verbal stimuli that varied on such dimensions as *familiarity, relatedness, relative frequency,* and *concreteness* or *abstractness.*
- A wide variety of explicit memory tasks have been developed. These include *serial learning, free recall, cued recall, paired-associate learning, forced-choice, yes-no, study-test,* and *single-item probe* techniques.

## IV. Newer Memory Tasks

- During the last twenty years, there has been a noticeable shift by memory researchers toward using much more diverse stimulus materials and tasks.
- This has occurred because it is now known that many memory phenomena are very task-specific.
- Another factor that led to this change was the finding that implicit remembering can occur in people (such as amnesics) who demonstrate no evidence of explicit remembering.
- This means that to adequately determine what a person truly remembers, it is necessary to assess the individual's memory using both explicit and implicit memory procedures.
- *Priming* is the term used to describe the influence of prior learning on subsequent behavior. Priming effects are apparent in both explicit and implicit memory tasks.
- To account for *dissociations* between explicit and implicit memory tests, some researchers have proposed that separate neural systems underlie the operation of explicit and implicit remembering.
- Others have argued that explicit and implicit memory tests rely on different types of cognitive processing. Specifically, explicit memory tests are primarily *conceptually driven,* while implicit tests of memory are largely *data-driven.*
- Recent research suggests that both positions may be correct; there may be different neural systems for explicit and implicit remembering, and these systems may employ different types of processing.

## V. Interpreting Memory Phenomena

- Constant reexamination of observations and conclusions is the best way to discover valid and reliable facts about memory.
- To appreciate and understand the subtleties of memory phenomena, it is necessary to read widely in your areas of interest, especially from *primary* sources.

# PART 2

# Memory Processes

# 3

# *Models of Memory*

———— ❖ ————

*Did you drink orange juice at breakfast?*
*Can a rabbit play golf?*
*Who sang the song "I Want to Hold Your Hand"?*
*What South American Country begins with an S?*
*How many eggs are in a dozen?*
*What is Julius Caesar's telephone number?*
*Is* welderly *an English word?*
*Do all birds fly?*

If you are like most people, some of the above questions are very easy for you to answer, while others might prove more troublesome. For instance, you probably knew instantly that rabbits don't play golf, that there are 12 eggs in a dozen, that Julius Caesar never had a telephone number, and that *welderly* is probably not a real English word. It might take you a little longer to remember that you didn't drink orange juice today, that the Beatles sang the 1964 smash hit "I Want to Hold Your Hand," and that not all birds fly. And you may never remember (if you ever even knew it) that *Suriname,* a country slightly larger than the state of Georgia, is on the east coast of South America.

The fact that we can answer so quickly and confidently a multitude of dissimilar questions indicates that our memory must be highly organized and that we must possess ways to effectively and efficiently analyze, manipulate, and search memory. These processes are often so effortless and automatic that we may not even be aware that we are using them. Many of us would be hard-pressed to describe how we knew that rabbits don't play golf or that *welderly* isn't likely to be a proper English word. We generally become consciously aware of the need to engage our vast store of knowledge only when presented with more vexing questions or problems. For example, if the name *Suriname* didn't immediately come to mind, many people would resort to the strategy of trying to visualize a map of South America and then "looking" for the right answer.

To fully understand the nature of memory, one must examine both the structure of memory and the strategies or processes that we use to manipulate or explore it. The rest of this chapter will concentrate on how memory might be organized and the different forms that memory may take.

# JUST HOW MANY MEMORY SYSTEMS ARE THERE?

There has been a long, continuing (and sometimes bitter) debate over whether there is a single memory system or multiple systems. Although there are certainly other points of contention, the debate has usually centered on the need for postulating a separate system or store for *short-term memory* (STM) phenomena and one for *long-term memory* (LTM) phenomena. The STM system supposedly retains small amounts of information for about 30 seconds. This can be new information (such as when you remember some of the exact wording of the last sentence you read), or it can be information retrieved from LTM (such as when you consciously recall your own date of birth when filling out a job application). If this information is given special attention, such as when it is rehearsed, then it can remain in STM indefinitely. In contrast, the LTM system is presumably capable of storing vast amounts of information, without the need for continuous rehearsal, essentially forever. Researchers in favor of a single system argue that there is neither a theoretical need nor convincing empirical evidence to warrant separate memory systems. Obviously, those favoring a multiple-memory-system approach disagree. In this chapter we will consider the arguments and evidence that each side has put forward in support of its position.

At least as far back as the ancient Greeks (Herrmann & Chaffin, 1988), many people have believed that STM phenomena differed fundamentally in nature from LTM phenomena. Personal introspection alone often leads people to believe in the need for such a distinction. For instance, to many people it just seems obvious that there is a difference between the fleeting and ephemeral nature of information just encountered (e.g., the name of a new acquaintance) and the much more enduring and permanent nature of information repeatedly encountered over long periods of time (e.g., your father's name).

William James (1890), one of America's most famous and influential early psychologists, wrote eloquently about this dualistic quality of memory. He distinguished between what he called *primary* and *secondary* memory. James said that primary memory consisted of the contents of consciousness and therefore contained information that was actively under consideration. And since the contents of our consciousness changed frequently, this meant that primary memory was transitory and fleeting. In contrast, secondary memory contained information that was *not* in conscious awareness; instead, it was in an inactive state that could often be brought into consciousness at will (in other words, it would enter primary memory). Information in secondary memory was considered to be much more permanently etched into the mind. James's conceptualization of primary and secondary memory is similar to how STM and LTM, respectively, are sometimes thought of today.

Notwithstanding the great influence that William James has had on psychology, the predominant view in this country until the late 1950s was that memory could best be viewed as a single system (Melton, 1963; Melton & Irwin, 1940). This was largely because psychology was deeply committed at the time to the principles of associationism. Most learning was thought of as the building up of stimulus-response (S-R) pairings, and remembering was held to be the recollecting of a response when presented with a stimulus. Our ability to remember something was primarily affected by the strength of the initial S-R bonding and the *similarity* of both prior and subsequent learning of other S-R pairings.

If initial learning was weak and a lot of similar pairings were learned, interference would occur and lead to memory failures. There were two forms the interference could take—when prior learning acts forward in time to cause *proactive interference* (PI; the prefix *pro* means "forward"), or when newer information acts backward in time to cause *retroactive interference* (RI; hence the prefix *retro*). On her honeymoon, if a previously married woman cried out her *first* husband's name while making love with her new husband, this would be an example of PI (and, we might add, an inauspicious way to start a new marriage). An instance of RI would be if you tried to remember your former phone number but your current one kept coming to mind instead. We will have more to say about the effects of PI and RI later. The important point to emphasize now is that according to *interference theory*, there's no need to postulate separate STM and LTM systems or components. Like all other unitary theories of memory, interference theory claims that memory processes do not work any differently as a function of when the material was learned.

## The Rise in Popularity of the Multiple-Memory-System Approach

What happened in the late 1950s and early 1960s that led most memory researchers to abandon the unitary view of memory and to embrace the multiple-system approach? It is interesting that one of the most important influences was really outside the realm of traditional psychology. It was the advent of the computer age, and it led memory researchers to think about memory in new ways (Houston, 1991). For instance, flowcharting became a popular technique. This involved the drawing of boxes on paper to represent the flow of information in a computer program or the sequence of steps that needed to be executed. It quickly became fashionable for psychologists to adopt the terms and concepts of the information-processing approach used by computer scientists. After all, great strides were being made in computer science at this time, so why not incorporate such things as STM buffers, LTM storage units, flowcharts, processing components, subroutines, and so forth, into human memory models?

At least two other developments played a major role in helping to usher in the multiple-memory-system approach. First, as described in more detail below, in the late 1950s some amazing new data appeared concerning the tiny capacity of STM and the huge amount of forgetting that can rapidly occur in STM if rehearsal is prevented. Second, the work of George Sperling in the early 1960s (described later in detail) convincingly showed that a *sensory memory* store exists that contains a vast amount of information that decays very quickly. These two experimental findings were seized upon by those favoring a multiple-storage view as evidence that memory is organized into separate components that probably obey different principles of operation.

## The Brown-Peterson Distractor Technique

In 1958, John Brown in England, and in 1959, Lloyd and Margaret Peterson, a husband-and-wife team in the United States, independently published similar data that absolutely *startled* many memory researchers. What these psychologists discovered was that if subjects were distracted from rehearsing a small amount of new information, in a matter of just seconds the information would often be completely forgotten! Since their results and paradigms were similar, and they published their findings within a few months of each other, it has become customary to call the procedure they developed the *Brown-Peterson Distractor Technique*.

Their paradigm is very simple to use and understand. For example, in the Peterson and Peterson (1959) study, subjects were given three consonant letters (with no obvious meaning) to remember and were asked to recall the letters after varying periods of delay (usually up to 18 seconds later). To prevent the subjects from just rehearsing the three letters during the retention period, which would have made it easy to have virtually perfect recall, the subjects were required to perform a distractor task. Immediately after the three letters were presented, a random number also was given. The subjects had to repeat the number and start counting backward by threes until the experimenter gave the signal to stop. At this point the subjects would try to recall the three letters. Each subject would be given many trials with different letter combinations to remember and different numbers from which to count backward. If you were a subject in such an experiment, your first trial (with a retention interval of 12 seconds) might look like this:

The experimenter says: "W T K" and "701"
Your response: "701, 698, 695, 692, 689, 686" (this takes 12 seconds)

FIGURE 3.1
Like human memory, a library's resources must be highly organized to be useful.
*Virginia Blaisdel/Stock, Boston.*

The experimenter says: "Recall"
Your response: "R P K"

Although subjects in such an experiment can do quite well for the first trial or two, after they have been through many trials, their performance is nothing short of atrocious. This can be seen in Figure 3.2, which illustrates typical performance in recalling the three-letter combinations after many trials. For instance, after only 18 seconds of the distractor task, only about 1 in every 10 trigrams will be correctly remembered! This means that 90 percent of the material is forgotten in a very short period of time.

These results generated tremendous excitement. Over the next few years, literally hundreds of studies were done using variations of the Brown-Peterson distractor task. The major reason that these results caused such a stir was that they provided, at least at the time, what seemed like strong evidence that there must be at least two different memory systems. One memory system (STM) was fragile, of small capacity, and greatly affected by whether or not a voluntary process such as rehearsal was allowed, while the other (LTM) was

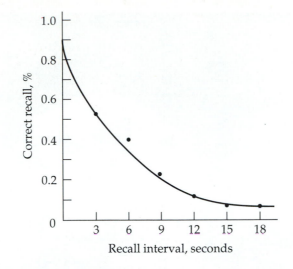

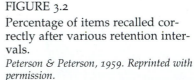

FIGURE 3.2

Percentage of items recalled correctly after various retention intervals.

*Peterson & Peterson, 1959. Reprinted with permission.*

much more durable, of immense capacity, and not subject to the whims of rehearsal procedures.

In addition, the Petersons attributed the rapid forgetting they saw to *trace decay* and not to *interference effects,* such as PI and RI. A theory of forgetting based on trace decay assumes that unless something is done with the material (such as rehearsing it), its trace will automatically fade away over time. A memory trace is also called an *engram* (see Chapter 7), and this is what is presumably present in the brain after something is learned. The Petersons' interpretation had a galvanizing effect on the debate between the unitary- and multiple-memory-system camps. Almost everybody believed that interference was the major cause of forgetting long-term memories. If it could be demonstrated that forgetting of short-term information was due to a different process (in other words, trace decay), then this would be a very compelling reason to believe in multiple memory systems. At the time, the Brown-Peterson task appeared to do this.

A few years later, however, Keppel and Underwood (1962) provided good evidence that the short-term forgetting observed in the Brown-Peterson task was due primarily to the buildup of proactive interference. They accomplished this by showing that on the first trial, when there would have been no proactive interference, subjects had no trouble remembering the three letters after completing the distractor task. After a few trials, proactive interference would develop, and people would have trouble distinguishing between letters presented earlier and those on the current trial. Baddeley and Scott (1971), using sequences longer than three letters, were able to demonstrate a small amount of forgetting on the first trial. They concluded that there was some trace decay occurring in the Brown-Peterson task, but considerably less than what the Petersons had assumed.

## The Atkinson-Shiffrin Memory Model

The stage was now set for someone to propose a memory model that used an information-processing approach and that included multiple memory systems or stages. Although there were other significant separate-stage models [in particular, the one developed by Waugh and Norman (1965)], by far the most influential model was the one developed over a series of years by Richard Atkinson and Richard Shiffrin (1965, 1968, 1971). This model was so influential and emblematic of the information-processing approach that it is often referred to as the "modal model."

As seen in Figure 3.3, the Atkinson-Shiffrin model proposes that incoming information first enters the *sensory register*. This is conceived of as a large-capacity storage system for sensory memory. The information contained in the sensory register is a relatively faithful record of the information obtained from each of the senses. The vast majority of sensory information never gets beyond the sensory register, and it decays away in a matter of seconds.

FIGURE 3.3

The stages of memory in the Atkinson-Shiffrin model.
*Atkinson & Shiffrin, 1968. Reprinted with permission.*

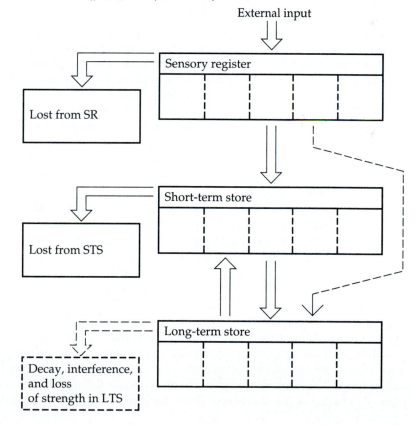

Information from the sensory register that is selected for further processing generally next enters the *short-term store* (what is generally referred to today as STM). On occasion, information can skip this stage altogether and go directly to the third stage (this information is represented by the dashed arrow in the figure). The third, and final stage, the *long-term store* (which is now usually called LTM), has an extremely large capacity, and memories are considered much less likely to be lost from it. Information flows back and forth between the short-term and long-term stores. The form in which information was usually encoded was thought to differ between these two stages. Information was believed to be encoded mostly in terms of its sounds (*acoustically* encoded) when in the short-term store but encoded mostly in terms of its meaning (*semantically* encoded) when in the long-term store.

Compared with the sensory register, the short-term store has a very limited capacity, on the order of only a few items. However, information lasts longer in the short-term store (up to 30 seconds), and in contrast to information in the sensory register, information in the short-term store can be maintained indefinitely if the person rehearses it. Rehearsal not only will keep the information "alive" but also will increase the probability that the information will enter the long-term store. Information not rehearsed will soon decay or be displaced by new information entering the short-term store. (Upon being presented with an unfamiliar telephone number, probably everyone has learned to rehearse the digits over and over until he or she can dial the number. Not doing so often means having to resort to looking up the number in the telephone book!) Atkinson and Shiffrin considered the short-term store as not only a temporary repository of information but also a workplace for processing information, controlling the flow of it, and making decisions.

What determines which information gets additional processing and which is left to decay? According to the Atkinson-Shiffrin model, the transferring of information between stages, and the type and amount of processing that certain information receives, is largely under the voluntary control of the individual. This notion of voluntary control is a hallmark of the Atkinson-Shiffrin model. To explain such control, the model distinguishes between *structural features* (e.g., the fast decay from the sensory register or the severe capacity limitations of the short-term store) and *control processes.*

Control processes can be thought of as flexible strategies a person can choose to use for selecting, manipulating, and transforming information. For instance, if when scanning the information available in the sensory register a person discovers something of interest, the person can intentionally decide to transfer the information to the short-term store. This illustrates the active role a person can exercise in the processing of information. Deciding whether or not to engage in rehearsal, determining what material should receive special attention, and deciding what information (if any) should be retrieved from the long-term store are additional examples of control processes that an individual can employ. The control processes themselves are thought to use some of the limited capacity of the short-term store. Each person decides how much of this limited capacity to "spend" on control processes and how much to "spend" on the storage of information. In essence, the Atkinson-Shiffrin model assumes that there is a trade-off between processing capability and storage space.

## Immediate Impact of the Atkinson-Shiffrin Model

As might be guessed, those who favored the idea of multiple memory stores generally embraced the model, while those who held steadfastly to a unitary view of memory were equally fervent in their opposition of it. Although some researchers questioned the need for a separate sensory memory component, the major controversy surrounding the model focused on the need to distinguish between STM and LTM. Early in this chapter we indicated that this was the major issue of debate between those who thought that memory was a single system and those who did not. In the following sections we will explore what is currently known about sensory memory and decide whether or not there is good support for a distinction between STM and LTM.

# SENSORY MEMORY

The purpose of *sensory memory* (also called the *sensory register*) is to keep a highly accurate record of what each of our senses has just experienced for a brief period of time. Estimates of the duration of sensory memory vary from less than 1/2 second to several seconds, depending on the sense involved and the physical conditions.

There are important reasons for having a sensory memory. First, it takes time to recognize the stimuli impinging on each of our senses. We must compare the newly arrived information with information already existing in our brains (presumably in something akin to STM or LTM) to see if we can recognize the pattern. This pattern recognition process usually occurs quite quickly, but it does take some time, and this time is supplied by the sensory memory. Second, we are constantly being bombarded with sensory information, and we can't possibly process all of it at once. Oftentimes, we are not even consciously aware of this bombardment. For example, if you close your eyes and focus on your sense of hearing, you may now become aware of the buzz from the overhead fluorescent lights or the ticking of a clock. Sensory memory allows us to have additional time to choose which sensory information we wish to give fuller attention to and process. Third, there are times when we cannot immediately devote attention to a stimulus that appears and then disappears very quickly. For instance, if you are deep in thought, you might not notice a mosquito landing on your skin looking for a good place to bite you. However, your chances of detecting the critter (and then squashing it!) are enhanced because you have a sensory memory for touch. This keeps the feeling of the mosquito's landing "active" for a little longer than would be the case if you had to depend only on the sensory receptor for touch still remaining activated. A fourth important reason to have a sensory memory is that it provides continuity from one moment to the next so that people can interpret their constantly changing environment correctly. As an example, speakers of English usually end their spoken questions with a rise in pitch. To use this cue, we must remember the pitch of earlier words. Consider, for instance, the question "Can we go today?" The "ay" sound of "today" rises in pitch, but to appreciate this, we must remember for a brief period of time exactly the pitch of the earlier words.

## How Much Can You See in a Single Glance?

In 1859, the philosopher Sir William Hamilton tried to answer this question by conducting a series of simple experiments with marbles. Hamilton threw varying numbers of marbles in front of himself, glanced at them briefly, looked away, and then estimated how many marbles had been presented. He was struck by the fact that although he was usually aware that several marbles had been presented, he could not accurately apprehend or count them all at one viewing.

About 100 years later, George Sperling (1960) tried to answer the same question while doing his doctoral dissertation at Harvard University. But instead of using marbles, Sperling presented his subjects with different arrays of letters, often consisting of three rows of four letters each. These letter arrays were presented for only 50 milliseconds (a millisecond equals one-thousandth of a second) and looked like this:

W K L P

R B C U

X V T D

Presenting the letters so quickly ensured that the subjects would get only one glance at them. The results indicated that subjects could recall only 4 or 5 of the 12 letters. However, the subjects complained to Sperling that they really "saw" more letters but that they forgot them while in the midst of recalling the first few. Being an alert experimenter, Sperling tested this introspection by now requiring that his subjects report only a part of the letter array. This *partial-report* procedure involved presenting a tone right after the 50-millisecond display. If a high-pitched tone was presented, subjects were expected to report only the top row of letters; a medium-pitched tone meant to report the middle row; and a low-pitched tone indicated that the bottom row should be reported. Sperling found that subjects could usually report 3 of the 4 letters from any randomly selected line.

How did he interpret this finding? Well, he reasoned that since subjects could report 3 letters from any given line, this suggested that they really could "see" approximately 9 letters in a single gaze. This was about twice the number reported when using a *whole-report* procedure. Further experiments found that if the tone was not presented immediately, the ability to remember what had been seen quickly deteriorated. For instance, if the tone was delayed for 1/2 second, subjects could recall only 1 or 2 letters per row. This suggested that only 3 to 6 letters were still available to them: an amount similar to what they could recall without any cueing during the whole-report procedure.

What made Sperling's work so exciting was that it provided the first empirical evidence that there was a form of memory that decayed far more rapidly than anyone had previously thought. For instance, Sperling demonstrated that the duration of sensory memory was considerably briefer than the duration of James's primary memory. Sperling's work had a major influence on the thinking of Atkinson and Shiffrin when they formulated the characteristics of their sensory register and on Neisser (1967), who later called this form of memory *iconic* and each individual visual image an *icon*. After literally hundreds of experiments, it is now known that iconic memory has a fairly large capacity and that it renders a relatively true or faithful representation of the stimuli that impinge at the receptor level.

In Sperling-type studies it has been found that the icon typically lasts from 200 to 400 milliseconds (Van der Heijden, 1981). However, the duration of the icon can be manipulated to some degree. For instance, the brighter the icon is, the slower it fades (Long & Beaton, 1982). Having an abnormally long icon has even been implicated in some types of reading disorders. There is some evidence that icons last longer for people who have dyslexia (DiLollo, Hanson, & McIntyre, 1983; Stanley & Hall, 1973), a condition in which people have difficulty with processing written letters and words. If this is true, then the physical images from one icon may persist too long and interfere with the processing of information from the next icon. Usually, however, the interplay between the timing of icons and their decay works smoothly so that there is continuity in our visual world.

## Sensory Memory for Other Senses

Although sensory memory systems are predicated for all the senses, only a little work has been done on the senses of smell, taste, and touch (Hill & Bliss, 1968). Cowan (1988) has suggested that the sensory memory component for each sense modality may actually consist of two distinct phases. The first phase extends sensation for several hundred milliseconds, and the information in this phase is unanalyzed. The second phase can hold material for several seconds, and this material can be partially analyzed. Not everyone is convinced that Cowan's two-phase proposal is correct, and Cowan himself acknowledges that the second phase may only reflect the operation of what is traditionally called STM.

Most of the sensory memory research has concentrated on the major senses of vision (iconic memory) and hearing [dubbed by Neisser (1967) as *echoic memory*]. Experiments have shown that echoic memory is similar to iconic memory in many of its characteristics. In terms of similarities, the *echo* (the name for the individual sound image) also contains raw sensory information that is held in faithful form before fading away. The capacity of echoic memory, however, may be considerably smaller than that of iconic memory (Houston, 1991). Furthermore, it is now believed by most researchers that the echo lasts for several seconds, substantially longer than does the icon (although if Cowan is correct, then this alleged difference might really just be an artifact of the different techniques used to measure echoic and iconic memory).

# SHORT-TERM MEMORY

Traditionally, memory researchers have proposed that there are several major features that distinguish STM and LTM. Many of these presumed differences were highlighted in the Atkinson-Shiffrin memory model. As shown in Table 3.1, a memory trace that was not rehearsed was thought to last only about 30 seconds in STM, but it could last indefinitely in LTM (some believed for a lifetime). The capacity of STM was also considered to be woefully limited when compared with the capacity of LTM. In addition, the code in which the information was primarily stored was assumed to differ—acoustic coding for STM and semantic coding for LTM. Furthermore, information retrieval from STM was supposed to be qualitatively different from information retrieval from LTM. For STM, information was presumably accessed in a *serial* fashion (i.e., one item after another), but for LTM, information could be retrieved in *parallel* (i.e., many items simultaneously). And finally, the major cause of forgetting was thought to be trace decay for STM but interference for LTM. In this section we will examine the evidence pertaining to the characteristics of STM and, where appropriate, compare and contrast these characteristics with those believed to be representative of LTM.

## Duration of Memory Trace

Everyone knows that recently presented material, if unrehearsed, is usually soon forgotten. This observation has been confirmed in many well-designed experiments. A common experience for many freshmen is to look up the telephone number of a local pizza parlor near campus, only to forget the full number before dialing it. Why? Possibly because a friend distracted the person from rehearsing the number (perhaps by reminding him or her to get extra cheese but not anchovies). Dozens of studies using a Brown-Peterson distractor-type task have provided uncontested and dramatic evidence that unrehearsed material is forgotten in about 30 seconds.

**TABLE 3.1** MAJOR FEATURES THAT WERE THOUGHT TO DISTINGUISH
BETWEEN STM AND LTM

|  | *STM* | *LTM* |
| --- | --- | --- |
| Duration of trace | 30 seconds (without rehearsal) | Indefinitely without rehearsal |
| Capacity | Very limited | Essentially unlimited |
| Code of memory | Acoustic | Semantic |
| Retrieval process | Serial | Parallel |
| Cause of forgetting | Trace decay | Interference |

## Capacity of STM

Look at the following string of letters, and try to memorize the letters in correct order:

ATTI BMCIAFB ISOSI OU

Not easy to do, is it? This illustrates that the capacity of STM is quite limited. In 1956, George Miller wrote one of the most famous and compelling articles in the annals of psychology, and he gave it the whimsical title "The Magical Number Seven, Plus or Minus Two: Some Limits on Our Capacity for Processing Information." Miller tested many people on their ability to recall, in order, various lists of digits, letters, and words. He repeatedly found that normal adults could typically remember only about seven items (give or take a couple). What Miller was testing is known as a person's *memory span* (defined in Chapter 2 as the maximum number of items correctly recalled in order). Because performance on memory span tasks is highly correlated with a person's powers of concentration and attention, such tasks are often used to gauge the working capacity of STM or to detect memory disorders. As an aside, the telephone company was also aware of Miller's finding that people can hold only about seven items in STM at a time. Putting this knowledge to practical use, and hoping to cut down on the customer's need to use operator assistance, the phone company decided to make standard telephone numbers seven digits long (Ellis & Hunt, 1993).

Miller coined the term *chunk* and used it to refer to the basic unit of information stored in STM. He claimed that people can store seven (plus or minus two) chunks in STM. But what exactly is a chunk? Well, according to Miller, a chunk is some meaningful grouping of information, and the process of combining information into chunks for storage in STM is called *chunking*. A chunk can be a single letter (like *Z*) or a group of letters that forms something meaningful to the person (like *Zebra*). One of the reasons why you probably had trouble remembering the letter string ATTI BMCIAFB ISOSI OU is that it contains 18 letters. This is well beyond the normal memory span. However, if you noticed the pattern of the letters closely, you would have been able to chunk these 18 individual items into the following six chunks: ATT IBM CIA FBI SOS IOU. Remembering these six chunks would not have overtaxed your STM capacity, and you would have been more successful in recalling all the letters. In Chapter 13 we describe an individual who increased his memory span for unrelated digits to over 80 through a complicated chunking process. Chunking is a way that we can greatly increase the amount of information that can be held in STM.

Another way that people have suggested measuring STM capacity is by examining which items people tend to recall during free recall. A typical experiment involves giving subjects a long list of items to study and then asking them to recall as many as possible in any order they want. If you plot the probability of recall as a function of the position in which the item was first studied (first, third, tenth, etc.), you create what is called a *serial-position curve* (Glanzer & Cunitz, 1966; Murdock, 1962; Postman & Phillips, 1965). This curve has a characteristic shape, which is shown in Figure 3.4.

Notice that the first few items and the last few items have a higher probability of being recalled. This is referred to as the *primacy effect* and the *recency effect*, respectively. Why do they occur? It has been proposed that the primacy effect occurs because the first items to be studied are given sufficient rehearsal to allow them to enter LTM. The middle items are not likely to receive as much rehearsal because they enter STM when it is already full and hence do not receive much attention. Finally, the last few items are well remembered, not because they receive extra rehearsal but because they are still in STM at the time of recall and can be quickly "spit" out. If this is the correct explanation of the recency effect, then the capacity of STM can be estimated by noting the size of the recency effect. With this method, STM capacity is estimated to be two to five items (Matlin, 1989), an amount smaller than Miller's estimate of seven plus or minus two. The existence of primacy and recency effects, along with the proposition that they seem to reflect the operation of two separate storage

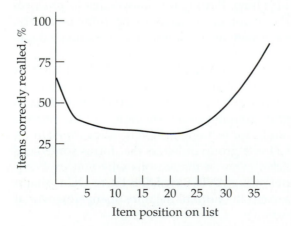

FIGURE 3.4
A typical serial-position curve.

systems, has been cited as strong evidence by those favoring a distinction between STM and LTM. However, we will have more to say about this presumed difference shortly.

Others have suggested that the capacity of STM is defined not in terms of a fixed number of items or chunks but rather in terms of a fixed amount of time (around 1.5 to 2 seconds) before the verbal trace fades (Baddeley, 1990; Ellis & Hennelly, 1980; Hoosain & Salili, 1988; Naveh-Benjamin & Ayres, 1986; Schweickert & Boruff, 1986). For example, Schweickert and Boruff (1986) tested people's memory spans for the digits 0 to 9, shape names (like *oval* and *semicircle*), consonants, nonsense syllables, three-letter words, and color names. They consistently found that the memory span for these different items equaled the number of items that people could pronounce in about 1.5 seconds.

Using time to pronounce items rather than number of chunks to measure STM capacity may offer an explanation as to why Welsh-speaking children seemed to have lower digit span scores on the Wechsler Intelligence Scale than did their English-speaking counterparts. Ellis and Hennelly (1980) noticed that it takes longer to pronounce digits in Welsh than in English. They then tested subjects who were bilingual in Welsh and English on digit span tasks using each language. What they discovered was that although their digit spans were smaller in amount in Welsh than in English, they were the same size when measured in terms of the amount recalled in a given time interval. Research by Naveh-Benjamin and Ayres (1986) has shown that similar relationships exist between memory span and rate of articulation in other languages as well. Taken together, these results support the view that STM capacity might be better measured in terms of the time it takes to pronounce items than in terms of the number of chunks recalled. However measured, STM capacity is very small.

## Coding of Information

The Atkinson-Shiffrin memory model proposed that information in short-term storage was acoustic in nature, while information in long-term storage was semantically encoded. There's a great deal of evidence that information in STM is generally encoded in terms of sounds (Adams, 1967; Baddeley, 1966; Conrad, 1963, 1964; Conrad & Hull, 1964; Kintsch & Buschke, 1969; Schweickert, Guentert, & Hersberger, 1990; Wickelgren, 1965). For example, Conrad (1964) visually presented subjects with a list of letters and then noted the types of errors they made during immediate recall. Even though the letters were presented visually, overwhelmingly, when the subjects made errors, they were of an acoustic nature. A typical error would be an acoustic confusion, like substituting a *V* for an *E*; much more rarely would a visual confusion occur, such as substituting a *V* for a *U*.

Nevertheless, there is also good evidence that nonacoustic codes can be used in STM. For instance, it is now well accepted that information in STM can be coded visually (e.g., Brooks, 1968; Conrad, 1972; Posner & Keele, 1967;

Shepard & Metzler, 1971; Sternberg, 1966). In fact, the same person who had been so instrumental in helping to establish the view that STM coding was largely acoustic showed convincingly that visual codes in STM were also possible. Conrad (1972) found that congenitally deaf subjects made visual confusion errors when performing Brown-Peterson distractor tasks. Since the subjects were deaf from birth, they could not store items acoustically, and so they relied on visual codes in STM.

It is also evident that semantic codes are used in STM (Shulman, 1971, 1972; Wickens, 1970, 1972). To cite one example, Shulman (1972) showed subjects lists of 10 words, with each word being presented for $1/2$ second. Following the tenth word, a probe word would appear. The task was to determine if the probe word matched another word from the list. Sometimes the term *match* meant that the probe had to be identical with a word on the list, while on other trials, *match* meant that the probe word was a synonym of a list word. Subjects were not informed before each trial what type of match would be expected. Instead, immediately prior to the presentation of the probe, either an *I* or an *S* would appear to indicate an identical or synonym match, respectively.

Now if subjects have only acoustic information stored in STM, then on trials in which an identical match is required, no added confusion or mistakes should occur when the probe word is only a synonym of a word on the list. However, this isn't what happened—the meaning of the probe word had an effect on performance. Subjects produced many more errors on identical match trials when the probe was a synonym of a list word than when the probe was not a synonym. This type of result provides strong evidence that semantic codes may be used in STM.

So although acoustic encoding of information may be the *preferred* way to store information in STM, it is clearly not the only way possible. The same can be said of LTM—although encoding of information is often based on meaning (semantic codes), it certainly doesn't have to be. For instance, in Chapter 9 we will review evidence that suggests that information in LTM can be visually encoded. There are also indications that LTM can encode information acoustically as well. Just consider how easy it is for you to recognize the sound of a familiar voice or know if a song is not being sung in the correct key.

## Retrieval from STM: The Sternberg Paradigm

Saul Sternberg (1966, 1967, 1975) developed and popularized a technique to explore how people retrieve information stored in STM. The procedure is very simple. The subject is given a list of items to remember (usually one to six digits or letters, so as not to exceed the STM span). This list is called the *memory set*, and it changes on every trial. After a few seconds, a test digit or letter (called the *probe item*) is presented, and the subject must indicate as fast as possible whether or not the probe item is a member of the memory set. This is usually done by pressing a "yes" or "no" key. Errors in this task are very low, so reaction time is the important dependent variable. Consider the following example:

*Trial 1*

1. Memory set presented: 6, 3, 5, 2, 7
2. Memory set encoded into STM
3. Probe item presented: 2
4. Subject's response: Press "yes" key

Sternberg found that as he varied the size of the memory set, the reaction time to respond increased as a linear function (straight line) of the number of items stored in STM (see Figure 3.5). For instance, for every digit added to the memory set, the reaction time increased by about 38 milliseconds. Sternberg interpreted the results as indicating that the probe item was *sequentially* compared with each item in STM and that this comparison process took about 38 milliseconds each time. He reasoned that if the search process had instead been done in parallel, in which case all the memory set items would have been compared simultaneously with the probe, then there would not have been a linear increase in reaction time with each additional memory set item. A simple parallel scanning procedure would predict no increase in reaction time as long as the memory set didn't exceed the STM span. Sternberg interpreted the results of his studies as not supporting a parallel scanning strategy.

However, there was another finding (that has also been replicated many times) that was very counterintuitive and surprising. Logically, one would think that as soon as a match was found, the subject would terminate the search. Imagine that you were a subject and were presented with Trial 1 above. If you sequentially compared the probe item (the 2) with the memory set, you would make a match after the fourth comparison. You would not have to continue the comparison process any further. But that is not what subjects typically do!

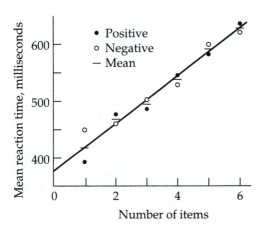

FIGURE 3.5

Sternberg's reaction time data as a function of the size of the memory set. *Reprinted by permission from S. Sternberg, "High-speed scanning in human memory," Science, Vol. 153 (1966), Fig. 1, pp. 652-654. Copyright 1966 by the AAAS.*

Instead of a *self-terminating serial search* that ends when a match is found, the data reveal that subjects conduct an *exhaustive serial search*. In other words, even though they don't have to do so to arrive at the correct response, subjects compare the probe with every memory set item in a sequential, exhaustive fashion.

Evidence of this exhaustive serial search can be seen in Figure 3.5—the reaction times for the "yes" (positive) and "no" (negative) responses are very similar. If a self-terminating search was being used, such reaction times would not be similar. The "yes" responses would be faster than the "no" responses because the subject would not have to scan the entire memory set except when the probe item matched the last item of the set. For "no" responses the entire memory set would always have to be searched. On the average, if a self-terminating serial search is used, then for any given memory set size, the "yes" responses should take half the time of the "no" responses. This means that the slope of the reaction time curves for the "no" responses should be twice as steep as for the "yes" responses. But this is not what is found. When many different populations of subjects (such as children, alcoholics, the mentally retarded, schizophrenics, the elderly, and even subjects stoned on marijuana) are used, the slopes for the "yes" and "no" responses are always found to be similar, although the rate of the exhaustive serial search varies considerably among the groups (Ashcraft, 1989).

At first blush, an exhaustive serial search strategy for STM seems crazy. Why would the subjects not stop as soon as they found a match? In answer to this question, Sternberg has proposed that while the comparison process occurs very rapidly (faster then $1/20$ second), the process to decide if a match is made may take considerably longer. Therefore, rather than take the time to make a decision after each comparison, it may be more efficient to make all the comparisons first and then make only one decision after the entire memory set has been scanned.

However, not everyone is convinced that retrieval from STM is best accounted for by an exhaustive serial search strategy. For instance, there's evidence that when the probe item matches the last item in a memory set, the reaction time for responding is faster than if the probe matched an item located earlier in the memory set (Burrows & Okada, 1971; Corballis, Kirby, & Miller, 1972). This should not happen if subjects are always using a serial search strategy. In addition, it has been found that well-practiced subjects can simultaneously scan STM for more than one probe item at a time (Simpson, 1972), which suggests that parallel processing is possible under certain circumstances. In fact, Townsend (1971, 1972, 1990) has been able to show that the typical Sternberg results, such as a linear increase in time as the memory set size increases, can be explained by resorting to fairly complex parallel processing models. If STM can be searched using parallel processing procedures, as now seems plausible on the basis of subsequent research and theorizing, then another distinguishing feature (i.e., retrieval mechanisms) that seemed to epitomize the differences between STM and LTM has lost much of its potency.

## Causes of Forgetting

Peterson and Peterson (1959) attributed the rapid decline in memory for un-rehearsed material to trace decay. Atkinson and Shiffrin also thought that decay was the principal way that forgetting occurred in short-term storage (along with displacement by new items entering the limited short-term storage buffer). It is now accepted that the buildup of proactive interference (PI) is largely responsible for the massive decline in performance observed by the Petersons and others using similar paradigms. It is likely that decay also plays some role in STM forgetting (Baddeley, 1990; Reitman, 1971, 1974). Interference effects are still assumed to be a major cause of forgetting in LTM, as you will see in Chapter 5. However, in Chapter 7, evidence is reviewed to indicate that aging and neurological factors may induce trace decay in LTM as well (Squire, 1987).

# EVALUATION OF THE STM-LTM DISTINCTION

From the last three sections it has become clear that neither the *coding of information*, the process of *retrieval of information*, nor the *causes of forgetting* furnish a sharp distinction between STM and LTM. Can we find more convincing evidence for a distinction between STM and LTM?

## The Recency Effect Revisited

Upon closer inspection, it turns out that the recency effect from free recall experiments does not necessarily provide strong evidence for a separate STM component. For instance, Wickelgren (1973) has argued that a single memory model can also explain the recency effect if one assumes that memory traces decay quickly at first but then more slowly. More damaging is the fact that some researchers have found recency effects when STM should not have played a role. For instance, Roediger and Crowder (1976) found both primacy and recency effects when subjects were given the free recall task of remembering the names of all the men who have been president of the United States. What makes this such an interesting finding is how the procedure for the task differs from the procedures for most other free recall tasks that show primacy and recency effects. The typical procedure involves having the subjects study a list of unrelated items just prior to free recall. In contrast, in the research by Roe-diger and Crowder, the subjects presumably had already stored the names of the U.S. presidents in LTM. Therefore, the recency effect they observed, which has been dubbed the *long-term recency effect*, can't be due to the "dumping" of STM. Using various techniques, others have also found evidence of long-term recency effects (e.g., Baddeley & Hitch, 1977; Bjork & Whitten, 1974; Glenberg, Bradley, Kraus, & Renzaglia, 1983; Koppenaal & Glanzer, 1990). As Baddeley (1990) notes, the existence of short- and long-term recency effects makes one wonder if there may not be a single mechanism that can account for both effects. If a single mechanism can explain both short- and long-term recency effects, then it obviously casts further doubt on the likelihood that a separate STM component is needed.

## Evidence from the Clinic

Potential support for the STM-LTM distinction has come from brain-damaged people who have memory disorders. Although the topics of memory consolidation and memory disorders are discussed in depth in Chapters 7 and 14, we will now briefly describe some of the findings relevant to the STM-LTM controversy. In the *classic amnesia syndrome*, the patient usually has both linguistic and general intellectual abilities intact. If not distracted or overly taxed, the person will not have difficulty in retaining new information for short periods of time. So these individuals appear to have a relatively intact STM system. They will, however, show some *retrograde amnesia* (a loss of memory for events prior to the cause of the onset of the amnesia), much of which dissipates with time. Memory for events occurring well before the brain damage causing the amnesia is essentially normal. This suggests that amnesics also possess a relatively intact LTM system. The major problem is a profound *anterograde amnesia* that doesn't improve with time. Anterograde amnesia refers to the inability to consolidate and remember new information for extended periods of time. This capsule picture of the classic amnesia syndrome implies that these people have both an STM and an LTM and that the problem is in transferring information from STM to LTM.

Further supporting the idea that there are separate STM and LTM components, Shallice and Warrington (1970) have observed a patient (K.F.) who had considerable difficulty retaining new information for short periods of time (i.e., he had a defective STM) but little problem with long-term learning (i.e., he had a nondefective LTM). Many other patients have been discovered who have selective recall deficits in what traditionally could be called STM or LTM (Basso, Spinnler, Vallar, & Zanobio, 1982; McCarthy & Warrington, 1990; Vallar & Shallice, 1990).

However, differences in ability to recall from STM or LTM do not necessarily favor the STM-LTM distinction. For example, as will be detailed in Chapter 14, people suffering from amnesia do *not* have a total inability to consolidate new information and to retain it for long periods of time. The deficit is selective. It is mainly apparent when patients are required to consciously recall or recognize information presented to them after the onset of the amnesia. They *can* learn new information and retain it if they are tested using *implicit memory tasks*. Such tasks do not require conscious recollection but show evidence of memory by affecting subsequent task performance (see Chapter 6).

For instance, one study (Jacoby & Witherspoon, 1982) took advantage of the fact that some words are homophones (they sound the same but have different spellings and meanings). An example of a pair of homophones is *reed* and *read*. When people are asked to spell homophones, they almost always respond by spelling the more frequently occurring instance of the two words. In Jacoby and Witherspoon's study, both normal and amnesic subjects were asked the question "What is an example of a reed instrument?" Afterward, when asked to spell "reed/read," both groups of subjects responded "reed," which is the less frequently encountered homophone. However, when later given a recognition test, only the normal subjects could recognize that they had earlier heard the word *reed*. So even though they had no conscious recollection of previously hearing the word *reed*, the amnesics revealed by their spelling that they were in fact influenced by (and therefore remembered) the question about musical instruments. The findings from studies using such implicit memory tasks demonstrate that anterograde amnesia may not be due to a disruption in transferring information between STM and LTM (as previously thought by many), largely negating support for the STM-LTM distinction.

Another troublesome aspect of the clinical literature is that patients who have a grossly defective STM but a normal LTM should be a paradox for those who believe in the STM-LTM distinction. According to the modal model in this area (Atkinson-Shiffrin), the vast majority of information that goes to LTM must first pass through STM. But how can LTM be normal if STM is defective? One would think these people would be seriously impaired, but in actuality, they often live an independent life with normal intellectual capabilities (Basso et al., 1982; Shallice & Warrington, 1970).

## Should the Distinction Be Abandoned?

There are people who believe that the answer to this question should be "yes." Some of them believe that it is time to abandon the multiple-memory-system approach altogether. Others, while perhaps accepting the notion of a separate sensory memory component, want to greatly deemphasize the distinction between STM and LTM. Few would deny that the empirical evidence supporting the STM-LTM distinction is no longer as firm as it once was believed to be. Many people are now more doubtful about the *necessity* of dividing memory processes into separate stages or components. The dissatisfaction with the Atkinson-Shiffrin model and similar approaches (e.g., Waugh & Norman, 1965) soon led to alternative memory models.

Nevertheless, as mentioned earlier, personal introspection still causes many people to believe (like William James believed) that qualitative differences exist between very recently acquired information and information that has been etched in the mind for a long time (perhaps decades). Because of this, and because it provides a convenient way to organize and present what is known about memory, most textbooks dealing with memory (especially introductory psychology books) still continue to use a multiple-memory-system approach. Of course, this will change if the evidence against it ever becomes incontrovertible.

# LONG-TERM MEMORY

You have just learned that some people doubt the existence of separate STM and LTM stores. Many memory researchers continue to use these terms, however, because they provide a useful way to present what is known about memory. Regardless of how you feel about the STM-LTM distinction, no normal person will deny having memories from years ago or that the capacity to store long-term memories is enormous. In future chapters we will see abundant evidence of the long duration and immense capacity of LTM. What is known and thought about LTM will be examined in these chapters in some detail. For instance, we will consider many methods for encoding information in and retrieving information from LTM, the probable biological mechanisms of LTM, how stress and emotion affect LTM functioning, techniques to improve LTM performance, and our autobiographical memory capability. (We will also consider many topics relating to STM.)

Therefore, in this section we will focus on a point made at the very beginning of this chapter. In trying to answer the opening list of questions, it became clear that LTM must be highly organized in order for us to be able to answer such questions so quickly. Let's examine some of the most widely used classifications for partitioning LTM. We will refer to them often in the rest of the book.

## Semantic Memory

People have long been interested in how we acquire *knowledge,* which can be defined as the storage and organization of information in memory (Solso, 1991). *Semantic* memory refers to general or generic knowledge about the world. As such, semantic memory encompasses an astounding amount of information stored in LTM. For instance, the meanings of all *words, symbols* (such as a "red" traffic light), *rules* (such as "Don't skip class"), and *facts* not tied to specific events (such as "Water boils when you see bubbles rising") are considered a part of semantic memory.

Semantic memory entails generic or general knowledge about the world that is not tied to specific experiences. A semantic memory is extracted from experience by noting the commonalities of many different experiences. For instance, one day a young child learns that the creature living next door is a "dog." After encountering several different dogs over a period of time, the child develops a generic understanding of the concept "dog." The child is said to have a semantic memory for the concept of "dog" if he can no longer remember the circumstances in which he learned about dogs.

Because so much of our knowledge is thought to reside in semantic memory, many models have been proposed to describe its organization. For instance, later in this chapter *propositional network models* and *connectionist models* will be discussed. These models attempt to explain how semantic memory is organized and how it operates. However, these are generally multipurpose models that try to account for a wide range of cognitive abilities (such as reasoning and language processing). In contrast to these more encompassing models, others have been developed that deal only with semantic memory. We will now briefly examine two types of these—feature-comparison models and network models of semantic memory.

**Feature-comparison models.** According to *feature-comparison* models of semantic memory, concepts are represented in memory in terms of lists of attributes or features. Probably the most well-known feature-comparison model is the one proposed by Smith, Shoben, and Rips (1974). The Smith et al. model distinguishes between two types of features: *defining features* and *characteristic features*. A defining feature is one that an object must possess to be considered an instance of a particular concept. In contrast, a characteristic feature is one that often is possessed, but does not have to be, by objects that are examples of a concept. For instance, the following subset of features might be stored for the generic concept *bird:*

Has feathers

Has wings

Can fly

Sings

Has two legs

Eats worms

Is food for cats

Some of these attributes are defining features, while others are only characteristic features. "Has feathers" is a defining feature, since all birds have feathers. However, "can fly," while being a characteristic feature of birds, is not a defining feature, since some birds (like roadrunners, emus, penguins, and ostriches) can't fly.

To determine whether or not a certain item is an instance of a particular concept, the model proposes that people compare the features of the item with the features stored in LTM for the concept. If there is little or no overlap of features, or if there is a very high correspondence, decisions can be quickly made. For example, people quickly respond "no" to the question "Is a beagle a bird?" and "yes" to the question "Is a pigeon a bird?" because of the difference in overlap of features. If there is only a moderate overlap between the item and the concept, then the decision process is slowed down until only the defining features can be checked. Asking people "Is a roadrunner a bird?" takes longer to answer because a roadrunner is not a typical bird and doesn't have many of the characteristic features of birds (it doesn't fly, sing, and eat worms; nor is it on a cat's menu). Therefore, a decision must be put off about roadrunners until the defining features (such as "has feathers") are checked.

Although feature-comparison models of semantic memory can explain some findings (e.g., that people respond faster for prototypical items, like "robin," than for nontypical items, like "roadrunner"), these models are unable to explain other findings. For instance, for some concepts (such as "chair") there do not appear to be defining features (Rosch, 1973).

**Network models of semantic memory.** Instead of assuming that knowledge is organized in LTM in terms of bundles of features, network models of semantic memory assert that information is stored in a network of interrelated nodes. For example, Collins and Quillian (1969) proposed a *hierarchical* network of concepts. As shown in Figure 3.6, each concept is represented by a node in the network, and each node has certain properties associated with it. This model is hierarchical because properties are stored only at the highest level to which

FIGURE 3.6

A part of a network model of semantic memory.
*Reprinted with permission.*

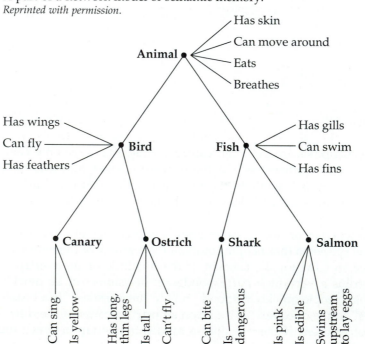

they apply. In other words, the fact that a canary can breathe is stored not at the canary node but instead at the highest node to which it applies, in this case the node "animal."

To better account for experimental data, Collins and Loftus (1975) introduced a revised version of the model. This new model abandoned the strict hierarchical nature of the previous model, proposed that there could be different kinds of links to connect concepts, and, perhaps most important, suggested that there would be *spreading activation* between nodes. Suppose that a concept was mentioned. The node that represented the concept would now become activated, and this activation would spread out to other nodes. The closer other nodes were, the more likely they would be activated. Once activated, these other nodes would also spread their activation to nearby nodes, and so forth. The spreading activation grows weaker the farther it travels, and eventually it ceases. If a node is activated, this means that the concept it represents can be processed better (perhaps it is more likely to be recalled or recognized) than would be true for an unactivated node. The closer the relationship between two concepts, the shorter the link between them, and the greater the likelihood that if one node is activated the other will be also.

Network models rapidly became popular (and still are). Part of the reason for this popularity is that they are very flexible and powerful. Ironically, these same traits have led some to question the real usefulness of such models (Johnson-Laird, Herrmann, & Chaffin, 1984). It has been argued that because these models are so flexible and powerful, they can be tinkered with to explain almost any new data. Furthermore, there is a concern that these models, although doing a commendable job in accounting for existing data, may not really represent how humans actually operate in the real world.

## Semantic and Episodic Memory

Although the specific terms were not used, the distinction between *semantic* and *episodic* knowledge has been noted by many scholars over the centuries (Herrmann, 1982). In modern times, Tulving (1972, 1983) is credited with making the most cogent case for the existence of these two types of knowledge.

Whereas semantic memories transcend the conditions in which they were formed, episodic memories explicitly refer to specific events and experiences in our life. In other words, episodic memory is tied to particular autobiographical events (such as remembering how you felt the first time you kissed your boyfriend or girlfriend, as opposed to how you typically feel when you kiss him or her). All memories start off as episodic; some remain this way, while others become divorced from individual experiences and become semantic memories.

Originally, Tulving considered episodic and semantic memory to be largely separate and parallel memory systems. However, owing to mounting evidence to the contrary, Tulving (1985, 1987) later suggested that episodic memory is probably a subset of semantic memory. In addition, he acknowledged the existence of a third type of LTM called *procedural memory*. Procedural memory or knowledge concerns learning that is obtained incrementally and that is inaccessible to conscious recollection. It typically involves learning how to perform a task or acquire a new skill (such as juggling a set of balls, riding a skateboard, or learning to knit). These are abilities that are difficult to describe how to do verbally; they are best taught by having them demonstrated and then practiced until mastered.

## Declarative and Nondeclarative Memories

Because semantic and episodic memory both involve the knowledge of facts, some people have preferred not to distinguish between them. Instead, they refer to memory for either kind of fact, semantic or episodic, as *declarative memory* (Cohen & Squire, 1980; Squire, 1987). Declarative knowledge has been defined as knowledge that deals with facts that can be acquired in a single trial (although sometimes more than one trial is needed) and that are directly accessible to conscious recollection. Examples of declarative knowledge are the definitions of new words learned in your Spanish class, the fact that the capital of Myanmar (formerly Burma) is Rangoon, and the exact circumstances (date, place, time, and so on) when you first met your present roommate.

Recently, some researchers have preferred to use the term *nondeclarative memory* rather than procedural memory (e.g., Squire, Knowlton, & Musen, 1993; Squire, Zola-Morgan, Cave, Haist, Musen, & Suzuki, 1990). This came about because the term *nondeclarative memory* seems to better capture the kinds of learning tasks that are preserved in many amnesic patients. These people can learn and remember motor and perceptual skills (such as showing improvements in the ability to track a moving light or to adapt to reading mirror-reversed words), which are instances of procedural memory. However, they can also show normal patterns of classical and operant conditioning, semantic priming effects (e.g., the homophone study described earlier in this chapter), and the ability to learn new cognitive tasks if their knowledge is tested in the right way (by implicit memory procedures—see Chapters 7 and 14). Because these additional abilities do not seem to really fit under the rubric of procedural memory, *nondeclarative memory* has gained in popularity as a term to describe these heterogeneous learning abilities.

# ALTERNATIVE MODELS OF MEMORY

## Levels-of-Processing Theory

In 1972, Craik and Lockhart published a paper in which they forcefully argued that too much attention and importance had been given to hypothetical structural components of memory. Although certainly not denying the existence of a separate STM and LTM, Craik and Lockhart proposed that in terms of the durability of a memory trace, it is much more meaningful to consider *how* information is processed rather than *where* it may be processed. Their model of how memories are formed, known as the *levels-of-processing* approach, became extremely influential during the 1970s. This approach deemphasizes structural components like sensory memory, STM, and LTM and stresses the essential role that encoding processes play in the formation of lasting memories. The durability of memories is seen as a direct function of the depth or level of processing that information receives. In essence, the deeper the processing, the more likely that the information will be remembered. A full discussion of the levels-of-processing approach will await until the next chapter, where encoding processes are considered in depth.

## The Working Memory Model

When describing the Atkinson-Shiffrin memory model, we noted that the model assumed that the short-term store had multiple functions. Not only did it hold information for short periods of time, but it also acted as a workplace for processing information, controlling its flow, and making decisions. In this model, the short-term store was thought of as being a single system. Baddeley and Hitch (1974) accepted the notion that STM could be a place where considerable processing and decision making took place. However, they challenged the idea that STM was a single system, proposing instead a new model of STM that has multiple, separate components. This new prototype of STM was referred to as the *working memory model*. Figure 3.7 depicts a simplified view of the model.

The heart of the working memory model is the *central executive*. This component is responsible for the coordination of attentional resources and the supervision of two slave systems known as the *phonological loop* and the *visuospatial sketch pad*. Unfortunately, very little is known about how the central executive actually works to control and coordinate its slave systems. Recently, it has been proposed that a breakdown in the normal functioning of the central executive may play an important role in the mental deterioration seen in Alzheimer's patients (Baddeley, 1992). (Alzheimer's disease is the most common form of senility suffered by older people and will be discussed in detail in Chapter 14.)

The phonological loop is responsible for manipulating speech-based information. It is theorized to have two components—a *phonological store* and an *articulatory control process*. It is proposed that our memory for a sound of speech is stored in the phonological store for about 1.5 to 2 seconds before fading away. However, if we perform subvocal rehearsal, such as by repeating over and over again the word *monster* silently to ourselves, the articulatory control process can "refresh" the acoustic memory trace of "monster" in the phonological store, allowing it to stay longer. The articulatory control process can also transform written language into a phonological code for storage in the

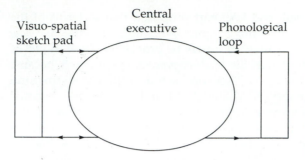

FIGURE 3.7
A conceptual view of Baddeley and Hitch's working memory model.
*From Alan Baddeley,* Human Memory: Theory and Practice. *Copyright © 1990 by Allyn and Bacon. Reprinted with permission.*

phonological store. Baddeley (1986, 1990, 1992) has shown that the phonological loop, as envisioned, can do a reasonable job in accounting for several factors that affect memory span. In addition, there is some evidence that the phonological loop aids in comprehending language, acquiring vocabulary, and learning how to read.

The visuo-spatial sketch pad is responsible for manipulating visuo-spatial images. As with the phonological loop, information can enter the visuo-spatial sketch pad directly (e.g., when you see a dog) or indirectly (e.g., when you generate an internal image from memory of a dog). This slave system is thought to be useful for planning spatial tasks and for helping to orient oneself in geographic settings. Much less is known about this component than is known about the phonological loop.

Overall, there is considerable evidence that the short-term processing of information is much more complex than anyone originally imagined. Some aspects of the working memory model (especially the phonological loop) have received good empirical support, although not all data are consistent with the model. Many aspects of the model need to be fleshed out, and the process should be considered an evolving one.

## Propositional Networks

As you will recall from our earlier discussion, network models of memory propose that related pieces of knowledge are linked together in a broad network. There are many different types of network models. One currently popular type is the *propositional network*. Each node in this kind of network represents a proposition. A *proposition* is a unit of knowledge that can be asserted as being either true or false. Consider the following example from Matlin's book *Cognition* (1989): the sentence *Susan gave a white cat to Maria, who is the president of the club* can be divided into these three propositions:

1.  Susan gave a cat to Maria.
2.  The cat was white.
3.  Maria is the president of the club.

Each of these three propositions can then be represented in a propositional network such as the one displayed in Figure 3.8. Each proposition is represented by a node (shown by the ellipses 1, 2, and 3), with the links (shown by arrows) indicating the relationships between the words (such as "Agent" and "Object").

Some very elaborate propositional networks have been developed. Two of the most prominent are HAM [Human Associative Memory (Anderson & Bower, 1973)] and ACT* [pronounced "act-star"—Adaptive Control of Thought (Anderson, 1983)]. The ACT* model is an extremely ambitious attempt to account for all forms of human cognition. So in addition to dealing with memory, it also tries to explain such abilities as language use, reasoning, learning, and decision making.

## Connectionist Models

While it has been said that network models were "computer-inspired," *connectionist* models have been said to be "neurally inspired." Network models of memory assume that knowledge, in the form of either concepts or propositions, is stored at single nodes in a network. These nodes are then activated in a serial fashion, one node at a time, often by spreading activation (e.g., Anderson, 1983; Collins and Loftus, 1975). Network models are guided by explicit rules that govern how information is learned and processed.

In contrast, connectionist models are patterned after the way the human brain works. These models assert that knowledge is not concentrated in single

FIGURE 3.8

An example of a propositional network for the sentence *Susan gave a white cat to Maria, who is the president of the club.*
*Figure from* Cognition, *Second Edition by Margaret W. Matlin, copyright © 1989 by Holt, Rinehart and Winston, Inc. Reprinted by permission of the publisher.*

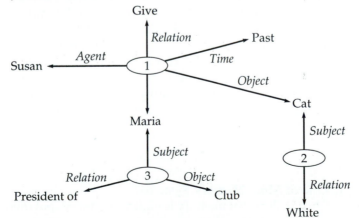

nodes, but as in the human brain, knowledge is distributed throughout the system. Furthermore, the carrying out of all cognitive processes (memory, learning, perception, language, thinking, reasoning, and so on) is thought to occur in parallel, just like it does in the brain. This means that many different nodes or units are interacting simultaneously.

As with the way neurons work (see Chapter 7), it is conceived that these units either excite or inhibit each other. Connectionist models also believe that knowledge is not stored in the individual units themselves but rather that knowledge is stored *within the connections* between the units. This is also analogous to how the brain works. All the "action" in terms of information processing and memory is thought to take place at the synapses (or connections) between neighboring neurons. In a connectionist model, learning and information processing are not guided by a set of explicit rules. In lieu of rules, it is contended that knowledge is learned and processed according to the *strength* of the connections between units. Because of the similarities to the way the brain functions, connectionist models are often referred to as *parallel distributed processing* (PDP) models or *neural networks*.

In the last few years, there has been a virtual explosion of interest in connectionist models, which are highly mathematical and complex in their various architectures. This enormous interest occurs for two major reasons. First, many people now believe that it makes intuitive sense to pattern a theory or model of semantic memory (or any other cognitive process for that matter) after the way the human brain appears to operate. Second, although the philosophical underpinnings of the connectionist movement occurred decades ago (e.g., McCulloch & Pitts, 1943; Pitts & McCulloch, 1947; Rosenblatt, 1962; Selfridge & Neisser, 1960), only with recent developments in computer hardware and software have a number of working connectionist systems been able to adequately simulate a large range of human behavior and performance (Bechtel & Abrahamsen, 1991; Estes, 1988; McClelland & Rumelhart, 1986, 1988; McCloskey, 1991; Morris, 1989; Seidenberg & McClelland, 1989; Smolensky, 1988).

Clearly impressive, and certainly popular, connectionist models will no doubt continue to capture the interest of cognitive psychologists, including memory researchers. But there are reasons to be cautious in how we interpret the results of these systems. For instance, McCloskey (1991), although certainly a proponent of their use, wisely urges caution in assuming that these models can really act as good theories of how human cognitive functions work. He convincingly argues that even though a particular connectionist model might do an excellent job in simulating some cognitive function (such as pattern recognition), this doesn't mean this is the way the human brain also performs the same function.

# SUMMARY

### I. One or More Memory Systems?
- It is clear that memory is highly organized, but there is an ongoing debate over whether there is a single memory system or multiple memory sys-

tems. The debate has centered on the need to postulate separate *short-term memory* (STM) and *long-term memory* (LTM) components.

- During the first half of this century, *interference theory* was dominant. This theory held that memory could best be viewed as a unitary system and that interference accounts for memory failures.
- By the late 1950s most memory researchers had abandoned the unitary view. The rise in popularity of the multiple-memory-system approach was due to the influence (and success) of the *information-processing approach* used by computer scientists, the dramatic effects of the *Brown-Peterson Distractor Technique*, and the work of Sperling on *iconic memory*.

## II. The Brown-Peterson Distractor Technique
- The Brown-Peterson paradigm showed that a massive amount of forgetting can occur in just seconds if people are not allowed to rehearse.
  - This result caused great excitement because it seemed to suggest the need to have separate STM and LTM components.
  - Forgetting of recently acquired information was assumed to be due to *trace decay* and not to *interference effects*.

## III. The Atkinson-Shiffrin Memory Model
- Introduced in the mid-1960s, the *Atkinson-Shiffrin memory model* became extremely influential. Using an information-processing approach, the model was composed of three separate components: *sensory register*, *short-term store*, and *long-term store*.
- An important aspect of the model was the distinction it made between *structural features* and *control processes* (the voluntary strategies a person uses to process information).

## IV. Sensory Memory
- *Sensory memory* provides us with a highly accurate record of the information impinging on our sensory receptors. Having a sensory memory allows additional time to recognize stimuli, to choose which sensory information to give full attention, and to process information that appears and disappears very quickly. Sensory memory also provides continuity from one moment to the next.
- Along with others, Sperling demonstrated the existence of a separate storage system for visual sensory memory (*iconic memory*). Iconic memory has a large capacity, renders accurate representations of the visual stimuli, and usually fades in less than a second.
- Each sense modality is thought to have its own sensory memory system, with characteristics broadly similar to those of iconic memory.

## V. Short-Term Memory
- Unless rehearsed, information in STM is forgotten within 30 seconds.
- By testing people's *memory span*, Miller claimed that the capacity of STM was seven (plus or minus two) *chunks*.

- Others have argued that STM capacity is defined not in terms of a fixed number of chunks but in terms of a fixed amount of time to pronounce items before the verbal trace decays.
- In a free recall task, people tend to best remember the first few items (*primacy effect*) and the last few items (*recency effect*). These effects were assumed to be due to the operation of LTM and STM, respectively.
- Although *acoustic encoding* of information seems to be preferred in STM, and *semantic encoding* in LTM, there's ample evidence that other types of codes can be used in short- or long-term memory tasks.
- The *Sternberg paradigm* has been extensively used to explore how people retrieve information from STM.
  - Sternberg concluded that information from STM is retrieved by means of a counterintuitive *exhaustive serial search* process.
  - However, others disagree with this explanation of the data and claim that information retrieval from STM is performed like retrieval from LTM—by means of *parallel processing*.
- Forgetting in both STM and LTM can occur because of either *trace decay* or *interference*.

## VI. Evaluation of the STM-LTM Distinction

- Much of the empirical evidence that once seemed to clearly suggest the existence of separate STM and LTM stores has eroded.
- Neither the coding of information, the method of information retrieval, the causes of forgetting, the recency effect, nor data obtained from patients with memory disorders provide unambiguous evidence that requires a separate STM and LTM.
- Many researchers, however, still hold to the distinction or at least prefer to use the terms *STM* and *LTM* as a way to help organize and present findings about memory.

## VII. Long-Term Memory

- LTM appears to have a virtually unlimited capacity and duration.
- An enormous amount of information in LTM is contained within our *semantic memory*. Semantic memory refers to all the general knowledge we have about the world. Different types of semantic memory models were described.
  - *Feature-comparison models* assume that concepts are represented in memory in the form of lists of attributes or features.
  - *Network models* of semantic memory propose that *concepts* are linked together in a broad network. Each concept is represented by a *node* in the network. The most powerful network models are those that assume there is *spreading activation* between nodes.
- LTM has been partitioned in different ways by different researchers. One popular classification system divides LTM into *episodic, semantic,* and *procedural* memory.

• Another popular system combines episodic and semantic memory under the rubric *declarative memory* (knowledge that deals with facts that can be acquired in a single trial and that are directly accessible to conscious recollection) and contrasts this type of memory with *nondeclarative memory* (knowledge that is obtained incrementally, like motor and perceptual skills, and that is not directly available to conscious recollection).

## VIII. Alternative Models of Memory

• Because of widespread dissatisfaction with the Atkinson-Shiffrin model, many alternative models of memory have been proposed.

  • The *levels-of-processing* approach asserts that it is much more meaningful to consider *how* information is processed than *where* the processing takes place.

  • The *working memory* model challenges the idea that STM is a single system. This model proposes that STM is composed of three separate, interrelated components—the *central executive,* the *phonological loop,* and the *visuo-spatial sketch pad.*

  • A *propositional network* assumes that each node represents a proposition (a unit of knowledge that can be either true or false). Some propositional networks, like ACT*, attempt to account for many types of human cognition.

  • *Connectionist models* are patterned after the way the human brain works. These models assume that as in the brain, knowledge is *distributed* throughout the system, all cognitive processing occurs in *parallel*, and knowledge is stored *within the connections* between nodes, not in single nodes. Connectionist models are often called *parallel distributed processing models* or *neural networks.*

# 4

# Encoding

———— ❖ ————

*I*n Chapter 2 you learned that the memory process can be divided into three successive phases: registration, retention, and remembering. The first phase, registration (often called *encoding*), involves transforming information into a form that a person can retain. When you intentionally try to register information, this is known as *explicit encoding*. Oftentimes, however, we register information incidentally—in other words, without any conscious, effortful attempt to do so. This is called *incidental learning.* If a friend asked you to remember the color of your Grateful Dead concert tickets, intentionally doing so would involve explicit encoding. However, if a month after the concert you can recall the color of the tickets, even though you didn't intentionally try to encode this information in the first place, this would be an example of incidental learning. As you might imagine, incidental learning usually results in poorer memory performance than does explicit encoding because less attention and effort are expended. Any student who has been caught by a "pop" quiz knows that a different form of studying would have been used the night before if he or she had expected the quiz.

Nevertheless, it is commonly thought that a tremendous amount of the information we learn and remember is registered through incidental learning. In fact, Hasher and Zacks (1979) believe that people encode environmental events that are very important to everyday life (such as the location of objects, the frequency of occurrence of events, and the temporal ordering of events) automatically, with little or no intentional effort or attention. In Chapter 9, we discuss at some length the evidence surrounding their proposal.

## THE FLEXIBILITY OF ENCODING

As described above, there's a great deal of flexibility in the amount of effort and attention a person can devote to the encoding process. For instance, if an individual desperately wants to remember some new information, the degree of concentration and effort involved in the explicit encoding process can reach heroic proportions. During final exams, students often study very intensely ("pulling several all-nighters") to help ensure that they will be able to recall certain facts for the exams. And even as exams are being passed out, many students frantically examine their notes or books, hoping to ferret out another fact or two before taking the test. Usually, however, less extreme effort is expended during explicit encoding (such as when a person is looking over a TV guide to decide what movies he or she might want to see this weekend). At the other end of the continuum, when we are not intentionally trying to pick up new information, we know that incidental learning can allow us to encode information without much effort at all.

## Selective Processing of Information

In addition to being flexible in terms of the amount of effort and intentionality expended during encoding, people can also be flexible in terms of the aspects of the stimulus they want to encode. A person is most likely to encode those aspects of a stimulus that are most important or significant at that instance. For example, when you see a grape, there are a variety of features that you may or may not encode about it. If you are selecting grapes for making wine, you may focus on features such as color (red, green, or purple), taste, and texture. But if you are the parent of a 2-year-old who is holding a grape in his or her hand, you will probably quickly encode the size of the grape and remember that grapes are a possible choking hazard. As you will read in Chapter 13, the famous Russian Shereshevskii (better known as S.) owed much of his remarkable ability to remember new information to the fact that he could encode stimuli in a number of different, often bizarre ways.

## Expectations

How people choose to encode information depends to a large extent on how they believe they will need to use that information in the future. A good example of this fact was nicely demonstrated in a study conducted by Frost (1972). Each of her subjects was presented with 16 drawings, one at a time, for 1.5 seconds each. The drawings depicted four animals, four articles of clothing, four vehicles, and four pieces of furniture. Figure 4.1 shows a sample of some of the drawings presented.

After seeing all 16 drawings, the subjects were given a 15-minute filler task (canceling out certain numbers from a booklet). Upon completing this task, the subjects were told that they would be presented with a new series of drawings to view. Their job was to decide, as fast as possible, if the object shown had the same *name* as one of the original drawings. If it did, the subjects were instructed to press a "yes" key that recorded their reaction time (RT).

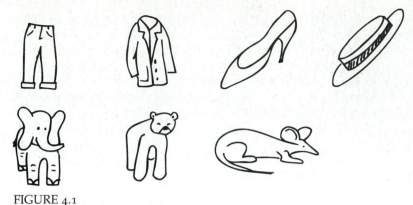

FIGURE 4.1
Example of stimuli used by Frost.
*From N. Frost, "Encoding and retrieval in visual memory tasks,"* Journal of Experimental Psychology, *Vol. 95 (1972), pp. 317–326. Copyright 1972 by the American Psychological Association. Reprinted by permission.*

Some of the new drawings were of objects that clearly had different names from those of the objects originally seen, while others were of objects that had the same names. Now here's the interesting twist: some of the objects with the same names were drawn exactly as they appeared in the original 16 drawings, but others were drawn from an orientation that differed from what was originally seen. Figure 4.2 shows examples of some of the test items. You can see for yourself that the first elephant (designated SS) has both the same name and the same orientation as one of the objects in Figure 4.1, that the second elephant (SD) has the same name but is pictured in a different orientation, and that the third object (a bunny) doesn't match the name of any of the objects. Given that the task was to decide if the new object had the same name as one of the old objects, the subject should hit the "yes" key for both elephant pictures.

Before we give you the results, there's one other crucial aspect that needs to be mentioned: there were actually two groups of subjects in the study, and one group was told the truth, while the other one was deceived. The subjects in the group given accurate information were told that they would later need to recognize the original 16 objects. Frost hypothesized that if there is flexibility in encoding, then it would make sense for these subjects to try to explicitly encode the visual characteristics of the drawings. The group given misleading information was led to believe that the later memory test would be a free-recall test of the objects' names. For these subjects, she hypothesized that it would make little sense for them to explicitly try to visually encode the drawings, since they were not expecting to have to recognize them again.

The results certainly seemed to confirm her hypothesis. Only the subjects expecting a recognition test responded faster to the drawings that were identical in both name and orientation to one of the original drawings. This is exactly what you would expect if the subjects expecting to recall the objects' names had not bothered to visually encode the first set of drawings. Results such as these strongly suggest that people can exert considerable voluntary

SS          SD          Bunny

FIGURE 4.2
Examples of test stimuli used in the recognition task.
*From N. Frost, "Encoding and retrieval in visual memory tasks," Journal
of Experimental Psychology, Vol. 95 (1972), pp. 317-326. Copyright 1972
by the American Psychological Association. Reprinted by permission.*

control over the encoding process. We will see more evidence of this flexibility
in encoding later in this chapter, particularly in the section describing the *levels-
of-processing* approach to memory formation (Craik & Lockhart, 1972).

# $S$TM AND LTM ENCODING

Please read the following brief story, and be prepared to have your memory
tested for one of the sentences.

> There is an interesting story about the telescope. In Holland, a man named Lipper-
> shey was an eyeglass maker. One day his children were playing with some lenses.
> They discovered that things seemed very close if two lenses were held about a foot
> apart. Lippershey began experimenting, and his "spyglass" attracted much atten-
> tion. He sent a letter about it to Galileo, the great Italian scientist. Galileo at once
> realized the importance of the discovery and set about to build an instrument of
> his own. He used an old organ pipe with one lens curved out and the other in. On
> the first clear night he pointed the glass toward the sky. He was amazed to find
> the empty dark spaces filled with brightly gleaming stars! Night after night Galileo
> climbed to a high tower sweeping the sky with his telescope. One night he saw
> Jupiter, and to his great surprise discovered near it three bright stars, two to the
> east and one to the west. On the next night, however, all were to the west. A few
> nights later there were four little stars.

Without referring back to the passage, decide which one of the following
four sentences was in the story.

A. He sent Galileo, the great Italian scientist, a letter about it.
B. A letter about it was sent to Galileo, the great Italian scientist.
C. Galileo, the great Italian scientist, sent him a letter about it.
D. He sent a letter about it to Galileo, the great Italian scientist.

If you are like most of the other people who have attempted this task, you
probably quickly eliminated choice C but then had some difficulty in deciding
between the other three choices. This is because choices A, B, and D all maintain

the correct meaning of the original sentence; they differ only in their surface form or structure. And after a short period of time, it is usually hard to remember the exact surface form or structure of what we encode. However, if you were asked to choose between the four sentences immediately after hearing the target sentence, you would likely have little trouble in correctly identifying choice D as the identical sentence.

The demonstration you just performed comes from an experiment conducted by Sachs (1967) in which she explored how well people could retain verbatim information over varying lengths of time. In her study, she had subjects try to identify the exact sentence they heard either immediately upon hearing it or after approximately 25 seconds (80 syllables of extra material) or 50 seconds (160 extra syllables). She observed that with no delay, subjects were highly accurate in making judgments about all four test sentences. But by the time that an additional 25 or 50 seconds had elapsed, their performance changed considerably. Their ability to choose between the three test sentences that differed superficially from each other (but not in meaning) now fell to almost chance levels. However, the ability to reject the test sentence that differed in *meaning* from the original (in this case, choice C) was still good (about 80 percent accuracy after 50 seconds).

Other studies have also found that people usually quickly forget verbatim information (e.g., Gernsbacher, 1985; Sachs, 1974), although not always entirely (Anderson & Paulson, 1977). So it seems that although we can, and often do, encode information in STM exactly as it was presented, we do not generally encode these surface characteristics into LTM. Instead, what is encoded into LTM is the meaning or gist of the information. This makes sense, since normally we do not need to remember the exact form in which information is presented. What is important is to encode the meaning for long-term storage.

Having said this, let's remember that in the last section we pointed out that a key characteristic of the encoding process is that it is a very flexible one. So if it is important to encode into LTM the exact surface structure of what is presented to us, we can readily do so. For example, when memorizing a poem, a quotation, or even a riddle, people will encode verbatim information into LTM.

# LIMITATIONS OF ENCODING

Unfortunately, even when we want to explicitly encode information, encoding processes do not function flawlessly. This, of course, leads to poor memory performance. Let's examine some of the limitations of the encoding process.

## Lack of Attention

The process of *attention* acts much like the focus on a camera. If a camera is not focused correctly, details are blurred. Similarly, if attention is less than complete, information is often only barely encoded. This suggests that many purported memory failures are not really memory failures at all. Instead, because of a lack of proper attention to the task or information (such as information presented in a dull lecture), the person never really learned (encoded) the material in the first place. And after all, you cannot be expected to remember what you never encoded.

## Incomplete Sensory Processes

Our sensory memories are constantly being bombarded with incoming information from our sensory receptors. The capacity to take in all this immense and constantly changing information is limited. Furthermore, information that does reach sensory memory decays rapidly, sometimes within a single second (this is especially true for the icon), and is gone forever. Therefore, most of the sensory information that bombards us never makes it past sensory memory. In addition, the amount of physical energy in the environment may make it difficult or impossible for our sensory receptors to respond adequately to the available information. For instance, if the intensity of the light, sound, or smell is very low, few details will be encoded.

## Personal Motivation

Even if the physical energy is sufficient to provide for excellent perception, the objects of our perception may be distorted because of what we are motivated to observe. For example, if you really want a certain person to be present at a party, then you may actually think that you see the person on the other side of the room. Only later, as you make your approach, do you discover that it is just someone else who closely resembles the sought-after person. So beware, because we often remember what we think we observed, even though this might not always correspond to reality.

In addition, there are times when people are motivated not to remember something. For instance, sometimes a person wishes to encode information just long enough to carry out some task but doesn't wish to remember the information for any longer. Consider the situation in which you want to call a restaurant or business that you have never called before and that you expect never to call again. You look the telephone number up and rehearse it only until you finish dialing. In such a situation, you want to maintain the number just long enough to use it, but not to learn it. In Chapters 8 and 14 we will discuss in detail the concept of *repression* (the process of banishing extremely unpleasant memories or experiences from conscious awareness), which is an extreme illustration of the power of motivated forgetting.

In some cases, a person does not wish to encode some information at all. For instance, many people refuse to listen to gossip because they don't want to hear bad things concerning their friends. The same is true about people who avoid becoming privy to secrets or incriminating information (perhaps as a protective measure so that later they won't have to become involved in some investigation). And some individuals actively avoid encoding what they consider to be trivia so as not to fill their memory with inconsequential things.

# WAYS TO ENHANCE ENCODING

Every memory begins with the encoding of information, either intentionally or incidentally. Because of this fact, a lot of attention has been devoted to exploring ways to enhance the encoding process. As you will learn in Chapter 15, many of the memory improvement techniques developed over the centuries specifically involve better ways for encoding information. In this section we will describe several factors that influence the encoding process.

## Organization

It's been said that "to organize is to memorize." George Mandler, one of the earliest and strongest adherents of this view, wrote in a very influential paper that "memory and organization are not only correlated, but organization is a necessary condition for memory" (1967, p. 328). Although this statement may be a bit too strong for some people, it certainly is true that one of the best ways to promote encoding is by organizing the material to be learned (Bower, 1970, 1972; Mandler, 1967). *Organization* is a process in which individual items are grouped together on the basis of some shared relationship. The relationship can be virtually anything that is meaningful or distinctive to the person. Items can be organized by their color, size, taste, meaning, pleasantness, hardness, funniness, sound, shape, and so forth. The process of *chunking*, discussed in the last chapter, essentially involves organizing the material to be remembered into larger, more meaningful units. Organizational processes such as chunking enhance encoding by reducing the amount of material that needs to be processed and stored.

The effects that organizational factors have on encoding have been studied most often with free recall tasks. These studies clearly demonstrate that organized material is easier to learn. For instance, subjects presented with word lists that are categorized in some fashion learn such lists faster than lists of unrelated words. Table 4.1 presents a list of 20 common objects. A quick inspection reveals that these objects can be organized into four semantic categories—animals, flowers, vehicles, and furniture. If, during a subsequent free recall test, a subject recalls all the animal names in a cluster, then all the flowers, and so on, then it can be assumed that he or she probably used an organizational strategy to encode the words. It has also been found that categorized lists are better remembered if they are presented in *blocked* form (all the items from one category are presented together) than if the items are randomly

**TABLE 4.1** COMMON OBJECTS THAT CAN BE REORGANIZED INTO FOUR
SEMANTIC CATEGORIES

Dog
Bus
Mouse
Chair
Tulip
Train
Table
Horse
Rose
Petunia
Airplane
Goat
Sofa
Pig
Bed
Boat
Lilac
Truck
Marigold
Dresser

presented (Ellis & Hunt, 1993). This is likely because the blocked presentation is more organized and fosters the encoding process.

Bousfield (1953) discovered that subjects will spontaneously organize items that were not presented in a blocked format. In his study, subjects were presented with a randomly composed list of 15 animal names, 15 professions, 15 boys' names, and 15 names of vegetables. During recall, people tended to organize the items into groups on the basis of their category membership. This effect has become known as *clustering*. Tulving (1962) has shown that people will try to impose a structure or organization on a list of words even when the words are unrelated to each other (at least as far as the experimenter is concerned). This subject-imposed organization becomes evident when, over a series of trials, subjects develop a consistency in the order in which they recall items. Tulving referred to this phenomenon as *subjective organization,* and further research has generally supported the idea that subjects will strive to build structure or organization into a list of items that appear at first blush to have little in common (Bousfield & Bousfield, 1966; Mandler & Pearlstone, 1966; Tulving, 1964).

Findings such as clustering in recall and subjective organization indicate that people will organize items even though they are not instructed to do so.

This suggests that just through daily living, people have learned the powerful, beneficial influence that organization can have on encoding (and hence memory).

## Warm-up

Encoding can be facilitated by familiarizing the person with the material to be learned or with the format of the memory task. By briefly performing a particular task with some sample materials, a person becomes more knowledgeable about what is to be expected later. For instance, before administering a list of 25 paired-associates to learn, it is wise to give subjects a few sample items to practice on. Learning is also made easier by providing people with overviews or outlines of the material. This allows the subjects to organize and place in context the material that needs to be learned.

## Distribution of Practice

It should come as no surprise that the more you study something, the more you learn about it. A brief exposure provides for minimal encoding operations, but continued exposure allows for more and deeper encoding. But did you know that *how* you decide to distribute your study time is an important factor? One of the earliest findings in the experimental study of memory was that the spacing of practice is a potent task variable (Ebbinghaus, 1885; Woodworth, 1938). In general, it is better to spread your practice over many trials than to mass the sessions together into one long session (for a recent review, see Payne & Wenger, 1992). Students who distribute study sessions over a week (e.g., studying 1 hour each day) learn more than students who study (cram!) the same number of hours all at one stretch. This is sometimes referred to as the *spacing effect*. Spacing your practice helps you avoid fatigue and inattention, which impair encoding effectiveness. The spacing effect may also work because, as has been proposed, each time we study or think about something, we make additional memory traces of it (Hintzman, 1978). The more copies, the greater the chances are of retrieving the information later.

The spacing effect, however, can't be applied in all situations, and it does have its limitations. Even though learning may be better if practice is distributed, sometimes there just isn't sufficient time to spread out practice or study sessions. If you just heard a rumor that your history teacher is going to give a surprise quiz on the last four chapters of the book later this afternoon, you have little choice but to engage in cramming! Also, in some situations, if the spacing interval is too great, forgetting can occur, and the person does worse than if he or she had used massed practice. This seems especially to be true for certain types of learning. A good example is the learning of intricate sequences of movement that are best acquired if a person puts in extended, continuous practice. So a new routine in gymnastics or a special shot in tennis may be learned faster if massed practice, rather than distributed practice, is used.

## Overlearning

A score on a memory test is not always a good measure of what someone knows. Even when the score is a perfect one! Consider a 3-year-old who, with much hemming and hawing, finally manages, after several attempts, to recall all the letters of the alphabet in order. Now you (we hope!) can also recall the letters of the alphabet flawlessly. Because both of you had the same score (no errors), do you want to concede that you and the 3-year-old know the alphabet equally well? Of course not. You know the alphabet much better, as can be easily shown by the fact that you can always recall it correctly and can do so much faster and with more confidence. The reason why you can do this is that you have *overlearned* the alphabet. Overlearning material is an easy way to enhance encoding; it will decrease the rate at which forgetting of the material will occur because it strengthens and embellishes the memory representation. In addition, your speed and confidence in remembering will increase. We often tell our students who are fearful about exams to overlearn the material. This improves their performance and dramatically cuts down their test anxiety.

## Knowledge Base

How well a person encodes something often depends on how much the person already knows about it (referred to as the person's *knowledge base;* see Chapter 12). Typically, the person who has the larger knowledge base will find it easier to encode new information about the relevant topic. A student who has studied French for several years will find it much easier to learn some new French vocabulary words than will a novice at French.

# *L*EVELS-OF-PROCESSING APPROACH

In the last chapter we introduced the *levels-of-processing* approach (Craik & Lockhart, 1972) as an alternative to theories that stressed the importance of multiple memory systems or stores. Since this approach emphasizes the vital role that encoding processes play in memory formation, we postponed a fuller discussion of it until this chapter. The levels-of-processing approach does *not* argue against the distinction between primary memory (STM) and secondary memory (LTM), as is popularly believed (Craik, 1990). However, in contrast to a structural model of memory (such as the Atkinson-Shiffrin model), the levels-of-processing approach assumes that there is only a single memory store. The part of this store that we can become consciously aware of is what Craik and

Lockhart call primary memory; the rest of the store is considered to be secondary memory. As Craik and Lockhart (1972) point out, their view of primary memory is synonymous with the way that William James had conceived of it—primary memory consists of the current contents of consciousness.

The levels-of-processing approach assumes that all incoming stimuli (sounds, sights, smells, etc.) can be processed at different levels of analysis. Some stimuli are processed at a very superficial, shallow level, with only physical or sensory features being noted. A person, for instance, may only note that a fire alarm is loud or that a word is typed in all CAPITALS. However, other stimuli may receive processing at a much deeper and meaningful level. An example of this more elaborate processing is determining the meaning and significance of an acrid smell (watch out—something spilled in chemistry lab!) or whether the adjective *kooky* is an apt description of your next-door neighbor. The hypothesis that different stimuli may be afforded differential amounts and types of processing should be familiar to you. This was a key point made earlier in the chapter, in the discussion about the inherent flexibility of the encoding process.

According to the levels-of-processing approach, the strength of memory formation is best thought of as being on a continuum. Memory strength is a by-product of the depth of encoding processes; the deeper the level of processing that a stimulus receives, the more likely it is that a lasting memory trace of it will form.

## Maintenance and Elaborative Rehearsal

As part of their levels-of-processing approach, Craik and Lockhart (1972) also proposed that there are two types of rehearsal, only one of which leads to long-term storage of information. One type is called *maintenance rehearsal* (also called *Type I rehearsal*), and its purpose is to simply maintain information in primary memory. This can be accomplished by just shallow processing of the information (such as repeating a telephone number over and over so that it remains in conscious awareness). Since maintenance rehearsal is such a low-level form of processing, Craik and Lockhart claimed that it would not lead to permanent retention of the information (e.g., once you stopped repeating the telephone number, it would fade from primary memory, and you would later have no memory of it).

The second type of rehearsal is called *elaborative rehearsal* (or *Type II rehearsal*). This type of rehearsal, as the names implies, involves a more elaborate or deeper analysis of the information. For example, to use elaborative rehearsal to remember a telephone number, a person should relate the digits to things that are meaningful. Suppose the number for a good friend is 212-5374. Perhaps if your friend is a swimmer, you can remember the "212" part of the number by recalling that it is the boiling point of water (in degrees Fahrenheit), the "53" because it is the number on his football uniform, and the "74" because he was born in 1974. Although initially it does take some time to think up meaningful associations, they really do work to help you remember. Craik and Lockhart proposed that only elaborative rehearsal would lead to long-term storage of information.

## Support for the Levels-of-Processing Approach

An excellent way to test the assumptions of the levels-of-processing approach is by using an *incidental* learning paradigm. In this kind of paradigm the subject receives no instructions to memorize any items. The subject is simply asked to make various judgments about the items being presented. Since the individual doesn't expect to receive a memory test later, the person presumably will only process the items in the way the experimenter intended. Therefore, the experimenter hopes it comes as a complete surprise to the subject when he or she is later asked to recall or recognize the original items.

To give you the flavor of a typical test of the levels-of-processing approach, try answering the questions in Table 4.2. Now try to recall the words about which the questions were asked. If you are typical, you will best remember the words that required you to analyze or think about their meaning or significance.

Many studies have supported the basic theme that deeper levels of processing lead to enhanced memory (e.g., Bellezza, Cheesman, & Reddy, 1977; Bower & Karlin, 1974; Craik & Tulving, 1975; Fisk & Schneider, 1984; Parkin, 1984). For example, Craik and Tulving (1975) performed an experiment very similar to the demonstration in Table 4.2. Subjects were presented with a lengthy list of words, each appearing separately on a screen for less than 1 second. They had to make one of three different judgments about each word: Was it typed in *capitals* (shallow encoding)? Did it *rhyme* with another word (intermediate encoding)? Or did the word *fit* into an empty space in a sentence (deep encoding)? After all judgments were made, a surprise recall test was given. Consistent with what the levels-of-processing approach would predict, the words that had undergone deep encoding (e.g., deciding if the word *rocks*

TABLE 4.2 SOME TYPICAL QUESTIONS THAT ARE USED IN INCIDENTAL LEARNING TASKS TO INVESTIGATE LEVELS OF PROCESSING

Answer "yes" or "no" to the following questions with respect to the target word.

| | |
|---|---|
| Is this a pleasant word? | happy |
| Is this word in capital letters? | CREAM |
| Does this word rhyme with jello? | hiccup |
| Would the word make sense in the following sentence? "I like to eat _____ for breakfast." | rocks |
| Is this word a type of music? | rap |

would make sense in the sentence) were recalled the best, followed by the words that were analyzed by how they sounded (e.g., deciding if *hiccup* and *jello* rhyme, an intermediate level of encoding); remembered the least well were the words that were processed only in terms of their physical appearance, a very shallow form of encoding (e.g., Is *CREAM* in capital letters?).

**The self-reference effect.** A study by Rogers, Kuiper, and Kirker (1977) provided strong additional support for the levels-of-processing approach. Using a typical incidental learning paradigm, they asked subjects to make judgments about 40 adjectives in terms of their physical appearance, their acoustic features, or their meaning. However, there was an additional condition: the subjects were also required to decide how well some of the adjectives applied to themselves. When people were later given a surprise free recall test, the best recall by far (as shown in Figure 4.3) was for the words that had been judged for personal descriptiveness. This has been called the *self-reference effect*, and it has been replicated many times (e.g., Brown, Keenan, & Potts, 1986; D'Ydewalle, Delhaye, & Goessens, 1985; Halpin, Puff, Mason, & Marston, 1984; Kahan & Johnson, 1992; Katz, 1987; Klein & Kihlstrom, 1986; Klein, Loftus, & Burton, 1989).

Apparently, deciding how a word might apply to oneself results in a deep level of encoding. And as we know, the levels-of-processing approach would expect such words to be highly memorable. Klein and Kihlstrom (1986) also provided evidence that people tend to *organize* self-reference words together, thinking how the traits the words represent might be interrelated. Such a view is consistent with what you learned earlier in the chapter—organization is a powerful variable that enhances encoding.

FIGURE 4.3
Results of the Rogers et al. study showing that the best memory
by far was for the self-reference words.

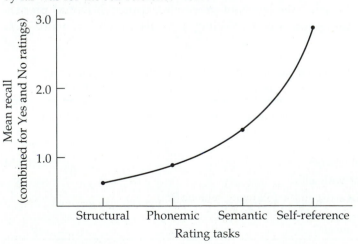

It turns out that the self-reference effect works just about as well if you make a judgment about someone other than yourself, as long as you know this person quite well (e.g., Bower & Gilligan, 1979). This indicates that there is nothing really unique about self-rating—a family member or close friend will suffice. Because of this, Matlin (1989) has humorously suggested that a more appropriate name for this phenomenon would be the "self-or-familiar-person-reference effect"! The important point to remember is that this research indicates that deep levels of encoding will occur only when the individual being considered is well known to you and that deeper levels of encoding increase the likelihood of remembering.

**More support: The generation effect.** Suppose that you are asked to generate a word that rhymes with each of the following words:

BANK—and your response is RANK
FLOWER—and your response is POWER
PICKET—and your response is TICKET
MOUSE—and your response is BLOUSE
COOK—and your response is ROOK
FLAKE—and your response is BAKE

Now another person is given the same list of six paired-associates to study. Notice that this other person just reads the list; he or she did not generate the second word of each pair. Later on, if you and this other person are each asked to recall or recognize the second word of each pair, you are very likely to do better. This superior memory for items that were self-generated has been dubbed the *generation effect* by Slamecka and Graf (1978), the researchers who first convincingly demonstrated the phenomenon.

Since their landmark study, an extensive amount of research has been devoted to this phenomenon (e.g., Donaldson & Bass, 1980; Gardiner, Gregg, & Hampton, 1988; Gardiner & Hampton, 1985; Graf, 1982; Hirshman & Bjork, 1988; Jacoby, 1978, 1983; Johnson, Raye, Foley, & Foley, 1981; McDaniel, Riegler, & Wadill, 1990; McDaniel, Wadill, & Einstein, 1988; McElroy & Slamecka, 1982; Naire & Widner, 1988; Slamecka & Fevreiski, 1983). The generation effect has been observed in tasks involving free recall, cued recall, and recognition, as well as in both intentional and incidental learning situations. In addition, a large variety of items (such as single words, word pairs, and sentences) and generation rules [e.g., rhyming, producing words in the same category (such as thinking up a word that is in the same category as the word *trout*), or producing either synonyms or antonyms] have all yielded generation effects.

Nevertheless, there have been some failures to find the effect (Donaldson & Bass, 1980; Graf, 1980; McElroy & Slamecka, 1982; Naire, Pusen, & Widner, 1985; Payne, Neely, & Burns, 1986). These null effects typically are found either when meaningless items (like nonwords) are used or if the subjects who did not generate the items are required to carefully consider the relationship between items or to think about the words they read.

How can we explain why the generation effect usually results in superior memory performance? And how do we account for the few failures to find it? Although this explanation is admittedly speculative, perhaps the generation effect is usually associated with better remembering because people pay more attention to items that they generate themselves than to items that are merely presented to them. If this is true, then the self-generated items are subjected to a deeper level of processing, and in keeping with the levels-of-processing approach, this deeper level of processing is the reason why they are remembered better. Supporting this hypothesis, when failures to observe the generation effect are noted, they occur either in situations in which the items to be remembered are meaningless (and hence hard to process deeply) or in situations in which the nongenerated items undergo considerable processing (Hunt, 1985).

The generation effect can be put to practical use during studying. As you probably have heard ad nauseam throughout your school years, teachers often implore their students to put what they read into their own words. Doing so *really* does help you to remember the material, because by using your own paraphrasing, you are, in essence, benefiting from the deeper processing that occurs when material to be learned is self-generated.

FIGURE 4.4
Attentiveness (or lack thereof) can have a major influence on the encoding process.
*Elizabeth Crews/The Image Works.*

## Why Do Deep Levels of Processing Promote Retention?

Many psychologists believe that the answer to this question involves two factors: *elaboration* and/or *distinctiveness* (Anderson & Reder, 1979; Craik & Lockhart, 1986; Walker & Jones, 1983). The elaboration hypothesis maintains that deep processing leads to a rich, complex encoding (an example of which would be the associations made earlier with your friend's telephone number). And a richer encoding should lead to better retention than the skimpier encoding that occurs with more shallow processing.

The distinctiveness hypothesis proposes that a deeper level of processing makes the item more distinctive from other memory traces. If the item is more distinctive, it will stand out and be easier to separate from other items at the time of recall. For instance, examine the following list of items for 15 seconds, and then try to recall as many of the items as possible:

cake
door
book
ring
help
7072
belt
rock
tree
head

It is quite likely that 7072 will be one of the items you recall. Why? Because it is different from all the other items. You may even spend some time wondering why it is on the list at all. This means it will receive a deep level of processing (perhaps more processing than any of the other items), making it distinctive and easy to remember. This phenomenon is quite robust and is called the *Von Restorff Effect*, named after the person who explored it in some detail (Von Restorff, 1933). If, however, 7072 were embedded among nine other four-digit numbers, it would not be distinctive and would have a smaller probability of being recalled than when placed among the nine words. It is probable that both elaboration and distinctiveness help account for why deeper processing is correlated with better memory.

## Criticisms of the Levels-of-Processing Approach

When the levels-of-processing approach was first proposed in 1972, it quickly won many adherents. Many factors were working in its favor. First, many people had grown dissatisfied with the multiple-memory-system theories proposed a few years earlier (particularly the influential Atkinson-Shiffrin model). So memory researchers were looking for something new. Second, Craik and Lockhart (1972) reexamined many previous studies and found that their results were quite compatible with the predictions of their model (e.g., Bobrow & Bower, 1969; Hyde & Jenkins, 1969; Johnston & Jenkins, 1971; Neisser, 1964; Treisman, 1964; Tresselt & Mayzner, 1960). Third, the first wave of research generated to test the assumptions of the levels-of-processing approach was mostly supportive. Fourth, the model of memory developed by Craik and Lockhart used an information-processing framework, and it was very fashionable at that time for psychologists of all stripes to embrace such an approach. Finally, on the surface at least, a levels-of-processing approach seemed to make good sense to many people.

These reasons may explain why it took several years before any substantial criticism of the levels-of-processing approach appeared. But by the late 1970s, several researchers had begun to seriously question the model or started to find data that were inconsistent with the basic tenets of the approach (e.g., Baddeley, 1978; Eysenck, 1978; D. L. Nelson & McEvoy, 1979; D. L. Nelson, Walling, & McEvoy, 1979; T. O. Nelson, 1977).

**Measurement of depth.** One of the most serious criticisms is that no adequate way has been found to *independently* measure the depth of processing. Without being able to measure processing depth separately from the amount of retention, the whole concept becomes circular. For instance, according to the levels-of-processing approach, if some material is well remembered, then it must have been encoded, or processed, "deeply." But how do you know it was processed "deeply"? Answer—because it is well remembered. This circularity issue has loomed as a major problem.

**Maintenance rehearsal and long-term retention.** A cornerstone of the levels-of-processing approach has been the distinction between maintenance rehearsal and elaborative rehearsal. It is asserted that only elaborative rehearsal can result in the long-term retention of information. However, several studies have convincingly demonstrated that this is *not* true. Maintenance rehearsal can lead to enhanced retention (Glenberg & Adams, 1978; Glenberg, Smith, & Green, 1977; Mechanic, 1964; Naire, 1983; Nelson, 1977; Woodward, Bjork, & Jongeward, 1973). For example, in one study Naire (1983) gave subjects a list of digits to remember. He told the subjects that to prevent rehearsal of the digits, he wanted them to engage in a filler task (rehearsing paired-associates) that was unimportant. So the subjects performed just a rote rehearsal of the paired-associates, which means that only maintenance rehearsal was operating. However, when the subjects were given a surprise test of their recall for the paired-associates, the result—contrary to the belief that maintenance rehearsal will not lead to long-term retention—was that they did, in fact, remember some of the paired-associates.

In addition, while others have found that simple repetition of items may not lead to much improvement in the ability to recall the items (supporting the levels-of-processing view), this type of maintenance rehearsal *can* markedly improve the *recognition* of items (Glenberg et al., 1977; Woodward et al., 1973). This nicely illustrates the importance of the form or type of memory testing (such as recall versus recognition) in determining what a person has or has not committed to memory. The value of utilizing different ways to measure memory is one of the themes of Chapter 5.

**Transfer-appropriate processing.** Another major assumption of the levels-of-processing approach is that if information is encoded, or processed, in a shallow, superficial manner, it will not be remembered as well as if it had been more deeply processed. But research has shown that this assumption isn't always true. The manner in which memory is assessed again proves to be a vital factor.

Consider a study conducted by Morris, Bransford, & Franks (1977). An experimenter read aloud 32 sentences that each had one word (the target) missing. The word *blank* was substituted for the missing word. Some of the subjects were asked to decide whether or not the target word rhymed with another word, and the other subjects were asked to decide if the target word was appropriate to fill the blank space. Below are some examples used by Morris et al.:

| Rhyming Task | Target word | Answer |
|---|---|---|
| "_____ rhymes with legal." | "Eagle" | Yes |
| "_____ rhymes with legal." | "Peach" | No |

| Semantic Task | | |
|---|---|---|
| "The _____ had a silver engine." | "Eagle" | No |
| "The _____ had a silver engine." | "Train" | Yes |

It was presumed that the rhyming task would require only a shallow level of processing. In contrast, the semantic task of judging if the target word could fit the context of the sentence should necessitate a deeper level of encoding. After the first phase of the experiment was completed, half of the subjects were given a recognition test in which they had to pick out the target words from among a number of similar words (called distractors). The results indicated that subjects did significantly better at selecting the target words if they had been presented in the semantic task rather than in the rhyming task. So far, so good—deeper processing led to better retention.

However, the other half of the subjects received a rhyming recognition task. In this memory test the subjects had to pick out words that rhymed with the original target words. For example, if an original target word was *Eagle,* then on the rhyming recognition test the subject should select the word *Regal* (from among distractors). The findings from the rhyming recognition test showed that subjects were better able to pick out the rhymes with the original target words if the original target words had been presented in the rhyming task rather than in the semantic task. In other words, the results were the opposite of what was found with the word recognition test. Memory was better, not worse, for target words that presumably received shallower processing.

These results reveal that a shallower level of processing—rhyming—does not necessarily lead to inferior retention. The term *transfer-appropriate processing* has been used to describe the fact that the "best" type of encoding critically depends on the type of retrieval required. The encoding processes that are most effective in any given situation are those that best match the retrieval conditions.

## Evaluation of the Levels-of-Processing Approach

Because of the nature of some of these criticisms, enthusiasm for the levels-of-processing approach has cooled considerably in recent years. In defense of the approach, Craik (1990) argues that the circularity issue (i.e., not being able to measure depth of processing separately from amount retained) is not as severe a problem as some people think. For instance, he maintains that, in fact, there is excellent agreement among independent judges as to what types of processing are deeper than others. He also points out that in other areas of psychology, there are concepts (such as reinforcement) that have been widely accepted and valued, even though they can't be measured independently of their effects either.

Craik (1990) also doesn't think that the phenomenon of transfer-appropriate processing is damaging at all to the levels-of-processing approach. Both can coexist without negating each other. Transfer-appropriate processing simply emphasizes that encoding and retrieval processes are closely tied, a notion that parallels the tenets of the *encoding specificity principle*, which will be discussed in Chapter 5. In general, deeper encoding *does* provide for better retention, but this can be overridden if the nature of the retrieval task requires a shallower level of processing for optimal memory performance.

# SUMMARY

### I. The Registration Process
- The registration process (encoding) involves transforming information into a form that can be retained.
- When a person intentionally tries to encode information, this is called *explicit encoding*. Encoding information without conscious intent is known as *incidental learning*.

### II. The Flexibility of Encoding
- People are very flexible in terms of the effort and intentionality expended during the encoding process.

- Not all features of a stimulus are encoded, only those that are judged to be most important at the time.
- How information is encoded depends on how a person *expects* to need to use the information in the future.

## III. STM and LTM Encoding
- Although information is often encoded *verbatim* into STM, this is not typical of LTM encoding. In LTM, it is much more likely that just the *meaning* of the information will be encoded.
- Nevertheless, given the flexibility of the encoding process, it is certainly possible to encode surface characteristics into LTM if a person so desires.

## IV. Limitations of the Encoding Process
- There are several limitations of the encoding process, including *lack of attention, incomplete sensory processing,* and *personal motivation.*

## V. Ways to Enhance Encoding
- *Organizing* the material to be learned is an excellent way to enhance encoding effectiveness. People will spontaneously attempt to organize items on the basis of some common characteristic that has meaning to them.
- Encoding can be facilitated through *warm-up* procedures that allow the subject to become familiar with the type of material to be learned and the format of the testing process and that provide a context for learning.
- How study time or practice is distributed can have a major impact on how much is encoded or learned. It is generally more beneficial to spread practice over many short sessions than to mass the practice into one or two long sessions. This is called the *spacing effect.*
- *Overlearning* material improves encoding. It also increases the likelihood and speed of retrieval, as well as the confidence of the individual in retrieving the information, and it decreases the rate of forgetting.
- The greater the *knowledge base* a person has about a topic, the easier it is to encode new relevant information.

## VI. Levels-of-Processing Approach
- The *levels-of-processing* approach assumes that memory strength is a by-product of the depth of the encoding process. Deeper levels of processing supposedly lead to longer-lasting memory traces.
- According to this framework there are two types of rehearsal—*maintenance rehearsal* (which is very shallow and doesn't lead to improvements in long-term storage) and *elaborative rehearsal* (which involves deeper, more meaningful analysis that does lead to better long-term storage).

*Support for the Approach*
- Tests of the levels-of-processing approach are typically conducted using *incidental learning paradigms* (subjects do not know there will be a memory

test later). Considerable support for the levels-of-processing approach has been found using such paradigms.

- Support includes the *self-reference effect*. This refers to the finding that when people are asked to relate words to themselves (or others they know well), they tend to remember these words very well. Presumably this is owing to the deep levels of encoding the words underwent.
- The *generation effect* (that self-generated items are better remembered than other nongenerated items) can also be seen as being consistent with the levels-of-processing framework.

### Possible Reasons Why the Approach Works

- Two related hypotheses have been proposed to explain why deeper levels of processing usually lead to better retention. The *elaboration hypothesis* asserts that deeper processing leads to a richer encoding and that a richer encoding should promote retention better than a skimpier encoding.
- The second hypothesis is known as the *distinctiveness hypothesis* and claims that deeper processing causes items to be more distinctive in memory. This makes them stand out at the time of retrieval. The *Von Restorff Effect* is an example of the power of distinctiveness to influence encoding processes and subsequent retrieval.
- It is currently believed that both elaboration and distinctiveness probably play a part in accounting for the levels-of-processing effect.

### Criticisms of the Approach

- The initial warm reception that the levels-of-processing approach received has cooled. Many people have complained that there is no adequate way to measure the *depth of processing* independently from the amount remembered, and so the approach has a *circularity problem.*
- Another problem for the levels-of-processing model is that maintenance rehearsal can lead to improved long-term retention. According to the levels-of-processing approach, this should not happen.
- The *transfer-appropriate processing* literature has also been cited as being contrary to the predictions of the levels-of-processing approach. These studies reveal that shallower levels of encoding do not always lead to inferior retention.

### Evaluation of the Approach

- In defense of the levels-of-processing approach, it has been suggested that the circularity issue is not as important as some people claim and that the transfer-appropriate processing work doesn't really cause problems for the model.
- It does make sense that deeper levels of encoding should *generally* lead to better retention.

# 5

# *Retention and Remembering*

———— ❖ ————

*I*t has been said that *death* and *taxes* are the only things we can really count on in life. But there is a third certainty—the frustrating fact that everyone forgets things. As was discussed in the last chapter, what sometimes passes as forgetting is not really a genuine retention loss at all. For example, people often fail to recall the name of a person to whom they have recently been introduced. These individuals then claim to have a poor memory for names. Typically, the source of the problem is that they have never properly encoded the name in the first place. When encoding fails, there's nothing to remember. Such instances are not examples of real forgetting. This chapter focuses on the processes of retention and remembering. When forgetting occurs, it will be assumed that it is not because encoding processes were unsuccessful or insufficient.

## ON THE PERMANENCE OF MEMORY

Read the following two statements, and decide which one you agree with the most:

1. Everything we learn is permanently stored in the mind, although sometimes particular details are not accessible. With hypnosis, or other special techniques, these inaccessible details could eventually be recovered.

2. Some details that we learn may be permanently lost from memory. Such details would never be able to be recovered by hypnosis, or any other special technique, because these details are simply no longer there.

Did you select number 1? If you did, then you have plenty of company. Loftus and Loftus (1980) conducted a survey in which they gave these same two choices to 75 people who had formal graduate school training in psychology and to 94 people who did not. They found that 84 percent of those with a psychology background and 69 percent of those without one agreed with statement 1. From these results, it appears that both people without a psychology background and those with specialized training in psychology generally believe that information stored in LTM exists permanently, even though this information may often be difficult to retrieve.

In their article, Loftus and Loftus went on to argue that this widespread belief in the permanence of memory may not be warranted. For instance, they reevaluated the fascinating work of Wilder Penfield and his colleagues that seemed to provide impressive evidence that brain stimulation could revive long-buried memories (Penfield & Perot, 1963; Penfield & Roberts, 1959). Penfield performed many operations in which he removed damaged areas of the brain in people who had severe forms of epilepsy. While doing these operations, he found that his patients often reported that vivid memories would spontaneously and involuntarily flash back to them when their brains were stimulated by electrodes in certain areas. This was interpreted as being very strong evidence that memory was permanently embedded in the brain. And, in fact, people with training in psychology who took part in the survey mentioned above often cited Penfield's work as one of the reasons why they believed that memory was permanently stored.

However, after Penfield's data were more carefully examined, psychologists started to question whether the brain stimulation work actually revealed anything important about the performance of memory (Loftus & Loftus, 1980; Neisser, 1967). For instance, only 40 cases out of 1132 provided any evidence that memory flashbacks may have occurred during brain stimulation. In addition, in those 40 cases, most of the patients' responses were vague, such as hearing some voice or singing, and were thus hard to classify as being related to a past memory. A detailed examination of these responses has led to the conclusion that most of them (if not all) were simply reconstructions or inferences and not the revival of real memories at all. On the basis of this reanalysis, it is now believed that Penfield's well-known findings should *not* be taken as good evidence that memory is permanently stored.

The *apparently* successful use of hypnosis to bring back long dormant memories has also been cited by many as a reason for their belief that memory is permanent. However, Loftus and Loftus (1980), along with many others, take exception to this notion. In contrast to what the average person typically believes about the power of hypnosis to uncover hidden memories, considerable research has convincingly demonstrated that using hypnosis as an enhancer of memory is fraught with difficulties (for an excellent review of this literature, we recommend the book *Hypnosis and Memory*, edited by Pettinati, 1988). For instance, while hypnotized, people are much more likely to succumb to suggestion and "leading" questions. This leads to an increased willingness to fabricate or construct new "memories" that can be shown to have never actually occurred. To make matters worse, these individuals usually have a great deal of confidence in these confabulations. Since hypnotized people have such a strong tendency to make up stories and memories, and then to experience a misplaced sense of confidence about them, many legal experts have vigorously opposed the use of hypnotically refreshed memory in court cases.

In trying to cast further doubt on the belief that memory is permanently stored, Loftus and Loftus (1980) also cited the research on eyewitness memory. They believe the research shows that eyewitness memory can be easily manipulated or distorted by supplying additional misleading information. Loftus and Loftus interpret such findings as indicating that original memories can be irrevocably lost from memory (but see Chapter 11 for other interpretations).

# EBBINGHAUS'S FAMOUS FORGETTING CURVE

Hermann Ebbinghaus was the first person to scientifically study remembering and its flip side, forgetting. As mentioned in Chapter 1, Ebbinghaus rightfully deserves credit for generating enormous interest in the *experimental approach* to studying memory. Using himself as his only subject, he painstakingly memorized list after list of nonsense syllables under very rigidly controlled testing situations. To provide the necessary data for his classic forgetting curve, Ebbinghaus undertook the Herculean task of first learning, and then relearning, over 1200 lists of nonsense syllables (13 syllables per list) to a criterion of two errorless recitations! He did this on 163 separate occasions between 1879 and 1880 (Zechmeister & Nyberg, 1982). Ebbinghaus used the method of *serial learning*, which means that he had to learn the nonsense syllables in each list in their correct order.

In order to measure the rate of forgetting (or, conversely, how much he had retained), Ebbinghaus varied the time interval between initial learning and his attempt to relearn the list. If the recall of a list was not perfect (and it rarely was, especially at the longer retention intervals), Ebbinghaus would restudy the list of syllables until he could again recite it without errors twice in a row. As shown in Figure 5.1, he relearned the lists using one of seven different intervals—20 minutes, 1 hour, 9 hours, 24 hours (1 day), 2 days, 6 days, and 31 days. To measure the amount of forgetting that had occurred since the initial learning phase, he calculated a *savings score*. This involved determining either how much *time* was saved in relearning the list or how many fewer *trials* were needed to regain mastery. For example, if after 2 days, it took 700 seconds to relearn a list that initially took 1400 seconds to learn, the savings score would be 50 percent. Or if after 31 days it took 24 trials to relearn a list that originally was learned in 30 trials, the savings score would be 20 percent. Whether time or trials is the dependent variable, the *higher* the savings score, the *greater* the amount of retention.

As revealed in Figure 5.1, the most rapid forgetting occurred soon after

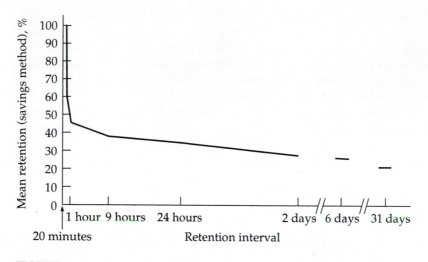

FIGURE 5.1
Ebbinghaus's forgetting curve.

learning. After just 20 minutes, there was a precipitous drop in retention—more than 40 percent of the material was forgotten. By 9 hours after learning, more than 60 percent was lost. The rate of forgetting slowed considerably as the retention interval increased. For instance, the drop in the savings score between 1 and 31 days was only about 12 percent. Ebbinghaus interpreted these data as indicating that forgetting appeared to be *logarithmic* in form. However, a recent reanalysis of Ebbinghaus's data suggests that a different mathematical function, a *power function*, may be a better description of the rate of forgetting (Wixted & Ebbesen, 1991). Regardless of what mathematical function may best fit the data, Ebbinghaus's findings suggest that the greatest amount of forgetting occurs in the first few hours after learning, with progressively less and less of a loss as time marches on.

## *H*OW REPRESENTATIVE IS EBBINGHAUS'S FORGETTING CURVE?

Today it is generally recognized that the rate of decay evident in Ebbinghaus's forgetting curve was atypically rapid. Even when nonsense syllables are employed, others have not found as steep a function of forgetting as Ebbinghaus (e.g., Luh, 1922). It is now believed that Ebbinghaus forgot at a more rapid rate because he used only one subject—himself. After all, to collect enough data to plot his forgetting curve, Ebbinghaus had to learn (and relearn) literally thousands of nonsense syllables. This would make it easy to become confused about which syllables were on any particular list. (The confusion would be due to massive amounts of proactive and retroactive interference; see Chapter 3 and a later section in this chapter.)

Obviously, people can remember meaningful material better than they can nonsense syllables. Ebbinghaus was aware of this too. He found that he could memorize and relearn poetry (Byron's *Don Juan*) much faster than he could a comparable amount of nonsense syllables. Nevertheless, except for being less steep, the general *shape* of forgetting curves in studies using words or sentences as stimuli is quite similar to that of Ebbinghaus's original function (for a review, see Slamecka & McElree, 1983). Typically, there is a large drop in memory shortly after learning, followed by a more moderate decline.

However, Ebbinghaus's forgetting curve does *not* describe how people forget in all circumstances. As you will learn in the next few sections, there are wide variations in the amount and form of forgetting. Much depends on the particular type of information to be retained, how long it took to acquire the information, and its personal significance.

## Do We Have a Permastore?

Have you ever wondered how long you will remember the foreign language you took in school? Harry Bahrick (1984) wondered and decided to find out. He discovered that the forgetting curve for knowledge of a foreign language is markedly different from Ebbinghaus's forgetting function. He tested 773 people who either had already finished studying Spanish in high school or college or were currently taking Spanish courses. All the subjects were given a battery of tests to determine their current knowledge of Spanish. Information was also obtained concerning how many years of formal training each person had received, what the individuals' grades were in their courses, and how much they practiced or used their Spanish during retention intervals that ranged over a 50-year period for some individuals.

Fortunately, from a memory researcher's standpoint but probably not from a Spanish teacher's, the vast majority of subjects used their Spanish very little (if at all) after completing their courses. This means that Bahrick's findings should be a relatively pure measure of what people can remember from such courses, without having to take into consideration the confounding (and difficult to weigh) factor of additional practice.

As expected, Bahrick found that the better Spanish was learned originally, the better retained it was. As seen in Figure 5.2, the greatest drop in retention occurred during the first 3 years after formal training had ceased. But then the retention of Spanish essentially ceased to decline during the next 25 to 30 years, after which there was evidence of some further decline in memory. It is gratifying to note that even after almost 50 years had elapsed, without any additional practice, some people still retained a large amount of knowledge about Spanish. Bahrick concluded that some knowledge of Spanish was held permanently in a memory storage system that he called a *permastore*. He likened

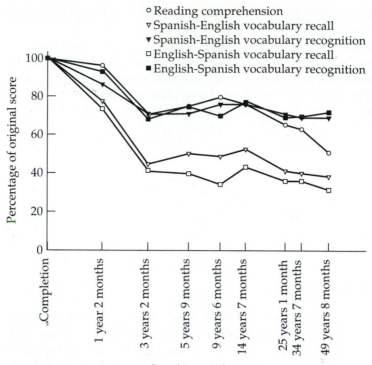

FIGURE 5.2

Retention curves for remembering Spanish with evidence suggesting
the existence of a permastore.

*From H. P. Bahrick, "Semantic memory content in permastore: Fifty years of mem-
ory for Spanish learned in school." Journal of Experimental Psychology: General, Vol. 113 (1984), pp. 1–29. Copyright 1984 by the American Psychological
Association. Reprinted by permission.*

this stable retention system to the *permafrost* of arctic regions, a layer that is
permanently frozen a few feet below the topsoil.

Bahrick, Bahrick, and Wittlinger (1975) investigated how well people can
remember old classmates. They tested the memory of 392 high school graduates
for their ability to remember the names and faces of classmates taken from old
class yearbooks. Even after decades had passed, subjects had a remarkable
ability to remember their old classmates. For instance, people who were tested
25 years after graduation could recognize the faces of past classmates or could
match their names with their faces at approximately the same very high level
of accuracy (about 90 percent) that other people obtained only 3 months after
graduating. Only at very long retention intervals (such as almost 48 years after
graduation) was there a noticeable drop-off in memory. But even at this very
long retention interval, memory was still quite good (75 to 80 percent accuracy).

More recently, Bahrick and Hall (1991) demonstrated that under certain conditions, many people can remember substantial amounts of high school algebra despite the passage of half a century in which they did not use any algebra. The critical factor was whether or not the person took additional math courses in college. If people did, then their retention levels were very high. However, for people who performed equally well in their high school algebra course but did not elect to take further math courses in college, retention of high school algebra was at near-chance levels. Bahrick and Hall (1991) attribute the superior memory performance of those who took additional math courses to the fact that they had the opportunity to relearn and use their knowledge of algebra over an extended period of years.

On the basis of the findings of such studies, Bahrick thinks that although some long-term information remains in memory only if occasionally rehearsed or used, there is also a large amount of information that achieves permastore status. This information, which is typically overlearned and acquired over considerable time periods through distributed practice, can remain in memory for decades.

## Autobiographical Events

In 1975, Linton reported the results of a study in which she recorded events each day from her personal life for six years. Each month she randomly selected events and then tried to remember specific details about them. How did her forgetting curve compare with Ebbinghaus's? Not well (see Figure 5.3). First of all, she had almost perfect retention for events that were tested within 1 year of their occurrence. This contrasts with Ebbinghaus's forgetting curve, which indicates a steep decline in memory shortly after learning. In addition, after the first year, events were forgotten at approximately a *linear* rate (resembling a straight line) of 5 to 6 percent each year. More of what we know about the fascinating area of autobiographical memory is described in Chapter 11. Further evidence will be presented to show that memory for personal events from one's life often does not resemble Ebbinghaus's forgetting curve.

## Nondeclarative Memories

In Chapter 3, we indicated that it was important to distinguish between *declarative* knowledge (facts that can sometimes be learned in a single trial and that are directly accessible to conscious awareness) and *nondeclarative* knowledge (learning that is obtained incrementally and that is not accessible to conscious recollection). Up until this point, we have only considered how declarative knowledge declines over time. What does the forgetting function look like for nondeclarative knowledge and skills?

You probably already know the answer on the basis of personal experience

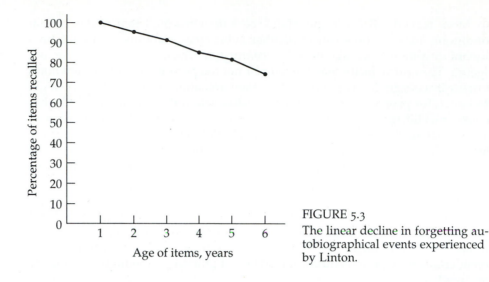

FIGURE 5.3
The linear decline in forgetting autobiographical events experienced by Linton.

(and, it is hoped, from your knowledge about the permastore). You will recall that the information most likely to enter the permastore is information that is both overlearned and acquired incrementally over long time periods. On a moment's reflection, you will see that this is also a very good description of how much of our nondeclarative knowledge is usually obtained. After all, people do not learn to ride a bicycle, swing a bat, swim, or play a musical instrument with any kind of reasonable ability in just one session. Instead, these skills and procedures are mastered by being overlearned and acquired through distributed practice over a time period often spanning weeks, months, or even years (remember all those piano lessons!).

The experimental evidence supports the idea that, in general, nondeclarative information is not forgotten like Ebbinghaus's forgetting curve would suggest. Even over long retention intervals, little forgetting of these types of skills occurs (Fleishman & Parker, 1962; Healy, Fendrich, Crutcher, Wittman, Gesi, Ericsson, & Bourne, 1992; Healy, Fendrich, & Proctor, 1990). This is especially true if a warm-up trial is given (Hammerton, 1963). For example, it is commonly believed that you never really forget how to ride a bicycle. In actuality, people do get rusty if they haven't gone riding for a while. But with very little effort, most people can easily regain their riding ability, often in a matter of minutes (even if it has been several years since their last ride).

There are important practical implications of this area of research. For instance, some types of nondeclarative knowledge are not overlearned, nor are they obtained through repeated practice over long time periods. Because of this, we should not expect this type of information to make it to the permastore. And there is evidence that it does not. In a study by McKenna and Glendon (1985), it was found that remembering how to correctly perform cardiopulmonary resuscitation (CPR) quickly fades if there is no practice of the procedures. CPR is a popular technique used especially to help heart attack and drowning victims, and it can greatly improve a person's chances of survival if it is performed quickly and correctly.

One of your authors took a CPR course some years ago and easily passed the written test and the performance tests (which involve showing the instructor how you would attempt to resuscitate various types of victims). However, because the training involved essentially massed practice over just two days, and the procedures were definitely not overlearned, the information faded amazingly (and embarrassingly) quickly. The moral is clear: People who want to retain their CPR skills (or almost any other physical or motor skills) should practice often and/or take refresher courses.

# REASONS WHY WE MAY FORGET

## Organic Disorders

Perhaps the strongest (and least controversial) evidence that memories are not always permanently stored comes from the clinic. It is now well accepted that certain diseases, types of head injuries, and toxic agents (such as alcohol) can lead to the destruction of nerve cells or change the balance of neurotransmitters in the brain (see Chapters 7 and 14). These factors can definitely result in the loss of specific memories.

## The Law of Disuse (Decay Theory)

For many years following Ebbinghaus's seminal work, it was widely thought that the simple passage of time caused memories and habits to fade and eventually decay away. Unless the information stored in memory was periodically

FIGURE 5.4

Cartoon showing the effects of alcohol on memory.

© *1989 King Features Syndicate, Inc. World rights reserved. Reprinted with special permission of King Features Syndicate.*

attended to or used in some fashion, it was asserted that our memories would become weaker and weaker as time went on. At some point, a memory would become so faded that it would cease to exist for all practical purposes. This theory was referred to as the *Law of Disuse* (Thorndike, 1914) or, more generally, *decay theory*. In Chapter 3 you learned that decay is still thought to be the principal mechanism for forgetting from sensory memory and probably is a contributing factor with regard to forgetting information from STM as well.

Although decay theory originally was intended to account for forgetting from LTM too, many current memory researchers reject the idea that time *per se* has much to do with forgetting of long-term memories. This change in opinion came about with the blistering attack on decay theory launched by McGeoch in 1932 (see the section on interference theory later in this chapter). From that time forward, it has generally been conceded that a much more compelling case can be made that forgetting from LTM depends not on how much time has passed since learning but rather on what occurs during the intervening time.

**A new theory of disuse.** In recent years an ambitious attempt has been made to recast decay theory, or the Law of Disuse, into a new *Theory of Disuse* (Bjork & Bjork, 1992). There are several key assumptions and implications of this new theory, and we will discuss a few of them here. One important assumption is that while there is no practical limit to how much information can be stored, there is a limit in our ability to retrieve information. A second assumption is that regardless of how well learned something is, the information will become increasingly inaccessible unless it is periodically retrieved. A good example of this is when we try to remember the combination of a lock that we have used dozens of times in the past but that we have not used recently. In such situations (particularly if we try to open the lock in a physical environment that is different from the typical one in which the lock has been used; see Chapter 9), people often become very frustrated over their inability to successfully access the right numbers from LTM.

In contrast to the original Law of Disuse, Bjork and Bjork would argue that the loss of retrieval access to the correct numbers is *not* due to the mere passage of time. Instead, it is a consequence of learning and/or retrieving other information that is similar (perhaps, in this case, the combinations of other locks). In other words, Bjork and Bjork propose that there is a competition for retrieval among items stored in LTM. Newly learned or recently retrieved items have an advantage over other items that are similar in some fashion but that have not been recently learned or retrieved. Compared with the former items, these latter items will become less accessible to retrieval.

According to Bjork and Bjork, their new Theory of Disuse has considerable practical adaptive value. For instance, one implication of the theory is that the information that has most recently been learned or retrieved will be the information most readily accessible. This has obvious adaptive consequences, since our current situation (where we are, whom we are with, what we are doing, etc.) is more likely to be related to our recent past situation than it is to more distant experiences. Another adaptive feature of the theory: older information that is no longer easily retrieved will not interfere with newer, but related, information. Bjork and Bjork use the example of a graduate student who moves from his or her undergraduate college to another school in a different part of the country. This person has to learn and remember lots of new information (telephone numbers, addresses, weather patterns, people's names, streets, restaurants, buildings, directions, and so forth). It would certainly be adaptive for this individual if all the similar corresponding information from undergraduate days (i.e., old telephone numbers, addresses, . . .) would lose retrieval strength and not interfere with the recall of the new information the person has to learn.

One final point. Because our capacity to store information is virtually unlimited, it makes sense that we would need a mechanism that helps us gain access quickly to the most relevant information stored in LTM. According to the Theory of Disuse developed by Bjork and Bjork, decreases in retrieval strength for information not recently retrieved can serve this very purpose.

## Interference Theory

In 1932, McGeoch published a very influential article that persuasively argued that the decay theory of forgetting, as envisioned by Thorndike (1914) and his followers, was wrong. McGeoch pointed out that except in cases when there is an immediate test of memory, there are always activities or events that occur between learning and retrieval. He maintained that these intervening events cause *interference* that disrupts our memories. In other words, it is not the mere passage of time that causes forgetting (as proposed by decay theory). Instead, forgetting occurs because of what happens during the time between learning and retrieval.

One of the earliest experiments that supported the interference theory of forgetting and that helped to discredit decay theory was performed by Jenkins and Dallenbach (1924). They arranged to have two college students from Cornell University learn lists of 10 nonsense syllables either early in the morning or just before bedtime at night. The students were then tested for their recall of the nonsense syllables at varying retention intervals. As shown in Figure 5.5, they were tested after either 1, 2, 4, or 8 hours. When the lists were learned in the morning, the subjects were simply instructed to come back to the laboratory at the specified time for testing. If they learned the lists just before bedtime, they were awakened during their sleeping period at the proper time.

As you can see, much more forgetting occurred when the subjects had been awake during the retention interval and engaged in daily activities than when they had been sleeping. This pattern of results is easy to explain for an interference theory of forgetting. After all, there are many intervening activities during the day that could disrupt or interfere with retrieval but many fewer that could potentially interfere while a person is sleeping (perhaps a little from

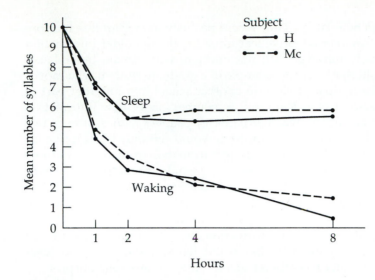

FIGURE 5.5
The mean number of nonsense syllables recalled by two sub-
jects after varying retention intervals of waking or sleep.
*From J. G. Jenkins and K. M. Dallenbach, "Obliviscence during sleep and*
*waking,"* American Journal of Psychology, *Vol. 35 (1924), pp. 605–612.*
*Reprinted by permission of the University of Illinois Press.*

dreaming?). The results, however, cannot be easily handled by decay theory.
Decay theory stipulates that the amount of forgetting is only a function of how
much time has transpired since the original learning. If the subjects were not
rehearsing the nonsense syllables during the retention interval (and they were
given strict instructions not to), then decay theory would have to predict an
equal amount of forgetting between daytime and nighttime learning. Clearly
this didn't happen. It should be noted, however, that there is evidence (see
Chapter 7) that during *rapid eye movement* (REM) sleep, memory consolidation
is strengthened. (Memory consolidation refers to the idea that memory traces
become more and more "fixed" in LTM as time goes on.) This could have also
helped account for the difference in recall between the sleepers and the non-
sleepers.

   In Chapter 3 we learned that the type of interference that McGeoch was
describing, and that presumably occurred in the Jenkins and Dallenbach (1924)
study, is known as *retroactive interference* (RI). You'll recall that this type of
interference occurs when newer information acts backward in time to inhibit
recall of older information. The other major type of interference is *proactive
interference* (PI), which occurs when previously learned information acts forward in time to inhibit recall of more recently learned material. In the laboratory, testing for the effects of PI and RI is usually done by having subjects learn
lists of words or paired associates. Table 5.1 shows the typical procedures for

**TABLE 5.1** PROCEDURES FOR TESTING RETROACTIVE AND PROACTIVE INTERFERENCE

|  | Step 1 | Step 2 | Step 3 |
|---|---|---|---|
| *Retroactive interference* | | | |
| Control group | Learn List A. | Do nothing. | Recall List A. |
| Experimental group | Learn List A. | Learn List B. | Recall List A. |
| *Proactive interference* | | | |
| Control group | Do nothing. | Learn List B. | Recall List B. |
| Experimental group | Learn List A. | Learn List B. | Recall List B. |

experimental and control groups used in these tests. If the experimental group's recall is inferior to the control group's, then interference has occurred.

It has been repeatedly demonstrated that PI and RI can have powerful effects on retrieval. One key factor in determining how much interference will occur is the amount of *similarity* between the tasks to be done or the information to be remembered. As you might imagine, the greater the similarity between two situations, the greater the likelihood of confusing the two. For example, if a new bank opens up and its telephone number is very similar to your old bank's phone number, you may well experience RI when you want to call the old bank and PI when you want to call the new one.

## Availability versus Accessibility

While being fully aware of the issues raised by Loftus and Loftus (1980) and others, many current memory researchers still think that there is little or no evidence that genuine *forgetting* (in the sense that there is an actual loss of information) occurs from LTM in healthy people (Ashcraft, 1989). This view of forgetting markedly differs from the view taken by those who favor the traditional *decay* and *interference* theories. These older theories maintain that forgetting of long-term memories can be due to a real loss from memory. However, while certainly not disproven, these theories have generally fallen out of current favor. They have been supplanted by the notion that (barring organic damage) all of our memories remain in LTM and that when forgetting occurs, it is really just a retrieval failure.

A distinction is usually made between the *availability* of a particular memory and its *accessibility*. It is widely believed that long-term memories are always available in healthy people (i.e., stored somewhere in memory) but that they may be inaccessible (unable to be retrieved, either temporarily or permanently). Some of the evidence that supports the distinction between availability and accessibility comes from work on *motivated forgetting, cue-dependent forgetting,* the *tip-of-the-tongue phenomenon,* and *context-dependent memory.*

FIGURE 5.6
Cartoon demonstrating motivated forgetting.
© *1989 MGN. Reprinted with special permission of North American Syndicate.*

**Motivated forgetting.** As poor Andy Capp discovers, people sometimes forget things because they *want* to forget them. This is called *motivated forgetting,* and it occurs whenever a memory that is available to the individual is made less accessible. There are two types of motivated forgetting—*suppression* and *repression.* If the person *consciously* tries to forget the memory (as the woman in the cartoon tried), then he or she is using suppression. Here is another example of suppression: As a star figure skater begins her routine at the Olympics, she deliberately tries to put out of her mind (suppress) the memory that she fell during her last performance. It has also been demonstrated in laboratory experiments that when subjects are instructed to forget information that has already been presented, they can do so (Bjork, LaBerge, & Legrand, 1968; Elmes, 1969; Weiner, 1968; Weiner & Reed, 1969). This is sometimes referred to as *directed forgetting.*

Repression is said to occur when a person *unconsciously* lessens (or sometimes eliminates) the accessibility to very unpleasant memories that are emotionally threatening. A person who is savagely beaten during a robbery may subsequently repress the whole disturbing event. The existence of repression is the very cornerstone of Sigmund Freud's psychoanalytic theory. Freud thought that the effects of repressing extremely intense memories could sometimes even lead to a loss of personal identity, called a *dissociative disorder* (see Chapter 14). The possible effects that repression has on memory for everyday events are discussed in more detail in Chapter 8.

**Cue-dependent forgetting.** Largely because of the research conducted by Endel Tulving and his colleagues, many memory researchers now believe that most memory failures are due to *cue-dependent forgetting* (Tulving, 1974; Tulving & Pearlstone, 1966; Tulving & Psotka, 1971; Tulving & Thomson, 1973). Cue-dependent forgetting is said to occur whenever retrieval cues are insufficient to rekindle previously encoded information.

In one of the earliest demonstrations of the powerful effects of retrieval cues, Tulving and Pearlstone (1966) had two groups of subjects learn lists of words from different categories. The category names (such as *sports* or *fruits*) preceded the items, although the subjects were told they did not have to remember them. At the time of testing, both groups of subjects were asked to recall the items, but one group was also supplied with the category names. The results were clear and important—the cued-recall group (those given the category names) far outperformed the free recall group. Since both groups were treated exactly the same, except that the cued-recall group was given good retrieval cues, the results strongly suggest that the subjects in the free recall group did not remember as many items as they had actually learned because they lacked sufficient retrieval cues. Tulving and Pearlstone interpreted these results as indicating that many additional items were probably *available* to subjects in the free recall group but that these items were not currently *accessible* and so failed to be recalled.

On a practical note, witnesses in court trials are often asked to remember things that have become inaccessible. When this happens, one effective way to help revive a memory is to use a procedure called *refreshing*. This involves presenting the witness with some or all of the information to be recalled. For example, if the person has difficulty remembering the details of a contract he or she signed, part of the contract may be presented to the person to prod the individual's memory. Refreshing works by helping the witness gain access to memories that are available but that may need some potent retrieval cue to be fully remembered.

**The tip-of-the-tongue phenomenon.** Take a minute and try to name all the dwarfs from the movie *Snow White and the Seven Dwarfs*. Did you have trouble recalling some of the names? If so, don't feel bad—most people can't recall all seven names without assistance (Meyer & Hilterbrand, 1984; Miserandino, 1991).

When attempting this task, you may have experienced the maddening *tip-of-the-tongue phenomenon*. This occurs whenever a person cannot immediately recall a word or name that the person is absolutely sure he or she knows. Subjectively, the correct answer seems to just about reach your conscious state, but it doesn't quite make it. Instead, recall is blocked, and so the response is aptly said to, figuratively, "be on the tip of your tongue." Although partial information about the blocked word or name is often known, the information is not enough to fully dredge it out of memory.

The tip-of-the-tongue phenomenon is another very good example of the need to distinguish between the availability and the accessibility of a memory. Most of these frustrating episodes are eventually successfully resolved (people usually *do* finally recall the correct word or name), particularly if enough good retrieval cues are supplied. For example, if someone mentions the correct response (obviously, a great retrieval cue), the tip-of-the-tongue phenomenon almost always ends quickly because the person can *recognize* the correct answer when it is given. This demonstrates that the information was clearly available and just needed the right cue to become accessible.

The tip-of-the-tongue phenomenon has been extensively studied (A. Brown, 1991; R. Brown & McNeill, 1966; Burke, MacKay, Worthley, & Wade, 1991; Read & Bruce, 1982; Reason, 1984b; Reason & Lucas, 1984). Table 5.2 presents a summary of some of the most consistent findings and conclusions. By the way, in case you are still wondering, the names of the seven dwarfs are *Sleepy, Grumpy, Dopey, Sneezy, Happy, Bashful,* and *Doc!*

**Context-dependent memory.** The amount and quality of information that a person later remembers greatly depend on two interrelated factors—how the information was encoded and the type of cues present at retrieval (Barclay, Bransford, Franks, McCarrell, & Nitsch, 1974; Morris, Bransford, & Franks, 1977). In Chapter 4, we introduced the term *transfer-appropriate processing* to refer to the fact that the "best" type of encoding depends on the type of retrieval required. For instance, if a word is encoded by considering how it sounds (e.g.,

**TABLE 5.2** SOME CONSISTENT FINDINGS ABOUT THE TIP-OF-THE-TONGUE PHENOMENON

- The phenomenon appears to be universal, spanning all ages.
- The tip-of-the-tongue state can be induced in many ways, such as by giving definitions and seeking the proper words, showing faces and seeking names, or asking people to identify odors.
- From diary studies it has been estimated that the experience occurs about once a week in daily life and that it increases with age.
- Naturally occurring tip-of-the-tongue states are most often triggered by names of personal acquaintances.
- Words that are related to the sought-after word often "come to mind." These words are usually either similar in meaning or, especially, similar in sound to the target word.
- During a tip-of-the-tongue experience, people can guess the first letter of the sought-after word about 50% of the time and also are accurate in guessing the number of syllables 50 to 80% of the time.
- About 50% of all tip-of-the-tongue instances are successfully resolved within about a minute from their start.

SOURCE: Taken from A. Brown, 1991.

does *car* rhyme with *jar*?), then it will be remembered best if the retrieval task requires the person to make a rhyming judgment.

The likelihood of retrieving information from LTM will be maximized if the conditions at retrieval match as closely as possible the conditions present during the original learning. This has become known as the *encoding specificity principle* (Tulving & Thomson, 1973; Tulving, 1983). Both transfer-appropriate processing and the encoding specificity principle emphasize that encoding and retrieval are closely intertwined.

A large amount of evidence supports the encoding specificity principle. For instance, in a well-known study by Light and Carter-Sobell (1970), each subject was shown 67 sentences at the rate of one sentence every 4 seconds. The task was to read each sentence aloud and to pay particular attention to an adjective-noun phrase that would be capitalized and underlined. A typical sentence might be the following: The <u>STRAWBERRY JAM</u> tasted great. The subjects were told to expect a memory test for the adjective-noun phrases after all the sentences had been presented.

Immediately following the last sentence, a recognition test was given in which 134 adjective-noun phrases were presented. Half of the nouns in these phrases were "old" ones (i.e., they had appeared in the original sentences), and half were "new" (acting as distractors). Now here's the really interesting part— some of the old nouns were presented with the original adjective (STRAW-BERRY JAM), and some were presented with a different adjective (e.g., TRAFFIC JAM). The subjects had to decide if just the *noun* part of the adjective-noun phrase was old or new. They did this by saying either "yes" or "no," respectively. In our specific example, the subjects should say "yes" to both STRAWBERRY JAM and TRAFFIC JAM, since JAM is a noun from one of the adjective-noun phrases in the original 67 sentences.

According to the encoding specificity principle, the closer the match between the conditions at encoding and those at retrieval, the better the memory performance. Therefore, on the basis of encoding specificity, one would predict that recognition would be superior for the nouns presented in the same context that occurred during encoding (STRAWBERRY JAM) than for the nouns that appeared in a different context (TRAFFIC JAM). And this is exactly what Light and Carter-Sobell observed. When the nouns were presented in their original context, subjects recognized the old nouns 65 percent of the time, but only 27 percent of the time when the nouns appeared in a different context.

The physical environment has also been shown to affect memory performance, as would be predicted by the encoding specificity principle. Researchers have demonstrated, for example, that ambient odors can serve as effective retrieval cues (Cann & Ross, 1989; Schab, 1990). In the study by Cann and Ross, some subjects were asked to recognize previously seen photographs while in the presence of an odor that was present during the original viewing of the pictures. Other subjects had to recognize the pictures while in the presence of an odor that was different from the original. The results indicated that signif-

FIGURE 5.7
Will she or won't she remember in time?
*Robert Houser/Comstock.*

icantly fewer errors were made when the odors matched during encoding and
retrieval.

In a very inventive study that showed the powerful effects of the context
on memory, Godden and Baddeley (1975) used deep-sea divers as their subjects.
Some of the divers studied a list of unrelated words while on a beach, while
others studied the same list while submerged 15 feet below the surface of the
water. The results clearly supported the encoding specificity principle: Significantly more words were remembered when the recall environment matched
the learning environment (e.g., being under water in both situations) than when
the two contexts were different (e.g., studying the list while under water and
trying to recall the words later while on the beach).

We know what you are probably thinking. If reinstating the context can
improve retrieval (presumably by making memories that are available become
more accessible), then maybe it would pay to study for your exams in the same
room in which the exams will be given. That's good thinking, and one study
did find evidence that college students recall more information if they are tested
in the same classroom in which they learned the material than if tested in a

different classroom (Smith, Glenberg, & Bjork, 1978). Unfortunately, this context-dependent effect has not always been found (Saufley, Otaka, & Bavaresco, 1985; Smith, Vela, & Williamson, 1988).

However, it is well established that the greater the differences in environmental context between learning and retrieval, the greater the chances are that memory will be hindered. Therefore, since there are no radios, stereos, or televisions playing during exams, and since you usually are not munching pizza or conversing with friends either, it might also be advantageous not to do these things while studying for exams. In this way you can keep the learning environment more similar to the environment in which you will be tested. This might be especially useful for exams that are highly dependent on having a good memory, such as tests of foreign language vocabulary or of art history.

Entire books (such as *Memory in Context: Context in Memory,* edited by Davies & Thomson, 1988) have been devoted to examining the close relationship between context and memory. In Chapter 8 we will examine the evidence for *state-dependent memory* (the idea that retrieval is best when the "state" of the person, such as being drunk, is the same at encoding and retrieval) and *mood-dependent memory* (i.e., the hypothesis that retrieval is most effective if the mood of the person at the time of encoding matches the mood at retrieval).

# *R*ETROSPECTIVE AND PROSPECTIVE MEMORY

Until now, when we have discussed the topic of forgetting, we have almost exclusively focused our attention on what is called *retrospective memory.* This is the ability to remember past events or information. Remembering what you ate for breakfast, the lyrics of a favorite song, which team won the World Series in 1992, the date you were born, that Napoleon was defeated at Waterloo, and that you lent your roommate $10 last week and she still hasn't repaid you are all examples of retrospective memory.

While no one will deny that retrospective memory is obviously of great importance to us, there is another type of memory that is also very relevant to our daily lives. This other type is called *prospective memory,* and it describes our ability to plan and remember to perform future tasks. As we all know, some people are very good at remembering to carry out future acts and intentions, while others are absolutely hopeless. There's even some evidence that your personality may predict whether or not you are likely to be good at prospective memory tasks. For example, Searleman and Gaydusek (1989) found evidence that people with a *Type A* personality (characterized, in part, by having a strong sense of time urgency, being highly competitive, being overly concerned with deadlines, and holding a perfectionist attitude) are more likely to remember to perform prospective memory tasks and to perform them quickly than those who are not considered to have a *Type A* personality. If you think of some of

**TABLE 5.3** COMMON PROSPECTIVE MEMORY TASKS THAT COLLEGE
STUDENTS OFTEN PERFORM

Remembering to:

- Take your umbrella today because rain is in the forecast.
- Leave for breakfast 15 minutes earlier than usual because you want to buy concert tickets at the bookstore before they sell out.
- Bring your library books with you to class and to take them to the library before it closes.
- Drop off your geology notebook at your friend's dorm room at least 2 hours before today's class (so she can copy the notes she missed).
- Keep your appointment with the career planning office at 2 p.m.
- Take your allergy pills after dinner.
- Call home tonight and wish your parents a happy anniversary (especially since you forgot to send them a card).
- Set your alarm clock at bedtime to wake you up an hour earlier than usual so you can get in some extra studying for a statistics exam tomorrow.

the memory tasks you might be expected to perform today, you will quickly realize that many of these tasks involve remembering to perform future actions (see Table 5.3).

Given the obvious importance of prospective memory in everyday life, you might imagine that memory researchers have devoted a considerable amount of their efforts to studying it. But this has not happened. In fact, it is only recently that memory researchers have begun to devote much attention to studying prospective memory. Why did most memory researchers so totally neglect and ignore the study of prospective memory?

The answer is that the *Zeitgeist* probably wasn't right for the study of prospective memory to blossom until the mid-1970s. *Zeitgeist* is a German word that means "the spirit of the time." Most memory researchers were not ready to study memory for future actions or intentions until the time was right for this to happen. What made the Zeitgeist change to favor the study of prospective memory in the mid-1970s? We believe that the change was due to the growth and popularity of the memory movements described in Chapter 1, especially the *everyday/applied* and *life-span* memory movements. These movements made it seem more "respectable" to explore memory tasks (like those in Table 5.3) that people needed to deal with every day. So researchers began investigating prospective memory by using nontraditional laboratory techniques, techniques such as giving subjects questionnaires to complete, asking subjects to keep diaries of their memory failures, and asking subjects to send postcards or make telephone calls at specified times. Much of the current research exploring prospective memory still has a distinctively naturalistic flavor to it.

## Distinguishing between Retrospective and Prospective Memory

The distinction between retrospective and prospective memory is not as clear-cut as it might at first seem (Baddeley & Wilkins, 1984). In fact, the two types of memory are often intertwined. For instance, successful completion of most prospective memory tasks requires some retrospective memory as well. Suppose you plan to make a videotape of your favorite television show tonight. In addition to remembering to do the taping (the main prospective task), you will also need to remember which tape you want to use, when the show is scheduled, and how to actually work the VCR (all needing retrospective memory).

If prospective tasks often contain elements of retrospective memory, perhaps there is a relationship between performance on one type of task and performance on the other. In other words, if a person is generally good at retrospective memory tasks, does this indicate that he or she will also perform well on tasks of prospective memory? Probably not, since several studies have not found a positive correlation between these types of memory tasks (Einstein & McDaniel, 1990; Kvavilashvili, 1987; Maylor, 1990; Meacham & Leiman, 1975/1982). In fact, Wilkins and Baddeley (1978) actually found a *negative* relationship between verbal recall and a simulated pill-taking task. In their study, 31 female subjects were asked to carry a small box with them for a week and to press a button on the box each day at 8:30 a.m., 1:00 p.m., 5:30 p.m., and 10:00 p.m. Whenever the button was pressed, the time was automatically recorded. This task simulates how well a person might remember to take prescribed pills, a task that obviously has important medical implications. Of primary interest to us, Wilkins and Baddeley reported that the subjects who were best at free recall of word lists (a retrospective task) tended to be the ones who were *least* accurate in the simulated pill-taking task (a prospective task).

Although it is true that retrospective and prospective memory tasks may overlap, making a distinction between the two murky at times, there are a number of ways to help distinguish between them (Baddeley, 1990; Baddeley & Wilkins, 1984; Cohen, 1989; Harris, 1984; Meacham & Leiman, 1975/1982; Munsat, 1966; Winograd, 1988). The most obvious distinguishing feature is that retrospective memory contains information about some previous experience or event, whereas prospective memory is concerned with planning and remembering to perform future tasks. In addition, retrospective memory is largely concerned with *what* is remembered, while prospective memory is mostly concerned with *when* (or *if*) something is remembered. Prospective memory tasks are also more vulnerable than retrospective ones to changing conditions. To be successful, prospective plans often must change in response to changing conditions. For example, if you intend to ask a certain person to go on a date Saturday night, but this person first mentions to you that he or she is going home for the weekend, your plans have to change.

When memory fails us, there are often consequences to pay, consequences that can affect our social interactions (Meacham, 1988). As you will learn in more detail in Chapter 10, people often develop memory reputations, and these reputations affect how the people are viewed and treated. These memory reputations depend largely on how well or how poorly people perform prospective memory tasks. If you fail to remember who was on the losing ticket for the last United States presidential election, the meaning of the word *nonplus,* or what your score was on the last psychology exam you took, your retrospective memory will be viewed as faulty. Only if these memory failures are very common, common enough to draw attention to you, will there likely be any social consequences (people may start to wonder about your health or even question your intelligence!). However, if you fail even a few prospective memory tasks, people will view you much more harshly. Why? Because prospective memory tasks often involve other people, whereas retrospective memory tasks generally do not. If you forget to pick up your date on time, to return borrowed items as promised, or to bring the drinks to the party, *you,* not your memory, will be blamed. The people involved will be angry and hostile, and if this forgetting of prospective memory tasks becomes a trademark of yours, you will be viewed and treated as an unreliable person. The social "costs" for failing prospective memory tasks are almost always greater than for failing retrospective tasks.

## Types of Prospective Memory Tasks

Since we have already devoted considerable space in this book to describing a wide assortment of retrospective memory tasks and procedures (especially in Chapter 2), this section will focus on prospective memory. All prospective memory tasks are goal-oriented, but they can vary enormously in important details. For example, some prospective memory tasks are self-imposed ("After dinner tonight, I am planning on going out with my friends"), and others are imposed on us ("You're part of this family, and I expect you to attend your grandparents' 50th wedding anniversary celebration this evening"). Some are of vital importance and should not be forgotten for any reason (your heart transplant operation is scheduled for tomorrow morning), while others we can safely let slide if need be (planning to read the Sunday comics before recycling the paper). Some require exact timing to be successful (the train leaves at 9:17 a.m. on Tuesday), and some do not (remembering to mow the lawn sometime before the neighbors start grumbling again). Some tasks involve only a single act (not forgetting to pay this month's phone bill on time), while others involve a whole series of interrelated steps (such as preparing to move permanently to a foreign country, which involves getting passport pictures taken, selling your car, saying good-bye to friends just before leaving, forwarding your bank account, remembering to cancel subscriptions, scheduling airline departure and arrival times, and so forth). As should be evident, many prospective memory tasks fit into one of two categories: either "remembering to keep appointments" or "remembering to do one thing before or after another" (Harris, 1984).

**Habitual and episodic tasks.** Another useful distinction to make is between *habitual* and *episodic* prospective memory tasks (Meacham & Leiman, 1975/1982). Habitual tasks are those that we engage in on a regular basis—for example, brushing your teeth when you wake up in the morning or routinely drinking orange juice at breakfast. Episodic tasks involve remembering to do things that we only rarely do (calling the veterinarian to schedule shots for your cat) or that we do only once (calling the veterinarian to finally have your cat neutered). The designation of a memory task as being either habitual or episodic depends not on the task but on the individual. Remembering to wash your hands after using the bathroom is an episodic task for most 4-year-olds, but (it is hoped) for an adult it should be habitual. Likewise, attending church services on Sunday mornings may be habitual or episodic, depending on the person involved. Little is known about the process by which a task graduates from being episodic to becoming habitual.

As you can probably guess, people forget to do episodic tasks more often than habitual ones. This is because habitual tasks are often embedded in a series of activities that are routinely performed in a certain order, and this order supplies the necessary cues for what to do next. For instance, many people have a fairly set routine upon awakening in the morning—they may first turn on the radio and then brush their teeth, take a shower, towel off, get dressed, have some breakfast, etc. Finishing one activity leads automatically into another; after all, you don't have to *actively* remember to get dressed after you finish drying yourself and are now standing around naked! In contrast, remembering to perform an episodic task often requires a break in the normal flow of daily activities, and unless we actively supply them, there are fewer cues available to remind us when to do something out of the ordinary.

## Factors Affecting Prospective Memory Performance

**Cues and reminders.** Whether or not a particular act of future remembering occurs often depends on the availability of appropriate cues in the immediate environment. If sufficient cues are present, at the right time, and the subject is properly motivated (see below), the task will be accomplished as planned. Chapter 15 describes numerous types of memory aids that people use to provide themselves with cues to aid their remembering of plans or obligations. In general, we know that most people prefer to use *external* memory aids (e.g., calendars, timers, or objects left in conspicuous places) rather than *internal* ones (e.g., rhymes or mental rehearsing) to prepare for future remembering (Intons-Peterson & Fournier, 1986). And this may be especially true for elderly people (Jackson, Bogers, & Kerstholt, 1988; Moscovitch & Minde, described in Moscovitch, 1982).

Meacham and Leiman (1975/1982) asked subjects to remember to mail postcards, one by one, on specified days. Half of the subjects were given colored tags to be placed on their key chains, with the idea being that these tags would act as external reminders to mail the postcards (up to 32 days later in some conditions). Although not overwhelming, there was some evidence that the tags increased the likelihood that the postcards would be mailed on the correct dates. Other research has shown unequivocally that reminders help people to remember future tasks or obligations. For instance, as you will learn in Chapter 15, many dentists and physicians have their secretaries call patients or mail them reminders of their scheduled appointments. Levy and Loftus (1984) estimated that such reminders increase the number of people who keep their medical appointments by 10 to 20 percent.

**Compliance, motivation, and commitment.** Successful completion of a prospective memory task is said to occur only if a person performs the correct task at the correct time. However, there's a complicating factor—a person may well remember that he or she needs to perform a task or keep an appointment (such as with the dentist) but for any number of reasons chooses not to (perhaps, in this case, because of fear of pain). If a person remembers the task but decides not to perform it, this is a failure in *compliance*, not a failure of prospective memory.

As will be evident many times in this book (especially in Chapter 8), *motivation* plays a key role in memory. This is as true for prospective memory as it is for retrospective memory. In a prospective memory task, if motivation is high enough, compliance won't usually be a problem. For instance, if someone promises you $1000 for calling him as soon as you know who has won the Kentucky Derby, you will undoubtedly try your best to remember to call him, even if you have to reach Kathmandu (the capital of Nepal) at 3 o'clock in the morning! Much less lavish incentives have been shown to increase motivation and hence compliance for prospective memory tasks. For example, Meacham and Singer (1977) discovered that being given the chance to be one of four persons out of approximately 40 to win $5 was enough to increase the accuracy of college students in mailing back postcards.

Another factor that can enhance compliance is making a *public commitment* that you will perform a future task (Levy, 1977; Levy & Loftus, 1984; Levy, Yamashita, & Pow, 1979; Wurtele, Galanos, & Roberts, 1980). Imagine stating to all your teammates, after personally having had a very poor season, that next year you will be in tip-top shape when soccer practice begins. After making such a public commitment, it is highly likely that you will strive to remember to work out during the off-season.

# Summary

### I. The Permanence of Memory
- Many people believe in the permanence of memory, even though information stored in LTM may be very difficult or impossible to retrieve.

- However, upon critical evaluation of the empirical evidence, some researchers have argued that the belief that everything we learn is permanently stored is unwarranted.

## II. Ebbinghaus's Forgetting Curve

- In order to measure how much information he had remembered over various retention intervals, Ebbinghaus invented the *savings score.*
- As displayed in his famous *forgetting curve,* Ebbinghaus found that the greatest amount of forgetting occurred shortly after the initial learning, followed by a much slower decline in retention.
- It is now recognized that Ebbinghaus's forgetting curve does not provide a universal description of the rate of human forgetting. Instead, the amount and form of forgetting greatly depend on the type of information, the length of time over which it is acquired, and its personal significance.
- Bahrick proposed that overlearned information acquired over a long time is held permanently in a memory storage system that he labeled *permastore.* Retention of information in the permastore shows little or no decline over very long time spans.
- Other research has also shown that the forgetting of *autobiographical* events and *nondeclarative* knowledge and skills does not follow the pattern suggested by Ebbinghaus's forgetting curve.

## III. Reasons Why People Forget

- Many reasons or mechanisms have been proposed to explain why we forget.
- It is known that certain *organic disorders,* such as head injuries or excessive alcohol intake, can destroy memories.
- *Decay theory* states that the simple passage of time causes our memories to grow weaker and weaker. Decay is the primary mechanism of forgetting from sensory memory and probably contributes to STM forgetting too.
  - Recently, a new *Theory of Disuse* has been formulated that suggests that retrieval failure can have adaptive value. This theory assumes that people have a limited capacity to retrieve information from memory, that even well-learned information will become increasingly inaccessible unless periodically retrieved, and that this inaccessibility is caused by the learning or retrieval of information that is similar to the sought-after material.
- *Interference theory* asserts that forgetting happens because other information or events disturb or interfere with retention.
  - There are two major forms of interference—*retroactive* (newer information acts backward in time to cause disruption) and *proactive* (previously learned information acts forward in time to cause disruption).

- Many current memory researchers subscribe to the view that little or no real forgetting of information occurs from LTM in healthy people. It is believed that long-term memories are always *available* (stored in memory) but that they may not be *accessible* (able to be retrieved).
  - *Motivated forgetting* occurs when a person wants to forget something. If done consciously, this is called *suppression;* if unconsciously, *repression.* In both suppression and repression an available memory is made less accessible.
  - The theory of *cue-dependent forgetting* maintains that forgetting occurs when there are insufficient retrieval cues. It is supposed that without good retrieval cues, available memories cannot become accessible.
  - The *tip-of-the-tongue* phenomenon can be considered a subset of cue-dependent forgetting. It occurs when someone is unable to immediately recall a word or name that the person definitely feels he or she knows.
  - People remember more when the conditions present at the time of encoding match the conditions present at retrieval. When similar conditions are ensured, available memories are made more accessible. This aspect of *context-dependent* memory is called the *encoding specificity principle.*

## IV. Retrospective and Prospective Memory

- *Retrospective memory* refers to our ability to remember past events or information. The vast majority of memory researchers have concentrated on investigating this type of memory.
- The ability to plan and remember to perform future actions is called *prospective memory.* Even though prospective memory tasks abound in everyday life, only recently have psychologists devoted much attention to studying them.
- The successful completion of a task may often require both prospective memory ability and retrospective memory knowledge.
- Since prospective memory tasks often affect other people, failure to adequately perform such tasks can have dire social consequences.
- A distinction is usually made between *habitual* and *episodic* prospective memory tasks. Habitual tasks (which are forgotten least often) are ones that are performed on a regular basis, while episodic tasks occur infrequently or only once.
- Using *external* cues and reminders, having a high level of *motivation* to ensure *compliance,* and making a *public commitment* can be useful ways to enhance the chances that a prospective memory task will be carried out successfully.

# 6

# Mental Representations and Memory

———— ❖ ————

You learned in Chapter 3 that a vast amount of sensory information constantly bombards us and that we have only a very limited ability to process it. In fact, only a tiny fraction of all this information is stored for a very brief time in our sensory memories. As you will recall, a major function of sensory memory is to preserve this information, in relatively raw or unanalyzed form, so that we can have additional time to decide which information will receive fuller attention and processing. But this immediately raises a very important question that was not addressed earlier: How do people decide which information should receive further attention and processing and which should be allowed to decay away?

A logical (and popular) answer is that people largely rely on their prior knowledge and experience about the world to help guide them. Not only does this general knowledge allow people to select the most relevant and important information to process, but perhaps of equal importance, this existing knowledge can also allow people to know which information can be safely disregarded. We will explore in this chapter how the mental representations that each of us has about the world around us influence how we encode, store, and retrieve information. While our mental representations are undeniably important and valuable in helping us to comprehend and remember complex events, they also have a down side—these same mental representations can also cause our memories to be incomplete or distorted.

123

# MAJOR TYPES OF SCHEMAS

A *schema* is a mental model or representation, built up through experience, about a person, an object, a situation, or an event. Essentially, a schema is simply an organized body of general information or beliefs, that may or may not be entirely accurate, about some topic or concept. We all have hundreds of different types of schemas (also called *schemata*). People experiencing similar situations and events will develop similar schemas. But since everyone has unique experiences in life, each of us acquires somewhat different schemas (and sometimes radically different ones).

## Person Schemas

You have probably developed schemas about all of your close relatives that you use to help in interpreting their actions. So if you come home one evening and find your father smoking a cigar, which he rarely does, you may quickly and accurately surmise that he is very worried. You can do this because you have developed what is called a *person schema* of your dad. A person schema contains general information and beliefs about consistent traits and characteristics of another person (Fiske & Taylor, 1984). This information can then be useful in helping to understand and later remember another person's behavior. The person schema you have for your father is activated upon seeing him or thinking about him, and in this instance, it reminds you that smoking is frequently a sign that your father is worried about something.

All of us have developed dozens of person schemas for others we know well. The person schema that you have for your best friend may include that he (or she) is often late for appointments, is usually witty, likes to wear hats, has a fondness for playing practical jokes, and writes funny limericks. If you meet someone who resembles your best friend in some fashion, there is evidence to suggest that the person schema for your best friend will become activated. This can then cause you to "remember" this new person as having some of the same personality characteristics that your friend has, even though you may have no good reason to assume this is true (Anderson & Cole, 1990).

## Self-Schemas

Each of us also has a *self-schema* consisting of general information that we believe to be true about our own traits, dispositions, abilities, goals, and so forth. In everyday situations, there is often an interplay between our self-schema and some of our person schemas. Consider the situation in which two friends (let's call them Sam and Peter) are squabbling over whose turn it is to leave a tip at their favorite restaurant. Sam is convinced that it's Peter's turn, but Peter is equally adamant that it is Sam's turn. Each is convinced that the other's memory is faulty.

Perhaps the reason why Sam and Peter have different recollections as to who left the tip last time is that neither of them can distinguish very well between the last time they ate at this restaurant and all the other times. If this is true, then each will have precious little recall of specific details of their last meal. This means that each of them must then depend almost entirely on his self-schema and his person schema of his friend to help reconstruct what probably happened at the last meal. Maybe Sam's self-schema is that he usually remembers to do things, and his person schema about Peter contains information that he is generally a forgetful person. Meanwhile, Peter's self-schema is that he is typically a generous person, while his person schema of Sam is that his friend often acts like a tightwad, one who hates to spend his money. Given their respective self-schemas and their person schemas of each other, it's not surprising that Sam and Peter each "remember" that it is the other's turn to pay.

## Scripts

A *script* is a particular type of schema that describes the kind of knowledge that people can abstract from a common, frequently occurring event (Abelson, 1981; Mandler, 1984; Schank & Abelson, 1977). For example, we have scripts for going shopping, riding a bus, visiting a friend in the hospital, attending birthday parties, and eating at a restaurant. Scripts are not composed of memories for any one particular event, such as your last visit to the local bowling alley; instead, they contain generic knowledge or memory about what usually happens when, for example, you go to any bowling alley. The following is a script that most of you will quickly recognize as being a good description of what people typically do upon their arrival at a fast-food restaurant:

> A person will get into the shortest line available that leads to a person taking food orders. Then the person will scan the menu listed on the front wall and make a decision as to what to order. As people ahead of the person get their orders completed, the individual moves up in the line. Upon reaching the front of the line, he or she tells the person standing at the cash register what food and/or drinks are wanted. After waiting for the order to be processed, the person then pays for the food. After making sure the change returned is correct, the person puts it away. At this point, if the person is alone, he or she will look for an unoccupied table and consume the meal. Upon finishing, the person puts the trash into a receptacle and then leaves.

Sometimes scripts, like the one above, provide a general structure for the sequence of events during routine activities. This will have a dual advantage. Not only will it allow a person to encode incoming information according to a well-known sequence, but it will also permit someone to anticipate that certain information should be forthcoming. For instance, if your script for eating at a fast-food restaurant is like ours, you will know to expect that the person would have to pay *before* eating (which is not true in a traditional restaurant that has waiters or waitresses). Some scripts, however, do not suggest a canonical (or fixed) order of events. All of us have a script for going to high school, yet each of us did different things at different times during a typical school day. While you may have had chemistry, history, and Spanish in a row before lunch, someone else could have had these same courses in the reverse order in the afternoon. For these types of scripts there is no set order in which activities will occur.

A major benefit of having a script is that it allows a person to fill in missing or omitted details. So, without having to be explicitly told, most of you can probably guess correctly that the person in the fast-food restaurant mentioned above does not leave a tip. You can do this by activating your own fast-food script; by fast-forwarding to the end, you can decide if tips in such restaurants are generally expected. (They aren't.)

Is there evidence that people actually form and use scripts? The answer is unequivocally yes, and the use of scripts starts at a very early age (e.g., Bauer & Mandler, 1990; Bower, Black, & Turner, 1979; Fivush & Hamond, 1990; Hudson, 1990; Hudson & Nelson, 1986; Mandler, 1984; Nelson, 1978, 1986; Nelson & Gruendel, 1981, 1986; Nelson & Hudson, 1989; Owens, Bower, & Black, 1979; Rabinowitz & Mandler, 1983; Ratner, Smith, & Padgett, 1990). Substantial research has demonstrated that scripts are even used by toddlers. For example, on the basis of careful interviews, Hudson and Nelson (1986) found that 3-year-olds had scripts for familiar events such as "eating dinner at home." And as most parents can attest, even 2-year-olds can develop and follow scripts: Try to vary the routine for getting ready to go to bed (such as by forgetting to turn on the night-light or forgetting to find a particular blanket or stuffed animal that the child *absolutely* must have before going to bed), and all hell breaks out!

An early example of the psychological reality of scripts was provided by Bower et al. (1979). College students were asked to list, in order of occurrence, about 20 activities associated with visiting a doctor, attending a lecture, getting up in the morning, going grocery shopping, and eating at a fancy restaurant.

| Visiting a doctor | Attending a Lecture |
| --- | --- |
| Check in with receptionist | Enter room |
| Sit down | Find seat |
| Read magazine | Sit down |
| Nurse tests | Take out notebook |
| Doctor examines | Listen to professor |
| Leave office | Take notes |
| | Check time |
| | Leave |

Overall, there was considerable agreement among the subjects concerning both the order of the activities and the activities themselves. About 6 or 7 activities were listed for each script by at least half of the subjects. And, on the average, another 5 or 6 activities were cited by 40 to 50 percent of the participants. Listed on page 126 are the most frequently mentioned activities for the "visiting a doctor" and "attending a lecture" scripts.

Bower et al. (1979) also had subjects read different versions of the same script. As an example, some subjects read three different passages about a "visit to a health professional" (one was about a doctor, one about a chiropractor, and one about a dentist). After a 20-minute intervening task, the subjects were asked to recall each passage. It was found that the subjects often confused one version with another. This is good evidence that scripts were being used, because this is just what would be expected to occur if recall for each version was being guided by the same basic script.

## MOPs and TOPs

A computer program called SAM was developed that was able to use scripts to make inferences and predictions and to answer questions on a limited number of topics (Schank, 1982; Schank & Abelson, 1977). Using scripts, SAM did a very respectable job of going beyond the given information in the written story.

As the computer program evolved, Roger Schank and his colleagues developed higher-order forms of scripts called *memory organization packets* (MOPs) and *thematic organization points* (TOPs). These higher-order scripts were intended to make the program more flexible and dynamic. Instead of having prestored, static scripts, the program now could create new types of scripts. A MOP is a collection of various *scenes* (events that form one part of a script) that are all related. If you are planning a birthday party, one scene might involve the actions taken to invite the guests (such as making up a list of potential names and calling people on the phone). Another scene could involve the preparations necessary to get the food and drinks ready to serve. The same scene can be used in different MOPs. For instance, a scene for inviting people in a birthday party MOP could also be used for inviting guests in a wedding MOP. A MOP will often, but not always, specify the order in which the scenes will occur (e.g., preparing the food before getting the decorations finished).

At a higher level than a MOP is a TOP. A TOP is a script that represents a more abstract theme than does a MOP. TOPs also allow people to see the similarities between two seemingly different situations. For instance, finding a $20 bill on the ground and getting a raise in pay, while certainly different in their details, could both be considered examples of the TOP "What a great day I'm having." Do people have something like MOPs and TOPs to help them organize information and to aid memory? We don't know yet. However, the concepts do make sense, and regardless of the final outcome, Schank and his coworkers should be recognized for their efforts in trying to bridge the gap between those computer scientists and psychologists who are engaged in the study of memory and cognition.

# THEORIES OF HOW SCHEMAS AFFECT MEMORY

Joseph Alba and Lynn Hasher published a widely read paper in 1983 that described a prototypical model of how schemas should affect memory performance. This influential article critically evaluated the popular notion that the memory process was schema-driven. To accomplish this, they formulated what they considered to be a modal model of existing schema theories. And according to their model, when a schema is activated, information is encoded on the basis of the operation of the following four processes:

1. *Selection.* Only the aspects of the incoming information that are most relevant and important to the currently activated schema are encoded.
2. *Abstraction.* The selected information is stored not in terms of its surface structure (such as the specific wording or type font used) but rather in terms of its meaning.
3. *Interpretation.* Relevant prior knowledge is accessed from LTM to aid in comprehending the new information.
4. *Integration.* This is a process by which a single, integrated memory representation is formed and stored. It occurs as a product of the selection, abstraction, and interpretation processes that precede it.

After outlining their schema model, Alba and Hasher (1983) went on to describe several research findings that were consistent with the model's predictions. They also pointed out, however, a fairly substantial amount of research findings that they considered to be inconsistent with or contradictory to the model. Overall, they did not think that schema theory did a good job of accounting for what we know about human memory capabilities. On the basis of all the evidence that existed at that time, Alba and Hasher concluded that human memory representations were much richer and more detailed than any existing schema theory would predict.

However, not everyone agreed with this rather negative conclusion about the worth of schema theory. For instance, Jean Mandler (1984), who has done extensive research on schema theory, questioned a basic tenet of Alba and Hasher's model—that only one schema at a time is activated and that this one schema largely directs the entire encoding process. Instead, she believes that it is much more likely that several schemas are simultaneously active, helping to guide comprehension and encoding. If this is true, then some of the seemingly inconsistent research findings cited by Alba and Hasher are no longer really inconsistent. For example, Alba and Hasher cited research that appears to show that the activated schema does not always determine what features of the new information get selected for encoding. But if, in reality, there are many schemas activated at the same time, and the investigators are focusing their attention on only one of them (and the "wrong" one), then it may well appear that the information selected for encoding is not relevant to the schema under consideration.

In addition, the schema model of Alba and Hasher proposes that memory will be best for information that is consistent with, expected by, or relevant to the activated schema. Weakening the predictive power of the model, Alba and Hasher cited data showing that it is often the *inconsistent, unexpected,* or *irrelevant* things that are better remembered! But again, this does not necessarily mean that schema theory cannot account for these types of findings.

Mandler (1984) agrees with Alba and Hasher's proposal that activated schemas prepare a person to expect certain things to happen or to be present in a commonly experienced situation (like having a conversation with someone). However, and this is where she differs from them, it is just because of this preparation for the expected that the expected is *not* given much attention. This allows a person to spend his or her limited attentional resources on the more novel aspects of a situation. According to this view, since schemas really direct our attention to unusual details, it will be the more surprising and bizarre things that will stand out in memory, not the commonplace things. And upon some reflection, it does often seem that it is the weird or odd things in life that we most remember. If you strike up a conversation with a stranger wearing a business suit and are later asked to recall what he was wearing, you are more likely to remember the strange, fluorescent hat with feathers that he had on than the fact that his shoes were standard loafers. This is because his outrageous hat violates your schema of what a conservatively dressed businessman would wear, while his shoes do not.

In the next section we will examine some of the direct evidence that schemas influence memory. In particular, we will see how having or knowing the correct schema can sometimes dramatically facilitate memory performance.

# *F*ACILITATING EFFECTS OF SCHEMAS

## *Memory for the Bizarre*

In 1972, John Bransford and Marcia Johnson conducted two experiments that have become classics in the memory literature. Their experiments vividly demonstrated the importance of having the right schema at the right time. To get some firsthand knowledge of this yourself, read the following passage, and then try to recall as much of it as possible (without looking back).

> If the balloons popped the sound wouldn't be able to carry since everything would be too far away from the correct floor. A closed window would also prevent the sound from carrying, since most buildings tend to be well insulated. Since the whole operation depends on the steady flow of electricity, a break in the middle of the wire would also cause problems. Of course, the fellow could shout, but the human voice is not loud enough to carry that far. An additional problem is that the string could break on the instrument. Then there would be no accompaniment to the message. It is clear that the best situation would involve less distance. Then there would be fewer potential problems. With face to face contact, the least number of things could go wrong.

Hard to remember much, isn't it? One group of subjects who had to do what you did could recall only 3.6 ideas out of a maximum of 14. This was known as the *no context* condition. There were two other conditions in the experiment—a *context before* and a *context after* condition. The groups of subjects for these conditions were shown the picture in Figure 6.1, either before reading the passage or afterward. The group that saw the picture before reading the paragraph did much better. The subjects recalled about 8 ideas out of the 14. What about the subjects who saw the picture after reading the story? It is

FIGURE 6.1

Man serenading a woman.
*Reprinted with permission from Bransford & Johnson (1972).*

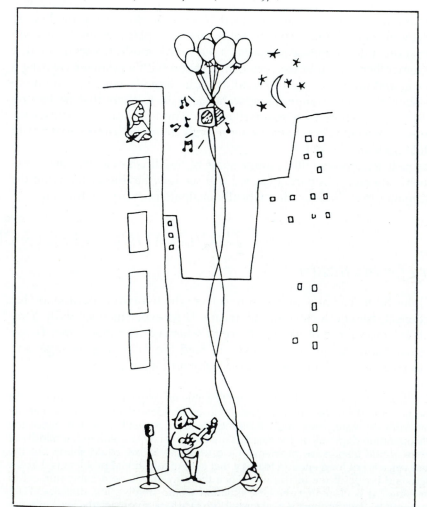

interesting that they did not benefit at all; the subjects in the context after condition recalled the same number of ideas (3.6) as did the subjects who were in the no context condition.

This study showed that having the right schema during the encoding stage can be crucial to understanding and remembering complex material. Seeing the picture allowed the subjects to make sense of what they were reading, in this case a story about a man serenading a woman who was in a high-rise building. But the picture only aided the subjects if they saw it *before* reading the passage; it didn't help at all if they saw it after. This indicates that the picture was helpful only if it was available during the encoding phase.

## Memory for the Commonplace

The previous study revealed the importance of having a schema that allowed comprehension of a bizarre and novel situation. Once comprehended, this complex passage could be reasonably encoded. It could still be argued that a schema is only really vital when a person is dealing with totally strange and novel events or situations. Perhaps the influence would be greatly diminished if a less bizarre, more familiar situation was presented. Bransford and Johnson (1972) tested this possibility by having subjects read passages such as the following and then asking them to recall as much as they could.

> The procedure is actually quite simple. First you arrange things into groups. Of course, one pile may be sufficient depending on how much there is to do. If you have to go somewhere else due to lack of facilities, that is the next step; otherwise you are pretty well set. It is important not to overdo things. That is, it is better to do too few things at once than too many. In the short run this may not seem important, but complications can arise. A mistake can prove expensive as well. At first the whole procedure will seem complicated. Soon, however, it will become just another facet of life. It is difficult to foresee any end to the necessity for this task in the immediate future, but one can never tell. After the procedure is completed, one arranges the materials into different groups again. Then they can be put into their appropriate places. Eventually they will all be used once more, and the whole cycle will have to be repeated. However, that is part of life.

For most people this passage is also difficult to comprehend and encode (unless you can guess the title while reading it). As in the first experiment, there were again three conditions: one group received *no title* at all, one received the *title before* reading the passage, and one received the *title after* reading the passage. In case you are still puzzled about what you read, go back and reread the passage, knowing that the title is "Washing Clothes," a familiar chore for most of us. The results of this experiment very closely paralleled those described earlier. Subjects without the benefit of the title recalled 2.8 ideas out of a maximum of 18, those supplied with the title before reading recalled 5.8 ideas, and those given the title after reading remembered 2.7 ideas.

## Homebuyer or Burglar: Effects on Memory

The two experiments by Bransford and Johnson (1972) illustrated the powerful effects that schemas can have on encoding processes. Their research suggests that knowing the proper schema only helps if the schema is available at the time of encoding. However, under certain conditions, it has also been shown that having a schema at the time of retrieval can enhance recall.

In a clever demonstration of this, Anderson and Pichert (1978) asked subjects to read a description of an old house from the perspective of either a potential homebuyer or a potential burglar. The passage contained information that was important for a homebuyer (such as the house having a "leaky roof" and a "damp and musty basement") and information of interest to a burglar (such as "a rare coin collection" and the fact that "no one is home on Thursdays"). Upon finishing the passage, all subjects recalled as much as they could. After a short delay, half of the subjects were asked to again recall as much as possible, but this time they were instructed to do it from the other perspective. In other words, the subjects who first read the passage from the perspective of a potential homebuyer now had to recall the passage from the perspective of a potential burglar, and those who first read it as a potential burglar were

FIGURE 6.2
The waiting room in the Brewer and Treyens (1981) study.
*Reprinted with permission from Brewer & Treyens (1981).*

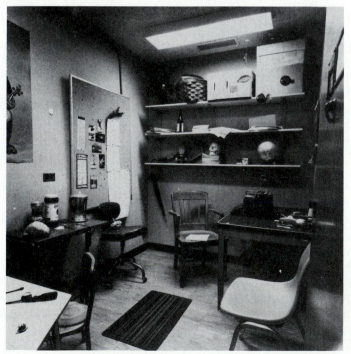

switched to a potential homebuyer. The other half of the subjects were simply asked to recall again as much as they could without any change in perspective.

If the effect of a schema is evident only at the time of encoding, then switching schemas at the time of retrieval should not help a person recall more facts. But, in fact, it does. Subjects who changed perspective at retrieval recalled more facts than did those who did not change perspective. Anderson and Pichert (1978) also showed that a change in schema was related to the *types* of facts remembered—recalling facts related to the new schema increased by 7 percent in one experiment and 10 percent in another. Furthermore, remembering facts associated with the old schema decreased by 7 percent and 21 percent, respectively, in the two experiments.

Although subjects reported that they tried to selectively encode facts relevant to the original perspective, they must have also encoded some facts unrelated to it that could be activated at the time of retrieval. So, then, why didn't the subjects in Bransford and Johnson's experiments show some enhancement in memory when they were given the correct schema at recall time? Cohen (1989) has suggested that the passages Bransford and Johnson used were so incomprehensible without the proper schema at the time of encoding that very little of the information was encoded at all. If this is true, then hardly any facts or ideas were stored by their subjects at the time of encoding, and hence, when the subjects were subsequently given the correct schema at the time of retrieval, there was virtually nothing in memory to be retrieved!

## Memory for Places

As we said in Chapter 2, much of our learning about the world occurs during episodes of incidental encoding. These are times when we are not actively trying to encode and remember information. Brewer and Treyens (1981) were interested in studying how schemas could affect the incidental encoding of information for places.

Each subject was taken into the room that is shown in Figure 6.2. The room was designed to look like the office of a graduate student in the psychology department. And, in fact, most of the items that appeared in the room would be appropriate ones for such an office—there was a Skinner box, a typewriter, a table, a coffee pot, posters, and so on. But there were some items intentionally omitted from the room (such as a telephone, pencils, and books) that would have been expected. Furthermore, a few items (such as a piece of bark, a toy top, and a skull) were placed in the room that would not be consistent with the average undergraduate's "office schema" for a graduate student.

An objective measure of how likely certain objects in the waiting room were to be in a graduate student's office was needed. So 14 subjects, not participating in the memory part of the experiment itself, rated 61 objects in the room for *schema expectancy*. They were asked to indicate on a 6-point rating scale "how likely the objects would be to appear in a room like this." In addition, another 14 subjects rated the objects for their *saliency* ["how noticeable the object is (or would be) in this room"].

Each subject in the actual memory part of the experiment was told by an experimenter to "wait in my office" for a few minutes until the experiment was to begin. The room lights were then turned on, and the experimenter asked the subject to have a seat in the room (only one chair did not have things on it). The experimenter closed the door of the room, and the subject was left alone in the room for 35 seconds. After the time elapsed, the experimenter reentered the room and told the subject that the true purpose of the study was to test his or her memory for the contents of the waiting room. Only about 1 minute elapsed between the time the subject left the waiting room and the start of the memory test (in a room deliberately chosen to be much different from the waiting room).

The 30 subjects in one group were asked to write down everything they could remember about the room in which they had waited. The results revealed strong independent correlations between the likelihood that objects would be recalled and their schema expectancy and salience ratings. This means that objects that were previously judged to "fit" into the office schema were more likely to be remembered as well as objects that had been judged to be high in saliency. So people tended to remember objects typical of a graduate student's office, such as chairs, desks, walls, and shelves, but they also remembered objects that were low in schema expectancy but high in salience (12 people remembered the toy top and 8 the skull). Objects judged to be low both in schema expectancy and in salience were not well remembered. Only 1 person remembered the fan, the umbrella, or the wrench.

A total of 88 objects were recalled by one or more of the subjects, and the average number of objects correctly recalled was 13.5. Of particular interest, 19 of the 88 objects were *inferred* objects. These were objects that were not actually present in the waiting room. Most of these objects (e.g., books were "remembered" by 9 people) were consistent with what people would expect to find in a graduate student's office.

Overall, this study provides strong evidence that schemas facilitate memory performance—in particular, memory for places and objects. Not only did subjects better remember the objects that were consistent with an office schema, but they also showed the power that an activated schema can have on memory: it was seen that a schema can produce errors in memory that are consistent with the schema. In the next section we turn our attention to examining in more detail some of the distorting effects that schemas can have on memory performance.

# DISTORTING EFFECTS OF SCHEMAS

We know that schemas provide a basis for making inferences about incoming information. In most circumstances, the inferences we make are correct, and they aid the encoding process by speeding up processing and by filling in missing gaps. Suppose you hear the sentence *The high school baseball game had to be postponed because of the weather.* Your schemas will help you make some reasonable inferences about why the game was postponed. First, because of your "high school baseball" schema, you can make the reasonable inference that the game would be played outdoors (only professional baseball teams sometimes play indoors). In addition, on the basis of your past knowledge about baseball games, you know that these games are postponed if the umpires decide that the weather will hinder play too much. This means that when you learned that the game was postponed because of the weather, your schema undoubtedly caused you to infer that the game was postponed because the weather was *bad* (probably owing to rain, since high school baseball is played in the spring), not because the weather was too *good* (in good weather the game could be postponed if everyone wanted to do something else on a fine, sunny day).

## Constructive and Reconstructive Changes

Unfortunately, sometimes our schemas lead us astray. We draw inferences that are incorrect and that distort the meaning of new information. When these distortions occur during the encoding stage, they are referred to as *constructive changes*, and when they occur during the retrieval stage, they are called *reconstructive changes*. It can often be very difficult to determine at what stage a particular distortion occurred, and in many situations distorting inferences are made at both encoding and retrieval (Kintsch, 1977).

One way that might help distinguish between constructive and reconstructive changes is to vary the timing of recall. Recall can be tested immediately after the presentation and then compared with what can be recalled after a delay has occurred. If there are differences in the type or amount of distortion between immediate and delay conditions, this would be evidence that both constructive and reconstructive changes took place. Distorting inferences drawn during the encoding stage should be evident immediately following the presentation of the new information. If after a delay has transpired there's evidence of other distortions, then it is likely that faulty inferences are causing reconstructive changes as well. Let's look at a specific example from the advertising literature.

**Pragmatic implications.** One method for investigating how people can fall prey to making false inferences on the basis of their schemas has been to use sentences that contain *pragmatic implications*. A pragmatic implication is a statement that leads a person to believe something that is neither explicitly asserted nor necessarily implied (Brewer, 1977; Harris, 1974, 1977). Presumably this occurs because there is an interaction between the actual information in the sentence and the person's knowledge of the world (i.e., his or her schemas). For instance, if you hear the sentence *The karate champion hit the cinder block*, this pragmatically implies that the block was broken (Brewer, 1977). However, this is an unwarranted inference, and it probably would not have been drawn if the word *swimming* had been substituted for the word *karate*. This can be contrasted with a logical implication, in which information is *necessarily* implied. A logical implication could be drawn from the statement *Joe coerced Fred into doing his homework for him*, which necessarily implies that Fred worked on Joe's homework.

Pragmatic implications have been used extensively in advertising to mislead people (Harris, 1983). Searleman and Carter (1988) selected four different types of pragmatic implications that are commonly found in real commercial advertising (see Table 6.1). They wanted to determine if there were differences in the effectiveness of different types of pragmatic implications for causing people to make false inferences about 16 fictitious products. Two commercials were prepared for each product—one that explicitly asserted a claim and one that only pragmatically implied the same claim. The subjects were divided into two groups, an immediate group and a short-delay group. In each group, half of the subjects listened to the explicitly asserted version of the commercial and half to the implied version.

The subjects were told that the purpose of the study was to investigate how information in commercials was understood. They were also instructed to accept that the commercials would be making accurate statements about their products. The subjects in the immediate group listened to each tape-recorded commercial (lasting only 15 to 20 seconds) and were then asked to judge the truthfulness of statements made about the product. On the basis of only what they heard, they were to judge if a statement was true, false, or of indeterminate truth value (for example, if the statement said the product came in a blue box,

TABLE 6.1  THE FOUR TYPES OF PRAGMATIC IMPLICATIONS USED BY SEARLEMAN AND CARTER (1988)

1. **Juxtaposing imperative statements** (e.g., "Get a good night's sleep. Buy Dreamon Sleeping Pills."). The juxtaposition of the two imperative statements can erroneously imply that the sleeping pills were responsible for the good night's sleep.

2. **Using comparative adjectives without a qualifier** (e.g., "Lackluster Floor Polish gives a floor a <u>brighter</u> shine."). This can lead to the false implication that this floor polish produces brighter shines than do other floor polishes. In actuality, this floor polish may only give a brighter shine than if only water is used.

3. **Using hedge words** (e.g., "Ty-One-On pain reliever <u>may</u> help get rid of those morning-after headaches."). The use of the hedge word *may* should weaken the assertion but can still leave a strong implication that the product will, in fact, relieve headaches.

4. **Reporting piecemeal survey results** (e.g., "John Doe Jeans are available in more colors than Gloria Vanderbilt's, are more sleekly styled than Sergio Valenti's, and are less expensive than Cheryl Tiegs's."). The unwarranted general conclusion could be reached that John Doe Jeans are better in all ways than the other jeans.

and no color was mentioned in the original commercial, the subject should indicate that the statement is of indeterminate truth value). One of the statements (called the *critical test statement*) was a paraphrase of the implied or asserted claim. Subjects in the short-delay group listened to all 16 commercials (which took about 5 minutes) before judging any of the critical test statements. Table 6.2 shows the asserted and implied versions of a sample commercial, along with the critical test statement to be judged.

Of primary interest to the present discussion, the results of the study showed that 50.6 percent of the implied claims were accepted as being true by the subjects in the immediate group. You'll recall that these individuals made their judgments only 15 to 20 *seconds* after hearing each commercial! This certainly suggests that faulty inferences were being drawn at the time of encoding. From this we can infer that schemas were causing constructive changes. But there was also evidence that reconstructive changes were occurring as well. After only a 5-minute delay, subjects in the short-delay group judged the implied claims as being true 74.4 percent of the time. In fact, for these subjects there was no significant difference in the percentage of "true" responses made to implied and asserted claims (85 percent). In this study, by varying the time of recall, it was possible to infer that both constructive and reconstructive changes occurred.

**The war of the ghosts.** Frederick Bartlett (1932) was one of the first memory researchers to champion the view that our schemas greatly affect the retrieval of long-term memories. He provided convincing evidence that when people attempt to recall stories, both constructive and reconstructive changes often take place.

In one famous series of experiments, Bartlett (1932) asked British subjects to read a short, somewhat bizarre passage from a North American Indian folktale (see Table 6.3). After the reading was completed, he asked the subjects to recall as many specific details as possible. Sometimes he asked people to retell the story to another person, who then had to retell it to another, and so on. This is similar to the game of "telephone" that children often play. And

TABLE 6.2 A JUXTAPOSED IMPERATIVE SAMPLE COMMERCIAL: ASSERTED AND IMPLIED VERSIONS

---

*Assertion version:* "Tossing and turning again? Having trouble getting to sleep? Take Dreamon Sleeping Pills to get a good night's sleep and feel refreshed in the morning. Dreamon Sleeping Pills, the ones in the purple package."

*Pragmatic implication version:* "Tossing and turning again? Having trouble getting to sleep? Get a good night's sleep and feel refreshed in the morning. Buy Dreamon Sleeping Pills. The ones in the purple package."

*Critical test statement:* "Dreamon Sleeping Pills will make you get a good night's sleep and feel refreshed in the morning."

---

**TABLE 6.3** "THE WAR OF THE GHOSTS" PASSAGE

One night two young men from Egulac went down to the river to hunt seals, and while they were there it became foggy and calm. Then they heard war-cries, and they thought: "Maybe this is a war-party." They escaped to the shore, and hid behind a log. Now canoes came up, and they heard the noise of paddles, and saw one canoe coming up to them. There were five men in the canoe, and they said:

"What do you think? We wish to take you along. We are going up the river to make war on the people."

One of the young men said: "I have no arrows."

"Arrows are in the canoe," they said.

"I will not go along. I might be killed. My relatives do not know where I have gone. But you," he said, turning to the other, "may go with them."

So one of the young men went, but the other returned home.

And the warriors went up the river to a town on the other side of Kalama. The people came down to the river, and they began to fight, and many were killed. But presently the young man heard one of the warriors say: "Quick, let us go home: that Indian has been hit." Now he thought: "Oh, they are ghosts." He did not feel sick, but they said he had been shot.

So the canoes went back to Egulac, and the young man went ashore to his house, and made a fire. And he told everybody and said: "Behold I accompanied the ghosts, and we went to fight. Many of our fellows were killed, and many of those who attacked us were killed. They said I was hit, and I did not feel sick."

He told it all, and then he became quiet. When the sun rose he fell down. Something black came out of his mouth. His face became contorted. The people jumped up and cried.

He was dead.

SOURCE: Bartlett, 1932.

just as children typically discover, after several retellings, Bartlett usually found that the original story was hopelessly garbled. Subjects would often make very systematic errors, such as trying to make the story more coherent than it really was, omitting details that seemed incomprehensible, or adding "new" details that were not in the original story.

Other times, Bartlett had the same individual make repeated attempts to recall the passage. The first attempt was usually about 15 minutes after reading the story, while other attempts occurred at intervals ranging from hours later to years later. Again, Bartlett observed that the passage underwent tremendous transformations over time. Bartlett attributed these omissions and additions to the fact that his British subjects did not have the proper schema to make sense out of the passage. They knew very little about North American Indian culture and so had great difficulty in processing the information. This led them to make faulty inferences during both encoding and retrieval. If Bartlett had tested Native Americans instead of British citizens, he almost certainly would have witnessed much better recall of the story.

**The distorting effects of labels.** Schemas can also influence our memory for visual stimuli. Carmichael, Hogan, and Walter (1932) demonstrated this by presenting subjects with a series of ambiguous line drawings. Before each drawing was presented, each subject was given a description, or verbal label, of what the drawing represented. Half the subjects were given one set of descriptions/labels and half were given a different set for the same drawings. As can be seen in Figure 6.3, subjects were clearly influenced by the assigned labels when later asked to reproduce the line drawings—many line drawings were distorted to look more like what the verbal labels suggested.

Now these distortions may be constructive changes (if they occurred during encoding) or reconstructive changes (if they happened during retrieval) or both.

FIGURE 6.3
Showing the effects of labels on the remembering of ambiguous visual stimuli.

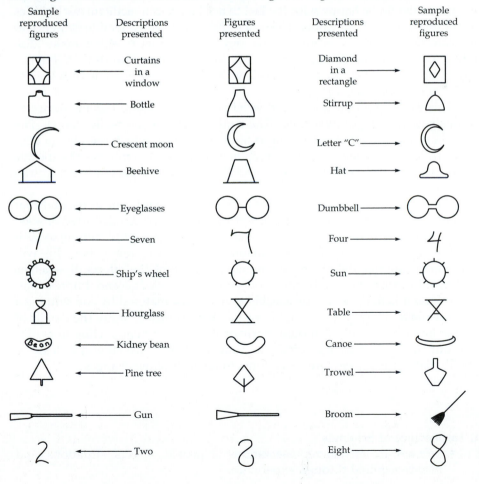

Hanawalt and Demarest (1939) provided evidence that at least some of the distortions were reconstructive in nature. They did this by repeating the experiment with one major difference—the descriptions/labels were supplied only at the time of retrieval. However, they still found that the subjects made distortions similar to the ones observed by Carmichael et al. (1932). In Chapter 11 you will learn about additional research that shows how easy it can be to induce changes in memory by asking "leading" questions and perhaps also by supplying subsequent misleading information.

## How Safe Are Our Memories?

In this chapter we have described the important role that schemas can play in determining the inferences we make (or don't make), what we select to encode and store, how this information is integrated with previous knowledge, and what we remember (Alba & Hasher, 1983; Mandler, 1984; Thorndyke, 1984). Everyone should be happy with the fact that schemas can facilitate our abilities to comprehend and remember. However, there's also considerable evidence to indicate that schemas can mislead us and can cause us to either make false inferences or remember inaccurately (e.g., Bartlett, 1932; Bransford & Franks, 1971; Carmichael et al., 1932; Hanawalt & Demarest, 1939; Searleman & Carter, 1988; Sulin & Dooling, 1974).

This raises an important question: How susceptible are our memories to reconstructive changes over time? The truth is that no one really knows. The process of remembering something is an active one in which the person tries to resurrect a past event. This resurrection is based on two things—the specific details (if any) still held in memory and the *schemas* the person has acquired that are relevant to the situation.

We do know that even memories that are very significant to us, and that are emotionally very arousing, still are prone to being wildly distorted or even completely forgotten (see Chapter 8). Perhaps the best way to minimize such memory errors is to overlearn the material we want to remember; this will leave many specific details in our memory and blunt the effects of schemas that would cause us to rely more on general knowledge and impressions. Sometimes it is not possible or feasible to overlearn material (if you witness a hit-and-run accident, you will not have the opportunity to study the details of it over and over again!). Although perhaps it is not very comforting to realize that our memories may not remain accurate over time, we should at least be aware that our memories are susceptible to reconstructive changes.

# SUMMARY

**I. Importance of Schemas**
- *Schemas* are mental representations of people, objects, situations, and events acquired through experience.

- How new information is integrated with previous knowledge, and the kinds of inferences that are made, can be greatly influenced by our schemas. Schemas also help us decide how information should be encoded, stored, and retrieved, and which information should receive this attention and processing.

## II. Major Types of Schemas

- Everyone has *person schemas* for others they know well. Person schemas consist of general knowledge and beliefs about other people's consistent traits and characteristics.
- A *self-schema*, as the name implies, consists of general knowledge that we believe is true about our own personality traits, abilities, goals, and so on.
- Another type of schema is called a *script*. Scripts, which start to develop at a very early age, contain generic knowledge that people have about common, frequently occurring events.
  - Some scripts provide a structure for the normal sequence of events during a routine activity. This allows an individual to anticipate what will happen next.
  - Scripts can often be useful for filling in missing details.
- It has been proposed that there are higher-order forms of scripts called *memory organization packets* (MOPs) and *thematic organization points* (TOPs).
  - A MOP is a collection of interrelated *scenes* (coherent segments of a script), while a TOP is a script that represents a high-level, often abstract theme.
  - The psychological reality of these two higher-order scripts has yet to be demonstrated.

## III. Theories of How Schemas Affect Memory

- Alba and Hasher proposed a model of how schemas should influence memory performance. The basic premise is that memory will be best for information that is consistent with, expected by, or relevant to the activated schema.
  - The model predicted that an activated schema would affect the encoding process by controlling the *selection, abstraction, interpretation*, and *integration* of information.
  - Although the research literature did provide some support for their prototypical schema model, Alba and Hasher believed that many research findings did not. This led them to conclude that schema theory was insufficient to account for the richness of human memory capabilities.
- Some researchers, however, have challenged the basic assumptions of the Alba and Hasher model, as well as Alba and Hasher's generally negative appraisal of the worth of schema theory.

· For instance, it can be argued that more than one schema is activated at any given time and, also in opposition to Alba and Hasher's model, that the actual function of schemas is to allow people to focus on the more novel and unexpected aspects of a situation. Views such as these can help account for many of the seemingly inconsistent or contradictory findings.

## IV. Facilitating Effects of Schemas

- Experiments such as the ones described by Bransford and Johnson clearly demonstrate the importance of having the right schema activated at the right time. To comprehend and remember complex information (especially if it is bizarre), the correct schema needs to be activated at the time of encoding.
- Research has also shown that having the proper schema at the time of retrieval can enhance memory performance.
- Schemas also affect the *incidental* encoding of information. Objects high in *schema expectancy* and *saliency* are likely to be remembered. As an illustration of the ability of schemas to lead us to fill in missing details, it was observed that people will often "remember" objects that were never present.

## V. Distorting Effects of Schemas

- Schemas can sometimes cause incorrect inferences to be made. If a distortion occurs at the encoding stage, it is called a *constructive change*, and if at retrieval, a *reconstructive change.*
- In many situations, both constructive and reconstructive changes will occur. One way to help distinguish between the two types of changes is by varying the time of retrieval. This was illustrated by citing research examining *pragmatic implications.* These are statements that lead people to believe something that is neither explicitly asserted nor necessarily implied.
- Bartlett's famous "War of the Ghosts" studies were among the first to clearly demonstrate the importance of having the proper schema for comprehending complex information.
- When ambiguous line drawings were assigned different descriptions, or labels, it was seen that schemas can also influence memory for visual stimuli.
- No one knows just how vulnerable our long-term memories are to reconstructive changes over time. A way to try to minimize the likelihood of such changes is to *overlearn* material.

# PART 3

———— ❖ ————

# The World Within Us

# 7

# *Biological Bases of Memory*

❖

*I*nvestigating the biological underpinnings of memory is a very hot research topic. And with good reason. While the topic is of great theoretical interest, if we had a thorough understanding of the biology of the memory process, there would be important practical benefits as well. As described later in this chapter (and in more depth in Chapter 14), there are many people who suffer memory disorders stemming from biological causes. With a better understanding of the biological processes involved, it is likely that both assessment of memory disorders and their treatment would markedly improve. It may also be possible to improve the memory capabilities of people with normal memory abilities through the use of drugs. In fact, as you will learn in this chapter, work is already progressing along these lines.

Many researchers have long sought to discover exactly *how* and *where* memory is stored in the brain. This has often been referred to as the "search for the engram." An *engram* is the term used to describe the memory trace that is presumably present in the brain after something has been learned. For many people interested in the area of memory, the search for the engram is their version of seeking the Holy Grail. Historically, there's been considerable debate over whether specific engrams are localized in discrete areas of the brain (Ramon y Cajal, 1911; Pavlov, 1927; Konorski, 1948; Hebb, 1949; Penfield & Jasper, 1954) or interwoven throughout the entire brain (Flourens, 1824; Koffka, 1935; Lashley, 1929, 1950).

It should be noted at the outset that not everyone is convinced that it is important (or even worthwhile) to search for the engram. For instance, Watkins (1990) has argued that memory theorizing using the notion of engrams, or memory traces, is misguided. He believes that to do so impedes our understanding of more important aspects of memory, such as context effects. Watkins's stance concerning the importance of knowing about memory traces, however, is clearly a minority viewpoint.

## THE EARLY SEARCH

Ivan Pavlov (1927) believed that during classical conditioning new connections were formed among neurons in the cerebral cortex of the brain. Although Pavlov himself never supplied any empirical evidence for this belief, in a classic series of studies Karl Lashley (1929) tried in vain to provide evidence that specific cortical connections are formed during conditioning procedures. In some of his studies, rats were trained to navigate through a maze with several blind alleys to find a goal box that contained food. After a rat had learned to run through the maze without error (typically for 10 consecutive trials), Lashley would destroy various parts of the rat's brain and then test the rat's ability to remember the correct pathways through the maze. In other experiments, to determine if it was possible to prevent learning from occurring in the first place, cortical tissue was destroyed before a rat was ever placed in the maze.

The results of Lashley's numerous studies indicated that removing parts of the cerebral cortex caused the rats to start making errors again and that the greater the cortical damage, the greater the number of errors. In addition, learning to traverse the maze flawlessly required many more trials if naive rats had parts of their cerebral cortex removed before conditioning started. However, much to Lashley's surprise (and disappointment), he found *no* evidence that destruction or removal of any *specific* area of the cerebral cortex could either erase the engram or cause learning to be prevented from occurring.

His results suggested that the amount of cortical tissue destroyed was far more important than the location of the damage. The results of his extensive series of studies forced him to reject, reluctantly, the *localizationist* position that he had originally set out to support. Instead, he came to champion the view that specific memories were diffusely distributed throughout the cerebral cortex and that all parts of the cortex were equally involved in learning. In summing up the results of his 30-year odyssey to find the engram, Lashley (1950) wrote the following famous lines:

> This series of experiments has yielded a good bit of information about what and where the memory trace is not. It has discovered nothing directly on the real nature of the engram. I sometimes feel, in reviewing the evidence on the localization of the memory trace, that the necessary conclusion is that learning just is not possible. (p. 477)

## THE MODERN VIEW OF THE ENGRAM

We now know that Lashley and others were wrong in thinking that the whole brain was involved in storing specific memories. Nevertheless, they were essentially correct with regard to their hypothesis that the information contained within an engram is interwoven throughout a neural unit. As Squire (1987) points out, the major difference between a localizationist and an antilocalizationist hypothesis centers on the issue of the *size* of the neural units involved. Today, it is widely believed that specific memories *are* localized in very discrete areas of the cerebral cortex. Some researchers have hypothesized that engrams are contained in functional units called *macrocolumns* that contain only a few dozen to a few hundred neurons (Mountcastle, 1979). Within each macrocolumn, an engram is supposedly distributed equally among the neurons, a proposition that's very similar to what Lashley and other antilocalizationists erroneously maintained occurred in the entire brain.

If all this is true, then why didn't Lashley find empirical evidence (that he doggedly sought in his maze experiments) that specific memories are highly localized? The answer is that Lashley probably didn't take into account the fact that a rat learns many things as it travels around the maze. For example, not only does it learn visual cues to find the correct paths to the goal box, but it also probably learns *kinesthetic* cues (information about where body parts are with respect to each other), *proprioceptive* cues (information about where we are and what each body part is doing), and *olfactory* cues (smell) as well. Therefore, many separate and widely dispersed engrams are laid down in the rat's cerebral cortex. When damage is done to one area—for example, the area containing the visual engrams—the rat can still find its way around the maze (although admittedly with more difficulty) by relying on the undamaged engrams from the other senses. The more cortex removed, the greater the likelihood that more sensory engrams will be lost, and so the greater the number of errors made. Had Lashley tested rats with damage in localized cortical areas for the effectiveness of *different* types of sensory cues, he would have discovered that specific areas of the cortex do indeed store specific sensory memories.

## *A* BRIEF OVERVIEW OF NEURONS AND THEIR FUNCTIONING

To appreciate much of what will be presented in the rest of this chapter, you will find that a brief discussion of the basic structure and functioning of neurons will be useful. As you probably already know, the neuron is the chief building block of the nervous system. In the central nervous system (comprising the brain and spinal cord) there are tens of billions of neurons. Every movement you make, every thought you have, every feeling you express, every memory you retrieve occurs because of the combined action of neurons communicating with each other.

The primary job of the neuron is to transmit information in the form of electrochemical impulses. Although neurons come in a variety of sizes, configurations, and degrees of complexity, they all have certain basic features and functions in common. As shown in Figure 7.1, each neuron has a *cell body,* multiple *dendrites,* and an *axon.* It is known that neurons do not physically touch each other; instead, a very small gap called a *synapse* separates them. Synapses measure only about 100 to 200 angstroms (an angstrom is one ten-

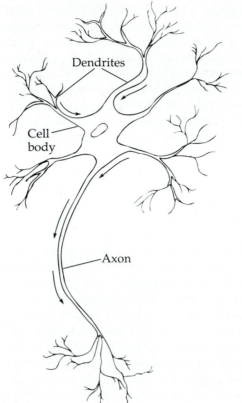

FIGURE 7.1
A typical neuron.

millionth of a millimeter) and can be found most typically between the axon of one neuron and the dendrite or cell body of another. A typical neuron has thousands of synapses with other neurons.

When a neuron is sufficiently stimulated, it produces an electrical impulse called an *action potential*. The action potential begins at the place where the axon is attached to the cell body and travels down the entire axon (which typically has several branches) at full force until it reaches the knoblike ends of the axon branches. These knoblike ends are called *terminal buttons*. The terminal buttons contain structures called *synaptic vesicles*, which are essentially bags full of *neurotransmitters*. When the action potential reaches the terminal buttons, the synaptic vesicles migrate to the *presynaptic membrane* (the membrane of the transmitting neuron) and release their neurotransmitters into the *synaptic cleft* (the gap that is also known as the synapse).

The neurotransmitters will then bind onto specific *receptor sites* that are embedded in the *postsynaptic membrane* (the membrane of the receiving neuron's dendrite or cell body). Similar to the way a key must have the right shape before it will work in a padlock, receptor sites (which are just complex molecules) will be activated only by those neurotransmitters that exactly fit their

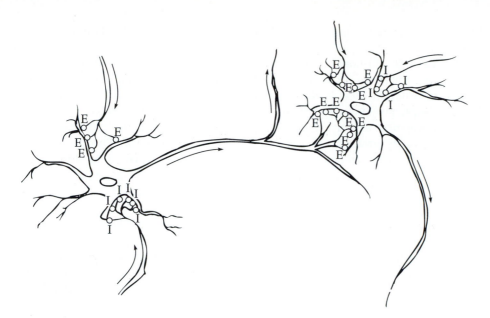

FIGURE 7.2
Two interacting neurons demonstrating excitatory (E) and inhibitory (I) impulses.

configuration. Dozens of different receptor-neurotransmitter combinations have been identified in recent years. Some of these combinations make it more likely that the receiving neuron will fire its own action potential (called an *excitatory synapse*), while others have the opposite effect, making it less likely that the receiving neuron will fire (called an *inhibitory synapse*). Since an individual neuron receives input from many different neurons at the same time, there are likely to be both excitatory and inhibitory synapses occurring simultaneously. If there are significantly more excitatory than inhibitory synapses, the receiving neuron will be stimulated to initiate its own action potential. If not, then the neuron will not fire (see Figure 7.2).

## BIOLOGICAL BASIS OF STM AND LTM

### A False Step

In the 1960s rapid advances were being made in understanding how chains of *deoxyribonucleic acid* (DNA) could act as the repository of genetic codes. And since genetic codes act something like memory traces (in that they both contain stored information), some researchers in the 1960s began to experiment with the idea that either *ribonucleic acid* (RNA) or *protein molecules* could be the biological code for storing individual memories. If memory storage was predominantly chemical in nature, and if a specific chemical coded for a specific memory, this suggested an interesting possibility. Perhaps memories could be "transferred" from a trained animal to a naive one by simple chemical injections.

So began the ill-fated "transfer" experiments of the 1960s and 1970s. A typical experiment might involve conditioning *planaria*, better known as flatworms, to constrict their bodies to a flashing light. Every time the light was flashed, the planaria were given an electric shock and would reflexively shrivel up. After learning to shrivel up in response to the light, the planaria were unceremoniously ground up and fed to untrained planaria. The previously naive planaria, who were turned into cannibals, would now also shrivel up when a light was presented (McConnell, 1962). Similar findings were reported if RNA from trained worms was directly injected into untrained worms (Jacobson, Fried, & Horowitz, 1966).

Ungar and his colleagues isolated and sequenced a 15-amino acid long peptide (a short fragment of a protein), which they dubbed *scotophobin,* meaning a "fear of darkness" in Greek. They found scotophobin in the brains of rats conditioned to avoid the dark but not in rats who were not so conditioned. When the scotophobin was injected into naive rats, they, too, avoided the dark (Ungar, Galvan, & Clark, 1968; Ungar, Ho, Galvan, & Desiderio, 1972).

As you might imagine, these results caused great excitement. They suggested that memory was stored as a chemical code that could be transferred from one animal to another. An unofficial journal was even published, called *The Worm Runners Digest,* to champion this view. The implications of this research were nothing less than astounding. Think about it—if specific memories could actually be transferred between trained and untrained animals, then it should be theoretically possible to artificially synthesize all sorts of memories. The possibilities would be almost limitless—if you wanted to learn about radio astronomy, then instead of spending years of hard work taking courses and reading books, all you might have to do is pay a visit to your local pharmacist and purchase the requisite series of pills, maybe even chocolate-flavored!

Unfortunately, because of the great difficulties that most researchers had in replicating the earlier work that showed the transfer of specific memories between planaria, the euphoria started to fade. And today, the general consensus is that such transfers are just not possible. The hypothesis that memory is stored in RNA or protein molecules and that extracts of these molecules can be transferred between animals is no longer accepted by most researchers. In the next section, however, we start to examine the types of changes that *do* occur as a result of experience.

## Anatomical Changes during Learning and Memory

Almost without exception, it is now taken for granted that the basis of all learning and memory must involve some anatomical changes in neurons or in their synaptic connections. Research has repeatedly shown that the chemistry and anatomy of the nervous system are changed in response to everyday experiences. Much of this work has been performed with newborn rats who were raised in radically different environments.

**Experience alters the brain of a rat.** In a series of studies started in the 1960s, groups of rats were raised in cages that provided either impoverished or enriched environments to determine if there would be any noticeable effects on brain growth and development. In an impoverished environment, a single rat was raised in a poorly illuminated cage with only food and water being available. In stark contrast, a rat raised in an enriched environment had a much larger cage and several litter mates with which to interact. Furthermore, the cage was equipped with ladders to climb, running wheels to turn, slides to go up and down, and various other "rat" toys that were periodically changed to increase variety.

After a suitable period of time in each environment, the rats were sacrificed, and their brains were inspected for differences. The inspections typically revealed clear evidence that differential experience altered the rats' brains. As might be expected, the changes all seemed to favor the rats who had lived in the enriched environments. Among other things, a rat raised in an enriched environment typically had a thicker cerebral cortex, a larger blood supply to the brain, an increased number of synaptic connections between neurons caused by greater branching of dendrites, and a greater number of glial cells, which are cells that support the metabolic activities of neurons (Rosenzweig, 1984; Rosenzweig & Bennett, 1972; Rosenzweig, Bennett, & Diamond, 1967; Rosenzweig, Krech, Bennett, & Diamond, 1962). The relevance of this type of research is that it clearly suggests that the type of environment that animals (including humans) are exposed to will have long-term biological effects on the brain.

**Simple learning in a simple organism: *Aplysia*, the sea snail.** Because of the great complexity of the nervous system of mammals, Eric Kandel and his associates decided to study the relatively simple nervous system of the sea snail *Aplysia californica*. There are only about 20,000 neurons in the *Aplysia* nervous system, and the individual neurons themselves are so large that they can be seen with the naked eye. This makes it much easier to examine in detail the synaptic basis of learning. Their hope was that by studying simple learning processes in a simple organism, they could learn something about how more complex systems (such as our own) worked as well. Largely owing to their exacting work, much has been learned in the last few years about the specific neural and chemical changes that occur during simple forms of learning in *Aplysia*.

As can be seen in Figure 7.3, a protective mantle shelf covers the gill of an *Aplysia*. At one end of the mantel shelf is a spout called the *siphon*. If either the mantel shelf or its siphon is touched, the sea snail will withdraw its gill into a cavity. This withdrawal reflex has been used to study the processes of *habitu-*

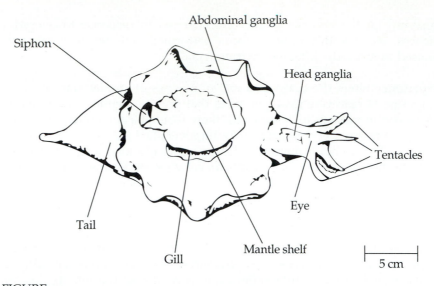

FIGURE 7.3
A sketch of *Aplysia*.
*Reprinted with the permission of McGraw-Hill, Inc. from A. Schneider and B. Tarshis,* An
Introduction to Physiological Psychology, *Third Edition, 1985, p. 509.*

*ation* and *sensitization*. Habituation is the *decrease* in responding to a repetitive
stimulus (discussed in Chapter 12 also), while sensitization is the *increase* in
responding to a repetitive stimulus. For example, the *Aplysia* will habituate, or
lessen, its withdrawal reflex to repeated light touches to its mantle shelf. However, if the *Aplysia* is first given an electric shock to its tail or head, this will
induce sensitization, and instead of weakening to the light touch to the mantle
shelf, the withdrawal reflex will become much stronger than it is normally.

The actual sets of neurons involved in learning habituation and sensitization in *Aplysia* have been discovered (Kandel & Schwartz, 1982). It has also
been found that habituation of the withdrawal reflex is caused by a lessening
of the excitatory postsynaptic potential of motor neurons involved in initiating
the withdrawal. This lessening of the excitatory postsynaptic potential makes
it less likely that the reflex will occur full force, which is exactly what one
would expect during habituation. Conversely, during sensitization, there is a
strengthening of the excitatory postsynaptic potential of the motor neurons.
This makes it more likely that a full-fledged withdrawal response will occur.

These changes in the excitatory postsynaptic potential have been traced to
changes in the ability of the presynaptic membrane to release neurotransmitters. During habituation there's a *decrease* in the release of neurotransmitters,
whereas during sensitization there's an *increase*. The rate of release of the neurotransmitters seems to be due to the number of calcium ions that enter the
presynaptic membrane. It is known that calcium causes synaptic vesicles to
move to the end of the presynaptic membrane and dump their neurotransmit-

ters into the synaptic cleft. The neurotransmitters then bind onto receptor sites on the postsynaptic membrane, causing an increase in the excitatory postsynaptic potential and thus making it more likely that the neuron will generate action potentials.

During habituation less calcium flows into the presynaptic membrane, which in turn means there's little release of neurotransmitters into the synaptic cleft. As a consequence, the excitatory postsynaptic potentials of the motor neurons are smaller. The end result is a lessening in the withdrawal reflex of the gill. During sensitization, however, more calcium ions flow into the presynaptic membrane, causing more neurotransmitters to be released, which then increases the excitatory postsynaptic potential. This finally results in an exaggerated withdrawal reflex, the hallmark of sensitization. Additional research has shown that classical conditioning of the withdrawal reflex is also possible and that similar processes are involved (Hawkins, Abrams, Carew, & Kandel, 1983).

It is truly remarkable how many intricate details are now known about basic learning and memory processes in *Aplysia* (Byrne, 1987; Carew, 1987; Carew, Marcus, Nolen, Rankin, & Stopfer, 1990; Mayford, Barzilai, Keller, Schacher, & Kandel, 1992). In addition to studying *Aplysia*, researchers have also studied simple associative learning in other invertebrates (animals without a backbone, or spinal column). For instance, much is known about the neuronal pathways and cellular changes involved in the classical conditioning of the marine snail *Hermissenda* to avoid moving toward light (Alkon, 1983; Crow & Alkon, 1978; Dudai, 1989).

It is still fair to ask what any of this has to do with the physiological basis of learning in higher animals. Does research on simple sea snails shed any light on how learning occurs in humans? Although unlikely, it is possible that the synaptic changes associated with learning in *Aplysia* and *Hermissenda* may apply only to invertebrates. Currently, the phenomenon known as *long-term potentiation* (described below) is the leading candidate to account for synaptic changes underlying learning in mammals such as us.

**More action at the synapse: Long-term potentiation.** If brief bursts of high-frequency electrical stimulation are applied to certain pathways in the hippocampus of animals such as rabbits, rats, or guinea pigs, this produces long-lasting increases in excitatory presynaptic or postsynaptic potentials in the affected neurons (Bliss & Lomo, 1973; Brown, Chapman, Kairiss, & Keenan, 1988; Huang, Colino, Selig, & Malenka, 1992; Lynch, 1986; Lynch & Baudry, 1984; Teyler & DiScenna, 1987; Zalutsky & Nicoll, 1990). This increase can last for weeks or months and is called *long-term potentiation* (LTP). The "potentiation" refers to the fact that the next time the affected neurons receive stimulation, their response is bigger than if they hadn't previously been exposed to bursts of high-frequency stimulation. What makes this line of research especially exciting is that the hippocampus, a part of the limbic system of the brain, plays a major role in the formation of most human long-term memories.

There are several different types of LTP (Lynch, Granger, & Staubli, 1991), and LTP has been observed in many areas of the brain other than just the hippocampus (Abraham, Corballis, & White, 1991; Iriki, Pavlides, Keller, & Asanuma, 1989; Teyler, 1991). In addition, there is still considerable controversy over the exact mechanisms leading to the increases in synaptic conductance observed between neurons. One proposed mechanism suggests that induction of LTP involves the influx of calcium ions into the postsynaptic membrane. The calcium then activates an enzyme that causes more receptors for the excitatory neurotransmitter *glutamate* to become functional. The increased number of receptors results in greater uptake of glutamate from the synaptic cleft. This, in turn, produces increases in the excitatory postsynaptic potentials (Lynch & Baudry, 1984).

It is important to remember that there are other proposed mechanisms for LTP and that some people believe that LTP depends on presynaptic as well as postsynaptic changes (e.g., Schuman & Madison, 1991). Furthermore, it is also clear that many additional factors (such as the action of several types of neurotransmitters and hormones) influence the induction, maintenance, and modulation of LTP (Dudai, 1989). An important goal for researchers is to show that LTP, which is induced by *artificial* stimulation of neurons, involves processes that are similar to ones that operate when action potentials are produced *naturally* during the learning process. Although much further work needs to be done in this regard, there's already some promising evidence that there are significant links between normal learning procedures and LTP (Berger, 1984; Landfield & Deadwyler, 1988; McNaughton, Barnes, Rao, Baldwin, & Rasmussen, 1986; Morris, Anderson, Lynch, & Baudry, 1986; Roman, Staubli, & Lynch, 1987).

**Hebb's two-stage process of memory formation.** In 1949, the Canadian psychologist Donald Hebb proposed a two-stage process of memory formation that is still considered by some researchers to be the best model of how short-term memories are maintained and how these memories can eventually become engrained in LTM. There are two basic stages of the model. In the first stage, environmental events or stimuli cause groups of interconnected neurons called *cell assemblies* (or *neural nets*, the currently more fashionable term) to set into motion a reverberating electrical signal. Figure 7.4 shows how this reverberation is maintained in a neural net containing only a few neurons. In actuality, there are undoubtedly many more neurons involved in a series of circuits, with each neuron receiving inputs from several other neurons simultaneously. Notwithstanding the additional complexity, the principle remains essentially the same as shown in Figure 7.4: the short-term memory for an event or stimulus is achieved for as long as the neural net continues to reverberate.

What about LTM? This is where the second stage of Hebb's model is important. Hebb believed that if uninterrupted for a long enough period of time, the reverberations during the STM stage would cause anatomical changes in the neurons themselves or their synaptic connections. These physical changes

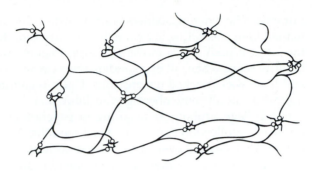

FIGURE 7.4
An example of a reverberating circuit of interacting neurons.

could take many different forms. For example, more receptors in the postsynaptic membrane could become active to bind with neurotransmitters; synaptic membranes could become larger, making the synaptic cleft smaller; synaptic strength between neurons could increase (in other words, it might become easier for one neuron to excite neighboring neurons to fire); new synapses could form between neurons; and so forth. Some of these proposed changes (such as more receptor sites or increased synaptic strength) are similar to ones that reportedly happen during the process of LTP. Indeed, the phenomenon of LTP and the mechanism by which it is achieved fit nicely with Hebb's model.

A particular memory, according to Hebb, would remain fragile and vulnerable to disruption during the first stage (i.e., during the reverberating part) and would remain so until completion of the second stage, when the anatomical changes were complete and the memory became a permanent one. There are likely to be several different (and probably overlapping) circuits of neurons to represent the same or similar memories. This provides for a needed degree of redundancy, since individual neurons often die. Hebb's model, however, probably doesn't apply to all forms of learning. Some forms of learning do not seem to progress from STM to LTM. For example, many incremental forms of learning such as classical conditioning may not involve an STM stage at all. Instead, the anatomical changes produced by learning seem to lead directly to LTM.

## CONSOLIDATION THEORY OF MEMORY FORMATION

Today it is widely accepted that the transformation from STM to LTM is usually a progressive one and that while a particular memory is in transition, it is susceptible to disruption or even erasure. This is known as the *consolidation theory of memory*. This theory maintains that most events and stimuli are *not* immediately placed into LTM; instead, only gradually, and only under certain circumstances, do they become consolidated, or relatively fixed, in our memory.

The most dramatic evidence supporting consolidation theory comes from humans who have sustained brain injuries. For instance, suppose a person named John was riding in a car driven by his sister Elise. They had just watched the latest Woody Allen movie at a local theater, and Elise was describing her favorite scene when, all of a sudden, their car was hit broadside by another car and Elise was knocked unconscious. Upon regaining consciousness, Elise had no trouble at all remembering who John was, or where she lived, or that she was a college sophomore majoring in psychology. However, Elise had absolutely no recollection that she had just seen the Woody Allen movie or, for that matter, that she had even been in a car accident.

This is a very common scenario, one that unfortunately happens regularly whenever one loses normal consciousness for an extended period of time. What Elise was suffering from is called *retrograde amnesia*—a loss of memory for events occurring prior to the onset of the disturbance causing the amnesia. Events experienced somewhat prior to the trauma are at least temporarily lost; events occurring at the actual time of the trauma are lost forever. Rarely is there any loss of memory for events that occurred much earlier than the trauma, explaining why Elise could still recognize her brother, recall where she lived, and remember that she was a psychology major. With the passage of sufficient time most of the events initially lost will be recovered, with the more distant memories coming back first. So Elise will probably first recall that she drove with her brother John to the movie theater; then she will remember that she saw the Woody Allen movie and, finally, that on the drive home an accident occurred. However, with regard to the actual impact of the crash, it is unlikely that Elise will ever be able to recall it.

Consolidation theory can account for much of what happened to Elise. When she was knocked unconscious, the trauma she experienced interfered with the neural activity (perhaps in the form of a Hebbian reverberating circuit described earlier) that was maintaining her STM. The material in STM at the time of the accident (in this case, the actual impact of the crash and perhaps also the fact that Elise was recalling her favorite scene from the movie) was erased completely and will never be retrievable. This happened because there was insufficient time for any anatomical changes to occur in the neurons maintaining the memory traces in STM or in their synaptic connections. Therefore, the memory traces never made it to LTM. The complete erasure of STM at the time of a head injury is the reason why people rarely can recall the actual impact of *any* injury that results in an appreciable length of unconsciousness.

Why were more distant memories not affected at all? What about the memories that were only temporarily lost and then slowly came back? Why do chronologically older memories come back first? Although definitive answers to these questions can't be stated with authority yet, consolidation theory can offer some reasonable explanations. The more distant memories (e.g., Elise's recognition of John) had likely already reached a point of stability in LTM such that they were quite resistant to disruption and therefore could be easily retrieved. On the other hand, memories that were temporarily lost but eventually recovered (e.g., Elise's remembering that she went to the movies) may have been in the process of becoming long-term memories at the time of the accident, but since consolidation was still incomplete, those memories became more difficult to retrieve for a period of time.

The types of memory problems that our fictitious Elise experienced are common for those who have had head injuries resulting in a period of unconsciousness. Research suggests that such brain injuries may have at least two effects on the memory system. First, the trauma may effectively erase what is currently in STM, and second, it may also interfere with the retrieval of memories still being consolidated into LTM. And there is a likely corollary for this second effect: retrieval is easier for memories that are further along in the consolidation process. If this is true, then it can explain why chronologically older memories are the ones most likely to recover the quickest.

In the rest of this chapter, we will describe how the consolidation process can be studied experimentally by artificially inducing amnesia; how the degree of neural arousal is related to memory consolidation; how various drugs, neurotransmitters, hormones, and stimulants can influence consolidation processes; the relationship between sleeping and consolidation; the brain areas most involved in the process of consolidation; and, finally, why it may be beneficial to have a lengthy consolidation period.

## Experimentally Induced Amnesia and Consolidation

Since the 1930s it has been known that supplying brief pulses of electricity to the temples of the brain will produce convulsions. When people suffering from deep depression are given *electroconvulsive therapy,* the convulsions can greatly reduce depressive symptoms. However, upon awakening from the convulsions, people also experience retrograde amnesia. They have, for instance, no memory of the treatment itself and often little memory for other events that happened earlier that day. Voluminous amounts of additional data supporting consolidation theory have been obtained by *experimentally* inducing retrograde amnesia in lower animals through *electroconvulsive shock* (ECS, as it is called when not used in a therapeutic setting).

A classic study by Chorover and Schiller (1965) will be used to give you the flavor of these experiments. Prior to their experiment, a set of wires was attached to the head of each rat so that the rat could be given ECS whenever the experimenter wished. Chorover and Schiller then conditioned groups of rats to learn a passive avoidance task in a single trial. On the first day of testing, when the rats stepped off a raised platform, they received a brief but painful footshock. In this kind of conditioning, if the rats are now placed back in their cages and left otherwise undisturbed, then upon being placed on the raised platform the next day, they will refuse to step off, evidently remembering the previous day's shock.

Using different groups of rats, Chorover and Schiller varied the time interval between giving rats the footshock and giving them a dose of ECS. When

"Do you still remember I owe you fifty dollars?"

FIGURE 7.5
A cartoon showing the amnesic effects of ECS.

they tested the rats the following day, they found that whether or not a rat remembered to stay put on the platform was a direct function of how soon after the footshock the ECS had been given. The shorter the time between the footshock and the ECS, the more likely it was that the rat would step off the platform, suggesting that memory for the aversive footshock was forgotten. Amnesia was greatest if only 1/2 second separated the footshock and the onset of ECS. However, if the interval between the footshock and the ECS was at least 10 seconds, significantly less amnesia was found, and if the ECS was administered about 30 seconds after the footshock, there was no evidence of any amnesia at all.

In addition to rat studies, numerous variations of this type of consolidation experiment have been conducted on such diverse animals as bees, monkeys, birds, and fish. The general finding from all these studies is basically the same: the shorter the time interval between the initial learning of a task and the disrupting situation (such as the administration of ECS), the less likely it will be that the task will be recalled. What has historically been controversial is not whether or not consolidation of memory takes place but rather how long the process takes. Some researchers believe that consolidation is normally completed in a matter of seconds or minutes, while others (especially those who work with human amnesics) hypothesize that consolidation can sometimes take years before completion (Squire, 1987).

## The Arousal Hypothesis of Memory Consolidation

It has been hypothesized that the amount of memory consolidation that occurs in a given situation is related to the degree of neural activity in certain areas of the brain directly following learning. This neural activity, or arousal, is believed either to make chemical reactions occur in the brain that encode the memory (chemically or by producing neural changes) or to reflect chemical, electrical, or anatomical changes that occur during learning. In this chapter the physiological evidence that arousal is important for memory consolidation will be described, while in Chapter 8, the effects that arousal has on what we choose to attend to and encode will be presented.

According to the arousal hypothesis of memory consolidation, if neural activity is low or if it is disrupted, there will be *less* consolidation. The retrograde amnesia that is evident after ECS in lower animals and that occurs naturally following certain brain injuries in humans is certainly consistent with this arousal hypothesis. However, there's another interesting implication of this hypothesis. If retrograde amnesia presumably is the result of lower or disrupted neural activity, then it should also be possible to demonstrate *retrograde facilitation* by increasing neural activity. Furthermore, this facilitation (or increased memory performance) should be most evident if the neural activity increases right after learning has occurred.

Is there any evidence to support the notion of retrograde facilitation? Yes; in fact, the evidence abounds. For instance, if rats are given direct electrical stimulation in areas of the brain that are known to be involved in neural arousal (e.g., the hippocampus, the amygdala, or the reticular formation), then recall of information is enhanced. As would be expected, given the importance of the timing of a disruption in the appearance of retrograde amnesia, the effects of brain stimulation on facilitating retention occur only when the stimulation is given soon after the initial learning. If there is a delay in administering the stimulation, there will be no evidence of enhanced recall (McGaugh & Gold, 1976). As with many other things in life, too much of a good thing is not beneficial: if too much stimulation is given, it results in disruption, and retention is impaired.

## Effects of Drugs, Neurotransmitters, Hormones, and Stimulants

There is a vast and complex literature on the effects that various drugs and chemicals have on cognitive functioning, including memory (for recent reviews, see Gold, 1987; Hock, 1987; Martinez, 1986; Martinez, Schulteis, & Weinberger,

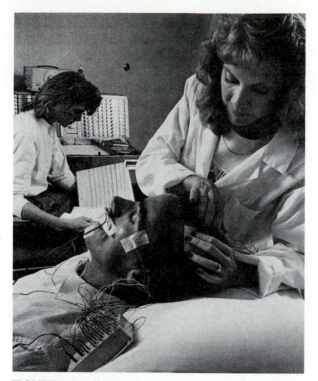

FIGURE 7.6
Scientists use many methods to probe the biological workings of memory.
*Grant LeDuc/Monkmeyer.*

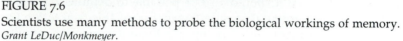

1991; McGaugh, 1989, 1990; Squire, 1987). The specific effect that a given substance will have on learning and/or memory usually is a function of many
factors. For instance, whether there is an enhancing or an inhibiting effect or
no effect at all will often critically depend on the exact nature of the task learned,
how well the task was learned, how arousing the task itself was, when the
substance was given (i.e., before or after learning, and how long before or
after), the dosage level, how fast the substance was metabolized, and so forth.
In our thumbnail sketch below of this highly technical area, you will see that
in spite of all these complicating factors, there is very good evidence that a
large number of substances that affect the arousal level of the nervous system
also affect memory consolidation.

**Benzodiazepines.** Probably the most widely prescribed psychoactive
drugs (drugs that alter consciousness, mood, and cognitive processing) over
the last 20 or 30 years have been the *benzodiazepines* (BZs). The BZs are sold
under a variety of different trade names (popular ones you may be familiar
with include Librium and Valium) and are prescribed to treat such problems
as sleeping disorders, anxiety, depression, epilepsy, panic, and muscular ten-
sion (Stephens, Duka, & Andrews, 1991). It has been repeatedly observed that

a side effect of many BZs is that they markedly impair memory ability. Specifically, while STM and LTM appear to be largely unaffected, the ability to encode new information is often greatly disrupted by certain BZs (Stephens et al., 1991). In fact, because of this selective memory dysfunction, some BZs have deliberately been given to patients to induce amnesia for the pain and unpleasantness surrounding surgery. The BZs are known to have a sedative effect on the nervous system. And a lower arousal level, coupled with a disrupted ability to encode new information into LTM, certainly is consistent with the arousal theory of memory consolidation described in the last section.

**Neurotransmitters.** There's an extensive literature showing that, depending on exactly when they are administered and in what doses, drugs that affect the ability of neurons to secrete the neurotransmitter *acetylcholine* into their synapses can either improve or retard memory (Squire, 1987). Typically, drugs that interfere with the normal use of acetylcholine prevent the formation of new memories. One such drug is *scopolamine,* which appears to primarily interfere with the central executive of working memory (see Chapter 3). Put another way, scopolamine disrupts the active processing of information (Frith, 1991; Rusted, 1988). Some naturally occurring plants contain scopolamine, and for centuries, knowledgeable people have used these plants for their memory-disrupting effects. For example, in Haiti, there is a plant called the "zombie's cucumber" that contains scopolamine, and because of its disorienting and amnesic properties, it is frequently used in ceremonies in which a person is turned into a zombie (Davis, 1988). As we will discuss in greater detail in Chapter 14, the tremendous loss of acetylcholine-secreting neurons is a hallmark of the devastating *Alzheimer's disease,* a fatal disorder in which memory loss is a prominent initial feature.

It has also been discovered that the neurotransmitter *norepinephrine* can enhance memory performance when given in the proper dosage immediately following learning. Likewise, the injection of drugs that increase the level of norepinephrine will have similar beneficial effects. In addition, drugs administered soon after learning that decrease the amount of norepinephrine lead to memory impairment. Research has further shown that drugs that block the receptors for the neurotransmitter *gamma-amino butyric acid* (GABA) enhance retention, whereas drugs that activate GABA receptors impair retention (Breen & McGaugh, 1961; Brioni & McGaugh, 1988; Brioni, Nagahara, & McGaugh, 1989; Castellano, Brioni, Nagahara, & McGaugh, 1989).

In general, the research on the effects of neurotransmitters on memory performance supports the arousal theory of memory consolidation. Increased levels of acetylcholine and norepinephrine are associated with higher levels of neural activity (and better memory performance), while increased levels of GABA are linked to lower levels of neural activity (and poorer memory performance).

**Hormones and stimulants.** There are also a variety of hormones and stimulants, such as *adrenocorticotrophic hormone* (ACTH), *epinephrine* (commonly known as adrenaline), *vasopressin*, and *amphetamines*, that are correlated with high arousal levels or stress. In general, to enhance memory these chemicals usually need to be administered within a few minutes of the original learning and in low doses. Similar to the effects of excessive electrical stimulation, if the dose is too high, memory is usually impaired (perhaps because the neural activity level is raised too high, causing disruption in the consolidation process). In addition, if other drugs are given that either increase or deplete the levels of these hormones and stimulants, memory will be enhanced or impaired, respectively. Also consistent with the arousal theory of memory consolidation is the finding that memory performance will be negatively affected only by antidepressants that are *also* sedatives; antidepressants that are not sedatives will not adversely affect memory (Curran, Sakulsriprong, & Lader, 1988).

**Interactions.** There's also good evidence that drugs, hormones, opiates, and neurotransmitters interact with each other, and with other ongoing metabolic or cognitive processes, to influence memory. For instance, it has been suggested that the massive release of hormones during highly emotional or stressful events is responsible for the establishment of vivid, long-lasting recollections of the events. These have been called *flashbulb memories* (Brown & Kulik, 1977) and will be discussed in more detail in Chapter 8.

As another example of the types of interactions that can occur, memory is apparently affected by the ability of the hormone epinephrine to influence the release of the neurotransmitter norepinephrine within the *amygdala,* a part of the limbic system that we will soon see has an important part to play in memory consolidation (Liang, Juler, & McGaugh, 1986; McGaugh, 1990, 1991). It has also been found that opiates (such as *B-endorphin*) that are released in times of stress or pain generally impair memory by inhibiting the release of norepinephrine in the amygdala (McGaugh, 1990). In addition, when epinephrine is released during times of stress or high arousal, the amount of glucose in the bloodstream dramatically increases. Glucose, which is a very simple sugar and one of the major sources of energy for the brain, can itself apparently influence memory consolidation.

**Effects of glucose.** In several studies, elderly people were asked to drink lemonade that was sweetened with either saccharin or glucose. Performance on subsequent memory tests revealed that those people who had glucose in their lemonade did better than those who had saccharin (Gold, 1987; Hall, Gonder-Frederick, Chewning, Silveira, & Gold, 1989; Manning, Hall, & Gold, 1990). It was also discovered that, in general, the elderly people who displayed a poor memory ability also had poor regulation of blood glucose (Hall et al., 1989). It has also been reported that glucose administration can enhance memory in aged rats and mice as well (Gold & Stone, 1988). The results from these glucose studies provide further support for the arousal theory of memory consolidation, because glucose is vital for maintaining a high level of brain activity, and increases in glucose are correlated with increases in memory performance.

## REM Sleep and Memory Consolidation

Sleep is an altered state of consciousness that is composed of a number of different stages. One particularly important stage is called the *rapid eye movement* (REM) stage. During a REM episode (there are usually four or five REM episodes during a normal night), a person is soundly sleeping and is typically dreaming. Paradoxically, although the major muscles of the body are effectively paralyzed during REM sleep (perhaps so that we will not be able to act out our dreams), there are also signs of nervous system arousal. For example, the brain wave patterns, blood pressure levels, evidence of sexual arousal, and breathing and heartbeat rates during REM sleep all resemble those of an excited and awake person, not what would be expected from a person who is deeply asleep.

Because of the arousal of the nervous system during REM episodes, it has been hypothesized that REM sleep can play a central role in producing memory consolidation. Several studies have shown, in both lower animals and humans, that when REM sleep is disrupted, recall of previously learned material drops significantly (Bloch, Hennevin, & Leconte, 1979; Cartwright, Lloyd, Butters, Weiner, McCarthy, & Hancock, 1975; Pearlman & Becker, 1973; Scrima, 1982; but see Schoen & Badia, 1984, for when REM sleep disruption did not interfere with memory).

It is interesting to note that newborn infants spend up to 50 percent of their sleep time in REM sleep, while older children spend about 30 to 40 percent, college-age people about 20 to 25 percent, and elderly people only about 5 percent. If REM sleep does aid memory consolidation, then it makes good sense that so much of newborn infants' sleep time is devoted to REM sleep; their need to acquire new information is much greater than it is for older people.

## Brain Areas Important for Consolidation

It should be clearly recognized that many areas of the brain need to act in concert for learning and memory to occur. Nevertheless, there are two major brain areas highly interconnected with each other that seem to be particularly vital to memory consolidation. These areas are the *medial temporal regions* (which are the inner areas of the two temporal lobes of the cerebral cortex) and the *diencephalon region* (which is a more central area of the brain composed of the thalamus and the hypothalamus).

Within the medial temporal regions, the *hippocampus* and the *amygdala* have been shown to be particularly important for memory consolidation. The most important structures within the diencephalon region are the *mammillary bodies* (which are structures in the posterior part of the hypothalamus) and the *dorsomedial thalamic nuclei* (collections of similarly shaped neurons on the upper part of the thalamus). Figure 7.7 shows where these structures are in the brain.

Largely on the basis of work with human amnesics who have suffered organic brain damage and models of human amnesia in monkeys, it is now

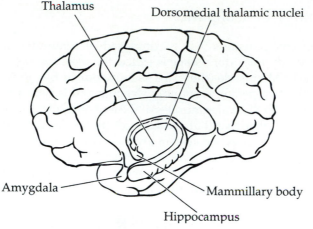

Thalamus

Dorsomedial thalamic nuclei

Amygdala

Mammillary body

Hippocampus

FIGURE 7.7
A diagram of the brain showing the position of the hippocampus, amygdala, mammillary body, and dorsomedial thalamic nuclei.

well accepted that these regions of the brain, particularly the medial temporal regions (e.g., Squire & Zola-Morgan, 1991), are responsible for the consolidation of certain types of memories but not others. What is not well accepted, however, is how to classify the type of learning that is preserved and the type that is impaired. One of the more popular ways of trying to capture the distinction has been to suggest that *declarative* knowledge (see Chapter 3) is largely lost but not *nondeclarative* knowledge (Cohen & Squire, 1980; Squire, 1986, 1987; Squire, Cohen, & Nadel, 1984; Squire, Knowlton, & Musen, 1993). As will be seen in Chapter 14, there are some problems with conceptualizing the memory abilities and disabilities of amnesics into these two categories (McCarthy & Warrington, 1990). However, none of the other popular divisions of memory (such as *semantic* versus *episodic*) or types of memory processing (such as *explicit* versus *implicit*) can fully account for the memory capabilities of amnesics either.

Are the medial temporal and diencephalic regions the actual sites of short- and long-term declarative memories? The answer is probably no. Unless it is overly taxed (see Chapter 14), short-term declarative memory is largely intact in people with amnesia caused by damaging either the medial temporal regions or the diencephalic region. Therefore, it seems highly unlikely that the STM engrams that exist following the onset of amnesia are stored in these regions of the brain. It also doesn't seem reasonable to believe that long-term memories are normally stored in these two areas, because after a person becomes amnesic following damage to either of these areas, it is well known that memories from the distant past are still readily retrievable. Now if the medial temporal and diencephalon regions were normally the repository of long-term declarative memories, a substantial proportion of these memories would be expected to perish during bouts of amnesia. But this rarely happens.

If the medial temporal and diencephalon regions are not where short- and long-term declarative memories are stored, then where are they stored? Converging evidence suggests that there is an important link between the sensory

/perceptual processing areas of the cerebral cortex and short- and long-term storage of information (Squire, 1987; Squire, Knowlton, & Musen, 1993). Specifically, it is believed that the cortical areas that are responsible for processing particular types of sensory data (such as incoming visual or auditory information) are the same areas of the brain in which short-term and long-term memories for these types of information are stored. At a later time, the stored information is also represented more abstractly in other cortical areas, areas not specifically tied to the sensory modality from which the original information was obtained.

It is hypothesized that for a *limited* amount of time after the learning of declarative knowledge, the medial temporal and diencephalic regions establish a relationship with LTM sites in the cerebral cortex. This relationship facilitates the consolidation and retrieval of declarative but not nondeclarative memories. After a period of time (which may be several years, according to some researchers), declarative knowledge stored in the cerebral cortex eventually becomes sufficiently consolidated, or fixed; thus these memories finally achieve complete independence from the structures of the medial temporal lobes and diencephalon. But until this time occurs, damage to or destruction of these areas will preclude new declarative learning from starting the consolidation process and will also prevent recently obtained declarative information from completing consolidation.

Nondeclarative information or memories, however, are spared during amnesia because they are obtained *incrementally* and hence do not proceed from STM to LTM in the same fashion as do declarative memories. Therefore, it has been claimed that these types of memories do not rely on the integrity of the medial temporal and diencephalic regions to become well established (Squire, 1987). Instead, research has suggested that the *cerebellum*, shown in Figure 7.8, may be an important area of the brain for establishing nondeclarative memories.

For instance, it is possible to classically condition a rabbit to close its *nictitating membrane* in response to a tone that is immediately followed by a puff

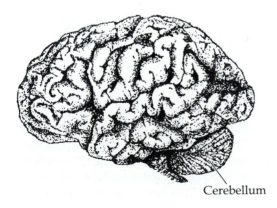

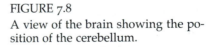

Cerebellum

FIGURE 7.8
A view of the brain showing the position of the cerebellum.

of air. (A nictitating membrane is a protective "third eyelid" that reflexively closes when a stimulus suddenly threatens the eye; it is found in cats, rabbits, and certain kinds of fish and birds.) Thompson, Berger, and Madden (1983) showed that a lesion to a certain part of the cerebellum of a classically conditioned rabbit will result in the abolishment of the conditioned response (i.e., the closing of the nictitating membrane when a tone sounds). Leaton and Supple (1986) have also discovered that removal of a part of the cerebellum disrupts the LTM for habituating to loud sounds in rats. The cerebellum is a very likely area for the storage of nondeclarative memories—it is heavily involved in our learning of coordinated movements (such as learning the backstroke or a new dance routine), exactly the kind of knowledge that makes up many of our nondeclarative memories.

## Reasons for Consolidation

The fact that the retention of a specific engram can be either inhibited or enhanced by post-learning events has led some memory researchers to prefer to use the term *modulation,* instead of *consolidation,* to refer to the establishment of long-term memories. Regardless of which term is used to represent the process, some fundamental questions still arise. For instance, isn't it a distinct disadvantage to have to wait long periods of time (some believe years) for many of our memories to become relatively fixed in LTM, all this time being susceptible to disruption? Wouldn't it be more efficient (and safer) to instantly, or at least within a minimum amount of time, have recent events, facts, and situations firmly placed within LTM?

Although we really don't know why from an evolutionary perspective the process of memory consolidation takes so long, we can offer a reason why it should not occur too quickly. You'll remember from Chapter 3 that all of us are constantly being bombarded with incoming sensory information. However, all animals (including humans) have only a limited capacity to process this massive amount of sensory input. Luckily, most of the information is only of momentary interest and will soon be of no real importance when the moment passes. So, we would definitely not want to preserve this inconsequential information in LTM. For example, if you're playing a game of Ping-Pong, it's certainly important to remember exactly where on the table your opponent hits the ball and with what type of spin, information that is stored for a second or two in your visual sensory register. But after you return the ball, you no longer need to maintain this specific information. What will be retained is general information acquired over time (e.g., that your opponent likes to use top spin a lot). Unless there is something particularly striking or vital about the previous play (remember that arousal improves the likelihood of consolidation), the very specific details quickly decay from the sensory register and are gone forever.

If memory consolidation happened too quickly, then countless millions of pieces of trivial information (such as all your plays and shots in every Ping-

Pong game you've ever played!) would end up being stored as permanent engrams. This would be an incredible waste of space and resources. However, *only* if you are aroused (e.g., your last shot wins the dorm championship) will what would otherwise have been a trivial piece of information, destined to vanish into the ether, be kept for further processing. In order to sort out the chaff from the wheat, so to speak, we may have to pay the price of having a long process of consolidation. However, why consolidation may extend for years is still a mystery awaiting an answer.

# SUMMARY

## I. Searching for the Engram
- An *engram* is a memory trace present in the brain after something has been learned.
- In the nineteenth century and the earlier part of this century, a debate raged over whether specific engrams were localized in discrete areas of the brain (a view championed by the *localizationists*) or interwoven throughout the whole brain (as believed by the *antilocalizationists*).
- The modern view is that specific engrams may be localized in small functional units called *macrocolumns* in the cerebral cortex. However, similar to the belief of the antilocalizationists, within each macrocolumn an engram is thought to be equally distributed.

## II. Overview of Neurons
- When sufficiently stimulated, a neuron will generate an *action potential*.
- An action potential causes various *neurotransmitters* to be released into the *synaptic cleft*, and when they bind onto *receptor sites*, they can either increase the probability that the receiving neuron will eventually fire an action potential of its own (called an *excitatory synapse*) or decrease the probability (called an *inhibitory synapse*).

## III. Biological Basis of STM and LTM
- At one time it was thought that *RNA* or *protein molecules* could code for specific memories. This led to the famous "transfer" experiments of the 1960s and 1970s.
- The notion that memory can be stored in complex molecules is no longer accepted by most people.

## IV. Anatomical Changes during Learning and Memory
- Most current memory researchers now believe that learning and memory involve anatomical changes in neurons or in their synaptic connections.
- Evidence to support this hypothesis can be found in studies showing brain alterations as a function of the environment in which an organism

has been raised, in the work on habituation and sensitization in the sea snail *Aplysia,* and in the exciting work being done on *long-term potentiation* (LTP) in mammals.

## V. Hebb's Two-Stage Model

- According to *Hebb's two-stage model of memory formation,* in the first stage short-term memories are represented and maintained by reverberating groups of interconnected neurons. The second stage involves anatomical changes in the neurons or their interconnections brought about by sufficiently long periods of the reverberations. The anatomical alterations result in the long-term storage of the information.

## VI. Consolidation Theory of Memory Formation

- The *consolidation theory of memory,* like Hebb's model, holds that the transformation from temporary memory to a more permanent memory is a progressive one. But unlike Hebb's model, consolidation theory doesn't necessarily believe that reverberating neural nets are responsible for temporary memory and, eventually, the establishment of relatively permanent memory.

- Evidence abounds in support of consolidation theory. For example, consolidation theory does an excellent job in accounting for the memory dysfunctions that accompany *retrograde amnesia* in victims of head trauma. It can also readily explain phenomena associated with experimentally induced amnesia.

## VII. The Arousal Hypothesis of Memory Consolidation

- The *arousal hypothesis of memory consolidation* maintains that the higher the levels of neural activity (within limits) directly following a learning episode, the greater the likelihood that memory consolidation will occur. This implies that *retrograde facilitation* should be possible by increasing neural activity following learning.

- Evidence supporting arousal theory comes from brain stimulation studies; from the effects of drugs, neurotransmitters, hormones, and stimulants that influence arousal levels; and from the relationship between memory performance and amount of REM sleep obtained.

## VIII. Brain Areas Important for Consolidation

- Brain areas particularly important for memory consolidation are structures in the *medial temporal regions* (especially the *hippocampus* and *amygdala*) and, to a lesser extent, structures in the diencephalon region (especially the *mammillary bodies* and the *dorsomedial thalamic nuclei*).

- One popular view holds that when these brain areas are damaged, the resulting amnesia adversely affects consolidation of *declarative memories* but not *nondeclarative memories.*

- The initial storage sites for short- and long-term declarative memories are probably not these brain areas; the sites are believed to be the *sensory modality* areas of the cerebral cortex. After a period of time has elapsed, this information is stored in more abstract form in other cortical areas.
- The *cerebellum* is believed to play an important role in the establishment of nondeclarative memories.

## IX. Reasons for Consolidation
- If memory consolidation occurred too quickly, then enormous amounts of trivial information would be stored as permanent engrams. This does not explain, however, why specific memories sometimes take years to reach complete consolidation.

# 8

# *Effects of Arousal, Stress, and Emotion*

❖

S uch emotional highs and lows as falling in love, witnessing the death of a close relative, or scoring the winning goal in a championship soccer game clearly reveal that our prevailing mood can have a profound influence on our cognitive functioning. During the last two decades there's been an explosion of research interest concerning the effects that arousal, stress, and emotional states can have on cognitive processes, especially on memory performance. In fact, a new scientific journal (*Cognition and Emotion*) was created in 1987 expressly to investigate these issues in depth. In this chapter we will explore the fascinating interrelationship between affective states and memory functioning. We will start by considering the influence that arousal has on memory functioning.

## *A*ROUSAL

In Chapter 7 we explained that changes in arousal can have a major impact on the likelihood of memory consolidation. And we know that arousal levels vary enormously, encompassing a continuum that goes from being trapped in a coma at one extreme to experiencing sheer terror or immense excitement at the other. Vast physiological changes, such as dramatic shifts in blood pressure, heart rate, breathing patterns, and hormonal production, are often associated with different levels of arousal. We also know that changes in arousal usually accompany changes in stress level and emotional states. Therefore, it is not surprising that researchers have been interested in the effects that differential arousal levels have on human performance for a long time.

## Yerkes-Dodson Law

One of the earliest (and still very influential) attempts to relate the effects of arousal to performance was the formulation of what is now commonly called the *Yerkes-Dodson Law* (1908). The two major assumptions of the Yerkes-Dodson Law are as follows:

1.  Optimal performance is associated with moderate levels of arousal or motivation.
2.  There's an inverse relationship between arousal or motivational level and task difficulty. Put another way, higher levels of arousal or motivation are associated with better performance for easy tasks but lower performance for hard tasks.

Eysenck (1982, 1984) explored in some detail the validity of the Yerkes-Dodson Law. He concluded that the evidence is strongest for the second assumption—that an optimal level of arousal is inversely related to task difficulty. Even so, Eysenck noted that one of the major shortcomings of the Yerkes-Dodson Law is that it is only *descriptive* in nature; in other words, it doesn't offer any explanation as to *why* there should be a relationship between arousal and performance. It is also now becoming increasingly evident that different types of arousers (such as stimulants, exercise, noise, incentives, anxiety, or amount of sleep deprivation) can have different effects on the same task. For instance, in terms of memory functioning, it appears that high arousal due to increased *incentives* tends to increase the capacity or efficiency of STM, while the addition of *noise* or increased *anxiety* decreases STM functioning. However, when LTM retrieval is considered, it has been observed that *incentives* often have no effect, while *noise* facilitates and *anxiety* hinders retrieval (Eysenck, 1984). Results such as these (and others to be discussed in the following sections) indicate that the Yerkes-Dodson Law greatly oversimplifies the very complex relationship that exists between arousal and human performance (including the effects of arousal on memory functioning).

## The Easterbrook Hypothesis

In 1959, Easterbrook developed a hypothesis that offered an explanation as to *why* the two assumptions of the Yerkes-Dodson Law might have some validity. He claimed that when an animal experiences a high state of arousal, emotionality, or anxiety, its focus of attention narrows to only a few cues in the environment. This narrowing of *cue utilization,* as he referred to the narrowing of attention, has the beneficial effect of decreasing the number of irrelevant cues that the animal uses. However, there is a down side too—when all the irrelevant cues have been excluded from attention, any further reduction in cue utilization will have the detrimental effect of eliminating relevant cues. The *Easterbrook*

*Hypothesis* explains the first assumption of the Yerkes-Dodson Law in the following way: performance is poor at low levels of arousal because attention is paid to many irrelevant cues, and it is also poor at high levels of arousal because some of the important cues (i.e., task-relevant ones) are ignored. The second assumption of the Yerkes-Dodson Law (that there is an inverse relationship between arousal and task difficulty) can be accounted for if the additional assumption is made that difficult tasks involve more relevant cues than do easy ones (Eysenck, 1984). If this is true, then according to the Easterbrook Hypothesis, task-relevant cues will start being ignored at lower levels of arousal for difficult tasks than for easier tasks. The result will be that as arousal levels rise, the more difficult the task, the greater the detriment in performance.

Is there evidence to support the Easterbrook Hypothesis? The answer is yes. Most of the supporting evidence has come from research paradigms in which two tasks are performed simultaneously. One of these tasks is designated to the subject as being the primary task (such as memorizing a list of words), while the other is relegated to only secondary importance (such as indicating whenever a high-pitched tone is presented). The Easterbrook Hypothesis predicts that under conditions of high arousal (which is often induced by threatening subjects with electric shock!), the performance on the secondary task will experience the most disruption. Why? Presumably because people experience a narrowing of attention during periods of high arousal, and this narrowing of attention will cause a person to concentrate on performing the primary task at the expense of the less important, subsidiary task. After reviewing the relevant literature, Eysenck (1984) concluded that high arousal does usually lead to increased attentional selectivity for the primary task. This is consistent with the Easterbrook Hypothesis's general prediction that as arousal levels increase, attention is allocated primarily to the most important aspects of the environment.

## The Weapon Focus Phenomenon

When eyewitnesses to violent crimes are later interrogated by police, they often have great difficulty recalling the details of the crimes. For instance, imagine that you are the intended victim of the knife-wielding slasher in Figure 8.1. Fortunately, you escape his clutches, and soon afterward you try to give a description of your assailant to police. What do you remember about him? Most likely, your attention was directed to the weapon being brandished about, and you probably won't immediately remember important information such as the person's facial features, hairstyle, or type of clothing. This is such a common phenomenon that it is not surprising that it has come to be known as *weapon focus* (Kramer, Buckhout, & Eugenio, 1990; Loftus, 1979a; Loftus, Loftus, & Messo, 1987; Maass & Kohnken, 1989; McCloskey & Egeth, 1983).

What causes weapon focus? Well, if it is reasonable to assume that most people are highly emotionally aroused when caught up in the commission of

FIGURE 8.1
A knife-wielding attacker (usually a statistics professor).

a violent crime, then the Easterbrook Hypothesis can provide the following explanation: the high level of emotional arousal leads to a narrowing of attention to the most critical stimulus—in this case, a weapon of some sort. If this is true, then it makes perfect sense to expect the typical person to pay close attention to the gun or knife being displayed and little attention to more peripheral details, such as whether the perpetrator was wearing shoes or sneakers!

There is good empirical support for the hypothesis that people experiencing high levels of emotional arousal encode only the most salient aspects of the situation and leave out the more peripheral details. However, the bulk of the evidence supporting the weapon focus effect comes from studies that have tested memory only a relatively short time (usually on the order of a few minutes to an hour) after the emotion-causing event. These studies consistently report that emotional arousal leads to inferior memory for peripheral information and, if further testing is done, often superior memory for central details (e.g., Christianson, 1984; Christianson & Loftus, 1991; Clifford & Scott, 1978; Deffenbacher, 1983; Kramer, Buckhout, Fox, Widman, & Tusche, 1991; Loftus & Burns, 1982).

**The action-decrement theory.** But if the retention interval was considerably longer, would there be an increase in memory for more peripheral details when the emotional reaction to the situation was much less or even absent? In other words, would you remember more details about the appearance of the person in Figure 8.1 (the person who attempted to knife you) after a few days or weeks had gone by? According to the *action-decrement theory* proposed by Walker (1958), the answer is yes. This theory assumes that an inhibitory process is established that protects a memory trace during the initial stages of memory consolidation. This inhibitory process also makes it more difficult to retrieve the trace soon after its formation. In addition, higher levels of arousal supposedly lead to higher levels of inhibition. Therefore, high arousal makes it more difficult for the trace to be recalled in the short term, but since the higher level of inhibition also leads to an increased probability of memory consolidation, the likelihood is increased that the trace will be recalled after a longer delay period.

The results of numerous studies have supported the action-decrement theory (e.g., Bradley & Baddeley, 1990; Christianson, 1984; Heuer & Reisberg, 1990; Kleinsmith & Kaplan, 1963, 1964; Parkin, Lewinsohn, & Folkard, 1982; Revelle & Loftus, 1990). For instance, Christianson (1984) tested subjects' memory for either a neutral story or an arousing one presented in a sequence of slides, which is a commonly used procedure in this line of research. When tested after only 12 minutes, subjects who viewed the neutral story performed better in a recognition test than did those who saw the emotionally arousing story. However, other subjects were tested after a 2-week interval, and for those subjects, the ones who had the better memory were the ones who had seen the arousing story, not the neutral one. This latter result is the opposite of what the weapon focus effect would have predicted, but it is exactly what would have been predicted according to the action-decrement theory.

However, three years later, in 1987, Christianson and Loftus tested a new group of subjects using the same slides and retention intervals employed earlier by Christianson. This time, in full support of the weapon focus effect, they discovered that subjects who saw the emotionally arousing slides had a poorer memory after *both* short and long retention intervals. And in a follow-up to the Heuer and Reisberg (1990) study, data more consistent with the weapon focus effect than with the action-decrement theory were found (Burke, Heuer, & Reisberg, 1992).

In summary, the weapon focus effect does a good job in predicting what people will remember (i.e., the central details but not the peripheral ones) when their memory is probed soon after the emotionally arousing event. But when longer retention intervals are employed, the data provide more support for the action-decrement theory than for the weapon focus effect.

# STRESS

Everyone experiences stress, often on a daily basis. Stress can be defined as a process of adjusting to or dealing with situations that produce mental or emotional upheavals. As stress increases, people are more likely to commit mistakes absentmindedly (Reason, 1988a; Reason & Lucas, 1984). For example, many people caught shoplifting claim that the crime was not intentional. They maintain that because of stressful events in their life, they were preoccupied with other thoughts and simply forgot to pay for certain items at the checkout counter (Reason & Lucas, 1984). In support of this possibility, the items involved in many instances of shoplifting are often trivial in terms of cost or are of no practical use to the person (e.g., an ink refill for a type of pen that the person doesn't even own).

The effect of stress on memory performance depends on the intensity of the stress. If the stress a person experiences is fairly minor (and certainly what is considered to be minor by one person may be considered much differently by somebody else), it may actually *facilitate* memory performance. In keeping with the Yerkes-Dodson Law, this is most likely to happen when the added stress raises the baseline level of arousal of the individual to a more optimal level. For instance, consider a person who usually doesn't make much of an effort to learn the names or interests of new acquaintances. Perhaps the person just doesn't want to devote the needed effort to do so. However, add a bit of stress to the situation to raise the person's arousal level (e.g., inform him that he is being introduced to his future in-laws), and most likely there will be an immediate improvement in memory.

If the stress experienced is more intense, this typically will also produce anxiety, and the combined effect of these two factors will be to hinder cognitive functioning, including memory performance. Again, this is consistent with the Yerkes-Dodson Law if one assumes that the increased level of stress and anxiety *overarouses* the person (as it certainly does Skyler in Figure 8.2). Consider the following three illustrative examples that all show the negative effects on memory of having too much stress.

In a study by Idzikowski and Baddeley (1987), novice sky divers were tested on a variety of performance tasks that included a digit span test (see Chapter 2), once on the day before they jumped and a second time just before entering the aircraft to make their first jump. Both subjective measures (based on self-reports) and objective measures (from heart-rate monitoring) indicated that subjects were significantly more anxious and stressed during the second testing session. And, as might be expected, there was a significant drop in

FIGURE 8.2

An example of what too much stress can do to a person.
*Reprinted by permission: Tribune Media Services.*

memory performance on the digit span task between the first and second testing sessions.

The following example has implications for eyewitness memory reports (see Chapter 11). Peters (1988) asked 212 adults to give physical descriptions of two people they briefly met and to pick them out from a series of photographs. One person was a nurse who had given the subjects an inoculation in the form of a shot in the arm. The other person was someone they met soon after the inoculation. Care was taken to expose each subject to each person for the same amount of time (approximately 15 seconds). As expected, the subjects experienced more stress and arousal during the time of the inoculation, as shown by elevated pulse rates and self-reports. When tested, the subjects were significantly poorer in describing the nurse's physical appearance and in recognizing her from a lineup than in demonstrating their memory for the other person.

One final example, one that many of us have personally experienced, is known as the *next-in-line effect* (Bond & Omar, 1990; Brenner, 1973; Brown & Oxman, 1978). This occurs when a person who is about to make a public presentation of some sort (such as a speech) must first listen to others making prior presentations. If the person is later tested for his or her memory of the earlier presentations, memory is particularly poor for the presentation made immediately prior to the subject's own presentation. Although other factors may play a role, it is likely that the memory deficit is at least partly due to the increased anxiety and stress experienced just before the individual's own time to present.

It is well known that novice sky divers show emotional and physiological reactions at the time of their jumps that indicate that they are terrified but that expert sky divers show little (if any) evidence of stress or anxiety (Solomon & Corbit, 1974). We expect that much the same is true for people who need to give blood samples often or to take injections (such as some diabetics) or for people who have had a great deal of practice in public speaking (such as experienced teachers or politicians). The moral is this: A little stress or anxiety will usually improve your performance or memory capability, but a lot will adversely affect you. An excellent way to help shield yourself from the negative effects of having too much stress or anxiety is to practice extensively those aspects of your life (whatever they may be) that now cause you to act like a novice. Acting like a novice invites stress and anxiety; when you become more experienced, the level of stress and anxiety drastically drops.

## Repression

What would happen to memory if the stress and anxiety associated with an event was extremely intense? Well, according to the Yerkes-Dodson Law, the memory for that event would be severely disrupted. Sigmund Freud (1915/1957), however, would have gone further. He believed that such events would be completely banished from consciousness through the process of *repression*. Repression is at the very heart of psychoanalysis and is said to occur when certain very unpleasant memories or events (often of an ego-threatening nature) are not allowed to enter conscious awareness. Some people have claimed that repression is common among people who commit crimes of great passion (such as when a man, in a jealous rage, murders his wife's lover). In fact, one estimate is that repression occurs in one out of every three crimes of passion (Bower, 1981).

This blockage of memory may be a permanent one, or it may be only temporary if the negative quality of the memory is subsequently diminished or removed. For instance, a person may initially repress what may have been perceived as a very embarrassing event at the time (e.g., ripping the back of your pants during recess in fifth grade, as one of your authors did), but years later, with a more mature perspective, the person may be able to recall the incident quite well and even laugh at it. If the disturbing events are powerful enough, then, according to Freud, repression causes a person to suffer a loss of personal identity. This results in the formation of a *dissociative disorder* (described more fully in Chapter 14), during which an individual becomes amnesic about important aspects of his or her life. The vast majority of modern clinical psychologists and psychiatrists (regardless of whether or not they have a psychoanalytic bent) would probably agree that events associated with extreme anxiety and stress can result in amnesia.

A recent and very well publicized court case has suggested that witnesses to a violent crime may repress the experience for years, but then they can somehow "recover" the memory when something seemingly inconsequential rekindles the heinous episode (Wortman, Loftus, & Marshall, 1992). In this particular case, George Franklin, Sr., 51 years old, was charged with sexually assaulting and murdering 8-year-old Susan Nason. The murder occurred on September 22, 1969, but the only witness (Franklin's daughter Eileen) repressed the episode for 20 years. Then in 1989, while playing innocently with her own children, Eileen had her first flashback of what happened that horrible day in September to Susan. Subsequently, she had many other flashbacks and she became convinced that her father was guilty of this terrible crime. Largely on the basis of the belief they had in Eileen's recovered memory, a jury in California convicted her father of murder in December 1990.

**The False Memory Syndrome.** In the last few years a large number of people (mostly women) have come forward to claim that they were sexually abused as children, that they had repressed the bad memories for years or even decades, and that they now remembered these hidden, vicious events. Many of these individuals have appeared on such national talk shows as Geraldo Rivera's and Oprah Winfrey's. Often with the help of a therapist, these individuals can now supposedly remember being assaulted by teachers, parents, priests, and so forth. As you might imagine, this has caused quite an uproar.

While not denying that it is certainly possible to recover repressed memories much later in life, many memory researchers and therapists are critical of what has been called the *False Memory Sndrome.* At a recent American Psychological Society symposium on the topic of remembering repressed abuse (June 20, 1992), the general consensus among the speakers was that many of these recovered memories probably never happened. Instead, it was believed that these "recovered" memories were more likely to have been induced by therapists who unwittingly encouraged troubled people to reconstruct or create fictitious tales of prior abuse and neglect. This seems to us to be a reasonable explanation for the recent spate of such cases, especially given all the attention this topic has received in the media and the fact that there are many books (such as the best-selling *The Courage to Heal*, 1988, by Ellen Bass and Laura Davis) and therapists actively promoting the idea that many women have repressed memories of childhood abuse.

In March 1992 a number of concerned individuals established the False Memory Syndrome Foundation in Philadelphia. The stated purposes of the foundation are (1) to better understand the reasons for the spread of the False Memory Syndrome, (2) to try to prevent new cases of the syndrome, and (3) to aid the victims—both those who make the allegations of abuse and those who are falsely accused. As of July 15, 1992, more than 650 families had contacted the foundation to describe stories of how adult children recovered "repressed memories" of sexual abuse while in therapy.

**Is everyday forgetting due to repression?** Is it true that normal, everyday forgetting is influenced by the act of repression, as Freud also maintained? If repression does play a role in normal forgetting, then we might expect that unpleasant memories would be remembered less well or less frequently than either neutral or happy memories. Evidence consistent with this prediction has been provided by two memory researchers, Marigold Linton and Willem Wagenaar, who each kept extensive diaries of their daily activities over a period of several years.

To conduct her study, Linton (1975) recorded at least two events from her personal life every day, accumulating more than 5500 items over a six-year period. Every month she would randomly select about 150 items from her ever-expanding pool of events and then attempt to recall specific details surrounding each item. For example, for each item selected, Linton would try to determine if she could actually recall the specific event and, if so, also provide a date for it. In all, she tested herself on about 11,000 items! Although Linton reported many intriguing findings with regard to forgetting autobiographical information, for our present purposes it is most interesting to note that she consistently found that she recalled more pleasant than unpleasant memories. Like Linton, Wagenaar (1986) also recorded daily events in his life for six years. He tested his recall of these personally experienced events by providing himself with various retrieval cues (such as whom he was with or when the event took place). Like Linton, Wagenaar also recalled pleasant events better than unpleasant ones. In one of the earliest studies to examine the memorability of pleasant versus unpleasant events, Meltzer (1931) asked his subjects to write down their experiences during a Christmas vacation. When they tried to recall those same experiences six weeks later, it was found that more of the unpleasant events were forgotten.

The studies cited above all dealt with naturally occurring events that were personally relevant. Would similar results be obtained, that is, a bias in favor of pleasant items being recalled, if the subjects simply had to learn lists of words varying in their affective quality? The answer appears to be yes. On the basis of a review of 52 studies involving the long-term memory of word lists, Matlin and Stang (1978) found that pleasant words were recalled significantly better than were neutral or negative words in 39 of the studies, and this was especially true if the delay between initial learning and subsequent testing was long. These authors suggested that the superior recall of pleasant words and events was a reflection of a broader phenomenon that they have called the *Pollyanna principle*: pleasant items are generally processed more accurately and efficiently than less pleasant ones. They believe that pleasant items may be stored in a more accessible fashion in memory, thereby allowing these items to be recalled more quickly and accurately.

We have seen that there is considerable evidence that negative or unpleasant items and memories are often less well remembered in everyday life. But does this mean that the Freudian concept of repression is responsible? Not necessarily, and it is probably not even likely, because there are good, plausible alternative explanations for the obtained results. For instance, instead of suggesting that repression is responsible, it may be reasonable to say that anxiety (which often accompanies unpleasant memories) interferes with a person's ability to recall unpleasant things by distracting the individual with competing thoughts. This has often been referred to as the *interference hypothesis* (D'Zurilla, 1965; Holmes, 1970, 1974). In addition, increases in anxiety are associated with a decreased ability to use strategies that will aid encoding and retrieval processes (Hertel, 1992; Williams, Watts, MacLeod, & Mathews, 1988).

It is also quite possible that people remember pleasant events better than unpleasant ones simply because they think about pleasant events more often. If this is true, then this increased rehearsal could help to explain why pleasant memories are recalled more often or more quickly than unpleasant memories. Furthermore, there are findings to suggest that the more critical factor may be the *arousal* level of the material and not whether the information to be remembered is unpleasant or upsetting. In fact, consistent with the action-decrement theory described earlier, data exist that show that *both* pleasant and unpleasant materials are more difficult to recall on a short-term basis (perhaps because of their tendency to raise a person's arousal level) but that on a long-term basis both types of materials may actually be easier to remember than neutral material (e.g., Bradley & Baddeley, 1990; Parkin et al., 1982). A repression model of forgetting would be hard-pressed to account for such findings. Whereas repression most assuredly plays an important role in many cases of clinical amnesia, its role in everyday forgetting is much more suspect.

# *E*MOTION

Like stress, emotions pervade our existence. Emotions can be defined as transitory states of feeling that vary in both intensity and quality. Emotional states almost always are associated with changes in arousal level, sometimes creating higher arousal and other times lower. All of us have experienced a wide gamut of pleasant and unpleasant emotional states: fear, happiness, surprise, mirth, sadness, depression, anger, zeal, and exhilaration, to name a few. And we have already learned that people tend to remember pleasant memories better than unpleasant ones.

In describing the effects that emotional states have on memory functioning, we will concentrate on the individual emotional state of *depression*. This is because of all the emotional states that we experience, *depression* has been (and continues to be) the one most often studied with regard to memory. The chief reason for this is that it ranks as one of the major types of memory disorders. In fact, our discussion of depression could just as easily have taken place in the chapter on memory disorders (Chapter 14). This section will also consider how the *context* of an emotional state can influence what people encode and remember. The chapter will conclude with a discussion of how intense emotional experiences influence memory.

## Depression and Memory Ability

People who are very depressed show a variety of telltale symptoms. These typically include low self-esteem; feelings of inadequacy, sadness, and hopelessness; loss of appetite; lack of interest in sex; sleep disturbances; and general fatigue marked by very low levels of arousal and energy. As if these symptoms are not bad enough, depressed people usually complain that their memory is worse than it used to be (Beck, 1967). And there is substance to these complaints—when depressed individuals are compared with either nondepressed people or even themselves (during times of remission), most studies show memory impairments (e.g., Johnson & Magaro, 1987).

The effects of depression on memory performance have been investigated by means of two different methods. One way involves studying people who are already in a depressed state (referred to as *natural depression*), while the other uses people who are artificially made to feel depressed in the laboratory (referred to as *induced depression*). How, you ask, do you experimentally induce depression? Table 8.1 describes the six most common ways that have been used to induce mood states (both positive and negative ones) in the laboratory. It is

**TABLE 8.1** THE SIX MOST COMMON MOOD-INDUCTION TECHNIQUES

1. *Velten procedure* (Velten, 1968): Subjects read a series of statements that suggest a particular mood state and then try to assume that mood. This procedure is the most common induction technique.

2. *Hypnosis:* Hypnotized subjects are asked to generate a particular mood, often by remembering episodes from their life in which they experienced the sought-after mood.

3. *Memory elicitation:* Subjects are asked to dwell on past events in which they experienced a particular mood.

4. *Success/failure:* Subjects experience either a series of successes or a series of failures (e.g., by playing computer games). The assumption is that people experiencing success will become happy, while those experiencing failures will become depressed.

5. *Music:* Subjects listen to affectively laden music.

6. *Mood posturing:* Subjects are instructed in how to make facial expressions and/or body postures consistent with particular moods. For example, a subject would frown and slump his or her shoulders to imitate the typical way a depressed person would look. It is assumed that by maintaining this position for a period of time, the subject actually begins to experience the imitated mood state.

important to note that although many studies have reported finding comparable memory impairments for people naturally depressed and for those in whom the depression was brought on through mood-induction techniques, this is not always the case (for recent reviews of this literature, see Blaney, 1986; Ellis & Ashbrook, 1988, 1989; Williams et al., 1988). In fact, it would be surprising if there were no differences between these two groups. After all, a naturally occurring depression differs from an artificial one in etiology, duration, and probably intensity. If one just considers the intensity factor alone, there's good evidence that the greater the severity of the depression, the greater the disruption of memory processes (Johnson & Magaro, 1987).

As you already know, in order to consciously commit something to memory (such as a list of items to buy at the store), a person must devote some effort and attention to the task. This usually entails organizing the material in a certain way (e.g., remembering all the vegetables in a single cluster) or elaborating on the material, perhaps by relating it to other things (e.g., keeping in mind which items to purchase by remembering the recipe of what you want to make for dinner). If such strategies are not used, then subsequent recall of the material is often poor. On the basis of this knowledge and the fact that depressed individuals lack energy and personal initiative, you can probably make an educated guess as to which types of memory tasks will prove to be the most onerous for a depressed person. That's right—memory tasks that require a fair amount of effort on the part of the individual are exactly the types of tasks that give depressed people the most trouble (Ellis & Ashbrook, 1988, 1989; Ellis, Thomas, & Rodriguez, 1984; Hasher & Zacks, 1979; Weingartner, Cohen, Murphy, Martello, & Gerdt, 1981; Williams et al., 1988).

For example, Weingartner et al. (1981) gave depressed and normal subjects word lists to remember. On each list there were words that could be grouped together by category—for instance, names of animals or flowers. Here's the interesting twist—sometimes the lists were unstructured (i.e., the words were randomly placed on the lists) and at other times the lists were already structured for the most efficient studying (i.e., all similar category items were grouped together). When both groups of subjects were given the structured lists to remember, there were no significant differences in the number of words recalled. However, when the lists were unstructured, the depressed subjects recalled significantly fewer words than did their normal counterparts.

The pattern of results displayed in the Weingartner et al. study (and many others) suggests that depressed people are either unwilling or unable to expend the necessary cognitive effort to maximize the chances for successful memory. Why is this true? A currently popular explanation, often called the *resource-allocation hypothesis* (Ellis & Ashbrook, 1988; Hasher & Zacks, 1979), rests on the logical (and empirically supported) assumption that there are always a limited number of available cognitive resources that a person can bring to bear on any mental endeavor. This hypothesis also maintains that depression reduces these available resources by inappropriately tying up attentional processes. This may occur because of attention being allocated either to irrelevant stimuli or to self-absorption. Therefore, according to the resource-allocation explanation, *any* memory task that makes significant cognitive demands will be performed less well by those suffering from depression. If, however, the memory task is already well-structured or otherwise organized for efficient remembering, or if explicit instructions are provided on how best to memorize the material, then differences in memory capabilities between depressed and nondepressed people should be minimal or nonexistent. Presumably this is because such memory tasks are now sufficiently easy and so can be carried out on "automatic pilot," thereby not overtaxing the diminished cognitive resources of the depressed.

We should note that there are other possible explanations for the poorer memory performance of depressed people. For instance, it is well known that depressed individuals are often wrapped up in their own thoughts and have little interest in activities unrelated to their own situation (like memory tests given to them by psychologists!). To the extent that this is true, these individuals simply may be unwilling, but not unable, to commit the necessary cognitive resources to do the task at hand, unless they find it personally relevant (Guenther, 1988).

In addition, there's evidence that depressed people often adopt response styles that can give one the impression that their memory is worse than it really is (Johnson & Magaro, 1987). For example, it has been demonstrated that depressed individuals often develop a response bias toward being very conservative when performing certain memory tasks. This response bias means that a depressed person may actually remember the correct answers but refrains from giving them because of being overly cautious. The result, of course, is to falsely conclude that the depressed person has an inferior memory.

Recently, it has been argued that the memory deficit typically seen in depressed subjects is not actually due to diminished cognitive resources; rather, it is due to a specific deficit in cognitive initiative (Hertel, 1992; Hertel & Hardin, 1990). In other words, this view holds that the real problem that depressed people have is their lack of ability to *spontaneously* initiate appropriate procedures and strategies to aid their memory. We believe it is likely that each of the different factors mentioned probably contributes to the memory impairments observed in depressed people.

## State-Dependent Memory

The term *state-dependent memory* refers to the idea that retrieval from memory will be best when the "state" of the person at initial encoding or learning matches the "state" of the person at the time of retrieval. What do we actually mean by the "state" of the person? Well, it can refer to any internal or external condition of a person's body or mind. The fundamental premise of state-dependent memory is that the closer the match between learning and retrieval, the better the retrieval will be. As you can see, state-dependent memory is really just a subset of the encoding specificity principle you learned about in Chapter 5.

**Drug-dependent memory.** Most of the early work on state-dependent memory (from around 1967 to 1976) involved using different kinds of drugs to induce changes in state (Eich, 1989). It has been shown, for instance, that if people are drunk during initial learning or studying, then best recall of the material occurs when they are again in a drunken state (Goodwin, Powell, Bremer, Hoine, & Stern, 1969). These results are consistent with anecdotal stories of alcoholics who hide important things, like money or bankbooks, while in a drunken state and then cannot remember where they hid the items when sober. However, once they again take to the bottle, they can recollect where the items were put. Besides alcohol, a large number of other drugs have been used to study drug-induced state-dependent memory, including marijuana and various stimulants and barbiturates. The results of these studies broadly support the existence of drug-induced state-dependent memory (for reviews of the drug literature, see Eich, 1977, 1980, 1989; Swanson & Kinsbourne, 1979; Tulving, 1983; Weingartner, 1978).

**Mood-dependent memory.** In part because of the success shown with studies of drug-dependent memory, around 1977 some researchers started to turn their attention to exploring whether or not mood states could also be important for state-dependent memory. After all, it seems reasonable to think that a particular emotion or mood (such as happiness or depression) may also provide a distinctive enough context to show state-dependent memory effects. And, in fact, in the late 1970s and early 1980s, the results from a number of studies seemed to provide good evidence that the mood of an individual could be sufficient to cause state-dependent memory (Bartlett, Burleson, & Santrock, 1982; Bartlett & Santrock, 1979; Bower, Monteiro, & Gilligan, 1978; Schare, Lisman, & Spear, 1984). For example, in the most influential of the early reports, Bower et al. (1978, experiment 3) used hypnotic suggestions to induce happy or sad moods in college students. Each subject learned two word lists, one while in a happy mood and one while in a sad mood. All subjects were later asked to recall the words while either in the same mood as in the original learning or in a different mood. The results indicated that recall was significantly better when there was a match in moods between learning and retrieval than if there was a mismatch (e.g., being in a happy mood both times as opposed to being happy during learning and sad during retrieval).

Things turned out not to be so simple, though. First of all, if subjects learned only one list instead of two and then had to recall the list in the same mood or in a different mood, mood-dependent memory usually didn't occur (Bower et al., 1978; Mecklenbräuker & Hager, 1984; Schare et al., 1984). This suggested that mood state would play a role in aiding retrieval only if there was some potential for confusing different memories (in this specific case, two word lists).

Consistent with this finding, it is also clear that a mood-dependent memory effect is strongest when other retrieval cues are weakest (Blaney, 1986; Bower, 1981; Eich, 1980, 1989; Gilligan & Bower, 1984; Kihlstrom, 1989; Singer & Salovey, 1988). This means that mood-dependent memory will typically occur only if subjects are asked to use free recall rather than either cued recall or recognition. Procedures for cued recall (such as providing a category name that helps the subject recall the specific items on a list) and recognition make retrieval tasks easier. Other limiting factors are that mood-dependent memory effects are more likely to be found when moods are positive rather than negative, only when intense moods are used, and when the material to be learned is related to real-life events (Blaney, 1986; Ellis & Ashbrook, 1989; Isen, 1985; Ucros, 1989). In addition, there is some evidence that mood-dependent memory effects will be evident only when the items to be recalled are internally generated by the individual, such as when the words to be remembered are generated by the subject rather than by the experimenter (Eich & Metcalfe, 1989).

Although some believe that it has been sufficiently demonstrated that mood-dependent memory is a real phenomenon that has a modest, yet significant, effect on retrieval under the right circumstances (Ucros, 1989), others seriously doubt the reliability of its effects (Ellis, 1983; Kihlstrom, 1989; Leight & Ellis, 1981; Marshall-Garcia & Beck, 1985; Wetzler, 1985). Also, Bower and Mayer (1985) attempted a direct replication of experiment 3 reported in Bower et al. (1978). The results were disappointing—they couldn't replicate the earlier positive findings. In a recent series of six experiments, Bower and Mayer (1989) again tried numerous procedures to provide solid evidence for mood-dependent retrieval. They failed.

Where does all this leave us? Well, we believe that the preponderance of evidence suggests that mood-dependent memory is certainly not an effective cue to aid remembering under most conditions, and even in ideal conditions for it to occur, the effects will be modest at best. Many doubt its usefulness at all. As you will see in the next section, however, there's much stronger evidence, and a greater consensus, that a different mood-related phenomenon does, indeed, have a marked effect on memory.

## Mood Congruence

After reviewing the literature concerning the relationship between mood and memory, Blaney (1986) concluded that the studies that initially *seemed* to support the existence of mood-dependent memory were actually more supportive of a different mood-related phenomenon known as *mood congruence*. Evidence for mood congruence occurs when a person's current mood causes selective or better encoding and/or retrieval of material that is consistent, or congruent, with the prevailing mood state. This means that mood congruency effects may be seen at either the time of encoding or the time of retrieval. Singer and Salovey (1988) have used the terms *encoding congruency* and *recall congruency* to distinguish between these two possibilities.

To investigate encoding congruency, a mood is typically induced by using one or more of the procedures in Table 8.1. Then the subject is asked to learn a list of words or to read a short story. These study materials contain a mixture of pleasant and unpleasant items or events. The subject now has to wait until the induced mood completely dissipates, at which point he or she is required to recall or recognize the words from the study list or various aspects of the story. For example, subjects could be put into a depressed mood by means of the Velten procedure and then asked to study the list of words in Table 8.2. As you can see, this list contains an equal number of pleasant and unpleasant words. Two hours later, when the subjects are in a neutral mood state again, they are asked to recall as many of the words as possible. If these subjects remember more unpleasant words (or remember them faster) when compared with a group of subjects who studied the list while in a neutral mood or in a happy mood, this is evidence to support encoding congruency. The opposite effect (i.e., remembering more pleasant words or remembering them faster) would be expected if the subjects had instead been placed in a happy mood at the study stage.

There are two common ways to examine recall congruency. One way involves first giving subjects some material to study, then putting them in a happy or depressed mood, and then asking them to recall or recognize the material. In this case, a person in a depressed mood who recalls more unpleasant material or recalls it faster than someone not in a depressed mood provides

**TABLE 8.2** A TYPICAL LIST OF PLEASANT AND UNPLEASANT WORDS THAT MIGHT BE USED IN MOOD-DEPENDENT MEMORY STUDIES

Friend
Pain
Injury
Promotion
Fight
Pretty
Defeat
Holiday
Gift
Torture
Gloom
Play
Horrible
Nasty
Success
Win
Death
Enjoy

evidence for recall congruency. A second way to study recall congruency is to ask people who are in a mood state (either a natural one or one that is induced) to recall autobiographical memories. Evidence supportive of recall congruency, for example, would be if a depressed person recalled more negative past events than a nondepressed person. Although there's evidence for both types of mood congruency, Singer and Salovey (1988) believe that the evidence is strongest for encoding congruency.

Unfortunately, many researchers have confounded encoding and recall congruency in their studies (Singer & Salovey, 1988). This problem occurs whenever mood state is not controlled during both learning and retrieval. For instance, confounding occurs when a researcher who is interested in examining encoding congruency doesn't make sure that the subjects are in a neutral mood during retrieval or, conversely, if interested in recall congruency, doesn't make sure that subjects are in a neutral mood at the time of learning. If such confounding happens, and if positive effects occur, then it is impossible to know whether to attribute them to encoding congruency or recall congruency (or both). Even allowing for the fact that many studies in this area are confounded, there's still considerable evidence for mood congruency effects for both naturally occurring and induced moods (Blaney, 1986; Gilligan & Bower, 1984; Singer & Salovey, 1988; Teasdale & Taylor, 1981; Teasdale, Taylor, & Fogarty, 1980).

**Asymmetry in mood congruency effects.**  There may also be an asymmetry in mood congruency effects that is similar to the one that occurs with mood-dependent memory. Mood congruency seems to occur with more regularity for *positive* moods than for *negative* moods (e.g., Isen, Shalker, Clark, & Karp, 1978; Nasby & Yando, 1982; Teasdale & Fogarty, 1979). One way to think about this is as follows: if you are in a happy mood, you are more likely to encode or retrieve pleasant items or memories, but if you are in a sad or depressed mood, the likelihood is not as great that you will encode or retrieve predominantly unpleasant things. This has been observed both in naturally depressed people and in people who were artificially made to feel depressed (for a comprehensive review, see Blaney, 1986).

Why should there be an asymmetry in mood congruency? Isen (1985) has put forth a reasonable explanation, at least for the mildly depressed. His reasoning is that people who are feeling happy wish to continue feeling happy, and one way to do this is by selectively encoding or remembering pleasant things. However, it would not make much sense for a depressed person to concentrate on negative items because this would only tend to exacerbate the depression. Isen thinks that many mildly depressed people may deliberately try to avoid reflecting on negative things so that they can regain a positive mood. This would account for the fact that negative moods do not lead to mood congruency effects as readily as do positive moods. The more seriously depressed people, however, may not be able to engage in such a process of "mood repair." For these people something else must account for asymmetrical mood congruency.

**The importance of self-awareness.** Recent evidence suggests that an individual's self-awareness of his or her current mood may help determine whether or not the person demonstrates mood congruency effects (Pyszczynski, Hamilton, Herring, & Greenberg, 1989; Rothkopf & Blaney, 1991). In their study, Rothkopf and Blaney (1991) had half of their subjects follow the usual procedure used in mood congruency studies—the subjects first completed a questionnaire that measured their current mood state, and then they generated autobiographical memories. It is very likely that this procedure causes each subject to focus on his or her current mood before generating past memories. For both males and females, it was found that subjects who were made self-aware of their moods showed good evidence of mood congruency effects (in this case, the more depressed you are, the more likely you are to recall depressing memories).

However, the other half of the subjects in the Rothkopf and Blaney study generated autobiographical memories *before* filling out the mood evaluation questionnaire. This means that for these subjects self-awareness of present mood was not guaranteed at the time they generated their past memories (since the mood questionnaire came later). The results revealed an interesting gender difference: the males showed no evidence of mood congruency effects, but the females did (but the females did not show as large an effect as did the females who had been made self-aware).

As pointed out by Rothkopf and Blaney (1991), these findings have potentially important consequences because almost all studies on mood congruency first make their subjects aware of their mood state before they are asked to recall past memories. Since in real life it is rare for someone to draw attention to your mood state (unless the mood is an extreme one), this means that the pervasiveness of mood congruency effects demonstrated in the laboratory may exaggerate what actually happens in everyday situations. Put another way, mood congruency (especially for males) may not play as large a role in the recall of memories in daily life as traditional laboratory research would lead us to believe.

## Intensity of Emotion: Flashbulb Memories

Take a moment and try to remember what you were doing and whom you were with during the daylight hours of January 28, 1986. Come on, you say, this is almost an impossible task. Most of you would probably draw a blank, unless you happened to remember that January 28, 1986, was the day of the tragic explosion of the space shuttle *Challenger*. Armed with this additional information, many of you would probably now claim to recall in vivid detail, and with great confidence, what you were doing when you first learned of the accident, whom you were with, how you learned about it, etc. If so, then you may have experienced what has been coined a *flashbulb memory* (Brown & Kulik, 1977).

A flashbulb memory is hypothesized to be an unusually detailed, vivid recollection of an event that was very surprising, emotionally arousing, and important. You probably have at least a few flashbulb memories. Some flashbulb memories are common to many people because they have national or international importance (the *Challenger* explosion, for example), while others are of a strictly personal nature (for example, remembrances of the unexpected death of a parent).

Because of the alleged clarity and durability of people's recollections, some researchers suggest that a special neural mechanism is responsible for the establishment of flashbulb memories (Brown & Kulik, 1977; Pillemer, 1984). Accordingly, it has been proposed that if an event exceeds a critical level of surprise and what has been called "consequentiality," this will trigger a special neural mechanism to "print" into permanent memory an astonishing number of details concerning the circumstances that occurred at the time the individual first learned of the dramatic event. It has also been assumed that the circumstances surrounding the shocking event will be accurate and largely immune to forgetting, in part because of frequent rehearsal of the relevant details.

The notion that flashbulb memories are in some way special may appeal to many of us who have experienced them. Nevertheless, the idea that flashbulb memories are established and maintained in a qualitatively different manner than is true for more "ordinary" memories has been seriously challenged in recent years. While it is true that some still argue that it is premature to abandon the possibility of there being a special flashbulb mechanism (e.g., Schmidt & Bohannon, 1988), many researchers now doubt the likelihood that any special neural mechanism is needed to explain the vivid quality of what have been called flashbulb memories (Brewer, 1992; Gold, 1992; McCloskey, 1992; McCloskey, Wible, & Cohen, 1988; Neisser, 1982; Neisser & Harsch, 1992; Rubin & Kozin, 1984). Instead, many psychologists believe that these memories are no different from other vivid memories and, furthermore, that they fall prey to the same types of problems that all other memories can experience—they can be wildly inaccurate, and they are not immune to forgetting over time.

A good illustrative example of the fallibility of flashbulb memories is provided by the work of Neisser and Harsch (1992). Believing that the *Challenger* disaster had all the earmarks for becoming a flashbulb memory, these fast-thinking investigators developed a questionnaire and administered it to 106 college students on the morning after the explosion. The students were requested to describe in their own words how they learned of the news and were also asked a number of specific questions. After 32 months, 44 of the original subjects agreed to fill out a similar questionnaire about the explosion. Finally, 6 months later, 40 of these 44 subjects participated in a brief individual interview.

The results of the study clearly showed that flashbulb memories were very prone to error and forgetting. Furthermore, it was discovered that the confidence that subjects had in their recollections was not significantly related to the accuracy of their recollections. For example, on the questionnaire given 32 months after the shuttle explosion, each subject's recall was scored on the basis of the following attributes: place, activity, informant, time, and others who may have been present at the time the person first heard the tragic news. Each subject's responses were compared with his or her morning-after questionnaire answers. After 32 months it was found that of 220 attributes recalled by subjects, 93 were completely wrong, 60 were partially wrong, and only 67 were essentially correct! In addition, one-fourth of the subjects were wrong on every "remembered" attribute. During the individual interviews that took place 6 months later, it was found that despite the use of prompts, cues, and even their own handwritten essays that they wrote the morning after the disaster, none of the inaccurate subjects could successfully retrieve their original memories. These kinds of results question the wisdom of imbuing flashbulb memories with special properties.

## Concentration Camp Experiences

It would seem reasonable to expect that people who were held captive in concentration camps during World War II would have many opportunities to form vivid memories of highly emotional events. Some of these experiences would probably be good candidates for consideration as flashbulb memories. And, in fact, many concentration camp survivors claim that they have great confidence in their memories of particularly heinous crimes (e.g., a murder or rape or personally being subjected to specific acts of brutal treatment) and of the perpetrators of these atrocities. However, in a recent trial of a suspected Nazi war criminal (Marinus De Rijke), doubt has been cast on the reliability of these accounts of long-lasting memory.

Although it was found that concentration camp survivors had generally good memory for certain aspects of camp life (such as the type of food they ate and the housing they were kept in), their memory for many important and dramatic details was quite poor or totally lacking after 40 years. Particularly interesting in this regard was a comparison of statements made by 15 witnesses between 1943 and 1948 and again between 1984 and 1988 (Wagenaar & Groeneweg, 1990). Table 8.3 clearly illustrates the vast amount of forgetting of important details of emotional events that occurred for many of these individuals. When these witnesses were later confronted with their own previous statements, only one failed to now remember the events in keeping with his original testimony taken in the 1940s.

Neither the intensity of an emotional experience nor the level of confidence that a person professes in his or her recollection can guarantee accuracy of recall. The effects of highly emotional events on memory are complex and do not always lend themselves to straightforward interpretations. It appears that memory for these events is certainly fallible, a conclusion that Wagenaar and Groeneweg (1990) also reached from their concentration camp study:

**TABLE 8.3** SOME EXAMPLES OF FORGETTING BY CONCENTRATION CAMP
SURVIVORS

"Witness P.C. reported how a man died in his crib. The next day De Rijke and Boxmeer came in to drag the body away in a most repulsive manner. In 1984 P.C. had
forgotten the incident, and De Rijke as well."

"Witness J. van D. was maltreated by Daalhuizen to such an extent that he was unable to do any work for a full year. In 1984 he had forgotten the name of Daalhuizen."

"Witness G.H.V. saw how a fellow-prisoner was maltreated by De Rijke and Boxmeer,
till the man died. In 1984 he had forgotten both names. In 1943 he reported how
another prisoner De V. was violently assaulted by Boxmeer. In 1984 he reported
that De V. was the perpetrator instead of the victim."

"Witness L. van der M. was beaten up by De Rijke, and was unable to walk for days.
In 1984 he remembered only receiving an occasional kick. He also witnessed the
murdering of a Jewish fellow-prisoner, but had forgotten all about it in 1984."

"Witness G.S. reported that the guards Diepgrond and Boxmeer had drowned a prisoner in a water trough. He did not remember this in 1984, and even denied having
said it."

SOURCE: Wagenaar & Groeneweg (1990, p. 84).

If the name and face of a person like De Rijke do not elicit any memories in his
victims, we must conclude that, for all practical purposes, De Rijke was lost from
memory. No matter how intensely the emotions were felt at the time of encoding,
no matter how clearly the images were engraved in the memories of the victims,
no matter how certain the survivors were that they would never forget, 40 years of
normal life in a modern Western society provided too many interfering experiences,
and apparently there was not a sufficient amount of overt or covert rehearsal to
counteract the interference. Life simply went on, and in many cases only the bare
backbone of the experience remained. (pp. 86–87)

## SUMMARY

I. **Arousal**
- Differential levels of *arousal* can have a marked effect on performance
  (including memory).
- The *Yerkes-Dodson Law* suggests that optimal performance is associated
  with moderate levels of arousal and that an inverse relationship exists
  between arousal and task difficulty.
  - Although there's good support for the assumption that arousal is
    inversely related to task difficulty, the Yerkes-Dodson Law is only
    descriptive in nature. It is also evident that different kinds of arousers
    can have different effects on the same task.
  - The *Easterbrook Hypothesis* offers an explanation as to why the Yerkes-

Dodson Law might work. Specifically, it claims that when an animal is in a state of high arousal, it will concentrate attention on only a few environmental cues.

- It has often been claimed that eyewitnesses to or victims of violent crimes concentrate only on (and hence remember) major details such as the weapon that was used. This has become known as *weapon focus phenomenon*, and it can be accounted for by the Easterbrook Hypothesis.

- In contrast, the *action-decrement theory* proposes that high arousal levels cause the memory for both central and peripheral details to be inhibited shortly after the emotionally arousing event, but that following longer retention intervals both types of details become easier to remember.

- Although there are some exceptions, the bulk of the available evidence suggests that the weapon focus phenomenon is most likely to operate after short retention intervals and that the action-decrement theory can better account for the data following long retention intervals.

## II. Stress

- The effects that *stress* has on memory depends largely on the intensity of it. Minor stress often boosts arousal to a more optimal level and facilitates memory; more intense stress usually overarouses the person (and causes high anxiety as well) and hinders memory functioning.

- *Repression* is said to occur when very unpleasant memories or events are not allowed to reach conscious awareness. If the repression is severe enough, it can lead to a *dissociative disorder* in which the individual becomes amnesic about important aspects of his or her personal life.

  - In recent years, many adults have come forward to claim that they have recovered repressed memories of childhood abuse. It is likely that most of these cases are instances of the *False Memory Syndrome,* in which therapists have induced or encouraged people under their care to create fictitious memories of abuse.

  - Freud thought that repression could explain many everyday memory losses. And there's considerable evidence that unpleasant items or memories are often less well processed and remembered in everyday life (the *Pollyanna principle*). However, there are a number of good explanations, other than repression, that can account for this. Today, most researchers do not think that repression plays much of a part in everyday forgetting.

## III. Emotion

- The effects of *depression* on memory functioning have been investigated either by examining people who are already in a natural state of depression or by examining people in whom depression has been artificially induced. Depressed people suffer from low levels of arousal and often complain about having poor memory abilities, which research has substantiated.

- Since depressed people usually lack energy and personal initiative, the memory tasks that prove to be most difficult for them are ones that require *effortful* processing.
- The most popular explanation to account for this lack of effortful processing is that depression reduces the number of available cognitive resources for performing any mental activity, including memory. This is called the *resource-allocation hypothesis*. However, there are likely to be multiple reasons why depression is linked to inferior memory capability.

- *State-dependent memory* refers to the idea that retrieval from memory is best achieved when the state of the person at the time of learning matches the state of the person at the time of retrieval (a subset of the *encoding specificity principle*).
  - Much of the early work investigating state-dependent memory was done by inducing various drug states. Many studies have shown that if learning occurs in a particular state (e.g., being drunk), then recall will be best when the same condition is reinstated during retrieval (i.e., being drunk again).
  - Starting in the late 1970s, people attempted to determine if *mood-dependent memory* also occurred. Although initial reports seemed promising, there have been many key failures to replicate mood-dependent memory. It is still a controversial topic; some people are convinced that mood-dependent memory occurs under the right conditions, while others are unconvinced and consider mood-dependent memory to be too unreliable and ephemeral a phenomenon.

- There's much greater consensus that a different mood-related phenomenon, called *mood congruence,* does markedly influence what we remember. Mood congruence occurs whenever a person's current mood state results in selective or better encoding and/or retrieval of material that is consistent (congruent) with the prevailing mood state.
  - Mood congruency may be asymmetrical in nature because the effect appears with more regularity for positive moods than for negative moods. This means that if you are happy, you will tend to encode or retrieve pleasant items or memories, but if you are unhappy, the likelihood is not as great that you will encode or retrieve primarily unpleasant items or memories.
  - Whether or not mood congruency effects are found may depend on your being made aware of your current mood state. This is especially true for males.

- A *flashbulb memory* is hypothesized to be a very detailed, vivid recollection of some important event that was very surprising and that caused a high level of arousal.

- · Some people have claimed that a special neural mechanism is responsible for the creation of flashbulb memories. It has also been assumed that because of this special mechanism, flashbulb memories are especially accurate and immune to forgetting.
- · Recent research has seriously challenged the idea that flashbulb memories are established and maintained in a qualitatively different way than is true for more "ordinary" memories. It now appears that flashbulb memories, just like other memories, are also prone to the ravages of forgetting and inaccuracy.

- Evidence from concentration camp survivors suggests that neither the intensity of an emotional experience nor the level of confidence in its recollection can guarantee accuracy of recall.

# PART 4

❖

# *The World Around Us*

# 9

# *The Environment and Memory*

———————— ❖ ————————

Certainly some of the important things we remember have to do with our own internal thoughts or dreams. However, we would argue that the vast majority of our memories involve events that occurred in the physical environment. And since the physical environment is part of the context of almost every memory task, aspects of the surrounding environment are often encoded with, and tied to, the memory traces that are established. For example, when people write lecture notes during a class, it is often done in ways that are quite unique to the individual. Some people write single words or short phrases, others try to compose full sentences, some include diagrams, and some even put mysterious scribblings in the margins of the page (that even they can't decipher later on, let alone the poor soul who borrows the lecture notes to study from). During a later exam, when trying to recall some key fact from the lecture notes, the author will often remember the actual physical layout of the page on which the fact occurs and might remember that the fact was circled twice in red and was near the bottom of the page (yet, and this causes great frustration, sometimes not quite remember the fact itself!).

## THE CUEING POWER OF PHYSICAL STIMULI

It is known that the physical presence of stimuli usually has a stronger effect on memory than does the mere thought of such stimuli. And as every good detective knows, the physical environment can provide very potent context cues to trigger dormant memories, even in a disinterested bystander, far better than mental efforts alone can do. (Remember that Sherlock Holmes would often direct a witness to "return to the scene of the crime" when the witness had

197

difficulty recalling the details of what had happened.) Because of this superiority of physical cues, as will be described in Chapter 15, people generally prefer to rely on physical stimuli rather than on internal strategies (using, for example, the method of loci first described in Chapter 1) to assist their memories.

The powerful cueing influence the physical environment can have on memory is well documented. Several times in the book we have presented evidence that one of the best ways to aid the retrieval process is to reinstate, as closely as possible, the original context in which the material was first learned. This, of course, is the basic premise of the *encoding specificity principle*. Consider the following personal experience:

> One of your authors has driven from his present home in Canton, New York, to where he grew up in Springfield, Massachusetts, at least 25 times during the last 10 years. He never has trouble getting there, nor does he ever need to resort to any maps. Yet if asked *before* he leaves to describe the route he will take, he knows he would give a pretty good imitation of being a moron! Although he can effortlessly drive from Canton to Springfield, he can't give but the broadest details of how he does it.

Rather than some form of creeping dementia befalling one of your authors, it is more likely that this is just an illustrative example of how important the physical environment can be for providing cues for retrieving information from LTM. The reason this person has so little trouble taking all the right roads and making the correct turns is that he has the cueing power of the immediate environment to help him. For example, when driving up to a particular crossroads in Springfield, he sees the McDonald's that he worked at 20 years earlier, and this automatically brings to mind that he has to make a sharp left and then almost an immediate right turn. If the McDonald's were to be torn down, the familiar environmental cues would be lost, and so would be one of your authors!

The powerful effect on memory of reinstating physical cues is most noticeable in situations where there are few other cues to trigger recall and when it would be very difficult for a person to *mentally* reinstate the same environment (Bjork & Richardson-Klavehn, 1989). A common situation that leads to such a state of affairs occurs when many years have gone by since you last visited some familiar place. Particularly dramatic instances of this happen when people return to former residences after having been away for a long time (S. Smith, 1988). A veritable flood of memories often spontaneously arises. If you think about it, you can probably find many times in your own life when such a rush of memories (often unbidden) came back to you when revisiting a familiar place after a long absence.

Since we have already devoted a fair amount of time to discussing the power of the environment to provide excellent cues to aid recall, the focus of this chapter will be on our memory for the environment itself. After all, people must encode, retain, and retrieve many elements of the environment just to cope with the demands of daily life (Gibson, 1979). We must be able to recall where we live and work; how to find our way around; what is safe to eat or drink and what is not; how to dress appropriately; and how to use or respond to countless objects and people encountered on a regular basis, such as traffic signs, stereos, medicines, tools, teachers, cousins, police officers, friends, enemies, and lovers (both current and past!). In fact, later in this chapter we will discuss the merits of a proposal (Hasher & Zacks, 1979, 1984) that maintains that there are certain fundamental aspects of the physical environment that are so vital for everyday functioning and survival that we *automatically* encode them.

## THE IMPORTANCE OF PAST EXPERIENCE

Research suggests that our memory for the physical environment is more like a sketch than a photograph. In other words, our memory for the environment typically contains gaps of information from the original scene much like a hastily made sketch would. For instance, the memory a person has of how to travel to a friend's house or how a beautiful sunset looked will often be dominated by only a few concrete images out of all the information actually available and perceived. Memory for the environment will usually involve a combination of perceptual memories for objects or events seen, heard, smelled, tasted, or touched and the meaning that we attribute to these perceptions.

Just as is true for other types of memory, a person's memory for a particular environment will be determined in large measure by how much past experience the person has had with it. In general, the information remembered from an environment will be a function of a person's awareness of that environment (Ittelson, 1973). Awareness is presumed to vary inversely with the degree to which a person has become adapted to the environment. Put another way, the *less* experience someone has had in a particular environment, the *more* likely it is that he or she will be aware of it and pay deliberate attention to it. For instance, the first time you visited the student union at your school, it is quite likely that you walked around fairly slowly as you tried to note special features for future reference (perhaps where the science fiction book club has an office). The more experience someone has had with a particular environment, the more adapted he or she becomes to it. With the increased adaptation, awareness of the surroundings often fades away, except when circumstances require close scrutiny. So by your eightieth visit to the student union, your pace has quickened quite a bit, and you may not even notice that the science fiction book club has moved to a new location (unless you are in need of finding the office to return a borrowed book).

While awareness tends to fade with experience, the physical environment can still implicitly elicit habits of memory in very predictable ways. As you know, people generally wash dishes in a kitchen sink, not in a bathroom sink. While washing dishes can be accomplished in either place, it rarely is, because the environments associated with kitchens and bathrooms elicit habits that are appropriate only for one environment or the other. It is not uncommon for a person to walk into a bathroom, start to wash his or her hands, and then suddenly remember that the real reason for entering the bathroom was to look for a magazine that might have been left there. Funny things like this occur frequently (especially to people who are prone to be absentminded) because certain environments become very associated with certain behaviors, and when these environments are encountered, particular habits are automatically triggered. This match between environmental conditions and human behavior is also due to the strong social value that our society places on performing certain behaviors only in particular places and at the right time. People know that screaming is permissible at a sporting event when the home team scores and perhaps even cursing when the other team does, but it is not deemed appropriate to scream or curse in a place of worship.

There are several different kinds of environmental memory. It is important to consider each kind separately because encoding, retention, and retrieval of each possess certain unique features. We will start with a discussion of memory for two-dimensional patterns and then move on to three-dimensional objects; finally, even though it is often neglected when environmental memory is considered, we will discuss memory for the fourth dimension—the timing of events.

# *T*WO-DIMENSIONAL MEMORY

Two-dimensional patterns confront us all the time. Magazines, newspapers, books, movies, and television are constantly presenting two-dimensional images and patterns for us to process and remember. In some cases this pattern recognition is important for our very survival—e.g., the recognition of traffic signs while driving. It appears that many two-dimensional patterns are acquired primarily through a *prototype* process. We are exposed to many variations of the same pattern, or we see the same pattern from different angles, distances, and luminances. In the process we develop a mental representation, or prototype, of the pattern that approximates the various perceptions of it that we have seen (Attneave, 1957; Posner & Keele, 1968; Rosch, Simpson, & Miller, 1976). For instance, after a lifetime of seeing various pictures of kangaroos, each of us has developed our own core image, or prototype, of a typical kangaroo.

Our ability to register and recognize complex two-dimensional scenes is extremely good. As many of us regrettably know, friends and relatives often take photos while on vacation and subject us to them on their return. Regardless of how exciting you find photos and slides of other people's vacations, there is evidence that we nevertheless remember them very well. Several researchers have explored our memory for pictures in formal laboratory experiments. In one study, subjects were initially presented with more than 600 different colored pictures. During a subsequent recognition test they were shown pairs of pictures, one a new picture and one that was an "old" picture (i.e., one presented earlier), and subjects had to pick out the "old" one. The subjects' performance was nothing less than phenomenal—they accurately picked out the "old" picture with *97 percent accuracy* (Shepard, 1967). In a similar study in which 2560 different slides were shown for 10 seconds each, subjects were later able to correctly recognize 90 percent of a subset of those slides (Standing, Conezio, & Haber, 1970). Apparently, our memory system for two-dimensional patterns is quite extraordinary.

Sometimes our memory for pictures approaches the faithfulness of detail that an actual photograph would contain (Shepard, 1984). More often, however, our memory for scenes will be less veridical, and we tend to remember objects or features of a scene that we expect to be there (remember the effects of having an "office schema" from Chapter 6).

# *T*HREE-DIMENSIONAL MEMORY

## *Memory for Objects*

The ancient Greeks believed that every object had an ideal form and that object perception simply consisted of recognizing the ideal form inherent in every object. The ability to recognize objects in this manner presumed that people were born with an innate understanding of the ideal form of objects. In modern times, the notion that we are born with knowledge of ideal forms (such as what an ideal chair or car looks like) is seen as ludicrous. Nevertheless, it is now well accepted that we are born with feature detectors in the brain that—while not attuned to highly complex forms like chairs—do respond to lines, curves, and angles (e.g., Hubel & Wiesel, 1965, 1979). These innate feature detectors, although certainly not what the ancient Greeks had in mind, do help people to quickly perceive and encode objects in the environment.

But our memory for objects is only as good as the attention we pay to them. Unless there is a good reason to do otherwise, people tend to encode only the most salient features of many objects that are used in daily life. How many times have you seen a penny or held a penny in your hand? Most college-age people would probably answer that they have seen or held a penny thousands of times. Thus it should be simple for an intelligent college student to simply recognize a penny, right? OK, then scan Figure 9.1 and pick out the real penny.

If you are like most other people, this is not the easy task that it seemed it would be. In fact, Nickerson and Adams (1979) presented each of the 15 drawings in Figure 9.1 to 36 college students and found that only 15 of the 36 (less than 42 percent) could correctly pick out the real penny. Other experiments by Nickerson and Adams further demonstrated that young adults often failed miserably when asked to draw the salient features of a penny from memory. Their results were replicated and extended by Rubin and Kontis (1983), who found that people were generally quite inaccurate in their drawings of a penny, nickel, dime, and quarter. A recent study by Jones (1990) has indicated that

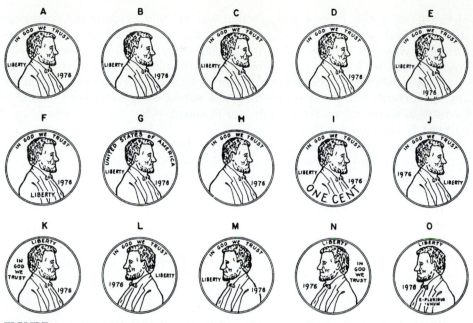

**FIGURE 9.1**
Pick out the real penny.
*Reprinted with permission from Nickerson & Adams, 1979.*

British college students are no better at remembering the critical features of their coins than are their American counterparts. For those of you who haven't yet fetched a penny out of your pocket to check if you were correct—Figure 9.1A is the picture of a real penny.

Examples abound to demonstrate that most people have little memory for even major details of common objects. Try writing down from memory the letter and number arrangement on the dial or buttons of a standard telephone. Now go and look at a telephone and check your performance. Again, if you are typical, even though you have used telephones for years, chances are good that you made major blunders in your recall. Although, as seen in the last section, our memory for two-dimensional patterns demonstrates that we have the *capacity* to pick up and remember a great deal of detailed information, our object memory shows that people often pick up only enough detail to deal with the immediate task at hand.

## Memory for Devices

Modern life presents us with numerous devices to be mastered and used. Such things as bicycles, appliances, automobiles, and VCRs all require us to determine how they function. Unfortunately, such devices are often poorly designed and therefore unnecessarily hard to use. Donald Norman, who has written a very interesting and informative book entitled *The Psychology of Everyday Things* (1988), proposes that a "user-friendly" device should possess certain characteristics. These characteristics include having visible controls, demonstrating a sensible conceptual basis (i.e., the operation is consistent with the effects), and providing continuous feedback for the operator.

Very often the disadvantageous characteristics of a device pertain to memory functioning. For example, many older-model cars don't provide any signal that you have left your headlights on when you turn off the ignition. Consequently, because they had forgotten to turn off their car lights, many people have experienced the utter joy of not being able to start their car later (more often than not in the dead of winter) because their car battery was drained of energy. Most newer-model cars now "know" enough to signal an auditory alarm if you should inadvertently forget to turn off your lights. In some cars, like Subarus, the headlights automatically go off as soon as the ignition is turned off. For many technical devices a critical issue is how much knowledge should be incorporated in the device itself and how much knowledge should presumably be in the user's head. Oftentimes, devices do not indicate whether or not any action is necessary on the part of the user, and the job of knowing or remembering what to do and when to do it is left entirely up to the individual (as in the case of turning off your car lights).

Some modern electronic devices are too complicated to learn to use easily. Many people do not bother to learn how to program their VCR because of the somewhat complicated procedures that need to be remembered each time the machine is programmed. Instead, these people will rely on another person (usually a family member or a friend) to do the task for them. This is also a good example of how social interactions can affect memory functioning, a topic that is considered in depth in Chapter 10. A computer is another prime example of a complicated device that requires a person to remember how to perform a series of operations in correct order. People who have been using typewriters for 20 or 30 years often resist learning how to use a word processor. They may feel overwhelmed by the magnitude of the task and even be a little fearful that they won't be able to remember all the necessary commands to operate the computer and printer.

Fortunately, in recent years, largely because of the tight economic times that have led to fierce competition for the consumer's dollar, manufacturers have started to make devices that are more user-friendly. Often this has taken the form of reducing the memory load the consumer needs to operate the device. For instance, recently made VCRs require much less rote memory than did their predecessors of just a few years ago.

## Spatial Memory

Edward Tolman (1948) argued that rats learn to traverse a maze by developing a *cognitive map* of the maze. A cognitive map is a mental representation of the spatial layout of an area. Tolman's suggestion that rats can form cognitive maps of their environment was a radical idea, and until his seminal work was finally accepted, most of his contemporaries scoffed at the idea. The prevailing notion was that rats learned a maze by positive reinforcement that linked specific responses to specific stimuli that occurred in different parts of the maze.

Modern research on spatial memory has been done primarily with humans, and this research has provided considerable evidence that people also develop and use cognitive maps (e.g., Finke, 1989; Levine, Jankovic, & Palij, 1982; McNamara, 1986). Everyday life requires us to move about our environments. In most situations (such as going to the movies or to the dentist's office) we do not have a physical map in our possession. Instead, we must rely on our cognitive maps to navigate these routes that contain various alleys, paths, roads, shortcuts, and landmarks. Often when people travel to a new area, they will seek directions from someone who has a better cognitive map than they do. But as shown in the cartoon in Figure 9.2, this does not always help much.

Before a person can develop a cognitive map of a new area, a key requirement is that the person must first get properly oriented to the new spatial arrangement. To help people obtain the proper orientation in places such as a

FIGURE 9.2
Problems in comprehending someone else's cognitive map.
*Drawing by Stevenson; © 1976 The New Yorker Magazine, Inc.*

large building, a college campus, or a national park, there are the famous (infamous?) you-are-here maps. An example of a typical you-are-here map is shown in Figure 9.3. These ubiquitous maps can be quite helpful, but only if they are properly aligned with the real world. As many of us regretfully know, misalignment is not uncommon. For instance, if an error is made in physically hanging a directory map of a mall, the little arrow that represents your present position will not properly orient you to what is actually in front of or behind you. Instead, the map may suggest that a clothing store is straight ahead, but in reality, if you walked straight ahead, you would end up in the bathroom! Research has shown that such misalignment will lead people to make such mistakes (Palij, Levine, & Kahan, 1984).

It is important to note that the mental representation gained from studying a map has different properties than the mental representation gained from

FIGURE 9.3
A you-are-here map showing some of the buildings of a college campus.

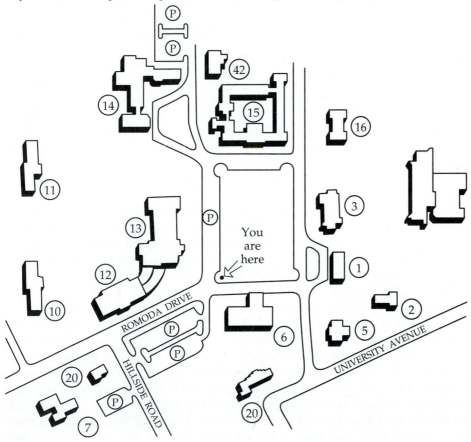

actual physical exploration of an area. In one study, college subjects learned the spatial arrangement of a complex building (the first floor of The Rand Corporation in Santa Monica, California) by means of a map, while others (a combination of secretaries and research assistants) learned the layout from working in the building varying amounts of time. The results indicated that the people who studied the map were superior in estimating straight-line distances and in judging the relative location of objects, while those who learned the spatial arrangement through experience were better at estimating route distances (other than straight-line ones) and at orienting themselves with respect to unseen objects (Thorndyke & Hayes-Roth, 1982). As might be expected, the subjects with the most extensive experience working in the building (from 1 to 2 years) performed the best. However, even these subjects were not superior in using their cognitive maps for object location judgments when compared with college students who had access to a map of the building for only an average of 20 minutes. This research suggests that by simply studying a physical map for a few minutes, a person can develop a cognitive map of an area that is in many important ways comparable (and sometimes even superior) to one that is obtained through extensive personal experience.

One's spatial knowledge of an area, even after extensive exposure or experience, can still possess some perceptual distortions (Moar & Bower, 1983; Shepard, 1984; Stevens & Coupe, 1978; Tversky, 1981). These distortions are often the result of higher-level mental processes interfering with specific details. As an example of this, answer the following question: Which city is farther west—Reno, Nevada, or Los Angeles, California? If you haven't checked a map recently (or if you don't live near either city), you probably answered Los Angeles (Stevens & Coupe, 1978). This certainly *seems* to be the correct answer, since we "know" that California is farther west than Nevada, but if you look at a map (see Figure 9.4), you will see that a large part of the state of Nevada (including Reno) is farther west than a sizable part of California (including Los Angeles).

From Chapter 6 you know that people remember features of the environment at least partly on the basis of schemas and expectations (e.g., Brewer & Treyens, 1981). People are also likely to "remember" that an object was in a certain place (e.g., a stoplight at a busy intersection), even though the object was never actually there (Biederman, Mezzanotte, & Rabinowitz, 1982). Fortunately, research has shown that with increased exposure to a spatial environment, distortions and biases are progressively eliminated (Craik & McDowd, 1987). The memorability of a place is also a function of well-known principles of perceptual organization. For instance, it has been demonstrated that items on a desk are better remembered if they are sensibly organized (Malone, 1983).

Before ending this section, it is important to note that there has been a lively debate as to whether or not it is even possible to store information in the brain in the form of mental images or cognitive maps (for good overviews of the debate, see Finke, 1985; Pinker, 1985; Solso, 1991; and Tye, 1991). This may seem surprising to you, since from a subjective point of view, most people

FIGURE 9.4
A map showing that Reno, Nevada, is actually farther
west than Los Angeles, California.

would certainly argue that they can encode images of objects, places, and
people quite easily. For instance, think about how you would answer the
following question: Are there more windows or tables in your current house?
To answer this question, most likely you generated a visual image of each room
of your house and then counted each window or table that you "saw."

Some theorists have maintained that our subjective feelings are wrong.
They believe that people store information not in the form of images but rather
in the form of abstract propositions (perhaps like the semantic networks discussed in Chapter 3) about physical objects and their interrelationships (e.g.,
Anderson & Bower, 1973; Pylyshyn, 1973, 1981). Although it would be difficult
to ever completely dismiss this possibility, there is abundant empirical evidence
that suggests that people can store information in the form of mental images
(Cornoldi & McDaniel, 1991; Finke, 1989; Kosslyn, 1973, 1975, 1981; Kosslyn &
Pomerantz, 1977; Paivio, 1969, 1971; Shepard, 1967, 1978; Shepard & Chipman,
1970; Shepard & Metzler, 1971) and that people can manipulate (e.g., mentally

rotate or visually scan) these mental images or cognitive maps in ways that are very similar to how they would perceive and manipulate actual physical objects and maps.

However, on the basis of a number of recent studies, there is also growing evidence that information about the physical environment is not encoded solely in terms of spatial features (Clayton & Habibi, 1991; McNamara, 1986; McNamara, Altarriba, Bendele, Johnson, & Clayton, 1989; Merrill & Baird, 1987; Sherman & Lim, 1991). The accumulated evidence strongly suggests that the same information can be encoded and stored in memory by means of different codes or modes of processing. This flexibility means that some of the key sensory or perceptual properties of the physical environment will be stored in the form of images in LTM, but in addition, some of this information will also be stored in a more abstract or propositional fashion.

## Memory for Object Location

In a very influential paper published in 1979, Lynn Hasher and Rose Zacks suggested that the ease of encoding information into memory varies as a function of attentional effort. They believed that some information could be encoded automatically, requiring little or no intentional effort or attention. At the other extreme, however, encoding other types of information would require intense effort and abundant attentional resources.

Hasher and Zacks suggested that the kinds of information that people encode automatically are those that involve fundamental aspects of the environment. According to their framework, *object location, frequency of occurrence,* and the *temporal order of events* are all automatically encoded into memory. Furthermore, they proposed that automatic encoding processes should not be affected by independent variables that are known to greatly influence effortful processing (Hasher & Zacks, 1984). The most important of these independent variables are presented in Table 9.1.

However, their belief in the automatic encoding of aspects of the physical environment has been seriously challenged in recent years. For instance, Naveh-Benjamin (1987, 1988) has provided evidence that the memory for the location of objects can vary as a function of competing activities, practice, intentionality, strategy use, age, and individual differences in ability. In spite of these results, Ellis (1990) still maintains that the encoding of object location is largely an automatic process. Even if memory for the location of objects turns out to be primarily an automatic process, this doesn't mean that memory for an object's location will always be correct. Automatic processing doesn't guarantee accuracy; it just means that some information about an object's location will be encoded in memory. While such information may often be sufficient, it makes sense to us that the use of voluntary, intentional efforts will increase the chances that people will remember the location of objects.

**TABLE 9.1** SOME INDEPENDENT VARIABLES THAT WILL NOT INFLUENCE THE AUTOMATIC ENCODING OF OBJECT LOCATION, FREQUENCY OF OCCURRENCE, AND TEMPORAL ORDERING OF EVENTS, ACCORDING TO HASHER AND ZACKS (1984)

Competing activities

Practice on a task

Feedback on performance

Varying of instructions

Intentionality to perform a task

Age differences (from school age to elderly)

Differences in arousal level, motivation, intelligence, and educational background

Accurate memory for object location can fail for a number of reasons. For instance, many people forget where they leave objects because they never properly encode their location in the first place. The more absentminded a person tends to be, the more likely this will be a continuing problem. But even if you are not often absentminded, if you are momentarily distracted by some event, this can interfere with encoding and lead to the misplacing of objects (Reason, 1984b; Reason & Mycielska, 1982). If the doorbell rings unexpectedly, most people will quickly put down any objects they are holding and go find out who is at the door. Later on, these individuals often will find it difficult to remember the location of the previously held items because of insufficient encoding of location information.

Some types of objects seem to be misplaced more often than others. For example, it is rare to misplace a bottle of milk, but it is frustratingly easy to misplace your reading glasses or a book. This is because there are only a few logical places where the bottle of milk can be placed (e.g., if it's not in the refrigerator, it most likely will be on the counter or table in the kitchen). In contrast, your glasses or book can be almost anywhere in, and even sometimes outside, the building. Again, as you read in Chapter 6, the memory people have for the position of objects in a room is highly influenced by their schemas and expectations.

Another reason that objects get misplaced is that many of them are continuously being picked up, used in some fashion, and then placed somewhere else. If a particular object can logically appear in a variety of different locations, and if a person has some recollection that he or she has, in fact, placed the object at various times in these different locations, then the problem can be one of faulty *updating* (Bjork, 1978). Updating is the process of remembering only the latest encounter one has had with an object. Suppose that you're reading a very interesting science fiction story. It is likely that you will carry it around with you at home and leave it in one of a multitude of places around your house (on the couch, on the kitchen table, on your pillow, or even on the sink in the bathroom) when you must leave for school or work. Upon arriving home again, if you haven't done a good job of updating your memory for the book's location, you will have to search lots of places before locating it.

Effective updating is very important for everyday living. If we didn't update our memories and erase outdated ones, we would have considerable problems with proactive interference (see Chapters 3 and 5). In addition, we would remember lots of useless information. After all, who needs to remember the birthday of a former lover, the combination of the locker you used in junior high school, the former telephone number of an aunt or uncle who has moved to a new city, or where the car was parked last week on a trip to the grocery store. Some astute people are aware of the problems involved with constantly updating their memories, and so they try to minimize the need for this updating. For example, these people will attempt to park their cars in the same spot every time they go to a large indoor parking garage or a shopping mall. This way they avoid having to update at all.

When an object cannot be quickly located, most people will try to mentally reconstruct the sequence of actions that occurred just before the object was placed down somewhere. This search strategy is often quite effective. It should be noted, however, that sometimes the reason an object isn't found is that the person searching for it doesn't really remember what it looked like, and upon seeing the actual object, he or she fails to recognize it. One of your authors has an embarrassingly difficult time recognizing all the hats, mittens, boots, and coats of his three children when picking them up at the baby-sitter's. On more than one occasion he has brought home the "wrong" stuff. At other times an object is not found simply because it is partially hidden or the person doing the searching is just not very thorough and misses the sought-after object, even though it is in plain sight.

## Frequency of Occurrence

Try answering the questions in Table 9.2. If you are like most other people, then with the exception of question 5, which we will consider shortly, you were probably quite accurate in your frequency estimates. By the way, there are billions more pennies in circulation than dollar bills, and there are usually dozens more types of magazines than types of beer in most supermarkets. A substantial amount of research has shown that people are sensitive to the rate of occurrence of many different types of stimuli and events. This includes the frequency of *single letters* (Attneave, 1953), *words* (Hasher & Chromiak, 1977; Hintzman, 1969; Howes, 1954; Shapiro, 1969), *verbatim sentences* (Gude & Zechmeister, 1975; Jacoby, 1972), *gist for sentences* (Gude & Zechmeister, 1975), *surnames* (Zechmeister, King, Gude, & Opera-Nadi, 1975), and *pictures* (Hintzman & Rogers, 1973). For example, a very high correlation (+.88) was found between the estimated frequency with which different English letters appeared in words and their actual frequency of occurrence (Attneave, 1953).

**TABLE 9.2** QUESTIONS ABOUT THE FREQUENCY OF OCCURRENCE OF VARIOUS EVENTS

1. Are there more pennies in general circulation or more dollar bills?
2. During the last year have you attended more musical concerts or birthday parties?
3. In the supermarket where you normally shop, are there more different kinds of beer or magazines?
4. Have you eaten more eggs or more candy bars in the last seven days?
5. Do more people die from floods or from asthma?
6. Have there been more rainy days this month or last month?

Three different methods are generally used to measure frequency knowledge (Hasher & Zacks, 1984). One method, called *frequency judgment,* involves asking people to give a direct estimate of the number of occurrences of a particular event or stimulus. For example, a subject may be shown a large group of pictures with some of the same pictures appearing several times. The subject's task is to estimate how many times each picture was presented. In the *frequency discrimination method* a person must choose either the more or the less frequently occurring item from a series of pairs of items. The third technique used to measure frequency knowledge is called the *ranking method.* This involves having the subject rank-order a list of items or events in terms of their frequency of occurrence.

Hasher and Zacks (1984) discovered an interesting phenomenon with regard to frequency judgments. Even though most people are very accurate when making such judgments, it was found that when first confronted with the need to make a frequency estimate, people generally have little confidence in their ability and even express surprise that they would be expected to have such information stored in their memories. Only after subjects have actually tried to perform frequency judgments do their initial doubts disappear. They soon realize that they do, in fact, have considerable knowledge about the frequency of occurrence of events. Findings such as these, however, are not at all surprising to Hasher and Zacks. In fact, it makes good sense to them that people encode information about frequency of occurrence without awareness or intention. This is because, as we learned earlier, Hasher and Zacks (1979, 1984) consider frequency information to be one of the aspects of the environment that is encoded automatically.

These claims, however, have been seriously questioned. For instance, there is evidence that frequency judgments do, in fact, vary with competing demands (Fisk & Schneider, 1984; Maki & Ostby, 1987; Naveh-Benjamin & Jonides, 1986; Sanders, Gonzalez, Murphy, Liddle, & Vitina, 1987); with nature of instructions, level of processing, and intentionality (Greene, 1984, 1986; Hanson & Hirst, 1988; Johnson, Peterson, Yap, & Rose, 1989; Jonides & Naveh-Benjamin, 1987; Maki & Ostby, 1987; Sanders et al., 1987; Williams & Durso, 1986); with age (Kausler, Lichty, & Hakami, 1984; Warren & Mitchell, 1980); and with physical condition (e.g., alcohol intoxication; Birnbaum, Taylor, Johnson & Raye, 1987). It has also been shown that if a person is just asked to *imagine* an object or event, this can increase the person's estimate of the frequency of occurrence for seeing the real object or event (Johnson, Taylor, & Raye, 1977). For example, if a person was presented with an actual picture of an apple three times and was also asked to *imagine* seeing an apple eight times, this person would later inflate his or her estimate of the frequency of occurrence for seeing the real picture of an apple (Johnson, Raye, Wang, & Taylor, 1979).

Even though the preponderance of evidence now suggests that the encoding of frequency information is certainly not just an automatic process unaffected by independent variables, this does not negate the fact that people are usually very good in their frequency estimations. But not always, as you will see for yourself if you ask a few friends the following question: Does the letter *V* occur more often in the first or third position in all English words of at least three letters? Your friends will probably try to answer this question by first determining how many words immediately come to mind that have a *V* as a first letter or a third letter. When they do this, almost inevitably they will generate more instances of words that start with a *V*, and because of this they will probably estimate that more words in English start with a *V* than have a *V* as a third letter. But they will be wrong! There are more words in the English language that have a *V* in the third position than in the first. And, in fact, the same relationship is true for the letters, *K, R, L,* and *N* (i.e., more words have these letters as the third letter than as the first letter).

Tversky and Kahneman (1973) conducted an experiment in which they found, after averaging the responses for all five of the previously mentioned letters, that subjects estimated that these letters appeared about twice as often in the first position as in the third. Why did subjects err so badly on this type of frequency task? The answer is that there are some situations in which people are especially prone to commit certain error-producing biases. According to Tversky and Kahneman (1973), people often judge the frequency of an event on the basis of how quickly or easily instances of the event can be remembered, using a strategy called the *availability heuristic.* A heuristic is a helpful rule of thumb that often, but not always, leads to a correct answer. Others have also shown that people will rely on an availability heuristic to make frequency judgments (Bruce, Hockley, & Craik, 1991; Williams & Durso, 1986). In many situations, the ability to think of appropriate instances (i.e., availability) and the actual frequency of occurrence of an event will be highly related. In such cases using an availability heuristic will lead to accurate frequency judgments.

However, using an availability heuristic doesn't always lead to correct frequency estimates (remember the difficulty in predicting the frequency of letter positions). The availability heuristic is also likely to be used, and to cause errors, when people are asked to estimate the frequency of real-life events that are rarely experienced directly (Lichtenstein, Slovic, Fischhoff, Layman, & Combs, 1978; Zechmeister & Nyberg, 1982). For instance, when subjects are asked to answer question 5 in Table 9.2, they usually estimate that more people die from floods than from asthma. In reality, just the opposite is true—deaths from asthma occur about nine times more frequently than do deaths from floods (Lichtenstein et al., 1978). Why are people so far off in their estimates? Probably because natural catastrophes like major floods make it into the head-lines, while, let's face it, a story about someone dying from asthma doesn't quite have the same pizzazz. Therefore, if a person is making a frequency estimate primarily on the basis of the availability of instances that quickly come to mind, he or she will recall more stories about floods than about killer asthma attacks, and an error in frequency judgment will be the result.

# MEMORY FOR THE FOURTH DIMENSION: THE TIMING OF EVENTS

Unless something bizarre has happened to you (like being locked up in solitary confinement or having to float around on a raft while lost at sea), the environ-ment in which you exist is in a constant state of flux. Not only do objects continuously come into and disappear from view, but also dozens of activities and events occur throughout the day. In order to give some coherence to this vast array of changes in our physical environment, people need to be able to order these changes in time. One way of doing this, as was already discussed in the previous section on memory for object location, is by *updating*. You'll remember that updating was a useful way to keep track of objects that were often moved around. Whenever we update our knowledge of movements and changes in the physical environment, we are also making temporal judgments.

Making accurate temporal judgments is crucial for successfully conducting daily life. It is so important, in fact, that the temporal order of events was one of the three fundamental aspects of the environment that Hasher and Zacks claimed were encoded automatically. However, as was also true for object location and frequency of occurrence, there is now good evidence that temporal information is affected by many of the same variables from which it was supposedly immune (Jackson, 1985; Naveh-Benjamin, 1990; Zacks, Hasher, Alba, Sanft, & Rose, 1984).

William Friedman (1990) described five different models (listed in Table 9.3) that have at one time or another been put forth to explain how people remember the timing of events. Let's examine each of these models.

## Time-Tagging Model

This model suggests that the time at which an event occurred is an attribute that is encoded into memory, just like attributes such as color, size, and form. When an event is recalled from memory, the time it occurred also is retrieved. It has even been suggested that the time-tagging of an event can be linked to a biological clock within the body.

**9.3** THE FIVE MODELS MOST OFTEN CITED TO ACCOUNT FOR THE MEMORY
OF THE TIMING OF EVENTS

*Time-tagging model:* The exact time an event occurred is encoded just like any other
attribute.

*Temporal sequencing model:* Events are stored sequentially, but without the precision
implied by the time-tagging model.

*Trace strength model:* The stronger the memory trace of an event, the more recently it is
estimated to have occurred.

*Inference model:* The timing of an event is estimated by reconstructing the situation and
then logically inferring when the event took place.

*Reminding model:* New experiences bring to mind previous related experiences, causing the relative temporal order of the experiences to be automatically stored.

On at least one level of analysis this model has some validity. After all,
normal people can easily tell the difference in time between an event that
occurred last weekend and one that occurred two years ago. However, with
some exceptions, our ability to remember the *exact* time when events occurred
is extremely poor. This argues against any strong version of a time-tagging
model. Consider the remarkable study conducted by Wagenaar on his ability
to remember events from his own life (this study was first mentioned in Chapter
8). Over a six-year period beginning in 1978, Wagenaar (1986) recorded one or
two of the most notable events or incidents that occurred each day. The information he recorded included what the event was about, who else was present,
where the event took place, and the exact date. When he later tested his recall
of this information by using various retrieval cues, he found that cues about
*who, what,* and *where* were helpful in allowing him to recall the details of an
event. However, when Wagenaar supplied himself with only the *date* of an
event, he found it to be "almost useless" as an aid for retrieving other relevant
information. In addition, when he was first given the *who, what,* and *where*
information and he had to remember the *date,* he found it extremely difficult
to do. As this and other research (as well as our own introspections) has shown,
memory for the timing of events can be very imprecise, especially as the event
recedes further into the past. Clearly, the evidence indicates that we do not
time-tag events as they are encoded into memory in a manner similar to the
way the post office stamps the date on a letter.

## Temporal Sequencing Model

This model suggests that events are stored sequentially in memory according
to their time of arrival. Murdock (1974) has suggested that an appropriate
metaphor for this model would be that of items moving along a conveyor belt.
Items placed on the conveyor belt at the same time are grouped together and
recede into the distance together. A rough estimate of how much time has
elapsed since the items first entered the conveyor can be made by noting their

distance away from the starting point or the number of intervening items between the starting point and the present location of the original items. As Friedman (1990) points out, such a model can account for the imprecise nature of our memory for the time of occurrence of events. It can also explain why it is more difficult to gauge the temporal ordering of events as time goes by (the farther down the conveyor belt you have to "look," the harder it is to "see" the items and their correct order).

Consistent with a temporal sequencing model (and the conveyor belt metaphor), it has been observed that subjects are most accurate in making order judgments about the last few words they saw in a list and that accuracy declines for ordering words that appeared earlier in the list (Friedman, 1990). Unfortunately, the data from numerous studies has also shown that the *first few* items can be very accurately placed in correct temporal order (Guenther & Linton, 1975; Hintzman & Block, 1971; Hintzman, Block, & Summers, 1973; Toglia & Kimble, 1976; Tzeng, 1976; Underwood, 1977). This consistent result poses a difficult problem for a temporal sequencing model of remembering time. Such a model would predict that the first few items of a list should be the ones hardest to place in correct temporal order. Furthermore, data from Wagenaar's study (1986) suggests that memory for events is rarely organized as a function of their time of arrival. For instance, he discovered that when two unrelated events occurred during the same day, the remembrance of one of them was not an effective retrieval cue for recalling the other.

## Trace Strength Model

The trace strength model for remembering temporal order rests on two assumptions. First, as time passes, the memory trace for an event decreases in strength. And second, people estimate the timing of an event by how strong its trace is—the stronger the trace, the more recent the event. This model has appeal because it seems to be consistent with some everyday experiences. When events are of roughly equal significance, the more recent event seems more vivid or stronger (Friedman, 1990). For instance, if you ate pizza last night in your favorite restaurant, the experience probably stands out more in your memory than does the experience you had eating pizza at the same establishment three months ago. In addition, many people probably use some variant of the trace strength model to help themselves get dressed in the morning. Since most of us don't want to wear exactly the same clothes each day to school or work, we stand in front of our closets looking at our clothes and pick out combinations that we don't remember wearing recently. The clothing items selected will be the ones that have little strength in our memories, because we assume that they haven't been worn lately; otherwise, we would have "remembered" them better.

However, a trace strength model (like the temporal sequencing model) also has trouble accounting for the fact that the first items of a list can be better ordered in time than can later-appearing items (especially those from the middle of the list). This is a problem because according to a trace strength model, more recently appearing items should be easier to place in proper order, since their traces should be stronger. Even more troubling is the finding that list items that are judged to be more memorable are not judged to have occurred more recently (Flexser & Bower, 1974; Tzeng, 1976; Tzeng, Lee, & Wetzel, 1979). A trace strength model for remembering the time of events would have predicted that more memorable items should have been judged to have appeared more recently. But this judgment doesn't appear to occur, and thus the appeal of a trace strength model is limited.

## Inference Model

This model assumes that the timing of an event is determined by using other pieces of information to logically infer when the event must have occurred. This often involves reconstructing aspects of the situation through the process of introspection. For example, suppose you were asked to remember the last time you went to a wedding. Unless the wedding had great personal significance for you (e.g., it was your own!), you would probably have to reconstruct the events and circumstances associated with the occasion to remember the date. Perhaps you might first recall that the wedding must have occurred on a very cold day, since you remember having had trouble with your car heater while driving to the ceremony. In addition, you also recall that the wedding ceremony was on a Friday night because you had to get permission to leave work early (you normally work the evening shift on Fridays). Finally, you can pinpoint the exact date by remembering that the wedding occurred on the weekend of the Super Bowl, and from general knowledge you know that football's annual extravaganza usually occurs on the third Sunday in January.

Lots of evidence exists that people do, in fact, engage in similar reconstruction processes to recall the timing of events (Baddeley, Lewis, & Nimmo-Smith, 1978; Brown, Shevell, & Rips, 1986; Friedman, 1987; Friedman & Wilkins, 1985). The inference model can also account for the surprising accuracy with which people remember the temporal order of the first few items of a list; the model assumes that subjects make a temporal landmark of the first items by associating them with the beginning of the list (Friedman, 1990).

**More support: Scale effects.** There are additional data that support the inference model. These data come from studies that have examined what are called *scale effects* (Friedman, 1987; Friedman & Wilkins, 1985). This term refers to the fact that some cues are useful for recalling some specific lengths or other aspects of time but not others. For instance, a cue might be helpful for determining what time of day something happened (e.g., the doorbell rang while you were showering, so your cousin must have arrived in the early morning) or the month in which it occurred (e.g., the love letter was delivered on Valentine's Day, so it must have been February), but it might not be helpful for reconstructing the day of the week or the year the event occurred.

A clever demonstration of scale effects was shown by Friedman (1987). At approximately 11:50 a.m. on Friday, January 31, 1986, a mild earthquake struck in northeastern Ohio, where Oberlin College is located. To many people who experienced the earthquake, it was a vibration of the ground that lasted for one or two seconds. Earthquakes are rare phenomena in that part of the country, so any occurrence would likely be a memorable event. At the end of September of the same year, Friedman sent a survey to Oberlin College employees asking them to estimate the hour, day of the week, day of the month, month, and year that the earthquake had occurred. In addition, the subjects were asked to rate their level of confidence for each estimate, and to "list the things you thought of in arriving at this estimate" (p. 518). Only those who had personally experienced the earthquake were asked to participate, and they were further told to give their estimates without consulting anyone else or any calendars.

As might be expected from the fairly short time period between the event and the survey (about eight months), subjects were generally quite accurate in terms of remembering that the earthquake hit earlier in the same year. More important, though, the results also provided strong evidence for both the inference model and scaling effects. For example, accuracy for the day of the week and day of the month estimates was not significantly different from what you would expect from pure guesses, and the month of occurrence estimates were off by nearly two months. However, subjects were much more accurate in their estimates of the hour at which the earthquake occurred. On the average, the hour estimate was off by only a little more than one hour, a level of accuracy significantly above what would be expected by chance. The subjects were also more confident about their hour estimates than about their estimates for day of the week, day of the month, and month. Why were subjects more accurate in the hour estimates? On the basis of their protocols, it was clear that subjects inferred that the earthquake must have struck around noontime because they were able to associate it with lunch. It was fortuitous that the earthquake struck near lunchtime because this provided people with an excellent cue for reconstructing the correct hour, but not for reconstructing the correct day of the week, day of the month, or month.

## Reminding Model

The last major model for remembering the timing of events assumes that new experiences bring to mind previous related experiences (Hintzman, Summers, & Block, 1975; Tzeng & Cotton, 1980; Winograd & Soloway, 1985). For instance, according to the reminding model, when the New York Giants won the Super Bowl in 1991, for many Giants' fans this brought to mind the previous Super Bowl victory by the Giants in 1987. When this occurred, the correct order of occurrence of the two victories was automatically stored in memory. The reminding model maintains that people continuously update the temporal ordering of an event each time they experience something that reminds them of it.

A key prediction of the model is that it should be easier to place in correct temporal order two related items than two unrelated items. Evidence consistent with this prediction has been found. For instance, Tzeng and Cotton (1980) showed that subjects were better at remembering the correct order for words that represented the same conceptual category (e.g., *arm* and *leg*) than for pairs of words representing different conceptual categories (e.g., *toad* and *pen*). The reminding model, however, can't explain the superior ability people have to recall the order of the first few words from a list, scaling effects, or people's ability to know the exact date of an event (Friedman, 1990).

## Choosing among the Models

In his evaluation of the five models, Friedman (1990) came to the conclusion that two of the models (time-tagging and temporal sequencing) are not well supported by the literature and have serious deficiencies. However, depending on the situation, each of the other three models (trace strength, inference, and reminding) are all probably used by people to order events in time. Overall, however, the inference model received the greatest support.

Friedman (1990, 1993) suggests that these models may have overemphasized our ability to remember events in *linear* time. *Linear time* refers to placing events in order from most distant to most recent and having knowledge of exact dates of occurrence. While people certainly can employ a linear approach to remembering the timing of events, and this is undoubtedly helpful to us, Friedman (1990, 1993) makes a good argument that people have also evolved a *cyclic* approach to remembering time as well. A cyclic approach involves relating cyclical patterns (the changing seasons, the rising and setting of the sun, the monthly changes in the appearance of the moon, the changes in tides, etc.) to the occurrence of events. Using a cyclic approach, it is not necessary to know the exact date of a prior event. All that would be needed is to know the relationship between the event and some cyclic pattern. For instance, our ancestors might have needed to know that they should plant their crops when certain types of birds migrated back to the area in the springtime. Depending on a calendar to find a specific date to start planting would not have been necessary (or perhaps even useful, given the variability of weather conditions year to year). As Friedman (1990, 1993) suggests, it may well be that a cyclical approach to remembering the timing of events may play a larger role in our lives than has been generally recognized.

# SUMMARY

**I. Cueing Power of Physical Stimuli**
- The physical environment provides powerful context cues to help people remember information.
- The beneficial effect of reinstating physical cues is most evident in situ-

ations in which few other retrieval cues are present and when it is difficult to mentally reinstate the environment.

## II. Importance of Past Experience
- Because of the wealth of information available and our limited processing abilities, our memories of the physical environment contain gaps and are selective.
- There generally exists an inverse relationship between awareness of the environment and adaptation—the less experience with an environment, the more attention will be paid to it.

## III. Two-Dimensional Memory
- People are quite good at encoding and remembering large numbers of complex two-dimensional patterns such as pictures, movies, and photographs.
- Through experience, people often acquire *prototypes* of frequently occurring patterns. This helps them to recognize such patterns quickly and accurately, even though they may appear in different guises.

## IV. Three-Dimensional Memory
- Although we have the capacity to remember an enormous amount of detail about objects, we usually encode only the most salient aspects. As a result, our ability to accurately recall the details of very common objects is surprisingly poor.
- Many modern-day devices are not "user friendly." A primary reason for this is that these devices often place unnecessary memory demands on people. As a result, some people resist learning or refuse to learn to use these devices.
- To navigate around the physical environment, people develop and use *cognitive maps* to aid their spatial memories.
    - Cognitive maps can be created either by studying a physical map or by having actual experience moving around in a particular environment.
    - Expectations and schemas can cause distortions in cognitive maps and in our ability to remember the features of the environment.
    - There is an ongoing debate by some researchers concerning whether or not it is even possible to store information in the brain in the form of mental images or cognitive maps.
    - On the basis of the available evidence, as well as powerful subjective experiences, most researchers think it is likely that people can store information in such a way that many of the sensory or perceptual qualities of the physical environment are preserved. However, this information can also be coded in a more abstract or propositional fashion.
- Hasher and Zacks proposed that certain fundamental aspects of the physical environment are automatically encoded into memory. This suppos-

edly meant that little or no intentional effort or attention was needed to process such information (and that such effort or attention would not even be useful).

- According to Hasher and Zacks, *object location*, *frequency of occurrence*, and the *temporal order* of events are all automatically encoded into memory.
- Evidence has accumulated, however, to indicate that each of these aspects of the environment can be affected by processes that influence effort and attention. Such evidence has seriously challenged the notion of automatic processing of environmental information.

- Even though people generally have good memory for object location, memory can fail for a variety of reasons. These include *inadequate initial encoding* of object location, being *absentminded* or *distracted, faulty updating, not being familiar* with objects, and *using poor search strategies*.
  - When memory for an object's location fails, a common strategy (one that often works) is to try to reconstruct the sequence of actions that occurred just before the object was placed down somewhere.

- Often much to their surprise, people are usually very astute at estimating the frequency of occurrence of various events. The three most common ways to measure frequency knowledge are the *frequency judgment method*, the *frequency discrimination method*, and the *ranking method*.
  - When people do err in making frequency judgments, it is often because they used some variant of an *availability heuristic*. This heuristic is used when a person judges the frequency of an event on the basis of how quickly or easily he or she can recall instances of the event. An availability heuristic often leads to correct estimates of frequency, but it can also lead people astray, especially if they are asked to estimate the frequency of events rarely experienced directly.

## V. Memory for the Fourth Dimension: Timing of Events

- To give coherence to daily life, people need to be able to order in time the vast array of changes that occur in the physical environment around them.

- Five different models of how people remember the timing of events were presented. These were the *time-tagging model*, the *temporal sequencing model*, the *trace strength model*, the *inference model*, and the *reminding model*.

- It was concluded that there was little evidence to support either the time-tagging model or the temporal sequencing model. Support was found for the trace strength and reminding models and especially for the inference model, which could explain certain phenomena that none of the other models could (such as *scale effects*).

- It was also suggested that too much attention has been given to how people process time in a *linear* fashion and not enough attention to how people use a *cyclic* approach to remembering the timing of events.

# 10

# *Social Interaction and Memory*

———— ❖ ————

For better or worse, our memory capability is constantly being used and displayed whenever we interact with other people. Whether we're having a casual conversation with a friend about an upcoming party or a serious discussion with a teacher concerning a grade on an exam, we often need to pick up information that will be needed in the future or to recall key information that was acquired in the past. Memory failures in social contexts can be embarrassing, and, as you will learn in this chapter, they can even incur the wrath of others (Goffman, 1961, 1969).

## *SOCIAL FACTORS AND MEMORY*

To appreciate the influence that social factors have on our memory, it is necessary to consider the relationship between the psychology of memory and social psychology (Shotter & Gauld, 1981). Researchers interested in social psychology investigate how our interactions with each other occur. For example, social psychologists explore how agreements, disagreements, and stalled negotiations depend on social variables, such as the *attitudes* that we and others hold toward the issue of dispute, the *roles* that we and others are playing at the time, and the kind of *impression* we want to make on others.

Social psychologists know that our personal relationships with others are highly dependent on memory. If someone is habitually forgetful, this person is destined to foul up relationships—sooner or later memory failures will insult or hurt others. Because of this awareness of the close interaction between memory and social relations, social psychologists have been paying increasing attention to the role that memory plays in a variety of social processes (Ostrom, 1989; Wyer & Srull, 1986, 1989).

As you know, the scientific study of memory involves investigating how we encode, retain, and retrieve memories. And although the psychology of memory certainly does not attempt to explain the origins of social interactions, it does recognize that memory processing can be markedly affected by social factors. For instance, one factor that affects our social interactions is *social information*. Social information is knowledge of the attitudes, roles, and means for impressing others that we need to be aware of when interacting with other people (Rothbart, 1981; Tetlock & Manstead, 1985).

This knowledge affects how we perform memory tasks in social settings. Some of this social information is implicitly ingrained in us by the culture we grow up in and dictates how we should behave in social interactions; the gender roles we are taught by society to accept as being appropriate for males or females are examples of such information. Other social information we acquire explicitly. For example, during a coffee break at work we learn from a coworker that the boss was arrested over the weekend for drunk driving. If you fail to remember this information and later launch into a discussion with the boss about a recent television documentary you saw concerning the stupidity of driving while intoxicated, you may find a smaller than expected raise in your salary the next time you are issued a contract!

A second social factor that affects memory processing is the *dynamics of social interaction*. Communicating with others takes thought, and that thought can limit the amount of cognitive resources we have at our disposal to either encode into memory important information spoken by others or retrieve information for use in the current conversation. Various social variables concerning the interaction between people (e.g., the pace of the conversation or the number and types of participants involved) will affect the accuracy and efficiency of such memory processing. Since memory performance is clearly affected by social variables, any account of memory performance must consider the impact of these variables.

Social factors affect memory performance by influencing which memory tasks individuals perform and their disposition to perform them. It is also true that different social groups or entities can have important, and sometimes unique, influences on memory performance. In addition, social factors can often affect the very credibility that people give to other people's memory. The important influences of these varying social factors on memory performance will be the main focus of this chapter.

## MEMORY TASKS TO BE PERFORMED

Most social situations require that you demonstrate that you know who others are, what they have done in the past, and what they are likely to do in the future. And different kinds of social situations tend to impose different kinds of memory tasks. For example, there are memory tasks that are required by society or culture, organized social events, the roles we adopt, casual conversations, intimate relationships, and pacts we make with others. Let's explore some of these tasks in more detail.

## Cultural Memory Tasks

Every culture has a body of knowledge that is transmitted to its members (Wegner, Guiliano, & Hertel, 1985). Some of this information pertains to government and religious institutions; other parts pertain to folklore and customs of behavior. The existence of this body of knowledge (sometimes referred to as a *collective memory*) imposes a task on the active members of a culture—they need to be aware of this information and to pass it on to the next generation.

Cultures also routinely convey *what* and *how* people should learn and remember. Over time, most cultures develop memory proverbs and sayings that help to guide the memory behavior of their members and the interpretation of the memory behaviors of others (Klatzky, 1984). These memory proverbs are often of a humorous or witty nature, as can be seen in Table 10.1, which presents some of the ones that evolved from our own western culture. In certain cultures, even ordinary people (but especially religious scholars) are expected to memorize prodigious amounts of information from religious texts such as the Koran, the Talmud, or the Bible. People who can perform such feats of memory are often greatly revered (and rewarded) by other members of the same culture.

**Symbolic reminders.** Cultures and subcultural groups require that their members perform memory tasks necessary for the activities or cohesiveness of

TABLE 10.1 A SAMPLING OF WESTERN CULTURE MEMORY PROVERBS

A liar needs a good memory.

One can forgive but not forget.

A person that has a good memory makes few loans.

That which is hard to endure is often pleasant to remember.

Sorrow remembered sweetens present joy.

There is no greater sorrow than to recall in misery the time when we were happy.

A person must get a thing before he can forget it.

Seldom seen, soon forgotten.

It is sometimes expedient to forget what you know.

Creditors have better memory than debtors.

Many people fail to become good thinkers for the sole reason their memory is too good.

A strong memory is usually accompanied with an informed judgment.

All complain of want of memory but not of want of judgment.

the culture or group. The way in which a culture endeavors to teach this information and the kinds of memory techniques taught to its members differ from one culture to another (Higbee & Kunihira, 1985). Different mechanisms are used to increase the likelihood that people will perform the necessary memory tasks. For example, one mechanism is the all-purpose *symbolic reminder*. This is a type of reminder that is intended as a signal to whoever notices it that something must be put in memory or remain in consciousness. Four such symbols (shown in Figure 10.1) are especially well known in western cultures. The *string-around-a-finger* symbol typically warns people to remember to perform some important chore, such as paying income taxes on time, or to act in some desirable manner, such as by putting litter in public containers. The picture of an *elephant* is similarly used to remind people of events they should attend, such as an upcoming school picnic. The *forget-me-not flower* and *Cupid* direct us annually to remember to do something nice for our valentine. These symbolic reminders are routinely used by governments, fraternal organizations, clubs, businesses, schools, and houses of worship to alert people that they should remember something. If you look around your dormitory or student center, you will likely find some of these symbols printed in newspapers and magazines and on posters and notices. When it is especially important that people remember certain information, the words *don't forget* are often written on or near the symbolic reminders and the pertinent information.

Some symbolic reminders are ritualized. For example, obituary columns in newspapers, tombstones, public monuments (such as the Vietnam War Memorial in Washington, D.C.), and a flag flown at half-mast serve to remind people to remember and think about certain events, certain people, and their

FIGURE 10.1
Internationally recognized symbols that direct a person not to forget something.

*Myosotis arvensis*
Common
forget-me-not

Cupid

deaths (Graumann, 1985). A ritualized symbolic reminder may involve a behavior that should be performed in a certain way. For example, if a prominent
person has recently died or if there's been a tragic local or national event, it is
customary to have a moment of silence before starting a sports event. Another
ritualized symbolic reminder (intended to have us reflect about our country)
is the obligatory playing or singing of the national anthem before professional
baseball games. Most religions are typically rich in symbols, and these symbols
are often used to help an individual remember things important to the practice
of a particular religion. For instance, rosary beads help Catholics remember the
proper sequence of their prayers.

Some memory tasks must be performed on precise days or dates. For
instance, people in every culture are required to honor certain holidays or
religious days. Observance of these days, typically shown by attending special
ceremonies, is explicitly taught by relatives (especially parents) and religious
leaders in the community. Reminders of their observance routinely appear in
the media. For certain days, observance is considered indicative of a person's
commitment to the cultural or religious group. Forgetting to publicly recognize
the day can sometimes lead to social rejection by others. In the United States,
a person who habitually refuses to celebrate the *4th of July* or who will not
behave properly when the flag goes by in a parade may be seen as unpatriotic
(and some may even argue that this person bears watching!). Likewise, a person
who refuses to partake in *Thanksgiving Day* activities may be considered antisocial. And a failure to remember to do things can sometimes elicit a very
formal social reaction, particularly by representatives of our legal system. Forgetting to pay a parking ticket may land you in court.

Finally, cultures establish ways to behave that are considered indicative of
appropriate attitudes for social interaction, and they also establish modes of
behavior that are considered to be indicative of antisocial attitudes (e.g., using
taboo language and gestures; Jay, 1992). In some cases, the prosocial behaviors
are taught explicitly ("Always say please," "Don't interrupt while others are
speaking," "Take turns"), while in other cases, the behaviors are expected to
be learned by more implicit means, such as by watching elders or other people
in positions of authority. A person who manifests antisocial behavior, even if
it is done unintentionally, is described as "forgetting his (or her) place." Every
culture imposes on its members the task of learning the prosocial behaviors to
be performed and the antisocial behaviors to be avoided (Cole & Scribner, 1974;
Lave, 1988). Later in this chapter we will discuss how antisocial behaviors may
interfere with memory performance.

## Social Events

Cocktail parties, meetings, high school reunions, and even informal get-togeth-
ers require people to remember several pieces of information before they attend.
For instance, deciding how to dress appropriately, what to bring, when to

*"Lucille, do we kiss the Friedlanders?"*

FIGURE 10.2
Cartoon illustrating the importance of memory for a
common social event.
*Drawing by Saxon; © 1974 The New Yorker Magazine, Inc.*

arrive, and even whom to kiss (see Figure 10.2) are all memory tasks of varying
importance that are implied by the invitation or the event. At the event itself,
a person must be able to quickly recall a variety of names and topics, and while
not appearing to be overburdened, the person must also be able to encode new
pieces of information during fast-moving conversations.

Consider the routine (but not easy) process of trying to remember the names of several people to whom you are introduced at a party. In addition to the person's name, during each introduction you are usually told a few facts about the person (e.g., "John Brown and his wife Sally just moved here from Tennessee, and she is working at the national public radio station, while he is doing substitute teaching in mathematics at the local junior high school."). Typically, you will pay attention to at least some of the facts mentioned and try to encode them in memory as you simultaneously try to be friendly and carry on at least a brief conversation with the new person or people. While you are being introduced, other people you already know will likely pass by, and this will require you to recall their names and interests, as well as how you usually respond to them. Minutes or hours later you may bump into one of the people you met earlier, whereupon you must try to recall the person's name and at least some of the pertinent facts about him or her. And before you leave the party, you need to remember to thank the host or hostess.

Such customary memory tasks constitute what are often called *memory rituals*. They demand continual encoding of new information and retrieval of old information (Hunter, 1957; Wagner, 1978). Some memory rituals require a person to play a starring role and can necessitate a massive amount of encoding and remembering. Testimonials, roasts, eulogies, and religious ceremonies are examples of events that often require people to put their memory ability on public display (sometimes for better, sometimes for worse).

## Role Expectations

Certain roles carry with them the responsibility to perform certain memory tasks. For instance, the officers of organizations are expected to recall more details pertaining to the organization than are other members. Likewise, certain occupations are known as requiring more reliance on memory than others. People aspiring to a particular role must be motivated for and become adept at the memory performances expected of the role. For example, experienced bartenders can remember drink orders and how to mix them much better and faster than can novice bartenders (Beach, 1988), and rug salespeople can remember rug patterns better than other people from the same culture (Wagner, 1978).

Even marital roles carry certain expectations about task performance. For example, Skowronski and Thompson (1990) found that women are generally better than men in estimating when autobiographical events happened. They speculate that at least part of the reason for this superiority is that women are more likely to be assigned the role of keeping track of important social events (like birthdays, anniversaries, and weddings) than are men. Likewise, as many husbands will probably attest, it is the wife who most often takes on the role of remembering to send invitations, Christmas cards, thank-you notes, and so forth.

## Personal Relationships

Like organized social events, maintaining good personal relationships also requires a person to perform many memory tasks. For instance, unless you want trouble, you had better remember your boyfriend's or girlfriend's birthday or the pet name your best friend likes to be called in private. If you walk outside your house and encounter a neighbor, you might have to be prepared to recall his or her hobbies, how this person's children are doing in school, and perhaps the latest sports scores for the local high school and college teams. And if you often confuse the names of your neighbor's kids or can't quite remember his or her favorite television programs, this person is not likely to consider you a good friend.

Success or failure at such memory tasks is often taken as revealing your personal regard for a person. Because the forgetting of personal information may be so important to one or both persons in a relationship, it is often said that this forgetting is *symbolic* of how one person feels about the other person. Although symbolic tasks may seem relatively trivial when they arise, their importance to other people can be crucial to continuing a close relationship. Table 10.2 lists several memory tasks that are symbolic of respect or affection (Herrmann, 1991).

As many business executives will ruefully admit, establishing good personal relationships between people from different cultural backgrounds is often difficult to do. Not bothering to learn (or remember) that there are cultural differences in greeting and recognizing people has soured many a relationship. Consider the following two examples. North Americans have typically been taught from an early age to shake hands with a firm grip when first meeting

**TABLE 10.2** SOME MEMORY TASKS SYMBOLIC OF RESPECT OR AFFECTION

Remembering a person's name and proper title

Remembering the details of a person's life and the person's important accomplishments

Remembering a person's areas of expertise and yielding to them

Remembering to keep appointments made with a person

Remembering an event shared with a person

Remembering a person's likes, dislikes, pet causes, hobbies, and projects at work or school

Remembering special acts to be performed for a person (such as giving a greeting or parting kiss, holding a door, serving breakfast in bed, or buying flowers or candy)

Remembering special occasions to be honored (including birthdays and anniversaries, as well as other traditionally special days, like Valentine's Day, Mother's Day, Father's Day, Secretary's Week)

Remembering tasks a person expects you to do

Remembering mannerisms of the person that signal a change in his or her needs or moods

SOURCE: Herrmann, 1991.

someone. However, people from the Middle East or the Orient have generally been taught to use a gentle grip when shaking hands. In their cultures a firm grip can be taken as a sign of aggression (Axtell, 1991). North Americans are also taught to look others directly in the eye when conversing. This is an indication of respect. But Korean and Japanese people are taught to do the direct opposite—to avoid looking directly at the person with whom they are speaking. To do otherwise may be taken as an intimidating gesture or even as a suggestion of sexual overtones (Axtell, 1991). Dramatic improvements in personal and business relationships can occur if people are willing to make an effort to remember some of the special behaviors and customs of people from foreign cultures.

**Personal obligations.** Daily life requires us to make appointments, keep appointments, repay favors, and do chores that others depend on us to do. Some of these tasks may be for friends or family; other tasks are necessary for one's job or are simply part of daily living (such as remembering to change the engine oil in your car every 3000 miles). Performance on such tasks helps to determine how others judge and treat a person. Failure to do well can lead family, friends, and acquaintances to make negative judgments about a person's caring, sensitivity, manners, or even intelligence.

It is important to remember to know when to perform our personal obligations. This remembering depends on several factors: the obligation's strength in memory, the importance of the obligation, how many other obligations must be remembered and kept, how many distractions occur at the time the obligation must be met, and so on (Doerner, 1986). To complicate matters, even if a person remembers that a task or obligation is to be performed, the individual may simply choose not to comply. For instance, if a friend recommends that you visit a mutual acquaintance who is in the hospital but whom you dislike, you may fail to visit the person because you don't want to—not because you forgot to do so. Another factor is the relationship that a person has with those to whom the obligation is owed (Meacham, 1988). Generally speaking, the greater the status of the person to whom the obligation is owed (and perhaps the perceived power this person has over us), the more likely it is that the obligation will be remembered and kept. Imagine that you had made two commitments for the same time. One was to your best friend, and the other was to a person you met once while standing in line to buy a bus ticket. The commitment you would most likely remember to honor is obvious.

**Memory pacts.** A special type of obligation is the *memory pact*. People form memory pacts with others to share the job of learning and remembering certain kinds of information or things to do. Explicitly stated memory pacts are especially common between people who live together because they often need to divide up chores. ("You remember to take out the trash, and I'll pick up some milk on the way home.") Pacts are also common between coworkers, who may similarly divide responsibilities for "keeping track" of different customers, orders, or inventory. Many memory pacts, however, are implicit in nature in

FIGURE 10.3
What can happen when you violate an implicit memory pact.
*Reprinted by permission: Tribune Media Services.*

that the parties involved never *explicitly* came to an agreement about each other's responsibilities. In these implicit agreements, one person may well forget or fail to carry out his or her part of the bargain. ("I thought *you* were going to pay the phone bill!")

Most people would be hard-pressed to recall all the explicit and implicit memory pacts that they share with others. However, when the appropriate situation arises, most people can recognize their obligations. When memory pacts are unilaterally broken or forgotten, heated arguments and upset feelings are a likely result. Just ask Broom Hilda.

# EFFECTS OF VARIOUS SOCIAL GROUPS OR ENTITIES

A social group or entity can be as small as yourself, or it can be a small group of people interacting together (such as some friends having a conversation), or it can be a large group or organization (such as a political convention or a college fraternity). These social groups or entities can not only affect people's beliefs and attitudes about memory tasks but also influence actual memory performance. Let's examine some of these effects.

## Oneself

People hold attitudes about which memory tasks they like or don't like to perform. These attitudes, in turn, affect memory performance. A person is likely to perform a memory task well when given positive feedback and to perform poorly when given negative feedback (Herrmann, 1984, 1991; Klatzky, 1984; Morris, 1984). For example, two groups of subjects were initially matched for performance in learning nonsense syllables. However, in a subsequent attempt at learning the same type of material, they differed in performance because the subjects in one group were told that they possessed superior ability for this memory task (this group did better this time), while the subjects in the other group were told that they were inferior (Sullivan, 1927).

A person's general level of self-esteem, derived in part from his or her history of social interactions, can also lead to a greater or lesser inclination to perform certain memory tasks (Borkowski, Carr, Rellinger, & Pressley, in press). Another important factor in determining what is attended to and encoded is an individual's self-concept (Greenwald & Banaji, 1989; Markus, 1980; Mischel, Ebbesen, & Zeiss, 1976). As you will recall from Chapter 4, people tend to remember adjectives best when they have to judge how well they apply to themselves (the *self-reference effect*).

A person's self-concept and memory for one's past are interdependent. And memory for the past appears to depend heavily on social events, since people keep track of such events because they are important to their personal identity (Neisser, 1988; Snyder & Uranowitz, 1978). Additionally, memory for our past depends on how active a role we have played in certain events. For instance, subjects sometimes remember themselves as being more involved in an activity than was actually true, but subjects who were merely observers do not usually show such a distortion in recall (Moore, Sherrod, Liu, & Underwood, 1979).

**Personal memory reputation.** In any circle of acquaintances or coworkers who have known each other for a while, each person will have developed a reputation for how often he or she succeeds or fails at particular memory tasks. And like reputations for other characteristics (such as loyalty, diligence, or discretion), *memory reputations* are based primarily on our past behavior patterns. These memory reputations often become a part of a person's self-concept.

The social consequences of a memory reputation are not as straightforward as you might think. It might seem that most people would regard a reputation for a good memory as desirable. However, a "good" reputation is also likely to bring extra responsibilities. If you are a person who is known for "always remembering details," people may ask you to remember more than your fair share. A "bad memory" reputation is usually regarded as a sign of incompetence or lack of caring. When a person's memory reputation is poor, others may simply consider the person unreliable. And if this individual then succeeds in remembering to actually do something that he or she had promised to do, it will be regarded as a fluke.

Nevertheless, a bad memory reputation can have its up side too, and some people actually try to cultivate just such a reputation (Baumeister, Cooper, & Skib, 1979; Gentry & Herrmann, 1990). People sometimes decide they are not able or willing to perform a memory task, and so they contrive to give the appearance that they are unable to perform it. If done on a regular basis, this quickly leads to a bad memory reputation. Although there is certainly a personal cost to doing these kinds of things (others will think less of you), it is also true that if you are thought to be absentminded or forgetful, people will be reluctant to rely on you, giving you extra free time or relief from normal obligations.

## Small-Group Interactions

Memory is often more likely to fail when one is with others than when one is alone. This is probably because memory performance can fail in a variety of ways when one is conversing with others. For example, the encoding of relevant new information (such as the name of the person with whom you are speaking) or the timely retrieval of stored information ("Who is the girlfriend of this person?") may not take place because the conversation you are having with another person is too involving or distracting. Even if a person has successfully encoded or retrieved some information, it may be that because of the dynamics involved in many social situations, the individual will fail to adequately communicate this information (Kimble, Hirt, & Arnold, 1985; Kimble & Zehr, 1982). In this section we will examine some of the factors that affect our memory performance when we are engaged in small-group interactions.

**Alterations in conversational flow.** All of us have, at one time or another, inadvertently repeated something that we had said only a few moments before. If the blunder is pointed out to you, you will feel embarrassed because it suggests either that you were not paying much attention to the conversation or, perhaps worse, that you are not a very intelligent person (Koriat, Ben-Zur, & Sheffer, 1988). At other times we recall something and quickly say it, but after a moment's reflection, we know that we remembered incorrectly. If others notice this error before a self-correction can be made, this will again lead to embarrassment.

But people can avoid inadvertent memory errors by using certain conversational techniques. One technique for avoiding inadvertent repetition involves reiterating out loud what you and others have just said. Such a strategy helps a person register who said what and also delays the input of new information. Obviously, you can't use this strategy all the time, because with frequent use it would quickly become tedious for you and the party with whom you are conversing, but used sparingly, it is a very effective tactic. Inadvertent recall errors can also be reduced by carefully monitoring and editing before *overtly* stating what you recall from memory.

It is also possible to buy time for retrieval of hard-to-remember information through the use of ploys that slow down a conversation or that restrict it to just one or two topics. Time needed for retrieval can also be secured by asking questions of the questioner or by referring questions to another person. Such stalling tactics are particularly effective when you're trying desperately to remember the name of the person with whom you're talking, and you don't want to let on that you can't recall the person's name. Thus, intelligent people can facilitate the performance of memory tasks in social contexts by simply controlling the rate of information exchange.

**The use of others as memory aids.** Sometimes people do not want to make much of an effort to remember a particular piece of information when in a conversation. So they may try to use someone else who is present as a memory aid (Intons-Peterson & Fournier, 1986; Intons-Peterson & Newsome, 1992). For instance, a person may ask another person to answer a question that the first person could have answered if a real effort was made. Or a person may ask another to encode and retain some information (such as the telephone number of the local theater) and to tell him or her about it later or ask to be reminded later when he or she is supposed to do something.

Unfortunately, there are disadvantages to using a friend or an acquaintance as a memory aid. First of all, the person who is being used as a memory aid has to be present when you need to use his or her information. In addition, the person who was entrusted with the memory task may not, in fact, remember accurately. This will often result in hurt feelings and recriminations on both sides. And even if the "helper" is physically present when needed and has a good memory, the helper will eventually expect to be paid back in like fashion.

**Feedback on memory performance.** People sometimes comment on their own memory performance or that of others. This "memory feedback," however, should not always be taken at face value. People will often deliberately contrive to make their own, or another person's, memory performance appear better or worse than it actually is. Why is this done? Because people often make statements about memory performance to achieve social goals. A person can flatter or insult someone, or show kindness or anger, by making certain comments about that individual's memory. And it is also not unusual for someone to make his or her own memory appear to be better or worse than it actually is as a means of protection from criticism and to get in good with others (Gentry & Herrmann, 1990).

If a person seems to forget more than usual when with a particular individual, it may be that he or she has feigned forgetting to let this other person demonstrate stored knowledge. A parent will often pretend that he or she cannot remember something so that a young child can showcase his or her ability. When teaching an adolescent to drive a car, a parent will resist (sometimes to an almost unnerving point!) saying where or how to steer the car so as to determine whether the son or daughter will remember correctly. And if someone attempts to gloss over a particular instance of forgetting, it may be that this person does not want the other person to be able to hold something against him or her. As you probably know from your own experience, memory performance in social interactions is not necessarily always what it seems to be.

It is obviously important to be able to distinguish contrived feedback from accurate and deserved feedback. In most everyday circumstances a person is best served by having an accurate memory self-concept, or what is often called *metamemory* (see Chapter 12). In other words, it is beneficial to have beliefs about your memory abilities that are accurate. If people believe negative contrivances about their memory, this will lower their confidence and may lead them to perform memory tasks less well. So that you can learn to spot memory contrivances in your own interactions with others, we list in Table 10.3 six of the most common types of memory contrivances.

It is well known that most people find it difficult to hold a lone dissenting view among well-respected friends or authorities (Asch, 1956). So if someone else confidently asserts that your memory is inadequate or wrong, this claim can cause you to start doubting yourself. This doubt can arise even if you are initially quite sure of your recollection. For example, if while reminiscing about a previous good time, you recall the event differently than several friends, you will tend to revise the memory to make it in line with your friends' version of it (Bregman & McAllister, 1982).

Many lawyers are aware of this tendency of people to doubt themselves when presented with statements that seem to run counter to their memory of an event. These lawyers can take advantage of this by asking witnesses *leading questions* (questions that suggest the "correct" way to answer). Research has shown that when this is done, a person is more inclined to "recall" facts consistent with the leading question, particularly if he or she has been led to believe that the questioner has better knowledge about what actually occurred (Smith & Ellsworth, 1987). (The research on the malleability of eyewitness memory is fascinating and will be covered in detail in the next chapter.)

**Proper memory etiquette.** A person's inclination to encode the details of a social interaction increases when he or she is interacting with others who are judged to have high status or attractiveness (DeBono & Hamish, 1988; Holtgraves, Srull, & Socall, 1989; Hovland & Weiss, 1951). One way to measure or

---

TABLE 10.3  CONTRIVANCES OF OTHERS ABOUT YOUR MEMORY

*Memory insult:* A person points out a memory failure of yours that otherwise might have been overlooked and claims that the failure is indicative of a "bad memory."

*Memory praise:* A person praises your success at a memory task far beyond what it deserves and claims that your success is indicative of a "good memory."

*Memory alibi:* A person makes excuses for a memory failure that you have.

*Memory responsibility charge:* A person claims that performing a memory task was your responsibility, not the responsibility of someone else (such as the person making the claim).

*Memory noncooperation:* A person fails to help you perform a memory task, although he or she is capable of cooperating.

*Memory fraud:* A person claims that your memory is in error on some point, although you both know that this claim is untrue.

SOURCE: Gentry & Herrmann, 1990.

gauge the current status of a personal relationship is to note the frequency with which the other person will comment on slight memory errors that you might make. For instance, if another person holds you in high regard, chances are that he or she will not give you much grief if your memory is less than fully accurate. However, as we all know from personal experience, if someone is angry with you, don't expect this person to let even little mistakes in recall go by without considerable objection. Our comments about the memory performance of others can greatly influence our future social interactions with them.

Some of the breaches in memory etiquette that we commit are simply bad habits that we have difficulty breaking. An example of a memory faux pas would be frequently calling someone by the wrong name because the person reminds you of someone else. We believe that it would soothe personal relationships considerably if people abided by certain rules of etiquette concerning other people's memory performance. And your show of respect or disrespect for another's memory ability will undoubtedly affect how the other person regards *your* memory ability. Some examples of what we think a social code of memory etiquette should include are provided in Table 10.4.

## Large-Group Interactions

Larger social groups also influence our memory beliefs, attitudes, and performance. In this section we specifically examine the possible effects that either identifying with or stereotyping a particular group or organization can have on memory.

**Group identification.** The accuracy of a person's recall for information can be affected by the types of groups to which he or she belongs or with which he or she identifies. Matters that are consistent with our religious, political, and

---

**TABLE 10.4** SOME RULES FOR GOOD MEMORY ETIQUETTE

1. Avoid commenting on another's lack of memory ability. If someone in a discussion forgets items just mentioned, then unless it is critical, this failure should not be pointed out.

2. If one must correct a memory error, the correction should be done politely. For example, when a person recalls some information incorrectly, he or she should be corrected in a considerate manner (e.g., "You meant XXX, didn't you?").

3. Unimportant memory errors, especially if they are made by a person who is a loved one, should be ignored.

4. It is impolite to point out unintentionally repeated recalls of some material or events (especially if the person is ill or elderly).

5. It is impolite to forget what another person was talking about in a conversation. Failure to remember indicates that one is disinterested.

6. It is impolite to recall another person's failures in life.

**FIGURE 10.4**
Social interactions can play an important role in memory.
*Owen Franken/Stock, Boston.*

social beliefs are learned better and retained better than matters inconsistent with these beliefs (Goethals & Reckman, 1973; Read & Rosson, 1982). For example, after reading a balanced passage that discusses the pros and cons of a political issue, most people initially learn more facts about the side they favor and fewer facts about the position they oppose. In addition, when tested again later, people show that they have more accurately retained the new facts about the side they favor (Greenwald, 1980; Levine & Murphy, 1943).

This phenomenon came to be known as *selective recall*. Subsequent studies sometimes failed to obtain the selective recall effect, and this even led some researchers to argue that no real relationship exists between opinion and memory. However, reviews of this literature have found that across many studies there is significant, though sometimes subtle, evidence that subjects do selectively recall material that is consistent with their attitudes (Read & Rosson, 1982; Roberts, 1985). And it should be remembered that Chapter 8 described in some detail how attitudes and emotional states can cause selective recall of information and past events.

The bias in memory due to selective recall can be reduced if a person is specifically told to examine the facts that are contrary to his or her own personal position. Besides having a more accurate memory for the facts of the matter, there's an additional beneficial by-product of this approach: people disinclined toward your point of view will often give you additional credit for being open-minded, simply because you possess an unusually accurate memory for the opposing point of view.

Peer group identification can sometimes lead to deliberate memory errors. For instance, it is well known that people will not recall certain information if doing so would associate them with an undesirable group. This is a tactic often used by spies, politicians, defendants in court, and members of unpopular organizations. A common example of this type of deliberate forgetting occurs in the classroom. A student may pretend not to remember some fact when asked by a teacher, so as not to be labeled a "nerd" or "bookworm" by his or her peers.

The way that people remember their acquaintances is also colored by their peer group. A change in the relevant peer group can result in a revision of how others are conceived and how they are remembered (Bond & Brockett, 1987; Hastie, Ostrom, Ebbesen, Wyer, Hamilton, & Carlston, 1980). A campus sports hero may be remembered in very positive ways by his or her coach and team-mates, yet this person may be remembered very differently by his or her teachers. Similarly, the class valedictorian may be remembered in different ways by the faculty, the athletic department, and classmates.

**Stereotypes.** A person's group identification can be based on a stereotype (e.g., pertaining to race, religion, gender, or age). Stereotypes are well known to unfairly suggest things about the behavior, civility, and intelligence of people to whom the stereotypes refer. But what is not generally recognized is that a stereotype can affect selective encoding of information in the same manner as described above for group identification (Bodenhausen, 1988; Hamilton & Trolier, 1986). It is well accepted, for example, that racism may affect encoding (Allport & Postman, 1945, 1947; Dovidio & Gaertner, 1986; Van Dijk, 1987).

For instance, in some of their classic studies of how rumors develop, Allport and Postman showed subjects a picture in which a white man holding a razor is confronting a black man in a subway car. After seeing the picture, a subject then had to describe the scene to another person, who then described it to another person, and so on, until six or seven people in a chain finally heard a description of the story. During the recounting of the scene, in over half of the chains of people, the razor was switched from being held by the white man to being held by the black man! Such a finding is consistent with the stereotype that many people held in the 1940s about black men: that black men were more likely to be involved in criminal or aggressive activities than were white men (Treadway & McCloskey, 1989).

Memory may be gender-biased as well. For example, boys and girls tend to better remember when to terminate an event if the event is consistent with their gender stereotype. Boys are better at remembering when to stop charging a motorcycle battery (a male stereotype activity) than at remembering when to stop baking cupcakes (a female stereotype activity), while girls are just the opposite (Ceci, Baker, & Bronfenbrenner, 1988; Ceci & Bronfenbrenner, 1985).

As another example of gender bias at work, male and female undergraduates were found to learn the *very same* ambiguous passage of directions differently, depending on whether the passage was given a "femalelike" title or a "malelike" title (Herrmann, Crawford, & Holdsworth, 1992). Subjects were given the following passage to read, which you may recognize as a clever takeoff on the famous "washing clothes" passage used by Bransford and Johnson (1972) (see Chapter 6).

> The procedure is actually quite simple. First, you rearrange the pieces into different groups. Of course, one pile may be sufficient depending on how much there is to do and the degree of design complexity. The next step is to get the necessary tools and implements. It is important not to overdo things. That is, work slowly and on one part at a time. In the short run this may not seem important but complications can easily arise. A mistake can be costly as well as time consuming. At first the whole procedure may seem complicated. However, after a while it will seem quite simple. Find the corresponding parts. Make sure that they are the right pieces and attach them. At first they may not seem to fit. Do not worry, they will if you are patient, work carefully, and follow our diagrams and directions. Once the smaller pieces are attached, the next step is to find which parts should now go together. Once you have done this, fit them together in the appropriate positions. Things should start to look good now. Add all remaining pieces and extras—you now have your finished product.

For half of the females and males, the above passage was titled "How to Make a Shirt" and for the other half "How to Make a Workbench." When later given 3 minutes to recall the passage, females remembered more ideas than males when it was thought that the passage was about shirt making, and males recalled more than females when the passage was thought to be about making a workbench (Herrmann et al., 1992).

Stereotypes associated with age also can negatively affect memory. As one example of this, it has been found that elderly people tend to learn less readily than younger adults because of beliefs that learning ability decreases with age (Best, 1992; Best, Hamlett, & Davis, 1992).

The same stereotypes that were described earlier as affecting our inclination to encode or remember information can also affect how others judge our memory ability. When someone's judgment of your memory capabilities is unrealistically high or low, it may be because this person holds stereotypical beliefs (associated with age, occupation, gender, etc.) that are being applied to you. For example, both males and females tend to expect other males to excel at remembering directions and females to excel at remembering shopping lists (Crawford, Herrmann, Randal, Holdsworth, & Robbins, 1989). As another example of stereotyping, college students were asked to rate the memory ability of people in different occupations. Among the findings it was discovered that airline pilots were judged to have the best memory overall, that college professors were judged to have the best memory for general knowledge, that plumbers and mechanics were seen as having the worst memory for personal experiences, and that salespeople were regarded as having the worst memory for following through on intentions (Herrmann, 1991).

The social pressure produced by stereotyping may even lead people to unwittingly conform to the stereotype. This can happen if the pressure to conform robs an individual of his or her self-confidence. Unfortunately, probably because most stereotypes are impressed over a lifetime, they usually are very resistant to change.

# JUDGING THE CREDIBILITY OF MEMORY PERFORMANCES

An accurate memory performance is useless if others don't trust the person involved, and a loss of confidence in a person's memory can be crucial. In 1988 Senator Joseph Biden of Delaware was campaigning for the presidency of the United States and doing quite well by most accounts. However, a story appeared in the media in which it was documented that Biden had given a speech that turned out to be very similar to one that the British Labor leader Neil Kinnock had given earlier. When confronted with this, Biden claimed that he had intended to give Kinnock credit but that he had simply forgotten to do so. This seemed innocent enough until additional news reports surfaced that indicated that Biden had also used the words of other politicians without giving them appropriate credit either. To make matters worse, Biden had also intimated that he had achieved good grades in law school, but when this claim was checked out, it was not supported by the records. Finally, Biden felt compelled to withdraw from the presidential race because both his memory and his veracity were in question. This last section will explore how expression, content, memory language, and nonverbal communication can affect the credibility given to a person's memory performance.

## Expression

Often, others may think that a person has failed at a memory task, while in truth, the person succeeded. For example, someone may accurately recall what took place at a certain party or meeting, whereupon someone else *emphatically* tells this person that his or her recall is wrong or incomplete. If someone else believes that his or her memory is rich and accurate (even when it isn't), that person is not going to believe another version of the event. One way that you can increase the likelihood that others will believe in what you recall is by expressing your recall with an appropriate degree of confidence.

Overstating or understating one's confidence in recall will likely hurt credibility. Considerable research has demonstrated that witnesses in a court of law will more likely be regarded as remembering the truth if they sit up and speak confidently. John Dean, of Watergate fame, was regarded as having an excellent memory, in part because he conveyed his recall of the events of Richard Nixon's presidency in a convincing fashion (later investigation, however, showed that

Dean's recall was actually full of inaccuracies; Neisser, 1981, discussed further in Chapter 11).

## Content

To be convincing, a person's memory claim should be internally consistent (Conway, 1990). Although inconsistencies appear in even highly accurate reports from memory, major contradictions between facts make a report appear illogical and suggest that the memory underlying the report is distorted. People you interact with will invariably discount what you recall if it contains obvious inconsistencies. Also, your recall will be better accepted if it has corroborating sources, such as newspapers, books, or memos. A particularly potent source is someone whose memory and truthfulness are trusted by all others and who can back up what you say.

## Memory Language

A person's recall will be more credible if the recall is couched in appropriate memory vocabulary. There are many terms and catch phrases used to describe our memory states. For instance, a large range of commonly used verbs can express varying degrees of certainty. People may indicate that they *suspect, believe, think, know, guarantee,* or even *swear* that something you remember is true or not true (Searle, 1969).

Different memory terms have subtly different meanings, and these nuances of meaning may influence the acceptance of your memory claims. For instance, after having forgotten to do something for a friend, a person may choose to excuse the oversight by saying that his or her memory was "overloaded." The success of this claim will depend on whether or not the person can actually demonstrate why his or her memory was overloaded. Or you may excuse yourself by saying that you have a memory "like a sieve." Whether this claim will be accepted will depend on whether your friend knows, or can be convinced, that your memory fails with unintentional and unusual frequency.

## Nonverbal Communication

Besides relying on appropriate verbal communication to convey the state of their memory processing, people effectively use (often unconsciously) nonverbal signals (Knapp, 1978). For instance, when a person recognizes a friend on the street, a smile or a raised eyebrow can be sufficient to signal recognition. Table 10.5 lists some common nonverbal indications of trying to remember something. Many of these nonverbal signals are probably universal. By consciously combining appropriate nonverbal signals with verbal claims, a person

**TABLE 10.5** NONVERBAL MEMORY LANGUAGE

*Indications of forgetting:* Blank stare, facial twitch, groans, look of guilt, look of surprise, open mouth, rolling one's eyes

*Indications of trying to remember:* Adjustment of posture, downward stare, faraway stare, head scratching, looking up, palm hitting forehead, pensive look, thinker's pose

*Indications of the tip-of-the-tongue state:* Crying "aha," nodding your head, repeated "ohs," snapping one's fingers, shaking one's fist

can often persuasively convince others that his or her memory is accurate, even when it is not.

# SUMMARY

## I. Social Factors and Memory

- It is becoming increasingly clear that our social interactions are highly dependent on our memory capabilities and, in turn, that our memory performance is often influenced by social factors.
- Perhaps the most important factor that affects our social interactions (and our memory processing) is *social information.* This is knowledge of the attitudes, roles, and means for impressing others that we use in our social encounters.

## II. Memory Tasks to Be Performed

- Most social situations require a person to demonstrate that he or she can remember considerable amounts of information.
- Every culture has its own body of knowledge that must be learned and remembered. *Symbolic reminders* are frequently used to signal people to remember something.
- During many social events a person needs to encode and retrieve a great deal of information and to do so quickly and while appearing to be at ease.
- The different roles or occupations we acquire come with responsibilities and expectations to perform certain memory tasks.
- Maintaining good personal relationships means that you have to perform many memory tasks and that you must honor your personal obligations to others. How successfully you fulfill these tasks and obligations is often viewed as being indicative of your personal regard for others.
  - A special type of personal obligation is the *memory pact,* which is an understanding between individuals that each will learn or remember certain information or to do certain things.

- Although sometimes *explicitly* stated, many memory pacts are agreed to *implicitly*. Breaking or forgetting a memory pact usually leads to hurt or upset feelings.

## III. Effects of Various Social Groups or Entities

- Different social groups or entities affect a person's beliefs and attitudes about memory tasks and can influence memory performance.
- An important social entity that affects memory is oneself. An individual's level of self-esteem or his or her self-concept can affect memory performance in predictable ways (e.g., the *self-reference effect*).
  - Most people acquire *memory reputations* that are based primarily on their track record for successfully performing various memory tasks.
  - Although most people strive to gain a good memory reputation, others actively seek to cultivate a bad memory reputation. A bad reputation can free a person from being entrusted to carry out memory obligations.
- Our ability to encode or retrieve memories and how we ultimately express them depends in large measure on the dynamics of our social interactions. People use a variety of ploys to control the flow of conversations and the number of memory tasks that must be performed. One technique, for instance, involves using another person as a memory aid.
- It is important to carefully monitor and assess the *feedback* that others give us concerning our memory performance. Oftentimes, people will knowingly exaggerate or even lie about another's memory performance to further their own ends. Several of the common *memory contrivances* that people use in daily life were presented.
- We presented some rules of proper *memory etiquette* that we believe can help keep social relationships from souring unnecessarily.
- A person's memory can be affected by the types of organizations or peer groups with which he or she identifies. Stereotypes that we or others hold about certain groups of people also color our memory and our expectations. *Selective recall* refers to the tendency to recall material that is consistent with one's attitudes.

## IV. Judging the Credibility of Memory Performances

- The credibility that people give to memory performances depends on several interrelated factors. People are more likely to believe you if you *express* yourself with the proper degree of confidence, make sure that your statements are *internally consistent*, use appropriate *memory vocabulary*, and are able to control the *nonverbal signals* that you are displaying.

# PART 5

# Individual Differences

# 11

# Autobiographical Experiences

❖

Having access to important autobiographical experiences is essential to living a normal life. Just imagine if you couldn't recall large portions of your personal past the way that many people suffering from amnesia cannot (see Chapters 7 and 14). How difficult life would be if you couldn't remember where you lived, who your friends and relatives are, what they look like, the types of skills or disabilities you may have, whether or not you have graduated from college (or even high school), where you work (and what you do for a living), and so forth.

In this chapter we will examine what is known about autobiographical memory and how malleable these memories can be, especially when people are asked to give eyewitness testimony in a court of law. Finally, we will briefly describe a relatively new (and controversial) area of autobiographical experiences—the memory that people may have for events that occurred while they were under the influence of anesthesia.

## AUTOBIOGRAPHICAL MEMORY

What did you do the night of your high school graduation? Who was your best friend when you were 10 years old? Can you remember the name of your first-grade teacher? What is the first personal memory that comes to mind when you think of the word *beach*? Researchers who ask such questions are interested in learning about *autobiographical memory* (Conway, 1990; Ross, 1991; Rubin, 1986). Perhaps the simplest definition of this term is the one offered by Brewer (1986); he states that autobiographical memory is "memory for information related to the self" (p. 26).

We have already described some notable findings concerning autobiographical memory. For instance, in Chapter 5 the possible existence of a *permastore* was discussed, and it was mentioned that the forgetting of autobiographical events does not follow the pattern suggested by Ebbinghaus's famous forgetting curve. From Chapter 8 we learned that for most people pleasant memories are more likely to be recalled than unpleasant memories, a phenomenon that was dubbed the *Pollyanna principle* by Matlin and Stang (1978). Some of the most powerful evidence in support of the Pollyanna principle was found by the diary studies of Linton (1975) and Wagenaar (1986). Linton and Wagenaar each tested their own memory for personal events they recorded in their diaries over a period of years. Diaries are often a rich source of information about many aspects of autobiographical memory (Cavanaugh & Hertzog, 1992). Also in Chapter 8, we described the controversial topic of *flashbulb memories*—highly detailed, accurate recollections of personally experienced events that were very surprising, emotionally arousing, and important; some researchers believe that these recollections are largely immune to forgetting over long periods of time. In Chapter 9 the issue of how people remember the timing of past personal events was discussed. It was learned that with some exceptions (see below), our ability to remember the exact timing of such events is usually quite poor. And in Chapter 12 the interesting and mysterious phenomenon of *childhood amnesia* will be presented. This term refers to the fact that most people have great difficulty remembering personal events that occurred during the first few years of life. In addition, although mentioned briefly in Chapter 7 and later in this chapter, we will wait until Chapter 14 to more fully discuss the loss of autobiographical memory for those suffering from *dissociative* and/or *organic* memory disorders.

Sir Francis Galton, an eminent British scientist and writer, is generally credited with initiating the empirical study of autobiographical memory (1879a, 1879b, 1883). One technique that he developed, the *cue-word method,* has become the most popular way to assess a person's autobiographical memory. Although there are many variations, the modern use of the cue-word method typically involves giving an individual a list of highly familiar concrete words and then asking the person to recall a personal memory associated with each word. Sometimes the instructions stress the importance of recalling the earliest memory or the most recent one, or the subject will be asked just to recall the first memory that is triggered by the word (as in the question above concerning the word *beach*). After supplying a personal memory for each word, the person is then asked to go back and date (as best as possible) when each memory occurred.

It should be noted that some researchers have questioned the wisdom of relying so extensively on the cue-word method. They argue that it produces a bias in the types of memories that are retrieved (e.g., Dritschel, Williams, Baddeley, & Nimmo-Smith, 1992; Rabbitt & Winthorpe, 1988). For instance, Rabbitt and Winthorpe (1988) reported that subjects recalled fewer personal memories when supplied with cue words, that these memories were of more recent origin, and that the memories tended to be less vivid and emotional when compared with the memories generated by subjects who were just given general instructions to recall past events.

Although the scientific study of autobiographical memory started over 100 years ago, hardly any additional research, except for a few scattered studies, was conducted on this topic until the mid-1970s. Then in 1974, Crovitz and Schiffman used the cue word method to elicit autobiographical memories from college students and rekindled interest in this area with the publication of a two-page article. Since the publication of this paper, hundreds of studies have been conducted on the ability of people to remember personal events, and there are no signs that interest in this aspect of memory, which affects us all, will soon slacken.

## Is There a Pattern to Autobiographical Memory Recall?

Perhaps the most fundamental question that researchers have tried to answer is this: When people try to recall the personal events of their lives, are there discernible patterns to this recall? We already know that the *Pollyanna principle* suggests that people are more inclined to remember pleasant memories than unpleasant ones. But are there other reliable patterns? For instance, do people tend to recall approximately the same number of events from all periods of their lives? This is sometimes called the *equal-sampling hypothesis* (Conway, 1990). Or do people recall more recent events? More remote events? Does the age of the person affect what memories are recalled?

To begin with, and to complicate matters, there is evidence from several studies that indicates that people can and do employ different strategies for searching their autobiographical memories (Brewer, 1986; Cohen & Faulkner, 1988; Linton, 1986; Rabbitt & Winthorpe, 1988; Reiser, Black, and Kalamarides, 1986; Rubin, Wetzler, & Nebes, 1986). And it is known that these different strategies can have a profound effect on the distribution of memories recalled from different periods of life. For example, given the cue word *beach*, some subjects may prefer to use a *backward-retrieval strategy* and will thus search their memory for the most recent association with the word *beach*. Others may prefer to use a *forward-retrieval strategy* and will start searching their earliest memories. These two strategies cause subjects to sample from different periods in their lives and therefore will produce widely different distributions of autobiographical memories.

Fortunately, the use of different search strategies can be minimized by giving subjects explicit instructions in how to search memory. It is also possible to reduce strategy differences by using cue words that are highly specific or meaningful for a given subject (Conway, 1990; Wagenaar, 1986). In other words, if a cue word relates directly to the subject's life, then he or she is less likely to engage in a backward- or forward-retrieval strategy. For instance, if a subject has been to Australia only once but has flown in an airplane many times, then the specific cue *koala bear* will better focus the person's retrieval process and minimize the influence of a backward- or forward-retrieval strategy than would the more general cue *airplane.*

On the basis of considerable evidence, it now appears that the equal-sampling hypothesis is surely wrong (Conway, 1990). People do not recall an equal number of personal events from the various periods of their lives. In addition, the age of the person doing the recalling also seems to influence the results. Rubin et al. (1986) compared the findings from several studies in which groups of people of different ages were asked to recall events from their lives. The results of their analysis suggest that everyone has a period of *childhood amnesia* for the first few years of life. Virtually no personal memories will be remembered from this time period. In addition, for both younger adults (less than about 35 years old) and older adults, a *monotonically decreasing retention function* can describe the distribution of memories recalled for personal events that took place during the last 20 to 30 years. In other words, within this time period, the personal memories most likely to be recalled will be the most recent ones, and the longer ago an event occurred, the less likely it will be remembered. Figure 11.1 illustrates the effect of the monotonically decreasing retention function on the recall of autobiographical memories.

These two factors, a childhood amnesia component and a monotonically decreasing retention function, seem to adequately describe the distribution of autobiographical memories recalled by young adults. A third component, however, must be included to account for the results of older subjects. This third component has been called *reminiscence.* Older adults show an increased ten-

FIGURE 11.1

Idealized illustration of the monotonically decreasing retention function for recalling autobiographical memories for the last 20 to 30 years.

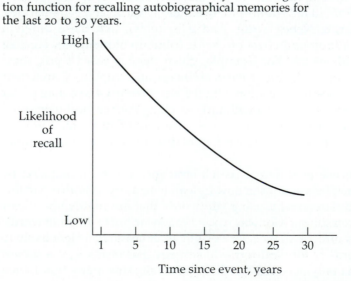

dency to recall events from their lives that occurred when they were 10 to 30 years old. This could be because these memories are often thought about by people (i.e., people like to reminisce about their youth) and are thus preferentially sampled by older adults during testing for autobiographical memory.

## Can We Believe Our Autobiographical Memories?

People who have sustained certain types of brain damage (especially bilateral damage to the frontal lobes) often resort to *confabulation* (see Chapter 14 also). Confabulation occurs when a person makes up a story (sometimes plausible and sometimes not) concerning a past event in his or her life. For example, Baddeley and Wilson (1986) describe a patient, R.J., who suffered a severe head injury at age 42 from a traffic accident. Examination of the patient revealed hemorrhages in both frontal lobes. A prominent behavioral feature of R.J. is that he now often confabulates stories that not only are quite implausible but also change with each retelling of the event! He tells his stories with great conviction, evidently believing that they are really true. When confronted with evidence that his story is false or irrational, he often still clings to his account. Commenting about R.J.'s great propensity to confabulate, Baddeley and Wilson (1986) report the following:

> R.J.'s confabulation is not limited to test situations. He confabulates in interacting with therapists, fellow patients, and his family. For example, one weekend while at home with his family he sat up in bed and turned to his wife, asking her, "Why do you keep telling people we are married?" His wife explained that they were married and had children, to which he replied that children did not necessarily imply marriage. She then took out the wedding photographs and showed them to him. At this point he admitted that the person marrying her looked like him but he denied that it was he. (p. 241)

Clearly, R.J. is suffering from a serious breakdown in accessing his autobiographical memories. To remedy the situation he resorts to confabulation. What about normal people? Are our autobiographical memories accurate accounts of what really transpired? Let's admit it, everyone lies on occasion, but we know when we are doing it, and it doesn't reflect what we truly believe is the truth. Probably most people think that by and large, their memories for personally experienced events are accurate. There may be a few minor discrepancies every so often, but in general, people believe their recall of autobiographical memories is reliable. After all, if our personal memories were not basically true, then people would have very distorted knowledge about themselves, and this would lead to great confusion (like what poor R.J. experiences). But just how veridical are our autobiographical memories?

It is now generally agreed that while the gist of most autobiographical memories is usually accurate, our personal memories are susceptible to systematic distortions, especially in terms of their fine details (Barclay, 1986; Brewer,

1986; Conway, 1990; Linton, 1986; Neisser, 1981). The major factor that is probably responsible for these distortions is one we have already discussed earlier in the book. In Chapter 6 it was seen that memory is often *reconstructive* in nature (Bartlett, 1932), and it is this reconstruction process that can lead to faulty remembrance of personal memories. So a person who can't quite remember the details of some past happening will likely fill in the gaps with details that he or she *believes* must have happened on the basis of plausible inferences.

The reconstruction of autobiographical memories is influenced by a process called *schematization* (Barclay, 1986). As described in detail in Chapter 6, people acquire schemas about activities or actions that occur repeatedly. The process of schematization starts in young children when memories for specific events merge into general scripts or schemas (see the next chapter also). These scripts or schemas then provide an organizational framework for the recall of everyday experiences (such as repeatedly visiting the same playmate's house). Schematization is very helpful in that it allows people to summarize the details of similar events or actions. But there is a price to be paid: specific details of any one episode, unless it is in some way unique, will likely be lost. Neisser (1981) has coined the term *repisodic memory* to refer to situations in which the recall of some event is really just the blending together of details from many similar episodes or events.

A good historical example of the distorting effects that repisodic memory can have on autobiographical memory occurred during the testimony given by John Dean, the former counsel to President Richard Nixon, during the Watergate hearings in 1973. When Dean was questioned about conversations he had with President Nixon and his senior staff concerning the cover-up that eventually led to Nixon's resignation, most members of the Watergate Committee were amazed by his detailed knowledge. Dean impressed many people with his seemingly remarkable memory for details (owing largely to the fact that he appeared confident in his speaking and to his use of persuasive verbal and nonverbal means to express himself, which are presentation tactics that, as you learned in Chapter 10, can add dramatically to the credibility given to someone's memory performance). However, when his testimony was later compared with the actual tape recordings of the conversations, it was revealed that he was wrong on many specific details and that he had confused different meetings and conversations. Nevertheless, the tapes did show that the *gist* of what he said was accurate. Apparently, when Dean tried to reconstruct what transpired during particular meetings or what was said in certain conversations, repisodic memory caused him to be inaccurate about many specific details while allowing him to still be relatively accurate about the major themes.

We also have *self-schemas* (Chapter 6), or particular ways in which we have come to view ourselves. These self-schemas can alter our autobiographical memories by causing us to "remember" an event in such a way that it is consistent with our self-concept (Barclay, 1986). For instance, if you truly believe that you are an honest person, then your self-schema may interfere with your ability to recall an episode in high school in which you cheated on an exam. This suggests an interesting possibility: if your self-schema should radically change over time, it may also affect what you remember from the past.

To summarize, it appears that for the most part our autobiographical memories are fairly accurate in their broad strokes. This is particularly likely for unique events that are not easily schematized and that are consistent with our self-schemas. However, especially over time, the specific details associated with individual events are often lost or distorted by the natural process of reconstruction. This is especially true for routine events. Therefore, be wary whenever anyone (including yourself) claims to remember specific details of a commonly occurring event that happened a long time ago.

# *E*YEWITNESS TESTIMONY

In the summer of 1979, things looked grim for Roman Catholic priest Father Bernard Pagano. He was on trial for committing several armed robberies in the Wilmington, Delaware, area. And although he maintained that he was innocent throughout the ordeal, seven eyewitnesses positively identified Father Pagano during the trial as being the "Gentleman Bandit," referring to the robber's polite manners and fine clothing. Miraculously for Father Pagano, the trial was suddenly halted when Ronald Clouser, knowing details that only the true robber could have known, came forward and confessed (Wortman, Loftus, & Marshall, 1992). Why was Father Pagano almost convicted of crimes that he didn't commit? As can be seen from their photographs in Figure 11.2, the two men do not strongly resemble each other. However, there were some powerful aspects of the case that worked to sway the judgment and memory of the witnesses against Father Pagano. For instance, before witnesses were shown pictures of possible suspects, the police suggested that the robber might be a priest. This would certainly be consistent with the fact that the robber had a relatively gentle demeanor. To make matters worse, Father Pagano was the only suspect who was shown wearing a clerical collar!

If not for the dramatic confession by Clouser, Father Pagano would almost certainly have been convicted of crimes he did not commit. It is regrettable that cases like Father Pagano's are not uncommon. A few years ago it was estimated that there were about 8500 wrongful convictions each year in the United States and that perhaps as many as half of them were due to faulty eyewitness testimony (Loftus, 1986). It is well known among trial lawyers and judges that having an eyewitness "take the stand" can greatly influence the outcome of a criminal trial. Juries usually place an inordinate amount of trust in eyewitness accounts. Apparently, jury members believe that eyewitness reports are highly accurate and that unless a witness is deliberately trying to mislead, eyewitness accounts should be considered almost as gospel.

Memory researchers, however, know better! For example, we saw in Chap-

FIGURE 11.2
Photographs of Father Pagano (right) and confessed robber Ronald Clouser (left).
*UPI/Bettmann.*

ter 8 that even when people's memories were tested for events that were vivid, highly emotional, and personally important and that they were extremely confident about (such as events in flashbulb memories), the memories for these events were often wildly inaccurate in many vital details. During the last 20 years, a large number of studies have examined just how veridical people's memories are for events they have witnessed. As you will learn in this section, these studies indicate that people (especially judges and members of juries) should be *much* warier about the trustworthiness of eyewitness testimony, even when given by well-meaning people of high integrity.

## The Misinformation Effect

After having witnessed an event, if misleading information about the event is later presented, people often have difficulty remembering the original event. This is often referred to as the *misinformation effect,* and there is extensive evidence for its existence (e.g., Belli, 1989; Ceci, Toglia, & Ross, 1987; Lindsay, 1990; Loftus, 1975, 1977, 1979a, 1992; Loftus, Donders, Hoffman, & Schooler, 1989; Loftus & Greene, 1980; Loftus, Miller, & Burns, 1978; McCloskey & Zaragoza, 1985; Tversky & Tuchin, 1989; Zaragoza, McCloskey & Jamis, 1987). To summarize when people are most susceptible to the misinformation effect, Loftus (1992) has proposed what she calls the *discrepancy detection principle.* According to this principle: "Recollections are more likely to change if a person does not immediately detect discrepancies between postevent information and memory for the original event" (p. 121).

As you might expect, research has typically shown (although not always, e.g., Zaragoza, 1987, 1991) that young children, perhaps owing to their greater suggestibility, are more susceptible to misleading information than are adults (e.g., Ceci, Ross, & Toglia, 1987a, 1987b; King & Yuille, 1987; Loftus, Levidow, & Duensing, 1992). The issue of how susceptible a young child is to leading questions or false information is of major importance to the legal system, especially given the recent rash of cases of alleged child abuse. If it is suspected that a young child is the victim of abuse, he or she is likely to be interviewed and questioned repeatedly by a whole host of people (such as parents, nurses, doctors, police, social workers, lawyers, and psychologists). Besides causing great stress and embarrassment for the child, each interview provides an opportunity, via leading questions, false information, and "coaching" in how to phrase answers by often well-meaning supporters, for the child's memory to become distorted. Because of the widespread belief that young children are highly vulnerable to suggestive or leading questions, at one time every state in the union required (and many still do) that the testimony of a child be confirmed by an older person before it could be accepted as evidence in a court of law (Ceci, Ross, & Toglia, 1987b).

To investigate the misinformation effect, most studies have used the following three-stage procedure:

*Stage 1:* All subjects experience an event. This usually involves viewing a series of slides, seeing a videotape, or witnessing a staged event (such as a person entering a classroom, arguing briefly with the teacher, and then storming out).

*Stage 2:* The subjects are divided into different groups on the basis of the type of postevent information to be presented to them. Some subjects are supplied with postevent information that is *consistent* with some detail of the witnessed event, some are presented with information that is *inconsistent* with that detail, and some are provided with no new information at all about the detail in question (a *neutral* condition). The additional postevent information is typically supplied to the subjects either when they are asked some questions about the event they witnessed or when they are asked to read a narrative account of the event.

*Stage 3:* The subjects are tested for their recall or recognition of the original event witnessed in Stage 1. Of course, of particular interest is how well the subjects remember the details of the original event for which additional postevent information (either consistent or inconsistent) was given. The testing is usually accomplished by having the subjects answer questions about the original event, or by having them make "Yes/No" decisions regarding whether or not particular events occurred or objects appeared in the original event, or by having them choose among pairs of slides the one slide in each pair that best corresponds to the original event.

For a concrete example of this three-stage procedure, consider the following classic study conducted by Loftus et al. (1978). In the study, subjects viewed 30 color slides (Stage 1) of a red Datsun getting into a car accident. In the sequence of slides, the Datsun stops at an intersection, turns a corner, and hits a pedestrian. Half of the subjects saw a *stop* sign at the intersection, and half saw a *yield* sign (see Figure 11.3). After seeing all 30 slides, subjects waited 20 minutes to 1 week before answering 20 questions about the accident (Stage 2). One question contained information that was either consistent, inconsistent, or neutral with regard to the type of traffic sign seen by the subjects. For instance, some subjects who had seen the yield sign were asked, "Did another car pass the red Datsun while it was stopped at the yield sign?" (consistent condition). Other subjects were asked, "Did another car pass the red Datsun while it was stopped at the stop sign?" (inconsistent condition). For a third group, the type of traffic sign was not mentioned at all (neutral condition). A similar pattern of questions was presented to subjects who had seen the stop sign in the original series of slides. In Stage 3, the subjects were given 15 pairs of slides and had to choose the slide from each pair that they had seen in Stage 1. As you can probably guess, the critical pair of slides showed the Datsun at an intersection, stopped at either a yield sign or a stop sign.

For those who answered the questions after 20 minutes, if the question they were asked in Stage 2 contained *consistent* information concerning the traffic sign they had seen, the correct sign in Stage 3 was chosen 75 percent of the time. However, if they were given *inconsistent* information in Stage 2, the correct sign was selected only 41 percent of the time. People in the neutral condition scored in between, choosing the correct sign around 59 percent of the time. If Stage 2 occurred a week after the subjects had first seen the original slide series, the effect of the inconsistent information was even more dramatic—while both the consistent and neutral groups showed some decline in accuracy,

FIGURE 11.3
The red Datsun at either a stop sign or a yield sign.

by far the greatest drop in accuracy (down to 20 percent) was for the subjects given the misinformation.

**Combating the misinformation effect.** Since the misinformation effect is so prevalent, researchers have tried to find ways to combat its effectiveness. It is comforting to know that research has found that people will be less susceptible to postevent misleading information if certain precautions are followed. For instance, Loftus (1977) has shown that if people first make a *public statement* about what they witnessed, this allows them to better resist the effects of being presented with subsequent misleading information. Another way to lessen the effects of postevent misleading information is to *forewarn* subjects that they may encounter misinformation (Greene, Flynn, & Loftus, 1982). The *timing* of presenting the misinformation is also an important factor. The longer the time interval between the witnessed event and the occurrence of the misleading information, the more likely it is that the original memory will be vulnerable (Loftus et al., 1978). This is probably because the false information will have a greater impact as the original memory fades away. There is also a limit to what people will believe. If the misleading information *blatantly* or *obviously* contradicts what was originally witnessed, people will not be influenced by it (Loftus, 1979b).

**What befalls the original memory?** Although no one doubts the existence of the misinformation effect, there's considerable disagreement concerning why it occurs. Initially, some researchers, especially Loftus and her colleagues (Loftus, 1975, 1977, 1979a; Loftus et al., 1978; Loftus & Greene, 1980; Loftus & Loftus, 1980), thought that postevent misleading information caused the original memory to be transformed, displaced, or overwritten. In other words, when people were misled by the new information, this resulted in the irrevocable loss of the original memory. In support of this belief, Loftus (1979a) found that offering subjects a $25 incentive to respond correctly did not lessen the effect of the misinformation effect, nor did it help to allow subjects the opportunity to make a second guess among several alternatives.

Others argued that the original memory was not really lost forever but that perhaps it was merely rendered inaccessible (Dodson & Reisberg, 1991), perhaps owing to retroactive interference (see Chapter 5) (Bekerian & Bowers, 1983; Bowers & Bekerian, 1984; Chandler, 1989; Christiaansen & Ochalek, 1983). Recently, Dodson and Reisberg (1991) found evidence of a misinformation effect when subjects were tested by means of a conventional recognition test (in other words, by means of an *explicit* memory test) but not if subjects were tested by means of an *implicit* memory test (these types of memory tests were first described in Chapter 2). This implies that at least some aspect of the original memory is still accessible and that this can be demonstrated if the subject's memory is probed by means or procedures that do not rely on the conscious recollection of events.

Whether the original memory is assumed to be lost completely or is believed to just be inaccessible to conscious recollection, both of these views suggest that there is some type of *memory impairment* for the original event. This memory impairment presumption still has many current adherents (e.g., Belli, 1989; Lindsay, 1990; Loftus et al., 1989; Tversky & Tuchin, 1989). Others, however, believe that there is no good evidence for the belief that any memory impairment occurs at all (McCloskey & Zaragoza, 1985; Zaragoza & McCloskey, 1989; Zaragoza et al., 1987). Instead, these researchers suggest that the misinformation effect is due to a *response bias* in favor of the false postevent information. Essentially, they maintain that the recognition test procedure often used to show the misinformation effect is really unsuited for assessing the effects of postevent misleading information on memory.

Their argument rests on the logical assumption that many of the subjects have forgotten the critical detail they witnessed in Stage 1 (e.g., the stop sign) by the time they are in Stage 2. Now, in Stage 2, some of these subjects are given false information about the critical detail (i.e., that a yield sign was originally presented). When tested in Stage 3, these subjects are forced to choose between a slide showing the stop sign and a slide showing a yield sign. It makes sense that their responses should be biased in favor of the incorrect choice (the yield sign), since they have no reason to doubt the false information received in Stage 2 (since they have forgotten the critical detail seen in Stage 1). Subjects who have forgotten the critical detail presented in Stage 1 but who do not receive misleading information in Stage 2 will not be biased in Stage 3 to guess in favor of the incorrect choice. Because of this inherent response bias, the subjects in the misled group will select the correct response less often than will others. Supporting this hypothesis, in several experiments using a *modified* recognition test in which the misleading false alternative was not offered as a choice in Stage 3 (thereby negating the possibility of any response bias), no significant differences were observed between the percentage of correct responses made by the misled subjects and the percentage for the nonmisled subjects (McCloskey & Zaragoza, 1985; Zaragoza et al., 1987).

So what does explain the misinformation effect? In spite of the work just cited, many researchers still believe that memory impairment is at least partly responsible (e.g., Loftus, 1992; Loftus & Hoffman, 1989). And they may be right! After all, as Cohen (1989) points out, there is no reason to expect that the original memory should always suffer the same fate. Perhaps sometimes the original memory is transformed or overwritten and is indeed lost forever; perhaps sometimes the memory is only rendered inaccessible; and perhaps sometimes all that is operating is a response bias that raises its head when people forget the original information and are exposed to additional, but misleading, information.

**Some practical implications of the misinformation effect.** Regardless of the cause(s) of the misinformation effect, the fact that it occurs has very important practical implications, especially legal ones. Let's consider a few of them.

- It is important for a judge or opposing attorney to guard against the use of leading questions because it is known that even subtle word changes can alter a witness's report. In one study, after seeing a film of a car accident, some subjects were asked, "About how fast were the cars going when they smashed into each other?" Other subjects were asked the same question except that the verb changed from *smashed* to either *hit*, *collided*, *bumped*, or *contacted*. Not only did the subjects who received the "smashed" version of the question estimate a higher speed, but they were also more likely to respond "yes" to the question "Did you see any broken glass?" even though there wasn't any broken glass shown in the film (Loftus & Palmer, 1974)!

- When people are interviewed by law-enforcement personnel (such as police detectives, polygraph specialists, or CIA and FBI investigators), more care should be taken to enhance the accuracy of eyewitness reports. It has been reported that one technique, called the *guided recall procedure*, produces more accurate eyewitness accounts than does the standard interviewing procedures used by law-enforcement personnel (Fisher, Geiselman, & Amador, 1989; Geiselman, Fisher, Firstenberg, Hutton, Sullivan, Avetissian, & Prosk, 1984; Geiselman, Fisher, MacKinnon, & Holland, 1985). The guided recall procedure gets the witness to mentally reinstate the environmental and personal context that prevailed at the time of the event in question. The witness is encouraged to recall every possible detail by employing different perspectives of the incident and by recalling the parts of the event in different orders. Questions are carefully phrased to reduce the possibility that the interviewer will inadvertently influence the witness's report.

- There is evidence that if witnesses are carefully instructed, they can, in fact, often identify the true source of their memories (Lindsay & Johnson, 1989; Zaragoza & Koshmider, 1989). Doing so can help a person distinguish between what was actually witnessed and what was subsequently learned about an event from other sources.

- Witnesses should view lineups and mug shots of possible suspects alone, thus eliminating the possibility of being influenced by the judgments of others (Loftus & Greene, 1980).

- Many judges (with the support of most trial lawyers) will not allow witnesses to use notes, forcing them to rely entirely on their own memories (Jacoby & Padgett, 1989). This certainly seems unwise, given what we now know about the vulnerability of eyewitness memory. And it also seems unfair—both lawyers and judges can use extensive notes, allowing them to remember exactly how they want to phrase their questions or give instructions to the jury.

- Perhaps it should be standard practice to have experts inform juries about the fallibility of eyewitness accounts, especially in cases where the verdict hangs (no pun intended), as it frequently does, on such testimony.

# MEMORY DURING ANESTHESIA

There are times when all of us feel sluggish. For many people this occurs just before falling asleep or after having eaten an especially large meal. During such times, our ability to focus attention is poor, and so our memory capabilities, which are so highly dependent on our ability to sustain attention, are also at a low ebb. In fact, in Chapters 7 and 8 the importance of having an adequate level of arousal for normal memory functioning and consolidation was repeatedly stressed. Therefore, it would be logical to predict that a person who has been anesthetized, and who therefore is at an extremely low level of arousal, will remember nothing at all from his or her stay in the operating room. And indeed, the majority of anesthesiologists emphatically claim that this is true, that none of their totally anesthetized patients ever remember anything that happens during surgery.

At the level of conscious awareness the anesthesiologists are undoubtedly correct, since a primary purpose of anesthesia is to make the patient amnesic during medical procedures. After all, no one wants to remember the pain and stress (and sometimes the embarrassment) associated with surgery. However, as you will learn, this lack of awareness on the part of the patient may not be as complete as many people have previously believed.

## The Fat Lady Syndrome

Apparently, it is not unusual for some medical personnel to make general comments about their patients during surgery. And sometimes these comments are of a disparaging nature. Especially likely targets are patients who are grossly overweight. Since some medical practitioners believe that a patient under full anesthesia will not be able to remember any such remarks postoperatively, insulting comments and "fat" jokes are not uncommon. There's good evidence, however, that such comments cannot always be made with impunity. Over the years, a number of reports have surfaced indicating that patients can sometimes remember the uttered remarks, sometimes not until days later, and then become furious during the recovery period. This is often referred to as the *Fat Lady Syndrome* (Bennett, 1988; Eich, Reeves, & Katz, 1985; Halfen, 1986).

A few years ago a lawsuit was even filed by a woman against her surgeon, who had referred to her as a "beached whale" during surgery. She suffered postoperative complications for several days and finally blurted out to her nurse, "That bastard called me a beached whale" (Bennett, 1988, p. 204). The lawsuit was settled out of court. Given the possible existence of the Fat Lady

FIGURE 11.4

A cartoon showing that it may be smart to try to head off a potential lawsuit even before the patient recovers from anesthesia.

© *1986, Washington Post Writers Group. Reprinted with permission.*

Syndrome and the lawsuits that can result, more medical personnel may start to do the kind of "debriefing" depicted in the cartoon in Figure 11.4.

## Is Memory Possible during Anesthesia?

The possibility that patients can still hear comments made while they are under anesthesia should be given serious credence, since it is well known that auditory functions are among the "last to go" (Bennett, 1988). If patients can actually hear and remember what goes on during surgery, this could have profound effects on their prognosis for recovery. Remarks that the operation is going poorly or that the patient is in much worse shape than was anticipated prior to surgery could have devastating effects.

In a series of experiments possibly involving some questionable ethics, Levinson (1965) provided early support for this possibility by fabricating mock "crises" during surgery. For example, in one study 10 dental patients were deeply anesthetized with ether before undergoing surgery. During the actual surgery, the following dire (but false) remarks concerning how things were going were made in the patient's presence by the attending anesthesiologist:

> "Stop the operation. I don't like the patient's colour. His/her lips are too blue. I'm going to give a little oxygen."
> After a few moments the anesthesiologist continued, "There, that's better now. You can carry on with the operation."

A month later, the patients were hypnotized and asked to reexperience the operation. Of the 10 patients, 4 could recall almost verbatim the traumatic words used during the fake crisis, while another 4 displayed great anxiety when trying to relive the operation.

Over the years, there have been many anecdotal reports of anesthetized patients being able to remember careless remarks made during surgery by the medical staff (e.g., Adam, 1979; Bennett, 1988). Critics have often dismissed such reports. They claim that these occurrences can easily be accounted for if one assumes that temporary decreases in the depth of anesthesia sometimes occur during operations. In such situations, a patient may have enough conscious awareness to retain some of what he or she hears. In addition, there were methodological flaws in many of the early experiments that were conducted, making it more difficult to interpret their results. For instance, in Levinson's (1965) study, no control group was used (i.e., patients who didn't hear false remarks about how badly their condition was during the operation), and Levinson may also have influenced the recall of his subjects through inadvertent cues given just prior to the hypnotic recall.

Nevertheless, these early tantalizing results spurred many researchers to more rigorously explore the possibility that people could later consciously recall or recognize auditory stimuli presented during deep anesthesia. To show you the dedication of some researchers, Elizabeth Loftus, a well-known and respected memory researcher whose work on eyewitness testimony was discussed earlier in this chapter, served as her own subject in such an experiment. Loftus needed to undergo abdominal surgery, so she arranged it so that a list of 100 unrelated words was read to her while she was anesthetized. Her recognition memory for the words was then tested three times—at 28, 53, and 82 hours after initial exposure. Her performance was always at chance levels (Loftus, Schooler, Loftus, & Glauber, 1985).

In addition to word lists, other researchers have used such auditory stimuli as poems, letter-word pairs, environmental sounds like fire bells, and music. The results of most of these studies were not seen as being very encouraging. In fact, reviews of much of this literature have led some researchers to conclude that there is little evidence, if any, that patients can later recall or recognize stimuli that were presented during deep anesthesia (Eich et al., 1985; Trustman, Dubrovsky & Titley, 1977).

## Implicit Memory during Anesthesia

Does this mean that surgical personnel can say whatever they like in an anesthetized patient's presence and be assured that the patient will be none the wiser or worse for it? Although this question is still controversial, the most likely answer is *no*. There's now a growing consensus that people can, indeed, remember what they heard while under the effects of anesthesia, but this memory is of a special type. Our current understanding suggests that recall or recognition on a verbal, *conscious* level normally does not occur under deep anesthesia. However, there's good evidence of remembering *without conscious awareness,* as shown by using *implicit memory* testing procedures (Bennett, 1988, 1990; Jelicic, 1990; Kihlstrom & Schacter, 1990; Kihlstrom, Schacter, Cork, Hurt, & Behr, 1990; Millar, 1988; Roorda-Hrdlickova, Wolters, Bonke, & Phaf, 1990;

Wolters & Phaf, 1990). Since the effects of this memory may be subtle and may be demonstrated only by sensitive measures, it's understandable that many surgeons and anesthesiologists have not personally seen evidence of this memory in their patients and so have remained skeptical.

Let's briefly examine some of the evidence that memory without conscious awareness is possible for things heard during anesthesia. In a clever experiment by Goldmann (1986), patients who were about to undergo surgery but who had not yet been anesthetized were given a pretest in which they were asked a number of arcane questions (e.g., "What is the blood pressure of an octopus?"). During surgery, when they were anesthetized, half of the patients heard the correct answers to these strange questions, while the other half did not. When the patients were tested on these same questions 1 or 2 days following surgery, there was a significant improvement in scores for the group that had heard the answers during surgery but no improvement for the group that had not. Yet when questioned, none of the patients in either group consciously recalled having heard anything during surgery!

In another example, Millar (1987) had groups of anesthetized patients listen to different tape-recorded lists of words. Each list contained eight words that were exemplars of a unique semantic category. For instance, if the category was vegetables, the words on the list might be *carrot, corn, squash,* etc. After recovery, the patients were asked to generate exemplars for different semantic categories. Similar to Goldmann's patients, none of the patients had any conscious recall of the prerecorded words heard while they were anesthetized. But Millar found that patients who had been exposed to a particular list of words while anesthetized would generate those particular words significantly more quickly than would patients who had not heard those words.

There's also evidence that patients who are unable to consciously recall instructions given to them while they were anesthetized may yet have their overt behavior altered in accordance with the instructions. For instance, in two separate studies, patients under anesthesia were told to touch their ears; later, when being interviewed, they did so significantly more often than did control patients, even though they were at a complete loss as to why they were tugging at their ears (Bennett, Davis, & Giannini, 1985; Goldmann, Shah, & Hebden, 1987).

## The Effects of Positive Statements during Anesthesia

We saw earlier that patients may respond negatively to what they hear in the operating room [e.g., the Fat Lady Syndrome and Levinson's (1965) work]. On the basis of such findings, it has even been suggested that patients should be fitted with earplugs during surgery so that the medical staff can converse with candor! But some enlightened people have taken just the opposite approach. Perhaps if patients can respond to negative comments, then maybe they can respond to positive statements as well. Their reasoning is that even though the patients will have no conscious recollection of the positive statements, their bodies may still react in a favorable, therapeutic way. Although not all studies have been supportive, there is considerable support for this hypothesis, some of it from even 30 years ago (Bonke, Schmitz, Verhage, & Zwaveling, 1986; Furlong, 1990; Hutchings, 1961; Mainford, Rath, & Barnett, 1983; McLintock, Aitken, Downie, & Kenny, 1990; Pearson, 1961; Rath, 1982; Wolfe & Millet, 1960).

To give you the flavor of some of this research, let's examine a recent study by Evans and Richardson (1988) that clearly shows that making positive statements to anesthetized patients can significantly aid their recovery. The patients were 39 women who were scheduled to have hysterectomies (partial or complete removal of the uterus). During the surgery, and while under anesthesia, 19 of the women listened to a tape recording that described normal postoperative procedures and explained how to best cope with them. The tape also contained direct therapeutic suggestions (e.g., "You will not feel any pain") and positive statements about the operation (e.g., "The operation seems to be going very well, and the patient is fine"). The 20 women in the control group listened to a blank tape. The results were impressive. Compared with the control group, the women in the suggestion group spent significantly less time in the hospital (1 1/3 fewer days), suffered from significantly shorter periods of pyrexia (fever), had significantly fewer gastrointestinal problems, and were rated as having a significantly better recovery on the basis of the nurses' assessment.

There was one more interesting aspect to the study. The researchers also asked each woman to describe any memories or dreams she had had since the operation and to guess whether she had listened to a suggestion tape or a blank tape during surgery. None of the patients could consciously recall any events that occurred during the operation, nor could the women in the suggestion group recall any of the statements. However, 18 of the 19 women in the suggestion group correctly guessed that they had heard the instruction tape during surgery, while only 11 of the 20 women in the control group accurately guessed that they had heard the blank tape. This result again demonstrates that auditory perception can occur during anesthesia and that memory for the auditory information may not be on a conscious level. Such results suggest that there may be very practical, beneficial effects of carefully monitoring what an anesthetized patient hears (and doesn't hear!) in the operating room. Future research could help to determine the most effective ways to aid postoperative recovery.

# Summary

## I. Autobiographical Memory

- Memory for information about one's past is called *autobiographical memory*. Although the scientific study of autobiographical memory began more than a century ago, relatively few studies were conducted for several decades. The modern resurgence of interest started in the mid-1970s, and interest has continued unabated.

- An especially popular method for investigating autobiographical memory has been the *cue-word method*. But people use many different strategies to search through their autobiographical memories, and these strategies can profoundly affect the types of memories recalled and the time periods from which they are sampled.

- Research has shown that almost everyone has a period of *childhood amnesia* for the first few years of life. Furthermore, recent personal memories are more likely to be recalled than are older memories. As people get older (especially beyond age 35), they have an increased tendency to *reminisce* about events that occurred during their youth.

- The gist of our autobiographical memories is usually accurate, but because memory is often *reconstructive* in nature and the reconstruction of memories is influenced by the *schematization process,* the specific details about events are often distorted or lost. This distortion or loss is least likely to occur for unique events that are not readily schematized and that are consistent with our own *self-schemas.*

## II. Eyewitness Testimony

- Although eyewitness accounts are very influential and are widely believed to be highly accurate, research suggests that people should be more suspicious of such reports.

- People frequently have difficulty remembering details of the original event if misleading information is subsequently presented. This is called the *misinformation effect.*

- Several factors can lessen the impact of the misinformation effect. These include having the person make a prior *public statement, forewarning* the person that false information may be presented, keeping the *time interval* as short as possible between the witnessed event and the misleading information, and having the false information *blatantly* or *obviously* contradict what was originally witnessed.

- There's great controversy over what happens to the original memory affected by the misinformation effect.
  - Some believe that the original memory is *displaced* by the new information and gone forever. Others believe that the memory still exists but is *inaccessible* (at least on a conscious level). Both of these viewpoints assert that some form of memory impairment occurs.
  - Other researchers maintain that the false postevent information doesn't impair the original memory at all. These researchers think that the misinformation effect is simply due to a *response bias.*
  - Since different memories can suffer different fates, it may be that all three factors may at times account for the misinformation effect.

- Six practical implications of the misinformation effect were presented. These included guarding against the use of leading questions, using special interviewing techniques, instructing witnesses to distinguish between what was actually witnessed and what was not, eliminating the influence of others during the viewing of lineups and mug shots, allowing the use of notes by witnesses, and informing juries about the fallibility of eyewitness testimony.

### III. Memory during Anesthesia

- Most anesthesiologists maintain that their patients never remember any events while properly anesthetized. However, this now appears to be true only at the level of *conscious* awareness.
- When *implicit* memory testing procedures are used, there's good evidence that remembering without conscious awareness is possible for events experienced during anesthesia.
- Although patients may be unable to consciously recall instructions given while they were anesthetized, upon recovery, their overt behavior may be influenced in accordance with the instructions.
- Perhaps most exciting of all, there's growing evidence that positive statements made during anesthesia may significantly aid recovery.

# 12

# Development of Memory across the Life Span

❖

We all know that having an accurate memory is crucial to living a normal life. But it may surprise you to learn just how soon in life our memory capabilities start to operate. As you will soon learn, there is good evidence that even *before* birth, humans have some capacity to learn and remember information. From personal experience we all know that tremendous changes occur in our memory capabilities as we get older. This chapter will explore how and why memory abilities change (sometimes for the better and sometimes not) as a function of increasing age and experience.

## MEMORY IN INFANCY

Clever and innovative research methods are often needed to assess the memory capabilities of human infants (especially newborns). Since infants typically do not speak any words until they are about a year old and speak only about 100 words by age 2, their memory cannot be tested by the most prevalent ways used to test memory in older children and adults (i.e., through verbal instructions and responses). After all, a 3-month-old infant can't describe his or her recollection of a picture presented the day before, nor will a 16-month-old infant obey instructions to rehearse a list of nonsense syllables.

### Remembering Visual Information

Perhaps the most common method developed to assess infant memory, one that doesn't depend at all on language ability, is the *habituation-dishabituation paradigm*, which is illustrated in Figure 12.1. In Chapter 7, *habituation* was

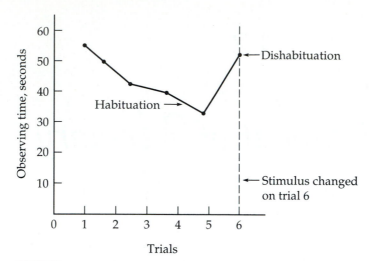

FIGURE 12.1

This shows the change in observing time if dishabituation occurs.

defined as a decrease in responding to a repetitive stimulus. The term *dishabituation* refers to the recovery from habituation; in other words, it means that responding returns to prehabituation levels. Visual recognition has proved to be the most popular type of memory assessed using the habituation-dishabituation method. A typical habituation-dishabituation procedure involves presenting an attentive infant with the same picture or pattern over a series of trials and observing the amount of time the infant fixates on the stimulus. Usually, the infant shows a decline in the amount of time spent looking at the stimulus over trials. This decrease is thought to reflect habituation; the infant recognizes the stimulus from previous trials and chooses to look at it less than before because it ceases to be novel and interesting. By varying the amount of time between trials and observing the extent of habituation that may occur, it is possible to estimate how long an infant can maintain his or her memory for the original stimulus. If a long enough delay occurs between successive showings, the infant will forget the stimulus upon subsequent presentation. When this happens, the infant will inspect the stimulus for an amount of time roughly equivalent to the infant's first encounter with it.

An excellent illustrative example of using the habituation-dishabituation paradigm is the now classic study by Friedman (1972) concerning the visual recognition memory of infants 1 to 4 days old. In his study, each infant was presented with a black-and-white checkerboard to look at for 60 seconds. Some infants saw a checkerboard with 4 squares, and some saw one with 144 squares. During each 60-second presentation, an observer recorded how long the infant looked at the checkerboard. Over a series of trials in which the same checkerboard was repeatedly presented, it was reliably found that the average looking time decreased significantly from about 60 seconds to 45 seconds.

To be certain that the decrease in looking time could really be attributed to habituation and not simply to fatigue, Friedman conducted a second experiment. This time, while some of the infants continued to see the same checkerboard pattern as before, others were now presented with a new pattern. Some of the infants who initially saw the 4-square pattern were now presented with the 144-square pattern, and some who had begun with the 144-square pattern were now presented with the 4-square pattern. If the earlier decrease in looking time had been due to fatigue rather than habituation, then the looking time should not be influenced by whether the infant was presented with the same checkerboard pattern or a novel one. However, if habituation was the cause of the decline, then the infants who continued to see the same repeated pattern should still show a decrease in looking time, while, in contrast, the infants seeing the novel pattern should show evidence of dishabituation (i.e., the looking time for these infants should increase). The results clearly supported the habituation explanation—the infants shown the same checkerboard pattern continued to depress their looking time; however, the infants shown the novel pattern increased their looking time significantly.

Using a variation of the habituation paradigm, Fagan (1973) has demonstrated that infants only 6 months old can recognize black-and-white photographs of human faces even after a two-week interval. There is now extensive evidence that recognition memory for visual objects is present very early in life and develops rapidly during the first 6 to 12 months (for reviews, see Daehler and Greco, 1985; Kail, 1990; Olson and Sherman, 1980; Werner and Perlmutter, 1979).

## Memory Ability for Other Senses

What about the development of memory ability for other senses? There is some fascinating research that suggests that memory for sounds may be present even before birth. For example, there is considerable evidence that a fetus probably learns to recognize its mother's voice. For instance, a study by DeCasper and Fifer (1980) showed that 3-day-old infants can distinguish their mother's tape-recorded voice from that of another female. This was accomplished by having each infant listen to recordings made by both his or her mother and an unfamiliar female as they read from Dr. Seuss's book *To think I saw it on Mulberry Street*. While an infant listened to the tape recordings, a nonnutritive nipple (i.e., one that does not give milk or juice when sucked) was placed in his or her mouth. By sucking on the nipple at different rates, the infants could learn to produce either voice. For instance, fast sucking might make the mother's voice come on, while slow sucking produced the voice of the stranger. Once they learned to control their environment in this way, the infants quickly learned to produce the mother's voice and produced it more frequently than that of the stranger. Since the infants spent no more than about 12 hours since their birth with their mothers (the infants were cared for primarily by the nursery personnel during their first 3 days of life), DeCasper and Fifer concluded that the infants preferred their mothers' voices because they had grown accustomed to them while still in the womb, not because of early postnatal experience.

This hypothesis is supported by converging evidence from several sources. First of all, it is known that hearing becomes functional for the fetus after around 32 weeks of gestation, so there would be ample time for the fetus to listen to and remember the mother's voice. In addition, Fifer (1981, cited in Spence and DeCasper, 1987) found no evidence that preference for the mother's voice over a stranger's was influenced by the amount of mother-infant contact during the first few days after birth. Consistent with these results, it has also been observed that early postnatal experience with the father's voice does *not* result in a preference for the father's voice over that of another male (DeCasper and Prescott, 1984). Research has shown that a fetus does not hear its father's voice as well as it hears its mother's voice, probably because the father is physically farther away (Querleu & Renard, 1981) and because the lower pitch of the father's voice doesn't carry as well. Even more convincing evidence that a fetus can remember its mother's voice comes from a study by DeCasper and Spence (1986). Mothers-to-be read the same children's story out loud, twice a day, during the last 6 weeks of their pregnancy. After birth, the infants preferred to listen to the particular story read to them while in utero rather than to novel stories.

In terms of the sense of smell, there is also some strong evidence that recognition abilities are present early in life. Much of the work in this area involves the use of breast pads, which are soft absorbent-cotton pads worn inside a brassiere to soak up excess milk from a nursing mother. Macfarlane (1975) found that infants only 6 days old prefer to turn in the direction of the breast pad worn by their mother rather than to a pad that had been worn by an unfamiliar nursing mother. Other research, however, has suggested that it takes about 6 weeks before infants will respond differently to breast pads worn by the mother or by a stranger (Russell, 1976). It has also been shown that breast-feeding infants, but not bottle-feeding ones, can recognize and will orient toward a pad that had been worn in another region of the body (such as the armpit) of their mother rather than a pad worn by an unfamiliar new mother (Cernoch & Porter, 1985). Why should breast-fed infants differ from bottle-fed ones? Perhaps owing to the direct contact while feeding, breast-fed infants are more likely than bottle-fed infants to learn what their mothers smell like.

The attentive reader may be wondering why the infants in the hearing and smell studies mentioned above showed a preference for the *familiar* stimulus (e.g., the mother's voice or smell) over the *novel* one. This seems to contradict the findings from the habituation-dishabituation research that assumes that infants prefer to attend to novel stimuli. Research has indicated, however, that this assumption is not always true. For example, it has been found that infants less than 2 months old often prefer familiar stimuli rather than novel ones (Weizmann, Cohen, & Pratt, 1971; Wetherford & Cohen, 1973), which is consistent with the data from the hearing and smell studies. There are also limitations that are inherent in the habituation-dishabituation procedure itself. As pointed out by Sophian (1980), if an infant does not show any preferential attention to a novel stimulus, this may indicate that the infant does not remember the original stimulus, or, alternatively, the infant may, indeed, remember the old stimulus but still may not choose to look longer at the novel one. And a very critical limitation of all habituation procedures is that only *recognition* memory can be assessed; nothing can be learned about the ability to *recall* information from memory or, perhaps of even greater importance, the ability to *use* the remembered information.

## The Conjugate Reinforcement Paradigm

Largely in an effort to overcome the limitations inherent in the habituation-dishabituation paradigm, Carolyn Rovee-Collier and her colleagues have developed a clever technique called the *conjugate reinforcement paradigm* to assess the memory ability of infants. As we will see, one of the major advantages of this new technique over the traditional habituation-dishabituation procedure is that it studies memory in infants who are *motivated* to remember their experiences. After all, it is reasonable to assume that if you want to fully test the memory capabilities of any organism, whether it be a frog, an infant, or a college freshman, it would be wise to try to make sure that the subject wants to remember.

The essence of the conjugate reinforcement procedure is really quite simple. As seen in Figure 12.2, one end of a ribbon is tied to the ankle of an infant who is lying on his or her back in a crib. The other end of the ribbon is tied to a mobile that is suspended over the crib. When the infant kicks with the ankle tied to the ribbon, the mobile starts to move. Infants apparently really like to kick the mobile into motion; as the mobile slows down, they will kick vigorously to get it going again, often vocalize loudly, and stare intently at the moving parts. This is called a conjugate reinforcement procedure because reinforcement (getting the mobile to move) is conjugated (or coupled) with a particular response (kicking).

The typical conjugate reinforcement procedure involves two or three 15-minute sessions that are 24 hours apart. Each 15-minute session has three phases. The first is a 3-minute baseline phase in which no reinforcement is obtained by kicking. Two mobile stands are suspended above the crib, one with an attached mobile and one without one. The ribbon is attached to the "empty" mobile stand. Although the infant can still see the mobile attached to one of the stands, kicking the foot with the ribbon tied to it will not set it in motion during this phase. When no reinforcement is available, a typical 3-month-old will kick 5 to 10 times a minute.

Following the baseline phase, there is a 9-minute acquisition phase in which the ribbon is now attached to the mobile stand that does have a mobile that can be activated by kicking. During this period the infant learns that he or she

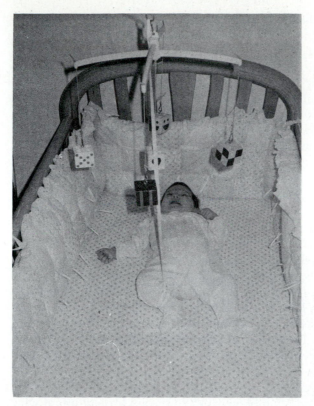

FIGURE 12.2
The apparatus used for training and testing infants for the
conjugate reinforcement paradigm.

can make the mobile move by kicking the foot with the ribbon on it. The same
3-month-old who was kicking only 5 to 10 times a minute during the nonreinforcement period will now often double his or her kicking rate. The last phase
is called the *immediate retention test*. During the last 3 minutes of each session,
the ribbon is again tied to the empty mobile stand, and the number of kicks
made is recorded. This nonreinforcement phase serves as a good measure of
the infant's final level of acquisition, since memory for the task is tested after
virtually no delay.

Memory performance should be at its maximum level during the immediate retention test. This level of performance can then be compared with
memory performance after varying amounts of delay have occurred. Testing
is performed under the exact conditions that occurred during the baseline phase
and the immediate retention test phase—a 3-minute nonreinforcement period
in which the infant can see the mobile, but kicking will not activate it. If an
infant completely forgets that kicking the foot with a ribbon on it was associated
with moving the mobile, then his or her performance should match that in the
initial 3-minute baseline phase. However, if an infant remembers the association
perfectly, then he or she should respond at the same high level as during the
immediate retention test. In other words, the more an infant forgets, the closer

performance will match the baseline level; the more an infant remembers, the closer performance will match the level shown during the immediate retention test.

**Results of the conjugate reinforcement procedure.** The results of such testing usually indicate that the memory of 2-month-old infants is significantly above the baseline level after a 1-day delay but is no longer significantly above baseline after a 3-day delay. For the typical 3-month-old, there's hardly any forgetting after a 3-day delay, memory performance is still significantly above the baseline level after an 8-day delay, and complete forgetting doesn't appear to occur until 13 days after training (Greco, Rovee-Collier, Hayne, Griesler, & Earley, 1986). It has also been found that the memories of even 2-month-old infants are very precise. For instance, if after a 24-hour delay period more than one object is changed on the mobile, the performance of these infants is no better than their baseline levels (Hayne, Greco, Earley, Griesler, & Rovee-Collier, 1986). This suggests that the only retrieval cues that will work are those that are highly specific to the initial training context. The infants are not remembering just general details about the mobile; they are remembering specific details (e.g., that the mobile originally had red bunnies on it and that they were later changed to yellow squares).

The importance of keeping the context the same between the initial training sessions and the subsequent testing sessions (a principle we have referred to as *encoding specificity* several times in the book) was also demonstrated in a study by Rovee-Collier, Griesler, and Earley (1985). In this study, two groups of 3-month-old infants were trained in the typical conjugate reinforcement procedure. For one group of infants the crib bumper (which is typically a colorful cloth liner that serves as a soft cushion and prevents the infant from getting his or her hands, feet, and sometimes head caught in the ribs of the crib) was the same during both training and testing. For the other group of infants the crib bumper was changed to one with a distinctly different colored pattern. When all the infants were tested after a 7-day delay, the infants tested in a crib with the same bumper demonstrated excellent memory (which is typical); however, in contrast, the infants tested with a different crib bumper showed no evidence of remembering to kick their foot.

**Memory reactivation.** What does it mean when an infant, after a long delay period, no longer kicks his or her foot significantly above a baseline level of kicking? Has the memory of what to do permanently vanished, or is it only currently inaccessible? (This should remind you of the important distinction between the *availability* and the *accessibility* of a memory trace discussed in Chapter 5). On the basis of studies using a *memory reactivation procedure,* there is now good evidence that apparently forgotten memories can be brought back by the use of some reminder of the original training sessions. It is very important that there be absolutely no chance for additional learning to take place during the time the reminder is presented—otherwise, it would be impossible to know if the reminder was responsible for reactivating an inaccessible memory or if the improved performance was just due to the chance for additional training to occur. Let's consider an example of how memory reinstatement can be achieved without additional learning.

Using the conjugate reinforcement paradigm, Sullivan (1982) demonstrated that memory can be reinstated in 3-month-old infants by means of memory reactivation. On the fourteenth day after the last training session, as expected, one group of infants showed no evidence that they remembered the association between foot kicking and making the mobile move. Exactly the same testing procedures were employed for a second group of infants with one difference— on the thirteenth day after the last training session each of these infants was given a brief reminder of his or her original training experience. The reminder consisted of watching the experimenter pull on the ribbon to make the mobile move. Note that the ribbon was never reattached to the infant's ankle; therefore, it was not possible for the infant to relearn that kicking causes the mobile to move. The effects of presenting the reminder were clear-cut: when tested the next day (which was the fourteenth day after the last training session), the infants in the second group responded at the same high level that they had displayed during the immediate retention test after the original training sessions.

It turns out that the effectiveness of the reminder to reactivate memory is not immediately apparent, perhaps reflecting the fact that it takes some time to achieve access to available—but, at the moment, inaccessible—memories (Fagen & Rovee-Collier, 1983). If infants are shown the reminder and then tested either 15 minutes or an hour later, there's no evidence that memory has, in fact, been reactivated. However, after about 8 hours, the reminder has a positive effect on memory for some infants, while after 24 hours retention is much improved. Further memory improvement is seen during the next 3 days after the reminder. It has even been found that memory can be reinstated by a reminder that occurs 34 days after the original training experience in about half of the infants tested (Greco et al., 1986). This means it is possible to get some 4-month-old infants to recall something they learned almost 5 weeks earlier!

**Other findings from testing the memory ability of infants.** The conjugate reinforcement paradigm has also shed some light on how infants remember information about places and on how infants form and use categories (Hayne, Rovee-Collier, & Borza, 1991; Hayne, Rovee-Collier, & Perris, 1987; Rovee-Collier, 1989). In addition, similar to the eyewitness-testimony literature discussed in the last chapter, this paradigm has shown that information given after the original training sessions can modify an infant's memory (Greco & Rovee-Collier, 1988). As you can see, the conjugate reinforcement paradigm has provided a wealth of new information about the memory abilities of young infants and will undoubtedly continue to do so.

Other research, not using the conjugate reinforcement paradigm, has shown that infants as young as 6 1/2 months old can retain information over a 2-year retention interval. Nancy Myers and her colleagues have evidence not only that these infants can remember a repeated event over a 2-year period (Myers, Clifton, & Clarkson, 1987) but also that even a *single* experience can be remembered after that length of time (Perris, Myers, & Clifton, 1990). Coupled with the conjugate reinforcement research, this work has forced many developmental psychologists to dramatically upgrade their assessment of the young infant's memory capabilities.

## Infant Memory Ability and Later Cognitive Ability

Is there a relationship between having a good memory as an infant and being more intelligent years later? As Kail (1990) points out, one would expect the answer to be yes, if it can be assumed that infants with good memory capabilities will be better able to take advantage of previous experiences compared with infants with less well developed memory skills. Consistent with this line of reasoning, some studies have found positive correlations to exist between recognition memory ability assessed during the first few months of life and having a larger vocabulary at 3, 4, 5, and 7 years (Fagan, 1984; Fagan & McGrath, 1981). Furthermore, Rose and Wallace (1985) reported that recognition memory ability at 6 months of age is positively related to intelligence test scores at 2, 3, 3 1/2, and 6 years. Although there is some evidence suggesting that infants' memory skills may be predictive of future cognitive capability, it should also be noted that there are studies in which no relationship has been observed (e.g., Fagan & Singer, 1983).

## Infantile Amnesia

As the cartoon on page 274 implies, Marvin is right; most adults simply cannot recall what it was like to be an infant. Think back to your own early childhood. What is your earliest memory, and when did it occur? While attempting to answer this question, try to be certain that you're actually remembering an event that happened, that you are not simply thinking about an event that your parents or siblings told you had occurred when you were small. If you are like most other people, you will not recall specific events that occurred before your third birthday (Sheingold & Tenney, 1982; Waldfogel, 1948; Wetzler & Sweeney, 1986). Research with adults has consistently shown that memory for personally experienced events typically begins between the ages of 3 and 4 (Pillemer & White, 1989; White & Pillemer, 1979). The inability to recall events that occurred during the early part of life is called *infantile amnesia* (or sometimes *childhood amnesia* when the focus is on humans only). This phenomenon is not just a frailty of human memory. Infantile amnesia has also been observed and studied in dogs, wolves, rats, mice, and even frogs (Spear, 1979).

This inability to remember events from our very early childhood is not

FIGURE 12.3

Marvin is pretty smart; he already knows about infantile amnesia.

*Reprinted with special permission of North America Syndicate.*

simply due to the substantial amount of time that has elapsed between the events and their recall. You learned in Chapter 11 that people can accurately recall autobiographical events many years after they have occurred, oftentimes even after several decades have passed. So what causes infantile amnesia? Sigmund Freud (1905/1953) believed that the experiences of the first years of life are not actually forgotten but instead are merely inaccessible to our conscious awareness owing to repression. According to Freud, many of our desires and fantasies are very erotic in nature at this age, and these sexual feelings come into conflict with the realities of everyday life. To resolve this conflict, we repress this whole period of our lives into the unconscious mind.

Most modern-day researchers would have trouble accepting this type of reasoning, especially since it would not explain why infantile amnesia also occurs in lower animals (unless one assumes that rats and frogs are subject to Freudian repression!). However, stripped of all its psychoanalytic trimmings, Freud's view basically maintains that infantile amnesia is due to a retrieval failure. It is supposed that a retrieval failure occurs because the context at the time of the original learning is much different from the context at the time of attempted retrieval (often decades later). A similar explanation was offered in 1947 by Schachtel, who, although a psychoanalyst himself, was one of the first to suggest that infantile amnesia was not a result of repression. His view was that the schemas of infants and young children do not correspond well to the schemas of adults, and this makes it very difficult for adults to retrieve their earliest memories. Information is probably organized, encoded, and stored by infants and young children in ways that are markedly different from how adults would handle the same information. For example, one major difference is that language is certainly used to a much greater extent by older children and adults than it is by infants. So if college students were asked to recall their second birthday party, they would probably have great difficulty because the memories were probably not originally encoded and stored verbally. In order to retrieve any information about their second birthday, the college students may have to reinstate some of the original context (e.g., by seeing a photograph of a tricycle received as a present or by viewing a home movie made of the party). This should again remind you of the encoding specificity principle.

Other general explanations for the phenomenon of infantile amnesia have been offered. One suggests that a major reason that early memories are so difficult to recall is that they get "disrupted," perhaps owing to normal maturational changes in the brain and central nervous system. If this hypothesis is correct, then infantile amnesia should not be as apparent in animals that have a relatively mature central nervous system at the time of birth. Just such an animal is the guinea pig, and providing some support for the disruption hypothesis, research has indicated that guinea pigs don't seem to exhibit infantile amnesia (Campbell, Misanin, White, & Lytle, 1974).

Another explanation for the phenomenon of human infantile amnesia rests on the assumption that specific episodes of routine events are not stored as separate events in a very young child's memory (Nelson & Ross, 1980). Instead, the memories for specific events merge into general scripts or schemas, which provide an organizational structure for the recall of everyday experiences (such as going grocery shopping). These general scripts or schemas make it difficult to remember specific circumstances surrounding any given event (see Chapter 6 also). Only those specific events that do not fit into an existing schema or script will be retained in memory, and perhaps only if the specific episode is rehearsed to oneself or retold to others will it become a part of one's long-term autobiographical memory (Nelson & Hudson, 1989).

Some researchers have suggested that infantile amnesia occurs because very early memories are not adequately processed and/or stored. Although it would be very difficult to show that inadequate processing is never a factor, on the basis of the memory reactivation work with the conjugate reinforcement paradigm and other studies (e.g., Myers et al., 1987; Nelson & Ross, 1980; Perris et al., 1990), we agree with Rovee-Collier (1989) that the human infant's inability to adequately encode information and store it for future use very likely is not a significant reason for infantile amnesia.

As we have seen, explanations to account for infantile amnesia are hardly in short supply. Unfortunately, current theories far outpace the available hard data. Much of child psychology teaches us that Freud was correct in believing that our experiences during the first few years of life have a great impact on us. Thus it is all the more surprising and bewildering that we seem to have such little conscious recollection of specific memories from this time period in our lives.

# MEMORY IN CHILDHOOD

As anyone who has spent some time around children of different ages will agree, as children get older, their ability to perform memory tasks dramatically improves. We're sure this does not come as a surprise to you. So the important question is not "*Does* memory improve?" (everyone knows that it does) but, rather, "*Why* does memory improve?" In this section we will try to provide some answers to this question; in addition, we will describe the capabilities and limitations of memory performance at various ages of childhood and early adolescence.

## Are There Sensory Memory Differences between Children and Adults?

Can differences in the earliest stages of the memory process account for memory differences between children and adults? In other words, is there any evidence of developmental changes in sensory memory functioning? No, there doesn't appear to be (Engle, Fidler, & Reynolds, 1981; Hoving, Spencer, Robb, & Schulte, 1978; Kail & Siegel, 1977). For instance, Kail and Siegel (1977) reported that the capacity and rate of decay of visual and auditory sensory memory are similar for 5-year-olds and for adults.

## What about STM and LTM Differences?

If there are no important sensory memory differences, perhaps there are differences in STM capacity that can account for the performance differences between children and adults. One of the most frequently used ways to measure STM capacity is with a *memory span* task (first described in Chapter 2). You recall that this task measures the number of items that can be recalled in order, either forward or backward, immediately following their presentation. The items usually are randomly presented digits, letters, or words. And it is well known that memory span dramatically increases between very early childhood and adulthood. For example, Dempster (1981) found that memory span for digits was only about two items for 2-year-olds but increased to five items for 7-year-olds and reached seven items for 12-year-olds.

What accounts for increases in memory span with age? One hypothesis is that memory span increases because STM capacity physically increases as humans mature neurologically (e.g., Pascual-Leone, 1970, 1978, 1987). In other words, this view holds that STM improves because there are more "slots" or spaces to temporarily hold information. Although it would be difficult to completely disprove the increased capacity hypothesis, there's no compelling evidence to support it, and it is generally not considered to be very likely (Dempster, 1985; Schneider & Pressley, 1989). In addition, some data would be very difficult to reconcile with the increased capacity hypothesis. For instance, if memory span increases were due to physical capacity limitations in very young children, then the types of stimuli used should not affect results—older children and adults should always do better. But they don't. Age effects are greatly attenuated when the stimuli used for testing have low familiarity or if the ability to rehearse the material is minimized (Dempster, 1985).

A more plausible hypothesis than increased physical capacity is that there is an increase in the functional capacity of STM. This presumed increase in functional capacity could simply be due to having more resources for mental effort available as one ages (Case, 1985). For example, it may well be that while the average number of chunks of information held in STM remains constant with age (remember George Miller and his magical number 7 + or − 2?), the amount of information contained in each chunk probably increases (Chi, 1976). Furthermore, as people get older, the speed with which information can be processed greatly increases (Kail, 1990; Siegler, 1991). In fact, with enough practice some tasks even become automatic (e.g., juggling) and seem to require hardly any conscious processing at all. This increase in the speed and efficiency of information processing suggests that there is less of a drain on the limited processing resources available for use in STM. As a consequence, these limited resources can be more effectively used by older people for storing information (Case, 1985; Case, Kurland, & Goldberg, 1982). Although a limited resources hypothesis has considerable intuitive appeal, not all researchers believe that differences in the amount of available processing resources (or their efficient use) can adequately account for age differences in memory performance (for recent reviews, see Brainerd & Reyna, 1990; Howe & Rabinowitz, 1990).

Long-term memory ability is typically assessed by examining a person's ability to either recall information or recognize it. As you have already learned (e.g., Chapter 2), it is widely known that it is usually easier for adults to recognize information than it is to recall it. This is particularly true for young children, who often have very good recognition memory but abysmal recall memory (Myers & Perlmutter, 1978; Perlmutter, 1984). Given that young children can recognize previously shown lists of pictures or words but have great difficulty recalling the items, this suggests that the problem is not one of properly encoding the information to be remembered. Instead, the problem seems to be that young children do not search their memories in a very proficient manner and are not good at providing prompts for themselves (Schneider & Pressley, 1989). In support of this hypothesis, a number of studies have found that recall can be significantly improved in 3- to 5-year-olds by providing helpful prompts (Ceci, Lea, & Howe, 1980; Emmerich & Ackerman, 1978; Sophian & Hagen, 1978). Examples of such prompts would be general category names (such as the cue "types of flowers" or "parts of an elephant") to help the children remember items from a list.

## The Effects of a Knowledge Base on Memory Development

For the next 20 seconds take a close look at the chessboard shown in Figure 12.4. If you were now provided with a blank chessboard and asked to place the various chess pieces on the squares in the same position you saw in the figure, could you do it? Most adults who try this task find it very difficult to reconstruct the exact position of all the pieces. On the basis of what you have

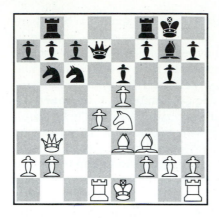

FIGURE 12.4
Try to memorize the placement of the chess pieces.

already read in this chapter, you would probably also guess that children would always be worse than adults at this task, since children have always been portrayed as having inferior memory capabilities, especially for difficult recall tasks. You would be wrong.

In 1978, Chi conducted a study in which children (average age was 10 years old) and adults were presented with brief exposures to chessboards that represented positions from real chess games. Tested immediately after being shown the chessboards, the children were much *better* than the adults at reconstructing the correct positions. This is surprising, and you might think that these were children who were specially selected because they had outstanding memories. Again, you would be wrong. When these same children were compared with the adults on a digit span test, the children performed as you would expect children to perform—they were inferior.

So why were these children superior to the adults at recalling the positions of chess pieces seen briefly on chessboards? The answer is that these children *were* specially selected, not for having extraordinary memory ability but because they were all expert chess players. On the other hand, the adults had much less experience playing chess. So it was easier for the children to reconstruct the chess positions because these positions represented configurations that were familiar to them, whereas in contrast, the pieces seemed almost randomly placed to the adults. The familiar configurations made it possible for the children to encode and store larger chunks of the chessboard positions during the brief time allowed for study. If the pieces had been randomly placed on the chessboards—i.e., if the positions had not been copied from real games—the advantage that the child experts had would have evaporated.

These results have usually been interpreted as showing the positive effects on memory that prior knowledge can exert. In other words, the more a person knows about a topic (referred to as a *knowledge base*), the easier it is to understand, integrate, and remember new information concerning that topic. It is also likely that in addition to the more direct influence of a substantial knowledge base, general interest in the area of expertise would make a person more motivated to learn and retain information. So it is probably a combination of both factors—a strong knowledge base and strong motivation—that is responsible for the impressive memory differences between experts and novices. Many studies have demonstrated the beneficial effects of having a strong knowledge base on memory performance (this will be discussed in much greater detail in the next chapter). Some researchers believe that it is primarily the growth in an individual's knowledge base that is responsible for superior memory performance with increasing age (e.g., Bjorklund, 1985, 1987).

To get an idea of the complexity of the knowledge base that a young child can have, take a look at Figure 12.5. This is a semantic network representation (see Chapter 3) of some of the knowledge that a 4 1/2-year-old boy had about 21 different dinosaurs (Chi & Koeske, 1983). Although many young children have an interest in and some knowledge about dinosaurs, this boy's knowledge bordered on the unreal. To help abet his consuming interest in the topic, his parents reportedly read dinosaur books to him about 3 hours per week for 1 1/2 years prior to his testing. He also had nine dinosaur books in his collection and many plastic dinosaur models to play with. This is how you create one of the world's youngest dinosaur experts!

## Metamemory

*Metamemory* refers to a person's general knowledge and awareness of his or her own memory processes as well as how one assesses one's own memory ability (Flavell & Wellman, 1977). Accurate metamemory is poor in very young children and slowly develops with age and greater experience in performing tasks. But even children of 3 or 4 demonstrate some metamemory; they are already aware that it is easier to remember a small group of items than a large group. As you will learn, however, differences in metamemory clearly account for some of the striking differences in the memory capabilities of people who are at different stages of life.

If asked to name the single greatest contributor responsible for memory differences between young children and either older children or adults, most memory researchers would chant the same litany—memory strategy differences. A *memory strategy* is often defined as a purposeful and deliberate attempt by an individual to enhance memory performance (Naus & Ornstein, 1983). Probably the most common memory strategy is the rehearsal of material that you want to remember. For example, to retain the correct order of all the digits of a telephone number just heard, most people rely on either overt or covert verbal rehearsal.

As children get older, they use such memory strategies as rote rehearsal (and much more elaborate ones) more often and more effectively. When poor memory performance occurs, it is often due to either a *production deficit* or a *mediation deficit* (Flavell, 1970). A production deficit is the failure to spontaneously generate an appropriate memory strategy to handle a particular mem-

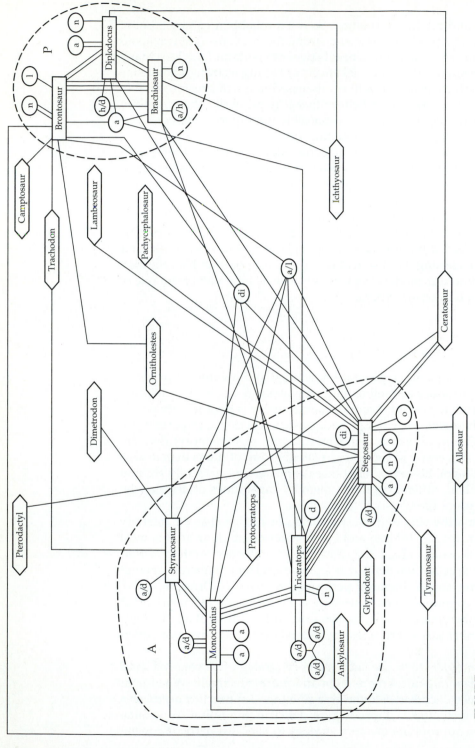

FIGURE 12.5

A semantic network representing one 4½-year-old's complex knowledge base about 21 dinosaurs. (A = armored, P = giant plant eaters, a = appearance, d = defense mechanism, di = diet, h = diet, h = habitat, l = locomotion, n = nickname, o = other.)

*From M. T. H. Chi and R. D. Koeske, "Network representation of a child's dinosaur knowledge," Developmental Psychology, Vol. 19 (1983), pp. 29–39. Copyright 1983 by the American Psychological Association. Reprinted by permission.*

ory task. In contrast, a mediation deficit occurs when an individual cannot make use of an appropriate memory strategy, regardless of whether it was spontaneously produced by the subject or supplied by the experimenter. In general, mediation deficiencies are found at younger ages than are production deficiencies.

While some researchers have found that the correlation between meta-memory and memory performance in children is often rather weak (e.g., Cavanaugh & Perlmutter, 1982; Flavell & Wellman, 1977), others have reported a stronger link (e.g., Borkowski, Milstead, & Hale, 1988; Schneider, 1985; Wellman, 1983). Because the metamemory of young children is underdeveloped, production deficits often occur and can be a contributing cause of inferior memory performance (along with having a poorer knowledge base and less ability to self-monitor their actions than either older children or adults have). For instance, it has been shown repeatedly that preschoolers, compared with elementary-school children, greatly overestimate their memory prowess (e.g., Flavell, Freidrichs, & Hoyt, 1970; Yussen & Levy, 1975). Now if a young child consistently overestimates his or her memory ability, then this child will incorrectly believe that there is no need for any special strategies to aid memory performance, even though this child may have the necessary intellectual capacity to profit from the use of such strategies. As a consequence, an older child or an adult without this false sense of security will outperform this child on a memory task because he or she knows that memory strategies are required and effective. In other words, older children and adults have more accurate metamemories.

A production deficit due to poor metamemory can also arise if a person simply doesn't realize that a memory strategy is even needed. If you ask a typical 4-year-old to remember a list of words as you read the words slowly, one at a time, the child will not engage in any obvious memory strategy to aid either encoding or retrieval (e.g., the child will usually try to recall the items in a random fashion rather than on the basis of some strategy such as alphabetic order). There's another way in which poor metamemory leads to a production deficit—the young child may realize that a memory strategy is needed but doesn't select an appropriate one. This could well account for the many "faulty" strategies that are adopted by preschoolers. With sufficient experience (translation: better metamemory) the child begins to mold these faulty strategies into effective ones (discussed more in the next section).

Mediation deficits are also certainly responsible for some of the age-related differences in memory performance. As one example, it is very easy for most adults to use mental imagery as a memory strategy to remember items on a list. Suppose you want to remember to buy peanut butter, milk, strawberry jelly, bread, and potato chips; an effective strategy would be to picture yourself eating a peanut butter and jelly sandwich with some potato chips and having a glass of milk to wash it all down. Now imagine the likelihood that a 3-year-old, also instructed to use mental imagery, will remember all five items as he or she strolls through the aisles of a grocery store with an adult. Without the child receiving some memory prompts from the adult, your chances of having that sandwich for lunch are almost nil!

## Development of Memory Strategies

When do children start to use memory strategies? Until about the mid-1970s, the predominant thinking was that memory strategies were infrequently used until around age 6 or 7 and that during the next few years their use increased and reached a high level of sophistication during adolescence. However, in the last 10 to 15 years this view has been successfully challenged, and it is now believed by most researchers that even very young children are trying to be strategic in their memory activities (Kail, 1990; Schneider & Pressley, 1989; Wellman, 1989). So upon reappraising many studies where it had originally appeared that preschoolers were not using memory strategies, it now seems clear that the children often were using memory strategies but that these strategies were simply not observed by the researchers.

Why were the strategies not observed? Probably because the strategies used by very young children are not the typical ones that older children or adults would most likely use (such as appropriate rehearsal of material to be remembered or the chunking of similar material during attempts at retrieval). Instead, these children often use what adults would probably consider to be faulty strategies (Wellman, 1989). Since these faulty strategies typically do not work, it would often appear that young children do not use any memory strategies at all. Wellman (1989) believes that the effective strategies used by older children and adults often evolve from what were initially faulty strategies. Here is an example of a faulty strategy: A 5-year-old writes herself a note to remember to watch her favorite television show tonight but then places it inside her piggy bank for safekeeping. So even when they have thought of a good strategy to aid remembering, young children frequently don't use the strategy effectively. In this case, the child is oblivious to the fact that to be a helpful reminder, a physical cue must be placed in a highly visible spot. As she gets older and has more experience with the proper use of physical cues, she will learn to leave them in places where they can be easily seen.

The search for strategic memory activities in children 2 to 5 is complicated by two factors that are not usually a concern when researchers are dealing with older subjects. First, it is often difficult to get them to understand what the memory task is, and second, and equally important, after they know what is expected of them, it can still be a chore to get them to comply (DeLoache, 1980). A common technique to discover the memory strategies of very young children has been to play a variant of the hide-and-seek game. The findings from a number of studies using this technique suggest that if the task is very simple, effective strategies to improve memory will be used even by 2-year-olds. For example, to help herself remember that the experimenter hid a doll in a toy refrigerator, a 2-year-old might point her finger at the refrigerator during the entire 2-minute retention interval. However, with more complicated tasks, effective strategies are not usually evident until at least 3 years of age (Schneider & Pressley, 1989).

A multitude of different memory strategies have been investigated as a function of age. We will briefly review two of the types of strategies that have been most extensively researched—*rehearsal strategies* and *organizational strategies*.

**Rehearsal strategies.** In a classic study by Flavell, Beach, and Chinsky (1966), children of 5, 7, and 10 were asked to recall out loud, either immediately or after a delay, the order in which the experimenter pointed to a series of pictures. The interesting twist in this study was that the experimenter was a trained lip-reader, thus making it possible to detect overt rehearsal of the names of the pictures. The results were clear-cut for both the immediate and delay conditions—while very few of the 5-year-olds rehearsed, more than half of the 7-year-olds did, and most of the 10-year-olds did. It is possible, however, that a child who wasn't observed to be overtly rehearsing the names of the pictures may have been doing so covertly.

Even when children begin to use rehearsal strategies on a frequent basis (this occurs around age 6 or 7), their use of such strategies is often unsophisticated. A typical 7-year-old will only rehearse a single word at a time (sometimes called *noncumulative rehearsal*), whereas an older child or an adult will spontaneously engage in a more beneficial strategy known as *cumulative rehearsal*, which involves rehearsing a set of words over and over again (Ornstein, Naus, & Liberty, 1975). The ability to modify rehearsal strategies to meet the demands of the task develops slowly. Even moderately sophisticated strategies often are not evident until adolescence is reached. For example, in one study, fifth graders, eighth graders, and college students were offered different amounts of money for correctly recalling words from a list (Cuvo, 1974). Some words were worth a penny, and some were worth a dime. The subjects were instructed to "think aloud" about the words they were trying to remember. Logically, to maximize your winnings, it would make sense to concentrate on rehearsing the "dime" words rather than the "penny" words. This is exactly what the college students did. And though it may be hard to believe, the eighth graders showed only a modest bias (it was not significant) in favor of rehearsing the dime words, while the fifth graders rehearsed and recalled approximately equal numbers of penny and dime words.

Another illustration of the naïveté of rehearsal strategies for children who haven't yet reached adolescence comes from studies in which subjects were told they would not have to remember certain information. For example, in two studies subjects were informed midway through seeing a sequence of pictures that they would not be asked to remember any of the pictures presented so far. One would expect that all subjects ceased rehearsal of the pictures already seen. This is what 15- and 18-year-old subjects did, but not 11-year-olds. Only the older subjects consistently showed selective rehearsal (Bray, Hersh, & Turner, 1985; Bray, Justice, & Zahm, 1983).

**Organizational strategies.** Another class of memory strategies that has been examined developmentally is known as *organizational strategies.* These are strategies in which items that are similar in some way are grouped together for encoding and/or retrieval. A common way to study the existence of organizational strategies is to give subjects a list of words or a series of pictures to remember that contains items that belong to a common category. For example, a list of words may include *arm, chin,* and *foot,* which are all body parts. Remembering the appropriate semantic categories during free recall improves retrieval of the list items.

Organizational strategies usually develop later than do rehearsal strategies, but if the lists contain highly associated items (such as *hot and cold* or *night and day,* then even young children will show some evidence of trying to organize similar items to aid recall (Myers & Perlmutter, 1978). In a study by Moely, Olson, Halwes, and Flavell (1969), it was found that if subjects as young as 5 or 6 years old were given explicit instructions to organize groups of pictures into categories, they could do so, and organization had a beneficial effect on their memory for the pictures. A different group of 5- and 6-year-olds, who were not given instructions to organize the pictures, did not spontaneously organize them, and their later memory performance was inferior to that of the first group. Therefore, younger children could effectively use an organizational strategy *if* it was provided for them, meaning that it probably was a production deficit and not a mediation deficit that was responsible for the inferior performance of the second group. Typically, organizational strategies don't occur spontaneously until about age 10 or 11 (Moely et al., 1969).

## Development of Prospective Memory

In Chapter 5 we defined *prospective memory* as the ability to plan and remember to perform future actions. Before we leave this section on children's memory capabilities, let's briefly consider how well children can perform prospective memory tasks.

In one of the earliest studies exploring prospective memory in children, Kreutzer, Leonard, and Flavell (1975) asked children how they could help themselves to remember to bring their ice skates to school tomorrow. They found that even kindergartners were usually able to think of some ways to help themselves remember. In addition, it was observed that the children (from kindergarten through fifth grade), just like most adults, also preferred to rely on external memory aids, such as leaving the skates next to the door or fastening a note to their clothes, rather than on internally created schemes to remember (such as composing a rhyme to aid recall). In another study, it was found that 6- and 8-year-old children could effectively use external retrieval cues to facilitate prospective remembering and that they profited from instructions in how best to use such cues (Meacham & Colombo, 1980).

Children generally have greater problems with prospective memory tasks than adults, largely because of their relatively poor metamemory. For instance, young children are frequently overconfident about their unassisted memory abilities; they fail to recognize prospective memory situations, and so they don't prepare for them properly (e.g., by providing themselves with an external reminder). And when they do recognize that a reminder would be helpful, they sometimes have difficulty in selecting a reminder that will be effective (Beal, 1985, 1988).

# MEMORY IN OLDER ADULTS

It is commonly believed that as a person grows older, memory capability declines markedly. As the media often show (see the cartoon in Figure 12.6), when older people forget things, they frequently blame their forgetfulness on the fact that they are aging. But as you will soon learn, only certain types of memory abilities decline noticeably as we age; other memory abilities either are unaffected or at most show only marginal decreases that have little practical importance. In addition, there's a great deal of individual variation among older adults—for some people memory functioning is hardly influenced at all by the aging process. For instance, in 1978, at the age of 60, a businessman named Stephen Powelson started to devote an hour each day to memorizing Homer's *Iliad* in the original Ancient Greek (Stone, 1990). The *Iliad* is composed of 24 books containing 15,693 lines of verse. By age 72, Powelson could recite from memory the first 22 books (with the exception of one 325-line list of ships and warriors in Book 2). Clearly, getting old doesn't have to mean having a failing memory.

## Factors Other than Aging That Can Cause Poor Memory Performance

In most studies examining the effects of aging on memory performance, 18- to 22-year-old college students are compared with older adults (typically at least 60 years old). If the older adults perform worse on a memory task than their younger counterparts, does this imply that the difference is due to advanced age? Not necessarily. Before concluding that age itself is the culprit for poor memory performance, make certain that a fair comparison is being made between age groups. It is vital to first make sure that the two groups being compared are approximately equivalent in such factors as health, amount of formal education, and motivation.

For example, older people are more likely to be taking prescription drugs

FIGURE 12.6

An example of how the media reinforce the notion that older adults are forgetful because of their advanced age.

*Reprinted by permission: Tribune Media Services.*

for health purposes, and we know that certain drugs can adversely affect memory performance. Also, younger adults are more likely to have had a greater amount of formal education and to have been exposed to this formal instruction more recently. Since schoolwork generally involves at least some explicit memorization (and sometimes a lot—remember that anatomy course or art history class you took!), younger subjects would have an obvious advantage in the practice of memorization.

In Chapter 8 we discussed how motivational factors play an important role in influencing memory ability. If the older subjects in a study are not as motivated as the younger ones, this alone can result in poorer performance. Furthermore, although it is true that older adults are more likely than younger adults to complain about faulty memory (Cavanaugh, Grady, & Perlmutter, 1983; Cutler & Grams, 1988; Dixon & Hultsch, 1983; Zelinski, Gilewswki, & Thompson, 1980), there is evidence that the self-ratings of memory disturbance by older people may be related more to their depressed mood than to actual poor memory performance (e.g., Bolla, 1991; Kahn, Zarit, Hilbert, & Niederehe, 1975; Larrabee & Levin, 1986; Niederehe & Yoder, 1989).

## Are There Age Differences in Sensory Memory?

The relatively few studies that have examined age differences in sensory memory have been centered on the visual (iconic) and auditory (echoic) modalities. Some studies have found no differences in the capacity or rate of decline of sensory memory as a function of age, while others have reported moderate deficiencies in older subjects (for reviews, see Craik, 1977; Crowder, 1980; Kausler, 1991). Some of the alleged deficiencies may be a function of attentional differences between younger and older subjects rather than indications of an actual decline in sensory memory functioning. However, even if there are some deficiencies for older adults, most memory researchers believe that sensory memory functioning changes little over the life span. Remember that earlier in this chapter we learned that the sensory memory capabilities of young children are largely comparable to those of young adults. It is now generally accepted that sensory memory differences resulting as a function of age play only a very minor role in the performance of everyday memory tasks.

## Are There Age Differences in STM and LTM?

If sensory memory differences are assumed to be small, what about age differences in STM and LTM? The party line among memory researchers used to be that STM remained largely unscathed in older adults and that it was LTM that suffered the most obvious decline. However, evidence continued to accumulate both from formal research studies and from just everyday observances of memory ability that this generalization wasn't very accurate. Rather than by searching for memory differences as a function of the length of the retention interval, it appears that a more fruitful answer to our question can be found by examining the *type* of memory task that is to be performed. In other words, the amount and type of memory processing involved are probably more important determinants of age differences than is making a distinction between STM and LTM (Craik, 1984).

## Tasks Least Likely to Cause Memory Problems for Older Adults

Memory differences between younger and older adults are *least* likely to be observed if the task involves meaningful, highly practiced, or well-learned material, regardless of whether short-term or long-term retention is being tested. For example, if older adults who were expert chess players were asked to reconstruct the chessboard position that was displayed earlier in this chapter (Figure 12.4), we would probably find that their memory performance would surpass that of younger, but less experienced, adult players. This would likely hold true if the reconstruction was performed after either a short- or a long-term retention interval.

Older adults are also not likely to show much of a deficit in memory if the task does not require any active manipulation or reorganization of the material to be remembered. Supporting this position is the finding that differences in digit span performance, Brown-Peterson distractor tasks (Chapter 3), or recency effects during free recall of lists are slight to nonexistent between older and younger adults (Craik, 1977). All three of these tasks require minimal active manipulation of the material that is being memorized. Consistent with this finding, there is also substantial evidence that *implicit memory* (which you'll remember involves tasks that do not require active manipulation or conscious recollection of past information) is much more likely to remain intact as one ages than is *explicit memory* (Kausler, 1991; Light, 1991; Russo & Parkin, 1993). [There are, however, some recent reports of small, but reliable, differences in implicit memory performance in favor of younger subjects (e.g., Chiarello & Hoyer, 1988; Hultsch, Masson, & Small, 1991).]

## Accounting for Age-Related Declines in Memory

There are a variety of theories that try to explain why older adults are less able to perform some memory tasks. Some people have suggested that age-related deficits are often the result of a reduction in the speed of the processing of information in working memory (e.g., Salthouse, 1991; Salthouse & Babcock, 1991). Others have proposed that memory in older people is impaired because, compared with younger people, older people have a diminished ability to inhibit information or thoughts that are not relevant to the task at hand (e.g., Gerard, Zacks, Hasher, & Radvansky, 1991; Hartman & Hasher, 1991; Hasher & Zacks, 1988).

The most popular theory is that there is a reduction in our attentional capacity to process information as we age. If true, this means that there will be a reduction in cognitive processing ability that will limit an older person's ability to use effective encoding and retrieval strategies to aid memory performance (Burke & Light, 1981; Craik, 1977, 1984; Guttentag, 1985; Welford, 1958). One implication of this hypothesis is that older adults should do more poorly than younger adults on memory tasks that require considerable attentional resources and mental effort. And there is good support for this hypothesis (for reviews, see Craik, 1977, 1984; Guttentag, 1985; Kausler, 1991). For example, if older and younger subjects are asked to do a *backward* digit span task (in which it is necessary to repeat the list of digits in reverse order) as opposed to the more typical forward task, older subjects usually do worse (Bromley, 1958;

Mueller, Rankin, & Carlomusto, 1979). Or if the task involves divided attention, as in a *dichotic listening procedure* in which several different letters are simultaneously presented to each ear, older subjects are again inferior to younger subjects in how many letters they can recall (Craik, 1977).

One of the most reliable age-related findings is that older subjects are particularly poor at tasks requiring free recall of information as opposed to tasks requiring just recognition (Botwinick & Storandt, 1974; Craik, 1977; Craik & McDowd, 1987). As mentioned earlier in the book, most people, young and old, are better at recognition tasks than at recall tasks. Just think for a minute how often you can recognize someone as being an acquaintance yet still be unable to dredge up (i.e., recall) his or her name from LTM. This is usually explained by the fact that recall requires more active retrieval processes and is a less "automatic" process than recognition (Kintsch, 1970).

If older people generally do have fewer processing and attentional resources than their younger counterparts, then it makes sense that older people would do less well on memory tasks that require more self-initiated efforts on their part, in other words, tasks like free recall. If this is so, then we would expect there to be much less of a difference in recognition memory ability as a function of age, since recognition is a more automatic process. This is exactly what has been observed (e.g., Craik, Byrd, & Swanson, 1987). Furthermore, consistent with this finding, there are significantly fewer differences in cued recall (in which the subject is given some help in retrieving the sought-after material) than in free recall as a function of age (Craik, 1977). To give you a concrete example, this means that your grandparents are probably unable to *recall* as many of the names of the state capitals as you can, but given a list of 200 possible city names to choose from, they should be just about as good as you are at *recognizing* the correct 50.

It has also been repeatedly found that older adults are less likely to *spontaneously* engage in appropriate mental strategies to aid their memory than are younger adults (Craik, 1977, 1984; Gregg, 1986; Guttentag, 1985; Schonfield & Stones, 1979; Zornetzer, 1986). Is this decrease in the spontaneous use of encoding and retrieval strategies by older people due to a production deficit or a mediation deficit? Put another way, are older adults not as capable of using effective memory strategies as younger adults (a mediation deficit), or is it that they simply don't usually think of good strategies to use (a production deficit)? With young children we found that sometimes their memory performance was inferior to that of older children or adults because of a production deficit, while it was also found that they sometimes performed more poorly because of mediation deficits. The same is generally true for older adults. Sometimes their inferior performance is due only to production deficits, while at other times it is probably due to real mediation deficits, which perhaps stem from a reduction in mental processing capability.

For example, older people are much less likely to use mental imagery spontaneously as a memory strategy than are younger people (Hulicka & Grossman, 1967; Rowe & Schnore, 1971). The inferior memory performance that results from this production deficit can be improved if older subjects are explicitly instructed or guided to use mental imagery strategies (Poon, Walsh-Sweeney, & Fozard, 1980). Nevertheless, it has also been demonstrated that a mediation deficit may also be partly responsible for the performance differences. After reviewing the mental imagery literature, Smith (1980) concluded that older people benefit less from mental imagery instructions than do younger people. But perhaps this is not really evidence of a mediation deficiency; maybe the older subjects can use mental imagery instructions as well as their younger counterparts, but they often decide not to do so because it takes too much mental effort.

We have seen that the situations that are most likely to show the largest age differences in memory performance are those that require an older person to use completely self-initiated processes and that involve the active manipulation or reorganization of the information to be remembered. Memory performance is further hindered if the task involves irrelevant information that should be ignored. Likewise, memory performance will be impeded if the person has to try to encode unfamiliar material, especially if it is presented in a way that typically can "overload" the processing capacities of even younger people (e.g., during dichotic listening).

On the basis of our current knowledge, we can offer a number of suggestions to help older individuals in their everyday memory tasks. Obviously, we think that these suggestions, which are presented in Table 12.1, can help improve the memory performance of anyone, young or old.

## Aging and Prospective Memory

Craik (1977) has suggested that prospective memory tasks should be particularly difficult for older adults, since he believes that aging interferes with self-initiated retrieval processes, the very processes that he contends are needed to

TABLE 12.1 SOME SUGGESTIONS FOR AIDING THE MEMORY OF
          OLDER PEOPLE

1. Present new information in a clear and organized way.
2. Suggest appropriate encoding and retrieval strategies.
3. Allow for self-paced memorization of the material.
4. Minimize distractions that could reduce processing resources or that the person may have trouble inhibiting.
5. Try to structure the task so that recognition rather than recall is needed.
6. Stress the importance of proper motivation, effort, and attention for doing well.
7. If the material to be remembered is very important, give instructions to *overlearn* the material so that its retrieval is "automatic."

perform prospective memory tasks well. The evidence, however, is mixed. Some studies have found little or no difference in prospective memory ability as a function of age (Einstein & McDaniel, 1990; Sinnott, 1986; West, 1988, Experiment 1), some have found that the ability declines with age (Cockburn & Smith, 1988; Dobbs & Rule, 1987; West, 1988, Experiment 2), and some have even found that older adults outperform their younger counterparts (Martin, 1986; Moscovitch, 1982; Poon & Schaffer, 1982).

Upon reflection, perhaps it shouldn't be too surprising that there are discrepancies in the literature on prospective memory and aging. After all, as mentioned in Chapter 5, there are many different types of prospective memory tasks, and it should be expected that some of these tasks will require more self-initiation than others. Einstein and McDaniel (1990, 1991) have recently suggested that many prospective memory tasks can be divided into two types—*event-based* and *time-based*. An event-based task involves a situation in which the action to be performed is done only when an external event occurs. For example, if you want to remember to invite your neighbor to a party, you will remember to do so only when you next see your neighbor. The event of seeing your neighbor acts as an external cue for remembering your intentions. In contrast, a time-based prospective task involves remembering to perform the task at a certain time (jogging at noon) or after a certain amount of time has elapsed (meet me in 20 minutes at the corner). For a time-based task there is no obvious or specific external reminder (like your neighbor!); instead, people must initiate the prospective task on their own. If Craik (1977) is correct that elderly people are less likely to do well on memory tasks that are highly dependent on self-initiation, then prospective memory deficits in the elderly should be evident only in time-based tasks, not in event-based ones. Einstein and McDaniel (1991) have reported finding exactly this outcome.

Maylor (1990) suggests that some of the discrepancies in the literature can be resolved by examining the type of reminder used. In her study, subjects ranged in age from 52 to 95 years old, and she found that the "younger" subjects were more likely to forget to make a telephone call if they depended on external retrieval cues, while the "older" subjects forgot more often if they used internal cues. Since internal cues require more self-initiation than external ones, Maylor's results are consistent with those of Einstein and McDaniel (1991).

# SUMMARY

## I. Memory in Infancy

- A traditionally popular way to assess infant memory ability is by using the *habituation-dishabituation paradigm*. Attending to a constant stimulus results in a decrease in responding (habituation) that can often be eliminated (dishabituation) if sufficient time has elapsed between successive presentations of the same stimulus.

- There is good evidence that newborns can recognize simple visual patterns, the sound of their mother's voice, and what their mother smells like.
- Although a great deal of useful information has been learned about infant memory abilities by using the habituation-dishabituation technique, it does suffer from some important limitations. For example, infants don't always prefer to attend to novel stimuli (a key assumption for the habituation-dishabituation paradigm). In addition, this procedure can only assess recognition memory; nothing can be learned about recall of information from memory or how to use remembered information.
- The *conjugate reinforcement paradigm* developed by Rovee-Collier and her colleagues overcomes many limitations of the habituation-dishabituation procedure. This new technique examines how well motivated infants can recall how to make a mobile move that is suspended over their crib.
  - Studies using the conjugate reinforcement technique have shown that 2- and 3-month-old infants can accurately recall information days after it was initially learned (especially if *memory reactivation* procedures are incorporated).
  - Research with this paradigm, as well as other recent work, has forced many researchers to markedly upgrade their assessment of the memory capabilities of young infants.
- *Infantile amnesia,* which is observed in many animal species, is the inability to recall events that occurred during the early part of life. For humans, this usually means that it is difficult or impossible to recall specific events that occurred before age 3.
  - Possible explanations for the cause of infantile amnesia are plentiful; however, none can adequately account for all the existing data. Freud thought that early events in life are not actually forgotten but instead are merely *repressed* from conscious awareness. A similar but more modern view hypothesizes that infantile amnesia is just an example of *retrieval failure* due to vastly different contexts occurring during the initial learning and the subsequent recall. Others have suggested that early memories are somehow *disrupted* during the maturation of the nervous system, that specific episodes usually are stored not as separate events but rather as *scripts,* or that early memories are simply just *not adequately processed or stored* for later recollection.

## II. Memory in Childhood
- There don't appear to be important differences in sensory memory functioning between young children and adults.
- *Memory span* increases dramatically from age 2 to adolescence. It is generally believed that this is due not to an increase in the physical capacity of STM but rather to an increase in functional capacity. In other words,

as children become older, they become more adept and efficient in using their available processing resources.

- In terms of LTM ability, the *recognition* ability of young children is often close to that of adults, but their *recall* ability is much inferior.

- The more a person knows about a particular topic (e.g., chess), the easier it is to understand, integrate, and remember new information about that topic. The information that a person knows about a topic is referred to as the person's *knowledge base.*

- *Metamemory* refers to a person's general knowledge and awareness of his or her own memory processes, as well as how one assesses one's own memory ability. Metamemory is poor in young children and slowly develops with experience.
    - As children get older, they use *memory strategies* more often and more effectively. A distinction is often made between *production* and *mediation* deficits. A production deficit occurs when a person fails to spontaneously generate an appropriate memory strategy, while a mediation deficit occurs when a person is unable to make use of an appropriate memory strategy.
    - Production deficits due to poor metamemory are very common in young children and result in inferior memory performance. Mediation deficits are also responsible for some of the observed differences in memory ability between children and adolescents or adults.

- Contrary to earlier beliefs, it is now generally accepted that even 2-year-olds will sometimes try to use memory strategies to improve their memory performance. These early strategies, however, are often faulty and not very effective. As children age, their use of specific memory strategies (such as *rehearsal* strategies and *organizational* strategies) becomes increasingly sophisticated.

- Young children do have some capacity to perform *prospective memory* tasks, but they often make mistakes largely because of poor metamemory.

## III. Memory in Older Adults

- Not all memory abilities decline as one gets older, and there's a lot of variability among people in terms of how much their memory functioning is affected by advancing age. Even when differences in performing a memory task are observed between younger and older people, the differences may not be directly attributable to age differences at all; rather, differences in factors such as general health, amount of formal education, and overall motivation may explain the differences in performance.

- For older adults, any deficiencies that occur in sensory memory functioning are not thought to have much of an effect on memory performance. In addition, it has not been found fruitful to make distinctions between STM and LTM as a function of advanced age.

- Memory differences are most pronounced between younger and older adults when the memory task requires the older person to use a completely self-initiated memory strategy, to actively manipulate or reorganize material, or to encode unfamiliar material.

- In addition, there's considerable evidence that attentional capacity declines as most people age, which means that there is a reduction in the ability to use efficient encoding and retrieval processes. If the memory task does not allow a person to process the material in an "automatic" fashion, or if the material is presented in such a way that it "overloads" the sensory capabilities (as in *dichotic listening*), older people will generally do worse than their younger counterparts.

- The evidence is mixed concerning whether or not elderly people perform worse on prospective memory tasks than do younger adults. Recent research suggests that elderly adults may have the most difficulty in prospective memory situations in which there are no obvious external reminders (such as *time-based* tasks) or in which a great deal of self-initiation is required.

# 13

# Exceptional Memory

———————— ❖ ————————

Some people amaze us with the ease with which they can learn and retain new vocabulary words in Russian or German, but they also annoy us because they have great difficulty keeping their appointments or remembering to purchase concert tickets. There are also people who have a remarkable ability to remember minute details about the lives of their favorite rock stars or the batting percentages for whole teams of baseball players, yet much to their chagrin, they can't seem to commit to memory important dates for a history exam. Many people also claim that they can encode, store, and retrieve instructions for a difficult task better if they are allowed to read the instructions themselves rather than having to listen to someone else read the instructions to them. And as you might have guessed, some people report just the opposite—they can deal with complex tasks better if they listen to instructions than if they read them.

We don't, however, have to depend just on anecdotal evidence to know that people differ widely in their memory capabilities. For instance, in 1978 Underwood, Boruch, and Malmi undertook what is still the largest study ever done to examine the variability of memory performance in normal people. Over a two-week period, 200 undergraduates at Northwestern University (86 males and 114 females) each earned $25 for participating in 10 sessions of 50 minutes each. During these sessions the students were tested in small groups ranging from 3 to 11. Each student was given 24 different learning and memory tests to perform.

The authors of the study were interested primarily in the pattern of correlations between various tasks (e.g., if you do poorly at free recall of a list of words, do you also do relatively poorly at remembering paired-associates?). For our purposes, however, the relevant data concern the degree of individual differences in performance. The results were clear: there were huge differences between individuals, all of whom were intelligent college students, as a function of the task demands. For example, some subjects learned and remembered abstract words much better than did others. Furthermore, there was considerable variability within subjects as well. In other words, the same individual who had no trouble learning paired-associates could easily be abysmal on memory span tasks.

The purpose of this chapter is to investigate individuals who have truly stupendous memory capabilities. These people have abilities that most of you would probably consider far beyond those which the average person would be capable of achieving. In fact, many of you would probably assume that these relatively rare individuals have or had vast intellectual skills. But with some notable exceptions, these assumptions are not true. Almost anyone can achieve phenomenal memory prowess (even a person who is mentally retarded!) if he or she has enough motivation to spend enormous amounts of time either practicing memory skills or obtaining expertise in a small area of study.

## EXPERT KNOWLEDGE

In the previous chapter, it was found that children are usually inferior to adults in terms of most memory functions and tasks. However, if you recall, there was one major exception to this general rule: if the children had special expertise in a topic (such as playing chess) that the adults did not have, and if memory was tested for this area of expertise, the children almost invariably outperformed the adults. Of course, the beneficial effect of being an expert is not limited to children. Anyone who possesses expert knowledge about a topic will find it easier to encode, store, and retrieve new information related to that topic than someone who does not.

The beneficial effect of having expert knowledge has been demonstrated in many different areas (e.g., Bedard & Chi, 1992; Chi, Glaser, & Farr, 1988; Ericsson & Smith, 1991a). For instance, Ceci and Liker (1986) investigated a group of 30 men who went to horse races almost every day of their adult lives. On the basis of their performance, 14 of these men were classified as being experts at handicapping harness races. It was discovered that these experts used highly sophisticated strategies in arriving at their decisions, often taking into account as many as seven variables at a time (e.g., the horse's closing speed, track conditions, purse size, and jockey ability). Obviously, these experts had to have excellent memories of what scores of horses (and their jockeys) did in past races. But what was surprising was that expert handicapping was not found to be related to general level of intelligence. In other words, while motivation and practice were of critical importance, how intelligent the person was did not correlate with his ability to perform a real-world task that required a great deal of cognitive complexity to perform at an expert level. As an example, one of the experts was a 62-year-old crane operator with an eighth-grade education and a tested IQ of 92!

It has been well documented that many famous composers and conductors had remarkable memories for music and musical composition. Consider the great conductor Toscanini. He was reputed to have memorized every note to be played by every instrument for about 250 symphonic works and all the words and music for about 100 operas (Marek, 1975). And the following amusing anecdote is often told about Mozart's phenomenal memory for music:

> Gregorio Allegri's *Miserere* was considered the exclusive property of the Vatican Choir and was so highly prized that no one was allowed to copy it, "on pain of excommunication." Mozart heard it once, went home, wrote the entire thing down from memory, went back, heard it a second time, made a few corrections scribbling secretly in his hat, and performed it later at a gathering at which the papal singer Christofori was present, who confirmed the absolute correctness of Mozart's "theft." (Marek, 1975, cited in Neisser, 1982, p. 414)

But undoubtedly, the area in which the effects of expert knowledge on memory have been most extensively studied is the realm of chess. There are some good reasons for this. First of all, cognitive psychologists (as well as computer scientists interested in artificial intelligence) have been studying how people play chess for decades (Chase & Simon, 1973a, 1973b; de Groot, 1965, 1966; Horgan & Morgan, 1990; Newell, Shaw, & Simon, 1963; Simon & Barenfeld, 1969; Simon & Gilmartin, 1973), so a great deal is known about how players at various skill levels evaluate chess positions and how they select moves to make. In addition, there is an objective rating system that provides a very good way to rate the playing strength of various chess players.

Most people would assume that a primary reason why a chess master is such a strong player is that he or she probably thinks ahead many more moves than do weaker opponents and considers a wider range of possible moves. Being both a trained psychologist and a recognized chess master, de Groot (1965, 1966) decided to explore this logical hypothesis. Partly because of his stature among highly rated chess players, he was able to convince some of the world's best chess players (such as international grandmasters) to allow him to study their thought processes while they were playing chess or evaluating specific chess positions. Each of the subjects in his studies, who usually varied in playing strength from strong amateurs to international grandmasters, was asked to think aloud while evaluating various chess positions. Much to de Groot's surprise, he generally observed that masters and grandmasters neither looked further ahead nor considered a wider range of moves when compared with players of much lower playing strength!

Well, if it is not depth of searching ahead for the best moves or considering more strategies, then perhaps marked differences in general intelligence can best account for why very few people achieve the rank of international master or grandmaster, even though millions of people throughout the world play the game on a regular and serious basis. But it turns out that intellectual differences are not likely to be a major factor either. For instance, although masters and grandmasters are often very adept at mathematics (de Groot, 1965) or have distinguished themselves in other intellectual arenas (Binet, 1966/

1893), a recent review of the available evidence concluded "that remarkable chess skill can exist in isolation, unaccompanied by other noteworthy intellectual abilities" (Cranberg & Albert, 1988, p. 161).

So what can account for the vast difference in playing ability between a grandmaster and a strong amateur player? The answer seems to be that the player with expert knowledge can much more readily size up a chess position and can identify potentially good moves considerably faster than can a player of lesser playing strength. The expert knowledge that a master or grandmaster possesses allows for very rapid *pattern recognition* of familiar arrangements of chess pieces. It has been estimated that because of the extremely large number of games that a grandmaster must play in order to achieve such a high level of proficiency, on the order of 50,000 unique patterns of meaningful chess configurations are stored in LTM by the typical grandmaster (Simon & Gilmartin, 1973).

In a series of studies by de Groot (1965, 1966), it was found that masters and grandmasters could reproduce from memory, with virtually no errors, a position from an actual chess game after viewing the position for only 5 seconds. In contrast, weaker players made considerably more errors in trying to reconstruct the position. This superior memory of very strong chess players for briefly presented chess positions (representing "real" games) has been replicated repeatedly (Charness, 1976; Chase & Simon, 1973a; Frey & Adesman, 1976; Horgan & Morgan, 1990; Lane & Robertson, 1979).

A plausible explanation for this memory performance difference is that superior chess players put fewer demands on their STM than do weaker players. You'll remember that STM capacity is very limited and that one way to effectively increase this limited capacity is to chunk two or more items together. And what's more, the bigger the chunks are, the greater the number of individual items that can be encoded for later retrieval. As you might have guessed, there's good evidence that superior players group chess pieces into larger chunks than do weaker players (e.g., Charness, 1989). So perhaps expert chess players can reconstruct chessboard positions better than their weaker counterparts because the stronger players, by virtue of their vastly greater storehouse of familiar chess patterns, can encode, store, and retrieve larger chunks of chess pieces.

If it is true that the superiority of masters and grandmasters in reconstructing a chess position after only a few seconds of viewing time is due to their huge repertoire of meaningful chess patterns, then you would predict that their advantage should be completely nullified if the chess position is composed of *randomly* placed pieces. You would make this prediction thinking that the chunking prowess of the superior player should only hold for meaningful game positions, not ones that are impossible or unfamiliar, as would be the case if pieces were haphazardly placed on the board. This is exactly what, in fact, happens. Chase and Simon (1973a) found no difference between a master-level chess player and a novice player in reconstructing from memory a chessboard that had pieces randomly placed on it. This provides strong evidence that it is the expert knowledge of the chess master, not some general visual memory superiority, that accounts for his or her remarkable memory for chess positions.

In fact, some think that the awesome pattern recognition capabilities of a master- or grandmaster-level chess player are at the very heart of chess mastery, not the ability to engage in deep analysis of complicated chess positions (e.g., Cranberg & Albert, 1988). Once a familiar pattern is recognized, likely moves seem to almost automatically suggest themselves. As Cranberg and Albert (1988) put it:

> Just as one fluent in a language generally does not need to stop and think before starting a sentence, so one fluent in the patterns of chess pieces does not need to engage in much conscious thought before generating a plausible move. The larger the storehouse of patterned piece configurations and the more that subtle differences among patterns are all included, the more likely the storehouse can be called upon to describe precisely a position at hand, and the more likely the moves it suggests will be appropriate to that specific position. Thus the large storehouse of patterns enables not only efficient memorization but also strong play. (p. 162)

Chess is certainly not unique in this regard. After only a few seconds of viewing time, expert bridge players can reproduce an organized bridge hand with much greater accuracy than can weaker bridge players (Charness, 1979; Engle & Bukstel, 1978). However, and this is also perfectly consistent with the chess data, both expert and novice bridge players are equally poor at reproducing from memory unorganized bridge hands. People with expert knowledge in nongame areas also have a much better memory for briefly presented data in their specific areas of expertise. For example, Egan and Schwartz (1979) have found that expert electronics technicians can recall brief exposures of meaningful circuit diagrams better than can less experienced technicians.

Experts are also likely to possess what are called *hierarchical knowledge structures* (Chase & Ericsson, 1982). Hierarchical knowledge structures presumably exist in LTM for the purpose of helping to organize a person's knowledge base so that he or she can respond quickly and appropriately to a given situation. The sophistication of these hierarchical knowledge structures will vary as a function of the individual's depth of knowledge of a topic. For example, a specific chess position can be recognized and encoded at different levels of analysis, which largely will depend on the strength of the player. A novice may only recognize that the position seems roughly even for both players, since each side has the same number and kinds of pieces left (such as two rooks, two knights, a bishop, four pawns, and a king). This is a relatively low-level analysis of the chess position. The chess master, too, can analyze the game at this low level; however, because of much greater knowledge and experience, the chess master will also be able to encode and process the chess position on a much higher plane. For instance, for those of you who are chess players, the master can also immediately recognize that the position comes from a minor variation of the Sicilian Defense and that black can sacrifice the king's rook for his opponent's bishop and obtain a winning endgame with his passed pawn.

We have seen that a person with expert knowledge in an area develops an impressive ability to quickly and automatically recognize an enormous number of meaningful patterns specific to the area of expertise. This knowledge is probably stored in a hierarchical fashion that facilitates initial encoding and aids responding. In a later section of this chapter, we will discuss the *Skilled Memory Theory* developed by the late Bill Chase and K. Anders Ericsson (1982). This theory does a good job in accounting for the development of many different types of expertise, ranging from the remarkable ability of a waiter (J.C.) to remember complete dinner orders for more than 20 people without having to write them down (Ericsson & Polson, 1988) to the skills of an expert figure skater (Deakin & Allard, 1991). It is clear that to become an expert, one must devote substantial amounts of time (and effort) to the chosen area or field, whether it be piano playing or Shakespearean scholarship. It is regrettable that there are no shortcuts to becoming an expert.

# THE MNEMONISTS

It is certainly impressive to watch a grandmaster play 50 chess games simultaneously against different players. As he or she arrives at each board, the opponent makes a move, and the grandmaster quickly reassesses the position (using the enormous storehouse of chess patterns engrained in his or her memory) and makes a move in response. This process is repeated for each of the 50 games, which on the average will last 20 to 25 moves. In the end, usually after 3 or 4 hours, the grandmaster will probably have won 45 to 48 of the games, with the remainder being draws. Oftentimes, the grandmaster will then play over the few games of the exhibition that were the most interesting and challenging. During this postmortem analysis, the grandmaster will reconstruct how the games were played and will suggest alternative moves (and the appropriate countermoves) that both players could have made. Non-chess-playing spectators are always extremely impressed that the grandmaster is able to remember so well the strategies and tactics used, especially just after having played 50 different games.

This demonstration of memory prowess by the grandmaster, phenomenal as it is, fits in well with the evidence reviewed in the previous section that people who develop expertise in a particular area will usually have a remarkable memory for patterns, facts, and new information related to their special area of knowledge. What is important to realize is that this increased memory ability is rarely if ever a primary goal of the people who acquire expert knowledge. Instead, the remarkable memory performance of these individuals is essentially an *unintentional* by-product that develops owing to the vast amounts of practice needed to obtain expertise.

In this section we will consider some individuals who have extraordinary memory abilities that are not just fortuitous by-products of being an expert in an area. These individuals are usually referred to as *mnemonists*—derived from the word *mnemonics,* which refers to the use of special tricks or devices to help a person remember things (Chapter 15 describes a number of common mnemonic techniques). Neisser (1982) has suggested that a better term for these individuals might be *memorists,* since not all people with excellent memories use mnemonic devices. Although Neisser is correct, we will continue to use the term *mnemonist,* since it is still the one used by the vast majority of researchers.

Some of you have probably seen professional mnemonists perform on stage or on television. They have prodigious memories for recalling long lists of unrelated numbers (such as serial numbers on dollar bills) or words called out rapidly by an audience. Some of these professional performers have written books describing the techniques they have used (e.g., a best-selling book published in 1974 that is still available in many bookstores is *The Memory Book,* by Harry Lorayne and former NBA basketball star Jerry Lucas).

Not all mnemonists become professionals or seek media publicity. Take, for example, "Bubbles P.," a man in his mid-thirties who makes his living mostly by playing poker and gambling (Ceci, DeSimone, & Johnson, 1992). Bubbles deals with numbers all the time, and numbers are what he is extremely good at remembering. To cite one example, his backward digit span has been measured; it is at least 15 digits and perhaps as high as 20. In contrast, the average for the typical adult is 4 digits. Having a prodigious memory for numbers has been very useful in his gambling exploits, and Bubbles further claims that he has sometimes used his memory tricks with numbers to pick up women in bars.

Throughout history there have been many well-documented reports of people who had phenomenal memories (Brown & Deffenbacher, 1975). By studying people with supernormal memory capabilities, we can learn about the limits of human memory and perhaps about techniques (such as those outlined by the Skilled Memory Theory) that we mere memory mortals can use to improve everyday memory. We will start our discussion of these individuals with an in-depth profile of probably the most celebrated of all the mnemonists, S. V. Shereshevskii.

## *S. V. Shereshevskii (S.)*

S. V. Shereshevskii (typically referred to simply as *S.* in the literature) was a Moscow newspaper reporter in his late twenties when his exceptional memory capabilities were first recognized. One day, the editor of the paper noted reproachfully that S. never took any notes during morning meetings when detailed assignments were being given out. S. told him there was no need to take notes, since he could remember everything the editor had said, whereupon S. proceeded to astound his editor by recalling verbatim all the instructions and assignments for that day. After witnessing this performance, the editor suggested that S. go to the local university and have his memory ability evaluated.

S. was completely taken aback by this suggestion. He was genuinely surprised to learn that others couldn't do what he could and that there was anything remarkable at all about his memory. So in the late 1920s, S. took his editor's advice and went to see psychologist A. R. Luria at the local university to get his memory tested. Thus began an almost 30-year association between the two men, with S. becoming the most famous mnemonist of modern times with the publication of Luria's book *The Mind of a Mnemonist* in 1968. Not much is known about S.'s family background. Luria only reported that "his father owned a bookstore, that his mother, an elderly Jewish woman, was quite well-read, and that of his numerous brothers and sisters (all of them conventional, well-balanced types) some were gifted individuals. There was no incidence of mental illness in the family" (p. 8).

Not expecting to find anything particularly unusual, Luria began to test S.'s memory span. However, Luria soon became flustered because, as he put it, he was "unable to perform what one would think was the simplest task a psychologist can do: measure the capacity of an individual's memory" (p. 11). What was so astounding about S.'s memory span? Just this: Luria found that he could give S. a list of 30, 50, or even 70 unrelated items and that S. was then able to recall all the items perfectly after only a single presentation. All that S. seemed to require was to be allowed 3 to 4 seconds to encode each item, during which time he would usually either close his eyes or stare at some point in space. Afterward, with equal ease, S. could recall the items in any order you requested: forward, backward, diagonally, you name it! It made no difference if the items were meaningful words, nonsense syllables, numbers, or other sounds, or if the items were presented orally or in written form.

As phenomenal as these findings are, it is perhaps even more incredible to note that S. could correctly recall such lists of items days, months, and even years later, all after only a single presentation. Even more unbelievable, he was able to do this even though he eventually became a professional mnemonist, which meant he had to remember these specific lists from the hundreds of other lists he memorized each year as part of his act. Luria eventually said he was forced to conclude "that there was no limit either to the *capacity* of S.'s memory or to the *durability of the traces he retained*" (p. 11).

So how did S. do it? What were the keys to his remarkable memory prowess? To start with, S. reported that he either would continue to "see" what he was asked to memorize after it was physically removed or could change the information to be remembered into graphic visual images that he could later use to recall the original items. For example, if S. was given a table of 50 numbers to remember, it would take him about 2 1/2 to 3 minutes to commit it to memory. When asked to reproduce the table, S. would invariably say that he could "see" the table before him and just had to "read it off" for errorless recall in correct order. It was in this way that he could just as easily recall the numbers in reverse order or by vertical, horizontal, or even diagonal rows. The occasional error he made was very instructive and lent support to his claim that he was actually "seeing" the numbers again just as they had originally been written. For instance, a mistake often consisted of recalling a 3 when, in fact, the correct number was an 8. An inspection of the original table would then usually reveal that the 8 had been written a little sloppily. This had led S. to "misread" it from his memory! His ability to continue to "see" an image after its removal suggests that S. had *eidetic imagery*, a topic that we will discuss in more detail later in this chapter.

Another factor that played a significant role in S.'s ability to remember so well was his large capacity for *synesthesia*. In its most robust form, this is an exceedingly rare phenomenon in which there is an involuntary joining of the senses. Sensory experiences in one modality simultaneously evoke sensory experiences in other modalities. For instance, people with strong synesthesia often report that they can hear colors or taste sounds. [For those of you who are intrigued by synesthesia, Richard Cytowic (1989) has written a fascinating book about it entitled *Synesthesia: A Union of the Senses*.] In S.'s particular case, every time he heard any type of sound, he would automatically produce vivid images of light and color that were often accompanied by sensations of taste and touch. Table 13.1 presents some of the synesthetic reactions that S. had when presented with pure tones of varying amplitude. Every time he heard the same tone or sound, he always had the identical synesthetic reaction. Even just listening to someone's voice would initiate a synesthetic reaction. After once speaking with L. S. Vygotsky (a famous Russian psychologist), S. remarked, "What a crumbly, yellow voice you have" (Luria, 1968, p. 24).

Whenever S. was given a list to memorize, graphic visual images were created for each item (along with an assortment of synesthetic components). In

**TABLE 13.1** SYNESTHETIC REACTIONS THAT S. HAD WHEN LISTENING TO SOME PURE TONES

Presented with a tone pitched at 30 cycles per second and having an amplitude of 100 decibels, S. stated that at first he saw a strip 12–15 cm. in width the color of old, tarnished silver. Gradually this strip narrowed and seemed to recede; then it was converted into an object that glistened like steel. Then the tone gradually took on a color one associates with twilight, the sound continuing to dazzle because of the silvery gleam it shed.

Presented with a tone pitched at 50 cycles per second and having an amplitude of 100 decibels, S. saw a brown strip against a dark background that had red, tongue-like edges. The sense of taste he experienced was like that of sweet and sour borscht, a sensation that gripped his entire tongue.

Presented with a tone pitched at 2,000 cycles per second and having an amplitude of 113 decibels, S. said: "It looks something like fireworks tinged with a pink-red hue. The strip of color feels rough and unpleasant, and it has an ugly taste—rather like that of a briny pickle. . . . You could hurt your hand on this."

SOURCE: Luria, 1968, pp. 22–23.

order to remember the order of the items, he would often use a common mnemonic technique called the *method of loci* (first mentioned in Chapter 1). To use this technique, you must first visualize a sequence of places that is very familiar and commit this sequence to memory. People often will use the rooms of their house or the path they take to work or school each day. Next you need to take a mental "walk" through the sequence of places and "put" an image of an item to be remembered in each place. For instance, while you are out shopping, suppose you want to remember to pick up a book at the library, get gasoline for your lawn mower, and go to the dry cleaner's to get your leather jacket. Using your house as the sequence of places committed to memory, you might mentally visualize "putting" an image of a book on the knob of the front door, "putting" an image of a lawn mower on the hatrack as you mentally enter the foyer, and "putting" an image of your jacket on the lamp in the living room. When you want to recall the items, just take a mental "walk" through your house and "see" the items you placed in various locations. It is important to use the same sequence of places each time if you want to remember the correct order of the items. In other words, make sure that you always mentally visualize the doorknob first, the hatrack second, and so on.

S. would often take a mental "walk" down Gorky Street in Moscow, with which he was very familiar, and place images of the items he wanted to remember at various landmarks along the way. To recall items in reverse order, all he had to do was "walk" in the other direction. As we learned earlier with the table of numbers, when S. made an error in recall, it was much more likely to be a perceptual error than a memory error per se. For example, on one occasion he forgot the word *egg* within a sequence of words. S. accounted for his mistake by recalling that he had carelessly "placed" the image of a white egg against a white wall. When he later took his mental "walk" down Gorky Street, he "walked" right by the egg without "seeing" it because it had blended in with the wall!

The synesthetic reactions that S. had were not voluntary occurrences by any means—they had apparently been forced on him since early childhood and could be tremendously distracting. Words that he read would often cause such graphic images to develop that he couldn't finish reading a sentence, or if he was listening to someone's voice, he would sometimes get so caught up with the multiple sensory effects it evoked that he couldn't concentrate on the content of what was being said. He dealt best with concrete images and had trouble manipulating abstract concepts and thoughts. Both his personal and professional life often suffered because S. had great difficulty separating fact from fantasy, perhaps because of his never-ending and unbidden synesthetic reactions. It is regrettable that the person who was arguably the best mnemonist ever identified ended his life in a Russian asylum for the mentally ill. However, strictly from a memory standpoint, it was these same synesthetic reactions and graphic images that enabled S. to have such phenomenal powers of recall. They provided him with numerous and vivid additional cues to aid his memory.

# V.P.

The mnemonist known as V.P. was born in 1934 in Riga, Latvia, and, what is interesting, grew up only about 35 miles from where S. did. He was an only child who at the age of 3 1/2 already knew how to read. By the age of 5 he had committed to memory a street map for a city of 500,000 people, and by age 10 he had memorized 150 poems for a contest. Because of World War II, he and his family were forced to leave Latvia; they found temporary refuge in Germany and eventually came to the United States, in 1950. Although V.P. graduated from college and even did some graduate work, it is surprising that he was satisfied with taking the relatively low-level job (for a person with his intelligence and education) of being a clerk.

V.P. had remarkable STM and LTM abilities for verbal material (Hunt & Love, 1972). For example, you'll remember (from Chapter 3) that most subjects who attempt the Brown-Peterson distractor task have difficulty remembering three consonants over an 18-second interval if they are required to count backward by threes during the interval. In addition, with the buildup of proactive interference over many trials, performance suffers even more. When V.P. was tested with this same paradigm, he showed hardly any forgetting of the three consonants even over an extended series of trials, when proactive interference should have been at a maximum.

To cite one example of his prodigious LTM for verbal material, Hunt and Love (1972) compared V.P.'s ability to recall Bartlett's famous "War of the Ghosts" story with that of college students. You will recall from Chapter 6 that this story is about 300 words long and is difficult to comprehend and remember unless one is well-versed in Native American customs and folklore. Distortions of the theme are common, and most college students quickly forget important names and details. However, V.P. is certainly not like most people. His retention level was remarkably high and showed little decline over intervals that ranged from 1 hour to 1 year later.

In contrast to Luria's mnemonist S., V.P. did not use graphic imagery or any synesthetic reactions to help him remember. He also denied that he used the method of loci, which S. frequently relied on. So how did V.P. memorize vast amounts of verbal material? Apparently he did it by using an amazing ability to quickly think of idiosyncratic verbal associations for the material to be remembered. Several factors helped him develop these verbal associations. First, he was well-read, and he could speak several languages, including Latvian, Estonian, French, German, Hebrew, Spanish, Russian, English, and even Latin. Second, standard intelligence tests revealed not only that his overall intelligence was quite high (136 IQ) but also that he had scored particularly well on scales that measure memory performance and the ability to rapidly notice small details. Finally, the schools that he attended as a child placed considerable emphasis on the rote learning of material, and this almost certainly influenced the development of his memory capabilities.

If V.P. was given a list of nonsense syllables to remember, he was able to quickly associate each nonsense syllable with some word or phrase in one of the languages he knew (undoubtedly capitalizing on his remarkable ability to quickly notice small details). The association might be with a Latin proverb, a Russian word, or the name of a relatively obscure political scientist. To remember lists of unrelated numbers, V.P. would quickly associate the numbers with various dates, ages, distances, and arithmetic relationships to form chunks of digits he could then encode and later recall.

## A Laboratory-Produced Mnemonist: S.F.

S.F. is unique among all mnemonists because he was the first one to be "created" explicitly for the purpose of studying how a person acquires an extraordinary memory. His historic achievement has been chronicled extensively (Chase & Ericsson, 1981, 1982; Ericsson, 1985; Ericsson, Chase & Faloon, 1980; Ericsson & Faivre, 1988). S.F. was an undergraduate at Carnegie-Mellon University in Pittsburgh, and his intelligence and memory abilities were average for a college student. Starting in May 1978 and continuing for more than 2 years, S.F. practiced increasing his memory span for unrelated digits for about 1 hour a day, 3 to 5 days a week.

The procedure he followed was a simple one: he read a sequence of random digits at the rate of one per second, and after completing the sequence, he tried to recall the digits in the correct order. If he made no errors, the next sequence was increased by one digit; however, if an error occurred, the sequence was decreased by one digit. Figure 13.1 shows the dramatic improvement in performance that S.F. achieved during the more than 250 hours of laboratory testing and training he underwent. As can be seen, his initial digit span was around 7 (which is an average value for most adults), but a truly remarkable expansion occurred as time went on. By the end of the training sessions S.F. had a digit span in excess of 80.

In order to learn about the techniques that S.F. developed to so dramatically increase his digit span, the researchers required him to make verbal reports describing how he tried to encode and recall all the digits in a sequence. The first strategy he discovered was to generate meaningful associations for groups of 3 or 4 digits in a row. He did this by relating these digits to running times for various races, ranging from the half-mile to the marathon. By chance, it just so happened that S.F. was a very good long-distance runner who competed in races throughout the eastern United States. This meant that he was quite familiar with expected running times for a number of races. He used this knowledge to help form meaningful chunks of digits, which had the beneficial effect of lessening the load placed on his STM. As an example of how he used this chunking strategy, when he was given the number 3492 as part of a sequence to be remembered, he encoded the number as "3 minutes and 49 point 2 seconds, near world-record mile time" (Ericsson et al., 1980, p. 1181).

During the first four months of practice, S.F. constructed an elaborate group

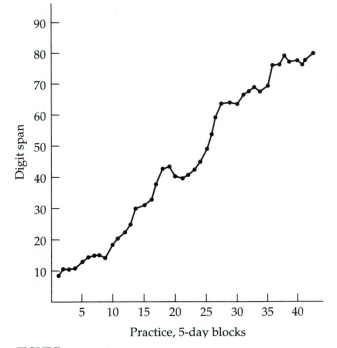

FIGURE 13.1
Average digit span for S.F. as a function of practice. Each
point represents the average digit span for five training
sessions of 1 hour each.
*Reprinted by permission of Guilford Publications from K. A. Ericsson &
I. A. Faivre (1988).*

of associations based on running times. However, he later started to develop
additional associations based on ages and dates, this being necessary because
some digit sequences couldn't easily be classified as representing running times
for races. These chunking strategies worked well until he tried to extend his
digit span above about 18 digits. Upon reaching this level, he began to have
trouble remembering the correct order of the three or four digit chunks he had
formed. He was eventually able to solve the problem by developing a retrieval
structure that allowed him to organize his groups of digits into larger "supergroups." Each of these supergroups could contain up to 4 digit groups (each
composed of 3 or 4 single digits). By learning to arrange these supergroups in
a hierarchical fashion, S.F. was able to extend his digit span past 80.

Tragically, S.F. died in 1981 from a chronic blood disorder. However, three
other people have followed the lead of S.F. and have also become laboratory-
produced mnemonists. They have each, after at least 100 hours of practice, been
able to increase their digit spans beyond 20. The most impressive of these
individuals is D.D., who is also a long-distance runner, just as S.F. had been.
Because he is also well-versed in knowledge about running times for various

races, Chase and Ericsson (1982) decided to train D.D. to use S.F.'s original chunking system. Although the chunking system D.D. eventually developed differed in some details from S.F.'s, the chunking systems were quite similar to each other and were both very successful. D.D.'s digit span has reached 106, the highest ever recorded (Ericsson & Staszewski, 1989).

**Skilled memory theory.** To try to explain the remarkable performance of their laboratory-produced mnemonists, Chase and Ericsson (1982) proposed the *Skilled Memory Theory;* they believe that it can account for most, if not all, individual differences in memory ability. A key premise of this theory is that exceptional feats of memory are not due to innate, possibly neurological, differences between people. In other words, one does not need to have an IQ that is astronomical or to have a brain that is somehow specially wired to be able to remember vast amounts of material. Instead, it is hypothesized that with sufficient practice and motivation, almost anyone can develop seemingly astounding memory capabilities. And there is now considerable evidence to indicate that the acquisition of exceptional memory skill is well within the capability of the average person (e.g., Ericsson, 1985; Ericsson & Smith, 1991b).

The Skilled Memory Theory is based on three principles. First, it is maintained that the material to be remembered must be encoded in a meaningful manner using previous knowledge to form associations. Second, it is necessary during the encoding or storage stage to attach specific retrieval cues to this material so that the material can be readily accessed at a later time from LTM by means of these cues. And finally, extensive practice greatly increases the speed of encoding and retrieval operations. Another key premise of the Skilled Memory Theory is that LTM can be utilized in a way that is usually thought to be reserved only for STM. For example, it is assumed that for most people, performance on a digit span task (or any other memory span task, for that matter) depends on the individual's ability to effectively use STM processes of encoding and storage. In fact, memory span tasks are one of the primary means by which STM is measured, and they are used extensively with clinical subjects to assess possible memory loss. However, in the case of people who have had a great deal of practice, proponents of the Skilled Memory Theory maintain that the material to be remembered in memory span tasks is encoded and stored directly into LTM.

Evidence to support this claim can be seen from an analysis of some of the data from S.F. At the end of each day's training session, S.F. always tried to recall as many of the digits as he could from all of the day's sequences. At first, he could hardly recall any of the digits presented, which suggests that he was using only STM to encode and store the digits. However, as he started to use his chunking techniques to increase his digit span, he was increasingly able to recall more digits. After 20 months of digit span practice he was able to remember more than 80 percent of the day's digits, which obviously means that the digits were making their way into his LTM.

Other data from S.F. are also consistent with the premise that the use of LTM is needed for prodigious recall of information. After having already practiced for three months, and with considerable gains to show for it in the length of his digit span, S.F. was given a surprise memory span test using letters of the alphabet instead of numbers. The result: his memory span for letters was a downright average score of 6! This is precisely what would have been predicted by the Skilled Memory Theory, for S.F. had no special chunking schemes devised to encode and store letters quickly into LTM. Therefore, like most other people, S.F. had to rely only on his STM processes, and so consequently his performance reflected the normal limits of STM.

## Rajan Mahadevan: A Numerical Mnemonist Par Excellence

A staff writer by the name of T. R. Reid published a story in *The Washington Post* Sunday newspaper on June 18, 1989, describing a recent interview that he had had with an individual named Rajan Mahadevan. The opening paragraphs of the article amply illustrate why Reid traveled all the way from Washington, D.C. to Manhattan, Kansas, to interview a 32-year-old psychology graduate student from India at Kansas State University.

> After I had spent a good deal of time with Rajan Mahadevan—after he had recited, from memory, the first 30 digits of Euler's constant, after he had written out, in his rapid-fire left-handed chicken scratch, a block of 50 random digits he had last seen at 9:15 a.m. on Oct. 5, 1987, after he had told me the row and seat number he was assigned on Air India's Flight 107 from Madras to Bombay nine years ago, after he had spun off the reservation numbers for Braniff, United, TWA, Delta, Southwest, American and Continental airlines, after he had laughed ruefully about the trouble he always had remembering the 31,812th digit of pi—after all that, he told me he'd like to chat again and asked for my telephone number.
>
> Mindlessly, reflexively, I reached in my pocket for a business card. A look of consternation creased Mahadevan's face. "No—I'm sorry! I'm sorry!" he said with alarm. "To use one of your cards for me, there is no need. Just tell me."
>
> Just tell him! Of course! Here I am talking to a living natural phenomenon, a research psychologist's dream come true, one of the most prodigious numerical memorists in the history of recorded science, and I had suggested that he couldn't even remember a telephone number. (p. F1)

Even as a young boy growing up in India, Rajan Mahadevan astounded people with his ability to remember anything numerical. Wanting to gain some fame and recognition for his numerical feats of memory, he contacted the editors of the *Guinness Book of World Records* to ask how he might make it into their book. They suggested that he try to memorize the digits of *pi*, a classic test of memory ability. As you probably already know, pi is the ratio of the circumference of a circle to its diameter. The first few digits of pi are 3.14159; the digits continue on forever, and it has been shown that there is no known pattern to them. On July 4, 1981, in his hometown of Mangalore, India, Mahadevan was able to correctly recite the first 31,811 digits of pi (it's reported that after the first 10,000 digits he paused for a Pepsi!) but could go no further. When asked why he stopped there, he replied, "The 31,812th digit, I don't know why, I am always stumbling over that one" (Reid, 1989, p. F2).

**TABLE 13.2** THE 6-BY-6 MATRIX OF RANDOM NUMBERS MADE UP BY THE NEWSPAPER REPORTER

| | | | | | |
|---|---|---|---|---|---|
| 1 | 1 | 1 | 4 | 6 | 7 |
| 7 | 8 | 3 | 1 | 2 | 4 |
| 1 | 8 | 0 | 2 | 7 | 9 |
| 6 | 1 | 7 | 4 | 5 | 3 |
| 3 | 9 | 1 | 6 | 5 | 5 |
| 3 | 2 | 6 | 7 | 8 | 9 |

SOURCE: Reid, 1989, p. F6.

To further demonstrate his memory for numbers, Mahadevan asked the newspaper reporter to write a 6-by-6 matrix of random digits on a chalkboard. The matrix that was made up is shown in Table 13.2. The reporter then copied the numbers down and erased the numbers on the board after 2 minutes had elapsed. Soon, Mahadevan began recalling all the numbers correctly—forward, backward, diagonally, and by horizontal rows.

As you will see from the following excerpt, Mahadevan encodes numbers into memory by quickly thinking up idiosyncratic semantic associations from LTM to chunk groups of digits together. If this technique sounds familiar, it should. This is essentially the same type of strategy used by V.P., S.F., and D.D.; it depends on having a vast knowledge base of associations that can be drawn on quickly.

> "I scan the entire thing and start to make associations," he said. "For example, there is '111'; that's called a 'Nelson' because Admiral Nelson had one eye, one arm and one leg. I see a '312' in there; area code of Chicago. There is '1802', which I reduce to 'plus 2' because John Adams occupied the White House in 1800. The '1745' I remember as 39, because Ben Franklin was 39 in 1745.
> "I don't know why I make those particular associations. These things come to me. They come to me naturally because I have an incredible *knowledge base*." (emphasis added; Reid, 1989, p. F2)

It is interesting to note that Rajan Mahadevan's phenomenal ability to remember numerical information does not extend to other domains. For instance, he seems to be below average for remembering faces; he constantly forgets where he put his keys, and on standard verbal memory tests, he scores only a little above average. We look forward to learning more about this fascinating person in the near future. In the next section, on eidetic imagery, we consider the remarkable ability that some people have to conjure up from memory amazing amounts of detail about visual scenes.

# EIDETIC IMAGERY

Look at Figure 13.2 for about 30 seconds, making sure that you scan the entire picture. Now avert your eyes from the picture, and try to recall as many details as possible.

FIGURE 13.2
Black-and-white version of a color picture shown to a 10-year-old
boy being tested for eidetic imagery.
*Reprinted from* Psychonomic Monograph Supplements, *Vol. 3, No. 3, pp. 25–
48, by permission of Psychonomic Society, Inc.*

If you're like most other people, you will indicate that you saw an Indian
boy holding a bow in one hand and a squirrel in the other. It is quite likely
that you will also report the presence of a deer in the background and maybe
some rabbits and birds. This would be typical of what most people could report
after seeing the picture for only 30 seconds. Contrast this rather sparse report
with the following transcript of what a 10-year-old boy recalled:

> Experimenter: Can you see it?
> Subject: Yes, I can see the white and blue sky, and the ground has two different
> shades of green in it with some blue on it . . . and I can see two different squirrels,
> one is gray and the Indian's holding him in his hand and he's eating a nut. The one
> on the ground—he's red with a white stripe on him. There are three birds in the
> air—they're green, orange—they've got some red on them.

Experimenter: Can you see the birds' mouths?

Subject: No—I can see the deer and the cloth on the Indian's belt, it has many colors on it, yellow is the biggest color—and I can see his bow he's holding, it's got zigzag red on it.

Experimenter: Anything else—any other animals?

Subject: There's three rabbits—two of them are brown and one of them is white—the one brown and white one are next to each other and there's another brown one in the right-hand corner.

Experimenter: What are they doing?

Subject: One over in the right-hand corner is jumping, and the other two are just standing around.

Experimenter: Tell me more about the Indian.

Subject: Well—

Experimenter: Start at the top and move down.

Subject: Well, he's got a headband on—he doesn't have a shirt on, he's got a belt on with a cloth hanging out which is red, yellow. He's got Indian moccasins on—I think they're brown.

Experimenter: Has he got anything else on?

Subject: No.

Experimenter: Anything else you can tell me—and tell me if any of the parts go away.

Subject: The rabbits and birds are going away (pause) and the sky (pause) that's it—it's all gone. (Leask, Haber, & Haber, 1969, p. 30)

The reason why the 10-year-old boy was so good at recalling the picture was that he was still able to "see" the picture even after it was removed from actual view. He has the rare ability to form *eidetic images*. The hallmark of eidetic imagery is that people who have it maintain that an image appears to be localized in front of them. They can then scan the image and examine different parts of it just as if the image were still physically present (which it is not).

The most common method to identify people with eidetic imagery is the *picture elicitation method,* which was just illustrated (Haber & Haber, 1964). This usually involves showing a subject an unfamiliar picture, which is placed on an easel for 30 seconds, and asking the subject to scan the entire scene. After the 30 seconds is over, the picture is removed from view, and the subject is asked to continue to look at the easel and to report anything that can be seen. If the subject starts to recall the details of the picture, the experimenter always asks whether the subject is actually "seeing" the picture again or is just remembering what the picture contained. A typical session involves showing four different pictures, and each session is tape-recorded.

An eidetic image differs from other forms of visual imagery in several important ways, besides the fact that the person confidently reports that the image still seems to be actually present when it is not (Haber, 1979a, 1979b; Haber & Haber, 1964, 1988; Leask et al., 1969). For instance, an eidetic image is not simply a long afterimage, because an afterimage moves around when you move your eyes and is usually a different color than the original image (think back to the last time someone took a picture of you with a flash camera—

the flash was bright white, but the afterimage was black, and it moved around as you moved your eyes). In contrast, an eidetic image doesn't move as you move your eyes, and it is in the same color as the original picture.

Now it is certainly true that many people can form good visual images from memory. For instance, it is not uncommon for a person who has studied hard to be able, when taking an exam, to conjure up a good visual image of a page in his or her textbook (it is hoped that the page contains the right answer to the current question!). Would this qualify as eidetic imagery? Probably not, since a common visual image created from memory (such as the image of a page in a well-studied book) would not have the following characteristics that are true of most eidetic images. Eidetic images usually fade away involuntarily, and this fading occurs part by part. Typically, it's not possible to control which part of the image fades away and which part remains visible. Unlike common visual images created from memory, most eidetic images last only from about half a minute to several minutes, and it is possible to voluntarily terminate an eidetic image forever by the simple act of blinking. Furthermore, once gone from view, an eidetic image can rarely be retrieved.

A common misconception is that eidetic imagery is synonymous with photographic memory. This is quite understandable. You might expect that a person who claims to still see a picture after it has been removed would be able to have a perfect memory of the original picture, and a perfect memory is what is implied by the term *photographic memory*. However, as it turns out, the accuracy of many eidetic images is far from perfect. In fact, besides often being sketchy on details, it is not unusual for subjects to alter visual details and even add some that were never in the original! This suggests that eidetic images are certainly not photographic in nature but are reconstructed from memory and can be influenced like other memories (both visual and nonvisual) by cognitive biases.

Who is most likely to have eidetic imagery? Most of the people identified as having the ability have been children. On the basis of the picture elicitation method, the incidence of eidetic imagery in the western hemisphere for elementary-school-aged children has ranged from less than 2 percent in some studies to about 15 percent in others (Haber & Haber, 1988). Males and females seem to be equally likely to have the ability to form eidetic images. Since many studies have found it more difficult to identify adults who have eidetic imagery, it has often been concluded that there is a negative correlation between age and incidence of occurrence—in other words, that children are much more likely to have the ability than are adults. In addition, on the basis of this premise, it is also often assumed that the ability vanishes in children who possess it as they begin to develop more abstract ways to think and to process incoming information.

There's a fair amount of evidence, however, that goes against the popular views that age and eidetic imagery are inversely related and that the ability vanishes with age. For instance, as Haber and Haber point out (1988), if there is a negative correlation with age, younger children should be more likely to have eidetic imagery than older children. This is not supported by the data; just as many 12-year-olds as 7-year-olds have been found to have eidetic imagery. Also, when a group of 12 children who ranged in age from 7 to 12 when first identified as having eidetic imagery was tested 7 years later, it was found that 11 of the 12 still had the ability, even though they all obviously had developed more abstract cognitive abilities over the years (Leask et al., 1969). Luria's famous mnemonist S., who was described earlier, also had eidetic imagery, and it started when he was a young child and persisted throughout his adult life. One study has even reported that nearly 25 percent of a group of 90-year-olds had eidetic imagery (Giray, Altkin, Roodin, Yoon, & Flagg, 1978); however, such a high percentage would be met with skepticism by most other researchers.

If the evidence supporting a negative correlation between age and likelihood of eidetic imagery is weak, then how can it be explained that most studies have found it easier to identify children as having eidetic imagery? The answer may be related to a rather obscure fact about the development of eidetic images. It has been found that if a person verbalizes during the 30 seconds when he or she is viewing the original picture, this interferes with the formation of an eidetic image. So perhaps the reason why significantly fewer adults are found with eidetic imagery is that when compared with children, adults are much more likely to try to both verbally and visually encode the picture into memory. If this is, in fact, true, then it means that adults are more likely to interfere with the formation of eidetic images and therefore are less likely to be identified as having eidetic imagery, even if they really do possess the ability (Leask et al., 1969).

The person who possesses the most amazing eidetic imagery ever identified is a woman called simply Elizabeth (to protect her identity). When first tested, she was a 23-year-old teacher at Harvard University and a very skilled artist (Stromeyer, 1970; Stromeyer & Psotka, 1970). One of her abilities, which few other artists can match, is that she can mentally project onto a canvas the precise scene she wants to paint, such as a beard on a beardless man or leaves on a barren tree, with remarkable detail and texture. In addition, after not having seen a poem that she had read years earlier in a foreign language, she can conjure up an exact image of the page of poetry she had read. Then she can accurately reproduce on paper the entire poem from the bottom line to the top line as fast as she can write.

Her most remarkable eidetic imagery involves her capacity to superimpose random arrays of dots to see common objects. Earlier we said that the picture elicitation method is the most common way to identify and measure eidetic imagery. Another technique is the *superimposition method*. This method requires a subject to scan an array of dots that is meaningless by itself and to try to form an accurate eidetic image of this dot pattern (see Figure 13.3). Then another seemingly meaningless dot pattern is presented (see Figure 13.4), which the subject can superimpose on the first dot pattern (which he or she already has an eidetic image of). The composite picture of the two dot patterns will contain

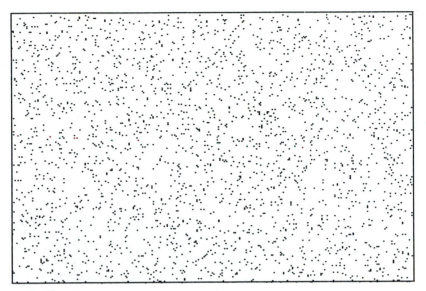

FIGURE 13.3
Try to form an eidetic image of this 1500-dot array.

a common object that the person will be able to see (see Figure 13.5 at the end of the chapter). However, if the person can't form an accurate eidetic image of the first dot pattern, then he or she will not see anything meaningful when the second pattern is presented. The superimposition method is a more difficult and exacting test of eidetic imagery; many people who do well on the picture elicitation task can't pass the superimposition one.

Elizabeth is the undisputed champion of superimposition tests. She was tested with random-dot stereograms, which are complex patterns of dots that are computer-generated. If a normal person views two random-dot stereograms presented one to each eye simultaneously through a special device called a stereoscope, the individual will see a three-dimensional figure. However, by itself each individual stereogram is meaningless. Here is what Elizabeth can do. She can view for 1 minute with her right eye a 10,000-random-dot stereogram and form an eidetic image of it. After a 10-second rest period, a different 10,000-random-dot stereogram is presented to her left eye. She can then superimpose her eidetic image of the pattern that was presented to her right eye on the actual 10,000-dot array being presented to her left eye and, finally, see a three-dimensional figure (e.g., a square floating in space or a "T" coming toward her).

Perhaps her greatest feat was forming an eidetic image of a 1,000,000-random-dot stereogram, holding the eidetic image in LTM for 4 hours, and then conjuring it back up and superimposing it on another 1,000,000-random-dot pattern to see three-dimensional objects. Some people are skeptical of Elizabeth's feats (and even of the very validity of eidetic imagery itself). Certainly,

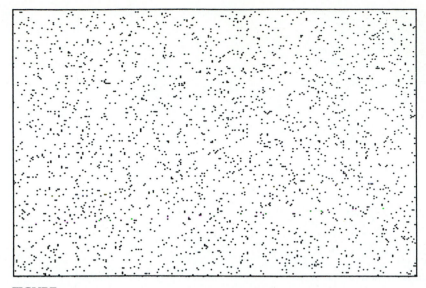

FIGURE 13.4
Try to mentally superimpose the image of Figure 13.3 onto this different 1500-dot array. Do you see anything familiar?

no one else has ever been found who even comes close to duplicating what Elizabeth can do. We have no idea how she developed her astonishing ability or how she can store such vast amounts of visual information.

In the last section of this chapter we consider individuals who truly astound most people. This is because, by almost all accounts, these individuals have severe intellectual and often emotional limitations or problems. Nevertheless, they can excel at certain things, especially tasks that require prodigious amounts of memorization.

# *I*DIOT SAVANTS

The term *idiot savant* has historically been used to identify individuals who have very low general intelligence but who possess some remarkable skill. This term, which is certainly a strange juxtaposition of words, was originally derived by combining the word *idiot* (which at one time was used as an actual level of classification to describe mentally retarded people) with the French word *savant* (which refers to a knowledgeable person). In recent years, largely owing to the pejorative nature of the word *idiot*, terms such as *mono-savant* (Charness, Clifton, & MacDonald, 1988), *savant* (Hill, 1978), and *savant syndrome* (Treffert, 1988) have become more fashionable to use. In keeping with this modern trend, we will use the term *savant* throughout the rest of this section to refer to these individuals.

A distinction is sometimes made between *talented savants* and *prodigious savants*. A talented savant is someone who performs a task at a level that is quite remarkable, given that the person is mentally retarded. In contrast, a prodigious savant has skills that are at such a high level that they would seem exceptional even for people with normal or higher-than-normal levels of intelligence. For example, a talented savant would be a person of low intelligence who has correctly memorized the names of all the state capitals and the names of all the state flowers and birds, while a prodigious savant would be a person who could correctly multiply five-digit numbers together in his or her head.

Finally, there is a category known as *autistic savants* that is reserved for people who demonstrate extraordinary ability in some area (such as music or art) but also suffer from the disorder of autism. Autism is a puzzling and debilitating condition that is usually identified during the first 2 1/2 years of life. Individuals with autism do not form close attachments with other people; they refuse to make eye contact, often have severe language disorders, do not like to be held or comforted, and are very self-centered. Although autistic people usually show an extreme disinterest in interacting with the external world, they often appear to have a need to preserve the sameness of the environment. They often engage in repetitive movements such as rocking back and forth or playing endlessly with inanimate objects like pencils or keys. A few years ago, in the movie *Rainman*, Dustin Hoffman starred as an adult autistic savant who could memorize vast numbers of names in telephone books and remember all the cards played in blackjack yet insisted that his environment not vary (for example, he absolutely had to watch *People's Court* with Judge Wapner, and he would wear only certain brands of underwear!). It has been estimated that about 10 percent of the autistic population show savant skills (for an excellent review of the autistic savant literature, see Rimland & Fein, 1988).

Finding savants among the mentally retarded is not nearly as common. A frequently cited estimate is that only 1 in every 2000 mentally retarded people qualifies as being a savant and that in this category of savants males outnumber females by a ratio of about 6 to 1 (Hill, 1978). The range of special talents or abilities displayed by savants is a narrow one. They almost always specialize in either music, art, lightning-fast arithmetic calculations, mechanics, or calendar calculations. Sometimes savants remember extraordinary details about very mundane things—for example, one savant could recall exactly, for every day in the last 25 years, what the temperature and humidity were at 3 p.m. in his hometown. Almost all savants share at least one quality: they have an exceptional memory in their area of expertise.

How can a person with quite meager intellectual skills develop extraordinary talent or ability in *any* area of expertise? Some researchers believe that these extraordinary abilities may simply be inherited (Goddard, 1914; Rife & Snyder, 1931) or that they may develop owing to damage to the left hemisphere of the brain, which then leads to both mental retardation and a compensatory development of the right hemisphere (Brink, 1980; Hauser, DeLong, & Rosman,

1975). Consistent with this last suggestion is the fact that the skills developed by most savants are those most often associated with the right hemisphere (such as music and art skills and mechanical ability). It has also been hypothesized that there may be abnormalities in the hippocampus and amygdala, areas of the brain known to be important sites for memory consolidation (Bauman & Kemper, 1985; Rimland & Fein, 1988). Here's how one researcher summarizes the quality of memory found in savants:

> Savant memory—so deep but so narrow, so vast but so emotionless, so limitless but so fixed—surely uses different circuitry than does ordinary memory, which is much more shallow but exceedingly wide, less vast but emotion-laden, and more limited but flexible, associative, and even creative. (Treffert, 1988, p. 571)

On the other hand, Ericsson and Faivre (1988) maintain that there's no need to postulate any special neural wiring, brain abnormalities, or compensatory right hemisphere mechanisms to explain how savants are able to develop their skills. Instead, they suggest that savants become experts in their area of interest in essentially the same way that people with higher levels of intelligence do it. In other words, savants have a great desire to excel at something and are willing to commit enormous amounts of time and effort to honing their skills and talents. This always involves a great deal of practice, much of which may be hidden from the casual observer. Ericsson and Faivre claim that Skilled Memory Theory, which is used to explain the development of exceptional memory (and other skills) in nonretarded individuals, is also an excellent theory to account for the development of special skills and talents in savants.

Since most mentally retarded people receive little praise or social reinforcement because of the obvious limitations that they possess, it is not surprising that some of them would purposefully seek to develop a talent or ability that brings them fame and notoriety. However, why is it the case that only 1 in every 2000 mentally retarded people develops an extraordinary skill? Are the other 1999 people simply lacking enough motivation to do what would be necessary according to Skilled Memory Theory to develop extraordinary memory or skill in a particular area? And why are the skills developed so narrow in range and often associated with the right hemisphere? Perhaps specific neurologic changes are, in fact, needed, coupled with an intense drive and motivation to practice and memorize. Certainly, there are no definitive answers to these questions yet; more research with these fascinating people is needed.

# SUMMARY

### I. Expert Knowledge
- People with *expert knowledge* can almost always encode, store, and retrieve new information related to their area of expertise better than can nonexperts.

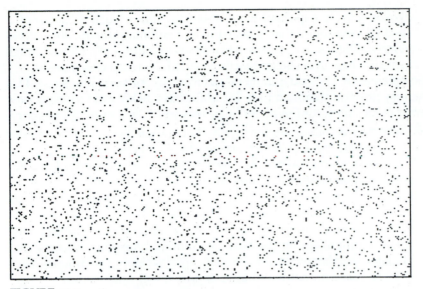

FIGURE 13.5
This 3000-dot array combines the dots of both Figure 13.3 and Figure 13.4.
If you had eidetic imagery you would have seen this diamond shape.

- A major advantage of expert knowledge is that it often allows a person to recognize familiar patterns very rapidly. These patterns then automatically trigger the most appropriate response.
- Experts also probably benefit from having superior *hierarchical knowledge structures* in LTM. These structures help people organize their knowledge bases in various domains and allow for quick and appropriate responses to new situations.

## II. The Mnemonists

- The term *mnemonist* is widely used to refer to individuals who have incredible abilities to remember new information.
- The most famous mnemonist was the Russian S.V. Shereshevskii (better known as S.). After almost 30 years of testing, the psychologist Luria claimed he was unable to find a limit to the capacity of S.'s memory or a limit to its durability.
  - There are several reasons why S. had such a phenomenal memory. First, it appears that he had *eidetic imagery* (which is the ability to continue to "see" an image after its physical removal). Second, S. could change the material to be remembered into graphic visual images that could later be used to recall the original information. Third, he possessed a great capacity for *synesthesia*. Synesthesia occurs when a sensory experience in one modality (such as vision) simultaneously

evokes sensory experiences in other modalities (such as hearing or smell). Every sound that S. heard would automatically produce vivid images of light and color and sometimes sensations of taste and touch as well. These synesthetic reactions aided his recall enormously.

- The mnemonist V.P. had a tremendous memory for verbal material. This memory prowess stemmed from his ability to quickly form idiosyncratic verbal associations for the material he was trying to commit to memory.
- S.F., who was a college student with average intelligence and memory abilities, became the first laboratory-produced mnemonist.
  - S.F. practiced increasing his memory span for unrelated digits for about 1 hour a day, 3 to 5 days a week, for a little more than 2 years. His digit span increased from a mediocre 7 to more than 80, an astounding increase.
  - The way he increased his digit span was by chunking numbers into meaningful groups on the basis of running times for various races. He later supplemented this strategy by developing additional associations based on dates and ages and by using "supergroups."
- The *Skilled Memory Theory* was proposed to account for the memory capabilities of mnemonists. A key premise of this theory is that individual differences in memory performance are not due to either neurological or intellectual differences between people. Instead, it is suggested that almost anyone with enough motivation and a willingness to endure extensive practice over long periods of time can perform exceptional feats of memory. There is considerable evidence in support of this theory.
- Rajan Mahadevan is a numerical mnemonist. His remarkable ability extends only to remembering sequences of unrelated digits. He remembers these numbers by using the same type of technique employed by V.P. and S.F.—he can quickly form idiosyncratic semantic associations to chunk together seemingly unrelated digits.

## III.  Eidetic Imagery

- *Eidetic imagery* is a rare phenomenon. People with this ability can still see an image of a picture after it has been removed, and they say that the image appears to be localized in front of them. This image, which usually lasts from 30 seconds to several minutes and then vanishes forever, can be scanned and examined as if it were an actual picture.
- Eidetic imagery is not simply an afterimage, nor is it synonymous with photographic memory.

## IV.  Idiot Savants

- The term *idiot savant* (it is now more common to use the term *savant*) or *autistic savant* has historically been used to refer to individuals who have low general intelligence or functioning but who, nonetheless, possess some truly astonishing skill or ability. The range of special talents displayed by most of these rare individuals is a narrow one, and these talents are often associated with the right hemisphere of the brain.

- Regardless of their particular talents, these people almost always possess an exceptional memory in their area of expertise.
- Various explanations have been offered to account for their extraordinary talents. These include heredity, damage to the left hemisphere of the brain and subsequent compensatory development of the right hemisphere, abnormalities in the hippocampus and amygdala, and Skilled Memory Theory. Future research is likely to indicate that a combination of these factors is responsible.

# PART 6

❖

# Changes in Memory Ability

# 14

# *Memory Disorders*

———— ❖ ————

Wall occasionally experience memory problems that can be bothersome and frustrating. Who among us hasn't ever misplaced the car keys, forgotten an important appointment, or been unable to pull out of memory the answer to an exam question? These everyday occurrences, while they can sometimes cause us grief or embarrassment, do not typically have a major effect on our lives.

However, there are some people who suffer from chronic lapses of memory. Episodes of forgetting occur so frequently that it is impossible to live a normal life. For some of these people the lapses are general in nature (i.e., forgetting occurs in a wide variety of situations), while for others the memory problems can be quite specific. An example of the latter type is a disorder called *prosopagnosia*, which occurs when the parietal and occipital lobes of the two hemispheres of the brain are damaged (Benton, 1980). Persons suffering from this disorder can no longer recognize familiar faces, while, in stark contrast, other areas of memory are unaffected. Now this certainly differs from the everyday experience of being unable to accurately place or recognize an acquaintance from the past—individuals with prosopagnosia can't recognize their mother's face or even their own face in a mirror!

Our discussion in Chapter 10 demonstrated that a good memory is important for having smooth social interactions. Therefore, it should not be surprising that a person suffering from a severe memory disorder is often at a real disadvantage in dealing with others. For instance, later in this chapter we will describe an individual (H.M.) who has great difficulty remembering new information. Consider how difficult and frustrating it would be for H.M. to become friends with you. Upon meeting you again, H.M. would not remember who you are, what your name is, your likes and dislikes, or what you had previously discussed. The embarrassment of forgetting the names and interests of longtime friends, relatives, and business associates can be devastating, not only to the individual involved but to his or her family as well. The social implications of having a severe memory disorder should never be underestimated.

The first part of this chapter will briefly describe some intriguing *memory anomalies* that normal people sometimes report experiencing. After this, the focus of the chapter will be on the assessment, diagnosis, and description of memory problems. The two major types of serious memory disorders will then be described: the *dissociative* and *organic disorders* of memory.

# SOME ANOMALIES OF MEMORY

There are a number of relatively benign anomalies of memory that sometimes occur among normal people. These anomalies do not typically signal the presence of any major disorder unless they occur very frequently and/or interfere with everyday life.

## Déjà Vu

This is perhaps the most well-known anomaly of memory. Translated from French, *déjà vu* literally means "already seen," which seems to be an apt description of this phenomenon. People who experience déjà vu report feeling *subjectively* that they have already experienced a situation, while *objectively* they know that they have never encountered this particular situation before. An example of déjà vu would involve a person who visits a dormitory room for the very first time and yet has the overwhelming sensation of having been there before. For most people this feeling would pass in a few seconds; however, in some instances it could last for minutes or hours.

Déjà vu episodes have been associated with injury to the temporal lobes of the brain and with some types of epilepsy. However, it occurs most often among normal people who have a propensity for daydreaming. Conditions most conducive to experiencing déjà vu include being in a state of heightened sensitivity or anxiety and being overly fatigued (Reed, 1979).

Several explanations have been proposed for the phenomenon. Mystical explanations suggest that déjà vu occurs because the person has experienced the situation in a previous life (reincarnation). Pseudoscientific accounts propose that people who experience déjà vu possess special abilities like telepathy or clairvoyance. Psychoanalytic theory assumes that déjà vu occurs because the current situation is associated with some event in the person's past that has been repressed into the unconscious. A more cognitive explanation maintains that déjà vu can simply be an instance of partial recognition. In other words, the reason why a person may have the subjective feeling that a new dormitory room is familiar, even though the person has never laid eyes on the room before, is that it resembles a similar but unidentifiable room the person has seen in the past.

## Jamais Vu

*Jamais vu* (also called *negative recognition*) is the converse of déjà vu. It occurs when an individual experiences a complete lack of familiarity in a particular situation when, in fact, he or she should not. Continuing with our previous example, a jamais vu episode would be occurring if a person enters a dormitory room in which he or she has lived for the past two semesters, and it seems totally alien and unfamiliar. It is also possible to have a jamais vu episode when meeting or seeing another person (Read, Vokey, & Davidson, 1991). On the basis of previous encounters, this person should seem familiar to you but is not. Most frequently this predicament occurs when the person is seen out of the normal context with which he or she is typically associated. So if you see one of your college professors in a sleazy topless bar holding a drink, you stand a good chance of not recognizing him or her (which would probably be fortunate for both of you). Jamais vu experiences are reported much less frequently than are déjà vu experiences, and they are most likely to happen in normal people who are fatigued or intoxicated (Reed, 1979).

## Time-Gap Experience

Many people have had the experience of driving a car for a length of time, arriving at their destination, and then suddenly realizing that they have no conscious recollection of having driven at all! They can't remember the turns they took and whether or not they obeyed the speed limit, stopped at red lights, and so forth. Reed (1972) coined the term *time-gap experience* to describe this happening. This form of highway hypnosis, as it has also been called (Khan, 1986), usually occurs when a person is driving for long stretches on a monotonous road or when someone is driving on a well-traveled route that requires little conscious attention.

## Cryptomnesia

Another term for *cryptomnesia* could be *unintended plagiarism*. As you know, plagiarism means stealing another's work and passing it off as your own. In cryptomnesia, an individual *honestly* believes that some work he or she has done is a novel creation, but in reality the work is not original. Instead, the work is based on earlier works of the individual or, more usually, of others. There have been a number of scandals in which famous individuals were charged with cryptomnesia. These people included the noted German philosopher, poet, and critic, Friedrich Nietzsche (Jung, 1905/1957); Sigmund Freud, the founder of psychoanalysis (Freud, 1901/1960); and the American author and lecturer Helen Keller, who was both deaf and blind (Bowers & Hilgard, 1986).

In more contemporary times, many lawsuits have been filed in the music industry in which claims were made that songwriters copied from earlier works without proper acknowledgment or compensation. Certainly, some of these cases probably involved outright plagiarism; others, however, may have been genuine examples of what is sometimes called *musical cryptomnesia*. Undoubtedly, one of the most famous cases of musical cryptomnesia involved the song "My Sweet Lord," written by George Harrison of the Beatles (Brown & Murphy, 1989). Because some people believed that this song bore an uncanny resemblance to a song recorded earlier by the Chiffons ("He's So Fine"), a lawsuit was filed against Harrison. Although during the trial Harrison admitted that he was familiar with "He's So Fine," he denied that he intentionally tried to copy it. The court agreed with him but ruled that there was an unintentional copywrite violation (in other words, that musical cryptomnesia had, in fact, occurred) and that Harrison was now legally responsible for the infringement.

Cryptomnesia is somewhat akin to jamais vu in that in both circumstances a person fails to recognize something or have any feeling of familiarity. We know very little about what causes cryptomnesia, but one way to guard against it is to very carefully search the relevant literature or music to make sure you are not unintentionally usurping someone else's creative work or ideas. How common is cryptomnesia in everyday life? This is very difficult to estimate because in everyday situations people rarely are confronted with evidence that their work or ideas are not original. Accusations of cryptomnesia typically arise only when people publish or perform their creative efforts, thereby drawing attention to what they have produced.

## ASSESSMENT OF MEMORY DISORDERS

Memory problems are one of the first telltale signs of organic brain damage. An accurate assessment of the patient's current memory abilities serves several important purposes. First, a proper assessment of remaining memory abilities will often be useful in helping to diagnose the severity, extent, and particular location of the brain injury. Second, changes in memory ability after the damage has occurred can indicate changes in the patient's overall condition. Third, a profile of the patient's enduring strengths and weaknesses with regard to memory processes can suggest the most appropriate rehabilitation procedures. Fourth, from a purely pragmatic perspective, sometimes it becomes imperative to know the everyday memory capabilities of the patient because of legal issues that may arise—for instance, issues involving the person's continued competency to manage life's affairs or the validity of disability claims for insurance purposes.

One confusing aspect of memory assessment is that the disciplines of neurology and psychology use different ways and terms to describe the subdivisions of memory. As we've seen throughout the book, psychologists often classify memory into three types (*sensory memory, STM,* and *LTM*) on the basis

FIGURE 14.1
A memory clinic you may want to avoid.

of how much time has elapsed since the material to be recalled or recognized was first learned. The discipline of neurology, however, typically dispenses with discussing or testing sensory memory functions, since it appears that these functions are not of much consequence for evaluating the effects of brain damage (Russell, 1981). Furthermore, in contrast to the classifications used by psychologists, the subdivisions that neurologists prefer to use are *immediate, recent,* and *remote* memory (Strub & Black, 1977).

The term *immediate memory* is equivalent to what psychologists refer to as STM. It is the retention span for recalling a series of events (e.g., a list of words or numbers) immediately after it has been presented. *Recent memory* and *remote memory* are finer subdivisions of what psychologists call LTM. Specifically, recent memory refers to a retention span for events that occurred only a few minutes ago (e.g., recalling the order in which six objects were touched by the examiner after a 10-minute delay) to several hours or even days ago (e.g., being able to recite what was eaten for breakfast yesterday morning). As may be surmised, remote memory is concerned with distant events in a person's own life or in the world in general (e.g., answering questions like "Who was your third-grade teacher?" or "What happened to the Middle East after World War II?").

## Memory Functions to Be Assessed

Table 14.1 summarizes several important aspects of memory functioning that should be considered in any thorough clinical assessment. To begin with, *immediate, recent,* and *remote* memory capabilities should each be examined. Although most organic disorders impair recent memory, some disorders affect the three memory spans, and differential impairment could provide useful information for the clinician. A good memory assessment will also separately examine the encoding, storage, and retrieval processes of the patient. In addition, it is important to determine the appropriateness of the types of memory strategies used by the individual. For instance, does the person try to use age-appropriate strategies for organizing and rehearsing material to be remembered?

When assessing memory functioning, it's wise to use a variety of stimulus materials, particularly if there's evidence that the organic damage is limited to one side of the head. Unilateral lesions or injuries (caused by a car accident, a stroke, or a gunshot, for example) typically result in the patient's having great difficulty with some types of materials but hardly any trouble with others. For instance, damage to certain areas of the left hemisphere of the brain will interfere with the processing and remembering of verbal stimuli but will have much less of an effect, if any, on visuospatial abilities (i.e., the perception, understanding, and remembering of shapes, orientations, and locations of objects) that are typically more the province of the right hemisphere (Springer & Deutsch, 1989).

Varying the type of dependent measure or response required is also important. For instance, as you learned in Chapter 12, normal elderly adults are more likely to show memory deficits in free recall than in recognition tasks. If recognition tests alone were used, the memory capabilities of elderly adults would be overrated. Erickson and Howieson (1986) also suggest using assessment procedures that can provide measures of both *quantitative* and *qualitative* memory performance. While just about all memory tests record quantitative performance, only a few take heed of qualitative aspects. And the qualitative aspects of a patient's answers can sometimes serve as revealing clues as to the nature of the organic disorder itself. For example, there is some evidence that

**TABLE 14.1** ASPECTS OF MEMORY TO BE CONSIDERED DURING A CLINICAL ASSESSMENT

1. Examine immediate, recent, and remote memories.
2. Evaluate encoding, storage, and retrieval processes.
3. Examine the types of strategies used for memory tasks.
4. Test memory with a variety of stimuli.
5. Require different types of responses.
6. Examine both quantitative and qualitative memory performance.
7. Determine if the memory tests relate to everyday memory demands.

making intrusion errors (e.g., recalling words during a free recall task that were not part of the original list) may be a distinguishing feature of people with *Alzheimer's disease* (Fuld, Katzman, Davies, & Terry, 1982), a disorder discussed later in this chapter.

A final consideration is whether or not the memory tests have any real relationship to everyday memory demands. Determining that a patient has difficulty in repeating a list of digits, in backward order no less, has probably little to do with his or her inability to remember to take pills on time or, upon boiling water, to shut off the burner.

## Memory Assessment Tests

Dozens of distinct memory assessment tests exist that an enterprising clinician can use to delve into the workings of a patient's memory (Herrmann, Schwartz, Rosse, & Deutsch, in press). Table 14.2 provides an overview of some of the techniques available. Because of both the enormous number of tests and the considerable overlap in the memory functions they examine, only a few of the more widely used ones will be described.

**Mental status examination.** During the initial session between a patient and an examiner, a *mental status examination* is usually given. This examination provides some preliminary insight into the patient's level of personal awareness, cooperativeness, and emotional state, as well as the individual's ability to communicate, attend, think, and remember (Lezak, 1983). Depending on the clinician's inclination, this examination can be performed either through a structured interview (i.e., an interview with a predetermined set of questions to be asked in a specified order) or by means of a more informal conversation with the patient. The mental status examination can usually detect gross problems in immediate, recent, and/or remote memory and will guide the clinician in selecting additional memory tests.

**Memory test batteries.** A number of memory test batteries have been developed, such as the *Guild Memory Test* (Gilbert, Levee, & Catalano, 1968), the *Randt Memory Test* (Randt, Brown, & Osborne, 1980), and the *Wechsler Memory Scale* (WMS) (Wechsler, 1945). These batteries contain individual verbal and nonverbal subtests that attempt to provide quick and accurate assessments of memory ability. Since the WMS is definitely the most well-known and fre-

**TABLE 14.2** MAJOR PROCEDURES FOR EVALUATING MEMORY ABILITY

| | |
|---|---|
| 1. Mental status examinations | 4. Brain imaging techniques |
| 2. Memory test batteries | 5. Questionnaires |
| 3. Neuropsychological test batteries | 6. Specific assessment scales |

quently used memory test battery, we will discuss this one to give you the flavor of this type of assessment tool.

The WMS consists of seven subtests: *Personal and Current Information, Orientation, Mental Control, Logical Memory, Digit Span, Visual Reproduction,* and *Associate Learning.* The first two subtests, similar to a standard mental status examination, are used to gather information. The subject is asked questions concerning his or her age and date of birth, current and recent public officials (e.g., "Who is the state governor?"), and time and place. The Mental Control subtest checks for accuracy and smoothness of automatisms (e.g., the reciting of a very well learned verbal pattern, such as the alphabet or months of the year) and simple conceptual tracking (e.g., counting from 1 to 53 by 4s). Logical Memory tests the ability to immediately recall verbal ideas from two paragraphs. The Digit Span subtest is similar to ones described earlier in this book. Visual Reproduction involves drawing designs from immediate or recent memory. Finally, the Associate Learning subtest involves verbal paired-associate learning ability. A single memory quotient is derived by combining the results of all the WMS subtests.

Notwithstanding its wide popularity, the WMS has been severely criticized for a number of reasons. For instance, some have questioned the reliability of some of its subtests, as well as the actual validity of the scale in distinguishing between normal and pathological memory (Chelune, Ferguson, & Moehle, 1986; Erickson & Scott, 1977; Prigatano, 1978). In addition, the subtests of the WMS are heavily weighted toward verbal memory assessment, and there is no testing of remote memory. Many researchers and clinicians also believe that deriving a single memory quotient is too simplistic, ignoring the multidimensional nature of memory.

In response to these criticisms, a revised form of the WMS has recently been released (The Psychological Corporation, 1987). The revision contains several new subtests to assess visual memory, has provisions for testing delayed recall, replaces the single memory quotient with five separate scale values, and has new sets of norms with which to interpret an individual's performance. Although it is still too early to adequately evaluate this revised version, and it has already been criticized as still being primarily a test of verbal memory, there's a general belief that the new version is superior to the original for assessing most memory dysfunctions (e.g., Loring, 1989; Spreen & Strauss, 1991).

**Neuropsychological test batteries.** Increasingly, when patients with known or suspected brain damage are referred to clinicians for evaluation, neuropsychological test batteries are the instruments of choice. The primary purpose of these batteries is to determine the type, extent, and location of any brain damage and the specific effects that this damage has on normal functioning. These test batteries are very comprehensive assessment instruments; they evaluate everything from simple sensory and motor skills (e.g., "Can you detect my touching your right cheek?'' or ''Can you write your name?'') to complex intellectual tasks (e.g., solving difficult math problems or verbal analogies).

The two most prominent instruments of this type are the *Halstead-Reitan Neuropsychological Battery* (HR) (Halstead, 1947; Reitan, 1955) and the *Luria-Nebraska Neuropsychological Battery* (LN) (Christensen, 1975a,b; Golden, Purisch, & Hammeke, 1985). From the perspective of a person whose main interest is in detecting memory disorders, the LN is to be preferred over the HR. Although Halstead was clearly interested in memory and has been credited with making some major contributions in the area (Goldstein, 1986), it is ironic that the test that bears his name contains little in the way of formal memory tests. By formal memory tests, we mean tests such as paired-associate learning and the recalling of stories. This is an important omission, since it is well known that people suffering from amnesia demonstrate their impairments most clearly on such formal tests of memory (Butters & Cermak, 1980). The LN contains 13 items that assess both immediate and recent verbal and nonverbal memory. It has nothing, however, to assess the functioning of remote memory.

**Brain imaging techniques.** Because of advances in computer technology, several new methods are now available to take detailed pictures of the living brain. These techniques hold great promise for diagnosing numerous types of brain disorders, many related to memory dysfunction. Prior to the advent of such techniques, in order to verify with precision the location and extent of brain injuries, it was typically necessary to do exploratory neurosurgery or await the results of an autopsy.

One of the oldest techniques is *computerized axial tomography* (CAT). As illustrated in Figure 14.2, this procedure involves sending a rapidly rotating X-

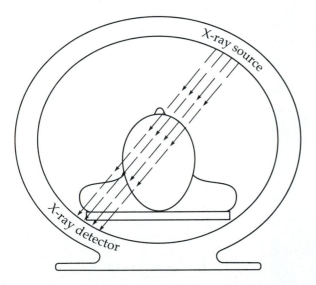

FIGURE 14.2
This shows a person undergoing a CAT scan.

ray beam through the patient's head to take thousands of pictures of the brain from different angles. A computer is used to process these pictures to get a three-dimensional, cross-sectional view of the brain.

A more recent and powerful technique, *magnetic resonance imaging* (MRI), uses strong magnetic fields, which surround the head, and radio-frequency pulses, which bombard it. As a response to the pulses, the brain emits signals, and these are processed by a computer to get pictures of the brain of much greater clarity than is possible with CAT. The top picture in Figure 14.3 shows an MRI view of a normal brain, while the bottom shows an MRI view of the brain of a patient suffering from Alzheimer's disease (a disorder in which memory failure is a major characteristic). It is evident that the hippocampus (marked "H") is considerably smaller in the Alzheimer patient. As you learned in Chapter 7, the hippocampus is a vital structure involved in the formation of long-term memories. MRI research has found that the hippocampus in Alzheimer's patients is about 40 percent smaller than it is in people with normal brains (Seab, Jagust, Wong, Roos, Reed, & Budinger, 1988).

Although both CAT and MRI can provide detailed anatomical pictures of the brain, a major disadvantage of both procedures is that neither can indicate anything about current neural activity or metabolic processes. Many important

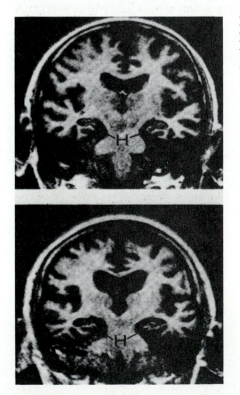

FIGURE 14.3
MRI views of a normal brain (top) and one with Alzheimer's disease (bottom).
*Reprinted with permission from J. P. Seab et al., 1988.*

brain functions, like memory, involve dynamic changes between interacting brain systems. What is needed is a procedure that is sensitive to this type of neural activity. Fortunately, there is a technique called *positron emission tomography* (PET) that can provide just this kind of information. Radioactively labeled glucose is injected into the bloodstream, and a highly sensitive radiation detector measures the amount of this glucose that has been taken up by different groups of neurons. The more active neurons absorb the most radioactive glucose. The level of radioactivity in different brain tissues is then measured by a computer, and a colored picture showing regional differences in metabolic activity of the brain is produced. Recently, neuroscientists have been able to combine MRI and PET scans into a single picture to produce three-dimensional images of the brain that contain structural information from MRI and indications of neural activity from PET (Levin, Xiaoping, Tan, Galhotra, Pelizzari, Chen, Beck, Chen, Cooper, Mullen, Hekmatpanah, & Spire, 1989).

A few words of caution, however, are necessary with regard to the brain imaging techniques. First, it should be noted that the area of brain imaging is very complex, and there are numerous disagreements concerning technical methods and the interpretation of results. Second, the results of studies in this area are often contradictory. Third, remember that the data obtained from all brain imaging techniques are correlational in nature only, meaning that no cause-and-effect conclusions can be safely drawn only on the basis of these data. Notwithstanding these concerns, the future for brain imaging techniques is rich with promise for providing new insights into memory dysfunctions.

**Questionnaire assessment.** Complaints about memory failures are common among people with organic brain damage. Therefore, many different questionnaires have been developed to gather data concerning self-assessments of memory ability. These questionnaires can usually be dichotomized into *memory questionnaires* (MQs) and *metamemory questionnaires* (MMQs). An MQ measures how well people can recognize or recall knowledge or events, whereas an MMQ determines what a person knows about the memory process or asks people to estimate how well they believe they can recognize or recall knowledge or events (Herrmann, 1983).

Some MQs specialize in assessing semantic memory (e.g., "Can you name the planets of the solar system?"), others concentrate on episodic memory (e.g., "What was the color of your first bicycle?"), and still others investigate both domains. There's also great variability among MMQs in the types of memory phenomena they examine. For instance, beliefs people hold concerning their memory prowess have been assessed for such phenomena as remembering to do routine acts (e.g., "Do you usually remember to lower the heat before going to sleep at night?"); keeping appointments; recognizing familiar people, music, or voices; following or remembering directions; recalling childhood memories; and remembering plots of books, television programs, and movies.

How reliable and valid are the responses from memory questionnaires? First the good news: the reliability of both MQs and MMQs seems to be fairly high. In other words, people do tend to give consistent and stable answers. The problem is with the validity of the answers. Although there isn't typically much of a problem when considering semantic memory, since it is a relatively easy task to determine the accuracy of the answers given, the validity of answers to episodic questions and of statements concerning memory aptitude is often suspect. With episodic questions, especially when remote memory is being investigated, it is sometimes difficult or impossible to verify the accuracy of the person's answers. Consider the question raised earlier concerning the color of a person's first bicycle. If the person answering the question is 92 years old, the likelihood of obtaining corroborating or noncorroborating evidence from a relative or friend is virtually nil. In terms of metamemory, the general finding is that people are not particularly good at assessing their own memory ability (Herrmann, 1982a). When the results of actual memory tasks are compared with a person's belief about how well he or she can do such tasks, the correspondence is often disappointingly low (e.g., Gilewski & Zelinski, 1986).

Given the concerns about the validity of MMQs, one might be tempted to think that this type of memory questionnaire is not useful in a clinical setting. However, this would be a wrong conclusion to draw. First, there's evidence that the number of memory complaints can vary as a function of the disorder. For instance, people suffering from depression often complain bitterly about their terrible memory, while people in the early stages of dementia often will not even admit they have a memory problem (Heston & White, 1983). So this differential assessment of memory aptitude can help distinguish the two disorders—even though, in some sense, it's completely irrelevant whether or not there's any real validity to any of the memory complaints. Second, if people have misconceptions about their memory ability, this can lead them to adopt poor strategies for remembering things. If you incorrectly believe that you can remember shopping lists easily, you probably won't write down all the ingredients you need to buy at the store for making lasagna tonight, and when you get to the store, you will likely forget some important items (like mozzarella cheese!). Knowing about a patient's false beliefs concerning his or her own memory capability may aid in rehabilitation procedures as well. A final benefit of using any type of questionnaire is that many people perceive questionnaires as being less threatening than standard memory tests given by note-taking neurologists or psychologists.

**Specific assessment scales.**  A number of specific scales or inventories have been developed to assess cognitive and noncognitive deficits in particular clinical populations. Two examples are the *Alzheimer's Disease Assessment Scale* (Rosen, Mohs, & Davis, 1984), for people with suspected dementia, and the *Boston Diagnostic Aphasia Examination* (Goodglass & Kaplan, 1972; revised 1983), intended for individuals who have language disturbances. Not only are these types of scales helpful in making the initial diagnosis, but they are also useful in assessing changes in ability over time. In this way they can serve to monitor the progression of the disorder or the effects of some treatment program.

# DISSOCIATIVE DISORDERS OF MEMORY

Major memory disorders are divided into two principal types on the basis of whether or not there is evidence of organic damage. If there's no evidence of physiological dysfunction (e.g., brain injury), and if it's obvious that there's been a marked and sudden alteration in the person's normal personality structure, then it is likely that the individual is suffering from what is referred to as a *dissociative disorder* (sometimes also called a *functional amnesia*). A dissociative disorder is a sudden splitting off (or dissociation) of a part of the person's personality. When this happens, there is a loss of personal identity that is believed to be due to the repression of very disturbing memories. There are three major dissociative disorders—*psychogenic amnesia, psychogenic fugue,* and *multiple personality*—and they all involve dramatic lapses of memory.

## Psychogenic Amnesia

*Psychogenic amnesia* is brought on by some extremely stressful or anxiety-provoking event in the individual's life (such as being raped). The person suddenly becomes unable to recall important personal information. This memory loss usually lasts for only a limited period of time (on the order of a few hours). However, there are many exceptions to this general pattern. For example, the amnesic episode can sometimes last for years, and its extent can encompass the person's entire past life. In other cases the memory loss will be highly specific, limited only to the most salient aspects of the triggering event.

What is interesting is that the person experiencing psychogenic amnesia can always remember some abilities from the past. For example, even though a woman may not be able to recognize any friends or relatives, she may still recall how to play a good game of poker (complete with bluffing). Regardless of the particular form that the memory loss takes, a defining characteristic of this type of amnesia is that the person is always aware of the inability to remember key personal information and is usually distressed by it. Typically, the amnesia will disappear with the same swiftness that marked its onset, and the recovery of lost personal memories will be complete, with little chance for a recurrence of the loss.

## Psychogenic Fugue

In a very small number of instances of intolerable stress or anxiety, a person will experience amnesia for personal memories and, in response, will move away from home and assume a new identity. If this occurs, the diagnosis will be *psychogenic fugue*. This state of fugue (from the Latin "to flee") can last for a few hours to several years. In extreme cases, the new identity that is assumed comes complete with a new name, set of personality characteristics, job, and group of friends. There are even cases on record of married people who, believing they are single because of their psychogenic fugue, marry another person and have children! During the fugue state the person doesn't seem concerned at all that the past is a complete mystery. When the fugue ends, the memory for the person's past life returns (although sometimes not completely). Recollection of events that took place during the fugue, however, is usually lost. Chronicling the plight of a person trapped in a fugue state has been the plot of more than one soap opera and novel. One of the most famous cases is the fugue state experienced by J. D. Salinger's hero Holden Caulfield, in *Catcher in the Rye.*

## Multiple Personality

In the most extreme form of dissociative disorder, a person's personality structure divides into two or more distinct identities. People who experience this type of dissociation are said to have the disorder of *multiple personality.* (Some people confuse multiple personality disorder with schizophrenia. The two disorders are quite distinct, though, with schizophrenia being a psychotic disorder in which the person displays a pattern of severely disturbed thinking, behavior, emotion, and perception.) Many clinicians believe that the disorder of multiple personality begins in childhood (although it is rarely diagnosed until at least adolescence) as a defense mechanism to banish extremely upsetting memories to an alternate self. This allows the original personality to free itself from overwhelming anxiety and stress (Confer & Ables, 1983). Evidence suggests that the majority of people with this disorder were forced to endure severe physical abuse (often of a sexual nature by a close relative) during their childhood years (Bliss, 1986).

Each identity, or personality, may be quite different from the other ones. The alternate identities can suddenly appear and take control of the person, and just as suddenly, they can disappear. It is not unusual for the subpersonalities to be different in sex, age, or race. A recent survey of 100 cases of people with multiple personality disorder indicated that the average number of alternate personalities was 13 (Putnam, Guroff, Silberman, Barban, & Post, 1986). A given personality will have its own likes and dislikes, behavior patterns, social relationships, and memories. In some cases, the various personalities are definitely aware of each other and may even carry on conversations. But in other cases, there is only a vague awareness of the other personalities—these people sometimes report hearing disembodied "voices" that reverberate in their head. Sometimes the person, who more often is a woman than a man, has no knowledge at all that there are different personalities inhabiting her or his body.

Although each personality is able to recall events that happened to him or her, there usually is no conscious recall for the events that transpire when another personality is dominant (Putnam et al., 1986). There is some evidence, however, that information obtained by one personality can sometimes influence the performance of another personality if implicit memory techniques are used. For example, in one 45-year-old woman with 22 distinct personalities, faces from a high school yearbook that one personality ("Alice") saw influenced another personality ("Bonnie") to select them as having been seen before (Nissen, Ross, Willingham, Mackenzie, & Schacter, 1988).

The general public probably has a distorted impression of how frequently cases of multiple personality arise. This is largely owing to the great publicity given to two women who were diagnosed as having this type of dissociative disorder. Best-selling books and widely seen commercial movies (*The Three Faces of Eve* and *Sybil*) graphically detailed the dramatic changes in outward personality that these women went through. In fact, multiple personality is a fairly rare disorder. The prognosis for complete recovery, unfortunately, is not as good as for psychogenic amnesia and psychogenic fugue.

# ORGANIC DISORDERS OF MEMORY

The other major type of memory disorder results from organic, or physiological, damage to the central nervous system (particularly the brain). Although sometimes it is possible to pinpoint the exact effect that a particular brain lesion or injury has on memory functioning, such limited effects are rare. A specific injury will more frequently disrupt a wide range of memory abilities. In addition, a particular memory ability (such as forward digit span) may be affected by damage sustained in many different parts of the central nervous system. This is because most cognitive functions depend, at least in part, on normal functioning of the entire brain. If one component of the brain malfunctions, it will cause multiple functions to suffer, even though that component may be only peripherally related to the function under study.

## Distinguishing Dissociative and Organic Memory Disorders

It is not always easy to distinguish dissociative memory disorders from organic ones. And as Mayes (1988) points out, an unknown proportion of people with dissociative memory disorders may also have some organic component that affects their memory capabilities. For instance, a person with multiple personality disorder may also have an organic brain dysfunction such as epilepsy (Benson, Miller, & Signer, 1986). Epilepsy is a disorder in which people suffer from recurrent brain seizures, and depending on how much and what parts of the brain are affected, there may or may not be an impairment of consciousness. If the epileptic seizures affect structures known to be important to memory processing (e.g., the hippocampus and amygdala), it becomes very difficult to separate out the individual effects of the dissociative disorder from those of the organic one (Mayes, 1988).

There are, however, several factors that can help distinguish between dissociative and organic memory disorders. First, sudden changes in personality resulting from a severe trauma or from anxiety-provoking events are hallmarks of only dissociative memory disorders. Second, in contrast to people with organic disorders, people with dissociative disorders usually show no obvious evidence of brain injury or tumors or disease. Third, the memory loss in dissociative disorders is primarily for personal past experiences. As we will see, the memory loss (and often continuing memory problems) of individuals with organically induced disorders are neither centered on nor limited to retrieval of personal memories. Fourth, people experiencing dissociative disorders (particularly psychogenic amnesia and psychogenic fugue) are much more likely than people with organic disorders to eventually have all (or nearly all) of their lost memories and memory functioning abilities restored.

## Causes of Organic Memory Disorders

Unfortunately, there are multiple kinds of organic damage that can adversely affect memory. Memory disturbances can occur when damage is done to the central nervous system from such things as head injuries; drug abuse; disruption of the blood supply to the brain; viral and bacterial infections, which can give rise to such illnesses as syphilis and meningitis, respectively; illnesses producing progressive dementia; and a variety of chronic diseases of the heart, liver, kidneys, lungs, and endocrine glands, which can lead to a lack of oxygenated blood or metabolic imbalances (Kapur, 1988; Khan, 1986; Mayes, 1988). Our discussion will focus on a few of the leading organic causes of memory failure.

Sustaining head damage is one of the leading causes of memory disorders. A blow to the head may or may not be serious. It may cause no loss of consciousness, a momentary loss of consciousness, or it may result in a coma that can last for months or even years. Even though a relatively mild head injury often does not cause a loss of consciousness, the blow may still be sufficient to disrupt consolidation of ongoing events. When this happens, the person can continue with normal activities; only later does it become apparent that the individual has absolutely no memory for what went on. This is a fairly common occurrence in contact sports when a person "gets his or her bell rung." For example, a football player may continue playing for several more downs after receiving a minor blow to the head, but upon subsequent questioning, it becomes clear that he has no recollection of what actually happened during those plays. Dan Marino, the quarterback for the Miami Dolphins, was unable to remember a touchdown pass he once threw in a game because he had earlier suffered a mild concussion while being tackled.

More substantial brain injury will cause a loss of consciousness that results in a coma. A general rule of thumb is that the longer the period of coma, the greater the amount of diffuse brain damage sustained. Upon recovery from a coma, there's usually a period of confusion and disorientation. During this time the patient will have a spotty memory for daily events, experiencing a condition that has been described as having "islands of memory" in a "sea of forgetfulness." As an example, a patient may remember a visit by her husband and children but not by her mother-in-law. To fill in the gaps, the person may resort to fabricating past events (confabulation). The term *posttraumatic amnesia* (PTA) refers to the loss of memory for the time interval from the onset of the coma to the recovery of continuous memory (i.e., remembering daily events in a coherent and chronological sequence as well as a noninjured person can). The duration of PTA can range from minutes to years, with greater durations usually occurring in cases of more severe brain damage.

After the PTA period, there is a selective loss of memory for events that occurred before the injury. As you first learned in Chapter 7, this is called *retrograde amnesia* (RA). Initially, the period of RA can be either relatively short (a few hours or days) or quite lengthy (memory is disrupted for decades), depending on the severity of the brain injury. However, regardless of the extent of memory loss, there's usually a gradual shrinkage of RA as time passes. Memories often come back in a haphazard order, but older memories typically return first. A point is finally reached where no further shrinkage occurs and a permanent memory loss remains for the events that transpired just before the injury. This permanent hole in memory is probably from a disruption in the consolidation process brought on by the head injury. To refresh your memory, in our fictitious example started in Chapter 7, Elise and her brother John were in a car accident on their way home from watching the latest Woody Allen movie. Elise was knocked unconscious and after a brief period awoke with a case of short-lasting RA. When Elise recovered consciousness, memory for recent past events slowly returned to her, but there was never a recollection of the actual collision itself.

Although it was not mentioned in Chapter 7 in our story about Elise, a much more devastating memory problem also occurs called *anterograde amnesia* (AA). This term refers to a brain-damaged person's inability to consolidate and remember new things. A person with AA will have immediate memory and *premorbid* (before the injury) remote memory still intact. The AA occurs because the brain no longer transfers information properly from immediate to recent memory. Fortunately, people with mild head traumas usually recover most of their past memories and also the ability to learn new things.

## The Classic Amnesia Syndrome

According to Squire (1987), the *classic amnesia syndrome*, which consists of both RA and AA episodes following a loss of consciousness, occurs only when there's bilateral damage to or destruction of certain areas of the brain. Bilateral damage refers to damage done to structures in both the left and right hemispheres. In Chapter 7 we indicated that the damage involves either the medial temporal lobes (especially the hippocampus and the amygdala) or areas of the diencephalon region (such as the mammillary bodies and the dorsomedial thalamic nuclei).

A controversy has developed over whether or not qualitatively different types of amnesia occur if damage is done to the diencephalic region versus the medial temporal regions (Butters, Miliotis, Albert, & Sax, 1983; McCarthy & Warrington, 1990; Parkin, 1987; Squire, 1987; Weiskrantz, 1985). For example, it has been hypothesized that medial temporal lobe amnesics forget information more rapidly than do diencephalic amnesics, that confabulation is more common in diencephalic cases, and that remote memory is more seriously disrupted in diencephalic amnesics.

A complicating factor in trying to settle the issue is that *Korsakoff's syndrome* (a disorder discussed more fully later in this chapter) is by far the most frequently studied type of diencephalic amnesia. The problem is that it is now highly suspected that many Korsakoff amnesics also have frontal lobe damage, and damage to the frontal lobes has been associated with a multitude of diverse problems (Butters & Stuss, 1989; Kapur, 1988; Mayes, 1988; Milner, McAndrews, & Leonard, 1990; Parkin, 1990; Petrides, 1989; Shimamura, Janowsky, & Squire, 1990; Squire, 1982). These include mood changes, a reduced ability to plan and monitor actions, impaired memory for temporal order, and several phenomena that would directly or indirectly influence memory performance, such as impairment of attentional control, increased distractibility, disruptions in metamemory, and increases in confabulation. So it may be that if different patterns of amnesic symptoms are sometimes observed between diencephalic and medial temporal patients (and this is still being debated; McCarthy & Warrington, 1990), it may be because of the additional frontal lobe damage that occurs in people who have Korsakoff's syndrome.

**The tragic case of H.M.**  To help you imagine what life is like for someone with the classic amnesia syndrome, the now famous case of H.M. will be highlighted (Corkin, 1984; Milner, Corkin, & Teuber, 1968; Ogden & Corkin, 1991; Scoville & Milner, 1957). In 1953, at age 27, patient H.M. had both medial temporal lobes removed to treat severe epilepsy. Because there are no pain receptors in the brain, H.M. was awake and talking during the operation. After H.M. recovered from the operation, his immediate memory and remote memory were intact, as was his overall intellectual ability. There was evidence of some RA, and at his last testing in 1989, this was found to occur primarily for the 11 years just prior to the operation (Ogden & Corkin, 1991). This means that only rarely can H.M. remember any events or information that he had experienced or learned from age 16 to age 27!

Without any doubt, the most devastating effect of the operation was profound AA, which has continued throughout his life. In other words, with some notable exceptions discussed below, H.M. could not (and still cannot) learn anything new. For instance, he doesn't recognize anyone he has met or seen since 1953 (he still doesn't recognize Suzanne Corkin, who has tested him every year for the last 20 years at MIT). H.M. can read the same magazine over and over again without awareness that he has ever seen the articles before, and he laughs with the same intensity every time he hears the same old jokes. When his family moved to a new house, he couldn't learn the route back to his new home, and so he would end up going to his former house time and time again. Conversations with H.M. can also be frustrating; if there's any distraction during the conversation (such as a blaring fire engine going by that captures his attention momentarily), H.M. will completely forget what was being talked about. He doesn't know how old he is, where he lives, what he was doing a few minutes ago, or what day, month, year, or season it is (Ogden & Corkin, 1991). He does show some very limited recall of famous events that occurred after 1953 (such as President Kennedy's assassination and the explosion of the space shuttle *Challenger*), but his knowledge of these events is often confused (Ogden & Corkin, 1991). This dense amnesia for new learning was completely unexpected by the medical staff at the time the operation was performed, and because of the tragic nature of H.M.'s memory loss, a similar operation has never again been done.

As noted above, H.M.'s inability to learn new things is not absolute. For instance, H.M. can learn new perceptual-motor skills such as those needed to perform mirror-tracing tasks. These tasks involve learning to accurately and quickly trace shapes (such as five-pointed stars), even though they are presented in mirror-reversed fashion (see Figure 14.4). Over a period of days H.M. showed steady improvement in mirror-tracing, yet he had no recollection of participating in any of the previous testing sessions, nor did he ever recognize the mirror-tracing apparatus (Milner, 1962)! This inability to remember previ-

FIGURE 14.4
A mirror-tracing task.

ous learning sessions is a common finding with other amnesics as well. This is often referred to as *source amnesia:* a person learns or remembers something but cannot remember the actual learning situation (i.e., the source of the information).

Over the years, additional testing of H.M. has indicated that he can learn and remember perceptual skills such as how to read mirror-inverted words and how to more quickly recognize incomplete drawings of objects with repeated exposures to them. H.M. has also learned more cognitive tasks such as solving complex puzzles. And it has been shown that H.M. can be influenced by various *priming procedures* (see Chapters 2 and 7). For instance, if he is shown a target word such as DEFINE and later given the stem DEF and asked to complete the stem with the first word that comes to mind, he will usually respond with the target word (Ogden & Corkin, 1991).

**What is preserved in classic amnesia?**  In addition to the abilities of H.M., the memory capabilities of many other amnesics have, of course, been studied. A fairly consistent pattern of memory abilities and disabilities has emerged. People exhibiting the *classic amnesia syndrome* will have a normal immediate memory (STM) but will show some RA that often shrinks with time and a profound AA that typically doesn't improve. Their learning and memory deficit is most clearly seen when they are asked to either recall or recognize verbal or nonverbal information that was presented to them after the onset of amnesia. They simply can't do it. Their linguistic and general intellectual abilities are largely intact. Very salient aspects of their life are also usually preserved, such as knowing their name, marital status, and close family members, and they can often give a brief outline of the major events of their life (except for the period covered by the RA). There are also certain types of tasks that these individuals can learn and remember. These include tasks requiring perceptual-motor skills, classical conditioning, priming tasks, and selective problem-solving tasks [such as learning a rule for generating numbers in a sequence (Kinsbourne & Wood, 1975) or how to solve complex puzzles or problems (Cohen, 1984)].

To account for these findings, as was mentioned in Chapter 7, some researchers believe that people with amnesia lose the ability to consolidate *declarative knowledge* into LTM but not *nondeclarative knowledge* (e.g., Squire, 1987; Squire, Zola-Morgan, Cave, Haist, Musen, & Suzuki, 1990; Squire, Knowlton, & Musen, 1993). You'll remember that declarative knowledge deals with facts and episodes acquired through learning that are directly accessible to conscious recollection, whereas, in contrast, nondeclarative knowledge is not readily accessible to conscious recollection and involves semantic priming effects, certain types of conditioning, and learning how to perform a task or acquire a skill over a period of time. Squire and his colleagues maintain that the types of learning that are preserved in amnesics are all aspects of nondeclarative memory.

However, it has been argued that the distinction between declarative and nondeclarative knowledge cannot fully account for what is preserved in memory and what is not (e.g., McCarthy & Warrington, 1990). For instance, there is evidence that amnesics *can* learn declarative knowledge after the onset of amnesia. One patient (H.D.) was able to become highly proficient in learning computer data entry techniques. This was accomplished by extensive repetitions of all the components of the task. But more impressive was that she was able to master new computer-related words and acronyms. This mastery clearly showed declarative learning (Glisky & Schacter, 1987). It should not be possible according to the declarative/nondeclarative model of preserved memory in amnesics.

Partly on the basis of findings such as these, others (e.g., Schacter, 1987) have suggested that whether or not amnesics show retention of information depends more on the type of testing procedure used than it does on the type of knowledge being processed. Specifically, it has been proposed that tasks given to amnesics that require *explicit* memory (such as free recall) will show no evidence of remembering, but tasks using *implicit* memory techniques (such as priming) will show good evidence of retention. The declarative/nondeclarative and explicit/implicit dichotomies greatly overlap and are the two most popular theories that current researchers use to try to provide a shorthand description of the memory capabilities of amnesics. Neither dichotomy, however, can fully account for the data.

## Transient Global Amnesia

As the name implies, *transient global amnesia* (TGA) involves a brief period of both RA and AA; it typically lasts for only a few minutes, hours, or days (Bender, 1956; Fisher & Adams, 1958; Kritchevsky, 1987, 1989). While there is some disorientation, the person's mental abilities seem relatively unaffected, and there is no loss of personal identity. What makes TGA such an intriguing disorder is that it appears quite suddenly and can be triggered by many diverse things, including taking a cold shower, experiencing physical stress, eating a large meal, and even engaging in sexual intercourse (Parkin, 1987)! A bizarre incident that took place in Japan has also been blamed for causing TGA. It is now known that certain drugs are associated with the onset of TGA, and one of these drugs, clioquinol, has sometimes been used to combat diarrhea. In 1966, clioquinol was distributed to large numbers of Japanese people to combat dysentery following a period of widespread flooding. The result—over 100 people reported having TGA symptoms (Parkin, 1987).

Recovery from TGA is just as sudden as its onset and is marked by a complete return of memory except for details during the attack itself. The disorder occurs most frequently in older people, doesn't seem to discriminate between men and women, and is believed by some people to be precipitated by a temporary lack of blood to regions of the brain important for proper memory functioning (like the hippocampus). Unfortunately, recurrent episodes of TGA are not uncommon.

## Specific Memory Disorders

The left and right hemispheres of the human brain differ in the types of memories they contain. These differences are most evident when the temporal lobe of either hemisphere is severely damaged or has to be surgically removed to prevent the spread of tumors or epileptic seizures. When the temporal lobe of the left hemisphere is nonfunctional or is removed, learning and remembering most types of verbal material is usually very difficult or impossible (Milner & Teuber, 1968). Lack of a well-functioning temporal lobe in the right hemisphere will typically result in poor learning and retention of visual and spatial information (Milner, 1968).

A very wide range of specific memory disorders can arise from localized or focal brain damage. Most of these specific memory disorders can be classified as being an instance of either *agnosia* (an inability to recognize sensory stimuli), *aphasia* (a disorder in which the person has difficulty in expressing and/or understanding either spoken or written language), or *apraxia* (an inability to perform purposeful movements in the absence of paralysis). Sometimes the damage is clearly limited to only one of the two hemispheres. For example, if damage occurs to certain areas of the left hemisphere, then *Broca's aphasia* can result. This is a disorder in which the individual has great difficulty in articulating words, presumably because the engrams for controlling the muscle movements involved in speech have been damaged or destroyed.

On the other hand, some apraxias occur primarily when damage occurs in parts of the right hemisphere. Consider the disorder known as *dressing apraxia*. People who have this problem have great difficulty putting on their clothes. Because of brain damage in the right hemisphere, they have forgotten how to carry out the body movements needed to get dressed (such as buttoning a shirt or tying shoelaces or a necktie). This is a very frustrating disorder: often after considerable time spent trying to get dressed, with perhaps only one arm making it into a sleeve or pants getting put on backward, the person gives up and throws the clothes into a heap on the ground! In other cases both hemispheres must be affected before the memory disturbance is evident (e.g., *prosopagnosia*, a type of agnosia for familiar faces, mentioned at the beginning of this chapter).

## Korsakoff's Syndrome

In 1887, a Russian physician named Sergei Korsakoff described a severe memory disorder that resulted from brain damage. This disorder, which now bears his name, is characterized by a major loss of recent memory. In other words, people with *Korsakoff's syndrome* (KS) have a severe AA and thus find it very difficult to learn and remember new things. This inability to learn and remember is especially evident when the memory task requires conscious recollection of the past. In addition, most KS patients exhibit extensive remote memory impairments, often losing decades' worth of memories.

Individuals with KS constitute the most widely studied group of people who have become amnesic after sustaining damage to the diencephalon region. Autopsies reveal that the brain damage is most often in the dorsomedial thalamic nuclei and the mammillary bodies (Butters & Cermak, 1975; Butters & Stuss, 1989; Squire & Zola-Morgan, 1991; Victor, Adams, & Collins, 1971). However, as mentioned earlier, it is generally accepted that the brain damage in these patients is usually very widespread, often extending to the frontal lobes. These patients are often described as being emotionally flat, rather apathetic, and surprisingly without much insight concerning their memory impairments (Squire & Zola-Morgan, 1991). There is also a marked tendency for confabulation, owing perhaps to the suspected frontal lobe damage. It is believed that a primary cause of KS is a severe deficiency of thiamine (vitamin B1). Many different conditions can give rise to a thiamine deficiency, thereby causing KS, but by far the most common cause is excessive alcohol intake over a period of years. Alcoholics typically have a poor diet and therefore a low intake of vitamins in general, and to make matters worse, alcohol appears to interfere with normal intestinal absorption of thiamine (Carlson, 1988).

## Dementia

People with *dementia* suffer from a deterioration of all intellectual abilities and undergo drastic changes in personality. There are three main types of dementia: *primary undifferentiated dementia, primary differentiated dementia,* and *secondary dementia* (Heston & White, 1983). The first two groups (known collectively as *progressive dementias* because the disorders worsen in a smoothly progressive way, without sharp declines) are caused by diseases that directly affect the brain, and they eventually result in death. The difference between the undifferentiated and differentiated dementias is that the former mainly affect the cerebral cortex, while the latter affect subcortical areas of the brain. Illnesses that cause primary differentiated dementias (e.g., *Huntington's disease*) are characterized by abnormal body movements, postures, or gaits; differentiated dementias can easily be distinguished from undifferentiated dementias.

Secondary dementias derive from illnesses that do not directly attack the brain. Certain drugs, poisons, vascular disorders, types of depression, and diseases of the heart and lungs can cause symptoms that mimic those of primary dementias. It is absolutely vital to determine whether the dementia-like symptoms a person may be displaying are due to primary or secondary dementia, because with proper treatment a secondary dementia can be cured, which, unfortunately, is not currently the case with primary dementias.

**Alzheimer's disease.** Undoubtedly the most common form of primary undifferentiated dementia—or, for that matter, of dementia in general—is *Alz-*

*heimer's disease* (AD). A diagnosis of AD used to be synonymous with *presenile dementia* (onset of dementia before age 65), with the term *senile dementia* reserved for people who developed dementia at or after age 65. Today, this age restriction no longer holds, since the same widespread neuropathological changes in the brain (e.g., *neurofibrillary tangles,* which are clumps of twisted nerve fibers, and patches of dead neurons called *senile plaques*) are evident in dementia patients before and after age 65. The incidence of AD increases with age, although it can begin when a person is still in his or her thirties. It has been estimated that more than 65 percent of people suffering from dementia have AD (Kolb & Whishaw, 1990). A great deal of publicity has surrounded this disorder in the last 10 to 15 years, even though the disorder has been known since antiquity. Perhaps this is because people are now living longer, and therefore a greater percentage of the population is falling prey to AD and similar dementias. Since the number of people in the United States living to age 85 or older is expected to rise from approximately 2.2 million to 16 million between the years 1980 and 2050 (Cohen, 1986), public health concerns about AD will probably continue to swell.

First clinically described by the German physician Alios Alzheimer in 1907, the disorder typically starts with the person showing unusual signs of forgetting. For instance, a previously punctual person will begin to miss appointments, or a person will stop at the dry cleaner's three times in one week, forgetting that all the clothes were picked up on the first visit. In addition to episodic memory failures, certain semantic memory deficits are also early signs of AD. For instance, people with AD typically have great difficulty in finding the right word to use in everyday speech (Nebes, 1989). The continual and worsening loss of memory is a defining characteristic of AD. In particular, recent memory is the first casualty, meaning that AA will be present. Both immediate and remote memories remain reasonably intact until the later stages of the disease. Eventually, however, all three types of memory greatly deteriorate. Similar to the memory losses of people with the classic amnesia syndrome, the memory failures of people with AD are most evident when conscious recollection of the past is required. A point is finally reached when the person can no longer speak intelligently, lacks all judgment or ability to use abstraction, has paranoid delusions, fails to recognize close family members, stares vacantly off into space, loses voluntary control of muscles, and becomes incontinent and bedridden. The afflicted person usually dies within 6 to 12 years after the onset of AD.

The brains of AD patients shrink considerably as the disease progresses. There is also considerable degeneration of the hippocampus and the frontal and temporal lobes, as well as a huge loss of acetylcholine-secreting neurons in the nucleus basalis of Meynert (a structure in the basal forebrain that sends axons to the hippocampus and the cerebral cortex; see Figure 14.5). Many attempts have been made to ameliorate the effects of AD or to slow its progression. For instance, since acetylcholine is in short supply in people with AD, and it is well known that this neurotransmitter is vital to normal memory

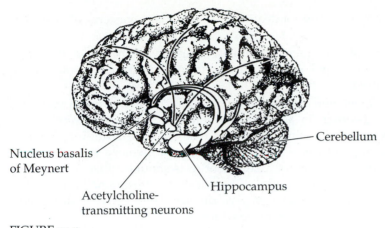

Nucleus basalis
of Meynert

Acetylcholine-
transmitting neurons

Cerebellum

Hippocampus

FIGURE 14.5
The acetylcholine pathways affected in Alzheimer's disease.

functioning (see Chapter 7), drugs have been administered to try to raise the level of acetylcholine in the brains of these people. Unfortunately, the results have been largely disappointing (Parkin, 1987). But rest assured, many drug companies are hard at work trying to develop effective drugs to treat (and, it is hoped, cure) AD.

One of the problems in developing treatments for AD is that the exact cause of it is still unknown. It is believed, however, that genetic predisposition plays a significant role (Breitner, 1988). In addition, researchers are investigating certain viruses, immune system dysfunctions, the fact that there may be excessive aluminum buildup in the brains of AD patients, and various neurotransmitter and hormone deficiencies and imbalances—all thought to be possible causative agents. Given the horrifying effects of the disease and its increasing incidence, considerable research efforts are being devoted to this tragic disorder.

## SUMMARY

### I. Anomalies of Memory
- Several anomalies of memory occur in normal people. These include *déjà vu, jamais vu, time-gap experience,* and *cryptomnesia.* Such anomalies are not usually indicative of any major disorder unless they occur often and/or interfere with normal life.

### II. Assessment of Memory Disorders
- An accurate assessment of a memory disorder is important for diagnosing the severity, extent, and location of brain damage; for determining changes in the patient's overall condition; for developing the best reha-

bilitation program; and for dealing with pragmatic concerns of everyday living.

- When a clinical assessment of memory capability is performed, the terms *immediate, recent,* and *remote* memory (borrowed from neurology) are generally used.

- Several different memory functions should be considered when assessing a memory disorder. In addition to examining immediate, recent, and remote memory, the clinician should also examine encoding, storage, and retrieval processes, as well as the types of memory strategies used by the individual. Memory assessment tests should utilize a variety of stimuli, require different types of responses, and examine both quantitative and qualitative memory performance. How the disorder affects everyday living should also be considered.

- A brief *mental status examination* is conducted in order to gain some insight concerning the person's current overall level of intellectual functioning. This will also provide a first glimpse of the specific memory problems that the person has.

- Many different types of procedures and tests are available to determine the extent of memory loss. These include *memory test batteries, neuropsychological test batteries, brain imaging techniques, questionnaire assessments,* and *specific assessment scales.*

### III. Dissociative Disorders of Memory

- *Dissociative disorders* involve a drastic and sudden change in personality and a loss of personal identity. The three major dissociative disorders are *psychogenic amnesia, psychogenic fugue,* and *multiple personality.* They are believed to occur when an individual cannot cope with some extremely stressful or traumatic personal event(s).

### IV. Organic Disorders of Memory

- *Organic disorders* of memory involve physiological damage to the central nervous system (the brain, in particular). Although usually not a problem, it is sometimes not easy to distinguish a dissociative memory disorder from an organic one.

- People recovering from a head injury resulting in a loss of consciousness often experience *posttraumatic amnesia* (PTA). These people experience confusion, disorientation, and bouts of both *retrograde amnesia* (RA) and *anterograde amnesia* (AA). For most people the PTA clears in a short period of time, but it can last for years in certain cases.

- The *classic amnesia syndrome,* in which there are episodes of RA and AA, occurs when there is bilateral damage to either the *medial temporal lobes* (especially the *hippocampus* and the *amygdala*) or the *diencephalon region* (especially the *mammillary bodies* and the *dorsomedial thalamic nuclei*).

- The RA gradually shrinks as time passes, but only up to a certain point. The AA does not improve with time. Immediate memory, as well as linguistic and general intellectual abilities, is basically normal. Memory deficits are most noticeable when the person is tested for conscious recollection of events or information presented after the onset of the amnesia.
- It is currently being debated whether or not the amnesia that occurs from medial temporal lobe damage is qualitatively different from that which occurs following diencephalic damage.
- People with the classic amnesia syndrome can learn and remember certain things (such as *perceptual-motor skills*) or later show the influence of certain procedures (such as *priming*). Some researchers have suggested that these individuals can no longer process and remember *declarative knowledge* but can handle *nondeclarative knowledge*. Others have suggested that a better way to capture the distinction between what is preserved and what is not is to propose that *explicit memory processing* is greatly disrupted but that *implicit memory processing* is still intact. However, neither dichotomy can adequately account for the complex pattern of memory abilities and disabilities of people with the classic amnesia syndrome.

- *Transient global amnesia* (TGA) occurs suddenly and results in a brief period of RA and AA. TGA may be caused by a temporary lack of blood to regions of the brain important for memory functioning. After the TGA attack, all memory functioning is restored. Memory for what transpired during the TGA episode is not recovered.

- Localized or focal brain damage can give rise to a large variety of specific memory disorders. These include *agnosias* (perceptual disorders), *aphasias* (language problems), and *apraxias* (problems with voluntary movement).

- *Korsakoff's syndrome* (KS), usually resulting from chronic alcoholism, is characterized by a major loss of recent memory and extensive remote memory loss. This is the most widely studied type of diencephalon amnesia. Yet it is not an example of a "pure" diencephalon disorder, because it is highly likely that there is also damage to other brain areas, especially the frontal lobes.

- *Dementia* is a deterioration of all mental abilities, and *Alzheimer's disease* (AD) is the most common type. Failure of recent memory is one of the first behavioral signs of the illness. Eventually, along with all other intellectual skills, immediate and remote memories also deteriorate.
  - The etiology of AD is not known, although there are several possible candidates. It is a fatal disorder marked by shrinkage of the brain, degeneration of the hippocampus and the frontal and temporal lobes, and a huge loss of acetylcholine-secreting neurons. AD is increasing in frequency owing to the aging of the population.

# 15

# *Memory Improvement*

❖

Memory experts have been astounding us with their feats for millennia. Undoubtedly, the best known of these early memory feats was accomplished by the Greek poet Simonides in 477 B.C. One day while Simonides was attending a large banquet, the roof of the building suddenly collapsed. Many of the guests perished, and their bodies were so badly damaged that it was impossible to identify them on the basis of their remains. Simonides, however, much to everyone's surprise, could correctly identify all the guests who had died. He could do this because earlier, before the roof gave way, he had paid attention to where each guest was sitting during the feast. When later asked to recall those present, he imagined all the seats around the banquet table, and each image of a seat enabled him to recall who had been sitting there. In other words, he used the *method of loci* to improve his memory, a technique that we have already described several times in this book.

It seems that people have always been interested in discovering ways to improve their memory performance. As was mentioned in the first chapter, some of the earliest written documents about memory were concerned primarily with practical ways to improve it. For example, it was already known by the sixth century B.C. that memory could be facilitated by means of rehearsal. Today, because there is still widespread interest in improving memory, commercial memory-improvement ventures in the form of books and courses have proliferated (e.g., Bellezza, 1982; Herrmann, 1991; Higbee, 1988; Lorayne & Lucas, 1974; West, 1985). In fact, many of you may have seen half-hour television "shows" (which are actually half-hour commercials) hyping these memory-improvement methods.

## MNEMONIC TECHNIQUES

The term *mnemonics* (discussed briefly in Chapter 13) refers to the use of internal strategies or methods to make it easier to encode, store, and/or retrieve information. Successful mnemonic techniques can be either visual or verbal in nature, and they often have several characteristics in common. For instance, the techniques often will focus attention on the attributes of the material to be remembered. Increasing attention to details can be a powerful way to improve memory. Mnemonic techniques also require increased effort on the part of the memorizer, and we already know that increasing the effort expended in a memory task usually results in better memory performance. Another common feature of effective mnemonic techniques is that the material to be remembered is organized in a way that makes it more meaningful to the person. For example, the person may elaborate on the material in some fashion or associate the material to be learned with material already stored in LTM. Let's look at some specific examples, some of which (especially those described in the next section) will probably already be familiar to you.

## Naive Mnemonics

An immense array of different mnemonic techniques have been discovered over the centuries. Many of these techniques can be called *naive mnemonics,* not because they are unsophisticated but because people naturally make use of them even without formal training or instruction (Bellezza, 1982). Examples of naive mnemonics include engaging in simple *rehearsal* or repetition (repeating a telephone number over and over until you dial it, keeping the information from fading from STM), using *rhymes* ("Thirty days hath September . . ." or "*i* before *e* except after *c*"), *chunking* items together (given an unstructured list of words, remembering all the fruit names as a cluster), and forming *images* to link items (if you want to remember to pick up your shirt at the cleaner's and to purchase some milk, form an image of carrying a milk bottle in your shirt pocket).

A major type of naive mnemonics is called the *first-letter mnemonic.* This memory aid involves using the first letter of each of the items to be remembered. The most common examples of the first-letter mnemonic technique are *acronyms* and *acrostics.* An *acronym* is a word that is composed of all the first letters of the items to be memorized. For instance, the word *HOMES* is frequently used as an acronym to remember the names of the Great Lakes: *H*uron, *O*ntario, *M*ichigan, *E*rie, and *S*uperior. An *acrostic* is a series of words, names, or lines (in a script or poem), the first letters of which are used to remind a person of something. Many a medical student has memorized the acrostic "*O*n *o*ld *O*lympus' *t*owering *t*op, *a* *F*inn *a*nd *G*erman *v*iewed *s*ome *h*ops" to learn the 12 cranial nerves (olfactory, optic, oculomotor, trochlear, trigeminal, abducens, facial, auditory, glossopharyngeal, vagus, spinal accessory, and hypoglossal).

Thousands of different acronyms and acrostics have been developed. An acronym that many beginning music students learn is *FACE,* which is useful for remembering the notes between the lines (F, A, C, and E). A common music acrostic is the sentence "*E*very *G*ood *B*oy *D*oes *F*ine." This helps a person to remember the notes (E, G, B, D, and F) on the lines in the treble clef.

"WHEN YOU'RE YOUNG, IT COMES NATURALLY, BUT WHEN YOU GET A LITTLE OLDER, YOU HAVE TO RELY ON MNEMONICS."

FIGURE 15.1
It seems that everyone has trouble remembering sometimes.
© *1978 by Sidney Harris—American Scientist Magazine.*

Sometimes people are formally instructed in the use of naive mnemonics or are taught to use specific examples of a class of naive mnemonics (such as the rhyme relating the number of days in each month). However, these mnemonics should still be considered naive ones, because even if there were no instructions given to use them, many people would still spontaneously develop such techniques, using their own self-generated examples.

## Technical Mnemonics

Unlike naive mnemonics, *technical mnemonics* are not spontaneously used by most people. The name is derived from the fact that these mnemonic techniques cannot be used until a person has first committed to memory certain *technical* information (Bellezza, 1982). This information is often a particular encoding scheme that is used to transform the to-be-learned information into another representational format. For example, the *method of loci* is considered a technical mnemonic because it requires a person to first commit to memory a physical expanse with distinct locations (e.g., a public park with water fountains, swings, a petting zoo, a baseball field, and so forth), which will later be used as a scheme for encoding information into memory.

There are many different types of technical mnemonics. One major class of these mnemonics is called *peg systems* because a person learns to use mental hooks, or pegs, on which to "hang" items to be remembered (Higbee, 1988). One widely known peg system is called the *peg-word* technique. This procedure teaches a person how to remember a list of items in order by first having the person learn a rhyme that associates a series of concrete nouns with the digits 1 to 10 (see Table 15.1).

After the rhyme is mastered, the person is instructed to form a vivid visual association between the first item to be remembered and the first peg word. For example, suppose you are going grocery shopping and you want to buy pistachio ice cream, oranges, and grape jelly. To remember the pistachio ice cream, recall the first line of the rhyme ("one is a bun"), and then form a vivid image associating a *bun* with the ice cream. For instance, you might picture in your mind a hot dog bun that is oozing green ice cream. To remember the oranges and the grape jelly, recall the second and third lines of the rhyme, retrieve the words *shoe* and *tree*, and then form vivid images associating these nouns with oranges and grape jelly, respectively. To later retrieve all three items on the shopping list in order, recall the first three lines of the rhyme, and you will remember the peg words and the items associated with them.

Another class of technical mnemonics is *translation schemes.* Probably the best-known translation scheme is the *number-letter mnemonic* (Higbee, 1988; Loisette, 1896). To use this mnemonic, a person must learn to associate each of the digits from 0 to 9 with a particular consonant sound. For example, the digit *1* has often been associated with the sound of the letter *t* because 1 and *t* are similar in shape, and the digit *3* has been associated with the sound of the letter *m*, which can be visualized as a 3 on its side. By adding vowels, which do not stand for any number, this system can be used to create peg words that can be used in the same manner as was described earlier. For instance, the peg word *tie* can be associated with the digit *1*, and the word *team* can represent the number *13*. Thus the number-letter mnemonic makes it relatively easy to code any number into a more meaningful word. Suppose you want to remember the digits 9 (associated with the consonant *p*, which is like a mirror image of

**TABLE 15.1** A COMMON PEG-WORD RHYME USING THE DIGITS *1* TO *10*

| | | |
|---|---|---|
| One is a bun | Five is a hive | Eight is gate |
| Two is a shoe | Six is sticks | Nine is line |
| Three is a tree | Seven is heaven | Ten is hen |
| Four is a door | | |

9), *1*, *3*, and *2* (associated with the letter *n*, which has two downstrokes). By adding vowels, you can create the name *Petman*, which will help you remember the number *9132*. In everyday life, we all need to remember strings of relatively random digits, such as social security numbers, telephone numbers, and combinations to locks. Using translation schemes can make remembering such numbers much easier.

Other popular technical mnemonics include the *link* and *story mnemonics* (Higbee, 1988). Briefly, the link system involves forming a visual image of each item to be learned and then visualizing a link between each successive item. In other words, the first item will be visually linked to the second, the second will be linked to the third, the third to the fourth, and so on throughout the list. According to the link system, if a person has formed visual associations between the items that are sufficiently vivid, then by recalling the image of the first item, the person will recall all the subsequent items in order. The story mnemonic is similar to the link system, but instead of using visual associations to connect the items, a person uses sentences that form a story (the sentences make use of all the items to be remembered).

**Are technical mnemonics really helpful?** With some notable exceptions (e.g., Herrmann, 1991), memory-improvement programs typically emphasize the use of technical mnemonics to aid memory performance. It is true that research has shown that using techniques such as the *method of loci, peg systems, translation schemes, link systems,* and *story mnemonics* can dramatically increase a person's ability to remember lists of words or objects (Bower, 1970; Higbee, 1988; McDaniel & Pressley, 1987). No one will deny that these types of technical mnemonics can work. Furthermore, these types of internal memory aids almost always account for how professional memory experts perform their remarkable feats on stage. Therefore, it may surprise you to learn that we *don't recommend* that you immediately start learning such techniques!

Why do we say this? First of all, most popular books and memory courses give the general impression that at least one of these methods can be employed for almost any memory task. This is not true. For example, it has been repeatedly observed that technical mnemonics are not readily applied to learning complex material such as poems or stories. They also don't help people to remember physical sequences, such as the physical movements performed by dancers, figure skaters, or gymnasts or the complex fingering required of musicians. In addition, research has also shown that these methods have limited usefulness for many everyday memory tasks. After all, rarely do people have to memorize long lists of unrelated words or objects (and in correct order). Even when people have a long list of items to remember, such as a huge grocery list for food needed to prepare a Thanksgiving Day dinner for a large gathering, they prefer to use simpler methods to keep track of the items (e.g., writing them down on paper). This illustrates an additional problem with most of the technical mnemonics—they usually require considerable effort to use, more effort than most people are willing to devote.

Two studies have investigated the memory strategies that people actually reported using in everyday life (Harris, 1980; Intons-Peterson & Fournier, 1986). In both studies, it was found that people hardly ever reported using internal memory strategies that required any formal prior training (i.e., technical mnemonics). It was found that people were much more likely to use *external* memory aids such as lists written down on paper and calendars on which the dates of appointments were marked. This does not mean that people don't use general, internal strategies to aid memory. They do, but these strategies are much more likely to be the naive mnemonics (e.g., rehearsal, chunking, or the formation of acronyms).

Perhaps technical mnemonics are not more popular for everyday use because most people don't know what they are or how to use them. If this is part of the reason for their lack of popularity, then we should find increased use of these techniques among people who are personally aware of their effectiveness. This hypothesis was explored by Park, Smith, and Cavanaugh (1990). In their study, they examined the self-reported use of memory strategies by psychologists who were memory researchers, psychologists who were not memory experts, and other professors who were not psychologists. The results were very revealing: memory researchers who were familiar with the use and effectiveness of technical mnemonics were *no more* likely to choose to use them than were other groups of highly educated people. In addition, all three groups of subjects reported that they rarely would use such techniques, that these techniques would be the ones that they would be *least* likely to recommend to others, and that their major memory aids were external aids and general internal strategies like rehearsal and better organization of the material to be remembered.

Most telling of all, and the most damaging for those who continue to promote the learning of technical mnemonics, are those studies that have investigated the memory strategies people choose to use *after* having been specifically trained to use technical mnemonics. These people are often well motivated to continue to use these techniques either because they have paid money to learn them or because they are people (often elderly) who have memory problems that they wish to correct. The results have been pretty consistent: after the initial training period is over, the people simply do not continue to use the techniques they learned in daily life (Bellezza, 1983; Higbee, 1988; Lapp, 1983; Roberts, 1983; Wood & Pratt, 1987). Why is this true? Because even in situations where the technical mnemonics would be appropriate to use (e.g., grocery shopping), the effort involved in using the techniques is too great or time-consuming. There are much less taxing ways to remember things—in particular, by using external memory aids. Think of it this way: Why would you want to use a peg system to remember 23 grocery items when it is so much easier to write them down on paper? In addition, after shopping you can just toss the paper away, since you no longer need or wish to remember the items. But can you just as easily "toss" away the 23 visual associations you made to memorize the list in the first place?

**When are technical mnemonics useful?** We are not declaring that technical mnemonics should play no role in learning or in memory improvement. It is our view that it *is* worthwhile to learn certain technical mnemonics, but only when they are particularly well suited for use and don't involve too great an investment in time or energy. Let's consider two examples, one concerned with the learning of foreign vocabulary words and the other involving how to quickly determine on what day of the week a particular date occurs.

*The Linkword Language System.* Some researchers have convincingly argued that one reason why technical mnemonics are rarely used, even by people who have learned how to use them, is that people have not been properly taught *when* to use them (e.g., Gruneberg, 1992). The point was previously made that technical mnemonics, even when they can be shown to be very effective, are not practical to use in many situations (look back at our question about using a peg system to remember 23 grocery items). Nevertheless, in some memory situations they may be highly appropriate and useful. An excellent case in point is the learning of foreign language vocabulary.

It has long been suggested that the use of imagery mnemonics can help people learn and remember foreign languages (Bacon, 1862; Loisette, 1896; Raugh & Atkinson, 1975). But the person who has been most responsible for promoting the use of imagery-based technical mnemonics to learn new foreign language words is Michael Gruneberg, who is a psychologist at the University College of Swansea in Wales (Gruneberg, 1985, 1987, 1992). Gruneberg has published a series of books and tapes in which he uses what he calls the *Linkword Language System.* Essentially, this system involves having people imagine an English word interacting with a foreign word that sounds like another English word. The idea is that when the words are linked with an image, the image will become a powerful retrieval cue for later recalling the two words. Try the following four examples from Gruneberg's books, allowing yourself to spend about 10 seconds considering each image before going on to the next:

The French for TABLECLOTH is NAPPE
Imagine having a NAP on a TABLECLOTH

The Italian for FLY is MOSCA
Imagine FLIES invading MOSCOW

The Spanish for SUITCASE is MALETA
Imagine MY LETTER in your SUITCASE

The German for LETTER is BRIEF
Imagine a BRIEF LETTER

Can you recall the Spanish word for suitcase or the French word for tablecloth? People who have tried the Linkword Language System (including one of your authors, who brushed up on his German) usually attest to its great effectiveness. Each book, and there are Linkword books available for learning French, Italian, Spanish, German, Greek, and Portuguese at this point, can be supplemented with a cassette tape that provides the proper pronunciation of each foreign word. The success of this technique underscores the fact that technical mnemonics can be highly effective in special situations. Let's consider another example, one that deals with calendar dates.

*A technical mnemonic for memorizing the calendar.* A simple technical mnemonic can be taught to people so that they never need to look at a calendar to determine on what day of the week a particular date occurs (Higbee, 1988). There are two parts to this mnemonic. The first is knowing which months have 31 days. As some of you may already know, you can determine this by counting the knuckles and valleys on your fists (thumbs don't count). As you can see in Figure 15.2, if you start with the knuckle on your left hand's littlest finger, this can represent the month of January. The valley between this finger and the next represents February, the next knuckle represents March, and so forth, until you finally reach the knuckle of the ring finger of your right hand (representing December). The months associated with a knuckle all have 31 days, while the "valley" months always have fewer than 31 days.

In order to fully memorize the calendar, you also need to commit to memory a 12-digit number and learn to associate each of the digits with a particular month of the year. This is essentially a peg system, one that is very easy to learn and use. The number you need to memorize for the 1994 calendar is 266-315-374-264. Each of these digits represents the date of the first Sunday in one of the 12 months of the year (see Table 15.2).

Once you have mastered this digit-month association, you can find the day of the week for any date by simply being able to add or subtract up to 7. For instance, on what day of the week will Christmas be in 1994? To answer this question you need to know that Christmas is always on December 25, and you need to remember that the first Sunday in December will be on the fourth. Knowing this, all you need to do is add 7 to get the date of the second Sunday (December 11), then add 7 again to get the date of the third Sunday (December 18), and finally add 7 more days, and you find that Christmas will be on Sunday in 1994. Suppose you want to know what day of the week your federal taxes will be due (April 15). If you know that the first Sunday in April will be on the third, then by adding 7 you know that the tenth will be a Sunday; therefore, your taxes will be due on a Friday. Try this one: Are there any months in 1994

**TABLE 15.2** DATE OF FIRST SUNDAY IN EACH MONTH FOR 1994

| | | | |
|---|---|---|---|
| January—2 | April—3 | July—3 | October—2 |
| February—6 | May—1 | August—7 | November—6 |
| March—6 | June—5 | September—4 | December—4 |

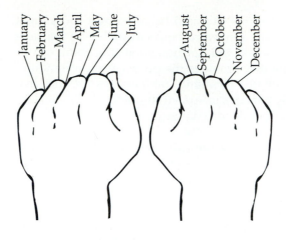

FIGURE 15.2
Months associated with knuckles have 31 days, and months associated with valleys do not.

in which there is a Friday the 13th? A little bit of thought (or looking at Table 15.2!) should convince you that Friday the 13th will occur only in months in which the first day is a Sunday (the month of May). The beauty of this technical mnemonic is that by learning a new 12-digit number each year (which shouldn't take more than a minute or two of your time), you can effectively memorize the entire 365-day calendar (and impress your friends and relatives as a bonus).

# EXTERNAL MEMORY AIDS

External memory aids are so ubiquitous that many of us don't fully appreciate how often we depend on them. For example, this morning a buzzer on your clock radio may have awakened you, helping you to remember to get up early to do some extra studying. If your clock radio has a "snooze button," you may have fallen back to sleep for a few more precious minutes, confident that you would soon be reminded again to get up. As you started to get dressed, you heard the whistle of the teakettle informing you that it was time to turn off the heat. The microwave oven "dinged" to indicate that you should now stir your oatmeal and then put it back in for one more minute. During breakfast, you scanned your appointment book or calendar to see the activities scheduled for today. A conspicuously placed *Post-it* note informed you of the items you need to purchase at the store. You set your watch to "beep" every four hours so that you won't forget to take some needed medication. Before leaving, you programmed the VCR so that you won't forget to tape your favorite television show. As you left the house, you grabbed your umbrella because you were clever enough to place it on the knob of your front door last night after hearing the weather forecaster predicted rain for the next day. Finally, you had to scamper across the grass because the automatic outdoor sprinkler had come on for 20 minutes, and you were thankful that you were relieved of the responsibility of having to remember to turn the sprinkler on and off, every morning and evening, during the hot weather.

During the last 10 to 15 years it has become increasingly apparent to memory researchers that external memory aids play a primary role in helping people to supplement their memories (Cavanaugh, Grady, & Perlmutter, 1983; Harris, 1978, 1980; Herrmann & Petro, 1990; Intons-Peterson & Fournier, 1986; Intons-Peterson & Newsome, 1992; Park et al., 1990; West, 1990). Some researchers have suggested that using external memory aids might result in the diminishment of a person's memory skills because these aids relieve the user of the need to develop such skills (Estes, 1980; Herrmann & Chaffin, 1988). On the other hand, it has also been suggested that using external memory aids might make people more aware of their memory abilities and limitations, thereby allowing them to use their memory capabilities more wisely. However, there are virtually no available data about how the use or disuse of these memory aids actually influences memory skill (if at all). We do know that to effectively use external memory aids, a person must first be aware that such aids are even needed; then he or she must be able to select an appropriate aid for the task at hand; finally, the individual must remember how to use the aid properly (Intons-Peterson & Newsome, 1992). In the next several sections we will briefly examine the major types of external memory aids. These can be classified as *noncommercial memory aids, commercial memory aids, reminding services,* and *external knowledge sources.*

## Noncommercial Memory Aids

There are many different kinds of noncommercial memory aids that people use. Some of these aids, which are mundane objects, are effective because people have devised novel uses for them. For instance, some people will place their wastebasket on the seat of their favorite chair as a reminder to do something important. By placing the wastebasket in such a conspicuous and inconvenient location, the person will focus attention on it (and, it is hoped, on the task it represents) whenever he or she is in the room.

Some people develop weird, idiosyncratic memory aids. For example, one of your authors is acquainted with a person who would put several coins in his mouth to remind himself to attend to important tasks. After completing each task, he would remove a coin. Although certainly strange, this strategy worked for this individual. Sometimes people develop superstitions that certain objects have a power to influence memory. They usually justify such beliefs on the grounds that these objects have brought them good luck on past memory tasks. For instance, some students will wear a special article of clothing to all major exams, use only a certain pen, or sit in a particular seat because they did especially well in the past while wearing or using these items. Before you scoff too much, keep in mind that there may be some validity to using superstitious memory aids. These aids may facilitate memory performance if they can elicit the same mental or emotional state while the person is taking the exam that was present during initial learning. This would be an example of state-dependent memory or mood congruence (discussed in Chapter 8).

There are many common noncommercial memory aids that almost everyone uses at least some of the time (such as calendars, appointment books, notes to yourself, and lists of things to do or buy). A favorite, it seems, especially among college students, is writing on your hand. Table 15.3 presents a number of examples of common noncommercial memory aids. Many of these are well-known symbolic reminders (such as a string tied around your finger). One problem with using such symbolic reminders is that all they do is remind you to do *something*; they often don't tell you *what* that something is. Still, using symbolic reminders works well for many people, and so they are among the most popular of external memory aids.

## Commercial Memory Aids

A commercial memory aid is a product that was specifically designed by the manufacturer to help a person with memory tasks. An example of such a device would be a pillbox that rings an alarm at specified times to remind a person to

**TABLE 15.3** SOME EXAMPLES OF NONCOMMERCIAL MEMORY AIDS

Asking someone to remind you

Bulletin boards

Calendars

Cue cards

A deliberate change in your routine

Diaries

Keeping records

Labeling to indicate that something was used

Labeling to organize

Mementos

Objects or notes put in special or unusual places

Shopping lists

Switching your ring or watch to the other hand or turning it over

Switching your wallet to another pocket

A string tied around your finger

A rubber band worn on your wrist

Wearing unusual clothes or accessories

Writing on your hand

SOURCE: Based on Harris (1980), Herrmann & Petro (1990), and Intons-Peterson & Fournier (1986).

take some prescribed medicine. Commercial memory aids have great potential for helping people with neurological problems (Fowler, Hart, & Sheehan, 1972; Jones & Adams, 1979; Klein & Fowler, 1981; Kurlychek, 1983; Naugle, Prevey, Naugle, & Delaney, 1988; Wilson, 1987; Wilson & Moffat, 1984), for helping the elderly who have memory deficits (Cavanaugh et al., 1983; McEvoy & Moon, 1988), and for helping normal people who want to improve their efficiency in specific memory tasks (Baddeley, 1982).

Herrmann and Petro (1990) have identified three different types of commercial memory aids. They labeled one type a *memory prosthetic* because its job is to facilitate memory performance. Examples would be the pillbox with the attached alarm and a parts cabinet that organizes nuts and bolts to facilitate subsequent retrieval. The second type of commercial memory aid was called a *memory corrector*. As you can guess, this device corrects memory errors. An example would be a credit-card holder that signals if a credit card is not replaced after a short period of time. They referred to the third type of commercial memory aid as a *memory robot* because this device performs memory tasks for the owner. A telephone that stores all your important numbers and that will dial any of them at the touch of a button would be considered a memory robot. The majority of currently available commercial memory aids are memory prosthetics.

It was also discovered that many items that at first blush appeared to be commercial memory aids turned out, on closer inspection, not to be (Herrmann & Petro, 1990). These items were instead called *memory-friendly products*. The major difference between a commercial memory aid and a memory-friendly product is that the primary function of a commercial memory aid is to aid memory, whereas aiding memory is only a secondary purpose of a memory-friendly product. For example, many calculators have a secondary function of reducing a person's need to use STM while performing complicated calculations. However, the primary function of a calculator is to calculate, so a calculator would be considered a memory-friendly device but not a commercial memory aid.

Table 15.4 presents many examples of commercial memory aids. As you can see, most of the aids are designed for a specific kind of memory task. Even the most general of devices (like an alarm clock) are limited to certain kinds of memory tasks. For instance, although an alarm can be used in many situations as a reminder, it would be useless as an aid to help a person remember how to tell a good joke. This task specificity of commercial memory aids, however, is quite consistent with the growing realization that memory processes are often task- and domain-specific (e.g., Baddeley, 1982; Chase & Ericsson, 1982; Davies & Thomson, 1988).

How well do commercial memory aids work? Unfortunately, research has not kept pace with the proliferation of these products. Most of the psychological research on memory improvement has focused on naive and technical mnemonics, and so very little is known about the effectiveness of commercial

**TABLE 15.4** SOME EXAMPLES OF COMMERCIAL MEMORY AIDS

**Shopping:**
Remembering to purchase certain items—shopping pads, memo stickers

**Dieting:**
Remembering what you have eaten—food-intake checklists, tables of caloric values of foods

Remembering what your weight has been—computerized scales with memory

**Keeping fit:**
Remembering how much you exercised—bicycle computers, pedometers

**Maintaining health:**
Remembering to take medication—organized pillboxes (with slots for the days of the week or times of the day), pillboxes with alarms

**Using the telephone:**
Remembering phone numbers—dialers (which automatically dial a number recorded in the dialer system), phones with redialing functions that remember the last number dialed, phone conversation recorders, telephone indexes

**Keeping track of possessions:**
Remembering object location—beeping key chains, desk organizers, eyeglass holders, sewing box, tackle box, tie and belt organizers

**Meeting obligations:**
Remembering to do things at a certain time—alarm systems, date books, card files, calendars

**Keeping track of finances:**
Remembering to pay bills—automatic bank payment systems, bill organizer, budget planners

**Traveling:**
Remembering to take everything you need—business materials kit, personal grooming kit

Remembering foreign languages—phrase books, translator calculators

Remembering currency rate of exchange—exchange-rate calculator

SOURCE: Adapted from Herrmann & Petro (1990).

memory aids (Herrmann & Petro, 1990; Intons-Peterson & Newsome, 1992). Much of what we do know has come only from anecdotal accounts made by consumers. It should not be assumed that commercial aids, perhaps because of their greater reliance on technology, are likely to be superior to noncommercial aids. For instance, key chains are available that beep when you clap your hands. For people who have a continual problem of forgetting where they left their keys, a beeping key chain can be a very useful device. However, these key chains have a nasty habit of beeping when random sounds are made (like from the radio or television), forcing people to retrieve them to shut off the beeper. This defect has so annoyed some people that they now refuse to use the key chain at all.

Many watches that sound alarms have also been criticized; they are said to be too hard for head-injured (or even normal) adults to use (Naugle et al., 1988; Wilson, 1987). For instance, the procedure for *setting* the alarm can be so complicated that many people will forgo the "convenience." Moreover, while evidence suggests that active reminders are better than passive ones (Harris, 1980), the number of active remindings that a person can handle in a day is probably limited. Buzzers frequently going off are bothersome and distracting, especially if you are trying to appreciate a musical concert or listen to an interesting lecture. Knowing the annoyance that some people experience when hearing such buzzers go off unexpectedly, many people (we are thankful) turn off their alarm watches when in a crowded situation. Of course, these people then run the risk of forgetting to do whatever the buzzer was supposed to remind them to do in the first place!

Certainly, noncommercial memory aids will continue to be used, for they work, are handy, and often cost far less than commercial aids. Nevertheless, it is likely that commercial aids will become more common in the future, particularly if their design takes account of our increasing knowledge of how the environment affects memory processing (see Chapter 9). More empirical research into the effectiveness of both commercial and noncommercial memory aids is definitely needed.

## Reminding Services

Many business executives have often relied on their secretaries to remind them of important business and personal obligations. Now there's even a company in Massachusetts that has a program called *The Reminders Club*. Its singular purpose is to remind people (for a fee, of course) about special occasions in their personal lives. Clients of this program supply the company with lists containing dates of birthdays, weddings, anniversaries, graduation days, and so on. Several days before an important occasion, the company will contact the individual to remind him or her about the upcoming obligation. This is an example of another type of external memory aid known as a *reminding service.* Such a service uses either the telephone or the mails to give its clients information about upcoming meetings, appointments, or obligations.

Many health providers (such as dentists and physicians) have their secretaries mail postcards or make phone calls to remind patients of their appointments. One review of the medical literature found that the compliance rate for keeping appointments was 10 to 20 percent higher for those patients who received telephone or mail reminders than for patients who did not receive such reminders (Levy & Loftus, 1984). However, since many reminding services involve social interaction over a telephone, it's unclear how much the service actually aids memory. A personal reminder may simply increase someone's motivation to keep an appointment already remembered.

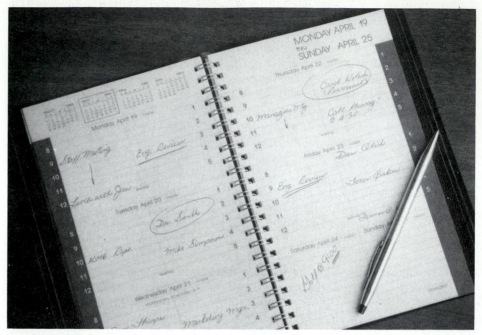

**FIGURE 15.3**
A common external memory aid used by busy people.

## External Knowledge Sources

*External knowledge sources* are the final type of external memory aid we will discuss. These are sources that contain information that you may have known at one time but have now forgotten, or they may contain information that you never knew. A dictionary is an excellent example of an external knowledge source. It can supplement a faulty memory (e.g., by reminding you how to spell the French word for appetizer, *hors d'oeuvre*), and it can also teach you the spelling and meaning of words that are new to you. There are many other external knowledge sources, such as reference books, thesauri, instructional videotapes, photographs, phone books, Rolodexes, books of quotations, business card files, and personal files (Hertel, 1988).

The external knowledge source that perhaps has the greatest potential for aiding memory is the personal computer. PCs are relatively inexpensive devices; they are widely available, can be used whenever a person so desires, and can provide an almost unlimited amount of information on any topic. While personal computers are able to provide information and memory prompts for normal people, it has also been demonstrated, as was briefly mentioned in the last chapter, that individuals with memory impairments can also profit from their use (e.g., Glisky & Schacter, 1987, 1988, 1989; Glisky, Schacter, & Tulving, 1986; Kirsch, Levine, Fallon-Kreuger, & Jaros, 1987). The use of personal computers to aid the memory of both normal and brain-injured people shows great promise.

# THE NEW APPROACH TO MEMORY IMPROVEMENT

So far, this chapter has described how naive mnemonics, technical mnemonics, and external memory aids have been used to facilitate memory processes. While these techniques and devices certainly have a role to play in memory-improvement programs, in recent years researchers and practitioners from a variety of backgrounds (e.g., psychologists, psychiatrists, gerontologists, speech pathologists, and physicians) have sought new ways to improve memory (Herrmann & Searleman, 1990; Herrmann, Weingartner, Searleman, & McEvoy, 1992).

## Content-Specific Memory Techniques

Part of this new approach involves employing new methods to mentally manipulate the information to be learned. In particular, this approach emphasizes the use of very content-specific techniques. As we have commented before, this makes good sense, since it is known that memory is often domain-specific. In other words, the memory skills to be taught should greatly depend on the nature of the specific memory task. An example of a content-specific technique is the *face-name imagery technique*, which helps people learn the names of individuals they meet. This technique requires a person to first transform someone's name into a concrete object. Having done so, the person now imagines this object and then mentally locates it somewhere on the other person's face.

Suppose you meet a Ms. Quackenbush at a party. To remember her name using the face-name imagery technique, think of an object that reminds you of her name. In this case, *Quackenbush* might remind you of Daisy Duck (Donald's girlfriend), because "quack" is the noise a duck makes. Now look for a prominent feature on Ms. Quackenbush's face (perhaps her high cheekbones), and imagine Daisy Duck sitting there waving to you. The next time you see Ms. Quackenbush, you should also see Daisy Duck, and this should remind you of her name. This method can substantially increase a person's ability to associate names with faces (McCarty, 1980; Morris, Jones, & Hampson, 1977; Sheikh, Hill, & Yesavage, 1986).

In Chapters 4 and 5 we discussed several ways to enhance the encoding of information. These included organizing the material to be learned, spacing (or distributing) your practice or study time, using elaborative rehearsal strategies, developing a large knowledge base, overlearning the material, and trying to make the conditions at the time of retrieval match as closely as possible the conditions that were present during encoding (the encoding specificity principle). All of these general procedures or techniques will help students better remember information needed for exams. But there are also some content-specific memory techniques that can help. For example, in terms of note-taking, Herrmann, Raybeck, and Gutman (in press) suggest that right after class, students should go over their notes from the lecture and generate questions about each paragraph or cluster of notes. This helps to reinforce what was said and can help point out quickly any areas of confusion. They also recommend taking notes on your notes. This will serve to condense your knowledge into more manageable pieces.

In his recent book on memory improvement, Herrmann (1991) describes more than 100 task-specific techniques that aid people in solving everyday memory problems. These techniques have been especially recommended for elderly people who often experience difficulty in remembering daily tasks. Examples include using plant alarms to remember when to water plants; singing along with others, which will allow a person to rehearse (and therefore remember) song lyrics; using a computerized spell-checker when possible; feeling the bristles of your toothbrush to tell if you have just brushed your teeth a moment ago; and putting objects that are used often (like car keys) always in the same place when at home. In the next section, we consider another aspect of the new approach to memory improvement.

## A Multimodal Approach

There is a growing awareness that memory performance is affected by many different psychological and physiological processes, or modes. As you already know, memory ability is clearly influenced by how a person mentally transforms material to be learned (e.g., by using mnemonic techniques), and memory is affected by how the physical environment is structured (e.g., by using external aids). However, an individual's memory capability also depends on his or her physiological condition, attitudes toward the memory task, emotional state, and even social skills. This fact has been largely overlooked or neglected until fairly recently (Herrmann & Searleman, 1992). In the next two subsections we will discuss how content-process and condition-process modes affect memory performance.

**Content-process modes.** The *content-process* modes directly affect the way that information is encoded and/or retrieved. These modes include *mental manipulations* of the information, manipulations of the *physical environment,* and manipulations of the *social environment.* Much of this chapter has already been devoted to describing, in some detail, the ways in which mental manipulations and changes in the physical environment can facilitate memory. Therefore, here we will review how social interactions can be structured to aid memory.

In Chapter 10 you learned that people can help themselves to encode or retrieve information in social encounters by using certain conversational skills or ploys. For instance, if you are having trouble remembering information during a conversation, there are ways to give yourself more time to think. One way this can be accomplished is by asking questions that force the other person to respond, thereby slowing the rate of the interchange between the two of you. Or if you can't readily answer a question from memory, an especially useful technique is to deflect the question entirely to a third party. You can also slow a conversation down by overtly reiterating what another has just said.

Conversational skills are primarily taught for social purposes, such as to enhance self-presentation. However, one of your authors has found that training college students in using specific conversational skills can also lead to improved memory performance. In addition, remedial work with brain-injured patients often includes giving specific instructions to the relatives of these people, instructions that describe ways to control the flow of a conversation with a person who has brain damage. And it has been demonstrated that skillful control of the conversational flow can lead to improvement in the patients' memory capabilities (Gervasio, 1988). The influence that social context exerts on memory functioning and performance is likely to be substantial, but only recently have researchers begun to really study this interesting interaction (Best, 1992; Wyer & Srull, 1989).

**Condition-process modes.** Condition-process modes indirectly influence memory functioning by changing the *physical condition* or *emotional state* of the person or by altering a person's *attitude* toward a memory task. The condition-process modes influence a person's overall condition to perform memory tasks without manipulating the content of the material to be learned. These modes primarily affect a person's alertness or motivation, which in turn influences the basic memory processes of encoding, storage, and retrieval. To manipulate memory performance by means of the condition-process modes, it is usually necessary to start *before* the memory task begins. You can prepare by monitoring what you eat, drink, or smoke before the memory task; by using relaxation techniques to improve your emotional state (right before or sometimes during the initial stages of the task); by getting enough sleep and rest; or by trying to foster a more positive or realistic attitude toward performing the memory task. It may be helpful to think of the content-process modes as affecting the "software" of the memory system, while the condition-process modes affect the "hardware."

*Physical condition.* A person's physical condition can affect memory performance, and at least some aspects of physical condition are under voluntary control. For instance, people can strive for a better memory by changing when they eat their meals during the day (Smith, 1988) and by using good eating habits (Logue, 1986; Michaud, Musse, Nicolas, & Mejean, 1991; Wurtman, 1981, 1982) to ensure that vitamins, minerals, and other nutrients are properly absorbed. You learned earlier that ingesting glucose can improve memory, especially in the elderly (Gold, 1987; Manning, Hall, & Gold, 1990). Studies also suggest that consistent exercise improves memory performance (Blomquist &

Danner, 1987; Blumenthal & Madden, 1988; Harma, Illmarinen, Knauth, & Rutenfranz, 1988; Stamford, Hambacher, & Fallica, 1974). A good memory can also be safeguarded by avoiding common substances that may impair memory, such as *alcohol* (Birnbaum & Parker, 1977; Hashtroudi & Parker, 1986); *tobacco* (Peeke & Peeke, 1984; Spilich, 1986); *marijuana* (Block & Wittenborn, 1984; Darley, Tinklenberg, Hollister, & Atkinson, 1973; Lister & Weingartner, 1987; Schwartz, 1991); *coffee,* under some circumstances (Bowyer, Humphrey, & Revelle, 1983; Eysenck & Folkard, 1980); and some *tranquilizers,* such as Valium (Parker & Weingartner, 1984). Furthermore, there's some evidence that people perform better on memory tasks if they don't attempt them right after waking up (Tilley & Statham, 1989).

*Emotional state.* As was reviewed in detail in Chapter 8, there is abundant evidence that one's emotional state can dramatically affect memory performance. Poor encoding and retrieval processes have been associated with negative emotions (Erdelyi & Goldberg, 1979; Matlin & Stang, 1978), very intense emotions (Freud, 1901/1960), situationally induced stress (Peters, 1988; Reason, 1988b), and clinical depression (Ellis & Ashbrook, 1988; Hertel, 1992).

Clinical research has tried to improve memory performance by using treatments that reduce extremes in emotionality or that lead to more positive emotional states. For instance, it is known that medications that alleviate depression are linked to improvements in memory ability (Wolkowitz & Weingartner, 1988). For most people instructions to relax per se don't seem to improve memory performance (Watts, MacLeod, & Morris, 1988), nor does routine practice of meditation or physical relaxation (Yuille & Sereda, 1980). Nevertheless, especially for elderly individuals, memory performance can be improved if training is given in relaxation techniques that can be used during the memory tasks (Yesavage, 1984; Yesavage & Rolf, 1984; Yesavage, Sheikh, Tanke, & Hill, 1988).

*Attitude.* A person's attitude toward a memory task can also greatly affect his or her performance. Attitudes influence a person's disposition to even attempt a memory task and, while the person is involved with the task, the efficiency and nature of responding. From Chapter 8, we learned that people learn more readily if they believe that they are superior at a given task (Rapaport, 1942; Sullivan, 1927); tend to acquire information that protects their ego or that is consistent with self-perceptions (Greenwald, 1980, 1981; Neisser, 1988; Sehulster, 1981a, 1981b, 1988); and are disinclined to perform memory tasks that they deem inappropriate for themselves owing to social stereotypes associated with age (Best, Hamlett, & Davis, 1992) or gender (Crawford, Herrmann, Randall, Holdsworth, & Robbins, 1989; Loftus, Banaji, Schooler, & Foster, 1987). In addition, if people have poor personal knowledge of their own memory abilities (metamemory), they may not approach a particular memory task appropriately when they are compelled to tackle it. For instance, if a child has the (mistaken) attitude that he or she can easily memorize a list of 25 words, then the child will probably not use a memory strategy (such as clustering together similar words to form meaningful chunks) that will increase performance.

Memory performance can definitely be enhanced by changing a person's attitude. For instance, increased self-esteem is correlated with better memory performance in normal children (Pressley, Borkowski, & Schneider, 1987), mentally retarded children (Borkowski, Carr, Rellinger, & Pressley, in press), and learning-disabled children (Zecker, 1988). And correcting stereotypical attitudes about being old has resulted in at least temporary facilitation of memory performance in the elderly (Best et al., 1992). But some people just don't want to make the effort to improve their memory performance (Cavanaugh & Morton, 1988). If only these people could be persuaded to have a more positive attitude toward everyday memory tasks, then probably their memory abilities would improve.

**The future of the multimodal approach.** Very little is known about how the various content-process and condition-process modes interact with each other to influence memory. However, like others, we believe that to fully understand the memory process (and to have the greatest chance to improve memory performance), researchers should devote much more attention to exploring a multimodal approach to memory functioning (Herrmann & Searleman, 1990; Jenkins, 1974; Perlmutter, 1988). The suggestion that memory is influenced by many different psychological and physiological processes, all acting simultaneously, is not really a new idea—more than a hundred years ago similar notions were being advanced (Feinaigle, 1813; Middleton, 1888).

# $S$UMMARY

## I. Mnemonic Techniques

- For thousands of years people have been interested in finding ways to improve memory performance. As evidence of this interest today, there are a multitude of memory-improvement books and courses available to the public.

- *Mnemonic techniques* are internal strategies or methods that are used to make it easier to encode, store, and/or retrieve material.
  - *Naive mnemonics* are strategies that normal people often use spontaneously. There's no need to have formal instruction in their use. Examples include *rehearsal, rhyming, chunking,* forming *mental images,* and using *acronyms* and *acrostics.*
  - *Technical mnemonics* are not spontaneously developed and used by most people. These methods can't be used until a person has first learned certain technical information, such as an encoding scheme. The major types of technical mnemonics are the *method of loci, peg systems, translation schemes, link systems,* and *story mnemonics.*

- Although technical mnemonics certainly work (e.g., the *Linkword Language System*) and can lead to remarkable feats of memory, we do not generally recommend their use. First, these methods are not well suited for handling many everyday memory tasks. Second, technical mnemonics usually require extensive training to use. Finally, most people typically find these techniques so taxing to use that they stop using them shortly after the initial training period is over.

## II. External Memory Aids

- *External memory aids* play a large role in helping people to supplement their memories for everyday tasks and appointments. *Noncommercial* and *commercial* aids are two major types of external memory aids. Although both types of aids are common, very little is known about how they influence, for better or worse, the development of memory skill.

- There are some noncommercial memory aids that almost everyone uses (such as lists, notes, and calendars). Some people use very idiosyncratic aids or develop ones based on superstitions. One problem with using the popular *symbolic reminders* (such as a rubber band worn on your wrist) is that these aids don't remind people of exactly what it is they are to remember.

- Commercial memory aids are products specifically designed to aid memory. The three main types are *memory prosthetics, memory correctors,* and *memory robots.* Most commercial aids are memory prosthetics and are very task-specific. Many products can be classified as being *memory-friendly.* They are not considered to be commercial memory aids, because aiding memory is a secondary purpose, not their primary function.

- A *reminding service* is another type of external memory aid. Its purpose is to remind people in advance about important obligations. Many health providers use reminding services to increase patients' compliance rate for keeping appointments.

- The fourth kind of external memory aid is called *external knowledge sources.* These sources contain information that a person has forgotten or information that a person never knew.

## III. The New Approach to Memory Improvement

- A new approach to memory improvement has been gaining favor in recent years. One aspect of this approach involves very content-specific mental manipulations of the material to be learned, as in the *face-name imagery technique.*

- The second major aspect of the new approach is the assumption that memory ability is affected by many different psychological and physiological processes, or modes. This *multimodal* approach suggests that memory functioning is simultaneously influenced by both *content-process* modes and *condition-process* modes.

- Content-process modes are thought to directly affect the way that information is encoded and/or retrieved. *Mental manipulations of material, manipulations of the physical environment,* and *manipulations of the social environment* are the three content-process modes.
- The condition-process modes indirectly influence memory functioning by affecting a person's alertness or motivation. As the name implies, these modes influence memory functioning by changing a person's *physical condition, emotional state,* or *attitude* toward the memory task.
- Little is currently known about how the content-process and condition-process modes simultaneously interact to influence memory functioning. A multimodal approach is likely to lead to a greater understanding of the memory process and to techniques that maximize memory performance.

# Epilogue

— ❖ —

We had several purposes in mind when we wrote *Memory from a Broader Perspective.* First and foremost, we wanted to present students with the most up-to-date research and theories concerning human memory. And we wanted to do this in a way that would convey the excitement and fascination of the field (you are the best judge as to whether or not we have succeeded in this purpose). Second, because we firmly believe that memory functioning and performance are influenced by a wide assortment of factors, we wanted to write a textbook that reflects this viewpoint. Therefore, this book contains not only the chapters you would expect to find in a traditional memory textbook (such as the chapters "Models of Memory" and "Encoding" but also chapters that have never appeared before in a book about memory that was designed for undergraduates (such as the chapters "Effects of Arousal, Stress, and Emotion" and "Social Interaction and Memory").

Another goal in writing this book was to showcase some of the ways in which memory research has been applied to everyday life, frequently through the use of nontraditional procedures and materials. Too often in the past, in our opinion, memory textbooks failed to present the practical aspects of memory research. The effect was that sometimes students were left wondering how the knowledge they had acquired really applied to their lives. So in this book we emphasized the relevance and importance of memory research.

# Glossary

❖

**Absentmindedness**  When a person intends to do one thing but unintentionally does another.

**Accessibility of a trace**  A trace is said to be accessible if it can be retrieved from memory with suitable retrieval cues. If the trace cannot be retrieved, it is considered to be inaccessible.

**Acetylcholine**  Increased levels of this neurotransmitter are usually associated with higher levels of neural activity and better memory performance.

**Acronym**  A word that is composed of all the first letters of the items to be memorized.

**Acrostic**  A series of words, names, or lines, the first letters of which help a person remember something.

**Action-decrement theory**  This theory assumes that an inhibitory process protects memory traces during the initial stages of memory consolidation. Because of this inhibitory process (which increases with higher levels of arousal), memory traces are supposedly more difficult to retrieve soon after their formation but easier to retrieve after a period of delay.

**Action potential**  An electrical impulse that travels down the axon at full force until it reaches the ends of the axon branches.

**Adrenaline (epinephrine)**  A hormone that in small doses may enhance memory.

**Adrenocorticotrophic hormone (ACTH)**  A hormone produced by the adrenal glands that in small doses may enhance memory.

**Agnosia**  An inability, due to brain damage, to recognize sensory stimuli.

**Alzheimer's disease**  A fatal form of dementia in which memory loss is a prominent initial feature.

**Amphetamine**  A stimulant that in the proper dosage may enhance learning and memory, especially when fatigue is present.

**Amygdala**  A structure within the medial temporal regions that is involved in the consolidation of declarative-type memories.

**Antecedent variables**  Independent variables that can alter a person's typical organismic level.

**Anterograde amnesia**  The inability to consolidate and remember new things.

**Aphasia**  A difficulty, due to brain damage, in expressing and/or understanding spoken or written language.

**Aplysia californica**  A sea snail which has been extensively studied and about which much is known concerning the neural and chemical bases of simple forms of learning (such as habituation and sensitization).

**Apraxia**  An inability, due to brain damage, to perform purposeful movements in the absence of paralysis.

**Arousal hypothesis of memory consolidation**  This hypothesis maintains that the amount of memory consolidation that occurs in a given situation is related to the degree of neural activity in certain brain areas immediately after learning. In general, the higher the level of neural activity, the more memory consolidation.

**Articulatory control process**  This theorized component of the phonological loop can supposedly refresh the acoustic memory trace and can transform written language into a phonological code for storage in the phonological store.

**Associationism/connectionism** The theoretical perspective that learning and memory involve the formation and storage of associations between items.

**Attention** The process of orienting to and/or observing the environment or the contents of working memory.

**Autistic savant** A person who demonstrates extraordinary ability in some area but who also suffers from autism.

**Autobiographical memory** Memory for the events of one's life.

**Availability heuristic** A strategy for judging the frequency of an event on the basis of how quickly or easily instances of the event can be remembered.

**Availability of a trace** Status of whether or not a trace is in memory.

**Axon** Neuronal fiber that transmits the action potential.

**B-endorphin** A natural opiate that is released in times of stress or pain and that generally impairs memory by inhibiting the release of norepinephrine in the amygdala.

**Backward-retrieval strategy** A procedure used to search autobiographical memory that involves starting with the most recent memories.

**Benzodiazepines (BZs)** Widely prescribed drugs that are used to treat a variety of ailments and that also impair a person's ability to encode new information.

**Bottom-up processing (data-driven)** This approach to processing information emphasizes the perceptual appearance of stimuli and does not involve the use of prior knowledge and expectations.

**Broca's aphasia** A person with this disorder has great difficulty in articulating words.

**Brown-Peterson Distractor Technique** Demonstrates how long unrehearsed information can remain in STM. After a stimulus is presented, the subject typically must count backward from some arbitrary number for a period of time. Afterward, the subject usually has great difficulty recalling the original stimulus because the counting eliminated effective rehearsal.

**Cell assemblies (neural nets)** Groups of interconnected neurons hypothesized to retain memories or to store knowledge. (See also *Macrocolumn*.)

**Cell body** A part of the neuron that contains the nucleus of the cell and that receives information from the dendrites.

**Central executive** The component of the working memory model that coordinates attentional resources and supervises the phonological loop and the visuo-spatial sketch pad.

**Cerebellum** A part of the brain that is involved in balance and movement coordination and that may also be a storage area for nondeclarative memories.

**Characteristic features** Features that often are possessed, but not always, by an object that is an example or instance of a certain concept.

**Childhood amnesia** See *Infantile amnesia*.

**Chunking** The process of combining information into meaningful clusters for storage in STM.

**Classic amnesia syndrome** This organic memory disorder is caused by bilateral brain damage to either the medial temporal lobes or the diencephalon region. The person has normal linguistic and intellectual abilities, as well as a relatively intact STM. However, the person suffers from both retrograde and anterograde amnesia. By using testing procedures that do not rely on conscious recollection, it has been shown that individuals with this disorder can learn and remember new information.

**Clustering** The tendency to organize items into groups on the basis of their category membership.

**Coding of information** Transforming the features or associations of a stimulus that are to be stored in memory. [See also *Encoding (registration)*.]

**Cognitive map** A mental representation of the spatial layout of an area.

**Commercial memory aid** A product that was specifically designed by the manufacturer to help a person with memory tasks. Examples are memory prosthetics, memory correctors, and memory robots.

**Computerized axial tomography (CAT)** A procedure that involves sending a rapidly rotating X-ray beam through the patient's head to take thousands of pictures of the brain from different angles.

**Conceptually driven**  See *Top-down processing*.

**Condition-process modes**  Manipulations of a person's physical condition, emotional state, and/or attitude in order to influence encoding, retention, and/or retrieval.

**Confabulation**  Making up a story concerning a past event in one's life.

**Conjugate reinforcement paradigm**  A procedure used to study the memory ability of infants. It involves determining how long an infant can remember that kicking a mobile will make it move.

**Connectionist models (parallel distributed processing models, neural networks)**  Computer models that are patterned after the way the human brain supposedly works (e.g., knowledge is distributed throughout the system, and many cognitive processes are performed simultaneously). These models assume that knowledge is stored within the connections between simple units and that these units can excite or inhibit each other by varying the strength of their interconnections.

**Consolidation theory of memory**  This theory maintains that most events and stimuli only gradually become fixed in LTM.

**Constructive changes in memory**  Distortions, often caused by drawing incorrect inferences from schemas, that occur during the encoding stage.

**Content-process modes**  Mental manipulations, physical environment manipulations, and social environment manipulations that influence encoding, retention, and/or retrieval.

**Context dependent memory**  The superior retrieval of information when retrieval occurs in the same context that was present during learning.

**Control processes**  Flexible strategies a person can choose to use to select, manipulate, and transform information.

**Cryptomnesia**  Unintended plagiarism.

**Cue-dependent forgetting**  An inability to remember something when sufficient retrieval cues are not present.

**Cued recall**  Providing a cue to help stimulate retrieval.

**Cue-word method for studying autobiographical memory**  Requiring a person to recall a personal memory that is associated with a certain word.

**Cultural memory tasks**  Memory tasks or obligations that are important for members of a specific culture to be aware of or to perform.

**Cumulative rehearsal**  Rehearsing a set of items over and over again.

**Data-driven**  See *Bottom-up processing*.

**Decay of a trace**  The physiological erosion or fading of a memory trace.

**Decay theory (Law of Disuse)**  This theory assumes that forgetting occurs owing to memories growing weaker and weaker with the passage of time. (See also *Theory of Disuse*.)

**Declarative memory**  Knowledge that can be acquired in a single trial and that is directly accessible to conscious recollection.

**Defining features**  Features that are always possessed by an object that is an example or instance of a certain concept.

**Déjà vu**  The subjective feeling that one has already experienced a situation while objectively knowing that the situation has never been encountered before.

**Dementias**  Disorders that result in a deterioration of all intellectual abilities and that produce drastic changes in personality.

**Dendrites**  Neuronal fibers that receive signals from the axons of other neurons and transit these signals to the cell body.

**Deoxyribonucleic acid (DNA)**  Chemical chains that contain genetic information.

**Dichotic listening procedure**  The simultaneous presentation of different messages to each ear.

**Diencephalon region**  A central region of the brain composed of the thalamus and hypothalamus. Important structures within this area for the consolidation of declarative-type memories are the mammillary bodies and the dorsomedial thalamic nuclei.

**Digit span task**  A memory span test using digits.

**Directed forgetting**  See *Suppression*.

**Discrepancy detection principle**  This principle states that people are most susceptible to the misinformation effect if they do not immediately detect discrepancies between postevent information and their memory for the original event.

**Dissociation**  The process by which one variable affects one type of test or process differently than it does another.

**Dissociative memory disorder (functional amnesia)**   A complete or partial forgetting of one's personal identity due to the repression of very disturbing memories.

**Distinctiveness hypothesis**   This hypothesis proposes that deeper levels of processing result in better retention because the deeper processing makes the information stand out (be distinctive) from other memory traces.

**Distribution of practice (spacing effect)**   The technique of spacing or distributing studying over time. It usually results in better retention than from massed practice.

**Dorsomedial thalamic nuclei**   An area in the diencephalic region that is composed of collections of neurons involved in the consolidation of declarative-type memories.

**Dressing apraxia**   Brain damage in certain areas of the right hemisphere causes a person to experience great difficulty in putting on clothes (the person has forgotten how to carry out the body movements necessary to get dressed).

**Drug-dependent memory**   The premise that if a person is placed in a drugged state (such as a drunken state) at the time of encoding certain information, recollection of this information will be best if the person is again placed in the same drugged state at the time of retrieval. (See also *State-dependent memory.*)

**Easterbrook Hypothesis**   This hypothesis proposes that attention is narrowed to only a few cues in the environment when an animal experiences a high state of arousal, emotionality, or anxiety.

**Echoic memory**   The sensory memory system for auditory stimuli.

**Eidetic imagery**   The ability to retain a very detailed visual image of a stimulus after it has been removed from actual view. Those who have this ability maintain that the image appears to be localized in front of them and can be scanned as if it were still physically present.

**Elaboration hypothesis**   This hypothesis proposes that deeper levels of processing result in better retention because the deeper processing results in a richer, more complex encoding of the information.

**Elaborative rehearsal (Type II rehearsal)**   Repetition of information in order to analyze it more deeply and to form a lasting memory of it. This is accomplished by relating the new information to information already stored in LTM.

**Electroconvulsive shock**   The administration of electrical stimulation to the brain that induces retrograde amnesia. When used to treat human depression, the procedure is called electroconvulsive therapy.

**Encoding (registration)**   The phase of the memory process that involves transforming information into a form that can be retained.

**Encoding congruency**   This occurs when a person's current mood causes selective or better encoding of material that is consistent, or congruent, with the prevailing mood state.

**Encoding specificity principle**   This principle states that the likelihood of retrieving information from LTM will be maximized if the conditions present at the time of retrieval match as closely as possible the conditions present at the time of initial encoding.

**Engram (memory trace)**   The record that is presumably present in the brain after something has been learned.

**Epilepsy**   A disorder in which people suffer from recurrent brain seizures that can affect memory functioning.

**Epinephrine**   See *Adrenaline.*

**Episodic prospective memory tasks**   Prospective memory tasks that we engage in rarely or just once.

**Explicit encoding**   The process by which a person intentionally tries to encode information.

**Explicit memory tasks**   Memory tasks that depend on the conscious recollection of prior learning.

**External knowledge sources**   Sources that contain information that a person may have known but has forgotten or that contain information that a person never knew.

**External memory aids**   Objects and devices that are used to aid memory.

**Everyday memory movement**   This movement emphasizes studying memory in naturalistic settings and exploring memory tasks that have an applied focus.

**Exhaustive serial search**   Before a decision is

made, memory is searched item by item until all the items have been searched for, even if the specific item of interest was found earlier.

**Explicit remembering**  The conscious recollection of previous experiences that occurs intentionally or unintentionally.

**Face-name imagery technique**  A mnemonic technique for learning a person's name that involves imagining a concrete object suggested by the name superimposed on the person's face.

**False memory syndrome**  After many years have elapsed, the fervent belief in the accuracy of recovered repressed experiences, even though they are not genuine.

**Fat Lady Syndrome**  A patient's later recollection of statements, especially when they are negative and directed toward the patient, made by surgical staff members while the patient is under anesthesia.

**First-letter mnemonic**  A naive mnemonic technique that involves using the first letter of each of the items to be remembered.

**Flashbulb memory**  This is an unusually detailed, vivid recollection of a surprising, emotionally arousing, and significant event that some people believe is always highly accurate and largely immune to forgetting.

**Forgetting curve**  The shape of the function describing the decrease in remembering over time.

**Forward-retrieval strategy**  A procedure used to search autobiographical memory that involves starting from the earliest memories.

**Free recall learning**  Allowing a person to recall list items in any order that he or she chooses.

**Functional amnesia**  See *Dissociative memory disorder*.

**Gamma-amino butyric acid (GABA)**  Increased levels of this neurotransmitter are associated with lower levels of neural activity and poorer memory performance.

**Generation effect**  The superior memory for items that are self-generated.

**Gestalt psychology**  The view put forth that context, organization, and meaning are important factors for perception, learning, and memory.

**Guided recall procedure**  A collection of retrieval strategies that reportedly produces more accurate eyewitness accounts than do more standard interviewing techniques.

**Habitual prospective memory tasks**  Prospective memory tasks that we engage in on a regular basis.

**Habituation**  The decrease in responding to a repetitive stimulus.

**Habituation-dishabituation paradigm**  Presenting a subject with the same stimulus over a series of trials and observing the amount of time the subject continues to attend to the stimulus. Subjects usually show a decline (habituation), but if a long enough delay occurs between trials, looking time may increase again (dishabituation).

**Halstead-Reitan Neuropsychological Battery (HR)**  This battery consists of a series of standardized cognitive tests that are often administered to people with known or suspected brain damage.

*Hermissenda*  A sea snail that has been extensively studied and about which much is known concerning the neuronal pathways and cellular changes involved during classical conditioning.

**Hippocampus**  A structure in the medial temporal regions involved in the consolidation of declarative-type memories.

**Huntington's disease**  An illness that causes primary differentiated dementia and that is characterized by abnormal body movements, postures, or gaits.

**Iconic memory**  The sensory memory system for visual stimuli.

**Idiot savant (mono-savant, savant, savant syndrome)**  A person who is mentally retarded but is, nevertheless, capable of performing some impressive memory and cognitive feats.

**Immediate memory**  See *Short-term memory*.

**Immediate retention test**  The nonreinforcement phase of the conjugate reinforcement paradigm designed to measure the infant's final level of acquisition.

**Implicit memory tasks**  Memory tasks that do not depend on the conscious recollection of prior learning.

**Implicit remembering** This occurs when someone has no conscious recollection of information or past events but is nevertheless affected by such material. (The influence is usually reflected in the performance of some task.)

**Incidental learning** The learning that occurs when a person does not intentionally try to encode information but nevertheless does so.

**Incremental learning** Learning that proceeds bit by bit, feature by feature, rather than all at once (as opposed to "all or none learning").

**Independent variables** Factors that influence memory performance.

**Infantile amnesia** The inability to remember events that occurred during the early part of life. This is sometimes called *childhood amnesia* when the focus is limited to humans.

**Information-processing/cognitive approach** The theoretical view that assumes that cognitive processes (like memory) involve a series of interrelated mental operations and that people are actively manipulating and using strategies to process information.

**Instructional variables** Independent variables that influence how someone performs a memory task by giving explicit or implicit instructions.

**Intentional forgetting** See *Motivated forgetting*.

**Interference hypothesis of anxiety** The claim that negative or unpleasant events are less well remembered because anxiety associated with these events interferes with a person's ability to recall them by distracting the person with competing thoughts.

**Interference theory of forgetting** This theory assumes that forgetting occurs because the memory trace to be remembered is confused with other memory traces that occurred either earlier or later. (See also *Proactive interference* and *Retroactive interference*.)

**Internal memory aids** Mental strategies that are used to aid memory.

**Jamais vu** A memory anomaly that occurs when a person experiences a complete lack of familiarity in a particular situation when he or she should not.

**Kinesthetic cues** Information about where body parts are positioned with respect to each other.

**Knowledge base** The information that someone knows about a topic.

**Korsakoff's syndrome** A memory disorder due to brain damage (often associated with prolonged alcoholism) that is characterized by severe anterograde amnesia and often extensive loss of long-term autobiographical memories.

**Law of Contiguity** Two events or experiences occurring closely in time will likely come to be associated with each other.

**Law of Disuse** See *Decay theory*.

**Levels-of-processing approach** This approach deemphasizes the structural components of memory (like STM and LTM) and stresses the role that depth of encoding plays in the formation of lasting memories.

**Lexical decision task** Quickly deciding whether or not a string of letters is a word.

**Life-span movement** This movement emphasizes the importance of examining the developmental changes that occur in memory functioning and ability throughout a person's entire life.

**Link mnemonic** A technical mnemonic that involves forming a visual image of each item to be learned and then visualizing a link between each successive item.

**Linkword Language System** A technical mnemonic for learning foreign language vocabulary that involves imagining an English word interacting with a foreign word that sounds like another English word. When the words are linked with an image, the image becomes a powerful cue for future retrieval.

**Localizationist position** The hypothesis that specific memories are stored in very discrete areas of the cerebral cortex of the brain.

**Long-term memory (LTM, secondary memory)** A component of the memory system that can hold vast amounts of information indefinitely.

**Long-term potentiation (LTP)** The increased sensitivity of neurons after having been exposed to brief bursts of high-frequency electrical stimulation.

**Long-term recency effect** The recency effect (the superior recall of the final few items of a list relative to the middle items during free recall) that occurs when the list is already stored in LTM.

**Luria-Nebraska Neuropsychological Battery (LN)** This battery consists of a series of standardized cognitive tests that are often administered to people with known or suspected brain damage.

**Macrocolumn** A collection of interconnected neurons in the cortex that acts as a functional unit to store engrams. (See also *Cell assemblies*.)

**Magnetic resonance imaging (MRI)** A scanning technique that uses strong magnetic fields, which surround the head, and radio-frequency pulses, which bombard it. In response, the brain emits signals, and these are computer-processed to get pictures of the brain.

**Maintenance rehearsal (Type I rehearsal)** Repetition of information with shallow processing in order to keep it active in consciousness.

**Mammillary bodies** Structures in the diencephalon region involved in the consolidation of declarative-type memories.

**Medial temporal regions** Inner areas of the temporal lobes of the brain containing the hippocampus and the amygdala, which are involved in the consolidation of declarative-type memories.

**Mediation deficit** The inability of an individual to make use of an appropriate memory strategy, either one that is spontaneously produced or one that is provided.

**Memorist** A person who has developed superior memory skills without the use of traditional mnemonic techniques.

**Memory anomalies** Memory disorders that are considered relatively benign (unless they occur very frequently and/or interfere with normal functioning).

**Memory blocks** Sudden cessations of thought when a person tries repeatedly to recall something but is unsuccessful.

**Memory contrivance** A deliberate distortion that a person uses to portray someone else's memory performance as better or worse than it actually is in order to achieve certain social goals.

**Memory corrector** A commercial memory aid that corrects memory errors.

**Memory drum** A device for presenting list items for a set amount of time in a precise and consistent fashion.

**Memory etiquette** Rules of behavior concerning how one should react when someone makes a memory error.

**Memory-friendly product** A product whose primary function is not to aid memory; aiding memory is only a secondary purpose.

**Memory language** Vocabulary and idioms that express memory states.

**Memory organization packet (MOP)** A collection of scenes that are highly related.

**Memory pacts** Agreements between individuals (sometimes explicit and sometimes implicit) to share the responsibility for performing certain memory tasks.

**Memory prosthetic** A commercial memory aid that facilitates memory performance.

**Memory proverbs** Cultural pearls of wisdom about how memory tasks should be performed and how the memory behavior of others is to be regarded.

**Memory questionnaire (MQ)** Measures how well someone can recognize or recall knowledge or events.

**Memory reactivation procedure** A way to determine whether or not an infant who is being tested with the conjugate reinforcement paradigm can remember apparently forgotten memories when supplied with some reminder of the original training sessions (such as the experimenter's making the mobile move by tugging on the ribbon).

**Memory reputation** The reputation a person earns for how often he or she succeeds or fails at particular memory tasks.

**Memory rituals** Memory tasks customarily expected of individuals in certain social situations.

**Memory robot** A commercial memory aid that performs memory tasks for the owner.

**Memory set** A list of items a subject is told to remember.

**Memory slips** Errors that occur when a person accidentally recollects something other than what was intended.

**Memory span** The number of items recalled in correct order from a serially presented list.

**Memory stereotypes** Beliefs people hold about the memory ability of others on the basis of group characteristics (such as gender or race).

**Memory strategy** A purposeful and deliberate attempt by an individual to enhance memory performance.

**Memory test battery**    A collection of standardized memory tasks used to develop a comprehensive account of an individual's memory functioning.

**Memory trace**    *See engram.*

**Mental status examination**    The initial session between a patient and an examiner to determine the patient's general level of awareness, cooperativeness, and emotional state, as well as the patient's ability to communicate, attend, think, and remember.

**Metamemory**    General knowledge and awareness of one's own memory processes, abilities, and interests.

**Metamemory questionnaire (MMQ)**    Measures what a person knows about the memory process or asks people to estimate how well they believe they can recognize or recall knowledge or events.

**Method of loci**    A technical mnemonic that requires a person to first memorize or call to mind a set of familiar locations. The person then mentally places each item to be remembered in one of those places. Retrieval of the items involves mentally "walking" through the locations and "seeing" the items.

**Minerva**    The Roman goddess of learning, memory, and wisdom (circa 1000 B.C.).

**Misinformation effect**    The difficulty that people have in remembering the original event after learning new information that is inconsistent with it.

**Mnemosyne**    The Greek goddess of memory (circa 1000 B.C.).

**Mnemonics**    The use of internal strategies or methods to make it easier to encode, store, and/ or retrieve information.

**Mnemonist**    Someone who possesses a superior memory because of using mnemonic techniques.

**Modulation**    Refers to the fact that the retention of specific memories can be either inhibited or enhanced by postlearning events.

**Mood-dependent memory**    The premise that if a person is experiencing a particular mood (such as happiness) at the time of encoding certain information, recollection of this information will be best if the person experiences the same mood

state at the time of retrieval. (See also *State-dependent memory.*)

**Mono-savant**    See *Idiot savant.*

**Motivated forgetting**    The forgetting that occurs because someone (consciously) suppresses or (unconsciously) represses a memory.

**Multimodal theoretical perspective**    The view that memory is best explained by taking account of all psychological processes, including memory and nonmemory processes (such as perceptual, motivational, physiological, emotional, and social processes).

**Multiple personality disorder**    An extreme form of dissociative disorder in which a person's personality structure divides into two or more distinct identities.

**Naive mnemonics**    Mnemonic techniques that people naturally use even without formal training or instruction.

**Network models**    Assert that information is stored in a network of interrelated nodes.

**Neural nets**    See *Cell assemblies.*

**Neural networks**    See *Connectionist models.*

**Neurofibrillary tangles**    Clumps of twisted nerved fibers, which are found in the brains of Alzheimer's patients.

**Neuron**    The basic unit of the nervous system; it consists of a cell body, dendrites, and an axon.

**Neurotransmitter**    A chemical released by a neuron into a synapse that can increase or decrease the likelihood that other neurons will fire action potentials.

**Next-in-line effect**    Because of stress associated with making an upcoming public presentation, an individual will have a poor memory for prior presentations (especially the one immediately prior to his or her own).

**Nictitating membrane**    The protective "third eyelid" of a cat, a rabbit, and certain kinds of fish and birds that reflexively closes when a stimulus threatens the eye.

**Noncommercial memory aid**    A product that was not specifically designed and sold as a memory aid but that effectively aids memory because people have devised a novel way to use it.

**Noncumulative rehearsal**    Rehearsing a single item at a time.

**Nondeclarative memory**  Knowledge obtained incrementally that is not directly accessible to conscious recollection. Many researchers now prefer to use the term *nondeclarative memory* rather than the term *procedural memory* because the former term seems to better capture the kinds of learning tasks that are preserved in many amnesic patients. For instance, amnesics show normal semantic priming effects, and such abilities would not be considered examples of procedural memory.

**Nonsense syllable**  A three-letter combination of a consonant, a vowel, and a consonant that is supposedly devoid of meaning. (Invented by Ebbinghaus.)

**Nonverbal memory communication**  Gestures, facial expressions, and nonverbal sounds that convey a person's state of memory processing.

**Norepinephrine**  A neurotransmitter that can enhance memory performance when given in the proper dosage immediately following learning.

**Number-letter mnemonic**  A technical mnemonic in which the digits 0 to 9 are associated with particular consonant sounds.

**Olfactory cues**  The smells present during learning and retrieval.

**Organic memory disorders**  Memory disorders with a clear physiological basis.

**Organismic variables**  Relatively permanent characteristics of a person that affect general memory performance (e.g., level of intelligence).

**Organization (organizational strategy)**  The process by which individual items are grouped together because of some shared characteristic. This process aids encoding, storage, and/or retrieval.

**Overlearning**  Continuing to study the material after complete recall has been demonstrated. This technique increases the likelihood that the material will be remembered.

**Paired-associate learning**  The learning of pairs of items with the result that one can recall the second item (called the response) when the first (called the stimulus) is presented.

**Parallel distributed processing (PDP)**  See *Connectionist models*.

**Parallel search**  A process by which multiple items can be accessed or retrieved from memory simultaneously.

**Partial-report procedure**  A procedure devised by Sperling in which only a randomly selected portion of the stimulus array was to be recalled.

**Peg system**  A technical mnemonic that requires a person to first memorize a series of number-object pairs, usually in a rhyme ("one is a bun, two is a shoe, . . ."); then the person mentally imagines each item to be remembered as interacting with one of the objects.

**Permastore**  A theoretical memory storage system containing information that was overlearned and acquired over considerable time periods through distributed practice. It is supposed that this information remains in LTM for decades, largely immune to forgetting.

**Person schema**  A mental representation that contains general information and beliefs about consistent traits and characteristics of another person.

**Phonological loop**  The component of the working memory model that is responsible for manipulating speech-based information. It contains an articulatory control process and a phonological store.

**Picture elicitation method**  A test for eidetic imagery that involves briefly presenting a visual picture, removing it from view, and then asking the subject to recall as many details as possible.

**Planaria**  A simple animal, better known as a flatworm, used in early conditioning studies.

**Pollyanna Principle**  This principle proposes that the reason why happy memories and pleasant words are usually better recalled than unhappy memories and less pleasant words is that the former items are generally processed more accurately and efficiently, which makes them more accessible for retrieval.

**Positron emission tomography (PET)**  To measure the metabolic activity of different areas of the brain, radioactively labeled glucose is injected into the bloodstream, and a radiation detector measures the amount of this glucose that has been taken up by different groups of neurons.

The level of radioactivity in different brain tissues is analyzed by a computer, and a colored picture of the brain is obtained.

**Postsynaptic membrane**   The membrane of the receiving neuron's dendrite or cell body.

**Posttraumatic amnesia (PTA)**   An amnesia for the time interval from the onset of a coma to the recovery of continuous memory.

**Pragmatic implication**   A statement that leads a person to believe something that is neither explicitly asserted nor necessarily implied.

**Presenile dementia**   A dementia that develops before age 65.

**Presentational variables**   Independent variables that affect memory performance by means of the way that stimuli are presented (e.g., varying the amount of time for studying a list of words).

**Presynaptic membrane**   The membrane of the transmitting neuron.

**Primacy effect**   The superior recall of the initial items of a list relative to the middle items during free recall. (See also *Serial-position curve*.)

**Primary differentiated dementia**   See *Progressive dementias*.

**Primary memory**   See *Short-term memory*.

**Primary memory measure**   Reflects the amount of information stored in memory.

**Primary undifferentiated dementia**   See *Progressive dementias*.

**Priming**   The effect that prior learning has on subsequent behavior or performance.

**Proactive interference (PI)**   Prior learning acts forward in time to interfere with the recall of something learned more recently.

**Procedural memory**   Knowledge obtained incrementally that is not directly accessible to conscious recollection. (See also *Nondeclarative memory*.)

**Prodigious savant**   An idiot savant who has skills that are at such a high level that they would seem exceptional even for people with normal or higher levels of intelligence.

**Production deficit**   The failure of an individual to spontaneously generate an appropriate memory strategy to handle a memory task.

**Progressive dementias**   These dementias, which worsen in a smoothly progressive way, are of two types: primary undifferentiated (which primarily affect the cerebral cortex) and primary

differentiated (which primarily affect subcortical areas of the brain).

**Proposition**   A unit of knowledge that can be asserted as being either true or false.

**Propositional network models**   Models of memory in which related pieces of knowledge are linked together in a broad network of nodes that each represent a proposition.

**Prosopagnosia**   A disorder (due to bilateral damage to the hemispheres of the brain) in which a person can no longer recognize familiar faces.

**Prospective memory**   The ability to plan and remember to perform future tasks.

**Proprioceptive cues**   Information about where we are and what each body part is doing.

**Prototype**   An instance or example of a concept that possesses all or most of the concept's characteristic features.

**Psychogenic amnesia**   A type of dissociative disorder in which a person forgets important personal information as a result of encountering an extremely stressful or anxiety-provoking event.

**Psychogenic fugue**   A type of dissociative disorder in which a person who has experienced intolerable stress or anxiety not only forgets important personal information but also moves away from home and adopts a new identity.

**Rapid eye movement (REM) sleep**   A stage of sleep in which the eyes move rapidly beneath closed lids and which has been associated with dreaming and the consolidation of memories.

**Reaction time (RT)**   The time interval between the onset of a stimulus and the beginning of a response made as quickly as possible.

**Recall congruency**   This occurs when a person's current mood causes selective or better retrieval of material that is consistent, or congruent, with the prevailing mood state.

**Recency effect**   The superior recall of the final few items of a list relative to the middle items during free recall. (See also *Serial-position curve*.)

**Recent memory**   A subdivision of LTM that refers to a retention interval for events that occurred a few minutes to a few days ago. (See also *Remote memory*.)

**Receptor site**   A complex molecule on the postsynaptic membrane that is affected by neurotransmitters that exactly fit its configuration.

**Reconstructive changes in memory**  Distortions, often caused by drawing incorrect inferences from schemas, that occur at the time of retrieval.

**Refreshing**  Providing a person with some or all of the information to be recalled as a way to revive a memory.

**Registration**  See *Encoding*.

**Reminding service**  A business whose purpose is to remind people about special occasions in their personal lives and to carry out personal memory tasks such as sending gifts and cards.

**Reminiscence**  The act or process of recalling past events.

**Remote memory**  A subdivision of LTM that refers to events that happened in a person's distant past. (See also *Recent memory*.)

**Repisodic memory**  Refers to situations in which the recall of some event is really just the blending together of details from many similar episodes or events.

**Repression**  An unconscious process that causes extremely unpleasant memories or experiences either to become less accessible or to be completely forgotten.

**Resource-allocation hypothesis of depression**  Maintains that there are always a limited number of available cognitive resources and that people suffering from depression have poorer memory performance because the depression reduces these resources (perhaps by inappropriately tying up attentional processes).

**Retention**  The storage of information.

**Retroactive interference (RI)**  Recently learned information acts backward in time to interfere with the recall of something learned previously.

**Retrograde amnesia**  A loss of memory for events occurring prior to the onset of the disturbance causing the amnesia.

**Retrograde facilitation**  Increasing memory performance by increasing the level of neural activity right after learning has occurred.

**Retrospective memory**  The ability to remember past events or information.

**Ribonucleic acid (RNA)**  Chemical chains that were once thought to store memories.

**Savant**  See *Idiot savant*.

**Savant syndrome**  See *Idiot savant*.

**Savings score**  A quantitative measure of the effort "saved" in relearning something owing to what was retained from the original learning.

**Scale effects**  Refers to the fact that some cues are useful for recalling some specific lengths or aspects of time but not others.

**Scene**  An event that forms one part of a script.

**Schema**  A mental model or representation, built up through experience, about a person, an object, a situation, or an event.

**Schematization**  The process by which memories for specific events merge into general scripts or schemas.

**Scopolamine**  A drug that appears to interfere with the normal use of acetylcholine and that prevents the formation of new memories by apparently interfering with the central executive of the working memory model.

**Scotophobin**  A protein found in the brains of rats conditioned with electric shock to avoid the dark. It was once believed that injecting scotophobin into naive rats would result in the "transfer" of the memory of the fear associated with getting shocked.

**Script**  A particular type of schema that describes the kind of knowledge that people can abstract from a common, frequently occurring event.

**Secondary dementias**  Dementias that derive from illnesses that do not directly attack the brain.

**Secondary memory**  See *Long-term memory*.

**Secondary memory measure**  Reflects aspects of memory other than the quantity of information correctly retrieved (e.g., speed of recall or confidence in being correct).

**Selective recall**  The superior recall of information that is consistent with a person's attitudes or beliefs.

**Self-reference effect**  The superior recall of information when people decide how well the information applies to themselves or to others they know well.

**Self-schema**  A mental model or representation of general information that we believe is true about our own traits, dispositions, abilities, and goals.

**Self-terminating serial search**  A process by which memory is searched item by item until the correct item is found, at which point the search ends.

**Senile dementia**   A dementia that develops at or after age 65.

**Senile plaques**   Patches of dead neurons found in the brains of Alzheimer's patients.

**Sensitization**   The increase in responding to a repetitive stimulus.

**Sensory memory (sensory register)**   A memory system for holding very briefly and accurately the sensory characteristics of a stimulus.

**Sensory register**   See *Sensory memory*.

**Serial learning**   Learning to recall a sequence of items in order.

**Serial-position curve**   A plot of the probability of retrieval (during free recall) as a function of the serial order in which items were first studied. Usually the first few items (primacy effect) and the last few items (recency effect) have a higher probability of being recalled.

**Short-term memory (STM, immediate memory, primary memory)**   The retention of information for about 30 seconds or less without rehearsal. Short-term memory is often considered a component of the memory system where information is stored and processed and is associated with conscious awareness.

**Single-item probe technique**   The subject first memorizes a short list of items and then is presented with a single probe item. The task is to decide as fast as possible if the probe was on the list.

**Skilled Memory Theory**   This theory proposes that exceptional feats of memory are due not to innate, possibly neurological, differences between people but instead to vast amounts of practice and a good dose of motivation.

**Social information**   Knowledge of the attitudes, roles, and means for impressing others that one should be aware of when interacting with others.

**Spacing effect**   See *Distribution of practice*.

**Spreading activation**   A type of mental excitement that supposedly moves from node to node in a network model.

**State-dependent memory**   The premise that retrieval from memory will be best when the "state" of the person at initial encoding or learning matches the "state" of the person at the time of retrieval. This is a subset of the encoding specificity principle.

**Stimulus variables**   The different types of material (such as letters and pictures) that a subject might be expected to remember.

**Story mnemonic**   A technical mnemonic that involves creating a story making use of all the items to be memorized.

**Structural features of memory**   Aspects of the memory process or of a memory component that are fixed or constant (such as the absolute capacity of STM).

**Study-test procedure**   Showing a subject a series of items, only half of which were presented during learning, and asking the subject to decide if the item is "old" or "new."

**Subjective organization**   The tendency of subjects to impose a structure or an organization on a group of items, even though the items seemingly are unrelated to each other.

**Superimposition method**   A test for eidetic imagery that requires a subject to scan an array of dots that is meaningless by itself and then mentally superimpose the image of this array on another dot pattern that is also meaningless by itself but that in combination with the first array produces a pattern that is, overall, recognizable.

**Suppression (directed forgetting)**   The conscious forgetting of a memory by deliberately trying not to think about it.

**Symbolic reminders**   Drawings or sketches of culturally established symbols (such as a string around a finger) that convey that something should not be forgotten.

**Synapse**   The very small gap that exists between neurons, sometimes called the synaptic cleft.

**Synaptic vesicles**   Structures within terminal buttons that contain neurotransmitters.

**Synesthesia**   A rare phenomenon in which sensory experiences in one modality simultaneously evoke sensory experiences in other modalities (e.g., hearing colors).

**Talented savant**   An idiot savant who can perform tasks at a level that is quite remarkable, given that the person is mentally retarded.

**Task variables**   The independent variables affecting a particular memory task or situation.

**Technical mnemonics**   Mnemonic techniques that require people to first memorize some encoding scheme (like a peg system) before it can be used to remember new information.

**Terminal button**   The knoblike end of an axon branch; it contains synaptic vesicles.

**Thematic organization point (TOP)**   A script that represents a more abstract theme than does a MOP and that often allows people to see the similarities between two seemingly different situations.

**Theory of Disuse**   A new explanation to account for forgetting that rejects the old idea that forgetting is due to the mere passage of time. This new Theory of Disuse assumes that people have a limited ability to retrieve information from memory and that even well-learned information becomes inaccessible when not periodically retrieved.

**Thoth**   The Egyptian god of learning, memory, and wisdom (circa 3000–4000 B.C.).

**Time-gap experience**   The subjective feeling that little or no time has elapsed when, in fact, a considerable lapse has occurred (often happens when one is driving for long stretches on a monotonous road or on a well-traveled route that requires little conscious attention).

**Tip-of-the-tongue phenomenon**   Occurs whenever someone cannot immediately recall a word or name that the person is absolutely sure he or she knows.

**Top-down processing (conceptually driven)**   This approach to processing information emphasizes the use of prior knowledge and expectations to help organize and elaborate on the information.

**Transfer-appropriate processing**   This principle suggests that the "best" type of encoding for a particular stimulus greatly depends on the type of retrieval later expected.

**Transient global amnesia (TGA)**   An amnesia that suddenly appears and that lasts only briefly (minutes, hours, or days).

**Type A personality**   A person who may be especially good at prospective memory tasks and who has a strong sense of time urgency, is highly competitive, is overly concerned with deadlines, and often holds a perfectionist attitude.

**Type I rehearsal**   See *Maintenance rehearsal*.

**Type II rehearsal**   See *Elaborative rehearsal*.

**Vasopressin**   A hormone that in small amounts can enhance memory.

**Visuo-spatial sketch pad**   The component of the working memory model that is responsible for manipulating visuo-spatial images, planning spatial tasks, and helping to orient a person in geographic settings.

**Von Restorff effect**   The superior memory for items that are perceptually or conceptually distinctive from other items studied.

**Warm-up**   The process of familiarizing a person with the material to be learned or with the format of a memory task so that the person will perform the memory task with greater speed and proficiency.

**Weapon focus phenomenon**   Occurs when eyewitnesses to a crime have great difficulty recalling various details of what happened because they focused their attention on the weapon used to commit the crime.

**Wechsler Memory Scale (WMS)**   Perhaps the best-known and most often used memory test battery.

**Whole-report procedure**   A procedure devised by Sperling in which the entire stimulus array was to be recalled.

**Word-fragments task**   An implicit memory test in which one attempts to identify a word from only letter fragments.

**Word-stem completion task**   An implicit memory test in which one attempts to complete a word when given only a few of the letters.

**Working memory model**   A model of memory that challenges the idea that STM is a single system. It is composed of three main components: the central executive, the phonological loop, and the visuo-spatial sketch pad.

**Yerkes-Dodson Law**   This law relates the effects of arousal and performance by assuming that optimal performance is associated with moderate levels of arousal and that there's an inverse relationship between arousal level and task difficulty.

# References

Abelson, R. P. (1981). Psychological status of the script concept. *American Psychologist, 36,* 715–729.

Abraham, W. C., Corballis, M. C., & White, K. G. (Eds.). (1991). *Memory mechanisms: A tribute to G. V. Goddard.* Hillsdale, NJ: Erlbaum.

Adam, N. (1979). Disruption of memory functions associated with general anesthetics. In J. F. Kihlstrom & F. J. Evans (Eds.), *Functional disorders of memory* (pp. 219–238). Hillsdale, NJ: Erlbaum.

Adams, J. A. (1967). *Human memory.* New York: McGraw-Hill.

Alba, J. W., & Hasher, L. (1983). Is memory schematic? *Psychological Bulletin, 93,* 203–231.

Albert, M. S., Butters, N., & Levin, J. (1979). Temporal gradients in the retrograde amnesia of patients with alcoholic Korsakoff's disease. *Archives of Neurology, 36,* 211–216.

Albert, M. S., Butters, N., & Levin, J. (1980). Memory for remote events in chronic alcoholics and alcoholic Korsakoff patients. In H. Begleiter (Ed.), *Biological effects of alcohol* (pp. 719–730). New York: Plenum Press.

Alkon, D. L. (1983). Learning in a marine snail. *Scientific American, 249,* 64–74.

Allport, G. W., & Postman, L. J. (1945). The basic psychology of rumor. *Transactions of the New York Academy of Sciences, 11,* 61–81.

Allport, G. W., & Postman, L. J. (1947). *The Psychology of Rumor.* New York: Holt.

Anderson, J. R. (1983). *The architecture of cognition.* Cambridge, MA: Harvard University Press.

Anderson, J. R., & Bower, G. H., (1973). *Human associative memory.* Washington, DC: Winston.

Anderson, J. R., & Paulson, R. (1977). Representation and retention of verbatim information. *Journal of Verbal Learning and Verbal Behavior, 16,* 439–452.

Anderson, J. R., & Reder, L. M. (1979). An elaborative processing explanation of depth of processing. In L. S. Cermak & F. I. M. Craik (Eds.), *Levels of processing in human memory* (pp. 385–403). Hillsdale, NJ: Erlbaum.

Anderson, R. C., & Pichert, J. W. (1978). Recall of previously unrecallable information following a shift in perspective. *Journal of Verbal Learning and Verbal Behavior, 17,* 1–12.

Anderson, S. M., & Cole, S. W. (1990). "Do I know you?": The role of significant others in general social perception. *Journal of Personality and Social Psychology, 59,* 384–399.

Asch, S. E. (1956). Studies of independence and conformity: I. A minority of one against a unanimous majority. *Psychological Monographs, 70*(9, Whole No. 416).

Ashcraft, M. H. (1989). *Human memory and cognition.* Glenview, IL: Scott, Foresman & Company.

Atkinson, R. C., & Shiffrin, R. M. (1965). *Mathematical models for memory and learning.* (Tech. Rep. 79). Stanford, CA: Stanford University, Institute for Mathematical Studies in the Social Sciences.

Atkinson, R. C., & Shiffrin, R. M. (1968). Human memory: A proposed system and its control processes. In K. W. Spence & J. R. Spence (Eds.), *The psychology of learning and motivation: Advances in research and theory* (Vol. 2, pp. 89–195). New York: Academic Press.

Atkinson, R. C., & Shiffrin, R. M. (1971). The control of short-term memory. *Scientific American, August,* 82–90.

Attneave, F. (1953). Psychological probability as a function of experienced frequency. *Journal of Experimental Psychology, 46,* 81–86.

Attneave, F. (1957). Transfer of experience with a class schema to identification learning of patterns and shapes. *Journal of Experimental Psychology, 54,* 81–88.

Axtell, R. E. (1991). *Gestures: The do's and taboos of body language around the world.* Chichester, England: John Wiley & Sons.

Bacon, J. H. (1862). *The science of memory.* London: Simpkin.

Baddeley, A. D. (1966). Short-term memory for word sequences as a function of acoustic, semantic and formal similarity. *Quarterly Journal of Experimental Psychology, 18,* 363–365.

Baddeley, A. D. (1978). The trouble with levels: A re-examination of Craik and Lockhart's framework for memory research. *Psychological Review, 85,* 139–152.

Baddeley, A. D. (1982). Domains of recollection. *Psychological Review, 89,* 708–729.

Baddeley, A. D. (1986). *Working memory.* Oxford: Clarendon Press.

Baddeley, A. D. (1990). *Human memory: Theory and practice.* Boston: Allyn and Bacon.

Baddeley, A. D. (1992). Working memory. *Science, 255,* 556–559.

Baddeley, A. D., & Hitch, G. (1974). Working memory. In G. H. Bower (Ed.), *The psychology of learning and motivation* (Vol. 8, pp. 47–89). New York: Academic Press.

Baddeley, A. D., & Hitch, G. (1977). Recency re-examined. In S. Dornic (Ed.), *Attention and performance* (Vol. 6, pp. 647–667). Hillsdale, NJ: Erlbaum.

Baddeley, A. D., Lewis, V., & Nimmo-Smith, I. (1978). When did you last . . . ? In M. M. Gruneberg, P. E. Morris, & R. N. Sykes (Eds.), *Practical aspects of memory* (pp. 77–83). London: Academic Press.

Baddeley, A. D., & Scott, D. (1971). Short-term forgetting in the absences of proactive interference. *Quarterly Journal of Experimental Psychology, 23,* 275–283.

Baddeley, A. D., & Wilkins, A. J. (1984). Taking memory out of the laboratory. In J. E. Harris & P. E. Morris (Eds.), *Everyday memory, actions and absentmindedness* (pp. 1–17). London: Academic Press.

Baddeley, A. D., & Wilson, B. (1986). Amnesia, autobiographical memory and confabulation. In D. C. Rubin (Ed.), *Autobiographical memory* (pp. 225–252). Cambridge, England: Cambridge University Press.

Bahrick, H. P. (1984a). Memory for people. In J. E. Harris & P. E. Morris (Eds.), *Everyday memory, actions and absent-mindedness* (pp. 19–34). London: Academic Press.

Bahrick, H. P. (1984b). Semantic memory content in permastore: Fifty years of memory for Spanish learned in school. *Journal of Experimental Psychology: General, 113,* 1–35.

Bahrick, H. P. (1991). A speedy recovery from bankruptcy for ecological memory research. *American Psychologist, 46,* 76–77.

Bahrick, H. P., Bahrick, P. O., & Wittlinger, R. P. (1975). Fifty years of memory for names and faces: A cross-sectional approach. *Journal of Experimental Psychology: General, 104,* 54–75.

Bahrick, H. P., & Hall, L. K. (1991). Lifetime maintenance of high school mathematics content. *Journal of Experimental Psychology: General, 120,* 20–33.

Banaji, M. R., & Crowder, R. C. (1989). The bankruptcy of everyday memory. *American Psychologist, 44,* 1185–1193.

Barclay, C. R. (1986). Schematization of autobiographical memory. In D. C. Rubin (Ed.), *Autobiographical memory* (pp. 82–99). Cambridge, England: Cambridge University Press.

Barclay, J. R., Bransford, J. D., Franks, J. J., McCarrell, N. S., & Nitsch, K. (1974). Comprehension and semantic flexibility. *Journal of Verbal Learning and Verbal Behavior, 13,* 471–481.

Bartlett, F. C. (1932). *Remembering.* Cambridge, England: Cambridge University Press.

Bartlett, J. C., Burleson, G., & Santrock, J. W. (1982). Emotional mood and memory in children. *Journal of Experimental Child Psychology, 34,* 59–76.

**Bartlett, J. C., & Santrock, J. W.** (1979). Affect-dependent episodic memory in young children. *Child Development, 50,* 513–518.

**Basso, A., Spinnler, H., Vallar, G., & Zanobio, E.** (1982). Left hemisphere damage and selected impairment or auditory verbal short-term memory: A case study. *Neuropsychologia, 20,* 263–274.

**Bauer, P. J., & Mandler, J. M.** (1990). Remembering what happened next: Very young children's recall of event sequences. In R. Fivush & J. A. Hudson (Eds.), *Knowing and remembering in young children* (pp. 9–29). New York: Cambridge University Press.

**Bauman, M., & Kemper, T. L.** (1985). Histoanatomic observations of the brain in early infantile autism. *Neurology, 35,* 866–874.

**Baumeister, R. F., Cooper, J., & Skib, B. A.** (1979). Inferior performance as a selective response to expectancy: Taking a dive to make a point. *Journal of Personality and Social Psychology, 37,* 424–432.

**Beach, K. D.** (1988). The role of external mnemonic symbols in acquiring an occupation. In M. M. Gruneberg, P. E. Morris, & R. N. Sykes (Eds.), *Practical aspects of memory: Current research and issues* (Vol. 1, pp. 342–346). Chichester, England: John Wiley & Sons.

**Beal, C. R.** (1985). Development of knowledge about the use of cues to aid prospective retrieval. *Child Development, 56,* 631–642.

**Beal, C. R.** (1988). The development of prospective memory skills. In M. M. Gruneberg, P. E. Morris, & R. N. Sykes (Eds.), *Practical aspects of memory: Current research and issues* (Vol. 1, pp. 366–370). Chichester, England: John Wiley & Sons.

**Beare, J. I.** (1906). *Greek theories of elementary cognition.* London: Oxford University Press.

**Bechtel, W., & Abrahamsen, A.** (1991). *Connectionism and the mind.* Cambridge, MA: Basil Blackwell.

**Beck, A. T.** (1967). *Depression: Clinical, experimental and theoretical aspects.* New York: Holber.

**Bedard, J., & Chi, M. T. H.** (1992). Expertise. *Current Directions in Psychological Science, 1,* 135–139.

**Bekerian, D. A., & Bowers, J. M.** (1983). Eyewitness testimony: Were we misled? *Journal of Experi-*

mental *Psychology: Learning, Memory, and Cognition, 1,* 139–145.

**Bellezza, F. S.** (1982). *Improve your memory skills.* Englewood Cliffs, NJ: Prentice-Hall.

**Bellezza, F. S.** (1983). Mnemonic-device instruction with adults. In M. Pressley & J. R. Levin (Eds.), *Cognitive strategy research: Psychological foundations* (pp. 51–73). New York: Springer-Verlag.

**Bellezza, F. S., Cheesman, F. L., & Reddy, B. G.** (1977). Organization and semantic elaboration in free recall. *Journal of Experimental Psychology: Human Learning and Memory, 3,* 539–550.

**Belli, R. F.** (1989). Influences of misleading postevent information: Misinformation interference and acceptance. *Journal of Experimental Psychology: General, 118,* 72–85.

**Bender, M. B.** (1956). Syndrome of isolated episode of confusion with amnesia. *Journal of Hillside Hospital, 5,* 212–215.

**Bennett, H. L.** (1988). Perception and memory for events during adequate general anesthesia for surgical operations. In H. M. Pettinati (Ed.), *Hypnosis and memory* (pp. 193–231). New York: Guilford Press.

**Bennett, H. L.** (1990). Influencing the brain with information during general anaesthesia: A theory of "unconscious hearing." In B. Bonke, W. Fitch, & K. Millar (Eds.), *Memory and awareness in anaesthesia* (pp. 50–56). Amsterdam: Swets & Zeitlinger.

**Bennett, H. L., Davis, H. S., & Giannini, J. A.** (1985). Nonverbal response to intraoperative conversation. *British Journal of Anaesthesia, 57,* 174–179.

**Benson, D. F., Miller, B. L., & Signer, S. F.** (1986). Dual personality associated with epilepsy. *Archives of Neurology, 43,* 471–474.

**Benton, A. L.** (1980). The neuropsychology of facial recognition. *American Psychologist, 35,* 176–186.

**Berger, T. W.** (1984). Long-term potentiation of hippocampal synaptic transmission affects rate of behavioral learning. *Science, 224,* 627–630.

**Best, D. L.** (1992). The role of social interaction in memory improvement. In D. J. Herrmann, H. Weingartner, A. Searleman, & C. L. McEvoy (Eds.), *Memory improvement: Implications for memory theory* (pp. 122–149). New York: Springer-Verlag.

Best, D. L., Hamlett, K. W., & Davis, S. W. (1992) Memory complaint and memory performance in the elderly: The effects of memory-skills training and expectancy change. *Applied Cognitive Psychology, 6,* 405–416.

Biederman, I., Mezzanotte, R. J., & Rabinowitz, J. (1982). Scene perception: Detecting and judging objects undergoing relational violations. *Cognitive Psychology, 14,* 143–177.

Binet, A. (1966). Mnemonic virtuosity: A study of chess players. *Genetic Psychology Monographs, 74,* 127–162. (Translated by M. L. Simmell and S. B. Barren from *Revue des Deux Mondes,* 1893, 117, 826–859.)

Birnbaum, I. M., & Parker, E. (Eds.). (1977). *Alcohol and human memory.* Hillsdale, NJ: Erlbaum.

Birnbaum, I. M., Taylor, T. H., Johnson, M. K., & Raye, C. L. (1987). Is event frequency encoded automatically? The case of alcohol intoxication. *Journal of Experimental Psychology: Learning, Memory, and Cognition, 13,* 251–258.

Bjork, R. A. (1978). The updating of human memory. In G. H. Bower (Ed.), *The psychology of learning and motivation* (Vol. 12, pp. 235–259). New York: Academic Press.

Bjork, R. A., & Bjork, E. L. (1992). A new theory of disuse and an old theory of stimulus fluctuation. In A. F. Healy, S. M. Kosslyn, & R. M. Shiffrin (Eds.), *From learning processes to cognitive processes: Essays in honor of William K. Estes* (Vol. 2, pp. 35–67). Hillsdale, NJ: Erlbaum.

Bjork, R. A., LaBerge, D., & Legrand, R. (1968). The modification of short-term memory through instructions to forget. *Psychonomic Science, 10,* 55–56.

Bjork, R. A., & Richardson-Klavehn, A. (1989). On the puzzling relationship between environmental context and human memory. In C. Izawa (Ed.), *The Tulane Flowerree Symposium on cognition* (pp. 313–344). Hillsdale, NJ: Erlbaum.

Bjork, R. A., & Whitten, W. B. (1974). Recency-sensitive retrieval processes. *Cognitive Psychology, 6,* 173–189.

Bjorklund, D. F. (1985). The role of conceptual knowledge in the development of organization in children's memory. In C. Brainerd & M. Pressley (Eds.), *Basic processes in memory development:*

*Progress in cognitive development research* (pp. 103–142). New York: Springer-Verlag.

Bjorklund, D. F. (1987). How age changes in knowledge base contribute to the development of children's memory: An interpretive review. *Developmental Review, 7,* 93–130.

Blaney, P. H. (1986). Affect and memory: A review. *Psychological Bulletin, 99,* 229–246.

Bliss, E. L. (1986). *Multiple personality, allied disorders, and hypnosis.* New York: Oxford University Press.

Bliss, T. V. P., & Lomo, T. (1973). Long-lasting potentiation of synaptic transmission in the denate area of the anaesthetized rabbit following stimulation of the perforant path. *Journal of Physiology (London), 232,* 331–356.

Bloch, V., Hennevin, E., & Leconte, P. (1979). Relationship between paradoxical sleep and memory processes. In M. A. B. Brazier (Ed.), *Brain mechanisms in memory and learning.* New York: Raven.

Block, R. I., & Wittenborn, J. R. (1984). Marijuana effects on semantic memory: Verification of common and uncommon category members. *Psychological Reports, 55,* 503–512.

Blomquist, K. B., & Danner, F. (1987). Effects of physical conditioning on information-processing efficiency. *Perceptual and Motor Skills, 65,* 176–186.

Blumenthal, J. A., & Madden, D. J. (1988). Effects of aerobic exercise training, age, and physical fitness on memory-search performance. *Psychology and Aging, 3,* 280–285.

Bobrow, S. A., & Bower, G. H. (1969). Comprehension and recall of sentences. *Journal of Experimental Psychology, 80,* 455–461.

Bodenhausen, G. V. (1988). Stereotypic biases in social decision making and memory: Testing process models of stereotype use. *Journal of Personality and Social Psychology, 55,* 726–737.

Bolla, K. I. (1991). Memory complaints in older adults: Fact or fiction? *Archives of Neurology, 48,* 61–64.

Bond, C. F., Jr., & Brockett, D. R. (1987). A social context-personality index theory of memory for acquaintances. *Journal of Personality and Social Psychology, 52,* 1110–1121.

Bond, C. F. & Omar, A. S. (1990). Social anxiety,

state dependence, and the next-in-line effect. *Journal of Experimental Social Psychology, 26*, 185–198.

Bonke, B., Fitch, W., & Millar, K. (Eds.). (1990). *Memory and awareness in anaesthesia.* Amsterdam: Swets & Zeitlinger.

Bonke, B., Schmitz, P. I. M., Verhage, F., & Zwaveling, A. (1986). Clinical study of so-called unconscious perception during general anaesthesia. *British Journal of Anaesthesia, 58*, 957–964.

Borkowski, J. G., Carr, M., Rellinger, E., & Pressley, M. (in press). Self-regulated cognition: Interdependence of metacognition, attributions, and self-esteem. In B. Jones (Ed.), *Dimensions of thinking: Review and research.* Hillside, NJ: Erlbaum.

Borkowski, J. G., Milstead, M., & Hale, C. (1988). Components of children's metamemory: Implications for strategy generalization. In F. E. Weinert & M. Perlmutter (Eds.), *Memory development: Universal changes and individual differences* (pp. 73–100). Hillsdale, NJ: Erlbaum.

Botwinick, J., & Storandt, M. (1974). *Memory, related functions and age.* Springfield, IL: Charles C. Thomas.

Bousfield, A. K., & Bousfield, W. A. (1966). Measurement of clustering and of sequential constancies in repeated free recall. *Psychological Reports, 19*, 935–942.

Bousfield, W. A. (1953). The occurrence of clustering in the recall of randomly arranged associates. *Journal of General Psychology, 49*, 229–240.

Bower, G. H. (1970). Analysis of a mnemonic device. *American Scientist, 58*, 498–510.

Bower, G. H. (1972). A selective review of organizational factors in memory. In E. Tulving & W. Donaldson (Eds.), *Organization of memory* (pp. 93–137). New York: Academic Press.

Bower, G. H. (1981). Mood and memory. *The American Psychologist, 36*, 129–148.

Bower, G. H., Black, J. B., & Turner, T. J. (1979). Scripts in memory for text. *Cognitive Psychology, 11*, 177–220.

Bower, G. H., & Gilligan, S. G. (1979). Remembering information related to one's self. *Journal of Research in Personality, 13*, 420–432.

Bower, G. H., & Karlin, M. B. (1974). Depth of processing pictures of faces and recognition memory. *Journal of Experimental Psychology, 103*, 751–757.

Bower, G. H., & Mayer, J. D. (1985). Failure to replicate mood dependent retrieval. *Bulletin of the Psychonomic Society, 18*, 39–42.

Bower, G. H., & Mayer, J. D. (1989). In search of mood-dependent memory. In D. Kuiken (Ed.), Mood and memory: Theory, research, and applications. [Special Issue]. *Journal of Social Behavior and Personality, 4*, 121–156.

Bower, G. H., & Monteiro, K. P., & Gilligan, S. G. (1978). Emotional mood as a context for learning and recall. *Journal of Verbal Learning and Verbal Behavior, 17*, 573–578.

Bowers, J. M., & Bekerian, D. A. (1984). When will postevent information distort eyewitness testimony? *Journal of Applied Psychology, 69*, 466–472.

Bowers, K. S., & Hilgard, E. R. (1986). Some complexities in understanding memory. In H. M. Pettinati (Ed.), *Hypnosis and memory* (pp. 3–18). New York: Guilford Press.

Bowyer, P. A., Humphrey, M. S., & Revelle, W. (1983). Arousal and recognition memory: The effects of impulsivity, caffeine and time on task. *Personality and Individual Differences, 4*, 41–49.

Bradley, B. P., & Baddeley, A. D. (1990). Emotional factors in forgetting. *Psychological Medicine, 20*, 351–355.

Brainerd, C. J., & Reyna, V. F. (1990). Gist is the grist: Fuzzy-trace theory and the new intuitionism. *Developmental Review, 10*, 3–47.

Bransford, J. D., & Franks, J. J. (1971). Abstraction of linguistic ideas. *Cognitive Psychology, 2*, 331–350.

Bransford, J. D., & Johnson, M. K. (1972). Contextual prerequisites for understanding: Some investigations of comprehension and recall. *Journal of Verbal Learning and Verbal Behavior, 11*, 717–726.

Bray, N. W., Hersh, R. E., & Turner, L. A. (1985). Selective remembering during adolescence. *Developmental Psychology, 21*, 290–294.

Bray, N. W., Justice, E. M., & Zahm, D. N. (1983). Two developmental transitions in selective remembering strategies. *Journal of Experimental Child Psychology, 36*, 43–55.

Breen, R. A., & McGaugh, J. L. (1961). Facilitation of maze learning with posttrial injections of picrotoxin. *Journal of Comparative and Physiological Psychology, 54,* 498–501.

Bregman, N. J., & McAllister, H. A. (1982). Eyewitness testimony: The role of commitment in increasing reliability. *Social Psychology Quarterly, 45,* 181–184.

Breitner, J. C. S. (1988). Alzheimer's disease: Possible evidence for genetic causes. In M. K. Aronson & R. N. Butler (Eds.), *Understanding Alzheimer's disease* (pp. 34–49). New York: Charles Scribner's Sons.

Brenner, M. (1973). The next-in-line effect. *Journal of Verbal Learning and Verbal Behavior, 12,* 320–323.

Brewer, W. F. (1977). Memory for the pragmatic implications of sentences. *Memory & Cognition, 5,* 673–678.

Brewer, W. F. (1986). What is autobiographical memory? In D. C. Rubin (Ed.), *Autobiographical memory* (pp. 25–49). Cambridge, England: Cambridge University Press.

Brewer, W. F. (1992). The theoretical and empirical status of the flashbulb memory hypothesis. In E. Winograd & U. Neisser (Eds.), *Affect and accuracy in recall: Studies of "flashbulb" memories* (pp. 274–305). New York: Cambridge University Press.

Brewer, W. F., & Treyens, J. C. (1981). Role of schemata in memory for places. *Cognitive Psychology, 13,* 207–230.

Bringmann, W. G., & Bringmann, N. J. (1986). Ebbinghaus and the new world. In F. Klix & H. Hagendorf (Eds.), *Human memory and cognitive capabilities* (pp. 45–50). Amsterdam: North Holland.

Brink, T. L. (1980). Idiot savant with unusual mechanical ability: An organic explanation. *American Journal of Psychiatry, 137,* 250–251.

Brioni, J. D., & McGaugh, J. L. (1988). Posttraining administration of GABAergic antagonists enhances retention of adversely motivated tasks. *Psychopharmacology, 96,* 505–510.

Brioni, J. D., Nagahara, A. H., & McGaugh, J. L. (1989). Involvement of the amygdala GABAergic system in the modulation of memory storage. *Brain Research, 487,* 105–112.

Bromley, D. B. (1958). Some effects of age on short-term learning and memory. *Journal of Gerontology, 13,* 398–406.

Brooks, L. R. (1968). Spatial and verbal components of the act of recall. *Canadian Journal of Psychology, 22,* 349–368.

Brown, A. S. (1991). A review of the tip-of-the-tongue experience. *Psychological Bulletin, 109,* 204–223.

Brown, A. S., & Murphy, D. R. (1989). Cryptomnesia: Delineating inadvertent plagiarism. *Journal of Experimental Psychology: Learning, Memory, and Cognition, 15,* 432–442.

Brown, A. S., & Oxman, M. (1978). Learning through participation: Effects of involvement and anticipation of involvement. *American Journal of Psychology, 91,* 461–472.

Brown, E., & Deffenbacher, K. (1975). Forgotten mnemonists. *Journal of the History of the Behavioral Sciences, 11,* 342–349.

Brown, J. (1958). Some tests of the decay theory of immediate memory. *Quarterly Journal of Experimental Psychology, 10,* 12–21.

Brown, N. R., Rips, L. J., & Shevell, S. K. (1985). The subjective dates of natural events in very long-term memory. *Cognitive Psychology, 17,* 139–177.

Brown, N. R., Shevell, S. K., & Rips, L. J. (1986). Public memories and their personal context. In D. C. Rubin (Ed.), *Autobiographical memory* (pp. 137–158). Cambridge, England: Cambridge University Press.

Brown, P., Keenan, J. M., & Potts, G. R. (1986). The self-reference effect with imagery encoding. *Journal of Personality and Social Psychology, 51,* 897–906.

Brown, R., & Kulik, J. (1977). Flashbulb memories. *Cognition, 5,* 73–99.

Brown, R., & McNeill, D. (1966). The "tip-of-the-tongue" phenomenon. *Journal of Verbal Learning and Verbal Behavior, 5,* 325–337.

Brown, T. H., Chapman, P. F., Kairiss, E. W., & Keenan, C. L. (1988). Long-term synaptic potentiation. *Science, 242,* 724–728.

Bruce, D. (1985). The how and why of ecological memory. *Journal of Experimental Psychology: General, 114,* 78–90.

Bruce, D., Hockley, W. E., & Craik, F. I. M. (1991). Availability and category-frequency estimation. *Memory & Cognition, 19,* 301–312.

Burke, A., Heuer, F., & Reisberg, D. (1992). Remembering emotional events. *Memory & Cognition, 20,* 277–290.

Burke, D., MacKay, D. G., Worthley, J. S., & Wade, E. (1991). On the tip of the tongue: What causes word finding failures in young and older adults? *Journal of Memory and Language, 30,* 237–246.

Burke, D. M., & Light, L. L. (1981). Memory and aging: The role of retrieval processes. *Psychological Bulletin, 90,* 513–546.

Burke, J. (1985). *The day the universe changed.* Boston: Little, Brown.

Burnham, W. H. (1888). Memory, historically and experimentally considered. *American Journal of Psychology, 2,* 39–90, 225–270, 431–464, 566–622.

Burrows, D., & Okada, R. (1971). Serial position effects in high-speed memory search. *Perception and Psychophysics, 10,* 305–308.

Butters, N., & Cermak, L. S. (1975). Some analyses of amnesic syndromes in brain-damaged patients. In R. L. Isaacson & K. H. Pribram (Eds.), *The hippocampus: Neuropsychology and behavior* (Vol. 2, pp. 377–409). New York: Plenum Press.

Butters, N., & Cermak, L. S. (1980). *Alcoholic Korsakoff's syndrome: An information processing approach to amnesia.* New York: Acadmic Press.

Butters, N., Miliotis, P., Albert, M. S., & Sax, D. S. (1983). Memory assessment: Evidence of the heterogeneity of amnesic symptoms. In G. Goldstein (Ed.), *Advances in clinical neuropsychology* (Vol. 1, pp. 127–159). New York: Plenum Press.

Butters, N., & Stuss, D. T. (1989). Diencephalic amnesia. In F. Boller & J. Grafman (Eds.), *Handbook of neuropsychology* (Vol. 3, pp. 107–148). Amsterdam: Elsevier.

Byrne, J. H. (1987). Cellular analysis of associative learning. *Physiological Review, 67,* 329–439.

Calkins, M. W. (1894). Association: I. *Psychological Review, 1,* 476–483.

Calkins, M. W. (1896). Association: II. *Psychological Review, 3,* 32–49.

Campbell, B. A., Misanin, J. R., White, B. C., & Lytle, L. D. (1974). Species differences in ontogeny of memory: Indirect support for neural maturation as a determinant of forgetting. *Journal of Comparative and Physiological Psychology, 87,* 193–202.

Cann, A., & Ross, D. A. (1989). Olfactory stimuli as context cues in human memory. *American Journal of Psychology, 102,* 91–102.

Carew, T. J. (1987). Cellular and molecular advances in the study of learning in Aplysia. In J. P. Changeaux & M. Konishi (Eds.), *The neural and molecular basis of learning* (pp. 177–204). New York: Wiley.

Carew, T. J., Marcus, E. A., Nolen, T. G., Rankin, C. H., & Stopfer, M. (1990). The development of learning and memory in Aplysia. In J. L. McGaugh, N. M. Weinberger & G. Lynch (Eds.), *Brain organization and memory: Cells, systems, and circuits* (pp. 27–51). New York: Oxford University Press.

Carlson, N. R. (1988). *Foundations of physiological psychology.* Boston: Allyn and Bacon.

Carmichael, L., Hogan, H. P., & Walter, A. A. (1932). An experimental study of language on the reproduction of visually perceived forms. *Journal of Experimental Psychology, 15,* 73–86.

Cartwright, R., Lloyd, S., Butters, E., Weiner, L., McCarthy, L., & Hancock, J. (1975). Effects of REM time on what is recalled. *Psychophysiology, 12,* 561–568.

Case, R. (1985). *Intellectual development: Birth to adulthood.* Orlando, FL: Academic Press.

Case, R., Kurland, D. M., & Goldberg, J. (1982). Operational efficiency and the growth of short-term memory span. *Journal of Experimental Child Psychology, 33,* 386–404.

Castellano, C., Brioni, J. D., Nagahara, A. H., & McGaugh, J. L. (1989). Posttraining systemic and intra-amygdala administration of GABA-b agonist baclofen impairs retention. *Behavioral and Neural Biology, 52,* 170–179.

Cavanaugh, J. C., Grady, J. G., & Perlmutter, M. (1983). Forgetting and use of memory aids in 20 to 70 years olds everyday life. *International Journal on Aging and Human Development, 17,* 113–122.

Cavanaugh, J. C., & Hertzog, C. (1992). Use of diary data in cognitive and developmental research. In R. L. West & J. D. Sinnott (Eds.), *Everyday memory and aging: Current research and methodology* (pp. 22–38). New York: Springer-Verlag.

Cavanaugh, J. C., & Morton, K. R. (1988). Older adults' attributions about everyday memory. In M. M. Gruneberg, P. E. Morris, & R. N. Sykes (Eds.), *Practical aspects of memory: Current research and issues* (Vol. 1, pp. 209–214). Chichester, England: John Wiley & Sons.

Cavanaugh, J. C., & Perlmutter, M. (1982). Meta-memory: A critical examination. *Child Development, 53,* 11–28.

Ceci, S. J., Baker, J. G., & Bronfenbrenner, U. (1988). Prospective remembering, temporal calibration, and context. In M. M. Gruneberg, P. E. Morris, & R. N. Sykes (Eds.), *Practical aspects of memory: Current research and issues* (Vol. 1, pp. 360–365). Chichester, England: John Wiley & Sons.

Ceci, S. J., & Bronfenbrenner, U. (1985). "Don't forget to take the cupcakes out of the oven": Prospective memory, strategic time-monitoring, and context. *Child Development, 56,* 152–164.

Ceci, S. J., & Bronfenbrenner, U. (1991). On the demise of everyday memory: "The rumors of my death are much exaggerated." *American Psychologist, 46,* 27–31.

Ceci, S. J., DeSimone, M., & Johnson, S. (1992). Memory in context: A case study of "Bubbles P.," a gifted but uneven memorizer. In D. J. Herrmann, H. Weingartner, A. Searleman, & C. L. McEvoy (Eds.), *Memory improvement: Implications for memory theory* (pp. 169–186). New York: Springer-Verlag.

Ceci, S. J., Lea, S. E. G., & Howe, M. J. A. (1980). Structural analysis of memory traces in children from 4 to 10 years of age. *Developmental Psychology, 16,* 203–212.

Ceci, S. J., & Liker, J. K. (1986). A day at the races: A study of IQ, expertise, and cognitive complexity. *Journal of Experimental Psychology: General, 115,* 255–266.

Ceci, S. J., Ross, D. F., & Toglia, M. P. (1987a). Age differences in suggestibility: Narrowing the uncertainties. In S. J. Ceci, M. P. Toglia, & D. F. Ross (Eds.), *Children's eyewitness testimony* (pp. 79–91). New York: Springer-Verlag.

Ceci, S. J., Ross, D. F., & Toglia, M. P. (1987b). Suggestibility of children's memory: Psycholegal implications. *Journal of Experimental Psychology: General, 116,* 38–49.

Ceci, S. J., Toglia, M. P., & Ross, D. F. (Eds.). (1987). *Children's eyewitness memory.* New York: Springer-Verlag.

Cernoch, J. M., & Porter, R. H. (1985). Recognition of maternal axillary odors by infants. *Child Development, 56,* 1593–1598.

Chandler, C. C. (1989). Specific retroactive interfer-ence in modified recognition tests: Evidence for an unknown cause of interference. *Journal of Experimental Psychology: Learning, Memory, and Cognition, 15,* 256–265.

Charness, N. (1976). Memory for chess positions: Resistance to interference. *Journal of Experimental Psychology: Human Learning and Memory, 2,* 641–653.

Charness, N. (1979). Components of skill in bridge. *Canadian Journal of Psychology, 33,* 1–16.

Charness, N. (1989). Expertise in chess and bridge. In D. Klahr & K. Kotovsky (Eds.), *Complex information processing: The impact of Herbert A. Simon* (pp. 183–208). Hillsdale, NJ: Erlbaum.

Charness, N., Clifton, J., & MacDonald, L. (1988). Case study of a musical "mono-savant": A cognitive-psychological focus. In L. K. Obler & D. Fein (Eds.), *The exceptional brain: Neuropsychology of talent and special abilities* (pp. 277–293). New York: Guilford Press.

Chase, W. G., & Ericsson, K. A. (1981). Skilled memory. In J. R. Anderson (Ed.), *Cognitive skills and their acquisition* (pp. 141–189). Hillsdale, NJ: Erlbaum

Chase, W. G., & Ericsson, K. A. (1982). Skill and working memory. In G. H. Bower (Ed.), *The psychology of learning and motivation* (Vol. 16, pp. 1–58). New York: Academic Press.

Chase, W. G., & Simon, H. A. (1973a). Perception in chess. *Cognitive Psychology, 4,* 55–81.

Chase, W. G., & Simon, H. A. (1973b). The mind's eye in chess. In W. G. Chase (Ed.), *Visual information processing* (pp. 215–281). New York: Academic Press.

Chelune, G. J., Ferguson, W., & Moehle, K. (1986). The role of standard cognitive and personality tests in neuropsychological assessment. In T. Incagnoli, G. Goldstein, & C. J. Golden (Eds.), *Clinical applications of neuropsychological test batteries* (pp. 75–119). New York: Plenum Press.

Chi, M. T. H. (1976). Short-term memory limitations in children: Capacity or processing deficits? *Memory & Cognition, 4,* 559–572.

Chi, M. T. H. (1978). Knowledge structure and memory development. In R. S. Siegler (Ed.), *Children's thinking: What develops?* (pp. 73–96). Hillsdale, NJ: Erlbaum.

Chi, M. T. H., Glaser, R., & Farr, M. J. (Eds.). (1988). *The nature of expertise.* Hillsdale, NJ: Erlbaum.

Chi, M. T. H., & Koeske, R. D. (1983). Network representation of a child's dinosaur knowledge. *Developmental Psychology, 19*, 29–39.

Chiarello, C., & Hoyer, W. J. (1988). Adult age differences in implicit and explicit memory: Time course and encoding effects. *Psychology and Aging, 3*, 358–366.

Chorover, S. L., & Schiller, P. H. (1965). Short-term retrograde amnesia in rats. *Journal of Comparative and Physiological Psychology, 59*, 73–78.

Christensen, A. L. (1975a). *Luria's neuropsychological investigation.* New York: Spectrum.

Christensen, A. L. (1975b). *Luria's neuropsychological investigation: Manual.* New York: Spectrum.

Christiaansen, R. E., & Ochalek, K. (1983). Editing misleading information from memory: Evidence for the coexistence of original and postevent information. *Memory & Cognition, 11*, 467–475.

Christianson, S-A. (1984). The relationship between induced emotional arousal and amnesia. *Scandinavian Journal of Psychology, 25*, 147–160.

Christianson, S-A., & Loftus, E. F. (1987). Memory for traumatic events. *Applied Cognitive Psychology, 1*, 225–239.

Christianson, S-A., & Loftus, E. F. (1991). Remembering emotional events: The fate of detailed information. *Cognition and Emotion, 5*, 81–108.

Clayton, K. N., & Habibi, A. (1991). Contribution of temporal contiguity to the spatial priming effect. *Journal of Experimental Psychology: Learning, Memory and Cognition, 17*, 263–271.

Clifford, B., & Scott, J. (1978). Individual and situational factors in eyewitness testimony. *Journal of Applied Psychology, 63*, 352–359.

Cockburn, J., & Smith, P. T. (1988). Effects of age and intelligence on everyday memory tasks. In M. M. Gruneberg, P. E. Morris, & R. N. Sykes (Eds.), *Practical aspects of memory: Current research and issues* (Vol. 2, pp. 132–136). Chichester, England: John Wiley & Sons.

Cohen, G. (1989). *Memory in the real world.* Hillsdale, NJ: Erlbaum.

Cohen, G., & Faulkner, D. (1988). Life span changes in autobiographical memory. In M. M. Gruneberg, P. E. Morris, & R. N. Sykes (Eds.), *Practical aspects of memory: Current research and issues* (Vol. 1, pp. 277–282). Chichester, England: John Wiley & Sons.

Cohen, G. D. (1986). Foreword. In T. Crook, R. Bartus, S. Ferris, & S. Gershon (Eds.), *Treatment development strategies for Alzheimer's disease.* Madison, CT: Mark Powley Associates.

Cohen, N. J. (1984). Preserved learning capacity in amnesia: Evidence for multiple memory systems. In L. R. Squire & N. Butters (Eds.), *Neuropsychology of memory* (pp. 83–103). New York: Guilford Press.

Cohen, N. J., & Squire, L. R. (1980). Preserved learning and retention of pattern analysing skill in amnesia: Dissociation of "knowing how" and "knowing that." *Science, 210*, 207–209.

Cole, M., & Scribner, S. (1974). *Culture and thought: A psychological introduction.* New York: John Wiley & Sons.

Collins, A. M., & Loftus, E. F. (1975). A spreading-activation theory of semantic memory. *Psychological Review, 82*, 407–428.

Collins, A. M., & Quillian, M. R. (1969). Retrieval time from semantic memory. *Journal of Verbal Learning and Verbal Behavior, 8*, 240–247.

Confer, W. N., & Ables, B. S. (1983). *Multiple personality: Etiology, diagnosis, and treatment.* New York: Human Sciences Press.

Conrad, R. (1963). Acoustic confusions and memory span for words. *Nature, 197*, 1029–1030.

Conrad, R. (1964). Acoustic confusions in immediate memory. *British Journal of Psychology, 55*, 75–84.

Conrad, R. (1972). Short-term memory in the deaf: A test for speech coding. *British Journal of Psychology, 63*, 173–180.

Conrad, R., & Hull, A. J. (1964). Information, acoustic confusion and memory span. *British Journal of Psychology, 55*, 429–432.

Conway, M. A. (1990). *Autobiographical memory: An introduction.* Philadelphia: Open University Press.

Corballis, M. C., Kirby, J., & Miller, A. (1972). Access to elements of a memorized list. *Journal of Experimental Psychology, 94*, 185–190.

Corkin, S. (1984). Lasting consequences of bilateral medial temporal lobectomy: Clinical course and experimental findings in H.M. *Seminars in Neurology, 4*, 249–259.

Cornoldi, C., & McDaniel, M. A. (Eds.). (1991). *Imagery and cognition.* New York: Springer-Verlag.

**Cowan, N.** (1988). Evolving conceptions of memory storage, selective attention, and their mutual constraints within the human information-processing system. *Psychological Bulletin, 104,* 163–191.

**Craik, F. I. M.** (1977). Age differences in human memory. In J. E. Birren & K. W. Schaie (Eds.), *Handbook of the psychology of aging* (pp. 384–420). New York: Van Nostrand Reinhold.

**Craik, F. I. M.** (1983). On the transfer of information from temporary to permanent memory. *Philosophical Transactions of the Royal Society of London, B302,* 341–359.

**Craik, F. I. M.** (1984). Age differences in remembering. In L. R. Squire & N. Butters (Eds.), *Neuropsychology of memory* (pp. 3–12). New York: Guilford Press.

**Craik, F. I. M.** (1990). Levels of processing. In M. E. Eysenck (Ed.), *The Blackwell dictionary of cognitive psychology* (pp. 213–215). London: Blackwell.

**Craik, F. I. M., Byrd, M., & Swanson, J. M.** (1987). Patterns of memory loss in three elderly samples. *Psychology and Aging, 2,* 79–86.

**Craik, F. I. M., & Lockhart, R. S.** (1972). Levels of processing: A framework for memory research. *Journal of Verbal Learning and Verbal Behavior, 11,* 671–684.

**Craik, F. I. M., & Lockhart, R. S.** (1986). CHARM is not enough: Comments of Eich's model of cued recall. *Psychological Review, 93,* 360–364.

**Craik, F. I. M., & McDowd, J. M.** (1987). Age differences in recall and recognition. *Journal of Experimental Psychology: Learning, Memory and Cognition, 13,* 474–479.

**Craik, F. I. M., & Tulving, E.** (1975). Depth of processing and the retention of words in episodic memory. *Journal of Experimental Psychology: General, 104,* 268–294.

**Cranberg, L. D., & Albert, M. L.** (1988). The chess mind. In L. K. Obler & D. Fein (Eds.), *The exceptional brain: Neuropsychology of talent and special abilities* (pp. 156–190). New York: Guilford Press.

**Crawford, M., Herrmann, D. J., Randal, E., Holdsworth, M., & Robbins, D.** (1989). Self perception of memory performance as a function of gender. *British Journal of Psychology, 80,* 391–401.

**Crovitz, H. F., & Schiffman, H.** (1974). Frequency of episodic memories as a function of their age. *Bulletin of the Psychonomic Society, 4,* 517–518.

**Crow, T. J., & Alkon, D. L.** (1978). Retention of an associative modification in Hermissenda. *Science, 201,* 1239–1241.

**Crowder, R. G.** (1980). Echoic memory and the study of aging memory systems. In L. W. Poon, J. L. Fozard, L. S. Cermack, D. Arenberg, & L. W. Thompson (Eds.), *New directions in memory and aging: Proceedings of the George A. Talland Memorial Conference* (pp. 181–204). Hillsdale, NJ: Erlbaum.

**Curran, H. V., Sakulsriprong, M., & Lader, M.** (1988). Antidepressants and human memory: An investigation of four drugs with different sedative and anticholinergic profiles. *Psychopharmacology, 95,* 520–527.

**Cutler, S., & Grams, A. E.** (1988). Correlates of self-reported everyday memory problems. *Journal of Gerontology: Social Sciences, 43,* 582–590.

**Cuvo, A. J.** (1974). Incentive level influence on overt rehearsal and free recall as a function of age. *Journal of Experimental Child Psychology, 18,* 167–181.

**Cytowic, R. E.** (1989). *Synesthesia: A union of the senses.* New York: Springer-Verlag.

**Daehler, M. W., & Greco, C.** (1985). Memory in very young children. In M. Pressley & C. J. Brainerd (Eds.), *Cognitive learning and memory in children* (pp. 49–79). New York: Springer-Verlag.

**Darley, C. F., Tinklenberg, J. R., Hollister, T. E., & Atkinson, R. C.** (1973). Marijuana and retrieval from short-term memory. *Psychopharmacologia, 29,* 231–238.

**Davies, G. M., & Thomson, D. M.** (Eds.). (1988). *Memory in context: Context in memory.* Chichester, England: John Wiley & Sons.

**Davis, W.** (1988). *Passage of darkness: The ethnobiology of the Haitian Zombie.* Chapel Hill, NC: University of North Carolina Press.

**Deakin, J. M., & Allard, F.** (1991). Skilled memory in expert figure skaters. *Memory & Cognition, 19,* 79–86.

**DeBono, K. G., & Hamish, R. J.** (1988). Source expertise, source attractiveness, and the processing of persuasive information: A functional approach. *Journal of Personality and Social Psychology, 56,* 541–546.

**DeCasper, A. J., & Fifer, W. P.** (1980). Of human bonding: Newborns prefer their mothers' voices. *Science, 208,* 1174–1176.

**DeCasper, A. J., & Prescott, P. A.** (1984). Human newborns' perception of male voices: Preference, discrimination and reinforcing value. *Developmental Psychobiology, 17,* 481–491.

**DeCasper, A. J., & Spence, M. J.** (1986). Prenatal maternal speech influences newborns' perception of speech sounds. *Infant Behavior and Development, 9,* 133–150.

**Deffenbacher, K.** (1983). The influence of arousal on reliability of testimony. In S. Lloyd-Bostock & B. Clifford (Eds.), *Evaluating witness evidence* (pp. 235–252). New York: Wiley.

**de Groot, A. D.** (1965). *Thought and choice in chess.* The Hague: Mouton.

**de Groot, A. D.** (1966). Perception and memory versus thought: Some old ideas and recent findings. In B. Kleinmutz (Ed.), *Problem solving: Research, method, and theory* (pp. 19–50). New York: John Wiley & Sons.

**DeLoache, J. S.** (1980). Naturalistic studies of memory for object location in very young children. In M. Perlmutter (Ed.), *New directions for child development: Children's memory* (pp. 17–32). San Francisco: Jossey Bass.

**Dempster, F. N.** (1981). Memory span: Sources of individual and developmental differences. *Psychological Bulletin, 89,* 63–100.

**Dempster, F. N.** (1985). Short-term memory development in childhood and adolescence. In C. Brainerd & M. Pressley (Eds.), *Basic processes in memory development: Progress in cognitive development research* (pp. 209–248). New York: Springer-Verlag.

**DiLollo, V., Hanson, D., & McIntyre, J. S.** (1983). Initial stages of visual information processing in dyslexia. *Journal of Experimental Psychology: Human Perception and Performance, 9,* 923–935.

**Dixon, R. A., & Hultsch, D. F.** (1983). Structure and development of metamemory in adulthood. *Journal of Gerontology, 38,* 682–689.

**Dobbs, A. R., & Rule, B. G.** (1987). Prospective memory and self-reports of memory abilities in older adults. *Canadian Journal of Psychology, 41,* 209–222.

**Dodson, C., & Reisberg, D.** (1991). Indirect testing of eyewitness memory: The (non)effect of misinformation. *Bulletin of the Psychonomic Society, 29,* 333–336.

**Doerner, D.** (1986). Intention memory and intention regulation. In F. Klix and H. Hagendorf (Eds.), *Memory and cognitive capabilities: Mechanisms and performances* (pp. 929–939). Amsterdam: North Holland.

**Donaldson, W., & Bass, M.** (1980). Relational information and memory for problem solutions. *Journal of Verbal Learning and Verbal Behavior, 19,* 26–35.

**Dovidio, J., & Gaertner, S.** (1986). *Prejudism, discrimination and racism.* New York: Academic Press.

**Dritschel, B. H., Williams, J. M. G., Baddeley, A. D., & Nimmo-Smith, I.** (1992). Autobiographical fluency: A method for the study of personal memory. *Memory & Cognition, 20,* 133–140.

**Dudai, Y.** (1989). *The neurobiology of memory: Concepts, findings, trends.* New York: Oxford University Press.

**D'Ydewalle, G., Delhaye, P., & Goessens, L.** (1985). Structural, semantic, and self-reference processing of pictorial advertisements. *Human Learning, 4,* 29–38.

**D'Zurilla, T.** (1965). Recall efficiency and mediating cognitive events in "experimental repression." *Journal of Personality and Social Psychology, 3,* 253–256.

**Easterbrook, J.** (1959). The effect of emotion on cue utilization and the organization of behavior. *Psychological Review, 66,* 183–201.

**Ebbinghaus, H.** (1885). *Über das Gedächtnis: Untersuchugen zur Experimentellen Psychologie.* Leipzig: Dunker & Humbolt. Translated by H. A. Ruger & C. E. Byssenine as *Memory: A contribution to experimental psychology.* New York: Dover, 1913.

**Ebbinghaus, H.** (1908). *Abris der Psychologie.* Leipzig: Dunker & Humbolt. Translated by M. Meyer as *Psychology: An elementary textbook.* Boston: Heath, 1908.

**Edgell, B.** (1924). *Theories of memory.* London: Oxford University Press.

**Egan, D. E., & Schwartz, B. J.** (1979). Chunking in recall of symbolic drawings. *Memory & Cognition, 7,* 149–158.

**Eich, J. E.** (1977). State-dependent retrieval of information in human episodic memory. In I. M. Birn-baum & E. S. Parker (Eds.), *Alcohol and human memory* (pp. 141–157). Hillside, NJ: Erlbaum.

Eich, J. E. (1980). The cue-dependent nature of state-dependent retrieval. *Memory & Cognition, 8,* 157–173.

Eich, J. E. (1989). Theoretical issues in state depen-dent memory. In H. L. Roediger III & F. I. M. Craik (Eds.), *Varieties of memory and conscious-ness: Essays in honour of Endel Tulving* (pp. 331–354). Hillsdale NJ: Erlbaum.

Eich, J. E., & Metcalfe, J. (1989). Mood dependent memory for internal versus external events. *Jour-nal of Experimental Psychology: Learning, Memory, and Cognition, 15,* 443–455.

Eich, J. E., Reeves, J. L., & Katz, R. L. (1985). Anes-thesia, amnesia, and the memory/awareness dis-tinction. *Anesthesia and Analgesia, 64,* 1143–1148.

Einstein, G. O., & McDaniel, M. A. (1990). Normal aging and prospective memory. *Journal of Exper-imental Psychology: Learning, Memory, and Cogni-tion, 16,* 717–726.

Einstein, G. O., & McDaniel, M. A. (1991, Novem-ber). *Aging and time- versus event-based prospective memory.* Paper presented at the annual meeting of the Psychonomic Society, San Francisco, CA.

Ellis, E. A. (1983). *Emotional mood as a context for state-dependent retention: Some limitations of the phenomenon.* Unpublished senior honors thesis, University of Toronto, Canada.

Ellis, H. C., & Ashbrook, P. W. (1988). Resource allocation model of the effects of depressed mood states on memory. In K. Fiedler & J. Forgas (Eds.), *Affect, cognition and social behavior* (pp. 25–43). Toronto, Canada: Hogrefe.

Ellis, H. C., & Ashbrook, P. W. (1989). The "state" of mood and memory research: A selective re-view. In D. Kuiken (Ed.), Mood and memory: Theory, research, and applications [Special is-sue]. *Journal of Social Behavior and Personality, 4,* 1–21.

Ellis, H. C., & Hunt, R. R. (1993). *Fundamentals of cognitive psychology* (5th ed.). Dubuque, IA: Wm. C. Brown Publishers.

Ellis, H. C., Thomas, L., & Rodriguez, I. A. (1984). Emotional mood-states and memory: Elabora-tive coding, semantic processing, and cognitive effort. *Journal of Experimental Psychology: Learn-ing, Memory, and Cognition, 10,* 470–482.

Ellis, N. C., & Hennelly, R. A. (1980). A bilingual word-length effect: Implications for intelligence testing and the relative ease of mental calculation in Welsh and English. *British Journal of Psychol-ogy, 71,* 43–52.

Ellis, N. R. (1990). Is memory for spatial location automatically encoded? *Memory & Cognition, 18,* 584–592.

Elmes, D. G. (1969). Cueing to forget in short-term memory. *Journal of Experimental Psychology, 80,* 561–562.

Emmerich, H. J., & Ackerman, B. P. (1978). Devel-opmental differences in recall: Encoding or re-trieval? *Journal of Experimental Child Psychology, 25,* 514–525.

Engle, R. W., & Bukstel, L. H. (1978). Memory pro-cesses among bridge players of differing exper-tise. *American Journal of Psychology, 91,* 673–689.

Engle, R. W., Fidler, D. S., & Reynolds, L. H. (1981). Does echoic memory develop? *Journal of Experimental Child Psychology, 32,* 459–473.

Erdelyi, M. H., & Goldberg, B. (1979). Let's not sweep repression under the rug: Toward a cog-nitive psychology of repression. In J. F. Kihl-strom & R. J. Evans (Eds.), *Functional disorders of memory* (pp. 355–402). Hillsdale, NJ: Erlbaum.

Erickson, R. C., & Howieson, D. (1986). The clini-cian's perspective: Measuring change and treat-ment effectiveness. In L. W. Poon, T. Crook, K. L. Davis, C. Eisdorfer, B. J. Gurland, A. W. Kasz-niak, & L. W. Thompson (Eds.), *Handbook for clin-ical memory assessment of older adults* (pp. 69–80). Hyattsville, MD: The American Psychological Association.

Erickson, R. C., & Scott, M. L. (1977). Clinical mem-ory testing: A review. *Psychological Bulletin, 84,* 1130–1149.

Ericsson, K. A., (1985). Memory skill. *Canadian Jour-nal of Psychology, 39,* 188–231.

Ericsson, K. A., Chase, W. G., & Faloon, S. F. (1980). Acquisition of a memory skill. *Science, 208,* 1181–1182.

Ericsson, K. A., & Faivre, I. A. (1988). What's ex-ceptional about exceptional abilities? In L. K. Ob-ler & D. Fein (Eds.), *The exceptional brain: Neuro-psychology of talent and special abilities* (pp. 436–473). New York: Guilford Press.

Ericsson, K. A., & Polson, P. G. (1988). A cognitive analysis of exceptional memory for restaurant orders. In M. T. H. Chi, R. Glaser, & M. J. Farr (Eds.), *The nature of expertise* (pp. 23–70). Hillsdale, NJ: Erlbaum.

Ericsson, K. A., & Smith, J. (Eds.) (1991a). *Toward a general theory of expertise*. Cambridge, England: Cambridge University Press.

Ericsson, K. A., & Smith, J. (1991b). Prospects and limits of the empirical study of expertise: An introduction. In K. A. Ericsson & J. Smith (Eds.), *Toward a general theory of expertise* (pp. 1–38). Cambridge, England: Cambridge University Press.

Ericsson, K. A., & Staszewski, J. (1989). Skilled memory and expertise: Mechanisms of exceptional performance. In D. Klahr & K. Kotovsky (Eds.), *Complex information processing: The impact of Herbert A. Simon* (pp. 235–267). Hillsdale, NJ: Erlbaum.

Estes, W. K. (1980). Is human memory obsolete? *American Scientist, 68,* 62–68.

Estes, W. K. (1988). Toward a framework for combining connectionist and symbol-processing models. *Journal of Memory and Language, 27,* 196–212.

Evans, C., & Richardson, P. H. (1988). Improved recovery and reduced postoperative stay after therapeutic suggestions during general anaesthesia. *The Lancet, #8609*(II), 491–493.

Eysenck, M. W. (1978). Levels of processing: A critique. *British Journal of Psychology, 69,* 157–169.

Eysenck, M. W. (1982). *Attention and arousal: Cognition and performance*. Berlin: Springer.

Eysenck, M. W. (1984). *A handbook of cognitive psychology*. Hillsdale, NJ: Erlbaum.

Eysenck, M. W., & Folkard, S. (1980). Personality, time of day, and caffeine: Some theoretical and conceptual problems in Revelle et al. *Journal of Experimental Psychology: General, 109,* 32–41.

Fagan, J. F. (1973). Infants' delayed recognition memory and forgetting. *Journal of Experimental Child Psychology, 16,* 424–450.

Fagan, J. F. (1984). The relationship of novelty preferences during infancy to later intelligence and later recognition memory. *Intelligence, 8,* 339–346.

Fagan, J. F., & McGrath, S. K. (1981). Infant recognition memory and later intelligence. *Intelligence, 5,* 121–130.

Fagan, J. F., & Singer, L. T. (1983). Infant recognition memory as a measure of intelligence. In L. P. Lipsitt (Ed.), *Advances in infancy research* (Vol. 2, pp. 31–78). Norwood, NJ: Ablex.

Fagen, J. W., & Rovee-Collier, C. (1983). Memory retrieval: A time-locked process in infancy. *Science, 222,* 1349–1351.

Fechner, G. T. (1860). *Elemente der Psychophysik*. Leipzig: Breitkopf & Harterl. Translated by H. E. Adler, D. H. Howes, & E. G. Boring as *Elements of psychophysics*. New York: Holt, Rinehart, and Winston, 1966.

Feinaigle, M. G. von (1813). *The new art of memory* (2nd ed.). London: Sherwood, Neely, and Jones.

Finke, R. A. (1985). Theories relating mental imagery to perception. *Psychological Bulletin, 98,* 236–259.

Finke, R. A. (1989). *Principles of mental imagery*. Cambridge, MA: The M.I.T. Press.

Fisher, C. M., & Adams, R. D. (1958). Transient global amnesia. *Transactions of the American Neurological Association, 83,* 143–145.

Fisher, R. P., Geiselman, R. E., & Amador, M. (1989). Field test of the cognitive interview: Enhancing the recollection of actual victims and witnesses of crime. *Journal of Applied Psychology, 74,* 722–727.

Fisk, A. D., & Schneider, W. (1984). Memory as a function of attention, level of processing, and automatization. *Journal of Experimental Psychology: Learning, Memory, and Cognition, 10,* 181–197.

Fiske, A. D., & Taylor, S. E. (1984). *Social cognition*. Reading, MA: Addison-Wesley.

Fivush, R., & Hamond, N. R. (1990). Autobiographical memory across the preschool years: Toward reconceptualizing childhood amnesia. In R. Fivush & J. A. Hudson (Eds.), *Knowing and remembering in young children* (pp. 223–248). New York: Cambridge University Press.

Flavell, J. H. (1970). Developmental studies of mediated memory. In H. W. Reese & L. P. Lipsitt (Eds.), *Advances in child development and behavior* (pp. 181–211). New York: Academic Press.

Flavell, J. H. (1977). *Cognitive development*. Englewood Cliffs, NJ: Prentice-Hall.

Flavell, J. H., Beach, D. H., & Chinsky, J. M. (1966). Spontaneous verbal rehearsal in a memory task as a function of age. *Child Development, 37,* 283–299.

Flavell, J. H., Friedrichs, A. G., & Hoyt, J. D. (1970).

Developmental changes in memorization processes. *Cognitive Psychology, 1,* 324–340.

Flavell, J. H., & Wellman, H. M. (1977). Metamemory. In R. V. Kail, Jr., & J. W. Hagen (Eds.), *Perspectives on the development of memory and cognition* (pp. 3–33). Hillsdale, NJ: Erlbaum.

Fleishman, E. A., & Parker, J. F., Jr. (1962). Factors in the retention and relearning of perceptual motor skill. *Journal of Experimental Psychology, 64,* 215–226.

Flexser, A. J., & Bower, G. H. (1974). How frequency affects recency judgments: A model for recency discrimination. *Journal of Experimental Psychology, 103,* 706–716.

Flourens, P. (1824). *Researches experimentales sur les propriétés et les fonctions du systeme nerveux dans les Animaux Vertebres.* Paris: Balliere.

Flugel, J. C. (1933). *A hundred years of psychology.* London: Duckworth.

Fowler, R., Hart, J., & Sheehan, M. (1972). A prosthetic memory: An application of the prosthetic environment concept. *Rehabilitation Counselling Bulletin, 15,* 80–85.

Freud, S. (1953). Three essays on the theory of sexuality. In J. Strachey (Ed. and Trans.), *The standard edition of the complete psychological works of Sigmund Freud* (Vol. 7, pp. 135–245). London: Hogarth. (Original work published 1905.)

Freud, S. (1957). Repression. In J. Strachey (Ed. and Trans.), *The standard edition of the complete psychological works of Sigmund Freud* (Vol. 14, pp. 28–160). London: Hogarth Press. (Original work published 1915.)

Freud, S. (1960). The psychopathology of everyday life. In J. Strachey (Ed. and Trans.), *The standard edition of the complete psychological works of Sigmund Freud* (Vol. 6, pp. 1–289). London: Hogarth Press. (Original work published 1901.)

Freud, S., & Brill, A. A. (1916). *Psychopathology of everyday life.* New York: Macmillan.

Frey, P. W., & Adesman, P. (1976). Recall memory for visually presented chess positions. *Memory & Cognition, 4,* 541–547.

Friedman, S. (1972). Habituation and recovery of visual response in the alert human newborn. *Journal of Experimental Child Psychology, 13,* 339–349.

Friedman, W. J. (1987). A follow-up to "Scale effects in memory for the time of events": The earthquake study. *Memory & Cognition, 15,* 518–520.

Friedman, W. J. (1990). *About time: Inventing the fourth dimension.* Cambridge, MA: The M.I.T. Press.

Friedman, W. J. (1993). Memory for the time of past events. *Psychological Bulletin, 113,* 44–66.

Friedman, W. J., & Wilkins, A. (1985). Scale effects in memory for the time of events. *Memory & Cognition, 13,* 168–175.

Frith, C. (1991). Has neurochemistry told us anything about human memory? In J. Weinman & J. Hunter (Eds.), *Memory: Neurochemical and abnormal perspectives* (pp. 129–138). Chur, Switzerland: Harwood Academic Publishers.

Frost, N. (1972). Encoding and retrieval in visual memory tasks. *Journal of Experimental Psychology, 95,* 317–326.

Fuld, P. A., Katzman, R., Davies, P., & Terry, R. D. (1982). Intrusions as a sign of Alzheimer's dementia: Chemical and pathological verification. *Annals of Neurology, 11,* 155–159.

Furlong, M. (1990). Positive suggestions presented during anaesthesia. In B. Bonke, W. Fitch, & K. Millar (Eds.), *Memory and awareness in anaesthesia* (pp. 170–175). Amsterdam: Swets & Zeitlinger.

Galton, F. (1879a). Psychometric experiments. *Brain, 2,* 149–162.

Galton, F. (1879b). Psychometric facts. *Nineteenth Century, 5,* 425–433.

Galton, F. (1883). *Inquiries into human faculty and its development* (1st ed.). London: Macmillan.

Gardiner, J. M., Gregg, V. H., & Hampton, J. A. (1988). Word frequency and generation effects. *Journal of Experimental Psychology: Learning, Memory, and Cognition, 14,* 687–693.

Gardiner, J. M., & Hampton, J. A. (1985). Semantic memory and the generation effect: Some tests of the lexical activation hypothesis. *Journal of Experimental Psychology: Learning, Memory, and Cognition, 11,* 732–741.

Geiselman, R. E., Fisher, R. P., Firstenberg, I., Hutton, L. A., Sullivan, S., Avetissian, I., & Prosk, A. (1984). Enhancement of eyewitness memory: An empirical evaluation of the cognitive interview. *Journal of Police Science and Administration, 12,* 74–80.

Geiselman, R. E., Fisher, R. P., MacKinnon, D. P., & Holland, H. L. (1985). Eyewitness memory enhancement in the police interview: Cognitive retrieval mnemonics versus hypnosis. *Journal of Applied Psychology, 70,* 401–412.

Gentry, M., & Herrmann, D. J. (1990). Memory contrivances in everyday life. *Personality and Social Psychology Bulletin, 18,* 241–253.

Gerard, L., Zacks, R. T., Hasher, L., & Radvansky, G. A. (1991). Age deficits in retrieval: The fan effect. *Journal of Gerontology, 46,* 131–136.

Gernsbacher, M. A. (1985). Surface information loss in comprehension. *Cognitive Psychology, 17,* 324–363.

Gervasio, A. H. (1988). Barriers to memory improvement in neurological populations: An adherence model. *Neuropsychology, 2,* 161–171.

Gibson, J. J. (1979). *The ecological approach to visual perception.* Boston: Houghton Mifflin.

Gilbert, J. G., Levee, R. F., & Catalano, F. L. (1968). A preliminary report on a new memory scale. *Perceptual and Motor Skills, 27,* 277–278.

Gilewski, M. J., & Zelinski, E. M. (1986). Questionnaire assessment of memory complaints. In L. W. Poon, T. Crook, K. L. Davis, B. J. Gurland, A. W. Kaszniak, & L. W. Thompson (Eds.), *Handbook of clinical memory assessment of older adults* (pp. 93–107). Hyattsville, MD: The American Psychological Association.

Gilligan, S. G., & Bower, G. H. (1984). Cognitive consequences of emotional arousal. In C. E. Izard, J. Kagan, & R. Zajonc (Eds.), *Emotion, cognition and behavior* (pp. 547–588). New York: Cambridge University Press.

Giray, E. F., Altkin, W. M., Roodin, P. A., Yoon, G., & Flagg, P. (1978, August). *The incidence of eidetic imagery in adulthood and old age.* Paper presented at the 86th annual meeting of the American Psychological Association, Toronto.

Glanzer, M., & Cunitz, A. R. (1966). Two storage mechanisms in free recall. *Journal of Verbal Learning and Verbal Behavior, 5,* 351–360.

Glaze, J. A. (1928). The association value of nonsense syllables. *Journal of Genetic Psychology, 35,* 255–269.

Glenberg, A. M., & Adams, F. (1978). Type I rehearsal and recognition. *Journal of Verbal Learning and Verbal Behavior, 17,* 455–463.

Glenberg, A. M., Bradley, M. M., Kraus, T. A., & Renzaglia, G. J. (1983). Studies of the long-term recency effect: Support for a contextually guided retrieval hypothesis. *Journal of Experimental Psychology: Learning, Memory, and Cognition, 9,* 231–255.

Glenberg, A. M., Smith, S. M., & Green, C. (1977). Type I rehearsal: Maintenance and more. *Journal of Verbal Learning and Verbal Behavior, 16,* 339–352.

Glisky, G. L., & Schacter, D. L. (1987). Acquisition of domain-specific knowledge in organic amnesia: Training for computer-related work. *Neuropsychologia, 25,* 893–906.

Glisky, G. L., & Schacter, D. L. (1988). Long-term retention of computer learning by patients with memory disorders. *Neuropsychologia, 26,* 173–178.

Glisky, G. L., & Schacter, D. L. (1989). Models and methods of memory rehabilitation. In F. Boller & J. Grafman (Eds.), *Handbook of neuropsychology* (Vol. 3, pp. 233–246). Amsterdam: Elsevier.

Glisky, G. L., Schacter, D. L., & Tulving, E. (1986). Computer learning by memory-impaired patients: Acquisition and retention of complex knowledge. *Neuropsychologia, 24,* 313-328.

Goddard, H. H. (1914). *Feeble-mindedness.* New York: Macmillan.

Godden, D., & Baddeley, A. D. (1975). Context-dependent memory in two natural experiments: On land and under water. *British Journal of Psychology, 66,* 325–331.

Goethals, G. R., & Reckman, R. F. (1973). The perception of consistency in attitudes. *Journal of Experimental Social Psychology, 9,* 491–501.

Goffman, E. (1961). *Encounters.* Indianapolis: Bobbs-Merrill.

Goffman, E. (1969). *The presentation of self in everyday life.* London: Allen Lane.

Gold, P. E. (1987). Sweet memories. *American Scientist, 75,* 151–155.

Gold, P. E. (1992). A proposed neurobiological basis for regulating memory storage for significant events. In E. Winograd & U. Neisser (Eds.), *Affect and accuracy in recall: Studies of "flashbulb" memories* (pp. 141–161). New York: Cambridge University Press.

Gold, P. E., & Stone, W. S. (1988). Neuroendocrine effects on memory in aged-rodents and humans. *Neurobiology of Aging, 9,* 709–717.

Golden, C. J., Purisch, A. D., & Hammeke, T. A.

(1985). *Luria-Nebraska Neuropsychological Battery: Forms I and II Manual.* Los Angeles: Western Psychological Services.

Goldmann, L. (1986). *Awareness under general anaesthesia.* Unpublished doctoral dissertation, Cambridge University, Cambridge, England.

Goldmann, L., Shah, M. V., & Hebden, M. W. (1987). Memory of cardiac anaesthesia. Psychological sequelae in cardiac patients of intra-operative suggestion and operating room conversation. *Anaesthesia, 42,* 596–603.

Goldstein, G. (1986). An overview of similarities and differences between the Halstead-Reitan and Luria-Nebraska Neuropsychological Batteries. In T. Incagnoli, G. Goldstein, & C. J. Golden (Eds.), *Clinical applications of neuropsychological test batteries* (pp. 235–275). New York: Plenum Press.

Goodglass, H., & Kaplan, E. (1972). *Assessment of aphasia and related disorders.* Philadelphia: Lea & Febiger.

Goodglass, H., & Kaplan, E. (1983). *Assessment of aphasia and related disorders* (rev. ed.). Philadelphia: Lea & Febiger.

Goodwin, D. W., Powell, B., Bremer, D., Hoine, H., & Stern, J. (1969). Alcohol and recall: State dependent effects in man. *Science, 163,* 1358–1360.

Graf, P. (1980). Two consequences of generating: Increased inter- and intraword organization of sentences. *Journal of Verbal Learning and Verbal Behavior, 19,* 316–327.

Graf, P. (1982). The memorial consequences of generation and transformation. *Journal of Verbal Learning and Verbal Behavior, 21,* 539–548.

Graf, P., & Mandler, G. (1984). Activation makes words more accessible, but not necessarily more retrievable. *Journal of Verbal Learning and Verbal Behavior, 23,* 553–568.

Graf, P., & Schacter, D. L. (1985). Implicit and explicit memory for new associations in normal and amnesic subjects. *Journal of Experimental Psychology: Learning, Memory, and Cognition, 11,* 501–518.

Graf, P., Squire, L. R., & Mandler, G. (1984). The information that amnesic patients do not forget. *Journal of Experimental Psychology: Learning, Memory, and Cognition, 10,* 164–178.

Graumann, C. F. (1985). Memorabilia, mementos, memoranda: Towards an ecology of memory. In F. Klix and H. Hagendorf (Eds.), *Human memory and cognitive capabilities* (pp. 63–69). Amsterdam: North Holland.

Greco, C., & Rovee-Collier, C. (1988, April). *Post-event bonding: The time window for the malleability of infant memory.* Paper presented at the meeting of the International Conference on Infant Studies, Washington, DC.

Greco, C., Rovee-Collier, C., Hayne, H., Griesler, P., & Earley L. (1986). Ontogeny of early event memory: 1. Forgetting and retrieval by 2- and 3-month-olds. *Infant Behavior and Development, 9,* 441–460.

Greene, E., Flynn, M. S., & Loftus, E. F. (1982). Inducing resistance to misleading information. *Journal of Verbal Learning and Verbal Behavior, 21,* 207–219.

Greene, R. L. (1984). Incidental learning of event frequency. *Memory & Cognition, 12,* 90–95.

Greene, R. L. (1986). Effects of intentionality and strategy on memory for frequency. *Journal of Experimental Psychology: Learning, Memory, and Cognition, 12,* 489–495.

Greenwald, A. G. (1980). The totalitarian ego. *American Psychologist, 35,* 603–618.

Greenwald, A. G. (1981). Self and memory. In G. H. Bower (Ed.), *The psychology of learning and motivation* (Vol. 15, pp. 201–236). New York: Academic Press.

Greenwald, A. G., & Banaji, M. R. (1989). The self as a memory system: Powerful, but ordinary. *Journal of Personality and Social Psychology, 57,* 41–54.

Gregg, V. H. (1986). *Introduction to human memory.* London: Routledge & Kegan Paul.

Gruneberg, M. M. (1985). *Computer Linkword: French, German, Spanish, Italian, Greek, Russian, Dutch, Portuguese, Hebrew.* Penfield, NY: Artworx.

Gruneberg, M. M. (1987). *Linkword French, German, Spanish, Italian, Greek, Portuguese.* London: Corgi Books.

Gruneberg, M. M. (1992). The practical application of memory aids: Knowing how, knowing when, and knowing when not. In M. M. Gruneberg & P. Morris (Eds.), *Aspects of memory* (2nd ed.) (pp. 168–195). London: Routledge.

Gruneberg, M. M., Morris, P. E., & Sykes, R. N.

(Eds.). (1978). *Practical aspects of memory*. London: Academic Press.

**Gruneberg, M. M., Morris, P. E., & Sykes, R. N.** (Eds.). (1988). *Practical aspects of memory: Current research and issues* (Vols. 1 & 2). Chichester, England: John Wiley & Sons.

**Gruneberg, M. M., Morris, P. E., & Sykes, R. N.** (1991). The obituary on everyday memory and its practical applications is premature. *American Psychologist, 46,* 74–76.

**Gude, C., & Zechmeister, E. B.** (1975). Frequency judgements for the "gist" of sentences. *American Journal of Psychology, 88,* 385–396.

**Guenther, R. K.** (1988). Mood and memory. In G. M. Davies & D. M. Thomson (Eds.), *Memory in context: Context in memory* (pp. 57–80). Chichester, England: John Wiley & Sons.

**Guenther, R. K., & Linton, M.** (1975). Mechanisms of temporal coding. *Journal of Experimental Psychology: Human Learning and Memory, 97,* 220–229.

**Guttentag, R. E.** (1985). Memory and aging: Implications for theories of memory development during childhood. *Developmental Review, 5,* 56–82.

**Haber, R. N.** (1979a). Twenty years of haunting eidetic imagery: Where's the ghost? *The Behavioral and Brain Sciences, 2,* 583–594.

**Haber, R. N.** (1979b). Eidetic imagery still lives, thanks to twenty-nine exorcists. *The Behavioral and Brain Sciences, 2,* 619–629.

**Haber, R. N., & Haber, L. R.** (1988). The characteristics of eidetic imagery. In L. K. Obler & D. Fein (Eds.), *The exceptional brain: Neuropsychology of talent and special abilities* (pp. 218–241). New York: Guilford Press.

**Haber, R. N., & Haber, R. B.** (1964). Eidetic imagery: 1. Frequency. *Perceptual and Motor Skills, 19,* 131–138.

**Halfen, D.** (1986, March 12). What do "anesthetized" patients hear? *Anesthesiology News*, p. 12.

**Hall, J. L., Gonder-Frederick, L. A., Chewning, W. W., Silveira, J., & Gold, P. E.** (1989). Glucose enhancement of memory in young and aged humans. *Neuropsychologia, 27,* 1129–1138.

**Halpin, J. A., Puff, C. R., Mason, H. F., & Marston, S. P.** (1984). Self-reference and incidental recall by children. *Bulletin of the Psychonomic Society, 22,* 87–89.

**Halstead, W. C.** (1947). *Brain and intelligence*. Chicago: The University of Chicago Press.

**Hamilton, D. L., & Trolier, T. K.** (1986). Stereotypes and stereotyping: An overview of the cognitive approach. In J. Dovidio & S. Gaertner (Eds.), *Prejudice, discrimination and racism* (pp. 127–163). New York: Academic Press.

**Hamilton, W.** (1859). *Lectures of metaphysics and logic* (Vol. 1). Edinburgh: Blackwood.

**Hammerton, M.** (1963). Retention of learning in a difficult tracking task. *Journal of Experimental Psychology, 66,* 108–110.

**Hanawalt, N. G., & Demarest, I. H.** (1939). The effect of verbal suggestion in the recall period upon the reproduction of visually perceived forms. *Journal of Experimental Psychology, 25,* 159–174.

**Hanson, C., & Hirst, W.** (1988). Frequency encoding of token and type information. *Journal of Experimental Psychology: Learning, Memory, and Cognition, 14,* 289–297.

**Harma, M. I., Illmarinen, J., Knauth, P., & Rutenfranz, J.** (1988). Physical training intervention in female shift workers: II. The effects of intervention on the circadian rhythms of alertness, short-term memory, and body temperature. *Ergonomics, 31,* 51–63.

**Harris, J. E.** (1978). External memory aids. In M. M. Gruneberg, P. E. Morris, & R. N. Sykes (Eds.), *Practical aspects of memory* (pp. 172–179). London: Academic Press.

**Harris, J. E.** (1980). Memory aids people use: Two interview studies. *Memory & Cognition, 8,* 31–38.

**Harris, J. E.** (1984). Remembering to do things: A forgotten topic. In J. E. Harris & P. E. Morris (Eds.), *Everyday memory, actions and absentmindedness* (pp. 71–92). London: Academic Press.

**Harris, R. J.** (1974). Memory and comprehension of implications and inferences of complex sentences. *Journal of Verbal Learning and Verbal Behavior, 13,* 626–637.

**Harris, R. J.** (1977). Comprehension of pragmatic implications in advertising. *Journal of Applied Psychology, 62,* 603–608.

**Harris, R. J.** (Ed.). (1983). *Information processing research in advertising*. Hillsdale, NJ: Erlbaum.

**Hart, J. T.** (1965). Memory and the feeling of knowing experience. *Journal of Educational Psychology, 56,* 208–216.

Hartman, M., & Hasher, L. (1991). Aging and suppression: Memory for previously relevant information. *Psychology and Aging, 6,* 587–594.

Hasher, L., & Chromiak, W. (1977). The processing of frequency information: An automatic mechanism? *Journal of Verbal Learning and Verbal Behavior, 16,* 173–184.

Hasher, L., & Zacks, R. T. (1979). Automatic and effortful processes in memory. *Journal of Experimental Psychology: General, 108,* 356–388.

Hasher, L., & Zacks, R. T. (1984). Automatic processing of fundamental information. *American Psychologist, 39,* 1372–1388.

Hasher, L., & Zacks, R. T. (1988). Working memory, comprehension, and aging: A review and new view. In G. H. Bower (Ed.), *The psychology of learning and motivation* (Vol. 22, pp. 193–225). New York: Academic Press.

Hashtroudi, S., & Parker, E. S. (1986). Acute alcohol amnesia: What is remembered and what is forgotten. In H. D. Cappell, F. B. Glaser, Y. Israel, H. Kalant, W. Schmidt, E. Sellers, & R. C. Smart (Eds.), *Research advances in alcohol and drug problems* (pp. 179–209). New York: Plenum.

Hastie, R., Ostrom, T. M., Ebbesen, E. B., Wyer, R. S., Jr., Hamilton, D. L., & Carlston, D. E. (1980). *Person memory.* Hillsdale, NJ: Erlbaum.

Hauser, S. L., DeLong, G. R., & Rosman, N. P. (1975). Pneumographic findings in the infantile autism syndrome. *Brain, 98,* 667–688.

Hawkins, R. D., Abrams, T. W., Carew, T. J., & Kandel, E. R. (1983). A cellular mechanism of classical conditioning in *Aplysia*: Activity-dependent amplification of presynaptic facilitation. *Science, 219,* 400–405.

Hayman, C. A. G., & Tulving, E. (1989a). Contingent dissociation between recognition and fragment completion: The method of triangulation. *Journal of Experimental Psychology: Learning, Memory, and Cognition, 15,* 228–240.

Hayman, C. A. G., & Tulving E. (1989b). Is priming in fragment completion based on a "traceless" memory system? *Journal of Experimental Psychology: Learning, Memory, and Cognition, 15,* 941–956.

Hayne, H., Greco, C., Earley, L., Griesler, P., & Rovee-Collier, C. (1986). Ontogeny of early memory: 2. Encoding and retrieval by 2- and 3-month-olds. *Infant Behavior and Development, 9,* 461–472.

Hayne, H., Rovee-Collier, C., & Borza, M. A. (1991). Infant memory for place information. *Memory & Cognition, 19,* 378–386.

Hayne, H., Rovee-Collier, C., & Perris, E. E. (1987). Categorization and memory retrieval by 3-month-olds. *Child Development, 58,* 750–767.

Healy, A. F., Fendrich, D. W., Crutcher, R. J., Wittman, W. T., Gesi, A. T., Ericsson, K. A., & Bourne, L. E. (1992). The long-term retention of skills. In A. F. Healy, S. M. Kosslyn, & R. M. Shiffrin (Eds.), *From learning processes to cognitive processes: Essays in honor of William K. Estes* (Vol. 2, pp. 87–118). Hillsdale, NJ: Erlbaum.

Healy, A. F., Fendrich, D. W., & Proctor, J. D. (1990). Acquisition and retention of a letter-detection skill. *Journal of Experimental Psychology: Learning, Memory, and Cognition, 16,* 270–281.

Hebb, D. O. (1949). *The organization of behavior.* New York: Wiley-Interscience.

Herrmann, D. J. (1982a). Know thy memory: The use of questionnaires to assess and study memory. *Psychological Bulletin, 92,* 434–452.

Herrmann, D. J. (1982b). The history of memory typologies and the semantic-episodic distinction. *Bulletin of the Psychonomic Society, 20,* 207–210.

Herrmann, D. J. (1984). Questionnaires about memory. In J. E. Harris & P. E. Morris (Eds.), *Everyday memory, actions and absentmindedness* (pp. 133–151). London: Academic Press.

Herrmann, D. J. (1991). *Super memory.* Emmaus, PA: Rodale Press.

Herrmann, D. J., & Chaffin, R. (1987). Memory before Ebbinghaus. In D. Gorfein & R. R. Hoffman (Eds.), *Learning and memory: The Ebbinghaus centennial* (pp. 35–55). Hillsdale, NJ: Erlbaum.

Herrmann, D. J., & Chaffin, R. (1988). *Memory in historical perspective: The literature before Ebbinghaus.* New York: Springer-Verlag.

Herrmann, D. J., Crawford, M., & Holdsworth, M. (1992). Gender-linked differences in everyday memory performance. *British Journal of Psychology, 83,* 221–231.

Herrmann, D. J., & Petro, S. J. (1990). Commercial memory aids. *Applied Cognitive Psychology, 4,* 439–450.

Herrmann, D. J., Raybeck, D., & Gutman, D. (in

press). *Improving student memory*. Toronto: Hogrefe & Huber.

Herrmann, D. J., Schwartz, B. L., Rosse, R. B., & Deutsch, S. I. (in press). Memory assessment. In E. D. Peselow (Ed.), *The effects of medication and psychopathology on memory*. Washington, DC: The American Psychiatric Association.

Herrmann, D. J., & Searleman, A. (1990). The new multimodal approach to memory improvement. In G. H. Bower (Ed.), *The psychology of learning and motivation* (Vol. 26, pp. 175–205). San Diego: Academic Press.

Herrmann, D. J., & Searleman, A. (1992). Memory improvement and memory theory in historical perspective. In D. J. Herrmann, H. Weingartner, A. Searleman, & C. L. McEvoy, *Memory improvement: Implications for memory theory* (pp. 8–20). New York: Springer-Verlag.

Herrmann, D. J., Weingartner, H., Searleman, A., & McEvoy, C. L. (Eds.). (1992). *Memory improvement: Implications for memory theory*. New York: Springer-Verlag.

Hertel, P. T. (1988). Monitoring external memory. In M. M. Gruneberg, P. E. Morris, & R. N. Sykes (Eds.), *Practical aspects of memory: Current research and issues* (Vol. 1, pp. 221–226). Chichester, England: John Wiley & Sons.

Hertel, P. T. (1992). Improving memory and mood through automatic and controlled procedures of mind. In D. J. Herrmann, H. Weingartner, A. Searleman, & C. L. McEvoy (Eds.), *Memory improvement: Implications for memory theory* (pp. 43–60). New York: Springer-Verlag.

Hertel, P. T., & Hardin, T. S. (1990). Remembering with and without awareness in a depressed mood: Evidence of deficits in initiative. *Journal of Experimental Psychology: General, 119*, 45–59.

Hertzog, C. (1992). Improving memory: The possible role of metamemory. In D. J. Herrmann, H. Weingartner, A. Searleman, & C. L. McEvoy (Eds.), *Memory improvement: Implications for memory theory* (pp. 61–78). New York: Springer-Verlag.

Heston, L. L., & White, J. A. (1983). *Dementia: A practical guide to Alzheimer's disease and related illnesses*. New York: W. H. Freeman.

Heuer, F., & Reisberg, D. (1990). Vivid memories of emotional events: The accuracy of remembered minutiae. *Memory & Cognition, 18*, 496–506.

Higbee, K. L. (1988). *Your memory* (2nd ed.). New York: Prentice-Hall.

Higbee, K. L., & Kunihira, S. (1985). Cross-cultural applications of Yodai Mnemonics. *Educational Psychologist, 20*, 57–64.

Hill, A. L. (1978). Savants: Mentally retarded individuals with special skills. In N. R. Ellis (Ed.), *International review of research in mental retardation* (Vol. 9, pp. 277–298). New York: Academic Press.

Hill, J. W., & Bliss, J. C. (1968). Modeling a tactile sensory register. *Perception & Psychophysics, 4*, 91–101.

Hintzman, D. L. (1969). Apparent frequency as a function of frequency and the spacing of repetitions. *Journal of Experimental Psychology, 80*, 139–145.

Hintzman, D. L. (1978). *The psychology of learning and memory*. San Francisco: W. H. Freeman.

Hintzman, D. L., & Block, R. A. (1971). Repetition and memory: Evidence for a multiple-trace hypothesis. *Journal of Experimental Psychology, 88*, 297–306.

Hintzman, D. L., Block, R. A., & Summers, J. J. (1973). Contextual associations and memory for serial positions. *Journal of Experimental Psychology, 97*, 220–229.

Hintzman, D. L., & Rogers, M. K. (1973). Spacing effects in picture memory. *Memory & Cognition, 1*, 430–434.

Hirshman, E., & Bjork, R. A. (1988). The generation effect: Support for a two-factor theory. *Journal of Experimental Psychology: Learning, Memory, and Cognition, 14*, 484–494.

Hock, F. J. (1987). Drug influences on learning and memory in aged animals and humans. *Neuropsychobiology, 17*, 145–160.

Hoffman, R. R., Bringmann, W., Bamberg, M., & Klein, R. (1987). Some historical observations on Ebbinghaus. In D. Gorfein & R. R. Hoffman (Eds.), *Learning and memory: The Ebbinghaus centennial* (pp. 57–75). Hillsdale, NJ: Erlbaum.

Holmes, D. S. (1970). Differential change in affective intensity and the forgetting of unpleasant personal experience. *Journal of Personality and Social Psychology, 15*, 234–239.

Holmes, D. S. (1974). Investigations of repression: Differential recall of material experimentally or naturally associated with ego-threat. *Psychological Bulletin, 81*, 632–651.

Holtgraves, T., Srull, T. K., & Socall, D. (1989). Conversation memory: The effect of speaker status on memory for the assertiveness of conversation remarks. *Journal of Personality and Social Psychology, 56,* 149–160.

Hoosain, R., & Salili, F. (1988). Language differences, working memory, and mathematical ability. In M. M. Gruneberg, P. E. Morris, & R. N. Sykes (Eds.), *Practical aspects of memory: Current research and issues* (Vol. 2, pp. 512–517). Chichester, England: John Wiley & Sons.

Horgan, D. D., & Morgan, D. (1990). Chess expertise in children. *Applied Cognitive Psychology, 4,* 109–128.

Houston, J. P. (1991). *Fundamentals of learning and memory* (4th ed.). San Diego: Harcourt Brace Jovanovich.

Hoving, K. L., Spencer, T., Robb, K., & Schulte, D. (1978). Developmental changes in visual information processing. In P. A. Ornstein (Ed.), *Memory development in children* (pp. 21–68). Hillsdale, NJ: Erlbaum.

Hovland, C. I., & Weiss, R. (1951). The influence of source credibility on communication effectiveness. *Public Opinion Quarterly, 15,* 635–650.

Howe, M. L., & Rabinowitz, F. M. (1990). Resource panacea? Or just another day in the developmental forest. *Developmental Review, 10,* 125–154.

Howes, D. (1954). On the interpretation of word frequency as a variable affecting speed of recognition. *Journal of Experimental Psychology, 48,* 106–112.

Huang, Y. Y., Colino, A., Selig, D. K., & Malenka, R. C. (1992). The influence of prior synaptic activity on the induction of long-term potentiation. *Science, 255,* 730–733.

Hubel, D. H., & Wiesel, T. N. (1965). Receptive fields and functional architecture in two nonstriate visual areas (18 & 19) of the cat. *Journal of Neurophysiology, 28,* 229–289.

Hubel, D. H., & Wiesel, T. N. (1979). Brain mechanisms of vision. *Scientific American, 241,* 150–163.

Hudson, J. A. (1990). The emergence of autobiographical memory in mother-child conversation. In R. Fivush & J. A. Hudson (Eds.), *Knowing and remembering in young children* (pp. 166–196). New York: Cambridge University Press.

Hudson, J. A., & Nelson, K. (1986). Repeated encounters of a similar kind: Effects of familiarity on children's autobiographic memory. *Cognitive development, 1,* 253–271.

Hulicka, I. M., & Grossman, J. L. (1967). Age-group comparison for the use of mediators in paired-associate learning. *Journal of Gerontology, 22,* 46–57.

Hultsch, D. F., Masson, M. E., & Small, B. J. (1991). Adult age differences in direct and indirect tests of memory. *Journal of Gerontology: Psychological Sciences, 46,* 22–30.

Hunt, E., & Love, T. (1972). How good can memory be? In A. W. Melton & E. Martin (Eds.), *Coding processes in human memory* (pp. 237–260). Washington, DC: Winston & Sons.

Hunt, M. (1982). *The universe within.* New York: Simon & Schuster.

Hunt, R. R. (1985, November). *No generation effect, but source information facilitates event retrieval.* Paper presented at the annual meeting of the Psychonomic Society, Boston.

Hunter, I. M. L. (1957). *Memory.* Baltimore: Penguin Books.

Hutchings, D. D. (1961). The value of suggestion given under anesthesia: A report and evaluation of 200 cases. *American Journal of Clinical Hypnosis, 4,* 26–29.

Hyde, T. S., & Jenkins, J. J. (1969). The differential effects of incidental tasks on the organization of recall of a list of highly associated words. *Journal of Experimental Psychology, 82,* 472–481.

Idzikowski, C., & Baddeley, A. D. (1987). Fear and performance in novice parachutists. *Ergonomics, 30,* 1463–1474.

Intons-Peterson, M. J., & Fournier, J. (1986). External and internal memory aids: When and how often do we use them? *Journal of Experimental Psychology: General, 115,* 267–280.

Intons-Peterson, M. J., & Newsome, G. L. (1992). External memory aids: Effects and effectiveness. In D. J. Herrmann, H. Weingartner, A. Searleman, & C. L. McEvoy (Eds.), *Memory improvement: Implications for memory theory* (pp. 101–121). New York: Springer-Verlag.

Iriki, A., Pavlides, C., Keller, A., & Asanuma, H. (1989). Long-term potentiation in motor cortex. *Science, 245,* 1385–1387.

Isen, A. M. (1985). Asymmetry of happiness and sadness in effects on memory in normal college students: Comments on Hasher, Rose, Zacks,

Sanft, & Doren. *Journal of Experimental Psychology: General, 114,* 388–391.

Isen, A. M., Shalker, T. E., Clark, M., & Karp, L. (1978). Affect, accessibility of material in memory, and behavior: A cognitive loop? *Journal of Personality and Social Psychology, 36,* 385–393.

Ittelson, W. H. (1973). *Environment and cognition.* New York: Seminar Press.

Jackson, J. L. (1985). Is the processing of temporal information automatic or controlled? In J. A. Michel & J. L. Jackson (Eds.), *Time, mind, and behavior* (pp. 179–190). Berlin: Springer-Verlag.

Jackson, J. L., Bogers, H., & Kerstholt, J. (1988). Do memory aids aid the elderly in their day to day remembering? In M. M. Gruneberg, P. E. Morris, & R. N. Sykes (Eds.), *Practical aspects of memory: Current research and issues* (Vol. 2, pp. 137–142). Chichester, England: John Wiley & Sons.

Jacobson, A. L., Fried, C., & Horowitz, S. D. (1966). Planarians and memory: I. Transfer of learning by injection of ribonucleic acid. *Nature, 209,* 599–601.

Jacoby, L. L. (1972). Context effects on frequency judgments of words and sentences. *Journal of Experimental Psychology, 94,* 255–260.

Jacoby, L. L. (1978). On interpreting the effects of repetition: Solving a problem versus remembering a solution. *Journal of Verbal Learning and Verbal Behavior, 17,* 649–667.

Jacoby, L. L. (1983). Remembering the data: Analyzing interactive processes in reading. *Journal of Verbal Learning and Verbal Behavior, 22,* 485–508.

Jacoby, L. L. (1984). Incidental versus intentional retrieval: Remembering and awareness as separate issues. In L. R. Squire & N. Butters (Eds.), *Neuropsychology of memory* (pp. 145–156). New York: Guilford Press.

Jacoby, L. L. (1988). Memory observed and memory unobserved. In U. Neisser & E. Winograd (Eds.), *Remembering reconsidered: Ecological and traditional approaches to the study of memory* (pp. 145–177). Cambridge, England: Cambridge University Press.

Jacoby, L. L., & Kelley, C. M. (1987). Unconscious influences of memory for a prior event. *Personality and Social Psychology Bulletin, 13,* 314–336.

Jacoby, L. L., & Witherspoon, D. (1982). Remembering without awareness. *Canadian Journal of Psychology, 32,* 300–324.

Jacoby, T., & Padgett, T. (1989, August). Waking up the jury box. *Newsweek,* 51.

James, W. (1890). *Principles of psychology* (Vol. 1). New York: Holt.

Jay, T. (1992). *Cursing in America.* Philadelphia: John Benjamins.

Jelicic, M. (1990). The possibility of memory for events occurring under general anaesthesia: A theoretical viewpoint. In B. Bonke, W. Fitch, & K. Millar (Eds.), *Memory and awareness in anaesthesia* (pp. 64–69). Amsterdam: Swets & Zeitlinger.

Jenkins, J. G., & Dallenbach, K. M. (1924). Obliviscence during sleep and waking. *American Journal of Psychology, 35,* 605–612.

Jenkins, J. J. (1974). Remember that old theory of memory? Well, forget it! *American Psychologist, 29,* 785–795.

Johnson, M. H., & Magaro, P. A. (1987). Effects of mood and severity on memory processes in depression and mania. *Psychological Bulletin, 101,* 28–40.

Johnson, M. K., & Hasher, L. (1987). Human learning and memory. *Annual Review of Psychology, 38,* 631–668.

Johnson, M. K., Peterson, M. A., Yap, E. C., & Rose, P. M. (1989). Frequency judgements: The problem of defining a perceptual event. *Journal of Experimental Psychology: Learning, Memory, and Cognition, 15,* 126–136.

Johnson, M. K., Raye, C. L., Foley, H., & Foley, M. (1981). Cognitive operations and decision bias in reality monitoring. *American Journal of Psychology, 94,* 37–64.

Johnson, M. K., Raye, C. L., Wang, A. Y., & Taylor, T. H. (1979). Fact and fantasy: The roles of accuracy and variability in confusing imaginations with perceptual experiences. *Journal of Experimental Psychology: Human Learning and Memory, 5,* 229–240.

Johnson, M. K., Taylor, T. H., & Raye, C. L. (1977). Fact and fantasy: The effects of internally generated events on the apparent frequency of externally generated events. *Memory & Cognition, 5,* 116–122.

Johnson-Laird, P. N., Herrmann, D. J., & Chaffin, R. (1984). Only connections: A critique of semantic networks. *Psychological Bulletin, 96,* 292–315.

Johnson, C. D., & Jenkins, J. J. (1971). Two more

incidental tasks that differentially affect associative clustering in recall. *Journal of Experimental Psychology, 89,* 92–95.

Jones, G., & Adams, J. (1979). Towards a prosthetic memory. *Bulletin of the British Psychological Society, 32,* 165–167.

Jones, G. V. (1990). Misremembering a common object: When left is not right. *Memory & Cognition, 18,* 174–182.

Jonides, J., & Naveh-Benjamin, M. (1987). Estimating frequency of occurrence. *Journal of Experimental Psychology: Learning, Memory, and Cognition, 13,* 230–240.

Jung, C. G. (1957). Cryptomnesia. In *Collected works* (Vol. 1, pp. 95–106). Princeton, NJ: Princeton University Press. (Original work published 1905.)

Kahan, T. L., & Johnson, M. K. (1992). Self effects in memory for person information. *Social Cognition, 10,* 30–50.

Kahn, R. L., Zarit, S. H., Hilbert, N. M., & Niederehe, G. (1975). Memory complaint after E.C.T.: Assessment with a new self rating instrument. *Archives of General Psychiatry, 32,* 1569–1573.

Kail, R. (1990). *The development of memory in children* (3rd ed.). New York: W. H. Freeman.

Kail, R. V., Jr., & Siegel, A. W. (1977). The development of mnemonic encoding in children: From perception to abstraction. In R. V. Kail, Jr., & J. W. Hagen (Eds.), *Perspectives on the development of memory and cognition* (pp. 61–88). Hillsdale, NJ: Erlbaum.

Kandel, E. R., & Schwartz, J. H. (1982). Molecular biology of learning: Modification of transmitter release. *Science, 218,* 433–442.

Kapur, N. (1988). *Memory disorders in clinical practice.* London: Butterworths.

Katz, A. N. (1987). Self-reference in the encoding of creative-relevant traits. *Journal of Personality, 55,* 97–120.

Kausler, D. H. (1991). *Experimental psychology, cognition, and human aging.* New York: Springer-Verlag.

Kausler, D. H., Lichty, W., & Hakami, M. K. (1984). Frequency judgments for distractor items in a short-term memory task: Instructional variation and adult age differences. *Journal of Verbal Learning and Verbal Behavior, 23,* 660–668.

Keppel, G., & Underwood, B. J. (1962). Proactive inhibition in short-term retention of single items. *Journal of Verbal Learning and Verbal Behavior, 1,* 153–161.

Khan, A. U. (1986). *Clinical disorders of memory.* New York: Plenum Medical Book Co.

Kihlstrom, J. F. (1989). On what does mood-dependent memory depend? In D. Kuiken (Ed.), Mood and memory: Theory, research, and applications [Special issue]. *Journal of Social Behavior and Personality, 4,* 23–32.

Kihlstrom, J. F., & Schacter, D. L. (1990). Anaesthesia, amnesia, and the cognitive unconscious. In B. Bonke, W. Fitch, & K. Millar (Eds.), *Memory and awareness in anaesthesia* (pp. 21–44). Amsterdam: Swets & Zeitlinger.

Kihlstrom, J. F., Schacter, D. L., Cork, R. C., Hurt, C. A., & Behr, S. E. (1990). Implicit and explicit memory following surgical anesthesia. *Psychological Sciences, 1,* 303–306.

Kimble, C. E., Hirt, E. R., & Arnold, E. M. (1985). Self-consciousness, public and private self-awareness, and memory in a social setting. *Journal of Psychology, 119,* 59–69.

Kimble, C. E., & Zehr, H. D. (1982). Self-consciousness, information load, self-presentation, and memory in a social situation. *Journal of Social Psychology, 118,* 39–46.

King, M. A., & Yuille, J. C. (1987). Suggestibility and the child witness. In S. J. Ceci, M. P. Toglia, & D. F. Ross (Eds.), *Children's eyewitness memory* (pp. 24–35). New York: Springer-Verlag.

Kinsbourne, M., & Wood, F. (1975). Short-term memory processes in the amnesic syndrome. In J. A. Deutsch (Ed.), *Short-term memory* (pp. 258–291). New York: Academic Press.

Kintsch, W. (1970). Models for free recall and recognition. In D. A. Norman (Ed.), *Models of human memory.* New York: Academic Press.

Kintsch, W. (1977). *Memory and cognition.* New York: Wiley.

Kintsch, W., & Buschke, H. (1969). Homophones and synonyms in short-term memory. *Journal of Experimental Psychology, 80,* 403–407.

Kirkpatrick, E. A. (1894). An experimental study of memory. *Psychological Review, 1,* 602–609.

Kirsch, N. L., Levine, S. P., Fallon-Kreuger, M., & Jaros, L. A. (1987). The microcomputer as an orthotic device for patients with cognitive deficits. *Journal of Head Trauma Rehabilitation, 2,* 77–86.

Klatzky, R. L. (1984). *Memory and awareness*. New York: W. H. Freeman.

Klein, R. M., & Fowler, R. S. (1981). Pressure relief training device: The microcalculator. *Archives of Physical and Medical Rehabilitation, 62*, 500–501.

Klein, S. B., & Kihlstrom, J. F. (1986). Elaboration, organization, and the self-reference effect in memory. *Journal of Experimental Psychology: General, 115*, 26–38.

Klein, S. B., Loftus, J. B., & Burton, H. A. (1989). Two self-reference effects: The importance of distinguishing between self-descriptive judgements and autobiographical retrieval in self-referent encoding. *Journal of Personality and Social Psychology, 56*, 853–865.

Kleinsmith, L. J., & Kaplan, S. (1963). Paired associate learning as a function of arousal and interpolated interval. *Journal of Experimental Psychology, 66*, 190–196.

Kleinsmith, L. J., & Kaplan, S. (1964). Interaction of arousal and recall interval in nonsense syllable paired-associate learning. *Journal of Experimental Psychology, 67*, 124–126.

Klix, F. (1986). On paradigm shifts in memory research. In F. Klix and H. Hagendorf (Eds.), *Human memory and cognitive capabilities* (pp. 45–50). Amsterdam: North Holland.

Knapp, M. L. (1978). *Nonverbal communication in human interaction*. New York: Holt, Rinehart, and Winston.

Koffka, K. (1935). *Principles of Gestalt psychology*. New York: Harcourt Brace Jovanovich.

Kohler, W. (1947). *Gestalt psychology*. New York: Liveright.

Kolb, B., & Whishaw, I. Q. (1990). *Fundamentals of human neuropsychology* (3rd ed.). New York: W. H. Freeman.

Konorski, J. (1948). *Conditioned reflexes and neuron organization*. Cambridge, England: Cambridge University Press.

Koppenaal, L., & Glanzer, M. (1990). An examination of the continuous distractor task and the "long-term recency effect." *Memory & Cognition, 18*, 183–195.

Koriat, A., Ben-Zur, H., & Sheffer, D. (1988). Telling the same story twice: Output monitoring and age. *Journal of Memory and Language, 27*, 23–39.

Kosslyn, S. M. (1973). Scanning visual images: Some structural implications. *Perception & Psychophysics, 14*, 90–94.

Kosslyn, S. M. (1975). Information representation in visual images. *Cognitive Psychology, 7*, 341–370.

Kosslyn, S. M. (1981). The medium and the message in mental imagery. *Psychological Review, 88*, 46–66.

Kosslyn, S. M., & Pomerantz, J. R. (1977). Imagery, proposition, and the form of internal representations. *Cognitive Psychology, 9*, 52–76.

Kramer, T. H., Buckhout, R., & Eugenio P. (1990). Weapon focus, arousal, and eyewitness memory: Attention must be paid. *Law and Human Behavior, 14*, 167–184.

Kramer, T. H., Buckhout, R., Fox, P., Widman, E., & Tusche, B. (1991). Effects of stress on recall. *Applied Cognitive Psychology, 5*, 483–488.

Kreutzer, M. A., Leonard, C., & Flavell, J. H. (1975). An interview study of children's knowledge about memory. *Monographs of the Society for Research in Child Development, 40*(1, Serial No. 159).

Kritchevsky, M. (1987). Transient global amnesia: When memory temporarily disappears. *Postgraduate Medicine, 82*, 95–100.

Kritchevsky, M. (1989). Transient global amnesia. In F. Boller & J. Grafman (Eds.), *Handbook of neuropsychology* (Vol. 3, pp. 167–182). Amsterdam: Elsevier.

Kuhn, T. S. (1962). *The structure of scientific revolutions*. Chicago: University of Chicago Press.

Kurlychek, R. T. (1983). Use of a digital alarm chronograph as a memory aid in early dementia. *Clinical Gerontologist, 1*, 93–94.

Kvavilashvili, L. (1987). Remembering intention as a distinct form of memory. *British Journal of Psychology, 78*, 507–518.

Landfield, P. W., & Deadwyler, S. A. (Eds.). (1988). *Long-term potentiation: From biophysics to behavior*. New York: Liss.

Lane, D. M., & Robertson, L. (1979). The generality of the levels of processing hypothesis: An application to memory for chess positions. *Memory & Cognition, 7*, 253–256.

Lapp, D. (1983). Commitment: Essential ingredient in memory training. *Clinical Gerontologist, 2*, 58–60.

Larrabee, G. J., & Levin, H. S. (1986). Memory self-ratings and objective test performance in a normal elderly sample. *Journal of Clinical and Experimental Neuropsychology, 8*, 275–284.

Lashley, K. S. (1929). *Brain mechanisms and intelli-*

*gence: A quantitative study of injuries to the brain.* Chicago: The University of Chicago Press.

Lashley, K. S. (1950). In search of the engram. *Symposia of the Society of Experimental Biology, 4* (pp. 454–482).

Lave, J. (1988). *Cognition in practice.* Cambridge, England: Cambridge University Press.

Leask, J., Haber, R. N., & Haber, R. B. (1969). Eidetic imagery in children: 2. Longitudinal and experimental results. *Psychonomic Monograph Supplements, 3,* 25–48.

Leaton, R. N., & Supple, W. F. (1986). Cerebellar vermis: Essential for long-term habituaton of the acoustic startle response. *Science, 232,* 513–515.

Leight, K. A., & Ellis, H. C. (1981). Emotional mood states, strategies, and state-dependency in memory. *Journal of Verbal Learning and Verbal Behavior, 20,* 251–266.

Levin, D. N., Xiaoping, H., Tan, K. K., Galhotra, S., Pelizzari, C. A., Chen, G. T. Y., Beck, R. N., Chen, C. T., Cooper, M. D., Mullen, J. F., Hekmatpanah, R., & Spire, J. P. (1989). The brain: Integrated three-dimensional display of MR and PET images. *Radiology, Sept.,* 786.

Levine, J. M., & Murphy, G. (1943). The learning and forgetting of controversial material. *Journal of Abnormal and Social Psychology, 38,* 507–517.

Levine, M., Jankovic, I. N., & Palij, M. (1982). Principles of spatial problem solving. *Journal of Experimental Psychology: General, 111,* 157–175.

Levinson, B. W. (1965). States of awareness during general anaesthesia. *British Journal of Anaesthesia, 37,* 544–550.

Levy, R. L. (1977). Relationship of an overt commitment to task compliance in behavior therapy. *Journal of Behavior Therapy and Experimental Psychology, 8,* 25–29.

Levy, R. L., & Loftus, G. R. (1984). Compliance and memory. In J. E. Harris & P. E. Morris (Eds.), *Everyday memory, actions and absentmindedness* (pp. 93–112). London: Academic Press.

Levy, R. L., Yamashita, D., & Pow, G. (1979). Relationship of an overt commitment to the frequency and speed of compliance with decision making. *Medical Care, 17,* 281–284.

Lewandowsky, S., Dunn, J. C., & Kirsner, K. (Eds.). (1989). *Implicit memory: Theoretical issues.* Hillsdale, NJ: Erlbaum.

Lezak, M. (1983). *Neuropsychological assessment* (2nd ed.). New York: Oxford University Press.

Liang, K. C., Juler, R. G., & McGaugh, J. L. (1986). Modulating effects of posttraining epinephrine on memory: Involvement of the amygdala noradrenergic system. *Brain Research, 368,* 125–133.

Lichtenstein, S., Slovic, P., Fischhoff, B., Layman, M., & Combs, J. (1978). Judged frequency of lethal events. *Journal of Experimental Psychology: Human Learning and Memory, 4,* 551–578.

Light, L. L. (1991). Memory and aging: Four hypotheses in search of data. *Annual Review of Psychology, 42,* 333–376.

Light, L. L., & Carter-Sobell, L. (1970). Effects of changed semantic context on recognition memory. *Journal of Verbal Learning and Verbal Behavior, 9,* 1–11.

Lindsay, D. S. (1990). Misleading suggestions can impair eyewitnesses' ability to remember event details. *Journal of Experimental Psychology: Learning, Memory, and Cognition, 16,* 1077–1083.

Lindsay, D. S., & Johnson, M. K. (1989). The eyewitness suggestibility effect and memory for source. *Memory & Cognition, 17,* 349–358.

Linton, M. (1975). Memory for real-world events. In D. A. Norman & D. E. Rumelhart (Eds.), *Explorations in cognition* (pp. 376–404). San Francisco: Freeman.

Linton, M. (1986). Ways of searching and the contents of memory. In D. C. Rubin (Ed.), *Autobiographical memory* (pp. 50–67). Cambridge, England: Cambridge University Press.

Listen, R. G., & Weingartner, H. J. (1987). Neuropharmacological strategies for understanding psychological determinants of cognition. *Human Neurobiology, 6,* 119–127.

Loftus, E. F. (1975). Leading questions and the eyewitness report. *Cognitive Psychology, 7,* 560–572.

Loftus, E. F. (1977). Shifting human color memory. *Memory & Cognition, 5,* 696–699.

Loftus, E. F. (1979a). *Eyewitness testimony.* Cambridge, MA: Harvard University Press.

Loftus, E. F. (1979b). The malleability of memory. *American Scientist, 67,* 312–320.

Loftus, E. F. (1986). Ten years in the life of an expert witness. *Law and Human Behavior, 10,* 241–263.

Loftus, E. F. (1992). When a lie becomes memory's truth: Memory distortion after exposure to misinformation. *Current Directions in Psychological Science, 1,* 121–123.

Loftus, E. F., Banaji, M. R., Schooler, J. W., & Foster, R. A. (1987). Who shall remember? Gender differences in memory. *Michigan Quarterly Review, 26,* 64–85.

Loftus, E. F., & Burns, T. (1982). Mental shock can reproduce retrograde amnesia. *Memory & Cognition, 10,* 318–323.

Loftus, E. F., Donders, K., Hoffman, H. G., & Schooler, J. W. (1989). Creating new memories that are quickly accessed and confidently held. *Memory & Cognition, 17,* 607–616.

Loftus, E. F., & Greene, E. (1980). Warning: Even memory for faces may be contagious. *Law and Human Behavior, 4,* 323–334.

Loftus, E. F., & Hoffman, H. G. (1989). Misinformation and memory: The creation of new memories. *Journal of Experimental Psychology: General, 118,* 100–104.

Loftus, E. F., Levidow, B., & Duensing, S. (1992). Who remembers best? Individual differences in memory for events that occurred in a science museum. *Applied Cognitive Psychology, 6,* 93–107.

Loftus, E. F., & Loftus, G. R. (1980). On the permanence of stored information in the human brain. *American Psychologist, 35,* 409–420.

Loftus, E. F., Loftus, G. R., & Messo, J. (1987). Some facts about "Weapon Focus." *Law and Human Behavior, 11*(1), 55–62.

Loftus, E. F., Miller, D. G., & Burns, H. J. (1978). Semantic integration of verbal information into a visual memory. *Journal of Experimental Psychology: Human Learning and Memory, 4,* 19–31.

Loftus, E. F., & Palmer, J. C. (1974). Reconstruction of automobile destruction: An example of the interaction between language and memory. *Journal of Verbal Learning and Verbal Behavior, 13,* 585–589.

Loftus, E. F., Schooler, J. W., Loftus, G. R., & Glauber, D. T. (1985). Memory for events occurring under anesthesia. *Acta Psychologica, 59,* 123–128.

Logue, A. W. (1986). *The psychology of eating and drinking.* New York: Freeman.

Loisette, A. (1896). *Assimilative memory or how to attend and never forget.* New York: Funk & Wagnalls.

Long, G. M., & Beaton, R. J. (1982). The case for peripheral persistence: Effects of target and background luminance on a partial-report task. *Journal of Experimental Psychology: Human Perception and Performance, 8,* 383–391.

Lorayne, H., & Lucas, J. (1974). *The memory book.* New York: Ballantine.

Loring, D. W. (1989). The Wechsler Memory Scale—Revised, or the Wechsler Memory Scale—Revisited? *Clinical Neuropsychologist, 3,* 59–69.

Luh, C. W. (1922). The conditions of retention. *Psychological Monographs, 31* (3, Whole No. 142).

Luria, A. R. (1968). *The mind of a mnemonist.* New York: Avon.

Lynch, G. (1986). *Synapses, circuits, and the beginnings of memory.* Cambridge, MA: A Bradford Book, The M.I.T. Press.

Lynch, G., & Baudry, M. (1984). The biochemistry of memory: A new and specific hypothesis. *Science, 224,* 1057–1063.

Lynch, G., Granger, R., & Staubli, U. (1991). Long-term potentiation and the structure of memory. In W. C. Abraham, M. C. Corballis, & K. G. White (Eds.), *Memory mechanisms: A tribute to G. V. Goddard* (pp. 3–26). Hillsdale, NJ: Erlbaum.

Maass, A., & Kohnken, G. (1989). Eyewitness identification: Simulating the "weapon effect." *Law and Human Behavior, 13,* 397–408.

Macfarlane, A. (1975). Olfaction in the development of social preferences in the human neonate. *Ciba Foundation Symposium, 33* (New Series), 103–117.

Madigan, S. (1983). Picture memory. In J. C. Yuille (Ed.), *Imagery, memory, and cognition: Essays in honor of Allan Paivio* (pp. 65–89). Hillsdale, NJ: Erlbaum.

Mainford, W. A., Rath, B., & Barnett, F. (1983, August). *Anesthesia and suggestion.* Paper presented at the meeting of the American Psychological Association, Los Angeles.

Maki, R. H., & Ostby, R. S. (1987). Effects of level of processing and rehearsal on frequency judgments. *Journal of Experimental Psychology: Learning, Memory, and Cognition, 13,* 151–163.

Malone, T. W. (1983). How do people organize their desks? Implications for designing office automation systems. *ACM Transactions on Office Automation Systems, 1,* 99–112.

Mandler, G. (1967). Organization in memory. In K. W. Spence & J. T. Spence (Eds.), *The psychology of learning and motivation* (Vol. 1, pp. 327–372). New York: Academic Press.

Mandler, G., & Pearlstone, Z. (1966). Free and constrained concept learning and subsequent recall. *Journal of Verbal Learning and Verbal Behavior, 5,* 126–131.

**Mandler, J. M.** (1984). *Stories, scripts, and scenes: Aspects of schema theory.* Hillsdale, NJ: Erlbaum.

**Manning, C. A., Hall, J. L., & Gold, P. E.** (1990). Glucose effects on memory and other neuropsychological tests in elderly humans. *Psychological Science, 1,* 307–311.

**Marek, G. R.** (1975). *Toscanini.* London: Vision Press.

**Markus, H.** (1980). The self in thought and memory. In D. M. Wagner & R. R. Vallacher (Eds.), *The self in social psychology* (pp. 102–130). New York: Oxford University Press.

**Marshall, J. C., & Fryer, D. M.** (1978). Speak, memory! An introduction to some historical studies of remembering and forgetting. In M. M. Gruneberg & P. E. Morris (Eds.), *Practical aspects of memory* (pp. 1–25). London: Methuen.

**Marshall-Garcia, K. A., & Beck, R. C.** (1985). Mood and recognition memory: A comparison of two procedures. *Bulletin of the Psychonomic Society, 23,* 450–452.

**Martin, M.** (1986). Aging and patterns of change in everyday memory and cognition. *Human Learning, 5,* 63–74.

**Martinez, J. L.** (1986). Memory: Drugs and hormones. In J. L. Martinez & R. P. Kesner (Eds.), *Learning and memory: A biological view* (pp. 127–163). New York: Academic Press.

**Martinez, J. L., Schulteis, G., & Weinberger, S. B.** (1991). How to increase and decrease the strength of memory traces: The effects of drugs and hormones. In J. L. Martinez & R. P. Kesner (Eds.), *Learning and memory: A biological view* (2nd ed.) (pp. 149–198). San Diego, CA: Academic Press.

**Matlin, M. W.** (1989). *Cognition* (2nd ed.). New York: Holt, Rinehart, and Winston.

**Matlin, M. W., & Stang, D. J.** (1978). *The Pollyanna Principle: Selectivity in language, memory, and thought.* Cambridge, MA: Schenkman.

**Mayes, A. R.** (1988). *Human organic memory disorders.* Cambridge, England: Cambridge University Press.

**Mayford, M., Barzilai, A., Keller, F., Schacher, S., & Kandel, E. R.** (1992). Modulation of an NCAM-related adhesion molecule with long-term synaptic plasticity in Aplysia. *Science, 256,* 638–644.

**Maylor, E. A.** (1990). Age and prospective memory. *The Quarterly Journal of Experimental Psychology, 42,* 471–493.

**McCarthy, R. A., & Warrington, E. K.** (1990). *Cognitive neuropsychology: A clinical introduction.* San Diego, CA: Academic Press.

**McCarty, D. L.** (1980). Investigation of a visual imagery mnemonic device for acquiring name-face association. *Journal of Experimental Psychology: Human Learning and Memory, 6,* 145–155.

**McClelland, J. L., & Rumelhart, D. E.** (Eds.). (1986). *Parallel distributed processing: Explorations in the microstructure of cognition* (Vols. 1 & 2). Cambridge, MA: The M.I.T. Press.

**McClelland, J. L., & Rumelhart, D. E.** (1988). *Explorations in parallel distributed processing: A handbook of models, programs, and exercises.* Cambridge, MA: The M.I.T. Press.

**McCloskey, M.** (1991). Networks and theories: The place of connectionism in cognitive science. *Psychological Science, 2,* 387–395.

**McCloskey, M.** (1992). Special versus ordinary memory mechanisms in the genesis of flashbulb memories. In E. Winograd & U. Neisser (Eds.), *Affect and accuracy in recall: Studies of "flashbulb" memories* (pp. 227–235). New York: Cambridge University Press.

**McCloskey, M., & Egeth, H.** (1983). Eyewitness identification: What can a psychologist tell a jury? *The American Psychologist, 38,* 550–563.

**McCloskey, M., Wible, C. G., & Cohen, N. J.** (1988). Is there a special flashbulb-memory mechanism? *Journal of Experimental Psychology: General, 117,* 171–181.

**McCloskey, M., & Zaragoza, M. S.** (1985). Misleading postevent information and memory for events: Arguments and evidence against memory impairment hypotheses. *Journal of Experimental Psychology: General, 114,* 1–16.

**McConnell, J. V.** (1962). Memory transfer through cannibalism in planarians. *Journal of Neuropsychiatry, 1*(Suppl. 3), 542–548.

**McCulloch, W. S., & Pitts, W.** (1943). A logical calculus of the ideas immanent in nervous activity. *Bulletin of Mathematical Biophysics, 5,* 115–133.

**McDaniel, M. A., & Pressley, M.** (Eds.). (1987). *Im-*

*agery and related mnemonic processes*. New York: Springer-Verlag.

**McDaniel, M. A., Riegler, G. L., & Wadill, P. J.** (1990). Generation effects in free recall: Further support for a three-factor theory. *Journal of Experimental Psychology: Learning, Memory, and Cognition, 16,* 789–798.

**McDaniel, M. A., Wadill, P. J., & Einstein, G. O.** (1988). A contextual account of the generation effect: A three-factor theory. *Journal of Memory and Language, 27,* 521–536.

**McElroy, L., & Slamecka, N.** (1982). Memorial consequences of generating nonwords: Implications for theories of the generation effect. *Journal of Verbal Learning and Verbal Behavior, 21,* 249–259.

**McEvoy, C. L., & Moon, J. R.** (1988). Assessment and treatment of everyday memory problems in the elderly. In M. M. Gruneberg, P. E. Morris, & R. N. Sykes (Eds.), *Practical aspects of memory: Current research and issues* (Vol. 2, pp. 155–160). Chichester, England: John Wiley & Sons.

**McGaugh, J. L.** (1989). Modulation of memory storage processes. In P. R. Solomon, G. R. Goethals, C. M. Kelly, & B. R. Stephens (Eds.), *Memory: Interdisciplinary approaches* (pp. 33–64). New York: Springer-Verlag.

**McGaugh, J. L.** (1990). Significance and remembrance: The role of neuromodulatory systems. *Psychological Science, 1,* 15–25.

**McGaugh, J. L.** (1991). Neuromodulation and the storage of information: Involvement of the amygdaloid complex. In R. G. Lister & H. J. Weingartner (Eds.), *Perspectives on cognitive neuroscience* (pp. 279–299). New York: Oxford University Press.

**McGaugh, J. L., & Gold, P. E.** (1976). Modulation of memory by electrical stimulation of the brain. In M. R. Rosenzweig & E. L. Bennett (Eds.), *Neural mechanisms of learning and memory* (pp. 549–560). Cambridge, MA: The M.I.T. Press.

**McGeoch, J. A.** (1932). Forgetting and the law of disuse. *Psychological Review, 39,* 352–370.

**McKenna, S. P., & Glendon, A. I.** (1985). Occupational first aid training: Decay in cardiopulmonary resuscitation (CPR) skills. *Journal of Occupational Psychology, 58,* 109–117.

**McLintock, T. T. C., Aitken, H., Downie, C., & Kenney, G. N. C.** (1990). The effect of intraoperative suggestions on postoperative analgesic re-

quirements. In B. Bonke, W. Fitch, & K. Millar (Eds.), *Memory and awareness in anaesthesia* (pp. 96–100). Amsterdam: Swets & Zeitlinger.

**McNamara, T. P.** (1986). Mental representations of spatial relations. *Cognitive Psychology, 18,* 87–121.

**McNamara, T. P., Altarriba, J., Bendele, M., Johnson, S. C., & Clayton, K. N.** (1989). Constraints on priming in spatial memory: Naturally learned versus experimentally learned environments. *Memory & Cognition, 17,* 444–453.

**McNaughton, B. L., Barnes, C. A., Rao, G., Baldwin, J., & Rasmussen, M.** (1986). Long-term enhancement of hippocampal synaptic transmission and the acquisition of spatial information. *Journal of Neuroscience, 6,* 563–571.

**Meacham, J. A.** (1988). Interpersonal relations and prospective remembering. In M. M. Gruneberg, P. E. Morris, & R. N. Sykes (Eds.) *Practical aspects of memory: Current research and issues* (Vol. 2, pp. 354–359). Chichester, England: John Wiley & Sons.

**Meacham, J. A., & Colombo, J.** (1980). External retrieval cues facilitate prospective remembering in young children. *Journal of Educational Research, 73,* 299–301.

**Meacham, J. A., & Leiman, B.** (1982). Remembering to perform future actions. (Paper presented at the annual meeting of the American Psychological Association, Chicago, September 1975.) In U. Neisser (Ed.), *Memory observed: Remembering in natural contexts* (pp. 327–336). San Francisco: Freeman.

**Meacham, J. A., & Singer, J.** (1977). Incentive effects in prospective remembering. *Journal of Psychology, 97,* 191–197.

**Mechanic, A.** (1964). The responses involved in the rote learning of verbal materials. *Journal of Verbal Learning and Verbal Behavior, 3,* 30–36.

**Mecklenbräuker, S., & Hager, W.** (1984). Effects of mood on memory: Experimental tests of mood-state dependent retrieval hypothesis and of a mood-congruity hypothesis. *Psychological Research, 46,* 355–376.

**Melton, A. W.** (1963). Implications of short-term memory for a general theory of memory. *Journal of Verbal Learning and Verbal Behavior, 2,* 1–21.

**Melton, A. W., & Irwin, J. M.** (1940). The influence of degree of interpolated learning on retroactive inhibition and the overt transfer of specific responses. *American Journal of Psychology, 53,* 173–203.

**Meltzer, H.** (1931). Sex differences in forgetting pleasant and unpleasant experiences. *Journal of Abnormal Psychology, 25,* 450–464.

**Merrill, A. A., & Baird, J. C.** (1987). Semantic and spatial factors in environmental memory. *Memory & Cognition, 15,* 101–108.

**Meudell, P. R., Northen, B., Snowden, J. S., & Neary, D.** (1980). Long term memory for famous voices in amnesic and normal subjects. *Neuropsychologia, 18,* 133–139.

**Meyer, D. E., & Schvaneveldt, R. W.** (1971). Facilitation in recognizing pairs of words: Evidence of a dependence between retrieval operations. *Journal of Experimental Psychology, 90,* 227–234.

**Meyer, D. E., & Schvaneveldt, R. W.** (1976). Meaning, memory structure, and mental processes. *Science, 192,* 27–33.

**Meyer, G. E., & Hilterbrand, K.** (1984). Does it pay to be ''Bashful''?: The seven dwarfs and long-term memory. *American Journal of Psychology, 97,* 47–55.

**Michaud, C., Musse, N., Nicholas, J. P., & Mejean, L.** (1991). Effects of breakfast-size on short-term memory, concentration, mood and blood glucose. *Journal of Adolescent Health, 12,* 53–57.

**Middleton, A. E.** (1888). *Memory systems: New and old.* New York: G. S. Fellows.

**Millar, K.** (1987). Assessment of memory for anaesthesia. In I. Hindmarch, J. G. Jones, & E. Moss (Eds.), *Aspects of recovery from anaesthesia* (pp. 75–91). Chichester, England: John Wiley & Sons.

**Millar, K.** (1988). Memory during anaesthesia. In M. M. Gruneberg, P. E. Morris, & R. N. Sykes (Eds.), *Practical aspects of memory: Current research and issues* (Vol. 2, pp. 230–235). Chichester, England: John Wiley & Sons.

**Miller, G. A.** (1956). The magical number seven, plus or minus two: Some limits on our capacity for processing information. *Psychological Review, 63,* 81–97.

**Milner, B.** (1962). Les troubles de la memoire accompagnant des lesions hippocampiques bilaterales. In P. Passouant (Ed.), *Physiologie de l'hippocampe* (pp. 257–272). Paris: Centre National de la Recherche Scientifique.

**Milner, B.** (1968). Visual recognition and recall after right temporal-lobe excision in man. *Neuropsychologia, 6,* 191–209.

**Milner, B., Corkin, S., & Teuber, H. L.** (1968). Further analysis of the hippocampal amnesic syndrome: 14-year follow-up study of H.M. *Neuropsychologia, 6,* 215–234.

**Milner, B., McAndrews, M. P., & Leonard, G.** (1990). Frontal lobes and memory for the temporal order of recent events. *Cold Spring Harbor Symposia on Quantitative Biology, 55,* 987–994.

**Milner, B., & Teuber, H. L.** (1968). Alteration of perception and memory in man. In L. Weiskrantz (Ed.), *Analysis of behavioral changes* (pp. 268–375). New York: Harper & Row.

**Mischel, W., Ebbesen, E. B., & Zeiss, A. M.** (1976). Determinants of selective memory about the self. *Journal of Consulting and Clinical Psychology, 44,* 92–103.

**Miserandino, M.** (1991). Memory and the seven dwarfs. *Teaching of Psychology, 18,* 169–171.

**Mitchell, J. M.** (1911). Mnemonics. In *Encyclopaedia Britannica,* Vol. 18. Cambridge: Cambridge University Press.

**Moar, I., & Bower, G. H.** (1983). Inconsistency in spatial knowledge. *Memory & Cognition, 11,* 107–113.

**Moely, B. E., Olson, F. A., Halwes, T. G., & Flavell, J. H.** (1969). Production deficiency in young children's clustered recall. *Development Psychology, 1,* 26–34.

**Moore, B. S., Sherrod, D. R., Liu, T. J., & Underwood, B.** (1979). The dispositional shift in attribution over time. *Journal of Experimental Social Psychology, 15,* 553–569.

**Morris, C. D., Bransford, J. D., & Franks, J. J.** (1977). Levels of processing versus transfer appropriate processing. *Journal of Verbal Learning and Verbal Behavior, 16,* 519–533.

**Morris, P. E.** (1984). The validity of subjective reports on memory. In J. E. Harris & P. E. Morris (Eds.), *Everyday memory, actions and absentmindedness* (pp. 153–172). London: Academic Press.

**Morris, P. E., Jones, S., & Hampson, P.** (1978). An imagery mnemonic for the learning of people's names. *British Journal of Psychology, 69,* 335–336.

**Morris, R. G. M.** (Ed.). (1989). *Parallel distributed processing: Implications for psychology and neurobiology.* Oxford: Clarendon Press.

**Morris, R. G. M., Anderson, E. Lynch, G., &**

**Baudry, M.** (1986). Selective impairment of learning and blockade of long-term potentiation by an N-methyl-D-aspartate receptor antagonist, AP5. *Nature, 319,* 774–776.

**Moscovitch, M.** (1982). A neuropsychological approach to memory and perception in normal and pathological aging. In F. I. M. Craik & S. Trehub (Eds.), *Aging and cognitive processes* (pp. 55–78). New York: Plenum Press.

**Moscovitch, M.** (1984). The sufficient conditions for demonstrating preserved memory in amnesia: A task analysis. In L. R. Squire & N. Butters (Eds.), *The neuropsychology of memory* (pp. 104–114). New York: Guilford Press.

**Mountcastle, V. B.** (1979). An organizing principle for cerebral function: The unit module and the distributed system. In F. O. Schmitt & F. G. Worden (Eds.), *The neurosciences* (pp. 21–42). Cambridge, MA: The M.I.T. Press.

**Mueller, J. H., Rankin, J. L., & Carlomusto, M.** (1979). Adult age differences in free recall as a function of organization and method of presentation. *Journal of Gerontology, 34,* 375–380.

**Müller, G. E., & Pilzecker, A.** (1900). Experimentelle Beitrage zur Lehre vom Gedächtnis. *Zeitschrift für Psychologie, Erganzungsband, 1,* 1–300.

**Munsat, S.** (1966). *The concept of memory.* New York: Random House.

**Murdock, B. B., Jr.** (1962). The serial position effect for free recall. *Journal of Experimental Psychology, 64,* 482–488.

**Murdock, B. B., Jr.** (1974). *Human memory: Theory and data.* Potomac, MD: Erlbaum.

**Murdock, B. B., Jr.** (1982). Recognition memory. In C. R. Puff (Ed.), *Handbook of research methods in human memory and cognition* (pp. 1–26). New York: Academic Press.

**Murray, D. J.** (1976). Research on memory in the nineteenth century. *Canadian Journal of Psychology, 30,* 201–220.

**Myers, N. A., Clifton, R. K., & Clarkson, M. G.** (1987). When they were very young: Almost-threes remember two years ago. *Infant Behavior and Development, 10,* 123–132.

**Myers, N. A., & Perlmutter, M.** (1978). Memory in the years from two to five. In P. A. Ornstein (Ed.), *Memory development in children* (pp. 191–218). Hillsdale, NJ: Erlbaum.

**Naire, J. S.** (1983). Associative processing during rote rehearsal. *Journal of Experimental Psychology, 9,* 3–20.

**Naire, J. S., Pusen, C. P., & Widner, R. L., Jr.** (1985). Representation in the mental lexicon: Implications for theories of the generation effect. *Memory & Cognition, 13,* 183–191.

**Naire, J. S., & Widner, R. L., Jr.** (1988). Familiarity and lexicality as determinants of the generation effect. *Journal of Experimental Psychology: Learning, Memory, and Cognition, 14,* 694–699.

**Nasby, W., & Yando, R.** (1982). Selective encoding and retrieval of affectively valent information: Two cognitive consequences of children's mood states. *Journal of Personality and Social Psychology, 43,* 1244–1253.

**Naugle, R., Prevey, M., Naugle, C., & Delaney, R.** (1988). New digital watch as a compensatory device for memory dysfunction. *Cognitive Rehabilitation, 6,* 22–23.

**Naus, M. J., & Ornstein, P. A.** (1983). Development of memory strategies: Analysis, questions, and issues. In M. T. H. Chi (Ed.), *Trends in memory development research* (Vol. 9, pp. 1–30). Basel, Switzerland: Karger.

**Naveh-Benjamin, M.** (1987). Coding of spatial location information: An automatic process? *Journal of Experimental Psychology: Learning, Memory, and Cognition, 13,* 595–605.

**Naveh-Benjamin, M.** (1988). Recognition memory of spatial location information: Another failure to support automaticity. *Memory & Cognition, 16,* 437–445.

**Naveh-Benjamin, M.** (1990). Coding of temporal order information: An automatic process? *Journal of Experimental Psychology: Learning, Memory, and Cognition, 16,* 117–126.

**Naveh-Benjamin, M., & Ayres, T. J.** (1986). Digit span, reading rate, and linguistic relativity. *Quarterly Journal of Experimental Psychology, 38,* 739–751.

**Naveh-Benjamin, M., & Jonides, J.** (1986). On the automaticity of frequency coding: Effects of competing task load, encoding strategy, and intention. *Journal of Experimental Psychology: Learning, Memory, and Cognition, 12,* 378–386.

**Nebes, R. D.** (1989). Semantic memory in Alzheimer's disease. *Psychological Bulletin, 106,* 377–394.

Neisser, U. (1964). Visual search. *Scientific American, 210*, 94–102.

Neisser, U. (1967). *Cognitive psychology*. New York: Appleton-Century-Crofts.

Neisser, U. (1976). *Cognition and reality*. San Francisco: Freeman.

Neisser, U. (1981). John Dean's memory: A case study. *Cognition, 9*, 1–22.

Neisser, U. (1982). Memorists. In U. Neisser (Ed.), *Memory observed: Remembering in natural contexts* (pp. 377–381). San Francisco: Freeman.

Neisser, U. (1985). The role of theory in the ecological study of memory: Comment on Bruce. *Journal of Experimental Psychology: General, 114*, 272–276.

Neisser, U. (1988). Time present and time past. In M. M. Gruneberg, P. E. Morris, & R. N. Sykes (Eds.), *Practical aspects of memory: Current research and issues* (Vol. 2, pp. 545–560). Chichester, England: John Wiley & Sons.

Neisser, U., & Harsch, N. (1992). Phantom flashbulbs: False recollections of hearing the news about Challenger. In E. Winograd & U. Neisser (Eds.), *Affect and accuracy in recall: Studies of "flashbulb" memories* (pp. 9–31). New York: Cambridge University Press.

Nelson, D. L., & McEvoy, C. L. (1979). Encoding context and set size. *Journal of Experimental Psychology: Human Learning and Memory, 5*, 292–314.

Nelson, D. L., Walling, J. R., & McEvoy, C. L. (1979). Doubts about depth. *Journal of Experimental Psychology: Human Learning and Memory, 5*, 24–44.

Nelson, K. (1978). How young children represent knowledge of their world in and out of language. In R. S. Seigler (Ed.), *Children's thinking: What develops?* (pp. 255–273). Hillsdale, NJ: Erlbaum.

Nelson, K. (1986). Event knowledge and cognitive development. In K. Nelson (Ed.), *Event knowledge: Structure and function in development* (pp. 1–19). Hillsdale, NJ: Erlbaum.

Nelson, K., & Gruendel, J. (1981). Generalized event representations: Basic building blocks of cognitive development. In M. E. Lamb & A. L. Brown (Eds.), *Advances in developmental psychology* (Vol. 1, pp. 131–158). Hillsdale, NJ: Erlbaum.

Nelson, K., & Gruendel, J. (1986). Children's scripts. In K. Nelson (Ed.), *Event knowledge: Structure and function in development* (pp. 21–46). Hillsdale, NJ: Erlbaum.

Nelson, K., & Hudson, J. A. (1989). Scripts and memory: Functional relationships in development. In F. E. Weinert & M. Perlmutter (Eds.), *Memory development: Universal changes and individual differences* (pp. 147–167). Hillsdale, NJ: Erlbaum.

Nelson, K., & Ross, G. (1980). The generalities and specifics of long-term memory in infants and young children. In M. Perlmutter (Ed.), *Children's memory: New directions for child development* (pp. 87–101). San Francisco: Jossey Bass.

Nelson, T. O. (1977). Repetition and depth of processing. *Journal of Verbal Learning and Verbal Behavior, 16*, 151–171.

Newell, A., Shaw, J. C., & Simon, H. A. (1963). Chess-playing programs and the problem of complexity. In E. A. Feigenbaum & J. Feldman (Eds.), *Computers and thought* (pp. 39–70). New York: McGraw-Hill.

Nickerson, R. S., & Adams, M. J. (1979). Long-term memory for a common object. *Cognitive Psychology, 11* 287–307.

Niederehe, G., & Yoder, C. (1989). Metamemory perceptions in depressions of young and older adults. *Journal of Nervous and Mental Disorders, 177*, 4–14.

Nissen, M. J., Ross, J. L., Willingham, D. B., Mackenzie, T. B., & Schacter, D. L. (1988). Memory and awareness in a patient with multiple personality disorder. *Brain and Cognition, 8*, 21–38.

Norman, D. A. (1988). *The psychology of everyday things*. New York: Basic Books.

Ogden, J. A., & Corkin, S. (1991). Memories of H. M. In W. C. Abraham, M. C. Corballis, & K. G. White (Eds.), *Memory mechanisms: A tribute to G. V. Goddard* (pp. 195–215). Hillsdale, NJ: Erlbaum.

Olson, G. M., & Sherman, T. (1980). Attention, learning, and memory in infants. In M. Haith & J. Campos (Eds.), *Handbook of child psychology* (Vol. 2, pp. 1001–1080). New York: Wiley.

Ornstein, P. A., Naus, M. J., & Liberty, C. (1975). Rehearsal and organizational processes in children's memory. *Child Development, 46*, 818–830.

Ostrom, T. M. (1989). Three catechisms for social memory. In P. R. Solomon, G. R. Goethals, C. M. Kelley, and B. R. Stephens (Eds.), *Memory: Interdisciplinary approaches* (pp. 198–220). New York: Springer-Verlag.

Owens, J., Bower, G. H., & Black, J. B. (1979). The "soap-opera" effect in story recall. *Memory & Cognition, 7*, 185–191.

Paivio, A. (1969). Mental imagery in associative learning and memory. *Psychological Review, 76*, 241–263.

Paivio, A. (1971). *Imagery and verbal processes.* New York: Holt, Rinehart, and Winston.

Palij, M., Levine, M., & Kahan, T. (1984). The orientation of cognitive maps. *Bulletin of the Psychonomic Society, 22*, 105–108.

Park, D. C., Smith, A. D., & Cavanaugh, J. C. (1990). Metamemories of memory researchers. *Memory & Cognition, 18*, 321–327.

Parker, E. S., & Weingartner, H. (1984). Retrograde facilitation of human memory by drugs. In H. Weingartner & E. S. Parker (Eds.), *Memory consolidation: Psychobiology of cognition* (pp. 231–251). Hillsdale, NJ: Erlbaum.

Parkin, A. J. (1984). Levels of processing, context, and facilitation of pronunciation. *Acta Psychologica, 55*, 19–29.

Parkin, A. J. (1987). *Memory and amnesia: An introduction.* New York: Basil Blackwell.

Parkin, A. J. (1990). Recent advances in the neuropsychology of memory. In J. Weinman & J. Hunter (Eds.), *Memory: Neurochemical and abnormal perspectives* (pp. 141–162). Chur, Switzerland: Harwood Academic Publishers.

Parkin, A. J., Lewinsohn, J., & Folkard, S. (1982). The influence of emotion on immediate and delayed retention: Levinger and Clarke reconsidered. *British Journal of Psychology, 73*, 389–393.

Parkin, A. J., Reid, T. K., & Russo, R. (1990). On the differential nature of implicit and explicit memory. *Memory & Cognition, 18*, 507–514.

Pascual-Leone, J. (1970). A mathematical model for the transition rule in Piaget's developmental stages. *Acta Psychologica, 63*, 301–345.

Pascual-Leone, J. (1978). Compounds, confounds, and models in developmental information processing: A reply to Trabasso and Foellinger. *Journal of Experimental Child Psychology, 26*, 18–40.

Pascual-Leone, J. (1987). Organismic processes for neoPiagetian theories: A dialectical causal account of cognitive development. *International Journal of Psychology, 22*, 531–570.

Pavlov, I. P. (1927). *Conditioned reflexes: An investigation of the physiological activity of the cerebral cortex.* London: Oxford University Press.

Payne, D. G., Neely, J. H., & Burns, D. J. (1986). The generation effect: Further tests of the lexical activation hypothesis. *Memory & Cognition, 14*, 246–252.

Payne, D. G., & Wenger, M. J. (1992). Improving memory through practice. In D. J. Herrmann, H. Weingartner, A. Searleman, & C. L. McEvoy (Eds.), *Memory improvement: Implications for memory theory* (pp. 187–209). New York: Springer-Verlag.

Pearlman, C., & Becker, M. (1973). Brief posttrial REM sleep deprivation impairs discrimination learning in rats. *Physiological Psychology, 1*, 373–376.

Pearson, R. E. (1961). Response to suggestions given under general anesthesia. *American Journal of Clinical Hypnosis, 4*, 106–114.

Peeke, S. C., & Peeke, H. V. (1984). Attention, memory and cigarette smoking. *Psychopharmacology, 84*, 205–216.

Penfield, W. W., & Jasper, H. (1954). *Epilepsy and the functional anatomy of the human brain.* Boston: Little, Brown.

Penfield, W. W., & Perot, P. (1963). The brain's record of auditory and visual experience. *Brain, 86*, 595–696.

Penfield, W. W., & Roberts, L. (1959). *Speech and brain mechanisms.* Princeton, NJ: Princeton University Press.

Perlmutter, M. (1984). Continuities and discontinuities in early human memory paradigms, processes, and performance. In R. Kail & N. E. Spear (Eds.), *Comparative perspectives on the development of memory* (pp. 253–284). Hillsdale, NJ: Erlbaum.

Perlmutter, M. (1988). Research on memory and its development: Past, present, and future. In F. E. Weinert & M. Perlmutter (Eds.), *Memory development: Universal changes and individual differences* (pp. 353–380). Hillsdale, NJ: Erlbaum.

Perris, E. E., Myers, N. A., & Clifton, R. K. (1990). Long-term memory for a single infancy experience. *Child Development, 61*, 1796–1807.

Peters, D. P. (1988). Eyewitness memory and arousal in a natural setting. In M. M. Gruneberg, P. E. Morris, & R. N. Sykes (Eds.), *Practical aspects of memory: Current research and issues* (pp. 89–94). Chichester, England: John Wiley & Sons.

Peterson, L. R., & Peterson, M. J. (1959). Short-term retention of individual verbal items. *Journal of Experimental Psychology, 58*, 193–198.

Petrides, M. (1989). Frontal lobes and memory. In F. Boller & J. Grafman (Eds.), *Handbook of neuropsychology* (Vol. 3, pp. 75–90). Amsterdam: Elsevier.

Pettinati, H. M. (Ed.). (1988). *Hypnosis and memory.* New York: Guilford Press.

Pillemer, D. B. (1984). Flashbulb memories of the assassination attempt on President Reagan. *Cognition, 16,* 63–80.

Pillemer, D. B., & White, S. H. (1989). Childhood events recalled by children and adults. In H. W. Reese (Ed.), *Advances in child development and behavior* (Vol. 21, pp. 297–340). San Diego: Academic Press.

Pinker, S. (Ed.). (1985). *Visual Cognition.* Cambridge, MA: The M.I.T. Press.

Pitts, W., & McCulloch, W. S. (1947). How we know universals: The perception of auditory and visual forms. *Bulletin of Mathematical Biophysics, 9,* 127–147.

Poon, L. W. (Ed.). (1986). *Clinical memory assessment of older adults.* Washington, DC: American Psychological Association.

Poon, L. W., Rubin, D. C., & Wilson, B. A. (Eds.). (1989). *Everyday cognition in adulthood and later life.* New York: Cambridge University Press.

Poon, L. W., & Schaffer, G. (1982, August). *Prospective memory in young and old adults.* Paper presented at the annual meeting of the American Psychological Association, Washington, DC.

Poon, L. W., Walsh-Sweeney, L., & Fozard, J. L. (1980). Memory skill training for the elderly: Salient issues on the use of imagery mnemonics. In L. W. Poon, J. L. Fozard, L. S. Cermak, D. Arenberg, & L. W. Thompson (Eds.), *New directions in memory and aging* (pp. 461–484). Hillsdale, NJ: Erlbaum.

Posner, M. I., & Keele, S. W. (1967). Decay of visual information from a single letter. *Science, 158,* 137–139.

Posner, M. I., & Keele, S. W. (1968). On the genesis of abstract ideas. *Journal of Experimental Psychology, 77,* 353–363.

Postman, L., & Phillips, L. (1965). Short-term temporal changes in free recall. *Quarterly Journal of Experimental Psychology, 17,* 132–138.

Pressley, M., Borkowski, J. G., & Schneider, W. (1987). Cognitive strategies: Good strategy users coordinate metacognition and knowledge. In R.

Vasta & G. Whitehurst (Eds.), *Annals of child development* (Vol. 5, pp. 89–129). New York: JAI Press.

Pressley, M., & El-Dinary, P. B. (1992). Memory strategy instruction that promotes good information processing. In D. J. Herrmann, H. Weingartner, A. Searleman, & C. L. McEvoy (Eds.), *Memory improvement: Implications for memory theory* (pp. 79–100). New York: Springer-Verlag.

Prigatano, G. P. (1978). Wechsler Memory Scale: A selective review of the literature. *Journal of Clinical Psychology, 34,* 816–832.

Putnam, F. W., Guroff, J. J., Silberman, E. K., Barban, L., & Post, R. M. (1986). The clinical phenomenology of multiple personality disorder: 100 recent cases. *Journal of Clinical Psychiatry, 47,* 285–293.

Pylyshyn, Z. W. (1973). What the mind's eye tells the mind's brain: A critique of mental imagery. *Psychological Bulletin, 80,* 1–24.

Pylyshyn, Z. W. (1981). The imagery debate: Analogue media versus tacit knowledge. *Psychological Review, 88,* 16–45.

Pyszczynski, T., Hamilton, J. C., Herring, F. H., & Greenberg, J. (1989). Depression, self-focused attention, and the negative memory bias. *Journal of Personality and Social Psychology, 57,* 351–357.

Querleu, D., & Renard, K. (1981). Les perceptions auditives du foetus humain [Auditory perception of the human fetus]. *Medecine et Hygiene, 39,* 2101–2110.

Rabbitt, P., & Winthrope, C. (1988). What do old people remember? The Galton paradigm reconsidered. In M. M. Gruneberg, P. E. Morris, & R. N. Sykes (Eds.), *Practical aspects of memory: Current research and issues* (Vol. 1, pp. 301–307). Chichester, England: John Wiley & Sons.

Rabinowitz, J. C., & Mandler, J. M. (1983). Organization and information retrieval. *Journal of Experimental Psychology: Learning, Memory, and Cognition, 9,* 430–439.

Ramon y Cajal, S. (1911). *Histologie du systeme nerveux de l'homme et des vertebres* (Vol. 2). Paris: Maloine.

Randt, C. T., Brown, E. R., & Osborne, D. P. (1980). A memory test for longitudinal measurement of mild to moderate deficits. *Clinical Neuropsychology, 2,* 184–194.

Rapaport, D. (1942). *Emotions and memory.* Baltimore: Williams & Wilkins.

**Rath, B.** (1982). *The use of suggestions during general anesthesia.* Unpublished doctoral dissertation, University of Louisville.

**Ratner, H. H., Smith, B. S., & Padgett, R. J.** (1990). Children's organization of events and event memories. In R. Fivush & J. A. Hudson (Eds.), *Knowing and remembering in young children* (pp. 65–93). New York: Cambridge University Press.

**Raugh, M. R., & Atkinson, R. C.** (1975). A mnemonic method for learning a second language vocabulary. *Journal of Educational Psychology, 67,* 1–16.

**Read, J. D., & Bruce, D.** (1982). Longitudinal tracking of difficult memory retrievals. *Cognitive Psychology, 14,* 280–300.

**Read, J. D., Vokey, J. R., & Davidson, M.** (1991, November). *Knowing who's new: The phenomenon of jamais vu.* Paper presented at the 32nd annual meeting of the Psychonomic Society, San Francisco.

**Read, S. J., & Rosson, M. B.** (1982). Rewriting history: The biasing effects of attitudes on memory. *Social Cognition, 1,* 240–255.

**Reason, J. T.** (1984a). Absent-mindedness and cognitive control. In J. E. Harris & P. E. Morris (Eds.), *Everyday memory, actions and absent-mindedness* (pp. 113–132). London: Academic Press.

**Reason, J. T.** (1984b). Lapses of attention in everyday life. In R. Parasuraman & D. R. Davies (Eds.), *Varieties of attention* (pp. 515–549). San Diego: Academic Press.

**Reason, J. T.** (1988). Stress and cognitive failure. In S. Fisher & J. T. Reason (Eds.), *Handbook of life stress, cognition, and stress* (pp. 405–421). Chichester, England: John Wiley & Sons.

**Reason, J. T., & Lucas, D.** (1984a). Absent-mindedness in shops: Its correlates and consequences. *British Journal of Clinical Psychology, 23,* 121–131.

**Reason, J. T., & Lucas, D.** (1984b). Using cognitive diaries to investigate naturally occurring memory blocks. In J. E. Harris & P. E. Morris (Eds.), *Everyday memory, actions and absent-mindedness* (pp. 53–70). London: Academic Press.

**Reason, J. T., & Mycielska, K.** (1982). *Absent-minded? The psychology of mental lapses and everyday errors.* Englewood Cliffs, NJ: Prentice-Hall.

**Reed, G.** (1972). *The psychology of anomalous experience: A cognitive approach.* London: Hutchinson University Library.

**Reed, G.** (1979). Everyday anomalies of recall and recognition. In J. F. Kihlstrom & F. J. Evans (Eds.), *Functional disorders of memory* (pp. 1–28). Hillsdale, NJ: Erlbaum.

**Reid, T. R.** (1989, June 18). The man with the endless memory. *The Washington Post,* pp. F1, F6.

**Reiser, B. J., Black, J. B., & Kalamarides, P.** (1986). Strategic memory search processes. In D. C. Rubin (Ed.), *Autobiographical memory* (pp. 100–121). Cambridge, England: Cambridge University Press.

**Reitan, R. M.** (1955). An investigation of Halstead's measures of biological intelligence. *Archives of Neurology and Psychiatry, 73,* 28–35.

**Reitman, J. S.** (1971). Mechanisms of forgetting in short-term memory. *Cognitive Psychology, 2,* 185–195.

**Reitman, J. S.** (1974). Without surreptitious rehearsal, information in short-term memory decays. *Journal of Verbal Learning and Verbal Behavior, 13,* 365–377.

**Revelle, W., & Loftus, D. A.** (1990). Individual differences and arousal: Implications for the study of mood and memory. *Cognition and Emotion, 4,* 209–237.

**Richardson-Klavehn, A., & Bjork, R. A.** (1988). Measures of memory. *Annual Review of Psychology, 39,* 475–543.

**Rife, D. C., & Snyder, L. H.** (1931). Studies in human inheritance: VI. A genetic refutation of the principles of "behavioristic" psychology. *Human Biology, 3,* 547–559.

**Rimland, B., & Fein, D.** (1988). Special talents of autistic savants. In L. K. Obler & D. Fein (Eds.), *The exceptional brain: Neuropsychology of talent and special abilities* (pp. 474–492). New York: Guilford Press.

**Roberts, J.** (1985). The attitude-memory relationship after 40 years. *Basic and Applied Social Psychology, 6,* 221–241.

**Roberts, P.** (1983). Memory strategy instruction with the elderly: What should memory training be the training of? In M. Pressley & J. R. Levin (Eds.), *Cognitive strategy research: Psychological foundations* (pp. 75–100). New York: Springer-Verlag.

**Roediger, H. L., III.** (1990). Implicit memory: Retention without remembering. *American Psychologist, 45,* 1043–1056.

Roediger, H. L., III, & Blaxton, T. A. (1987). Retrieval modes produce dissociations in memory for surface information. In D. Gorfein & R. R. Hoffman (Eds.), *Memory and cognitive processes: The Ebbinghaus Centennial Conference* (pp. 349–379). Hillsdale, NJ: Erlbaum.

Roediger, H. L., III, & Crowder, R. G. (1976). A serial position effect in recall of United States presidents. *Bulletin of the Psychonomic Society, 8,* 275–278.

Rogers, T. B., Kuiper, N. A., & Kirker, W. S. (1977). Self-reference and the encoding of personal information. *Journal of Personality and Social Psychology, 35,* 677–688.

Roman, F., Staubli, U., & Lynch, G. (1987). Evidence for synaptic potentiation in a cortical network during learning. *Brain Research, 418,* 221–226.

Roorda-Hrdlickova, V., Wolters, G., Bonke, B., & Phaf, R. H. (1990). Unconscious perception during general anaesthesia, demonstrated by an implicit memory task. In B. Bonke, W. Fitch, & K. Millar (Eds.), *Memory and awareness in anaesthesia* (pp. 150–155). Amsterdam: Swets & Zeitlinger.

Rosch, E. (1973). Natural categories. *Cognitive Psychology, 4,* 328–350.

Rosch, E., Simpson, C., & Miller, R. S. (1976). Structural bases of typicality effects. *Journal of Experimental Psychology: Human Perception and Performance, 2,* 491–502.

Rose, S. A., & Wallace, I. F. (1985). Visual recognition memory: A predictor of later cognitive functioning in preterms. *Child Development, 56,* 843–852.

Rosen, W. G., Mohs, R. C., & Davis, K. L. (1984). A new rating scale for Alzheimer's diseases. *American Journal of Psychiatry, 14,* 1356–1364.

Rosenblatt, F. (1962). *The principles of neurodynamics.* New York: Spartan.

Rosenzweig, M. R. (1984). Experience, memory, and the brain. *American Psychologist, 39,* 365–376.

Rosenzweig, M. R., & Bennett, E. L. (1972). Cerebral changes in rats exposed individually to an enriched environment. *Journal of Comparative and Physiological Psychology, 80,* 304–313.

Rosenzweig, M. R., Bennett, E. L., & Diamond, M. C. (1967). Effects of differential environments on brain anatomy and brain chemistry. In J. Zubin & G. Jervis (Eds.), *Psychopathology of mental de-velopment* (pp. 45–56). New York: Grune & Stratton.

Rosenzweig, M. R., Krech, D., Bennett, E. L., & Diamond, M. C. (1962). Effects of environmental complexity and training on brain chemistry and anatomy: A replication and extension. *Journal of Comparative and Physiological Psychology, 55,* 429–437.

Ross, B. M. (1991). *Remembering the personal past: Descriptions of autobiographical memory.* New York: Oxford University Press.

Rothbart, M. (1981). Memory processes and social beliefs. In D. L. Hamilton (Ed.), *Cognitive processes in stereotyping and intergroup behavior* (pp. 134–145). Hillsdale, NJ: Erlbaum.

Rothkopf, J. S., & Blaney, P. H. (1991). Mood congruent memory: The role of affective focus and gender. *Cognition and Emotion, 5,* 53–64.

Rovee-Collier, C. (1989). The joy of kicking: Memories, motives, and mobiles. In P. R. Solomon, G. R. Goethals, C. M. Kelly, & B. R. Stephens (Eds.), *Memory: Interdisciplinary approaches* (pp. 151–180). New York: Springer-Verlag.

Rovee-Collier, C., Griesler, P. C., & Earley, L. A. (1985). Contextual determinants of retention in 3-month-old infants. *Learning and Motivation, 16,* 139–157.

Rowe, E. J., & Schnore, M. M. (1971). Item concreteness and reported strategies in paired associate learning as a function of age. *Journal of Gerontology, 24,* 470–475.

Rubin, D. C. (1986). *Autobiographical memory.* Cambridge, England: Cambridge University Press.

Rubin, D. C., & Kontis, T. C. (1983). A schema for common cents. *Memory & Cognition, 11,* 335–341.

Rubin, D. C., & Kozin, M. (1984). Vivid memories. *Cognition, 16,* 81–95.

Rubin, D. C., Wetzler, S. E., & Nebes, R. D. (1986). Autobiographical memory across the lifespan. In D. C. Rubin (Ed.), *Autobiographical memory* (pp. 202–221). Cambridge, England: Cambridge University Press.

Rundus, D. (1971). Analysis of rehearsal processes in free recall. *Journal of Experimental Psychology, 89,* 63–77.

Russell, E. W. (1981). The pathology and clinical examination of memory. In S. B. Filskov & T. J. Boll (Eds.), *Handbook of clinical neuropsychology* (pp. 287–319). New York: John Wiley & Sons.

Russell, M. J. (1976). Human olfactory communication. *Natural (London), 260,* 520–522.

Russo, R., & Parkin, A. J. (1993). Age differences in implicit memory: More apparent than real. *Memory & Cognition, 21,* 73–80.

Rusted, J. M. (1988). Dissociative effects of scopolamine on working memory in healthy young volunteers. *Psychopharmacology, 96,* 487–492.

Rybash, J. M., Hoyer, W. J., & Roodin, P. A. (1986). *Adult cognition and aging.* New York: Pergamon.

Sachs, J. S. (1967). Recognition memory for syntactic and semantic aspects of connected discourse. *Perception and Psychophysics, 2,* 437–442.

Sachs, J. S. (1974). Memory in reading and listening to discourse. *Memory & Cognition, 2,* 95–100.

Salthouse, T. A. (1991). Mediation of adult age differences in cognition by reductions in working memory and speed of processing. *Psychological Science, 2,* 179–183.

Salthouse, T. A., & Babcock, R. L. (1991). Decomposing adult age differences in working memory. *Developmental Psychology, 27,* 763–776.

Sanders, R. E., Gonzalez, E. O., Murphy, M. D., Liddle, C. L., & Vitina, J. R. (1987). Frequency of occurrence and the criteria for automatic processing. *Journal of Experimental Psychology: Learning, Memory, and Cognition, 13,* 241–250.

Saufley, W. H., Otaka, S. R., & Bavaresco, J. L. (1985). Context effects: Classroom tests and context independence. *Memory & Cognition, 13,* 522–528.

Schab, F. R. (1990). Odors and the remembrance of things past. *Journal of Experimental Psychology: Learning, Memory, and Cognition, 16,* 648–655.

Schachtel, E. G. (1947). On memory and childhood amnesia. *Psychiatry, 10,* 1–26.

Schacter, D. L. (1987). Implicit memory: History and current status. *Journal of Experimental Psychology: Learning, Memory, and Cognition, 13,* 501–518.

Schacter, D. L., Cooper, L. A., & Delaney, S. (1990). Implicit memory for unfamiliar objects depends on access to structural descriptions. *Journal of Experimental Psychology: General, 119,* 5–24.

Schank, R. C. (1982). *Dynamic memory.* New York: Cambridge University Press.

Schank, R. C., & Abelson, R. P. (1977). *Scripts, plans, goals, and understanding.* Hillsdale, NJ: Erlbaum.

Schare, M. L., Lisman, S. A., & Spear, N. E. (1984). The effects of mood variation on state-dependent retention. *Cognitive Therapy and Research, 8,* 387–408.

Schmidt, S. R., & Bohannon, J. N., III. (1988). In defense of the flashbulb-memory hypothesis: A comment on McCloskey, Wible, and Cohen (1988). *Journal of Experimental Psychology: General, 117,* 332–335.

Schneider, W. (1985). Developmental trends in the metamemory–memory behavior relationship: An integrative review. In D. L. Forrest-Pressley, G. E. MacKinnon, & T. G. Waller (Eds.), *Cognition, metacognition, and human performance* (Vol. 1, pp. 57–109). New York: Academic Press.

Schneider, W., & Pressley, M. (1989). *Memory development between 2 and 20.* New York: Springer-Verlag.

Schoen, L. S., & Badia, P. (1984). Facilitated recall following REM and NREM naps. *Psychophysiology, 21,* 299–306.

Schonfield, D., & Stones, M. J. (1979). Remembering and aging. In J. F. Kihlstrom & F. J. Evans (Eds.), *Functional disorders of memory* (pp. 103–139). Hillsdale, NJ: Erlbaum.

Schuman, E. M., & Madison, D. V. (1991). A requirement for the intercellular messenger nitric oxide in long-term potentiation. *Science, 254,* 1503–1506.

Schwartz, R. H. (1991). Heavy marijuana use and recent memory impairment. *Psychiatric Annals, 21,* 80–82.

Schweickert, R., & Boruff, B. (1986). Short-term memory capacity: Magic number or magic spell? *Journal of Experimental Psychology: Learning, Memory, and Cognition, 12,* 419–425.

Schweickert, R., Guentert, L., & Hersberger, L. (1990). Phonological similarity, pronunciation rate, and memory span. *Psychological Science, 1,* 74–77.

Scoville, W. B., & Milner, B. (1957). Loss of recent memory after bilateral hippocampal leisions. *Journal of Neurology, Neurosurgery and Psychiatry, 20,* 11–21.

Scrima, L. (1982). Isolated REM sleep facilitation recall of complex associative information. *Psychophysiology, 19,* 252–259.

Seab, J. P., Jagust, W. J., Wong, S. T. S., Roos, M. S., Reed, B. R., & Budinger, T. F. (1988). Quantitative NMR measurements of hippocampal atrophy in Alzheimer's disease. *Magnetic Resonance in Medicine, 8,* 200–208.

Searle, J. R. (1969). *Speech acts.* Cambridge, England: Cambridge University Press.

Searleman, A., & Carter, H. (1988). The effectiveness of different types of pragmatic implications found in commercials to mislead subjects. *Applied Cognitive Psychology, 2,* 265–272.

Searleman, A., & Gaydusek, K. A. (1989, November). *Relationship between prospective memory ability and selective personality variables.* Paper presented at the annual meeting of the Psychonomic Society, Atlanta.

Sehulster, J. R. (1981a). Phenomenological correlates of a self theory of memory. *American Journal of Psychology, 94,* 527–537.

Sehulster, J. R. (1981b). Structure and pragmatics of a self theory of memory. *Memory & Cognition, 9,* 263–276.

Sehulster, J. R. (1988). Broader perspectives on everyday memory. In M. M. Gruneberg, P. E. Morris & R. N. Sykes (Eds.), *Practical aspects of memory: Current research and issues* (Vol. 1, p. 323–328). Chichester, England: John Wiley & Sons.

Seidenberg, M. S., & McClelland, J. L. (1989). A distributed, developmental model of word recognition and naming. *Psychological Review, 96,* 523–568.

Selfridge, O. G., & Neisser, U. (1960). Pattern recognition by machine. *Scientific American, 203,* 60–68.

Shallice, T., & Warrington, E. K. (1970). Independent functioning of verbal memory stores: A neuropsychological study. *Quarterly Journal of Experimental Psychology, 22,* 261–273.

Shapiro, B. J. (1969). The subjective estimation of relative word frequency. *Journal of Verbal Learning and Verbal Behavior, 8,* 248–251.

Sheikh, J. I., Hill, R. D., & Yesavage, J. A. (1986). Long-term efficacy of cognitive training for age associated memory impairment: A six month follow-up study. *Developmental Neuropsychology, 2,* 413–421.

Sheingold, K., & Tenney, Y. J. (1982). Memory for a salient childhood event. In U. Neisser (Ed.), *Memory observed: Remembering in natural contexts* (pp. 201–212). San Francisco: Freeman.

Shepard, R. N. (1967). Recognition memory for words, sentences, and pictures. *Journal of Verbal Learning and Verbal Behavior, 6,* 156–163.

Shepard, R. N. (1978). The mental image. *American Psychologist, 33,* 125–137.

Shepard, R. N. (1984). Ecological constraints in internal representation: Resonant kinematics of perceiving, imagining, thinking and dreaming. *Psychological Review, 91,* 417–446.

Shepard, R. N., & Chipman, S. (1970). Second-order isomorphism of internal representations: Shapes of states. *Cognitive Psychology, 1,* 1–17.

Shepard, R. N., & Metzler, J. (1971). Mental rotation of three-dimensional objects. *Science, 171,* 701–703.

Sherman, R. C., & Lim, K. M. (1991). Determinants of spatial priming in environmental memory. *Memory & Cognition, 19,* 283–292.

Shimamura, A. P. (1986). Priming effects in amnesia: Evidence for a dissociable memory function. *Quarterly Journal of Experimental Psychology, 38A,* 619–644.

Shimamura, A. P., Janowsky, J. S., & Squire, L. R. (1990). Memory for the temporal order of events in patients with frontal lobe lesions and amnesic patients. *Neuropsychologia, 28,* 803–813.

Shotter, J., & Gauld, A. (1981). *Memory as a social institution.* Leicester, England: British Psychological Society, Plymouth Polytechnic.

Shulman, H. G. (1971). Similarity effects in short-term memory. *Psychological Bulletin, 75,* 399–415.

Shulman, H. G. (1972). Semantic confusion errors in short-term memory. *Journal of Verbal Learning and Verbal Behavior, 11,* 221–227.

Siegler, R. S. (1991). *Children's thinking* (2nd ed.). Englewood Cliffs, NJ: Prentice-Hall.

Simon, H. A., & Barenfeld, M. (1969). Information-processing analysis of perceptual processes in problem solving. *Psychological Review, 76,* 473–483.

Simon, H. A., & Gilmartin, K. (1973). A simulation of memory for chess positions. *Cognitive Psychology, 5,* 29–46.

Simpson, P. J. (1972). High-speed memory scanning: Stability and generality. *Journal of Experimental Psychology, 96,* 239–246.

Singer, J. A., & Salovey, P. (1988). Mood and memory: Evaluating the network theory of affect. *Clinical Psychology Review, 8,* 211–251.

Sinnott, J. D. (1986). Prospective intentional and

incidental everyday memory: Effects of age and passage of time. *Psychology and Aging, 1,* 110–116.

Skowronski, J. J., & Thompson, C. P. (1990). Reconstructing the dates of personal events: Gender differences in accuracy. *Applied Cognitive Psychology, 4,* 371–381.

Slamecka, N. J. (1985). Ebbinghaus: Some associations. *Journal of Experimental Psychology: Learning, Memory, and Cognition, 11,* 414–435.

Slamecka, N. J., & Fevreiski, J. (1983). The generation effect when generation fails. *Journal of Verbal Learning and Verbal Behavior, 22,* 153–163.

Slamecka, N. J., & Graf, P. (1978). The generation effect: Delineation of a phenomenon. *Journal of Experimental Psychology: Human Learning and Memory, 14,* 592–604.

Slamecka, N. J., & McElree, B. (1983). Normal forgetting of verbal lists as a function of their degree of learning. *Journal of Experimental Psychology: Learning, Memory, and Cognition, 9,* 384–397.

Smith, A. (1988). Effects of meals on memory and attention. In M. M. Gruneberg, P. E. Morris, & R. N. Sykes (Eds.), *Practical aspects of memory: Current research and issues* (Vol. 2, pp. 477–482). Chichester, England: John Wiley & Sons.

Smith, A. D. (1980). Age differences in encoding, storage, and retrieval. In L. W. Poon, J. L. Fozard, L. S. Cermak, D. Arenberg, & L. W. Thompson (Eds.), *New directions in memory and aging* (pp. 23–46). Hillsdale, NJ: Erlbaum.

Smith, E. E., Shoben, E. J., & Rips, L. J. (1974). Structure and process in semantic memory: A feature model for semantic decisions. *Psychological Review, 81,* 214–241.

Smith, S. (1988). Environmental context-dependent memory. In G. M. Davies & D. M. Thomson (Eds.), *Memory in context: Context in memory* (pp. 13–34). Chichester, England: John Wiley & Sons.

Smith, S. M., Glenberg, A. M., & Bjork, R. A. (1978). Environmental context and human memory. *Memory & Cognition, 6,* 342–353.

Smith, S. M., Vela, E., & Williamson, J. E. (1988). Shallow input processing does not induce environmental context-dependent recognition. *Bulletin of the Psychonomic Society, 26,* 537–540.

Smith, V. L., & Ellsworth, P. C. (1987). The social psychology of eyewitness accuracy: Misleading questions and communicator expertise. *Journal of Applied Psychology, 72,* 294–300.

Smolensky, P. (1988). On the proper treatment of connectionism. *Behavioral and Brain Sciences, 11,* 1–74.

Snyder, M., & Uranowitz, S. W. (1978). Reconstructing the past: Some cognitive consequences of personal perception. *Journal of Personality and Social Psychology, 36,* 941–951.

Solomon, R. L., & Corbit, J. D. (1974). An opponent-process theory of motivation. *Psychological Review, 81,* 119–145.

Solso, R. L. (1991). *Cognitive psychology* (3rd ed.). Boston: Allyn and Bacon.

Sophian, C. (1980). Habituation is not enough: Novelty preferences, search, and memory in infancy. *Merrill-Palmer Quarterly, 25,* 239–257.

Sophian, C., & Hagen, J. W. (1978). Involuntary memory and the development of retrieval skills in young children. *Journal of Experimental Child Psychology, 26,* 458–471.

Spear, N. E. (1979). Experimental analysis of infantile amnesia. In J. F. Kihlstrom & F. J. Evans (Eds.), *Functional disorders of memory* (pp. 75–102). Hillsdale, NJ: Erlbaum.

Spence, M. J., & DeCasper, A. J. (1987). Prenatal experience with low-frequency maternal-voice sounds influence neonatal perception of maternal voice samples. *Infant Behavior and Development, 10,* 133–142.

Sperling, G. (1960). The information available in brief visual presentations. *Psychological Monographs: General and Applied, 74,* 1–29.

Spilich, G. L. (1986, August). Cigarette smoking and memory: Good news and bad news. In G. L. Spilich (Chair), *Symposium on cognitive and environmental agents: Theoretical and pragmatic implications.* New York: American Psychological Association.

Spreen, O., & Strauss, E. (1991). *A compendium of neuropsychological tests: Administration, norms, and commentary.* New York: Oxford University Press.

Springer, S. P., & Deutsch, G. (1989). *Left brain, right brain* (3rd ed.). New York: Freeman.

Sprung, L., & Sprung, H. (1986). Hermann Ebbinghaus: Life, work, and impact in the history of psychology. In F. Klix & H. Hagendorf (Eds.), *Human memory and cognitive capabilities* (pp. 23–34). Amsterdam: North Holland.

Squire, L. R. (1982). Comparison between forms of amnesia: Some deficits are unique to Korsakoff's syndrome. *Journal of Experimental Psychology: Learning, Memory, and Cognition, 8,* 560–571.

Squire, L. R. (1986). Mechanisms of memory. *Science, 232,* 1612–1619.

Squire, L. R. (1987). *Memory and brain.* New York: Oxford University Press.

Squire, L. R., & Cohen, N. J. (1982). Remote memory, retrograde amnesia, and the neuropsychology of human memory. In L. S. Cermak (Ed.), *Human memory and amnesia* (pp. 275–303). Hillsdale, NJ: Erlbaum.

Squire, L. R., Cohen, N. J., & Nadel, L. (1984). The medial temporal region and memory consolidation: A new hypothesis. In H. Weingartner & E. S. Parker (Eds.), *Memory consolidation* (pp. 185–210). Hillsdale, NJ: Erlbaum.

Squire, L. R., Knowlton, B., & Musen, G. (1993). The structure and organization of memory. In L. W. Porter & M. R. Rosenzweig (Eds.), *Annual Review of Psychology* (Vol. 44, pp. 453–495). Palo Alto, CA: Annual Review Inc.

Squire, L. R., & Zola-Morgan, S. (1991). The medial temporal lobe memory system. *Science, 253,* 1380–1386.

Squire, L. R., Zola-Morgan, S., Cave, C. B., Haist, F., Musen, G., & Suzuki, W. A. (1990). Memory: Organization of brain systems and cognition. *Cold Spring Harbor Symposia on Quantitative Biology, 55,* 1007–1023.

Stamford, B. A., Hambacher, W., & Fallica, A. (1974). Effects of daily exercise on the psychiatric state of institutionalized geriatric mental patients. *Research Quarterly, 45,* 35–41.

Standing, L., Conezio, J., & Haber, R. N. (1970). Perception and memory for pictures: Single-trial learning of 2560 visual stimuli. *Psychonomic Science, 19,* 73–74.

Stanley, G., & Hall, R. (1973). Short term visual information processing in dyslexics. *Child Development, 44,* 841–844.

Stephens, D. N., Duka, T., & Andrews, J. S. (1991). In J. Weinman & J. Hunter (Eds.), *Memory: Neurochemical and abnormal perspectives* (pp. 11–42). Chur, Switzerland: Harwood Academic Publishers.

Sternberg, S. (1966). High-speed scanning in human memory. *Science, 153,* 652–654.

Sternberg, S. (1967). Retrieval of contextual information from memory. *Psychonomic Science, 8,* 55–56.

Sternberg, S. (1969). The discovery of processing stages: Extensions of Donder's method. *Acta Psychologica, 30,* 276–315.

Sternberg, S. (1975). Memory scanning: New findings and current controversies. *Quarterly Journal of Experimental Psychology, 27,* 1–32.

Stevens, A., & Coupe, P. (1978). Distortions in judged spatial relations. *Cognitive Psychology, 63,* 390–397.

Stollery, B. (1988). Neurotoxic exposure and memory function. In M. M. Gruneberg, P. E. Morris, & R. N. Sykes, (Eds.), *Practical aspects of memory: Current research and issues* (Vol. 2, pp. 242–247). Chichester, England: John Wiley & Sons.

Stone, J. (1990). Homer's greatest hits. *Discover,* 85–87.

Stromeyer, C. F., III. (1970, November). Eidetikers. *Psychology Today,* 76–80.

Stromeyer, C. F., III, & Psotka, J. (1970). The detailed texture of eidetic images. *Nature, 225,* 346–349.

Strub, R. L., & Black, F. W. (1977). *The mental status examination in neurology.* Philadelphia: F. A. Davis.

Sulin, R. A., & Dooling, D. J. (1974). Intrusion of a thematic idea in retention of prose. *Journal of Experimental Psychology, 103,* 255–262.

Sullivan, E. B. (1927). Attitude in relation to learning. *Psychological Monographs, 36,* 1–149.

Sullivan, M. (1982). Reactivation: Priming forgotten memories in human infants. *Child Development, 53,* 516–523.

Swanson, J. M., & Kinsbourne, M. (1979). State-dependent learning and retrieval: Methodological cautions and theoretical considerations. In J. F. Kihlstrom & F. J. Evans (Eds.), *Functional disorders of memory* (pp. 275–299). Hillsdale, NJ: Erlbaum.

Teasdale, J. D., & Fogarty, S. J. (1979). Differential effects of induced mood on retrieval of pleasant and unpleasant events from episodic memory. *Journal of Abnormal Psychology, 88,* 248–257.

Teasdale, J. D., & Taylor, R. (1981). Induced mood and accessibility of memories: An effect of mood state or of induction procedure? *British Journal of Clinical Psychology, 20,* 39–48.

Teasdale, J. D., Taylor, R., & Fogarty, S. J. (1980). Effects of induced elation-depression on the accessibility of memories of happy and unhappy experiences. *Behavior Research and Therapy, 18,* 339–346.

Tetlock, P. E., & Manstead, A. S. R. (1985). Impression management versus intrapsychic explanations in social psychology: A useful dichotomy. *Psychological Review, 92,* 59–77.

Teyler, T. J. (1991). Memory: Electrophysiological analogs. In J. L. Martinez & R. P. Kesner (Eds.), *Learning and memory: A biological view* (2nd ed.) (pp. 299–327). San Diego, CA: Academic Press.

Teyler, T. J., & DiScenna, P. (1987). Long-term potentiation. *Annual Review of Neuroscience, 10,* 131–161.

Thompson, R. F., Berger, T. W., & Madden, J. (1983). Cellular processes of learning and memory in the mammalian CNS. *Annual Review of Neuroscience, 6,* 447–491.

Thorndike, E. L. (1914). *The psychology of learning.* New York: Teachers College.

Thorndike, E. L., & Woodworth, R. S. (1901). The influence of improvement in one mental function upon the efficiency of other functions. *Psychological Review, 8,* 247–261, 384–395, 553–564.

Thorndyke, P. W. (1984). Applications of schema theory in cognitive research. In J. R. Anderson & S. M. Kosslyn (Eds.), *Tutorials in learning and memory* (pp. 167–192). San Francisco: Freeman.

Thorndyke, P. W., & Hayes-Roth, B. (1982). Differences in spatial knowledge acquired from maps and navigation. *Cognitive Psychology, 14,* 560–589.

Tilley, A., & Statham, D. (1989). The effect of prior sleep on retrieval. *Acta Psychologica, 70,* 199–203.

Toglia, M. P., & Battig, W. F. (1978). *Handbook of semantic word norms.* Hillsdale, NJ: Erlbaum.

Toglia, M. P., & Kimble, G. A. (1976). Recall and use of serial position information. *Journal of Experimental Psychology: Human Learning and Memory, 2,* 431–445.

Tolman, E. C. (1948). Cognitive maps in rats and men. *Psychological Review, 55,* 189–208.

Townsend, J. T. (1971). A note of the identifiability of parallel and serial processes. *Perception and Psychophysics, 10,* 161–163.

Townsend, J. T. (1972). Some results concerning the identifiability of parallel and serial processes. *British Journal of Mathematical and Statistical Psychology, 25,* 168–199.

Townsend, J. T. (1990). Serial and parallel processing: Sometimes they look like Tweedledum and Tweedledee but they can (and should) be distinguished. *Psychological Science, 1,* 46–54.

Treadway, M., & McCloskey, M. (1989). Effects of racial stereotypes on eyewitness performance: Implications of the real and the rumoured Allport and Postman studies. *Applied Cognitive Psychology, 3,* 53–63.

Treffert, D. A. (1988). The idiot savant: A review of the syndrome. *American Journal of Psychiatry, 145,* 563–572.

Treisman, A. (1964). Monitoring and storage of irrelevant messages in selective attention. *Journal of Verbal Learning and Verbal Behavior, 3,* 449–459.

Tresselt, M. E., & Mayzner, M. S. (1960). A study of incidental learning. *Journal of Psychology, 50,* 339–347.

Trustman, R., Dubrovsky, S., & Titley, R. (1977). Auditory perception during general anesthesia—myth or fact? *International Journal of Clinical and Experimental Hypnosis, 25,* 88–105.

Tulving, E. (1962). Subjective organization in free-recall of "unrelated" words. *Psychological Review, 69,* 344–354.

Tulving, E. (1964). Intratrial and intertrial retention: Notes towards a theory of free recall verbal learning. *Psychological Review, 71,* 219–237.

Tulving, E. (1972). Episodic and semantic memory. In E. Tulving & W. Donaldson (Eds.), *Organization and memory* (pp. 381–403). New York: Academic Press.

Tulving, E. (1974). Cue-dependent forgetting. *American Scientist, 62,* 74–82.

Tulving, E. (1983). *Elements of episodic memory.* New York: Oxford University Press.

Tulving, E. (1985). How many memory systems are there? *American Psychologist, 40,* 385–398.

Tulving, E. (1987). Multiple memory systems and consciousness. *Human Neurobiology, 6,* 67–80.

Tulving, E., & Pearlstone, Z. (1966). Availability versus accessibility of information in memory for words. *Journal of Verbal Learning and Verbal Behavior, 5,* 381–391.

Tulving, E., & Psotka, J. (1971). Retroactive inhibition in free recall: Inaccessibility of information available in the memory store. *Journal of Experimental Psychology, 87,* 1–8.

Tulving, E., & Schacter, D. L. (1990). Priming and human memory systems. *Science, 247,* 301–306.

Tulving, E., & Thomson, D. M. (1973). Encoding

specificity and retrieval processes in episodic memory. *Psychological Review, 80,* 352–373.

Tversky, A., & Kahneman, D. (1973). Availability: A heuristic for judging frequency and probability. *Cognitive Psychology, 4,* 207–232.

Tversky, B. (1981). Distortions in memory for maps. *Cognitive Psychology, 13,* 407–433.

Tversky, B., & Tuchin, M. (1989). A reconciliation of the evidence on eyewitness testimony: Comments on McCloskey and Zaragoza. *Journal of Experimental Psychology: General, 118,* 86–91.

Tye, M. (1991). *The imagery debate.* Cambridge, MA: The M.I.T. Press.

Tzeng, O. J. L. (1976). A precedence effect in the processing of verbal information. *American Journal of Psychology, 89,* 577–599.

Tzeng, O. J. L., & Cotton, B. (1980). A study-phase retrieval model of temporal coding. *Journal of Experimental Psychology: Human Learning and Memory, 6,* 705–716.

Tzeng, O. J. L., Lee, A. T., & Wetzel, C. D. (1979). Temporal coding in verbal information processing. *Journal of Experimental Psychology: Human Learning and Memory, 5,* 52–64.

Ucros, C. G. (1989). Mood state-dependent memory: A meta-analysis. *Cognition and Emotion, 3,* 139–167.

Underwood, B. J. (1977). *Temporal codes for memories: Issues and problems.* Hillsdale, NJ: Erlbaum.

Underwood, B. J., Boruch, R. F., & Malmi, R. A. (1978). Composition of episodic memory. *Journal of Experimental Psychology: General, 107,* 393–419.

Underwood, G. (1978). *Strategies of information processing.* London: Academic Press.

Ungar, G., Galvan, L., & Clark, R. H. (1968). Chemical transfer of learned fear. *Nature, 217,* 1259–1261.

Ungar, G., Ho, I. K., Galvan, L., & Desiderio, D. M. (1972). Isolation, identification, and synthesis of a specific behavior-inducing brain peptide. *Nature, 238,* 196–197.

Vallar, G., & Shallice, T. (Eds.). (1990). *Neuropsychological impairments of short-term memory.* Cambridge, England: Cambridge University Press.

Van der Heijden, A. H. C. (1981). *Short-term visual information forgetting.* London: Routledge & Kegan Paul.

Van Dijk, T. (1987). *Communicating racism.* Newbury Park, CA: Sage Publications.

Velten, E. A. (1968). A laboratory task for induction of mood states. *Behavior Research and Therapy, 6,* 473–482.

Victor, M., Adams, R. D., & Collins, G. H. (1971). *The Wernicke-Korsakoff syndrome.* Philadelphia: F. A. Davis.

Von Restorff, H. (1933). Uber die Wirkung von Bereichsbildungen im Spurenfeld. *Psychologische Forschung, 18,* 299–342.

Wagenaar, W. A. (1986). My memory: A study of autobiographical memory over six years. *Cognitive Psychology, 18,* 225–252.

Wagenaar, W. A., & Groeneweg, J. (1990). The memory of concentration camp survivors. *Applied Cognitive Psychology, 4,* 77–87.

Wagner, D. A. (1978). Memories of Morocco: The influence of age, schooling and environment on memory. *Cognitive Psychology, 10,* 1–28.

Waldfogel, S. (1948). The frequency and affective character of childhood memories. *Psychological Monographs: General and Applied, 62*(Whole No. 291).

Walker, E. L. (1958). Action decrement and its relation to learning. *Psychological Review, 65,* 129–142.

Walker, N., & Jones, P. (1983). Encoding processes and the recall of text. *Memory & Cognition, 11,* 275–282.

Warren, L. R., & Mitchell, S. A. (1980). Age differences in judging the frequency of events. *Developmental Psychology, 16,* 116–120.

Warrington E. K., & Weiskrantz, L. (1968). New method of testing long-term retention with special reference to amnesic patients. *Nature, 217,* 972–974.

Warrington, E. K., & Weiskrantz, L. (1970). Amnesic syndrome: Consolidation or retrieval? *Nature, 228,* 628–630.

Warrington, E. K., & Weiskrantz, L. (1974). The effect of prior learning on subsequent retention in amnesic patients. *Neuropsychologia, 12,* 419–428.

Watkins, M. J. (1990). Mediationism and the obfuscation of memory. *American Psychologist, 45,* 328–335.

Watkins, M. J., & Gardiner, J. M. (1982). Cued recall. In C. R. Puff (Ed.), *Handbook of research methods in human memory and cognition* (pp. 173–195). New York: Academic Press.

Watkins, M. J., & Tulving, E. (1975). Episodic memory: When recognition fails. *Journal of Experimental Psychology: General, 104,* 5–29.

Watts, F. N., MacLeod, A. K., & Morris, L. (1988). A remedial strategy for memory and concentration problems in depressed patients. *Cognitive Therapy and Research, 12,* 185–193.

Waugh, N. C., & Norman, D. A. (1965). Primary memory. *Psychological Review, 72,* 89–104.

Wechsler, D. (1945). A standardized memory scale for clinical use. *Journal of Psychology, 19,* 87–95.

*Wechsler Memory Scale-R.* (1987). San Antonio: The Psychological Corporation.

Wegner, D. M., Guiliano, M., & Hertel, P. (1985). Cognitive interdependence in close relationships. In W. J. Ickes (Ed.), *Compatible and incompatible relationships* (pp. 253–276). New York: Springer-Verlag.

Weiner, B. (1968). Motivated forgetting and the study of repression. *Journal of Personality, 36,* 213–234.

Weiner, B., & Reed, H. (1969). Effects of the instructional sets to remember and to forget on short-term retention: Studies of rehearsal control and retrieval inhibition (repression). *Journal of Experimental Psychology, 79,* 226–232.

Weingartner, H. (1978). Human state dependent learning. In B. T. Ho, D. W. Richards, & D. L. Chute (Eds.), *Drug discrimination and state dependent learning* (pp. 361–382.). New York: Academic Press.

Weingartner, H., Cohen, R. M., Murphy, L., Martello, J., & Gerdt, C. (1981). Cognitive processes in depression. *Archives of General Psychiatry, 38,* 42–47.

Weiskrantz, L. (1985). On issues and theories of the human amnesic syndrome. In N. M. Weinberger, J. L. McGaugh, & G. Lynch (Eds.), *Memory systems of the brain* (pp. 380–415). New York: Guilford.

Weiskrantz, L. (1987). Neuroanatomy of memory and amnesia: A case for multiple memory systems. *Human Neurobiology, 6,* 93–105.

Weiskrantz, L. (1989). Remembering dissociations. In H. L. Roediger III & F. I. M. Craik (Eds.), *Varieties of memory and consciousness: Essays in honour of Endel Tulving* (pp. 101–120). Hillsdale, NJ: Erlbaum.

Weizmann, F., Cohen, L. B., & Pratt, J. (1971). Novelty, familiarity and the development of infant attention. *Developmental Psychology, 4,* 149–154.

Weldon, M. S., & Roediger, H. L. III. (1987). Alter-

ing retrieval demands reverses the picture superiority effect. *Memory & Cognition, 15,* 269–280.

Welford, A. T. (1958). *Aging and human skill.* London: Oxford University Press.

Wellman, H. M. (1983). Metamemory revisited. In M. T. H. Chi (Ed.), *Trends in memory development research* (pp. 31–51). Basel, Switzerland: Karger.

Wellman, H. M. (1989). The early development of memory strategies. In F. E. Weinert & M. Perlmutter (Eds.), *Memory development: Universal changes and individual differences* (pp. 3–29). Hillsdale, NJ: Erlbaum.

Werner, J. S., & Perlmutter, M. (1979). Development of visual memory in infants. In H. W. Reese & L. P. Lipsitt (Eds.), *Advances in child development and behavior* (Vol. 14, pp. 1–56). New York: Academic Press.

Wertheimer, M. (1912). Experimentelle studien uber das Sehen von Bewegung. *Zeitschrift fur Psychologie, 61,* 161–265.

Wertheimer, M. (1986). The annals of the house that Ebbinghaus built. In F. Klix & H. Hagendorf (Eds.), *Human memory and cognitive capabilities* (pp. 35–43). Amsterdam: North Holland.

West, R. L. (1985). *Memory fitness over forty.* Gainesville, FL: Triad Publishing.

West, R. L. (1988). Prospective memory and aging. In M. M. Gruneberg, P. E. Morris, & R. N. Sykes (Eds.), *Practical aspects of memory: Current research and issues* (Vol. 2, pp. 119–125). Chichester, England: John Wiley & Sons.

West, R. L. (1990). Planning practical memory training for the aged. In L. W. Poon, D. C. Rubin, & B. A. Wilson (Eds.), *Everyday cognition in adulthood and late life* (pp. 573–597). Cambridge, England: Cambridge University Press.

Wetherford, M. J., & Cohen, L. B. (1973). Developmental changes in infant visual preferences for novelty and familiarity. *Child Development, 44,* 416–424.

Wetzler, S. E. (1985). Mood state-dependent retrieval: A failure to replicate. *Psychological Reports, 56,* 759–765.

Wetzler, S. E., & Sweeney, D. B. (1986). Childhood amnesia: An empirical demonstration. In D. C. Rubin (Ed.), *Autobiographical memory* (pp. 191–202). Cambridge, England: Cambridge University Press.

White, S. H., & Pillemer, D. B. (1979). Childhood

amnesia and the development of a socially accessible memory system. In J. F. Kihlstrom & F. J. Evans (Eds.), *Functional disorders of memory* (pp. 29–73). Hillsdale, NJ: Erlbaum.

Wickelgren, W. A. (1965). Acoustic similarity and intrusion errors in short-term memory. *Journal of Experimental Psychology, 70,* 102–108.

Wickelgren, W. A. (1973). The long and short of memory. *Psychological Bulletin, 80,* 425–438.

Wickens, D. D. (1970). Encoding categories of words: An empirical approach to meaning. *Psychological Review, 77,* 1–15.

Wickens, D. D. (1972). Characteristics of word encoding. In A. W. Melton & E. Martin (Eds.), *Coding processes in human memory* (pp. 191–215). Washington, DC: Winston.

Wilkins, A. J., & Baddeley, A. D. (1978). Remembering to recall in everyday life: An approach to absentmindedness. In M. M. Gruneberg, P. E. Morris, & R. N. Sykes (Eds.), *Practical aspects of memory* (pp. 27–34). London: Academic Press.

Williams, J. M. G., Watts, F. N., MacLeod, C., & Mathews, A. (1988). *Cognitive psychology and emotional disorders.* New York: Wiley.

Williams, K. W., & Durso, F. T. (1986). Judging category frequency: Automaticity or availability? *Journal of Experimental Psychology: Learning, Memory, and Cognition, 12,* 387–396.

Wilson, B. A. (1987). *Rehabilitation of memory.* New York: Guilford Press.

Wilson, B. A., & Moffat, N. (1984). *Clinical management of memory problems.* Rockville, MD: Aspen Systems.

Winograd, E. (1988). Some observations on prospective remembering. In M. M. Gruneberg, P. E. Morris, & R. N. Sykes (Eds.), *Practical aspects of memory: Current research and issues* (Vol. 1, pp. 348–353). Chichester, England: John Wiley & Sons.

Winograd, E., & Soloway, R. M. (1985). Reminding as a basis for temporal judgments. *Journal of Experimental Psychology: Learning, Memory, and Cognition, 11,* 262–271.

Wixted, J. T., & Ebbesen, E. B. (1991). On the form of forgetting. *Psychological Science, 2,* 409–415.

Wlf, E. (1922). Über die veränderung von vorstellungen: Gedächtnis und Gestalt. *Psychologische Forschung, 1,* 333–373.

Wolfe, L. S., & Millet, J. B. (1960). Control of post-operative pain by suggestion under general anesthesia. *American Journal of Clinical Hypnosis, 3,* 109–112.

Wolkowitz, O. M., & Weingartner, H. (1988). Defining cognitive changes in depression and anxiety: A psychobiological analysis. *Psychiatry & Psychobiology, 3,* 1–8.

Wolters, G., & Phaf, R. H. (1990). Explicit and implicit measures of memory: Evidence for two learning mechanisms. In B. Bonke, W. Fitch, & K. Millar (Eds.), *Memory and awareness in anaesthesia* (pp. 57–63). Amsterdam: Swets & Zeitlinger.

Wood, L. E., & Pratt, J. D. (1987). Pegword mnemonic as an aid to memory in the elderly: A comparison of four age groups. *Educational Gerontology, 13,* 325–337.

Woodward, A. E., Bjork, R. A., & Jongeward, R. H. (1973). Recall and recognition as a function of primary rehearsal. *Journal of Verbal Learning and Verbal Behavior, 12,* 608–617.

Woodworth, R. S. (1938). *Experimental psychology.* London: Methuen.

Wortman, C. B., Loftus, E. F., & Marshall, M. E. (1992). *Psychology* (4th ed.). New York: Knopf.

Wurtele, S. K., Galanos, A. N., & Roberts, M. C. (1980). Increasing return compliance in a tuberculosis detection drive. *Journal of Behavioral Medicine, 3,* 311–318.

Wurtman, R. J. (1981). The effects of nutritional factors on memory. *Acta Neurologica Scandinavica, 89*(Suppl.), 145–154.

Wurtman, R. J. (1982). Nutrients that modify brain function. *Scientific American, 246,* 50–59.

Wyer, R. S., & Srull, T. K. (1966). Human cognition in its social context. *Psychological Review, 93,* 322–359.

Wyer, R. S., & Srull, T. K. (1989). *Memory and cognition in its social context.* Hillsdale, NJ: Erlbaum.

Yates, F. A. (1966). *The art of memory.* Chicago: The University of Chicago Press.

Yerkes, R. M., & Dodson, J. D. (1908). The relation of strength of stimulus to rapidity of habit formation. *Journal of Comparative and Neurological Psychology, 18,* 459–482.

Yesavage, J. A. (1984). Relaxation and memory training in 39 elderly patients. *American Journal of Psychiatry, 141,* 778–781.

Yesavage, J. A., & Rolf, J. (1984). Effects of relaxation and mnemonics on memory, attention, and anxiety in the elderly. *Experimental Aging Research, 10,* 211–214.

Yesavage, J. A., Sheikh, J., Tanke, E. D., & Hill, R. (1988). Response to training and individual differences in verbal intelligence and state anxiety. *American Journal of Psychiatry, 145,* 636–639.

Young, M. N. (1961). *Bibliography of memory.* Philadelphia: Chilton.

Yuille, J. C., & Sereda, L. (1980). Positive effects of mediation: A limited generalization? *Journal of Applied Psychology, 65,* 333–340.

Yussen, S. R., & Levy, V. M. (1975). Developmental changes in predicting one's own span of short-term memory. *Journal of Experimental Child Psychology, 19,* 502–508.

Zacks, R. T., Hasher, L., Alba, J. W., Sanft, H., & Rose, K. C. (1984). Is temporal order encoded automatically? *Memory & Cognition, 12,* 387–394.

Zalutsky, R. A., & Nicoll, R. A. (1990). Comparison of two forms of long-term potentiation in single hippocampal neurons. *Science, 248,* 1619–1624.

Zaragoza, M. S. (1987). Memory, suggestibility and eyewitness testimony in children and adults. In S. J. Ceci, M. P. Toglia, & D. F. Ross (Eds.), *Children's eyewitness memory* (pp. 53–78). New York: Springer-Verlag.

Zaragoza, M. S. (1991). Preschool children's susceptibility to memory impairment. In J. Doris (Ed.), *The suggestibility of children's recollections: Implications for eyewitness testimony* (pp. 27–39). Washington, DC: American Psychological Association.

Zaragoza, M. S., & Koshmider, J. W., III. (1989). Misled subjects may know more than their performance implies. *Journal of Experimental Psychology: Learning, Memory, and Cognition, 15* 246–255.

Zaragoza, M. S., & McCloskey, M. (1989). Misleading postevent information and the memory impairment hypothesis: Comment on Belli and reply to Tversky and Tuchin. *Journal of Experimental Psychology: General, 118,* 92–99.

Zaragoza, M. S., McCloskey, M., & Jamis, M. (1987). Misleading postevent information and recall of the original event: Further evidence against the memory impairment hypothesis. *Journal of Experimental Psychology: Learning, Memory, and Cognition, 13,* 36–44.

Zechmeister, E. B., King, J. F., Gude, C., & Opera-Nadi, B. (1975). Ratings of frequency, familiarity, orthographic distinctiveness and pronounciability for 192 surnames. *Behavior Research Methods and Instrumentation, 7,* 531–533.

Zechmeister, E. B., & Nyberg, S. E. (1982). *Human memory: An introduction to research and theory.* Monterey, CA: Brooks/Cole.

Zecker, S. (1988, April). The role of motivation in memory remediation of brain damaged adults. In D. Payne & D. J. Herrmann, *Symposium on the new approach to the improvement of memory performances and memory ability.* Buffalo: Eastern Psychological Association.

Zelinkski, E. M., Gilewski, M. J., & Thompson, L. W. (1980). Do lab tests relate to self-assessment of memory ability in young and old? In L. W. Poon, J. L. Fozard, L. S. Cermak, D. Arenberg, & L. W. Thompson (Eds.), *New directions in memory and aging* (pp. 519–544). Hillsdale, NJ: Erlbaum.

Zornetzer, S. F. (1986). Applied aspects of memory research: Aging. In J. L. Martinez & R. P. Kesner (Eds.), *Learning and memory: A biological view* (pp. 203–233). New York: Academic Press.

# Name Index

# Subject Index